Musical Comedy in America

Ethel Waters in a visionary moment of *Cabin in the Sky*.

Musical Comedy in America

From *The Black Crook* to *South Pacific*
by CECIL SMITH

From *The King and I* to *Sweeney Todd*
by GLENN LITTON

THEATRE ARTS BOOKS

New York

Published by
THEATRE ARTS BOOKS
153 Waverly Place, New York, N.Y. 10014

Library of Congress Catalog No. 80-51638
ISBN-0-87830-564-5 (Paperbound)

Designed by Bernard Schleifer

Manufactured in the United States of America
by Murray Printing Company

PHOTO CREDITS:

Theatre Collection, N.Y. Public Library—Cover, I, II, 1, 2, 4, 5.
Vandamm Collection, N.Y. Public Library—III, IV, 8, 10, 14, 15.
The Fred Fehl Collection, The Hoblitzelle Theatre Arts Library,
Humanities Research Center, University of Texas at Austin—frontispiece.
The Joseph Abeles Collection—V, 13, 16. Martha Swope—VI, 17. John
Swope—12. Harvard Theatre Collection—3. Ben Pinchot—7. George
Karger-Pix, Inc.—9. Lucas & Monroe Studio—11. Colophon from
Sweeney Todd: The Demon Barber of Fleet Street used with permission of
Richard Barr and Charles Woodward.

to my mother, affectionately
CECIL SMITH

to my parents and Lucy
GLENN LITTON

CONTENTS

FOREWORD TO THE FIRST EDITION ix

FOREWORD TO THE SECOND EDITION xi

PART ONE: 1864–1907

I	*Before The Black Crook*	2
II	*The Black Crook*	7
III	*The Death of Pantomime*	13
IV	*The Bleached Blondes*	16
V	*Evangeline and Edward E. Rice*	19
VI	*The Kiralfys*	28
VII	*Farce-Comedy*	31
VIII	*Comic Opera: The First Decade*	39
IX	*Comic Opera: The Second Decade*	55

PART TWO: 1908–25

X	*The Gaiety Girls, The Passing Show, and Weber and Fields*	64
XI	*The Turn of the Century*	73
XII	*The Merry Widow and the Ziegfield Follies*	87
XIII	*Before and During the First World War*	93
XIV	*A New Era*	102
XV	*New Art and Old Formulas*	114
XVI	*The Postwar Revue*	125
XVII	*Musical Comedy from 1919 to 1925*	136

PART THREE: 1925–50

XVIII	The Revue Becomes Civilized	144
XIX	Musical Comedy Discovers Contemporary Life	155
XX	The Depression Decade	160
XXI	The New Audience	170
XXII	War and Postwar Years	182
XXIII	The Past, The Present, and The Future	201

PART FOUR: THE 1950s

| XXIV | The Book Musical Refined | 208 |

PART FIVE: THE 1960s

| XXV | Trouble | 252 |

PART SIX: THE 1970s

| XXVI | An Uncertain Comeback | 300 |
| INDEX | | 351 |

Illustration sections appear between pages 80–81 and 272–73.

Foreword to the First Edition

by Cecil Smith

THE PURPOSE OF this book—the first to recount the history of the popular musical stage on Broadway and its intersecting streets—is to tell what the various entertainments were like, how they looked and sounded, who was in them, and why they made people laugh or cry. The values employed in the book are changeable and inconsistent. Sometimes an affable smile is bestowed upon a musical comedy, burlesque, or revue that was really very bad. Sometimes a harsh verdict is brought in against an entertainment that received widespread approval and praise. I can only plead that the book itself, in the writing of it, refused to come out any other way.

If the descriptions and assessments of the pieces and people it deals with are offhand rather than scholastic, or opinionated rather than measured and impersonal, this is because the medium itself does not suggest *Wissenschaft* and the devices of the doctor's dissertation. I have sought to treat the works on their own level and in their own terms, which are ordinarily very friendly and gay. A mere rambling narrative, however, would have left matters scattered and confused. I have endeavored to show the position of individual works and of the categories to which they belong within the historical continuity that led to musical comedy as we know it today. My personal critical judgments are tangential to this main enterprise, and may as well remain inexplicable to those whose minds and tastes are different from mine.

Many people with special reasons to remember them will undoubtedly lament my failure to mention certain specific pieces and people anywhere in the course of the book. I do not think any of the missing items, ancient or modern, were omitted unintentionally, though a multitude of different reasons led to their exclusion.

For all important purposes, the history of musical comedy in America starts with *The Black Crook*, as everyone has always said it did. In order not to begin the story *in vacuo*, I have sketched in a brief memento of some of the theatrical enterprises that preceded it. But this is no more than a prologue, and the main tale, as far as it can yet be told, stretches from *The Black Crook* at one end to *South Pacific* and other contemporary musical comedies at the other. Five years hence I hope it will be necessary to add another chapter.

I did not prepare this book all by myself. Many of its materials result from the successive researches of Raymond Ericson, James Hinton, Jr., Arnold Rood, and George Yacker, all of whom manifested a degree of accuracy and discrimination that is uncommon in the human race, let alone research assistants. Paul Myers, of the Theatre Collection of the New York Public Library, was at all times a paragon of helpfulness. Leslie H. Bradshaw, who knows more about the subject at firsthand than most people, fixed an unflagging eye upon the manuscript, and pointed out some errors I was delighted to withdraw from public exhibition. Hermine Rich Isaacs, who was my colleague on the *Theatre Arts* magazine we both loved, read and improved the copy with tender inflexibility. Robert M. MacGregor, the publisher of the book, preserved an exemplary balance of patience and firmness during the irritating periods when I did other things instead of working on the manuscript, and supplied nothing but constructive suggestions from start to finish.

C. S.

Middlefield, Massachusetts
September, 1950

Foreword to the Second Edition

by Glenn Litton

TO SAY THAT musical comedy in America lives is an understatement. Having survived some of the roughest times since the end of World War II, it still dances, sings, struts, kicks, dazzles, and splashes. If there were a special Muse for the musical, she might sing, as Carlotta does in Prince and Sondheim's *Follies,*

> *"Good times and bum times,*
> *I've seen them all and, my dear,*
> *I'm still here.*
> *Plush velvet sometimes,*
> *Sometimes just pretzels and beer,*
> *But I'm here."*

Cecil Smith never got to add that chapter he predicted would be needed some five years after the first edition of this book—not because the addition wasn't warranted but because of his untimely death. This updating of his work is an acknowledgment, by Theatre Arts Books and the author, of our great debt—and the debt of all who have an interest in the musical—to Smith's pioneering work.

Without trying to imitate Smith's style, I've followed the pattern he set. The chronicle from 1950 to 1980 moves forward by decades, with enough meandering to allow for grouping of shows either where trends are evident or where logic requires that certain collaborators' efforts be gathered in one bundle.

When it comes to offering justifications for my criticisms, I can only refer the reader to Smith's Foreword. But on one point I would disagree with what he says there. Smith's critical judgments were not at all tangential to his history. His affection for musical comedy is evident in them, as well as his frustration when his reasonable expectations weren't fulfilled. Smith showed us that commentators have a responsibility to take musicals seriously but not solemnly.

Our musical theatre has grown up in the past thirty-five years. Its ambitions—and accomplishments—have often been pitched higher than anything normally conjured up by the words "musical comedy."

That's why I often use the term "musical theatre" rather than "musical comedy." There's still plenty of room for frivolity on our musical stage, but there's also room—and need—for daring and artistry.

Looking back on the great diversity of shows in the past thirty years, I'm only sorry that I've had to omit many productions. I've also had to pass over most revues, either quickly or in silence, not because they were irrelevant or uninteresting but because so much was happening to the book musical, the conceptual musical, and the theme musical.

A note on form. The names of cast members enclosed in parentheses are those of the actors and actresses who played in the musicals at their openings.

Ken Aptekar, Bob Chapel, Peter Cook, Margaret Eagle, Bernie Kaplan, Lew Lloyd, Ann Peck, and Roger Salomon have been inspiration and support.

George Eells and Lewis Maxwell Rosen wrote critiques of an early draft of the manuscript and prevented many errors from appearing in print.

Elaine Hallett patiently guided this edition through its final stages of publication.

William McCollom and John V. Falconieri helped get into print a portion of an early draft.

Paul Meyers, the staff of the Theatre Collection of the New York Public Library, the staff of the Freiberger Library at Case Western Reserve University, and the staff of the Boston Public Library aided in my research.

George Zournas has fostered this project with serenity and warmth.

I want to make a special dedication to the memories of John Reid Klein, who gave me my first opportunity in musical theatre, Marvin Felheim, who suggested the project, Leota Diesel, who edited the manuscript, and Robert M. MacGregor, the founder and publisher of Theatre Arts Books, who took a chance on an unknown.

Thanks to the following publishers for their permission to quote excerpts from the noted songs:

"ANOTHER HUNDRED PEOPLE" (Stephen Sondheim). © 1970 The Herald Square Music Company and Rilting Music, Inc. Used by permission. All rights reserved.

"BLACK AND BLUE" (by Fats Waller, Andy Razaf, and Harry Brooks). Copyright © 1929 by Mills Music, Inc. Copyright renewed. Waller's interest controlled by Chappell & Co., Inc. (Intersong Music, Publisher). From the Broadway musical *Ain't Misbehavin'*.

G.L.

Boston, Massachusetts
September, 1979

PART ONE
1864–1907

The hour-glass figure of Lillian Russell in *Pepita*.

I. Before The Black Crook

THE POPULAR musical stage in the United States reached major dimensions for the first time on the evening of September 12, 1866, when the curtain of Niblo's Garden, on the corner of Broadway and Prince Street in New York, rose on the opening performance of *The Black Crook*. Not that *The Black Crook* was, as has frequently been claimed, the "first musical comedy"; a far cry from George and Ira Gershwin or Richard Rodgers and Lorenz Hart, it was a splashy combination of French Romantic ballet and German Romantic melodrama, decidedly more retrospective than forward-looking in its style and materials. But on the evening of its première a genuinely metropolitan audience attended and applauded a costly musical spectacle produced at home, presented in the English language, and designed to appeal to sophisticated tastes. *The Black Crook* was the first major triumph of Broadway over the monopoly of Europe on the one hand, and the Bowery on the other. It attracted the carriage-trade audience that customarily supported Italian opera, French opéra-bouffe, and the serious spoken drama. Yet it also lured from their usual haunts the devotees of fleshly diversion who had previously sought their theatrical pleasures in the lower-caste theatres of the Bowery.

Before the advent of *The Black Crook*, popular musical entertainment was varied and copious in the New York theatres, but the modest scale on which it was conceived precluded the possibility that any attraction would attain the "hit" status of *The Black Crook*, which rolled up a total of 474 performances in its initial engagement at Niblo's Garden. Extravaganza, pantomime, variety, and the minstrel show (in descending order of pretentiousness and production cost) were the ruling types of entertainment. Each of these—the minstrel show perhaps least—ultimately contributed its share to the developing form we now call musical comedy, and each provided anticipations of materials and devices still to be found in such mid-twentieth-century pieces as *Oklahoma!* and *South Pacific*.

The minstrel show, the homeliest form of mid-nineteenth-century musical diversion, is often assumed to be more or less ageless. It was not until 1841, in point of fact, that New York was offered for the first time an entertainment cast in what later came to be considered the classic form of minstrelsy. From this time onward, the minstrel show enjoyed a life-span of about twenty-five years before fading from the New York scene, outmoded by such white-face variety shows as those presented by Tony Pastor in his Music Hall after 1864, and by the elaborate productions that followed on the heels of *The Black Crook*. On the road, minstrelsy retained its audience until well into the twentieth century, particularly in towns too small to merit regular visits from more pretentious troupes, though even New York continued to receive occasional visits from such groups as Lew Dockstader's Minstrels. Only the celluloid product of Hollywood was finally powerful enough to rout the minstrel show from its last naïve strongholds.

The bigger companies, such as Bryant's Minstrels and the San Francisco Minstrels, provided their customers with a generous assortment of amusements. A classic, if perhaps unusually lavish, bill of Bryant's Minstrels in 1857—the high noon of minstrelsy in New York—divided the performance into three clearly defined parts. The first part employed the characteristic minstrel lineup, with its interlocutor and end men, its tissue of gags and topical quips. In the second portion, described as "terpsichorean divertissement," the members of the company offered an "Ethiopian Fling, à la Polka"; a "Conga Cola Dance"; a cinquetemps; and a local-color production number, "Essence of Old Virginny, Unequalled Plantation Dance." Vocal solos and duets, and, at one point, a "burlesque violin duet" by the Mullenhowen brothers (of which, unhappily, no description survives) were interlarded among the "terpsichorean" items.

The final section (or act, as we should call it now) was called "Plantation Holiday Sports." Starting placidly with a banjo song and a "Southern Scene," the entertainment proceeded in a crescendo of excitement through a comic skit called "Three Hunters, The Challenge Dance," a spectacle, "On the Levee" (glorified beyond the bounds of mere local color by the introduction of a trained elephant), and a "Burlesque Circus," to a final "Terrific Horse Combat," designed to leave the audience breathless at the final curtain. That showmanship took precedence over geographic and ethnologic literalism is indicated not only by the presence of the elephant on the levee but also by the fact that popular dances of the time—quadrilles, galops, and jigs—shared equally with Negro dances in the "Southern Scene."

Though variety—which we now call vaudeville—ultimately sounded the doom of minstrelsy, it was still under a cloud in 1857 when Bryant's Minstrels appealed to the family audience with the items detailed above. At that time, variety bills were almost always presented in saloons to which no reputable gentleman could take a lady—or even, if he was really careful, himself. The irresistible allurement of these resorts, which dotted the Bowery and the neighboring streets, was not the mediocre assortment of song-and-dance acts the managements saw fit to offer. It was, instead, the young, pretty, and open-minded "waiter-girls," available in an inexhaustible supply, and advertised in aphrodisiac fashion in the daily papers. Now and again the police descended upon the variety saloons, and the waiter-girls were temporarily withdrawn from circulation. These reforms never lasted long, however; if his saloon was closed by the law, a manager usually found it a simple matter to reopen in a nearby location.

During the heyday of the waiter-girls, a few managers tried, with varying degrees of success, to present variety shows bereft of this blandishment. The shrewdest of these operaters was Tony Pastor, whose unwillingness to engage in the off-color aspect of the business was counterbalanced by an unusual gift for picking talent. He won an increasingly loyal patronage from those who approved his love of decency, and in 1864 opened his handsome new Music Hall, which remained for many years a popular rendezvous of the best family trade. The Music Hall soon became a celebrated showcase for promising talent. In the 1870s and 1880s, many graduates of Tony Pastor's—among whom the most famous was Lillian Russell—were numbered among the leading performers of the musical stage.

Against the counterclaims of variety and minstrelsy, of P. T. Barnum's circuses and Swedish prima donnas, of ballet and acrobatics, and of Italian grand opera and French opéra-bouffe, the art of pantomime—with characters dating back to Italian *commedia dell' arte* of the sixteenth century—maintained a steady following in the United States through the first three quarters of the nineteenth century. In the pre-*Black Crook* period no pantomime ever occupied an entire evening by itself; it normally shared a bill with two short, nonmusical pieces, either melodramas or farces. Only toward the end of its history, in the late 1860s and the 1870s, did pantomime expand into a full-length entertainment, encouraged by the example already set by the extravaganzas and burlesques of the time.

The basic procedure of every pantomime was essentially the same. The central participants were introduced at the outset, and very soon afterward—frequently at the instigation of a fairy's wand—were "transformed" into stock *commedia dell' arte* characters (Harlequin, Columbine, Clown, Pantaloon, Dandy), wearing the costumes and masks appropriate to their traditional functions. These conventionalized figures did not, however, constitute the entire cast of the play. Additional actors took part, as the plot might require, wearing realistic costumes and disdaining to employ the stylized manners of the pantomime performers. The representatives of the harlequinade acted entirely in dumb show, making their meaning clear by a simple and familiar language of gesture. The others were allowed to speak. Even the pantomime characters frequently regained their voices in order to sing.

The plots of the pantomimes were ordinarliy drawn from Mother Goose rhymes and other widely familiar sources, or else they were evocations of the ever-popular and seemingly inexhaustible doings of the fairy world. Whatever the subject matter of their plots, the pantomimes were seldom very faithful to it, since the pieces were intended to serve primarily as vehicles for the exploitation of any special talents the players might be lucky enough to have—for comedy, song, character impersonation, or dance.

The more expensive pantomime productions also sought to impress their audiences by spectacular scenic effects, "tricks," and "deceptions," accomplished by means of the elaborate machinery that inspired awe in mid-century audiences. As early as 1847, for example, a "pantomimic fairy play," *The Golden Ax* (produced at the Boston Museum), rejoiced in a final climactic scene described as "Stars and Stripes, American Colors, *warranted not to run*, Bunker Hill and Buena Vista! Lots of Patriotism."

Though pantomime was as much a run-of-the-mill feature of the theatrical scene of the 1840s and 1850s as comic opera became in the 1880s and 1890s, it produced only one great practitioner in this country—George L. Fox. The career of Fox, which epitomizes the rise, triumph, and rapid decline of this specialized art, may be reserved for its proper place later on, in connection with *Humpty Dumpty*, the first musical attraction to surpass the run record of *The Black Crook*.

The term "extravaganza," applied in France (where the type originated) to the balletic evocations of fairyland also known as *"féeries,"* was from the beginning much more loosely applied in this country. The word was first appropriated here by the Ronzani troupe, a ballet company of French and Italian performers who arrived in New York in 1857, and included in their first bill an "extravaganza," *Novelty, with the Laying of the Atlantic Cable*. The Ronzanis themselves made very little stir, and soon went back to Europe. But the term "extravaganza," as a description of an elaborate and frequently topical spectacle, became a long-lived member of American stage vocabulary, finally disappearing in the 1920s, after the revue, the elaborately staged musical comedy, and the motion pictures had divided its province among them.

Long before the arrival of the Ronzanis, mixed bills which might well have been called extravaganzas were already the stock-in-trade of the immensely popular Ravel Family. Specialists in French ballet, pantomime, and acrobatics, the Ravels catered to as many tastes as possible, and being top-level performers retained their hold over the New York public for more than twenty years, from the mid-1840s to the late 1860s. Toe dancing, still a fairly new feature of ballet (it was introduced in France in the 1830s), appealed to those members of the Ravels' audience who prided themselves on their cultivation, while aerial and gymnastic acts satisfied those with heartier predilections.

The Ravels' bill on February 17, 1847—to take a random specimen—opened with a short farce without music, called *Thumping Legacy*. (The use of a short curtain raiser was a habit that died slowly, persisting until after 1870.) This was followed by "the first act of the beautiful ballet of *La Sylphide*," featuring Mme. Léon Jomelli, the Ravels' perennial *prima ballerina*. The Sylphide and her companions were reasonably faithful to the layout of the ballet as Taglioni originally danced it; for their version, like Taglioni's, contained a *grand pas de deux*, a Scotch quickstep, a Grand Tableau, and "The Flight of the Sylphide." At the close of the ballet, several of the Ravels performed the tightrope act which was the troupe's most renowned accomplishment. After a comic pantomime entitled "The Milliners, or The Hungarian Rendez-vous" (if only the scenario still existed for curious eyes a century later!), Young Marchetti demonstrated "feats of agility," and Mme. Jomelli threw herself into "La Cachuca." The performance ended with a tableau vivant, "Italian Brigands, or the Midnight Assault."

Although the musical bills of this time made frequent appeals to both patriotism and provincialism, none had attempted to deal with an indigenous American story until John Brougham offered his *Pocahontas* in New York in 1855. Filling only half an evening, *Pocahontas*, which its author (who played the role of John Smith) described as a burlesque, endeavored to tell a historic American story without falling back upon the devices of either pantomime or ballet. It was a sober-sided imitation, in rather bleak terms, of the contemporaneous French extravaganzas, without any of their spectacular features. *Pocahontas* created no sensation in New York, nor did Brougham's sequel a year later, *Hiawatha, or Ardent Spirits and Laughing Waters*. Audiences on the road took more kindly to *Pocahontas*, and Brougham was able to tour in it for a decade or so, meanwhile writing more plays, which had no discernible influence on the development of the American theatre.

The most ambitious extravaganza before *The Black Crook* was Thomas de Walden's *The Balloon Wedding*, given its première in New York on January 15, 1866, in a refitted minstrel hall known as Wood's Theatre. (Niblo's Garden, soon to house *The Black Crook*, was the only theatre at this time adequately equipped to take care of pretentious musical productions.) Almost the sole source of pleasure in *The Balloon Wedding* was the marvelous exhibition of the Six Hanlon Brothers, a group of acrobats whose skill dimmed the brilliance of the Ravels' tightrope exploits as they performed "summersets in the air from the shoulders of one of the brothers to the shoulders of another, at eight or ten feet away." The efforts of Frank Chanfrau, a popular comedian who had appeared with the Ronzanis in 1857, to amuse the audience with his impersonation of an eccentric Frenchman were futile, for De Walden's script, according to *The Spirit of the Times*, was "so bad that not even the imbecile stock companies with which Mr. George Wood, from two theatres, nightly insults the intelligence of New York, could make it any worse."

Lacking an accomplished corps de ballet, *The Balloon Wedding* sought to replace beauty and charm with vacuous novelty. It provided, *The Spirit of the Times* reported, "any quantity of young ladies in the most eccentric ballet that was ever seen or *heard*, for this ballet *sing* as well as *dance*, and are perpetually saying or singing, 'tra, la, la, la' on the slightest provocation.

When anybody comes on the stage, they 'tra-la-la-la' him on—when he makes his exit, they 'tra-la-la-la' him off—they witness their lovers locked up, and remark 'tra-la-la-la'—they themselves are taken in arrest by blue-coated Policemen, and instead of entering a protest in the usual emphatic English, they merely remove their handkerchiefs from their mouths, and mention 'tra-la-la-la'—one faints away and falls down to it—and others whisper 'tra-la-la-la' and she 'comes to'—and somebody slaps somebody's face to the pleasant chorus of 'tra,' etc.—somebody steps on somebody's toes, and the threats of vengeance are drowned in the howls of 'tra,' etc."

At the end of its first week, *The Balloon Wedding* was enriched by a scene showing a "mysterious fairy illuminated fountain," which the critic of the same periodical thought "by all odds the best lively stage effect I have seen." But this spectacular addition did not save the show, and the girls tra-la'd their way into oblivion at the end of a fortnight. We may write this costly failure off as a symptom of the growing pains of the American musical stage, and as a preamble to the discovery of the species later known as the chorus girl. Its demise was not mourned; for only eight months later *The Black Crook* came along to inaugurate a new era.

II. The Black Crook

THE MEMBERS of the audience at the première of *The Black Crook* arrived at Niblo's Garden in time for a 7:45 curtain. They remained enthralled until 1:15, when the final curtain came down after the stupendous transformation scene that was the crown of the production. In these five and a half historic hours, they saw the most expert and the best routined dancing, by a ballet of more than a hundred girls, yet offered on this side of the Atlantic. They marveled at stage spectacles more elaborate and magnificent than any American producer had ever before devised. And the baldheads and Fifth Avenue fops in the front rows saw legs—beautiful legs, over a hundred pairs of them. To be sure, earlier entertainments—particularly the French ballets, with their brief costumes—had confirmed the suspicion that the female leg existed. But there had never been anything quite as revelatory as *The Black Crook*. In addition to five and a half hours of white tarlatan, the new piece threw in for good measure in the second act a *pas de démons*, in which four girls—given the pretext of a diabolical incantation—advanced to the front of the stage, wearing tights, without a vestige of anything remotely resembling a skirt.

This unprecedented blend of art and bodily allurement, this first of the great Broadway hits, came into being through one of the most curious accidents of American stage history. In the summer of 1866, Henry C. Jarrett (an aspiring young theatre manager) and Harry Palmer (a Wall Street broker who was willing to be Jarrett's backer) brought over a French ballet troupe, with the intention of presenting a Parisian success, the Romantic ballet *La Biche aux Bois,* in the Academy of Music. Before their production was ready to open, the Academy of Music burned down. Jarrett and Palmer were left with an expensive ballet company on their hands, and no theatre in which to present it.

Meanwhile, William Wheatley, the manager-producer of Niblo's Garden, the most fashionable New York home of large and spectacular theatrical attractions, had signed a contract with Charles M. Barras, an unknown author, for the production of his melodrama *The Black Crook.* In their extremity, Jarrett and Palmer proposed to Wheatley that they combine forces by adding the French ballet as an adornment to *The Black Crook,* whose original script did not envisage the use of music or dancers. Already harassed by doubts as to the merits of a melodrama he had purchased hastily, Wheatley readily agreed to the idea. Barras objected, saying that the French dancers would "ruin his beautiful play." But since he was on the verge of starvation, he was willing to be silenced by a down payment of $1,500 and a royalty contract. His silence proved to be golden; in subsequent years his income from royalties on *The Black Crook* enabled him to buy an elaborate country home near Cos Cob, Connecticut, where he lived most comfortably until the day he walked onto a New Haven Railroad trestle as a train approached from the opposite direction.

As soon as Barras had accepted his $1,500, Wheatley went to work. At a reported cost of $25,400—a staggering figure in 1866—he completely made over the stage of Niblo's Garden. Every board moved in grooves, and could be taken up, pushed down, or slid away. Any part of the stage, in other words, could be removed altogether. Trap doors could be introduced anywhere. The cellar below the stage was made so deep that entire scenes could be sunk out of sight by the use of relatively simple machinery.

Properties, scenery, costumes, and machinery Wheatley purchased in London, for a total of $3,000. (The bill for transporting the entire shipment, weighing 110 tons, across the ocean, was $500!) The newspapers estimated the aggregate production cost at sums ranging from $35,000 to $55,000. Inasmuch as this was the P.T. Barnum era of grandiose overstatement, the $35,000 estimate is certainly closer to the fact, since even this was a far larger amount than had been spent on any previous theatrical production.

After the opening of *The Black Crook,* the newspaper reviewers were rhapsodic over its novel enchantments, though some ventured to express lukewarm views about Barras' play. Outside the press, opinions were sharply divergent. Many were overcome by the beauty of the spectacle; but those of a moralistic turn of mind were offended by its frank enticements. It is difficult to say which group performed a greater service to the box office.

One clergyman, suspecting that *The Black Crook* constituted a threat to the virtue of his congregation, went to see it for himself, and reported back in the following fashion (quoted in a letter from Charles Burnham to the New York *Sun*, September 23, 1932):

". . . the immodest dress of the girls; the short skirts, undergarments of thin material allowing the form of the figure to be discernible; the flesh-colored tights, imitating nature so well that the illusion is complete; with the exceedingly short drawers, almost tight-fitting, extending very little below the hips; arms and neck apparently bare, and bodice so cut as to show off every inch and outline of the body above the waist. The attitudes were exceedingly indelicate—*ladies* dancing so as to make their undergarments spring up, exposing the figure beneath from the waist to the toe, except for such coverings as we have described."

This description, if it was widely circulated, must have been a source of incalculable satisfaction to Wheatley and his partners. More helpful still was the vigorous opposition of the New York *Tribune*. That newspaper had recently engaged in an altercation with P.T. Barnum, who not only withdrew all his advertising from the *Tribune* but persuaded other managers, Wheatley among them, to follow his example. Perhaps in retribution, the *Tribune* sometimes printed harsh attacks upon the unadvertised plays. When the paper singled out *The Black Crook* for special disapproval, the production became a *cause célèbre*, and nobody could hold his own in conversation unless he had seen it.

Barras' play, so quickly lost in the shuffle of two hundred female legs, had been written in Cincinnati in 1857. The author at that time was hot with the inspiration enkindled by a performance of Weber's *Der Freischütz*, given by a touring English opera company. Seeking to supply the company with the libretto for a new opera, he appropriated from *Der Freischütz* as much as he possibly could, and incorporated it into the text called *The Black Crook*. The opera company did not buy it. Nine years later, however, Wheatley did, though his lack of judgment staggers the imagination.

In justice to Barras, it must be admitted that *Der Freischütz* was by no means the only source of his script. His borrowing was more extensive than this. Goethe's *Faust* prefigured the basic situation of the plot, and a literary detective would have no trouble in spotting *Undine*, *The Naiad Queen*, *The Swiss Cottage*, and other pieces familiar to readers, playgoers, and balleto-manes of the period.

The *Freischütz* element was immediately apparent in the preliminary situation of the plot. Hertzog, the Black Crook, had made a compact with the Devil, agreeing to win over to the Devil's cause one human soul for each year of life vouchsafed to him. The account must be settled annually, just before midnight on New Year's Eve. Rudolph, the hero of the story, was a painter; Amina, the heroine, a rural beauty. A certain Count Wolfenstein used his feudal authority to take Amina captive and lock Rudolph in a dungeon. Planning to make Rudolph his victim for the year, Hertzog—by virtue of magical powers given him by the Devil—freed Rudolph from prison and persuaded him to go in search of the treasure said to be in a cave of gold in the forest. On the way, Rudolph saved the life of a dove, who was pursued by a serpent. The dove turned out to be the fairy queen Stalacta, who promptly exposed Hertzog's trickery. Count Wolfenstein was appropriately killed; Rudolph married Amina; and the Black Crook, like Kaspar in *Der Freischütz,* was carried off to hell by the Devil.

However questionable its originality and dramaturgical skill, the book of *The Black Crook* allowed ample room for spectacle and balletic display. Nearly everyone felt that the first act contained too much alleged drama and too little else. With the "Grand Ballet of the Gems" at the opening of the second act, however, the excitement began. Later in the act, "hurricanes of gauze" blew through the Harz Mountains, and "cascading girls poured down the wild glens." At the end of the act, in an eerie locale obviously suggested by the Wolf's Glen in *Der Freischütz,* an elaborate ritual of incantation came to a climax in the startling *pas de démons.*

Most breathtaking of all was the transformation scene at the close of the play. "One by one, curtains of mist ascend and drift away," wrote a nameless reporter. "Silver couches, on which the fairies loll in negligent grace, ascend and descend amid a silver rain. From the clouds drop gilded chariots and the white forms of angels. It is a very beautiful pageant."

As the run of *The Black Crook* progressed, new features were added. Audiences in the summer of 1867 saw a "Baby Ballet," in which more than a hundred children, ranging in height from twenty-five to forty-five inches, executed military evolutions, led by the five-year-old nephew of a member of the Ravel family. In September, a dazzling new ballroom scene was introduced, with a grand carnival and masquerade.

The Black Crook is remembered today for its total effect, rather than for the individual performers who appeared in it. But in 1866, Marie Bonfanti, the fifteen-year-old ballerina who danced the role of Queen Stalacta, and her colleagues of similar age, Riga Sangalli and Betty Rigl, stimulated an adulation comparable to that of theatregoers nearly seventy years later for Colonel Wassily de Basil's three "baby ballerinas" of the Ballet Russe de Monte Carlo—Tamara Toumanova, Irina Baronova, and Tatiana Riabouchinska.

In its first engagement, *The Black Crook* achieved a run of 474 performances in sixteen months, and grossed more than a million dollars. For more than twenty-five years afterward, it was nearly always being presented somewhere—either in New York or on the road (where, as late as 1906, it could still be discovered, no doubt in shrunken form, in so remote a Western outpost as Provo, Utah). In the entire nineteenth century, only *Uncle Tom's Cabin, Rip Van Winkle* (neither of which was a musical attraction), and Edward E. Rice's burlesque *Evangeline* equaled or surpassed its widespread and long-continued popularity. *The Black Crook* was revived in New York eight times in the nineteenth century—in 1868, 1871, 1873, 1879, 1881, 1884, 1889, and 1892. Christopher Morley and Cleon Throckmorton brought it back to life in 1929 in Hoboken, New Jersey, with Agnes de Mille as Queen Stalacta.

The successive revivals increasingly replaced the formal French ballets with popular dancing and topical variety entertainment. In the 1892 production, vaudeville dancing completely obliterated the bits of ballet that had remained until then. But a quartet of French music-hall dancers—La Sirène, Serpentine, Eglantine, and Dynamite—created a furore with a so-called quadrille, in which they combined "serpentine" dancing with high kicking. A notable feature of their performance was the split, a contortion that had never before been demonstrated on the polite stage. Once again, the "chappies" and baldheads were delighted, and the moral custodians were displeased. Describing the specialty dancers as "four coarse and ugly French women of mature years," one critic maintained that "their exploits exceeded in shamelessness anything before brought over from the French capital for display in a respectable theatre."

If Wheatley, Jarrett, and Palmer had been able to foresee the flexibility with which *The Black Crook* could be modified to fit changing tastes and fashions, they might have reconsidered their decision to close it early in 1868. But like so many successful producers in later years, they were obsessed by the desire to present a sequel. Accordingly, on January 17, 1868, *The Black Crook* relinquished Niblo's Garden to *The White Fawn*.

Though its stupid book was attributed to James Mortimer, *The White Fawn* was basically an attempt to derive a second *Black Crook* from *La Biche aux Bois*, the Parisian ballet Jarrett and Palmer had expected to give at the Academy of Music in 1866 when they first imported their French ballet troupe. The plot revolved about a princess who was changed into a white fawn; everything was made right at the end in the Realms of the Dragon Fly.

The première was even more of a drain upon the patience of the audience than the opening of *The Black Crook*. It lasted six hours, and even then the final transformation scene, requiring eighty carpenters and twenty gasmen, was too balky to be attempted on the first night. There were the expected ballets and spectacles, the most admired of which was an enchanted lake scene, featuring Signor Costa's "Firefly Ballet." But in spite of these allurements and the producers' attempt to make it an even more unqualified apotheosis of the female leg than *The Black Crook*, *The White Fawn* suffered the fate of most sequels and perished, on July 11.

To call *The Black Crook* the first example of the theatrical genus we now call musical comedy is not only incorrect; it fails to suggest any useful assessment of the place of Jarrett and Palmer's extravaganza in the history of the popular musical theatre. It was, to be sure, the first American musical entertainment to achieve the long-run prosperity upon which producers subsequently learned to pin their hopes. But in its first form it contained almost none of the vernacular attributes of book, lyrics, music, and dancing which distinguish musical comedy, as a type, from ballet and spectacular extravaganza. True, it thrust two hundred legs upon the gaze of the beholder. But the unabashed leg is by no means an indispensable feature of musical comedy, since dozens of musical comedies have enjoyed great success without revealing more than an occasional ankle or part of a calf; and, on the other hand, the undraped leg is not, and never has been, the sole property of musical comedy—as witness the can-cans in Offenbach's opéra-bouffes, or the heroines in nautical or military tights in some of the most high-minded comic operas of the 1880s.

Moreover, it is too soon to be talking about musical comedy in 1866. Neither the term nor the concept it represents existed as yet. We first encounter the term, loosely used to describe a piece involving both music and comedy, in connection with the burlesque *Evangeline*, which was produced in 1874. Later on, it was used in offhand fashion in connection with musical farce-comedies, farces with occasional interpolated songs, and comic operas. Not until the middle 1890s did a relatively standardized form begin to emerge, to which the name of musical comedy was given for the sake of distinguishing it from the more traditional and less vernacular productions known as comic opera and operetta.

Even though it discovered a new audience and hinted at a new world of musical entertainment, *The Black Crook* was really the swan song of early nineteenth-century Romanticism. Half German melodrama and half French ballet-extravaganza-*féerie*, both its content and its manner of presentation continued the fashions and traditions of European stagecraft of the 1840s and 1850s. Its subject matter was out of style before it was produced. Its only aspects of modernity and only lessons for productions that followed resided in its expert command of the machinery of illusion and uncommonly successful address to its audience. The failure of *The White Fawn*, which employed exactly the formulas of *The Black Crook* with the added advantage of previous experience, was to be expected, for the venerable and archaic materials in which Jarrett and Palmer traded deserved no further currency. Within the next few years Lydia Thompson, arriving from the London music halls, was able to offer a better leg show; the Kiralfy brothers devised even more breathtaking spectacles; and Edward E. Rice, with *Evangeline*, introduced homespun humor and plot elements that made *The Black Crook* and *La Biche aux Bois* seem very remote, very foreign, and very old-fashioned.

III. The Death of Pantomine

HUMPTY DUMPTY, which opened at the Olympic Theatre in New York on March 10, 1868, and ran for 483 performances—nine more than *The Black Crook*—in its initial engagement, signalized both the triumph and the farewell of traditional pantomime in the United States. Pantomime never became a deeply rooted theatrical institution in this country, as it did in England, where it is still in evidence, to the delight of British children during the Christmas holidays. In England an increased use of words soon brought pantomime near to the character of burlesque and extravaganza, the types that superseded it in the United States. After Edward E. Rice's trail-blazing production of *Evangeline* in 1874, American burlesque retained possession of practically all the features of pantomime except the dumb show and the stylized harlequinade. As a consequence, pantomime had no further *raison d'être*, except as a vehicle for the talents of those who performed in it.

George L. Fox, the producer and star of *Humpty Dumpty*, was the only pantomime performer with enough box-office power to keep the ancient art alive against the fresher and more informal appeal of burlesque. After his retirement, American pantomime died swiftly. In retrospect, indeed, the main history of American pantomime appears to have been contained in the history of Fox's career. One of the most gifted performers in the annals of our stage, Fox was frequently described in his own time as the greatest pantomime clown since Grimaldi. His fame was kept alive after his death by a wooden effigy in front of a drugstore in New Haven; the statue might be there still if an ebullient group of Harvard undergraduates, elated by the victory of their crew over Yale's, had not taken it away one evening in 1911.

Born in Boston in 1825, Fox began his professional career as an actor in one of the early *Uncle Tom's Cabin* companies. In 1850, he turned to comedy, calling himself Lafayette Fox at that time and taking part in various short burlesques, extravaganzas, and pantomimes—among them *The Frisky Cobbler* and *The Golden Ax*, in the latter of which he achieved a signal success in the character role of Farmer Gubbins.

Though he continued to act in various métiers, he soon decided that pantomime was his most promising field. Choosing to adopt the artistic style of the French performers rather than the crude, slapstick methods of the Italian school, Fox modeled his technique upon that of the Ravel family, whose potpourris of pantomime and other attractions were already in vogue in New York as Fox was beginning his pantomimic career.

As must be the case with every great clown, Fox concealed touching traits of human sympathy and understanding beneath his grotesque, painted exterior. The extraordinary control of his facial muscles made the technique of mugging famous; it would be interesting to know how much of the standard practices of today's and yesterday's comics might be traced back in a direct genealogical line to devices originated by Fox. For actually it was his mugging, far more than his command of the traditional gesture language and the roughhouse humor universally used by pantomime clowns, that accounted for his extraordinary popularity. "He was not content to please," one critic wrote, "merely by being knocked down numerous times and jumping over tables and through windows. His muteness and passivity were infinitely more ludicrous than the bustling antics of other clowns, as also was his affectation of ignorant simplicity and credulous innocence."

Fox grew rapidly in reputation and resources. In 1858, he became one of the managers of the Bowery Theatre, where he offered a long list of short pantomimes, in mixed bills with farces and melodramas. In 1862, his run of 150 consecutive performances in *Jack and the Beanstalk* established a New York record for a single performer.

Despite the warnings of friends who felt that he would be unable to compete with the established Ravel Family (who were not only masters of pantomime, but were also able to provide ballet and circus attractions), Fox ventured to move uptown from the Bowery to Broadway in 1866. These prophets of doom were mistaken, however, for after a few less epoch-making preliminary offerings, *Humpty Dumpty* brought Fox the supreme success of his career, outdrawing and outplaying anything the Ravels had ever presented, and shattering all run records before its time.

Humpty Dumpty was conceived as a show for the common people, even for lowbrows; it was not intended to serve as a diversion for the baldheads, fops, and aesthetes who sang the praises of *The Black Crook*. Without displaying any legs, it could stand competition with the contemporaneous *White Fawn* and Lydia Thompson's newly arrived company of bleached British blondes, and outdo them in longevity and box-office intake; for it appealed to a homelier, and therefore a larger, audience. For the première of *Humpty Dumpty*, Fox brought uptown a great many Bowery vulgarities he soon sloughed off, as he began to understand the demands of even the lowbrow uptown audience for proprieties and niceties that would have been wasted on Bowery patrons.

Humpty Dumpty was weakest in the elements in which *The White Fawn* was strongest. The ballets were feeble; Mlle. Rita Sangalli, a graduate of *The Black Crook*, "tried to be a grand ballet in herself," and did not repeat the impression she had made in the handsomer surroundings of the earlier piece. The spectacular effects in *Humpty Dumpty* and the inevitable final transformation scene, while conceived in broad and generous terms, were on the whole artistically unsatisfactory. When all was said and done, the pantomime was carried by the personality of Fox and by the simple, straightforward appeal of its naïve materials.

The title of *Humpty Dumpty* was as good as meaningless, for the pantomime had no real plot, and bore little discernible relationship to the Mother Goose rhyme. As with every other pantomime, the characters were introduced at the beginning, and marked time until the expected Fairy Queen came along to transform them. Goody Two-Shoes became Columbine; Old One-Two became Pantaloon; Tommy Tucker became Harlequin; Humpty Dumpty became Clown. For the rest of the evening, the dumb show of these pantomime folk was woven into an elaborate variety and spectacle show. A troupe of roller skaters (the first important stage appearance of skaters) shared the footlights with circus acts, singers who presented songs of the concert-saloon and minstrel-hall variety, and a "Baby Ballet," headed by the five-year-old niece of Gabriel Ravel. (The Ravel Family seemed to have on hand an inexhaustible supply of tiny relatives, ready and willing to appear in the productions of their rivals.) There were spectacle scenes depicting the Valley of Fertility; a subterranean grotto; a marketplace in Naples ("La Tarantella by full corps"); the Olympic Theatre by night; a skating pond by moonlight ("Polish National Dance"); the Dell of Ferns; and the Retreat of the Silver Sprites. The Neapolitan marketplace scene which came at the end of Act I culminated in a "Celebrated Trick Steamboat and Explosion." Great prominence was given in the program to the names of the two scene designers, Minard Lewis and J.A. Johnson; their names appeared after the titles of each scene, much as composers' names are printed opposite the titles of their works in contemporary musical programs. The music of *Humpty Dumpty* remained as negligible an element as it had been in *The Black Crook*, though in this instance a composer—A. Reiff, Jr.—was at least mentioned, though he apparently collected most, if not all, of his score from outside sources.

Subsequent revivals of *Humpty Dumpty* did not change the essential nature of the piece, though they sought to make it bigger and more expensive. The 1871 version was given in three acts instead of the original two, with the middle act devoted to a great array of variety and circus acts. Among the new additions were the "Tyrolean eccentricities" of the Martens Family; Signor Casselli in a balancing feat on wire; the Zig-Zags, grotesque comedians; Young Adonis, aged four and one-half, and Little Venus, aged two and one-half, riding bicycles; a "Cat Duett" by two of the Martens Family, which evoked sympathetic meows from the gallery; and a sensational Hungarian divertissement by the Kiralfy Brothers.

The 1871 revival of *Humpty Dumpty* was preceded by a short-lived sequel, *Hickory Dickory Dock*, mention of which is made only to add one more datum to the gloomy history of sequels. But the setback was a minor one for Fox, who was able to send *Humpty Dumpty* companies on the road without his personal services as Humpty, and to sell the English rights to the "merry Vokes Family."

In the course of a second return engagement at Booth's Theatre, New York, in 1873, Fox began to behave peculiarly. One day he abruptly started to chase his colleagues about the stage; he then leapt from the stage to a stage box and pummeled a decorous lady on the head with a loaf of property bread. As suddenly as he had left it, he returned to the stage, went back into his clown's character, and began mugging for dear life. This time he managed to carry the situation off, but the symptoms rapidly became worse. When he developed a fixation upon the notion of having a statue of himself erected in Union Square, his associates realized that the time had come when he must be taken to an institution. He survived only a few months longer.

Humpty Dumpty's momentum kept it going on the road for a few years, with Tony Denier, the Clown of the original road company, as its mainstay. The final revival in New York in 1880 was a confession of inadequacy, however. In order to bolster up a weak attraction, the management supplied the pantomime with two Harlequins, two Columbines, two Clowns, and two Pantaloons. There proved to be no safety in numbers, however, for the show was kept from a prompt closing chiefly by a novelty that was wholly irrelevant to its native character—the Spanish Students, who sang, danced, and played in an instrumental ensemble consisting of mandolins, guitars, and a solo violin. But there was no ducking the fact: Pantomime had died with George L. Fox. By 1880, it was already a specter from the grave, and its best assets had been bequeathed to burlesque, extravaganza, and the modest farce-comedies of Nate Salsbury's Troubadours.

IV. The Bleached Blondes

IT SEEMS RATHER to be desired that the points of a fine woman should be somewhat better known and more thought of than they have been." This measured opinion was expressed by a noted editor of Shakespeare's plays, Richard Grant White, in comment upon Lydia Thompson and her company of British blondes, who arrived from London to make their first American appearance in the burlesque *Ixion, or The Man at the Wheel*, at Wood's Museum in New York on September 21, 1868. Possibly White might have tempered his speech if he had been able to look into the future, for it was Lydia Thompson who gave burlesque the initial momentum in its seventy-year journey toward Minsky's and legal obliteration.

Before Lydia burst upon the American consciousness, with her "troupe of British blondes that put a golden hirsute girdle around the earth," burlesque had been a naïve diversion. It consisted of brief travesties of current plays, novels, and fashions, confined to a secondary position in mixed bills chiefly devoted to one- or two-act farces, comedies, and melodramas.

In *Ixion*, originally devised a year or so earlier for her more sophisiticated British admirers, Lydia found ways and means of expanding a burlesque of a familiar story into a diversified and racy entertainment that filled the better part of an evening. (*Ixion* was preceded by the farcical half-hour curtain raiser that was customary in those days, even in more serious branches of the theatre. In many of her subsequent bills, however, she followed the precedent of *The Black Crook* and devoted the evening to a single full-length piece.) The title of *Ixion*, suggesting cultivated subject matter of classical origin, imparted an air of spurious elegance to her first American offering. In the actual performance, however, the plot was the least of her worries. Neither Lydia nor her blondes (let it be recorded that two of the young ladies were brunettes, having refrained from the use of peroxide, which derived an early notoriety as a bleaching agent from the Thompson troupe) could act, nor did they pretend to. They did their duty by the incessant, unrelieved rhymed couplets that constituted the script, and they mouthed faithfully the laborious puns that passed for humor. No, it was neither the dramatic nor the literary qualities of *Ixion* that brought all of fun-loving New York to Wood's Museum. A few excerpts from the punning list of characters will serve as corroborative evidence:

"IXION (King of Thessaly)—but though a king with the prefix of an x, it does not alphabetically follow that he has a wise head on his shoulders.
"JUNO—fond of peacocks that sing pea-hens of joy while drawing her car.
"MARS—commander-in-chief, as Ma's usually are.
"THE NINE MUSES, including POLLY HYMNIA.
"Those Thessalians who would be these aliens if they weren't natives; dreadful Democrats, members of several secret societies who demand the right of free speaking in a state of free-dumb.
"Crowd of Red Republicans, unread Republicans, avengers, scavengers, Greeks, sneaks, and female furies."

It was the constant, unfettered romping of the girls, the frequent topical references to interests and foibles of the day, and, above all else, the extensive display of the female form that won the British blondes their loyal and considerable following. Lydia was the real discoverer of the tired businessman. She elevated to the Broadway level the well-tried saloon technique of passing intimate remarks to the baldheads in the first row. Nor did she and the girls neglect to establish a rapport with the wealthy young fops in the stalls, who sat "ogling with an amorous idiocy" that even the fairy coryphées of *The Black Crook*, in their more remote loveliness, had not induced. Oblivious of the demands of art for art's sake, *Ixion* kept its spectators happy with a kaleidoscopic variety of opéra-bouffe songs, topical "hits" (as gags were called), can-cans, snippets of ballet, specialty dances, spectacles, and transformation scenes. If the ballerinas failed to dim memories of the corps de ballet in *The Black Crook,* and if the spectacles and transformation scenes were neither lavish nor particularly skillful in their mechanical handling, nobody cared much. There was too much else to see.

To display their legs, Lydia Thompson and her girls resorted to a subterfuge that was both less indirect than the *pas de démons* in *The Black Crook* and much more wholehearted, since it lasted throughout the entire evening. Lydia merely put on male attire and played the title role of Ixion, and most of the other girls followed her example in their dress. Patently, no deception was intended, for the ideal mid-century feminine figure—with its transcendent bust and columnar calves and thighs—could scarcely conceal its gender. This device was by no means Lydia's invention, having long been a favored feature of burlesque when she first adopted it; but she gave it a new meaning, which was to influence stage fashions (in the more sedate comic opera as well as in burlesque) for forty years to come. This meaning became explicit when the girls sang a song with the refrain "How's that for high!" and all gave a high kick.

With the young women preempting the juvenile male parts, Lydia's company required little in the way of masculine support. But the seedy male comic, who in later burlesques was to adopt the red nose of the pantomime clown, had his place in *Ixion* in the form of a gawky rustic in blue overalls, whose presence in the celestial regions with such elevated characters as Juno and Jupiter would have been difficult to explain if Lydia had taken the plot more seriously.

At first Lydia was received with undivided approbation. E. F. House, the theatre critic of *The Spirit of the Times,* wrote in ecstasy that "jig-dancing is etherealized by her bewitching steps, and comic songs are sublimated by her modesty of manner and archness of expression." But a storm of public indignation soon began to gather, as the performance began to be the talk of the town. House himself, for reasons that are no longer discernible, jumped onto the moral bandwagon, and shortly afterward narrowly averted a physical attack by Lydia's manager, who called him a liar because he had impugned the propriety of the blonde charmer's deportment. House's paper did not abandon the battle, but continued, in its editorial columns, to take an agitated view of the British blondes' effect upon public morals:

"There are sad proofs enough that these gilded larvae breed to a vocation, and many a girl who months ago was modestly content with plain attire and an honest name now basks her nude limbs in the hot gaze of an abandoned crowd, or streams like a yellow meteor along the pavé, luring weak followers to her new ambition."

It was in Chicago, however, that the most flamboyant episode of Lydia Thompson's career took place, on the occasion of her first visit to that plain-speaking city, early in 1870. Intent upon a crusade, Wilbur S. Story, the editor of the Chicago *Times*, caused his paper to roar incessantly against the "immorality" on display at Crosby's Opera House. Finally Lydia got tired of his daily abuse. As he left his office one afternoon, she waylaid him on the sidewalk of Wabash Avenue, and administered a horsewhipping. At the theatre that evening she retaliated further by appending outrageous verses employing his full name to one of her songs, "If I Ever Ceased to Love." Story brought Lydia to court, where she was judged guilty and fined $100—a trifling price indeed for the national publicity the escapade brought her.

Wood's Museum, in which Lydia began her New York career, was a second-class house. Having established her reputation, she soon moved—on February 1, 1869—to the more fashionable and more capacious Niblo's Garden, which had housed both *The Black Crook* and its sequel, *The White Fawn*. Here she presented a new burlesque entitled *The Forty Thieves*, whose "dialogue evidenced glancing acquaintance with the higher author-ities—Mother Goose, Arabian Nights, Police Reports, Shakespeare, Dumas, and the La Crosse Democrat." This ran until May 28, when she embarked, "abundantly supplied with local allusions for openings in the provinces," on the tour that ultimately took her to the home city of Wilbur S. Story. At the close of her trial in Chicago, she returned to Niblo's Garden, on April 4, 1870, in *Pippin, or The King of the Gold Mines*. Her vogue proved to be relatively short-lived, however, and she soon returned to England. In 1891, she attempted an American comeback, but she looked pathetically middle-aged and her outmoded style appealed only to a few sentimentalists who had worshiped her in her heyday.

V. Evangeline and Edward E. Rice

UP TO NOW, the entrepreneurs of the American musical stage had concerned themselves chiefly with the attempt to turn Eurpean forms of entertainment into popular American currency. John Brougham's *Pocahontas*, as we have seen, was an endeavor to find an American parallel for the traditional French extravaganza, or *féerie*. *The Black Crook* was the resplendent finale of a long period of interest in French Romantic ballet and German Romantic melodrama. *Humpty Dumpty* was the dying triumph of the ancient harle-quinade. Lydia Thompson's burlesques clung to the classical references and stereotyped literary devices of old-fashioned English burlesque. Each of these entrants upon the American scene had something new to offer, it is true (legs, more often than not), but essentially each was the ending and summing-up of an older convention rather than the initiation of a fresh line of development.

With his production of *Evangeline* in 1874, Edward E. Rice created the first American musical show of a character so homespun that it could in no way be described adequately by reference to foreign fashions and procedures. *Evangeline* created a world of entertainment in which Rice continued to enjoy the utmost success with the public for more than twenty years. The format of his "American burlesque" was permissive rather than restrictive; he invented an informal manner of presentation that allowed burlesque to grow along with the tastes and fashions of the time, to develop new performers, and to take on new colorations.

A Bostonian by birth, Rice settled down in his middle twenties, after a brief fling at acting in a stock company, to what looked like a steady, promising desk job in the office of the Cunard Line. One night he went with his friend, J. Cheever Goodwin, a young Harvard graduate employed as a reporter on the Boston *Traveler,* to see a performance by Lydia Thompson and her high-kicking blondes.

Finding the evening "highly depressing because of the peculiar density of its British humor," Rice and Goodwin maintained that they could write a much better burlesque themselves, and immediately set out to do it. They seized upon Longfellow's *Evangeline* as a suitably familiar subject for an American travesty. Goodwin wrote the book and lyrics, and Rice composed the music. A natural musician, but not an educated one, Rice played the piano by ear, and wrote his score in "a kind of phonography which no one but he could decipher." As a result of his efforts, *Evangeline* became the first full-scale American stage production with an entirely original musical score. And it is not a bad score, as the printed edition testifies. One looks in vain for any national or local qualities in the musical idiom, to be sure; but Rice knew how to give life to a march and lilt to a waltz, and how to reduce the tune of a comic or topical song to a proper subservience to the words.

Since Rice and Goodwin had more enthusiasm than money, they were in no position to produce their show lavishly. They were able to persuade the management of Niblo's Garden to take it as a stopgap attraction for the midsummer doldrums, in July 1874. The production was economical—even cheap-looking—at every point. But it made an immediate hit, and when it was forced out of Niblo's Garden by other commitments for the house, Rice was able to obtain funds for a more sumptuous investiture for the Boston opening in the fall and an ultimate return to New York.

Since the initial booking at Niblo's Garden was a short one by foreordination, *Evangeline* could show no first-run record to rival those of *The Black Crook* and *Humpty Dumpty*. But by the time it had run its full course, *Evangeline* had remained alive for nearly thirty years, and was the only nineteenth-century musical production that rivaled, or perhaps surpassed,

The Black Crook in perennial, nationwide popularity. (It would be a hopeless task to try to gather definitive figures establishing the thirty-year grand totals of *Black Crook* and *Evangeline* performances; it is not likely that any twentieth-century musical attraction—even *Blossom Time*—has achieved a comparable record.)

Although *Evangeline* may properly be classified as a burlesque (in the pre-Minsky sense of a travesty on a familiar story, with the hero's part played by the leading lady in tights), Rice at first called it an "American opéra-bouffe," and later an "American extravaganza." His evasion of the accurate generic description was understandable, for he intended the piece as a diversion for the entire family, not merely for the roués, sophisticates, and black sheep who constituted an important portion of Lydia Thompson's audience. He dropped the term "opéra-bouffe" as soon as he realized that French comic opera, despite its support by many New Yorkers of means and advanced tastes, was discountenanced by thousands of simple, respectable people because of its devotion to double entendre and off-color situations. He sought, according to his own pronouncement when he became sole owner and producer of the show after its initial engagement at Niblo's Garden, "to foster a taste for musical comedy relieved of the characteristic and objectionable features of opéra-bouffe." (This, incidentally, appears to be the first incidence of the term "musical comedy" in connection with a popular piece on the American stage.)

Despite their contempt for Lydia Thompson's attainments, Rice and Goodwin (the latter of whom seems to have played second fiddle to his dynamic partner from the beginning) did not hesitate to appropriate any of her devices that looked serviceable to the new context. Since no better justification could be imagined in the 1870s for revealing the full constructional details of the female leg, they retained the artifice of putting the prima donna in tights and assigning the leading male role of Gabriel to her. They also managed to find reasons to clothe a good many of the other girls in similar fashion, and they introduced a corresponding transvestite character, a male comic who impersonated a maiden lady. George K. Fortesque, who created the role of "the ponderous Catherine," made this part his special property almost continuously from 1874 to 1901—with occasional excursions into other female impersonations, such as a burlesque, in the late 1880s, of Fanny Davenport's sensational performance in Sardou's *Fedora*, entitled *Well-Fed Dora*.

Two touches of particular originality were regularly praised wherever *Evangeline* was seen. One of these was a silent personage—whose debased descendant we have seen in our own day in the blasé individual who sat at the edge of the proscenium in *Hellzapoppin*—known as the Lone Fisherman. He had little connection with the plot, and maintained a serio-comic, pseudo-philosophic isolation from the people and events of the play. This mystifying mute figure won so firm a hold upon the fancy of the American public that

James S. Maffitt, who created the part, was able—like Fortesque as Catherine—to round out an entire career playing very little else.

Another winning feature of *Evangeline* was likewise a conceit that still has the power to evoke laughter today. Inasmuch as Longfellow had awarded Evangeline a milk-white cow, Rice and Goodwin thought it a good idea to include the cow among the dramatis personae of their burlesque. Accordingly they dreamed up a trick heifer whose movements were negotiated by one man in the front legs and another in the hind legs. To the ungainly creature they allotted an eccentric dance, which proved to be not merely an instantaneous success but one of the unwithering attractions of the show throughout its whole life. With the passage of the years, indeed, the *Evangeline* heifer came to be one of the best-known celebrities of the musical stage. As late as 1896, the critic of the New York *Journal*, reporting upon one of the last metropolitan reappearances of the extravaganza, bracketed its girls and its heifer as comparable features, referring to its "perennial limbs and immutable cow." (The same weary first-nighter described the twenty-two-year-old piece as "that primal extravaganza belonging neither to life nor to drama.")

It is a bit tiresome to say it about each successive production, but truthfulness again requires the observation that the plot of *Evangeline* was the least of its attractions. Goodwin's book bore astoundingly little relation to Longfellow's poem, or, for that matter, to anything coherent at all. Africa and Arizona were locales of the action as well as Acadia, and nobody ever arrived in Louisiana. With padded legs, blacked eyelashes, and rouged cheeks, the girls engaged in "the pedal calisthenics which carried *Evangeline* like a centipede on its hundred legs," and carefully avoided giving offense to the family audience, which marveled at the sprouting of the whales, the vertiginous balloon trip to Arizona (shades of *The Balloon Wedding*), and, beyond all else, the sphinxlike demeanor of The Lone Fisherman, whom one reviewer so aptly called "an original and incomprehensible embodiment."

Dancing, as we expect to find it in a reputable musical production today, was decidedly a secondary interest in *Evangeline*. The piece was devoid of the familiar trappings of extravaganza—the Fairy Queen, the tarlatan costumes, the coryphées on their *pointes*. Except for the dance of the milk-white heifer, the primordial kickings and cavortings of the young ladies of the chorus, and a military drill by the entire cast to the music of the "Evangeline March" in the finale, evidences of choreographic planning were lacking entirely. Some of the principals, however, performed jigs and other popular routines in connection with their songs and ballads.

The structure of *Evangeline*, as opposed to its content, clearly betrayed dependence upon the usages of French opéra-bouffe and pre-Gilbert-and-Sullivan English comic opera, though the musical and literary craftsmanship was far more naïve than that of Audran or Offenbach and their librettists.

The piece consisted of a series of songs and ballads, varied by an occasional duet or trio or chorus, with a connective tissue of rhyming, punning nonsensicalities. Some impression of the quality of its literary humor is afforded by the description of the character of Evangeline as an early program gives it: *"Our heroine,* a creature of *impulse* and an *impetuous pet,* pursued through love's *impatient* prompting, by Gabriel, and with a view to edacious contingencies— by a whale. "

Some of the more thoughtful observers of theatrical phenomena found the success of *Evangeline* as puzzling as later generations of critics found those of *Abie's Irish Rose* and *Tobacco Road*. The author of an unsigned review in the New York *Dramatic Mirror* in 1880 exclaimed, when it fell to his lot to deal with one of the frequent return engagements of *Evangeline:* "The vitality of the extravaganza is something wonderful, considering the length of time [six years] it has been before the public. Some of the old, pointless puns and gags have been eradicated, only to be replaced by new puns and gags just as witless and just as inane as their predecessors. . . . When it is all over, the question arises, What is there in *Evangeline* that should ever have gained for it the amount of public favor it has enjoyed?"

Nobody undertook to answer the *Dramatic Mirror's* query. But *Evangeline* continued to prosper, and Rice sent a multiplicity of companies out on the road, billed sometimes as Rice's Evangeline Combination and sometimes as Rice's Surprise Party. The puns finally disappeared from the printed programs, but they never vanished from the script; their deletion would have been as unthinkable as the banishment of the heifer or the Lone Fisherman.

The most famous revival of *Evangeline* occurred in 1885, when Rice was at the height of his affluence, thanks to the epoch-making success of his new *Adonis*. With revisions in the text (made by John J. McNally, since Goodwin and Rice had parted company soon after the first days of *Evangeline)* and some new music composed by Rice, the refurbished war horse played 251 times in New York before setting forth on the road. Rice himself conducted the fiftieth performance; for the hundredth performance, Henry E. Dixey, who owed his stardom to Rice's management, came over from *Adonis* to join in the dance at the end of the first act. Seventeen-year-old Fay Templeton, who was to remain a favorite on the musical stage until her final appearance in Jerome Kern's *Roberta* in 1932, came up from touring the South to make her first Broadway appearance as Gabriel—in tights, and with a Lillian Russell hourglass figure. Her new song, "I Don't—Do You?", became the hit number of the show, for a time rivaling the popularity of Lillian Russell's contemporaneous specialty, "The Silver Line." A group of acrobats vied for favor with the heifer and the Lone Fisherman.

Evangeline was the one constant in Rice's life during all these years—his life insurance, so to speak; for whenever other enterprises failed he could safely fall back upon the assured earnings of his firstborn. But he was tire-

lessly active in bringing out elaborate new productions and usually skillful
in finding ways to capture the public fancy.

At one early point, however, he made a bad guess, because, like
Brougham and Jarrett and Palmer and George L. Fox before him, he pinned
his hopes upon a sequel. In 1880, Rice's Surprise Party (whatever Rice's
surprise might be, one could apparently be sure it would involve Longfellow)
offered "a new and original American operatic extravaganza, *Hiawatha*,"
with the gracious Alice Atherton as the Indian brave, about whom "all lisping
ladies say 'He-aw-wath-a charming fellow.' " Chalk-faced, nervous little
Willie Edouin, who became one of the most popular comics of the 1880s,
was a member of the cast, and also young Henry E. Dixey, who developed
into a matinee idol in *Adonis* four years later, as well as a group of super-
numeraries described as "adjunct-conspirators who *add junk.*"

Again the entire score was composed by Rice, who dictated it to a
secretary "with suggestions about its instrumental effects"—a procedure that
has its counterpart in the methods of more than one contemporary musical-
comedy composer. Goodwin having departed from Rice's fellowship to devote his talents to the authorship of a long series of dubious comic-opera
librettos, Rice obtained the book of *Hiawatha* from Nathaniel Childs, who
appears not to have had the magic touch. Neither a costly production by
Arthur Voegtlin, who designed *The Black Crook*, nor a hit song called "Tea
and Toast and Kisses" could save *Hiawatha;* it closed after two weeks.

Rice's next important production, *Pop,* revealed at the Bijou Opera
House in New York in 1883, was described as "a new, highly sensational
melodramatic operatic comedy mélange." A hybrid entertainment, it consisted of burlesque and extravaganza elements, organized within a framework borrowed from the small farce-comedies—such as Nate Salsbury's *The
Brook* and William A. Mestayer's *The Tourists in the Pullman Palace
Car*—which suddenly became popular in 1879.

The main source of humor in *Pop* was the portly George K. Fortesque
(the Catherine of *Evangeline*) who appeared in this instance as Anthony
Belsize from Alabama, "a Wealthy Southerner, who is never in a hurry, and
who used to masquerade in female attire in his youth." The second act of
the entertainment—by far the longest—took place in the saloon of the
S. S. *Scythia*, en route from London to New York. The opening act merely
showed preparations for the trip in London, and the closing act saw the
members of the cast settled in New York.

The specialties in the second act were more diverse than those of *Evangeline*, for Rice drew upon the resources of the variety shows by including a
group of Tyrolean warblers, various imitations, and vocal duets in music-
hall style. The burlesque elements of *Pop* were confined chiefly to two
episodes—a scene showing the awakening of the statue, from *Pygmalion
and Galatea*, and a burlesque scene from *Romeo and Juliet*. In the third
week, Rice added a new number to strengthen the lact act—"The Dudes
and the Dude Princes"—in which a number of the girls engaged in a march,

dressed as dudes. This was an up-to-the-moment touch, for it was at precisely this time that the elegant dudes began their reign as the princes of New York's pavements, restaurants, and theatres. Their immediate predecessors, the mashers, were never—as far as the records indicate—similarly canonized in any theatrical entertainment.

Ten years after the first production of *Evangeline*, on September 4, 1884, Rice presented *Adonis* at the Bijou Opera House, initiating a record-breaking run of 603 consecutive performances. The New York opening was not the première of the piece, for it had been tried out at Hooley's Opera House in Chicago in July. For the first time, Rice was not listed as producer, but only as composer. William Gill was the producer, though there can be no doubt that Rice's money was generously involved. Gill was also coauthor of the book with Henry E. Dixey, the male lead.

With *Adonis*, Rice allowed the hush-hush term "burlesque" to be used for the first time in the official description of one of his attractions. He called it a "burlesque-extravaganza"; and it was, in point of fact, vaguely a burlesque of the Pygmalion and Galatea theme, which had already haunted Rice's fancy in *Pop*, the previous year.

The hyphenated description "burlesque-extravaganza" indicated that the earlier distinction between these two types of entertainment had now become blurred. Only the girls in tights, the puns, and the lip service to a familiar plot remained from the earlier conventions of burlesque; the hero was a handsome man rather than a woman in tights. The term "extravaganza" had by now been used to describe so many kinds of pieces endeavoring to be amusing through their diversity of materials and impressive by their spectacle that the word had come to mean almost anything, or perhaps nothing definitive at all. Rice apparently soon found the word a useless one, for except for *The Seven Ages*, in 1889, he abandoned it in the advertisements of the productions that came after *Adonis*, choosing to call them all burlesques, up to the last one of the kind, *Excelsior Jr.*, in 1895.

The long run of *Adonis* was partly explained by the inordinate popularity of the sleek Henry E. Dixey, who had made his start in *Hiawatha*. As Adonis, Dixey had ample opportunity to display his fine figure and his unusually shapely legs. He was also a nimble dancer, an adroit comedian, and a well-trained singer. In later years he remained one of the fixtures of the musical stage, seldom wanting for an assignment, though never again attaining the peak of popularity *Adonis* enabled him to reach.

Equally important to the success of *Adonis* was the way in which Rice—like Russel Crouse and Howard Lindsay many decades later in *State of the Union*—kept freshening the dialogue by bringing the topical references up to the moment. Since nobody could ever tell what new quips would add to the merriment, people went back again and again; the *Dramatic Mirror* observed that it was "an institution to be regularly patronized like the El railways or the Eden Musée."

While Rice continued to be an important producer for another quarter century, his formative influence upon the American musical stage decreased as he tended to repeat earlier formulas. His own creative contribution also became less. For *The Corsair*, presented in 1887, he composed only part of the score, delegating the lion's share of the musical responsibility to the English composer John J. Braham. In his later productions, Rice undertook to contribute very little, writing no music and taking almost no hand in the preparation of the books. *The Seven Ages*, staged in 1889 as a starring vehicle for Dixey, employed a plot based upon the Seven Ages of Man detailed by Jaques in Shakespeare's *As You Like It*. The piece offered a touch of novelty in the behavior of its chorus girls, who abandoned their wonted aloofness to enter into chatty conversation with the audience. *1492 Up to Date*, presented in 1893, a year too late for the quadricentennial but in time to capitalize upon the nationwide interest in the World's Columbian Exposition at Chicago, was a "musical, historical, mellow drama" that threw together bits of opéra-comique, comic opera, stereopticon projections, extravaganza, farce-comedy, vaudeville, local comedy, burlesque, and even minstrelsy.

Obviously Rice had now departed a great distance from his starting-point; though *1492 Up to Date* was moderately successful, its effort to encompass the entire known range of light musical diversion amounted to the admission that the days of burlesque, as he had once conceived it, were now as good as finished. In *Little Christopher Columbus*, produced in 1894, Rice moved a long step further away from burlesque by engaging two especially well-equipped comic-opera composers, Ivan Caryll and Gustave Kerker, to write the score and Kerker himself to conduct it. It was an elaborate show with a costly and stunning production, but it was no longer a burlesque, and it presaged Rice's complete abandonment of burlesque in favor of musical comedy.

Excelsior Jr., introduced at Hammerstein's Olympia Theatre in 1895, constituted one last reversion to the now historic burlesque type. Once again one of Rice's pieces depended upon Longfellow for its inspiration; the book by W. A. Barnett was blithely advertised as "a perversion of Longfellow's *Excelsior*." But in brashly announcing that the burlesque was a "perversion," Rice revealed the sophistication that had come over his own thinking and over that of the theatre public as well. No longer could the homely hokum of *Evangeline* be offered in a new piece without self-conscious apology; whatever the durability of the heifer and the Lone Fisherman, they were now recognized to be period pieces. *Excelsior Jr.* survived for six months, less on its own merits that upon those of Fay Templeton, who was still a charmer, though she had put on enough weight to make her tights bulge embarrassingly; Theresa Vaughan, who repeated from *1492 Up to Date* her artifice of singing local ballads with German words, strumming the guitar "somnolently"; and Arthur Dunn, who gave a raucous imitation of Paderewski, whose name was now beginning to be a household word.

Though Rice enjoyed a virtual monopoly of the field, two burlesques were introduced by a young actor-producer, Nat C. Goodwin. In *Little Jack Sheppard*, presented at the Bijou Opera House in 1886, on the heels of *Adonis'* closing, Goodwin acquainted the American audience with the skirt dancing of Loie Fuller. A sharper contrast to the prima donna in "trunks" could scarcely have been found. When Loie Fuller, with her voluminous yardage of swirling pleated skirts, demonstrated the pictorial possibilities of these neglected garments, the entire masculine sex found a new object of admiration, and the ladies in tights soon learned to fear and respect the competition of the growing tribe of skirt dancers.

Goodwin's second production, *Big Pony, or The Gentlemanly Savage*, was too weak a concoction to add new impetus to the skirt-dance enthusiasm, despite the continuing presence of Loie Fuller. It remained for a visiting English troupe—George Edwardes' Theatre Burlesque Company, who arrived at the Standard Theatre in New York on November 15, 1888, in *Monte Cristo Jr.*—to give impetus to the interest Goodwin had engendered. Though their visit was less successful financially than Lydia Thompson's tours two decades earlier, it exerted no less influence upon popular taste. The Edwardes company, whose London home was the Gaiety Theatre, offered a species of entertainment that differed radically both from Lydia Thompson's and from Rice's. The Gaiety burlesque abandoned the rhymed couplet and the pun, depending upon more spontaneous and swifter dialogue. Above all, it provided both the principal ladies and the members of the chorus with the long, swishy skirts that had been Loie Fuller's stellar prerogative in the Nat Goodwin burlesques. It is safe to assume that Loie Fuller had been impressed by the new uniform of the Gaiety Girls and had hastened to capitalize upon it before the Edwardes company could get to this country.

The Gaiety company brought one more burlesque to New York—*Faust Up to Date*—under the new and important management of Abbey and Grau, in 1889. The piece did not prosper, for the critics felt that Edwardes had sent a company inferior to that of *Monte Cristo Jr.* The next time a Gaiety troupe crossed the Atlantic it brought not a burlesque but a musical comedy. And burlesque itself, having won a new lease on life through the rediscovery of the skirt, soon fell under the capable guidance of Weber and Fields.

VI. The Kiralfys

THE BROTHERS Imre, Bolossy, and Arnold Kiralfy, Hungarian dancers and
pantomime performers, came to the United States in 1868. For a few years
they lived by picking up any jobs they could find: Arnold danced in the 1868
revival of *The Black Crook;* Imre and Bolossy were the two Harlequins in
the 1871 revival of *Humpty Dumpty*.

As they observed the tastes and reactions of the people of their new
country they discovered a provocative fact: The American audience was
completely overawed by the marvelous. Give any assembly of Americans
a series of realistic, large-scale reproductions of famous or familiar spectacles,
and it would remain rooted to the spot for an entire evening. One of the
most prosperous entertainment enterprises of the 1870s was the Colosseum,
erected at Broadway and Thirty-fifth Street, and modeled after the Colosseum in London as a home for impressive cycloramas. Its first attraction,
in 1874, entitled *London by Night*, exploited "wonderful effects of moving
water, clouds, storms and numerous other wonderful mechanical deceptions,
all devised by C. F. Brown, master machinist, imported from the Royal
Colosseum in London."

Observing the effect upon the audience not only of the cyclorama but
of the transformation scenes in *The Black Crook* and other musical attractions, the Kiralfy brothers determined to produce a spectacle of their own.
Seeking a subject that would offer opportunities for many striking and realistic mechanical effects, they hit upon the popular Jules Verne romance
Around the World in Eighty Days.

If they had been less sure of themselves, the Kiralfys might have abandoned their project before it reached the production phase, for two other
versions of the same story were presented in New York before theirs was
ready. One of these, without music or ballet, claimed attention with Ouina,
a "trained war elephant." The other employed music and the other customary resources of the musical stage, but was small, economical, and unimpressive.

The tameness of these two earlier efforts in the same year apparently
gave additional force to the Kiralfy production, which was revealed at the
Academy of Music (rebuilt after the fire that led to the staging of *The Black
Crook* at Niblo's Garden) on August 25, 1875. With shrewd theatrical imagination, the Kiralfys dwelt with special zeal upon the more exotic aspects
of the story, and themselves appeared as natives of Borneo. Great admira-

tion was bestowed by the public and the critics upon the scenes representing the places farthest from home—the Suez Canal, Calcutta, and the Taj Mahal. "Nothing so splendid as the scene at the Suttee and the ballet of the second act has ever been witnessed in this city," wrote one transported critic.

In their settings, which represented "the best French school of painting," the Kiralfys, or their unnamed designers, hit upon an important principle for the designing of spectacular scenes. They kept the backgrounds "in minor key and in pastel colors" to give an effect of atmosphere and space, and to throw the actors in the foreground into a vivid relief that would be lost if the backgrounds were too primary or too gaudy. Furthermore, they paid great attention to realistic detail. They were the first American producers, for instance, to make the cuts between the branches of trees naturalistic in shape and disposition, instead of using the monotonous, symmetrical holes which were customary in stage foliage at the time.

For a decade after their production of *Around the World in Eighty Days*, the Kiralfys remained unchallenged as promulgators of large pictorial pieces. Their supremacy rested upon their taste and discretion in the use of color and their unrivaled understanding of the potentialities of technical and mechanical effects. When the electric light was invented, they were quick to take advantage of its new possibilities. Their spectacle *Excelsior*, presented at Niblo's Garden in 1883 at an alleged cost of $75,000, boasted "novel electric effects by the Edison Electric Light Company, under the personal direction of Mr. Edison." The experimental nature of the lighting was indicated by the fact that Edison thought it important to be on hand to see that everything went well. Electricity by no means eliminated gas from the lighting of *Excelsior*. It was reserved for special effects; the program also advertised gas effects and electric-gas lighting. Nor, for that matter, was *Excelsior* the first production to make use of electricity, though it was the first and only one in which Edison himself participated. The Kiralfys themselves had already employed electric lights in the eerie incantation scene in their revival of *The Black Crook*.

It was not their technical ability alone that kept the Kiralfys at the top of the list of producers of spectacles. Having been trained as dancers, they were also aware of the requirements of spectacular theatre in this field. *Excelsior*, which proved to be their magnum opus, made use of the combined talents of the Parisian Eden Theatre Ballet Company, the Venetian Ballet Troupe, and "the most distinguished artists of the Scala Theatre of Milan."

In the course of the production, in which not a word was spoken, the entire rise and perfection of modern civilization was reviewed with relentless thoroughness. The cast of characters included such metaphorical figures as Light, Darkness, and Civilization, as well as representatives of practically every corner of the earth and every walk of life—Pepin, described as the inventor of the steamboat; Volta, the electrician; an Indian danseuse; an Arab merchant's daughter; a Chinaman; the chief of the Italian miners; a

Mexican; a Grand Turk; a French engineer; a brigand in the desert; an Englishman; and a lady known as La Cosmopolete. The countless dancers and extras appeared as genii of civilization, of constancy, of invention, of harmony, of renown, of power, of glory, of science, of agriculture, of industry, of valor, of union; and as boatmen, peasants, musicians, postillions, telegraph boys, engineers, miners, workers in the earth, Europeans, Africans, Asiatics, Americans, sailors, and officers.

The vast mélange led up to a great apotheosis, "The Triumph of Light Over Darkness and the Peaceful Union of Nations." To arrive at this desirable final tableau, three acts and twelve preparatory "great tableaux" were required. Despite its cosmic sweep, the scenario did not fail to keep up to date; not only was the discovery of electric power celebrated by example, but the invention of the telegraph was noted in a ballet in which the girls were dressed as telegraph messengers.

The Kiralfys followed *Excelsior* with a number of other grandoise endeavors, none of which duplicated its success. Only *Lagarde*, among these, warrants passing mention, because of the tangential fact that Maurice Barrymore was a member of its cast; the piece itself was a tiresome blowing-up of an old melodrama, *The Duke's Moot*, by Le Bossu, and offered as its central attraction a ballet based on the Seven Ages of Man, a subject which seemed to haunt the theatrical mind in the 1880s.

In 1888, Imre and Bolossy Kiralfy had a falling-out, and the firm disbanded. Arnold Kiralfy went back to dancing, with diminishing success, and died in 1908. Bolossy continued for two more seasons as a New York producer, achieving his only success in 1888 with another Jules Verne piece, *Mathias Sandorf*. Imre left the theatre altogether, and turned to the production of outdoor spectacles. In 1888, he presented *The Fall of Rome* on Staten Island, with a cast of two thousand, tons of armor, a leviathan ballet, and quantities of chariot racing and Roman wrestling. He then moved to England, where he produced an even larger spectacle involving 2,500 participants. He died in Brighton, England, in 1919. Bolossy, who had retired from theatrical activity in 1889, lived on obscurely in this country until 1932, when he died at the age of eighty-four.

Though the period of their ascendancy was relatively short and the total number of their productions was not large, the Kiralfys left an indelible mark upon the New York stage. Their vast enterprises were never rivaled until the flamboyant years of the Hippodrome in the early twentieth century. The source of strength in their first productions—their technical acumen—became a weakness when they tried merely to make their spectacles constantly bigger and more eye-filling, without developing new ideas to replace the ballet-extravaganza materials on which they had learned to depend in the atavistic days of *The Black Crook* and *Humpty Dumpty*.

VII. Farce-Comedy

A LIVELY LITTLE GROUP of five itinerant players known as Salsbury's Troubadours, newly arrived from Chicago, St. Louis, and other western points, brought a trifle called *The Brook* to New York on May 12, 1879. To the patrons of the San Francisco Opera House, *The Brook* constituted nothing more than a pleasant way of passing a spring evening in the theatre occupied throughout the winter by the popular San Francisco Minstrels. To us, gifted with hindsight, *The Brook*—despite its tiny budget and its brief engagement of two weeks—was one of the most important productions of its time, outweighing from the historian's viewpoint such costly offerings as the Kiralfys' *Around the World in Eighty Days* or Fox's *Humpty Dumpty*.

The Brook was the germinal cell out of which musical comedy ultimately grew. It was the first full-length musical piece to adopt the distinguishing formula of musical comedy by putting its central trust in the topical materials of the variety show and arranging these materials upon the framework of a plot. For musical comedy may be distinguished from such other forms of entertainment as comic opera and burlesque by its direct and essentially unstylized appropriation of vernacular types of song, dance, and subject matter; and it may be distinguished from its chief source of inspiration, the variety show, by its employment of a plot and, at least in some slight degree, of consistent characterization.

If *The Brook* did not possess a musical score of its own, or make any pretense at choreography, or display the urbanities of staging that later generations learned to expect of a musical comedy, it did offer—within its modest resources of talent and investiture—an evening's diversion suffused with an informal, friendly charm that no spectacular machinery, pantomimic stylizations, or red-nosed, red-wigged comics and buxom women in tights could duplicate.

It is important, in view of the unyielding provinciality of New Yorkers, to observe that the most natural and spontaneous musical entertainment New York had yet encountered was a product not of the metropolis itself but of the hinterland. New York, in fact, was the last city to make the acquaintance of the musical farce-comedy (as the type soon came to be called), after Nate Salsbury, its first native exponent, had spent four years on the road perfecting it. Only when half of America had already found it palatable was the New York audience permitted to sample it.

Nate Salsbury began his theatrical career in the 1860s, being entrusted, in his first job, with a single line in Brougham's *Pocahontas*, a piece long forgotten in New York but still persistent on the road. After various stock-company experiences, he formed his own company, and on May 1, 1875, Salsbury's Troubadours made their first appearance in Chicago in a "comic absurdity," *Patchwork*. For the format and subject matter of this half-length piece Salsbury was almost shamelessly indebted to a similar troupe of five English performers, the Vokes Family, whose touring bill contained a divertissement entitled *Belles of the Kitchen*. Ringing minor changes upon the plot of *Belles of the Kitchen*, Salsbury's script for *Patchwork* involved an antic group of kitchen servants. At 7:30 in the morning, while the family was still "in the arms of Morpheus," the servants donned some costumes worn by the guests at a masquerade the night before, and demonstrated their talents in various song and dance specialties. The lark was interrupted by the arrival of members of the family, who caused the servants to disappear through stove holes, windows, and chimneys as the final curtain descended.

The Brook, Salsbury's second composition, was scarcely longer than *Patchwork* when it was first presented in St. Louis in 1877. But as Salsbury's confidence in his product grew, its size expanded. At the New York première it was still preceded by a short, nonmusical curtain raiser, *Husband in Clover*, but the recitation of Tennyson's poem vouchsafed St. Louisans had now been abandoned. By the time the piece returned to New York in 1880 it occupied an entire evening.

The full title and subtitle of Salsbury's "laughable and musical extravaganza" (the rule still seemed to be: When in doubt call it an extravaganza) read:

THE BROOK
"For man may come and man may go, but I flow on forever"
Depicting the Pleasures of a Jolly Pic-Nic

The five Troubadours were cast as members of a theatrical company. In the first act they determined to take a boat trip down the river, for a "jolly picnic." The second act showed the picnic itself. The audience split its sides at an endless series of contretemps: fish bait was mixed with the coffee; the jam was saturated with salt; vinegar was spilled on the sandwiches—and a basket thought to contain watermelons proved to be filled with theatrical costumes. This last mistake provided a pretext for the chief entertainment of the evening, for the performers made use of the costumes for impersonations, eccentric dances, and specialty songs. When their repertory was exhausted, they reembarked on the boat. The brief third act merely showed their return home, exhausted but happy.

Whatever its shortcomings in music, humor, and talent, *The Brook* established an important precedent by its assumption that naturalness could be thoroughly entertaining—that the audience, in this instance, could have a good time by sharing in the familiar pleasures of a picnic. As one critic wrote, "*The Brook* appeals to the natural impulses of everybody, and all nature is held up to the mirror." Salsbury himself explained that the farce-comedy "claimed to be a novelty, in the sense that it is different in its motive and execution from any musical production of its kind thus far presented for public consideration. The main object which we strive to attain is the natural reproduction of the jollity and funny mishaps that attend the usual pic-nic excursion."

Like Edward E. Rice with *Evangeline*, Salsbury established his reputation by offering entertainment the entire family could accept, though there was passing criticism of a song in the repertory of Nellie McHenry, the leading woman, entitled "Pretty, Though Fragrant, as a Picture." After delighting family audiences from coast to coast, Salsbury took *The Brook* to the British Isles—the first American musical production, in all probability, ever to appear there. It was approved by everybody except a Dublin reviewer who objected that it "does not gratify those who desire to see some division between the stage and the music halls." He also took exception—not unfairly, perhaps—to humor that defined a kiss as "a lip tickle (elliptical)" and permitted Salsbury at one point to say to Miss McHenry, "If you are going to smother me, do it s'mother way," and at another to observe, when she fainted in his arms, "How heavy a young woman is when she faints, especially after lunch!"

Salsbury kept the Troubadours on the move, partly with the perennial *Brook* and partly with new pieces of similar genre, until 1887. The last of his farce-comedies was *The Humming Bird*, given at the Star Theatre in New York on February 7 of that year. John Webster and Nellie McHenry still remained from the original company, and the troupe had been expanded from five to seven. From this time forward, Salsbury devoted himself to other interests. Signing as manager of Colonel William F. Cody, otherwise known as Buffalo Bill, he became the first producer of the celebrated Wild West Show, the predecessor of the present-day rodeo. Salsbury last functioned in New York as producer of a large spectacle, *Black America*, in Madison Square Garden in 1895.

The Troubadours' discovery of farce-comedy quickly set a fashion, for it was too successful and profitable not to invite imitation. To begin with, a farce-comedy could be mounted at extremely small cost, with an infinitesimal company and minimal settings, properties, and machinery. In the second place, it was easy to cast and direct, since it required no specialized techniques of pantomime or burlesque, no chorus, no French ballets, no transformation scenes. The form gave free opportunity to each performer to exploit whatever talent he might possess. As time went on, the freedom of farce-comedy from fixed traditions enabled a number of original and gifted comics to develop their individual styles of performance.

The second successful farce-comedy, and the only real competitive threat to Salsbury's Troubadours on the road, was *The Tourists in the Pullman Palace Car*, billed as "an entertainment of fun and incident," and presented in New York for the first time at Haverly's Theatre on November 8, 1879, with William A. Mestayer as producer and J. H. Haverly as manager. A more pulse-quickening tale than *The Brook*, *The Tourists in the Pullman Palace Car* strung its specialties upon a plot involving the trip of a group of tourists to California on an emigrant train, and the confusion arising out of a diamond robbery and complications of mistaken identity.

It possessed no musical score of its own, and its choice of music, like that of *The Brook*, was nothing if not eclectic. Among the items employed, according to the printed program, were Sullivan's "Serenade" from *Box and Cox* [sic]; "Nursery Rhymes (Original with the Tourists)"—"Poor Cock Robin," and "The North Wind Doth Blow"; "Luncheon Chorus," from *The Chimes of Normandy;* "The Kentucky Home"; "The Telegraph Boy" (words by W. A. Mestayer, music by David Braham); *German Emigrants—Der Wasserfall;* Scene from *Il Trovatore;* Harrigan and Hart's latest sketch, "The Skids Are Out Today" (music by David Braham); General Finale and "Forward to Do or Die" from *Fatinitza;* and End of Route.

The heyday of farce-comedy in New York lasted only about five years, although "combinations," as the farce-comedy troupes were called, continued to tour the rest of the country for twenty years longer. In the first rush of production, too many farce-comedies were produced to warrant a full listing here. A few, however, possessed features of distinctive interest. *Hobbies* (1879) brought Nat C. Goodwin to the musical stage for the first time, in imitations—not unlike those for which Nate Salsbury was famous— of such celebrated tragedians as Booth, Barrett, and Jefferson. Goodwin soon became a very popular performer, and, as we have already seen, produced two burlesques in the late 1880s, in which he shared billing with Loie Fuller. *Minnie Palmer's Boarding School*, exploiting the gifts of the comedienne Minnie Palmer, was, apart from *The Tourists*, the most prosperous imitator of *The Brook*.

A variant on the initial farce-comedy pattern was provided by *Dreams, or Fun in A Photograph Gallery*, offered in 1880 by a group called Willie Edouin's Sparks. This piece, thrown together after the failure of Rice's *Hiawatha*, used burlesque materials within a farce-comedy framework that was suited to Edouin, Alice Atherton, and James T. Powers, all of whom were left unemployed by the swift closing of Rice's sequel to *Evangeline*. *Dreams* justified its burlesque elements by having the dances in the photographer's shop take place in the dreams of an old man who had fallen asleep.

Within five years, the popularity of these small-scale farce-comedies faded. The last one to make even a moderate impact was *We, Us and Company at Mud Springs*, produced by Mestayer in 1884. The locale was a hotel built on a railroad turntable, an architectural device that enabled the proprietress to give each new patron the impression that he would have a sunny room. A mischievous youth turned the turntable one night when various lovers were abroad on nocturnal adventures—with farcical intrigues that were held to justify the usual songs, dances, knockabout antics, puns, and musical specialties.

Like many another novelty, early farce-comedy wore out its welcome speedily because its practitioners could not find ways of renewing the interest of their audiences once the initial freshness of the form had worn off. Lacking real validity of plot or characterization and the integrity of presentation that specially composed musical scores might have provided, the farce-comedies were easily nudged out of the Broadway scene by the comic operas which poured into the theatres after the triumphant success of *H. M. S. Pinafore* in 1879. Though its vogue began in the same year as that of the farce-comedy, comic opera prospered because it offered more substance and kept on discovering new facets and new subjects, while farce-comedy, becoming sterile and repetitious, retreated to the road. In the 1890s, farce-comedy enjoyed a whirlwind revival, but it was then conceived in more elaborate terms of production, and soon became indistinguishable from musical comedy, which supplanted it.

Akin to the early farce-comedies in their homely naturalness and disdain for artifice were the *Mulligan Guard* plays, written and presented in rapid rotation by Edward Harrigan and Tony Hart between 1877 and 1885. These farces, bearing such titles as *The Mulligan Guard's Chowder* and *The Mulligan Guard's Picnic*, represented the first attempt on the New York stage to achieve quasi-realistic local color by employing as characters familiar Bowery figures, whose manners and locutions were fairly accurately reproduced, though with broad satire and travesty. Harrigan's own stock part was that of an Irishman, and Hart played female roles.

The *Mulligan Guard* farces do not, strictly speaking, fall within the proper purview of this narrative. They were straight plays, dotted with interpolated songs, and, on rare occasions, dances; and they were followed by an olio of variety acts. But the songs were some of the wittiest and most professional of their day, for Harrigan and Hart maintained David Braham, a deft and well-trained musician, as their staff composer and musical director. Nearly every Harrigan and Hart show nurtured at least one song hit that was sung and whistled all over town and (as in the instance of *The Tourists in the Pullman Palace Car*) frequently borrowed for use in farce-comedies and other musical entertainments. Though the Harrigan and Hart farces employed none of the other appurtenances of the musical stage, they established a vogue for local and topical songs which helped prepare the way for the Broadway-conscious musical comedies of George M. Cohan after the turn of the century.

Perhaps the best of the entire Harrigan and Hart output was *Cordelia's Aspirations* (1883). One of the Mulligan series, despite the absence of the familiar name from its title, the farce dealt with Dan Mulligan's rise in society and consequent social blunders. In a fit of jealousy his wife drank from a bottle that was labeled "poison," but actually contained whiskey—with a resulting drunk scene that made Annie Yeamans famous as a comedienne. Among the songs—by David Braham, of course—were "Just Across from Jersey," "My Dad's Dinner Pail," and "Sam Johnson's Cakewalk." The last of these called upon a group of Negro dancers. Harrigan and Hart were the first major producers to employ Negro performers, almost two decades before *A Trip to Coontown* and *In Dahomey* called for recognition of the talent of Negro artists. In *Cordelia's Aspirations*, the Negro performers were brought into the play as a stranded *Uncle Tom* troupe returning from Germany.

After *Cordelia's Aspirations*, bad fortune began to overtake Harrigan and Hart. In 1884 the Theatre Comique, in which they had been appearing, burned down, destroying the scores and parts of nearly all of Braham's music for the many *Mulligan Guard* farces. The following year the partners had a falling out; and although each tried to continue on his own, the great days were over. But they had made their contribution: They had discovered New York, and whether in *Forty-Five Minutes from Broadway* or in *On the Town*, the American musical stage never afterward completely forgot its home town.

Somewhat more elaborate in their entertainment features, but in many ways similar in structure, were the comedies with music written and produced by Charles Hoyt. The first successful venture in Hoyt's career was a "farrago" called *A Bunch of Keys*, presented by Willie Edouin's Sparks at the San Francisco Opera House (from which farce-comedies and cognate attractions had nosed out the minstrel shows soon after the appearance of Salsbury's Troubadours) in 1883. The action took place in a hotel; and Willie Edouin's nervous cry of "Front!" became a byword all over town.

In a production directed by Edouin and including in the cast his partners of *Hiawatha* and *Dreams*, it was obvious that the mannerisms of burlesques would predominate. But in his subsequent farces Hoyt abandoned burlesque. He translated minstrel-show music and dancing into fresh terms, eliminating the blackface aspects, but basing the essential style of his divertissements upon typical minstrel stunts and techniques. He showed little interest in finding pretexts to weave the music and dancing into the structure of his plays, as was customarily done—at least superficially—in the contemporaneous comic operas. The program of *A Tin Soldier*, presented in 1886, even went so far as to call the songs "musical interruptions," and the list of musical numbers in the printed program included the "Faust Waltz," "composed expressly by Chas. Gounod for another purpose."

In *A Rag Baby* (1884), Hoyt for the first time assigned the stage direction to Julian Mitchell, who had begun his professional career as a bit player in *A Bunch of Keys*. Mitchell remained Hoyt's sole stage director from this time forward. Later he served briefly in a similar capacity for George M. Cohan, whose musical comedies were indebted even more, perhaps, to the example of Hoyt's highly localized and vernacular scripts and routines than to the more primitive conceptions of Harrigan and Hart. Toward the end of his career, Mitchell received the supreme accolade when Florenz Ziegfeld, Jr., engaged him to stage several editions of the *Ziegfeld Follies*.

Under Mitchell's guidance, one Hoyt comedy after another made its way into public favor, each distinguished by the author's special trademark, an initial indefinite article: *A Rag Baby*, *A Parlour Match* (which introduced the comic team of Evans and Hoey, and ran to less plot and more specialty dances and songs than most of the other pieces), *A Tin Soldier*, *A Hole in the Ground*, *A Midnight Bell* (in which Maude Adams made her debut, with no great fanfare), *A Brass Monkey* (the creature which suffers when the weather gets very cold), *A Contented Woman* (a satire on woman suffrage), *A Texas Steer*, *A Runaway Colt*, *A Black Sheep*, *A Dog in the Manger*.

Hoyt reached the zenith of his career with *A Trip to Chinatown*, which opened on November 9, 1890, and continued until it had exceeded by 47 performances the run record held for sixteen years by *Adonis*. *A Trip to Chinatown* chalked up a tally of 650 performances in its first engagement. A return booking in the spring of 1894 brought the total well above 700. In 1908, a sumptuous revival was staged by Ziegfeld.

In *A Trip to Chinatown*, Hoyt's technique of constructing an entertainment was indistinguishable from the helter-skelter method of the compilers of other farce-comedies. The plot dealt with the difficulties of two slumming couples in San Francisco who were trying to avoid each other but chose to visit the same restaurant. The story, however, was Hoyt's least concern. His responsibility to his characters ended when he had branded them with such names as Welland Strong, Ben Gay, Rashley Gay, Willie Grow, Norman Blood, Noah Heap, and Hoffman Price.

A Trip to Chinatown swept into national popularity to the tune of the still unforgotten song, first sung by Harry Conor:

> *"The Bowery! the Bowery!*
> *They do such things, and they say such things*
> *On the Bowery; the Bowery!*
> *I'll never go there any more."*

In the course of the run a second hit of almost equal proportions was added—"Reuben, Reuben, I've Been Thinking." The musical numbers were continually changed, and new specialty acts—such as that of Loie Fuller, making butterfly's wings of her skirts, with appropriate colored lights—were frequently added.

At least as late as 1896, *A Trip to Chinatown* was still being revised, as it filled a prosperous itinerary on the road. In that year an unidentified reviewer in the Boston *Transcript,* whose dim view of the music left him in a unmistakable minority, wrote: "Everyone knows *A Trip to Chinatown.* Pieces of this sort are generally furbished up at the beginning of each fresh season, to be sure. But the piece is still recognizable and as funny as ever. With the exception of an excellent burlesque on an operatic terzet, the songs seemed to us an unwelcome interruption of the bubbling fun and humor of the play. . . . To be sure, Mr Hoyt's humor smacks far more of the barroom than of the drawing room . . . but . . . the use he makes of it has a conspicuous artistic side. But anything flatter than the songs is difficult to imagine." In justice to the author, it should be remarked that Hoyt, running true to form, endeavored to ward off criticism of the music by referring to *A Trip to Chinatown* as a "musical trifle."

With *A Trip to Chinatown,* farce-comedy approached its finish. Its possibilities were exhausted, for nothing more was likely to be achieved through the lackadaisical practices exemplified in the format of *A Trip to Chinatown.* Just around the corner were the new forms of musical comedy and revue, and already at hand was the Weber and Fields revivification of burlesque and extravaganza—fresh formulations that were to distinguish the new order from the old.

Subsequent farce-comedies accordingly came to seem like vestigial remains. Critics were invariably cynical about their merits, and the public, while it kept attending them for a while, turned more and more to fresher and better constructed types of entertainment. The reaction of the *Dramatic Mirror*'s anonymous reviewer to *A Straight Tip,* a farce-comedy with a book by John J. McNally and a compiled score from nameless sources, may be taken as typical of the growing disaffection toward such diversions:

"*A Straight Tip* made the public laugh, and it probably will put money in the pocket of its producer. There is no story to interest the spectator, but there is plenty of rough-and-tumble fun, catchy music, pretty girls, and . . . a number of old jokes which the farce comedian [James T. Powers] gets off in his best style." The high points of the show seem to have been the variety stunts of Powers, who offered a burlesque of the popular dancer Carmencita—a butterfly dance—and performed one of his standard routines, a caricature of a woman doing her hair. Riotously funny Powers may have been, but those alone were hardly the materials to keep farce-comedy alive in the face of the competition soon provided by the Gaiety Girls and *The Passing Show.* Having made its twenty-five-year contribution, farce-comedy left New York for the road, and finally for oblivion.

VIII. Comic Opera: The First Decade

THE ARRIVAL IN AMERICA of the first Gilbert and Sullivan opera, *H. M. S. Pinafore*, in the 1878-79 season, led to a veritable eruption of comic opera. Before Gilbert and Sullivan showed the English-speaking audience what it had been missing, comic opera had been largely the esoteric diversion of those who enjoyed hearing it performed in French or German. For fifteen years or more, French opéra-bouffe had been a source of special delight among connoisseurs, among whom it shared favor with Italian opera, and, in lesser degree, German light opera.

Maurice Grau, an indefatigable enthusiast for opéra-bouffe, gave New Yorkers in the late 1870s and early 1880s an opportunity to make an extensive acquaintance with this type of musical entertainment, in performances by visiting French companies, whose acting abilities and vocal endowments were considered the best the musical stage then offered. Lecocq's *Giroflé-Girofla* and *La Fille de Madame Angot* and works by Audran and Offenbach were regularly imported after they had been brought out in Paris, usually to the great satisfaction of Grau's discriminating but limited audience. The partisans of opéra-bouffe concurred in the opinion of the New York *Dramatic Mirror* that this Gallic form of musical pleasantry was superior to all others; the French composers alone, the *Mirror* argued, felt an adequate responsibility for keeping the plot and characterization of a good farce intact; and they were able to invest a piece with sparkling music and lively humors without sacrificing its dramatic features to the exigencies of musical art. Those who understood French of course took delight in the raciness of the dialogue, the double entendres, and the exposition of doubtful situations with a frankness that would have been inadmissible in an English-language libretto.

Thanks to the vitality of the works produced by French composers and librettists and to the high level of performance consistently maintained by Grau's imported companies, opéra-bouffe retained its popularity for more than twenty years. Even at the close of this period it did not die, for as the performance of foreign works in translation became more popular, many of the works of Lecocq, Audran, and Offenbach found their way into the repertories of English-speaking companies. Before 1879 and the Gilbert and Sullivan invasion, however, only *Giroflé-Girofla* and *Madame Angot's Daughter* had been given in English translation for those who were not attracted by Grau's French productions at Daly's Theatre.

German light opera was even less known to the English-language audience. The works of Marschner and Lortzing were given only for German-born and German-speaking audiences; and of the newer products of the Viennese operetta renaissance of the 1870s only von Suppé's *Fantinitza* had been brought forward in English.

The field was wide open, therefore, for *H. M. S. Pinafore* to reveal the joys of comic opera to a public whose sights were still leveled upon *Evangeline* and *Humpty Dumpty*. The spectacular success of *Pinafore* in England had led American managers to suspect that the nautical comedy would also win a cordial reception on this side of the Atlantic. Inasmuch as no reciprocal copyright arrangements existed with England at that time, *Pinafore* was the unquestioned property of anyone in America who chose to appropriate it. The race to get it on the stage involved the entire nation, as pirated productions were given in nearly every principal city from Boston to San Francisco, many months before Rupert D'Oyly Carte brought his company from England to acquaint us with the completely authentic version.

Boston stole a march on the rest of the country. The first American showing of *H. M. S. Pinafore* occurred at the Boston Museum (a theatre devoted to musical attractions, not the present fine arts museum) on November 25, 1878. Since the opera, like so many pieces of its time, was designed to be preceded by a one-act curtain raiser, the evening began with Tom Taylor's nonmusical farce, *Nine Points of the Law*. Three weeks later, however, Gilbert and Sullivan's *Trial by Jury* was substituted; this lampoon of Old Bailey has remained the regular companion of *Pinafore* up to our own day, and is so billed by the contemporary D'Oyly Carte company.

The success of *Pinafore* in Boston was enormous, surpassing the triumph of *Evangeline*, or of any other musical piece the city had ever seen. By August 1879, no fewer than 241 representations had been given in Boston by a variety of companies, including one composed of child actors. (Juvenile *Pinafore* troupes were excessively popular for a season or two, and sprang up all over the country. There was also a Church Choir Pinafore Company.)

New York finally saw *Pinafore* in February 1879 at the Standard Theatre, with Thomas Whiffen as the Right Honourable Sir Joseph Porter, K.C.B. The huge success of the production encouraged several other managers to get together competing companies, and all, in a measure, prospered.

Finally, more than a year after the first pirated performance in Boston, the D'Oyly Carte Opera Company deserted the Savoy Theatre in London long enough to undertake a month's engagement in New York, at the Fifth Avenue Theatre, beginning on December 1, 1879. Sir Arthur Sullivan conducted on the opening night, and W. S. Gilbert appeared on the stage as a sailor. Subsequent performances were conducted by Alfred Cellier, who himself was soon to become known as a capable composer of comic operas. By virtue of the distinction of its auspices, this authentic exhibition should have routed the pirated productions in disgrace. But it did not; the success of the D'Oyly Carte version was by no means as exceptional as we might assume it would have been, in view of the reputation the company has enjoyed for more than seventy years since that time. The audience and the critics found the performance satisfactory, but nobody found reason to praise it at the expense of the representation given ten months earlier at the same theatre.

In 1879, of course, there were no Savoyard purists capable of recognizing that the D'Oyly Carte company had exclusive access to the original orchestrations made by Sullivan, which are, as we now recognize, far finer examples of orchestral craftsmanship than the boiled-down or imitative scorings used by the rival companies and still used by touring Gilbert and Sullivan companies today. To be sure, odds and ends of the stage business invented for the English production gave new point and amusement to the book, but the force of these was lost in the general effect. A great personal success was achieved, however, by J. H. Ryley, as Sir Joseph Porter. He did not return to England with the company, but remained to continue his career in this country.

Gilbert and Sullivan and D'Oyly Carte were naturally deeply perturbed by the pirated performances of *Pinafore*, from which they received no royalties. When *The Pirates of Penzance* was ready for presentation, they determined that history should not repeat itself. Keeping their company in New York at the close of the month's engagement of *Pinafore*, they immediately—on New Year's Eve, 1879—gave the world première of the new piece at the Standard Theatre, relying on the British copyright law to protect their interests in London.

The Pirates of Penzance won acclaim from the critics, some of whom thought it superior to its predecessor. The public, however, did not quite recapture its earlier enthusiasm, and the run lasted only until March 6, 1880. Nor did any of the next four Gilbert and Sullivan operas, brought forward at an average rate of one a year—*Patience, Iolanthe, The Sorcerer*, and *Princess Ida* (written earlier than *The Sorcerer* but presented here later)—rekindle the *Pinafore* flame. All were well received and adequately supported, but the changeable public, having skimmed off the novelty of the Gilbert and Sullivan teamwork during the *Pinafore* craze, was eager to turn its attention in other directions.

Three elements accounted for the universal popularity of *Pinafore*—its wit, its workmanship, and its accessibility. The quips and rhymes and turns of phrase were really funny, surprisingly, outrageously funny; they are still funny today, and that is more than can be said of the jokes in *Evangeline* or *The Brook*. The high craft of both the librettist and the composer insured the full effectiveness of each individual conceit and thematic development; each lyric, passage of dialogue, song, and concerted number was a complete success in its particular way, and the audience was not expected to hunt out the good intentions behind professional inadequacy or incompetence. Words and music alike were written from the point of view of the audience; they were catchy and easy to learn, and fun to sing at home around a square piano in the evening. From *H . M . S . Pinafore* the American audience began to learn, whether it recognized the fact or not, the difference between hack work and first-class professional skill and integrity. Having sensed this difference, the public was now ready to listen to other works by first-class craftsmen, French and German as well as English, and to assume some responsibility for apprehending more complex musical and dramatic textures. Thus Gilbert and Sullivan won an audience not only for their own works in America, but for transatlantic light music generally.

With unprecedented vigor, the New York stage began in 1880 to devote itself to the presentation of almost every comic opera it could find. From the three principal sources—London, Paris, and Vienna—one comic opera after another was imported, fitted with an English translation (frequently of distressing crudity) and mounted as sumptuously as possible. The production of musical pieces quickly reached a volume that had never been known before. Indeed, the large-scale industry of musical production in New York dates from the discovery of English-language comic opera. Earlier, a season might bring forth a single *Black Crook* or *Around the World in Eighty Days*, but production was intermittent, and attractions appeared one at a time, usually at widely spaced intervals. But in 1880, in addition to the farce-comedies, burlesques, and pantomimes we have already encountered, ten comic operas were produced; in 1883 the total rose to thirteen. A lean year then followed, with only six. But the triumph in 1885 of *The Mikado*, which restored Gilbert and Sullivan to the pinnacle of popularity, and the comparable success of *Erminie* restored the faith of managers and investors, and comic opera took a new and long lease on life.

The sudden rise of comic opera in the 1880s need cause no mystification. No other period in the nineteenth century witnessed so great a concentration of European talent in this field. Gilbert and Sullivan, in England, were turning out pieces at the rate of one a year. Offenbach and Audran, at the height of their glittering powers, were writing with ebullience and technical assurance. Viennese operetta had moved into its "classical" period, as the effervescence of French opéra-bouffe was added to the sentiment of the traditional Singspiel in the works of Von Suppé, Millöcker, and the younger Johann Strauss. Never has the European musical stage been so amply supplied with composers of light music who possessed both artistic sensibility and sound musical and theatrical training. After the death of Offenbach, opéra-bouffe lost much of its sparkle. In the transition from Strauss to Lehár, Viennese operetta suffered a decline in intrinsic quality which was aggravated as Lehár later gave way to Stolz and the mechanical exploitation of *Drei Viertel Takt*.

Many years were to pass before American-made comic opera and operetta could begin to hold its own with audiences accustomed to the competence and fecundity of Offenbach, Millöcker, and their contemporaries. Nevertheless, a few native products were fabricated and staged in the very first flush of the comic-opera craze. The initial experiment was *The First Life Guards at Brighton*, by J. S. Crossey, a Philadelphia composer of surpassingly slight talent. First presented in Crossey's home city in November 1879, *The First Life Guards at Brighton* moved to Manhattan in January 1880, where it was instantly reviled for its weak libretto and simple-minded music, and forced to close for want of patronage at the end of a fortnight.

The second comic opera of native composition, while far more professional in musical stature, was an equal failure with the public. Entitled *Deseret* (1880), it was composed by Dudley Buck of Brooklyn, the most noted Episcopal church composer in America at that time, to a libretto dealing with the Mormons. As churchgoers brought up on his *Festival Te Deum* will recognize, Buck was a well-educated, if appallingly academic, musician, head and shoulders above most of his colleagues in compositional technique. *Deseret* was an elaborate affair requiring a chorus of sixty, and manifesting the routine clichés of German conservatory style. Buck's temperament kept him from understanding the needs of the stage, and he was unable to keep his score from sounding churchy and deadpan. Recognizing the composer's prestige in ecclesiastical circles, one reviewer observed unkindly that "the length of *Deseret's* run will depend largely upon the liberality of these Brooklynites." Apparently church and stage did not mix, for the supply of friends of the composer and of W. A. Croffut, the librettist, ran out quickly, and *Deseret* left the boards twelve days after its opening.

Two other pitiful efforts made by American composers in the next two years may be brushed in passing, for the sake of filling in the record. *Elfins and Mermaids* (1881), with book and music by Charles Brown of Albany, New York, was terrible enough to be "unconsciously funny." *L'Afrique* (1882) was devised in amateur fashion by Wayman C. McCreary of St. Louis, and performed by a cast as amateurish as the composer.

With *The Little Tycoon*, in 1886, American comic opera won its first modest toehold. Handsomely produced by Augustin Daly, its book and music were the work of an otherwise insignificant author, Willard Spencer. The sources of its success, unfortunately, lay largely outside Spencer's contributions to it, for it interested the audience more by its topical humor than by any intrinsic merits of plot or music. In a Philadelphia revival a year or two later, for instance, Digby Bell, who was not in the original New York cast, interpolated a topical song in ten stanzas, "What could the poor man do?", which was full of local allusions about the New Woman, "Billy" Penn, trolley cars, Napoleon, Trilby, and nearly every other subject people were talking about. The immediate influence of the Gilbert and Sullivan patter songs—particularly those in *The Mikado*—is obvious.

The Begum, described as a "Hindoo comic opera" and offered at the Fifth Avenue Theatre on November 21, 1887, marked the initial collaboration of Reginald de Koven and Harry B. Smith as composer and librettist. Despite the efforts of such adroit comedians as De Wolf Hopper, Digby Bell, and Jefferson de Angelis, it failed. The influence of *The Mikado* was again evident, this time in the Oriental setting. But the book and lyrics did not fit the setting, and were described as "cheap wit of the variety or minstrel stage." De Koven's music scarcely attracted passing mention.

Far more shrewdly calculated than any earlier American comic opera was *The Lady or the Tiger?*, given at Wallack's Theatre on May 7, 1888, with a book derived by Sydney Rosenfeld from Frank R. Stockton's popular story, and with music by Julius J. Lyons, scored by Adolph Nowak, conductor of the piece. Hopper and De Angelis were again on hand, along with Maud Wilson. Conceiving the piece as a "spectacular lyric comedy," Rosenfeld concocted a libretto of more than the usual credibility. His promise to find a solution for the famous enigma at the end of the Stockton story was given tremendous publicity before the opening. Unhappily, the solution was something of a dud. When the door of the arena opened, a comic old lady (played by Mathilde Cottrelly) emerged. In other words, it was neither the Lady nor the Tiger; the Tiger had been poisoned by a court official who was himself in danger of the creature's jaws. The chief fault of the book lay in the fact that Rosenfeld spent two acts staving off all possible eventualities and enlarging a story that might have been told in about ten words. Hopper carried the main burden of the piece as well as he could, in his exuberant, noisy way. The music, however, lacked force, the orchestration was thin and primitive, and the entire score was wretchedly sung. But it lasted seven weeks—almost four times as long as any of the preceding American comic operas—and was even revived in 1892, with Della Fox, Hopper's leading lady in *Wang*, as the threatened heroine.

In view of the vise-like grip of "O Promise Me" upon the affections of the American people, *Robin Hood,* presented at the Standard Theatre on September 28, 1891, after an initial run in Boston, by the repertory company known as The Bostonians, would seem to merit respectful attention. But this opera, though it was the first genuine hit by an American composer and librettist and later proved to be the only durable work in Reginald de Koven's extensive list, bore little significant relationship to the past, present, or future of the popular musical stage. Its aspirations were basically operatic. Even when it was first produced, *Robin Hood* was thought to be "both in subject and spirit a light dramatic opera rather than a comic opera in the English sense of the term," though De Koven's share in it was considered "creditable to his taste, if not to his originality." Except in the annals of the national box office, *Robin Hood* occupies no significant place in our story, for its stuffy manners led to nothing provocative in subsequent musical pieces—not even in those by De Koven and Smith.

Though *Fatinitza* had been given in English as early as 1874, the first Viennese work to profit from the new enthusiasm for comic opera was not by von Suppé, or, for that matter, by either of the other top-ranking Viennese composers, Karl Millöcker and Johann Strauss, Jr. It was *The Royal Middy* (1880), an adaptation of *Der Seekadett*, by Richard Genée, now remembered primarily as a librettist for Strauss rather than as a composer in his own right. *The Royal Middy* was the first comic opera given under the management of Augustin Daly, who quickly became one of the most active and reputable American producers of this form of entertainment.

Since it was inferior in musical quality, *The Royal Middy* demonstrated, by the warm response it received, a mounting interest on the part of the New York audience in the over-all effect of comic opera, rather than any musical discrimination. The music was the weakest attribute not only of the piece itself, but also of the performance. Except for Catherine Lewis, none of the performers sang well. Ada Rehan, a newcomer who was soon to develop a large following, had little to do except look pretty. The production was lavishly staged and costumed, and was well provided with unusually attractive girls, who caused a stir when they appeared as a chorus of middies, wearing "trowsers." An inventive production number, presaging the Ninette de Valois ballet *Checkmate* many years later, presented a game of chess, with gaily dressed children as pawns, castles, knights, and bishops. Later in the year a second version of *Der Seekadett* was advanced in New York under the title *The Sea Cadet*. Sydney Rosenfeld's slavish translation of the original German libretto served to prove that Fred Williams' free adaptation of *The Royal Middy* had greatly benefited a stupid book. The only advantage of the second production was one the audience did not appreciate: As in the case of the D'Oyly Carte production of *H. M. S. Pinafore*, the composer's original orchestration was used.

Daly hoped to create a sensation with a second Genée comic opera, *Zanina*, which he presented at his theatre in 1881. Long before the opening, an energetic campaign of publicity whetted the public appetite for a glimpse of the nautch girls, six in number, who arrived in ample season, expressed their dismay at the American climate and the American diet to reporters who descended upon them in their hotel, and duly displayed their dances at the opening performance. From this remote vantage point, it is impossible to guess how authentic the art of the nautch girls may have been. In any case the entire audience, wholly conditioned to the extensions and elevations of French ballet, found the more restricted and floor-bound movements of the little Indian dancers dull and uninviting. One critic wrote that their dance was "a monotonous, rhythmic movement of the hands and feet to the accompaniment of a drum and three-stringed sitar. They are not pretty and their faces were disfigured by ugly ornaments. There was nothing improper, suggestive or licentious in the dance." Another reviewer commented that however much the snake dance may have charmed the snake, it did not charm the audience.

Ill luck hounded Daly's nautch girls. One of them fell ill shortly before the première of *Zanina*, and died a few days later. All the girls really suffered from the rigors of New York winter weather, and their complaints about their diet were based on grounds far more legitimate than a mere desire to supply newspaper copy. It was many a long year before any more Indian dancers were brought to this country; it was easier to provide counterfeit Oriental art, and the audience preferred it.

The Merry War (1883) was the first comic opera by Johann Strauss, Jr., to reach the English stage in this country. While the piece made a pleasing impression with its well-trained chorus of a hundred voices and its Japanese ballet (antedating *The Mikado* by two years), *The Merry War* did not create a major stir. The operettas of Strauss, indeed, stubbornly failed to achieve as much popularity as the products of Von Suppé, Millöcker, Offenbach, Audran, and Gilbert and Sullivan. It is especially interesting to observe that no producer appeared to be interested in staging *Die Fledermaus*, which was to achieve a two-year run on Broadway more than half a century later, and which, from today's perspective, would seem to be the one work that might have catapulted Strauss to the fame we now feel he deserves.

The vogue of Vienna continued with Millöcker's *The Black Hussar* (1885), which achieved a run of 104 performances at Wallack's Theatre. An exceptional cast conspired with Millöcker's skillful score to make the piece a success. In it De Wolf Hopper, Digby Bell, and Mathilde Cottrelly sang a Gilbertian topical song, "Read the Answer in the Star," to which they constantly added new verses.

The greatest German comic-opera event of the 1880s, however, was the production of Genée's *Nanon*, which came to the Casino Theatre after runs of over 300 nights in both Berlin and Vienna (and, for that matter, a modestly successful engagement in German at the busy Thalia Theatre in New York). This time Genée, whose earlier music had been unimpressive, had provided a waltz serenade, "Anna, in Rapture I Come to Thee," which had become known all over central Europe, and instantaneously duplicated its European vogue in this country. The waltz appeared and reappeared again and again throughout the score of *Nanon*, and nobody ever got tired of it.

The production, one of the most forward-looking of its day, was conceived by Heinrich Conried, who later became manager of the Metropolitan Opera Association. In a sharp departure from the fashion of deploying the chorus in military drill formations (a technique habitually employed in the contemporaneous pieces of Edward Solomon), Conried sought to distribute the members of the chorus in a more naturalistic manner; he was one of the first to insist that chorus girls might be made to seem something more than brainless, identical mechanisms. Conreid's imagination, along with the luxuriant investiture, caused *Nanon* to be described as a "sensual delight."

Sydney Rosenfeld, the translator of the book, had now popularized his style. The wooden treatment of *The Sea Cadet* was replaced by a sense of freedom that permitted him to introduce references to Henry Ward Beecher and Robert G. Ingersoll, even though the action of *Nanon* took place during the reign of Louis XIV of France.

Most of the French opéra-bouffes made known in English in the 1880s were bright but conventional formula pieces, attractive enough at the time, but without much interest to posterity. Audran's *The Snake Charmer* (1881) deserves mention because a young graduate of Tony Pastor's Music Hall named Lillian Russell made her first appearance on the comic-opera stage in this otherwise forgotten work.

It is one of the persistent ironies of the musical stage that the most popular attractions are often the products of composers and authors of inferior gifts. Opéra-bouffe provided a striking instance of this disparity between popular taste and the soberer judgment of posterity. While Offenbach's brilliant *La Vie Parisienne* drew only a lukewarm response in 1883, and *La Belle Hélène* was not given in this period at all, a piece called *Falka* rode to great success at the Casino Theatre in 1884. With music by an all-but-unknown composer, François Chassaigne, and an English book by a well-meaning hack named H. B. Farnie, *Falka* again demonstrated a truth already made plain by Genée's *Royal Middy* and *Nanon*—that the best productions, rather than the best compositions, are likely to become hits. *Falka* suffered from the perennial malady of comic-opera books—a malady that continued, in later years, to afflict the books of musical comedies: All the good materials were used up before the beginning of the last act, which was weak and stale.

The tone of Farnie's adaptation was "of the street, rather than the drawing-room," and the fun, such as it was, lay in the contrived situations, the dialogue, and the well-executed farcical business—not, as in the best examples of Gilbert and Sullivan or Offenbach, in taut and witty plot construction or appositeness of the musical score to the dramatic situations and the idiosyncracies of the characters. There was a tremendously intricate argument, confusingly full of military people. (A military plot, in the 1880s, provided an excuse for the ever-popular military drills by the chorus, and for masculine uniforms that left their legs in full view.) The stock characters were typical of the period, and suggested that comic opera, when conceived on the mundane level of *Falka*, was none too far removed from burlesque, despite its claim to a superior cultural intention. There were the fat, bald, red-nosed comic; the gypsy-dancer soubrette, with her tambourines; the dashing hero, with a handle-bar mustache; the buxom heroine, whose figure approached the hour-glass contour Lillian Russell was about to immortalize; the testy old man, easily duped; the ridiculous middle-aged fop; and the unlovely, strong-minded maiden lady, of the Katisha type. The ladies of the chorus were mirrors of a fashion that was not approved by the *Dramatic Mirror,* which observed that they "would have looked very pretty if they had refrained from painting two inches thick with rouge, and from putting black under and on their eyelids, as if they were decorating a hearse." In the role of von Fulba, one of the memorable comics of the American stage,

Francis Wilson, made his comic-opera debut, offering an impersonation that had "neatness, a peculiar dryness, and an unconscious and immense comic force."

Among the satellite English composers who owed their audience to the vogue for Gilbert and Sullivan, the most gifted was Edward Solomon, some of whose comic operas made enough of an impression to threaten the Savoy Theatre duo with important box-office competition. Solomon, who a few years later became the first of Lillian Russell's three husbands, introduced his talents to this country in 1881 with *Billee Taylor*, produced by the curious and short-lived partnership of Rupert D'Oyly Carte and Edward E. Rice.

With a story set in 1800, *Billee Taylor* provided an opportunity for the exploitation of archaic customs and fashions in dress that seemed as quaint to the 1881 audience as 1881 customs and dress seem to us today. The musical score, written with confident professional command, might be described as halfway between *The Bohemian Girl* and *H. M. S. Pinafore* in style. The sentimental airs were afflicted with a mid-century, post-Mendelssohnian loginess (a little like the hymn tunes of the period) which Sullivan was able to avoid. The nautical tunes (for *Billee Taylor* was naval rather than military) were considerably better and had some of *Pinafore's* rakishness and bravado.

Upon *Billee Taylor* we must pin the responsibility—a grave one, when the stage routines of the 1880s are seen in retrospect—for popularizing those rigid and monotonous military drills which for a time eliminated nearly all dancing by the chorus girls from comic-opera performances. The chorus served as a mere utility, good for little except the construction of regular, foursquare group figures and rhythmic stepping. Certainly no noticeable effort was made to bring the girls into the development of the plot. Apparently this was entirely satisfying to the audience, however, for *Billee Taylor* ran for more than a hundred performances (an exceptional record for a standard-sized comic-opera production), reopened for a summer engagement at Niblo's Garden, and was revived in 1885 for Lillian Russell, who by that time had married its composer.

Solomon continued to produce comic operas as rapidly as his London contemporaries at the Savoy Theatre, though none of them were as good as those of Gilbert and Sullivan. After three mediocrities—*Claude Duval*, *The Vicar of Bray*, and *Virginia*—Solomon again struck pay dirt with *Polly, The Pet of the Regiment* (1885), produced by Rice without the assistance of D'Oyly Carte, who at that point was taken up with the imminent presentation of *The Mikado*.

Polly was the piece that turned Lillian Russell into a full-fledged star. In it she played a daughter-of-the-regiment role, and sang her way, as the press agents would say, straight into the hearts of her audience. Polly Pluckrose, the lovely orphan child of a British grenadier who lost his life in the Ashantee War, was adopted by the 200th Hussars, and grew to radiant young womanhood under the protection of that gallant regiment. The plot was a remarkably hard-boiled variant on the conventional comic-opera triangle. Polly's two competing suitors were Private Mangle and Major General Bangs. With a worldliness as refreshing as it was rare on the comic-opera stage of the 1880s, Polly persisted in preferring the major general, who offered a more tangible recompense for her affections, until she discovered that Private Mangle was in reality a German prince. As soon as the truth came out, she promptly decided to marry the private.

Any integrity Miss Russell's characterization may have possessed was largely accidental. She designed her own costumes, or at least took credit for their design, and they were anything but simple and demure. And to make sure that she held her public in the hollow of her hand, she introduced into the second act the popular ballad "The Silver Line," a sentimental ditty from the music halls, originally thrust into the context of Solomon's *The Vicar of Bray* by Marie Jensen in 1883, and forthwith appropriated by Miss Russell for use in both Gilbert and Sullivan's *Patience* and Offenbach's *The Princess of Trebizonde*.

To this day Lillian Russell remains one of the most deeply beloved and widely admired prima donnas of the American popular musical stage. Such latter-day celebrities as Marilyn Miller, Gertrude Lawrence, Ethel Merman, and Mary Martin have never received quite the same unbridled adulation; nor has any of them become the single, supreme, unchallenged symbol of all that was most desirable and most glamorous in her period.

"From early girlhood to the hour of her death," wrote Francis Wilson in 1922, "she moved in a court of beauty of which she was the undisputed queen." This beauty, which won her three husbands, the lifelong friendship of Diamond Jim Brady, and millions of advocates all over America, was combined with a temperament so generous that Lew Fields, after her death, called her "the dearest thing that ever was in show business."

Though she had little or no talent as an actress, she did not flaunt her beauty as a device to deflect attention from her dramatic shortcomings. She seemed almost unconscious of her physical endowments, apparently taking them for granted as gifts God intended her to preserve and cherish, but regarding them without vanity. Beyond argument, she was the best-dressed woman on the stage. She took her responsibility for the handsome and unblemished display of her expensive dresses so seriously that she bought substitute gowns of cheap fabric but identical color to wear at rehearsals, in order to preserve her wardrobe in complete freshness for the opening-night performance.

The daughter of an editor and a militant woman suffragist, Lillian Russell was born in Cleveland in 1861. In spite of all feminist leanings, her mother recognized Lillian's exceptional beauty, and reared her with a full appreciation for her loveliness and a sense of her duty to protect it. With Lillian's naturally sweet face went an equally sweet voice, which her mother placed under the care of Leopold Damrosch, one of the leading musicians of New York, when the time came to begin serious vocal training.

Her sumptuous beauty alone might never have carried Lillian Russell to the summit of success if she had been a less capable singer. Already in 1880, when Tony Pastor introduced her to his Music Hall audience as an "English ballad-singer," her voice was admirably schooled. After her death, W. J. Henderson, the most exacting critic of vocalism in the history of the New York press, wrote in the *Sun*, "Her voice was a clear, full lyric soprano of beautiful quality, but entirely without warmth or variety of color." She developed steadily in vocal prowess, until in *Princess Nicotine*, in 1893, she ventured to sing eight high C's at each performance, seven times a week. After one performance Nellie Melba went backstage to chide her, saying, "No prima donna sings fifty-six high C's a week." If the cautious, calculating Melba disapproved of so rash a vocal expenditure, she nevertheless admired Lillian Russell greatly (perhaps because she herself was a similarly perfect, cool, colorless singer) and remarked that she would have been an ideal Marguerite in *Faust*.

In 1886, the year after *Polly*, Lillian Russell lifted to prosperity another of her husband's works—*Pepita, or The Girl with the Glass Eyes*. In addition to Miss Russell, the cast included Chauncey Olcott, a fresh recruit from the minstrel shows, who was to remain the most popular Irish tenor of the American musical stage for nearly fifty years. *Pepita* was the last piece in which Solomon and Miss Russell were professionally associated. Shortly afterward, their marriage was dissolved, and Solomon returned to England amid printed rumors that he had already possessed a wife there at the time he married Miss Russell. Solomon's name figured in American playbills once more before it disappeared altogether. In 1889, *The Red Hussar* served as a vehicle for the American debut of Marie Tempest, who achieved more renown for herself than for the weak piece in which she appeared.

Lillian Russell moved from *Pepita*, after it closed, into another English comic opera, *Dorothy* (1887), which had a highly successful run. An importation from the renowned Gaiety Theatre in London, *Dorothy* was composed by Alfred Cellier, who conducted the D'Oyly Carte performances of *H. M. S. Pinafore* and *The Pirates of Penzance* in New York. The book was written by B. C. Stevenson. Cellier shared in the polite tradition of Edward Solomon, and, like him, imitated without essential originality the musical style of Sullivan, displaying an educated, well-bred, solid compositional technique. Stevenson's libretto was complimented by high-thinking critics for its refusal to employ the slangy diction characteristic of many American comic-opera books and adaptations.

But both Solomon and Cellier, when all was said and done, were scarcely more than pale counterfeits of the master team of British comic opera. Any loss of prestige Gilbert and Sullivan may have suffered as a result of their two most recent efforts, *The Sorcerer* and *Princess Ida*, was recovered a hundred times over by the triumph of *The Mikado* in 1885. It would be difficult to say which of three pieces was the greatest hit of the 1880s—*Adonis*, *The Mikado*, or *Erminie*. But *The Mikado* is still full of vitality, half a century after the permanent disappearance of *Adonis*, and thirty years after the last big revival of *Erminie*.

D'Oyly Carte and the authors of *The Mikado* ought to have learned a lesson from their unhappy experiences with the pirating of *H. M. S. Pinafore*, but they did not. The first American performance of the Japanese opera was again an unauthorized one, in Chicago instead of Boston this time, on July 6, 1885. The producer was Sydney Rosenfeld, the translator of *The Sea Cadet*, *Nanon*, and other German-language comic operas. On July 20, Rosenfeld brought *The Mikado* to the Union Square Theatre in New York. It was allowed to play only one performance before it was closed by law. The legal difficulties were soon straightened out, however, and the production resumed its run on August 17, with Henry C. Miner as manager in place of Rosenfeld. It was an inept performance and was mildly received, though the work itself was favorably regarded, and Roland Reed won a personal success as Ko-Ko.

Two days after the reopening of the pirated *Mikado*—on August 19—D'Oyly Carte presented the official version, with John Stetson as his appointed American managerial representative. Sullivan did not arrive in time to conduct the authentic première, but came for a special gala performance on September 24. The production manifested the highest excellence in every regard. Accordingly, justice was finally done, for the D'Oyly Carte version ran for 250 performances at the Fifth Avenue Theatre, which had ample time to change its name to the Standard and back to the Fifth Avenue again before the engagement ended. All of the United States and Canada quickly went *Mikado*-mad. The rage for Japanese art, whose currency in England had prompted Gilbert's satire in the first place, swept the country. Nearly the entire text of *The Mikado* became household words; in due season the quips and lyrics were passed down from one generation to the next, and even today half the audience at a *Mikado* performance usually knows what the next line is going to be. Probably no other piece in the entire history of the American musical stage has settled so deep in the affections of thousands of perennial, unshakable devotees.

Judged on the merits of its book and music, the triumph of *Erminie*, the year after *The Mikado*, is inexplicable. Certainly the erudite H. T. Parker of the Boston *Transcript* found it so when it was revived in 1920. To him it seemed "a thin and pretty sentimental balladry, with high notes here and there, klinking little choruses, lightly running little ensembles." But there is no blinking the facts. Edward Jakobowski's "sentimental balladry" and "klinking little choruses" were listened to attentively by capacity audiences at the Casino Theatre for five months after the première on May 10, 1886. Contracts made before the opening then forced *Erminie* to go on tour; but within six weeks it was back to continue its run for ten additional months. Like the other major hits of the nineteenth century, it was revived repeatedly, usually with great success. By the end of the century it had established a total of 1,256 performances in New York alone.

Even Rudolph Aronson, the producer of *Erminie*, was taken completely by surprise. Shortly before the opening, he declined to buy the exclusive American rights for $500. Subsequently, he claimed to have paid out $120,000 in royalties. We need not mourn his lack of foresight, however, for he reaped his full share of the benefits. On top of the Casino Theatre he built New York's first roof garden, and on pleasant nights during the run of *Erminie* presented an orchestra of thirty players "before crowds seated among blooming plants and green shrubs and flowing fountains."

Harry Paulton drew his libretto for *Erminie* from a nearly forgotten early nineteenth-century play, *Robert Macaire*. Originally devised in 1823 as a French melodrama, under the title *L'Auberge des Edrets*, the piece changed in its first Paris rehearsals from a blood-and-thunder tragedy to a comedy when its leading actor, Frédéric Lemaître, found himself unable to take it seriously. In its reoriented form, *Robert Macaire* traversed the theatre worlds of France, England, and America. Records of many performances in Greenwich Village and other downtown locations can be found in the early annals of the New York theatre. Years later, the story aroused the interest of Robert Louis Stevenson and William Ernest Henley, who wrote a joint version. Paulton's book for *Erminie*, however, did not undertake to borrow from Stevenson and Henley, but went directly to the historic farce. The plot, not worth recounting in detail, since it was not the source of *Erminie's* popular appeal, dealt with the adventures of two thieves, one dashing and brave, the other timorous and insecure.

The second act of *Erminie*, a ballroom scene done entirely in pink, was widely considered to be the most ravishing stage spectacle of the decade. The entire act was little more than a costumed ballad concert, ending with a dance. In rehearsal the scene was so spare that Aronson persuaded Jakobowski to interpolate a lullaby he had composed for an earlier, unsuccessful work. Sung at the première by Pauline Hall, and on later occasions by Isabel Urquhart and by Lillian Russell, this lullaby became the most popular tune in the entire score.

Pleasing as it was, the pink ballroom scene would not have been enough to account for the first-rate success of a third-rate comic opera. It was the performance of Francis Wilson as Cadeaux, the timid little thief, with his tattered clothes and omnipresent valise, that raised *Erminie* to its otherwise undeserved pedestal in the hall of fame. As touching as George L. Fox, as inspired in the invention of comic devices as Bobby Clark, Wilson was one of the memorable comedians of the American stage. With the adroit aid of his partner, William S. Daboll, who played Ravennes (the character modeled after Robert Macaire), Wilson saw to it that *Erminie* never suffered a moment of letdown when he was on the stage.

A graduate of minstrelsy and stock-company acting, Wilson turned to the legitimate musical stage in 1880, appearing with Mitchell's Pleasure

Party in a farce-comedy, *Our Goblins,* written by William Gill in the fashion established by Salsbury's Troubadours. Not long afterward, he acted in *H. M. S. Pinafore* on the West Coast, in Strauss' *The Queen's Lace Hand-kerchief* in Philadelphia and New York. With *Erminie* the shape of his career was established once and for all. The Jakobowski operetta became the major fact of his life, and he appeared in countless revivals, forming his own *Erminie* company in 1894. His last appearance on the stage was with De Wolf Hopper in the 1920 *Erminie* revival.

On this last occasion H. T. Parker described the attributes of comic art that Wilson already manifested at the beginning of *Erminie's* career in 1886: "His bright eyes twinkled, out of a face that alarm and relief, self-satisfaction and self-depreciation, were constantly and comically traversing. He was a picture of comic dilapidation as he sprawled or slipped on the staircase, a picture of comic bewilderment." Lewis C. Strang, in a captivating volume of firsthand impressions, *Famous Stars of Light Opera,* names Cadeaux as by far the best of Wilson's parts, "consistent, well-elaborated, keenly the-atrical, well-characterized, deceptively spontaneous, with nothing left to chance. He seems to have investigated the anatomy of merriment."

Instead of visualizing Robert Macaire's little friend in terms of Daumier's drawings, in which the artist drew upon the play for purposes of political satire, Wilson envisaged a Cadeaux who reminded old-timers of George L. Fox (who, as it happened, once played the role of Cadeaux, then known as Jacques Strop, in the original nonmusical *Robert Macaire*). Apart from a surface resemblance, however, Wilson was not at all like Fox, who was essentially a jovial, rollicking, mugging clown, despite the element of pathos in his style. Wilson's comedy and farce were rooted in his sense of char-acterization. He achieved much of the force of his humor by the unerring consistency with which successive bits of business built up a rounded and believable character.

With *Erminie,* comic opera of the 1880s reached its climax. The next few years marked a period of general sterility, as though the musical theatre were taking a nap before launching into the new and exciting experiments of the middle 1890s. Three more Gilbert and Sullivan operas came along to relieve the monotony—*Ruddigore, The Yeomen of the Guard,* and *The Gondoliers*—but none proved to be another *Mikado.* The list of Viennese and German operettas was swelled by a variety of mediocrities.

One piece of some interest was *Castles in the Air,* the first comic opera by Gustave Kerker, a German émigré who established himself successfully in this country, and ultimately attained great fame from his music for *The Belle of New York.* De Wolf Hopper, a rowdy comedian who maintained a long hold over a big popular audience, was starred for the first time in *Castles in the Air,* appearing opposite the vivid and petite Della Fox, who was shortly to share with Hopper the popular favor accorded the exotic *Wang.*

Just at the turn of the decade, *Poor Jonathan,* a Millöcker operetta presented in 1890, presaged the development in public taste the new decade was to witness. Though its music and many of its other features were shaped in the familiar mold of Viennese comic opera, *Poor Jonathan* was the first "dresscoat" piece—dealing with contemporary life and manners—to be staged at the Casino Theatre, the most fashionable home of traditional comic opera and operetta. Only the final scene, at West Point, allowed opportunity for the lavish colors and striking costumes which had always been considered a fundamental requisite of comic opera productions.

Poor Jonathan had a curious history. It was first produced in Germany, where its American locale at that time was thought to be the height of the exotic. Any resemblance it bore to life in the United States was purely accidental. The stage directions for the first act read: "Rubygold's plantation; happy darkies picking cotton along the Battery, New York." Since this scene could hardly be expected to elicit a favorable response from New York audiences, the setting was shifted, for local consumption, to West Point.

Lillian Russell was the leading lady in *Poor Jonathan*, a little out of her element in a piece which, unfortunately for her limited gifts, required a modicum of acting ability. Gustave Kerker was the musical director, and the stage director was Heinrich Conried.

The heaviest responsibilities of *Poor Jonathan* were carried by Jefferson de Angelis, who was by now fully established as one of the most popular comedians of the American musical stage. De Angelis had attained the status of a star by a long, hard route. Like most other comedians of his day, he received his basic training in variety, minstrel shows, and melodramas—largely in San Francisco. He appeared in the first San Francisco performance of *H. M. S. Pinafore*, though up to that time he had made his reputation as a Dutch comic, a species that was to become immortalized around the turn of the century by Weber and Fields, the Rogers Brothers, and Sam Bernard. In the course of a four-year tour (from 1880 to 1884) of Australia, China, India, and Africa, he developed his technique as a comic-opera comedian. Making his way finally to New York—where he had been only once before, briefly, as a youth—he found an opening with E. E. Rice's Surprise Party, in *A Bottle of Ink*. After a brief spell with W. A. Mestayer's combination, in *We, Us, and Company*, he was given his first big-time opportunity in Philadelphia, in *The Little Tycoon*. He next moved into the road company of *Ruddigore*, and from this point forward his career was assured. Though he had already appeared in New York in a variety of comic operas, *Poor Jonathan* was the first to bring him into major prominence. Three years later, in 1893, he took part in the first revue in the history of the New York stage, *The Passing Show*. In 1897 he produced one of his greatest successes, *The Wedding Day*, a comic opera in which he was co-starred with Lillian Russell and Della Fox. The later years of his career included an appearance as Ko-Ko in the memorable Shubert-Brady revival of *The Mikado* in 1910, with William Danforth as the Mikado, William Pruette as Pooh-Bah, Andrew

Mack as Nanki-Poo, Fritzi Scheff as Yum-Yum, Christie MacDonald as Pitti-Sing, Christine Nielson as Peep-Bo (later played by Alice Brady), and Josephine Jacoby as Katisha. His final appearances, in the late 1920s, were in two nonmusical plays, *The Royal Family* and *Apron Strings*.

Without De Angelis' exceptional gift for characterization, which won praise even from the rock-ribbed Philip Hale of the Boston *Herald, Poor Jonathan* might easily have collapsed. Yet it was an important experiment in the direction of dramatic verisimilitude. Largely devoid of the elaborate dances, picturesque groupings, and effective military marches and formations that were the stock-in-trade of the comic operas at the Casino, *Poor Jonathan* rested its case on its plot and characterizations, and on its topical songs and concerted numbers. Breaking away from many of the expected conventions of comic opera, it paved the way for later musical comedies that adopted the informality of farce-comedy, yet strove to reach the better musical standard of comic opera.

Perhaps more important still, *Poor Jonathan* proved that the comic-opera stage, the sole field of operation of the most cultivated and craftsmanlike authors, composers, and performers of the light lyric theatre, could now make way for a piece that showed no concern for European royalty and nobility, foreign regiments and navies, or exotic, historical, and legendary scenes of far away and long ago. The validity of American life as theatrical subject matter was beginning to be apparent to the proponents of upper-level musical entertainment, as it had been from the first to the sponsors of burlesque and farce-comedy. When the top-grade authors and producers discovered America, the dawn of musical comedy was at hand.

IX. Comic Opera: The Second Decade

THE MAJORITY LIKE HIM very much; the minority detest him beyond endurance," wrote Lewis C. Strang of De Wolf Hopper in 1900. It must have been a large majority and a small minority, for Hopper had been one of the busiest comic-opera comedians of the 1890s, having reached stardom in the Gustave Kerker comic opera *Castles in the Air* in 1890. The fact that his success in New York was something less than triumphant partially justifies Strang's acid comment for it was the road and not the metropolis that first gave Hopper his solid position in the American theatre.

His next piece, *Wang* (1891), was, however, quite as much of a hit in New York as on its elegant road tour in Wagner Palace Cars. (This trip is described in an illustrated booklet entitled *De Wolf Hopper's Wagner Tour*, a title that might lead the unwary to suppose that he went barnstorming as Wotan and Hans Sachs.) *Wang* was followed in quick succession by two more well-contrived vehicles, *Panjandrum* and *Dr. Syntax*, which managed to keep Hopper before the public somewhere in the United States nearly all the time.

Wang employed the petite Della Fox as its leading lady. Whether in tights or in skirts, both of which the plot entitled her to wear, she was one of the most admired charmers of the day. Time has dimmed her reputation, perhaps because her personal life was less colorful than that of Lillian Russell; but she was no less effective a performer, quite able to hold her own against Miss Russell's more buxom allurements and more operatic voice when they appeared together in *The Wedding Day* in 1897. Though Lillian Russell was the accepted queen of comic opera, Della Fox "had in her day," according to Jefferson de Angelis' autobiography, "as many women worshipers as Geraldine Farrar. It was nothing uncommon to see fifty or a hundred women and girls waiting at the stage door when she left the theatre." For the "conscious buffoonery" and "classified mannerisms" of Hopper her directness and simplicity served as an excellent foil, and a good half of the success of *Wang* could be credited to her.

A compound of familiar comic-opera materials with an admixture of burlesque, *Wang* took place in Siam. "It might equally well be laid in the interior of the dark continent," drily observed the *Dramatic Mirror*, which went on to say: "The book is by far the better half of *Wang*. The score is mediocre to a degree." For the book, the credit, if such it was, went to the untiring J. Cheever Goodwin, who nearly two decades earlier had collaborated with Edward E. Rice in the early monument of burlesque, *Evangeline*. In the succeeding years, having broken off relations with Rice soon after the production of *Evangeline*, Goodwin had devoted himself to a long list of comic-opera librettos, all neatly cut and tailored for the class trade. Away from Rice he lost some of his feeling for the simple verities that gave *Evangeline* its peculiar validity, and he turned into little more than a highgrade hack. The book of *Wang* reached the summit of its wit when the regent of Siam remarked, "I don't reign, I sprinkle." Other word plays, we are told, "were equally good."

The composer to Goodwin's "syllabic gymnastics" was a fellow Bostonian, Woolson Morse. Except for *Cinderella at School*, produced in Springfield, Massachusetts, in the late 1880s, and refurbished for New York purposes later on as *Dr. Syntax*, *Wang* was Morse's first important score. Trained in musical composition in Germany, he was one of the first wholly capable American comic-opera composers. Morse's talent so impressed W. S. Gilbert that he asked the American composer to become his collaborator after the split between Gilbert and Sullivan. Morse refused, however, and continued to compose pieces for New York production—many of them in conjunction with Goodwin—with the aid of the harmonium, at which he always wrote his music. The trouble with the score of *Wang* was not that it was incompetently written, but that it lacked freshness and originality in its musical ideas. Two or three pretty ballads and a topical song were all it offered to post-performance whistlers. Morse made little or no attempt to simulate Oriental color, except in the music for Wang's first entrance (on a full-scale imitation elephant) and for the wedding and coronation marches, of which it was said that for Morse "oriental equals loud cymbals plus cacophony." Another contemporary observer detected almost every kind of influence in the score, from Gilbert and Sullivan to the revivalist hymns of Moody and Sankey.

Wang was called an "operatic burletta" out of deference to the burlesque aspect that permitted Miss Fox to wear tights. But its conventions were those of comic opera, as was true of all Hopper's subsequent vehicles. His voice had been trained operatically, and his special talent was for a broad projection that required operatic singing and spectacular stage settings.

Almost exactly two years after the première of *Wang*, Goodwin and Morse provided Hopper and Miss Fox with their next piece, *Panjandrum*. It was described as an "olla podrida in two acts," as good a term as any for a work designed as a sequel to *Wang*. This time the Philippine Islands (a safe comic-opera locale, since nobody knew very much about the Philippines in 1893) provided the remote setting. The plot required Hopper to make his entrance with a toreador song, inasmuch as, "finding his sweetheart, Phiunta, has been attracted by the prowess of a matador, he resolves to regain her affection by himself fighting the bull." The resolution of the plot required a full evening: at the end of Act I, Hopper "returned to the stage tattered on the horns of a bull, after his expected victory."

A contemporary interview with Hopper's manager, Ben Stevens, gives some picture of theatrical finances in 1893. "Receipts for the first four weeks of *Panjandrum*," he reported, "have been $5,200 in excess of receipts of *Wang* during the first month at the same theatre. It may interest the theatrical profession to know how much *Panjandrum* cost. I will not give it in round numbers, but in exact figures—$23,870.86. I think you may say safely that that touches the topnotch of pecuniary investment in a light opera. I need simply say that *Wang* cost $12,600."

Edna Wallace Hopper, De Wolf Hopper's wife, was leading lady in *Dr. Syntax* (1894). The growing demand of audiences for comic operas with vaguely believable plots was reflected in the absence of an exotic locale, and in the comparatively tight construction of the libretto, which was based on Tom Robertson's play *Cinderella*. In a tradition kept alive today by the performances of Frederick Ashton and Robert Helpmann as the Ugly Sisters in the Sadler's Wells version of Prokofieff's ballet *Cinderella*, a schoolmistress was impersonated in grotesque transvestite fashion, and engaged in a comic duet and dance with Hopper. The piece ended with a boat race between Harvard and Columbia, which "would have been even more exciting if Mr. Hopper had not explained in his speech before the curtain after the first act that Columbia would win in New York, but that Harvard would beat Columbia when he played Boston." Hopper was already displaying the penchant for curtain speeches that made it impossible, in later years, for his audiences to escape hearing him recite "Casey at the Bat."

Hopper next appeared in *El Capitan* (1896), a piece memorable chiefly because its music was written by John Philip Sousa. Six years earlier, Sousa, already director of the United States Marine Band in Washington, had ventured into the comic-opera field by making the orchestrations for *The Merry Monarch*, a vehicle for Francis Wilson, with music partly by Emmanuel Chabrier and partly by Woolson Morse. Though he had functioned as orchestrator on one or two subsequent occasions, *El Capitan* was his first complete score. Sousa made later efforts to win success in the comic-opera field, but his destiny lay with his marches.

Morse's willingness to take over Chabrier's opéra-comique, *Le Roi Malgré Lui*, and adapt it to American uses typified the belief in the supremacy of foreign comic opera which still prevailed in the early 1890s. Some years were still to pass before the output of competent native composers became large enough to render the contributions of Europe relatively unessential to Broadway's needs. The works brought to the United States in the 1890s reflected, however, a slump in the quality of the products of Parisian and Viennese composers. In Paris, Offenbach and Lecocq were dead, Audran was near the end of his career, and no younger composers had come along to replace them. The Viennese movement of the 1870s—the inspired combination of Offenbach's gaiety with the remnants of the indigenous Singspiel of Lortzing and Flotow—which had swept Johann Strauss, Jr., von Suppé, and Millöcker to the summit of popularity, had lost its energy. By 1900 all three of these composers were dead; and most of the pieces they wrote in the 1890s were inferior to their earlier ones. Not until *The Merry Widow* (1907) ushered in the neo-Viennese period of the Hungarians Franz Lehár and Emmerich Kalman did Central European comic opera—despite the contributions of the Moravian Leo Fall—really take a new lease on life in the United States.

One of the few French successes of this period was *Miss Hellyett* (1891), with music by Audran and a book by Maxime Boucheron, rewritten by David Belasco for the benefit of Mrs. Leslie Carter, who made her only appearance in a musical work in the leading role. Audran's *La Cigale* (1891), in which Lillian Russell sang, included new music by Ivan Caryll, soon to become in his own right one of the important composers for the American musical-comedy stage.

The supply of Viennese and German comic operas was larger, but hardly more distingushed. In the United States, for some incomprehensible reason, Johann Strauss, Jr., never attained during his lifetime the popularity he enjoyed in Europe. When he came to America to conduct his dance orchestra in 1890 he enjoyed a considerable personal success, but *Die Fledermaus* did not fully capture the American imagination until more than forty years afterward, and *The Gypsy Baron* never really has up to this very day. It is not surprising, therefore, to discover that the works of Strauss did not figure on the boards in the 1890s, despite his visit. Lovers of Germanic comic opera, whose taste seemed to be indestructible, were regaled instead by Zeller's *The Tyrolean* (1891), in which Marie Tempest was the star. It would long since have been forgotton if it had not shared a double bill with Mascagni's *Cavalleria Rusticana*, which was new to New York and created quite a stir. (This production of *Cavalleria Rusticana*, incidentally, is the earliest precedent in New York for the plan, now frequently proposed, of presenting grand operas for extended runs in legitimate houses.) Marie Dressler, whose subsequent career was associated with anything but German operetta, appeared in Charles Puerner's *The Robber of the Rhine* (1892). Hellmesberger's *Apollo, or The Oracle of Delphi*, in which Lillian Russell sang in 1891, was marked by a beautiful production, Grecian manners, little vitality, and an unending supply of waltzes. Slightly more distinctive was Adam Itzel, Jr.'s *The Tar and the Tartar* (1891), because Helen Bertram ventured to perform a barefoot dance. Stahl's *The Lion Tamer*, orchestrated by Sousa, owed its success to the low comedy of Francis Wilson, who played the title role. The one Viennese work of any special merit was Millöcker's *Poor Jonathan*.

American composers of serious stripe accelerated their efforts to compete with their foreign colleagues in the early 1890s, but most of their products were stillborn. Reginald de Koven attempted vainly to reinforce his *Robin Hood* success with *The Fencing Master* (1892), with Marie Tempest in the cast. Edgar Stillman Kelley's *Puritania* dealt laboriously with Salem witchcraft, a vocation that was to return to the stage in grand-opera form in Charles Wakefield Cadman's *A Witch of Salem* (1926), produced by the Chicago Civic Opera Company, and Howard Hanson's *Merry Mount* (1934), produced by the Metropolitan. Salem witches do not seem to inspire American composers to their most inviting efforts, if the evidence of these three works may be regarded as indicative.

With so little to offer of either the homemade or the imported variety, comic opera slid out of favor considerably between 1890 and 1895. Its place in the affections of the public was largely usurped by extravaganzas and spectacle shows, which multiplied rapidly in that period of low production costs and ready spending-money. Such spectacles as those of the Kiralfy Brothers and Edward E. Rice had been a part of the American theatrical scene ever since *The Black Crook* set the original pattern of success. But they had been fairly widely spaced, on the assumption that not more than one or two at a time could succeed. Now, however, the rate of production was considerably accelerated, and for five years many of the interesting attractions of the New York musical stage were modernized variants of this elaborate form.

Chicago was a year late in opening its world's fair celebrating the four hundredth anniversary of Columbus' discovery of America, but the New York theatre was right on time. On May 15 of the appropriate year, *1492*, an extravaganza with a book by R.A. Barnett and music by Carl Pflueger, opened, heralded by publicity calling it "a musical, historical melodrama." But its music was nothing to hum the next day; its historical data were open to suspicion, to say the least; and its melodrama, or drama of any kind, was minimal. Perhaps, on reconsidering, it is wrong to dispose of its music so unfeelingly, for after the opening some additions to the score were made—pieces by Edward E. Rice, the producer of the show (and long ago the composer of *Evangeline*) and Anton Rubinstein. *1492* was no more than a big, undisciplined, spectacular variety show, with gaudy scenery and punning humor directly descended from that of *Evangeline*, but with none of the old-time breathtaking Kiralfy tricks and transformations. Though it passed as an extravaganza, it was quite as much a burlesque, and in addition it was a mixture of French opéra-comique, standard comic opera, farce-comedy, vaudeville, local comedy, minstrelsy, and stereopticon views.

An especially successful extravaganza was *Aladdin, Jr.*, produced by David Henderson in 1895. The prolific J. Cheever Goodwin provided the book, which meant that puns were its main form of humor. The music, such as it was, came from W.F. Batchelor, W.F. Glover, and Jesse Williams. Hannah Boyd and J.J. Burke headed the cast, whose performances, like Goodwin's story, were largely subordinate to spectacular effects. One reviewer, awed by what he had seen, wrote, "Mr. Henderson is regarded as the most eminent contriver of this sort of entertainment in this country, and there are few who, having seen his former efforts and taken into account this, his latest, will dispute his position as head of the managers who work in this field." The story was that of Aladdin, moved to Peking and Egypt and told serio-comically, with magnificent scenes representing "the grand square in Peking, the exterior and interior of the mystic gardens of the imperial palace, and a place on the banks of the Nile."

"In the third act," reported the voluble *Dramatic Mirror*, "is seen the cascade of the Golden Glen and the resort of the Silver Storks, where is descried the amber ballet, one of the finest features of the show. In the last act, a barbaric pageant is unfolded. The final scene is one of transformation called 'The Birth of the Butterfly.' " As for the plot, "symmetries of happening [what reviewer would not love to have coined that expensive phrase?] are lost sight of among entertaining details that please one or another sense of the person who finds pleasure in such displays."

Even the newspaper writers of the day used theatrical terms ambiguously. Although one critic announced in 1890 that "burlesque as a satirical medium is dead," producers continued in many cases to call their pieces burlesques, and to incorporate "satirical"—or as we should say today, parodistic—elements. Perhaps the chief feature of burlesque—one it shared with extravaganza and with certain comic operas—was the use of women who were really not performers at all, but merely exhibitors. To any of us who might be spirited back to see a comic opera of the 1880s, this might seem a distinction without a difference; but there actually was a difference in social caste and stage routines between the burlesque chorus girls in their exaggeratedly revealing tights and the more decorous comic-opera girls, even when the latter wore abbreviated military costumes for their eternal drills and marches. Not that the burlesque girls were indecent; the road to Minsky's was still a long one. But the dress and convolutions of the girls in genuine comic opera were handled with what, for want of a more precise description, might be called better taste.

And so some pieces were described as burlesques and others, not greatly unlike them, as extravaganzas and comic operas. Moreover, the more elaborate farce-comedies of the early 1890s were often hard to tell from comic operas on the one hand and from burleques on the other. To make matters worse, the term "musical comedy" began to appear in print with some regularity. If the reader is confused about these descriptive terms, so is the author; and so were the producers and critics of the day. It required the fresh viewpoint of Weber and Fields in the later 1890s to give burlesque a new specification and a new lease on life.

The last successful extravaganza of the 1890s was *The Man in the Moon*, presented in 1899 by George W. Lederer, who had now joined the front rank of musical producers. The music involved three well-known composers—Ludwig Englander, Reginald de Koven, and Gustave Kerker; the book was by Louis Harrison and Stanislaus Stange. The cast included Sam Bernard, who was later to crown his career as a Dutch comic with the *Potash and Perlmutter* farces, Marie Dressler, and Christie MacDonald, later one of the best loved of all leading women. The extent of popular interest in *The Man in the Moon* was indicated by the production of a burlesque version of it, *The Maid in the Moon*, which soon opened on the Casino Roof, and by the fact that it prompted a sequel, *The Man in the Moon, Jr.*, for which De Koven provided the entire score (and which, like all sequels, failed to repeat the success of the original).

The mixed genre of comic opera-burlesque-extravaganza was somewhat painfully exemplified by *Tabasco* (1894), which deserves to be put on record because it was the only light-minded essay of George Whitfield Chadwick, the Boston composer who was, along with Edward MacDowell, the Aaron Copland or the Virgil Thomson of his day—one of the most respected and most frequently performed American musicians of two generations ago. After *Tabasco*, Chadwick must have dreaded comic opera as a burned child dreads the fire. The *Dramatic Mirror*, apparently overlooking the composer's high station, considered *Tabasco* "hardly worthy of serious mention. Of late, almost anything that contains musical jingles, slangy witticisms and a variegated assortment of coryphées and multi-colored costumes is styled a comic opera on the American stage. But it is time to call a halt, and give the style of entertainment to which *Tabasco* belongs its proper classification. *Tabasco* is nothing more nor less than a musical hodge-podge of this, that, and the other."

The previous year, Hammerstein's version of *The Talisman*, a minor example of French opéra-comique, had introduced the elements of extravaganza more acceptably; but its lesson was wasted. In a period of skirt dances, barefoot dances of spring, and hefty high-kicking chorus girls, Hammerstein's attempt to revive French ballet as the *pièce de résistance* of *The Talisman* was ill-timed, even though his dancers substituted high kicks for some of their arabesques. The ballet of the Zephyrs and Bacchantes celebrating the rotation of the four seasons would have guaranteed the success of a production in the 1870s. But ballet was dead as dead could be in the 1890s, and only the innovations of the Ballets Russes twenty years later, interpreted for America by Gertrude Hoffman, reinstated ballet dancing—temporarily—in the esteem of American audiences. Fashions in dancing have always run in cycles in the American theatre. Successive exotic importations of the balletic variety have had to take their turn with all the vernacular dances that have worked their way up from variety and vaudeville, and with the more pretentious native styles, such as, in later years, the idealized ballroom dancing of the Castles, the modish pseudo-modernity of the Albertina Rasch girls, and the genuine modernism of Charles Weidman and Martha Graham. Even now, ballet is not a secure partner in musical comedy, and some recent productions have boasted proudly that they had none of it.

Out of the peculiarly meaningless welter of pieces spawned in what we nostalgically call the Gay Nineties, two other comic operas merit notice for purely tangential reasons. *The Rainmaker of Syria* (1893), a German importation with music by Leo Fall, which remained open for only a few days, is the earliest production in connection with which there appears the term "angels," as a description of its misguided backers. *A Daughter of the Revolution* (1895), by J. Cheever Goodwin and Ludwig Englander, represented a new low in historical drama, for it made the mistake of taking its subject seriously, and actually contained a scene showing Washington crossing the Delaware. It is easy to see why George P. Scannell, writing in 1894, had already decided that comic opera had declined in favor of more exhibitionistic musical shows.

The one really unique and unclassifiable item of the mid-1890s was an unbelievable entertainment called *Hamlet II*. Given in the guise of burlesque, the play combined Shakespeare's poetry with "the language of the Rialto with a speed and dexterity as amusing as it is clever." The hero, Laertes, Rosencrantz, Guildenstern, and Osric were all girls in tights, and Hamlet danced a skirt dance.

PART TWO

1908—25

Ethel Jackson in *The Merry Widow*.

X. The Gaiety Girls, The Passing Show, and Weber and Fields

CREATING A TIDAL WAVE of enthusiasm comparable only to that rolled up a generation earlier by Lydia Thompson and her bleached blondes, the Gaiety Girls disembarked in New York in the late summer of 1894. George Edwardes, the manager of the Gaiety Theatre in London, presented his English charges at Daly's Theatre on September 18, 1894, in a so-styled comic opera, *A Gaiety Girl*. But it was not *A Gaiety Girl* which "became the talk of the town" and kept the piece running until it had to leave because of the players' commitments back home in England. It was the Gaiety Girls themselves, who now occupy a special page in the theatrical memory book along with their American successors, the Florodora Girls and the Follies Girls. An audience jaded by the standardized come-ons of padded burlesque queens and empty-headed comic-opera chorus girls performing empty-headed drills fell wholeheartedly in love with the vivacity, the superior attractiveness of face and figure, and the good breeding and grooming of the pert visitors. Unlike the sirens of Lydia Thompson's troupe, the Gaiety Girls moved the entire genus chorine one step up the ladder toward the position of respectability and social acceptance musical-comedy girls enjoy today.

George Edwardes was one of the great showmen of his time. The London theatre to whose name he brought immortality was built in 1868. Under the first manager, John Hollingshead, the Gaiety was at first devoted to a variety of attractions. The opening bill offered a one-act operetta, a comedy-drama, and a short extravaganza with a book by W.S. Gilbert, who had not yet entered into partnership with Arthur Sullivan. In the first five seasons alone, Hollingshead presented a miscellaneous assortment of some 150 pieces (which meant about fifty complete bills)—comedies, dramas, burlesques, and comic operas. In 1876, stimulated by the example of Lydia Thompson, who had popularized the full-length burlesque in England, Hollingshead turned his theatre over to that form of entertainment exclusively, beginning with *Little Don Caesar*. He improved on the quality of Miss

Thompson's productions, and engaged performers whose abilities were sufficient to build and hold a loyal following.

In *G. G.*, a book of memoirs, George Grossmith—a later manager of the Gaiety—recalls these halcyon years in connection with his decision to try a revival of old-fashioned burlesque there in 1921:

"Why not again put the Gaiety to the use for which it was built? Burlesque. . . .[Grossmith's nostaligia carried him away from the facts; the Gaiety was not actually built for burlesque, but took it on as an acquired characteristic.]

"Relight the 'Sacred Lamp'! The idea kept me awake for nights. . . .Burlesque . . . I doubt if the description were applied to a new production today whether ninety-nine percent of playgoers would know what sort of entertainment they were invited to see. In America the term had become attached to a cheap and coarse type of continuous vaudeville. The old burlesque of the Gaiety, Strand, and the Avenue and a few other theatres was the predecessor of musical comedy and revue—much like the English pantomime minus the harlequinade and fairy element. In my boyhood its reigning stars were Edward Terry, Nellie Farren, Kate Vaughan, Fred Leslie, Florence St. John, Arthur Roberts, Charles Danby, Millie Hylton and many others. Fred Leslie was in those days what Jack Hulbert is today. Nellie Farren, though entirely different in method and personality, was the prototype of Gracie Fields. The play consisted of a musical and rhyming travesty on some well-known romance, play, opera or legend, often with a punning title such as *Faust and Loose, Knife and Falka*, or else *Little Jack Sheppard, Carmen Up-to-Date*, followed by *Cinderella Up-Too-Late*.

"The hero was always played by a girl, and the chorus, like the hero, were mostly clad in tights. The comedians wore costumes and wigs and almost inevitably red noses."

For the record, Grossmith's "new old burlesque," called *Faust-on-Toast*, was a flat failure in London, even with Jack Buchanan in the cast. The rhymes and puns irritated the audience, and the girls looked "hideous" in their tights and high boots.

The Gaiety Theatre was always up-to-date, whether with its *Carmen* or with its swiftness to install arc lights (in 1878) and incandescent bulbs (in 1879), improvements with which it set an example for all other London theatres. When Fred Leslie died and Nellie Farren fell ill and there were no reigning favorites to replace them, George Edwardes, now the manager, determined to strike out on a new course. He eliminated the red-nosed comics and the girls in tights, but retained the informality of burlesque presentation. He festooned a comic-opera plot with embellishments and variety acts, in the fashion of the American farce-comedies. With shrewd directorial skill, he brought order out of chaos, gave his mélange a production that was "spirited, tasteful, and almost recklessly elaborate," and in 1893 offered to the public what he called a "musical comedy," *A Gaiety Girl*. The application of the term "musical comedy" to a modernized, dressed-up, popularized variant of comic opera was not, however, Edwardes' invention. A piece of similar plan but more moderate scope, *In Town*, had been given at the Prince of Wales Theatre a year earlier.

If any single moment can be elected as the moment of the birth of modern musical comedy, this was it. American farce-comedy, from its humble beginnings with Salsbury's Troubadours, had grown up and, so to speak, taken a trip to England, where it entered into a liaison with British comic opera and burlesque. *A Gaiety Girl* was the result of that union; she was part English and part American in parentage. When she came to this country in 1894, the American audience recognized her, despite the heavily British strain in her makeup, and took her to its heart.

In 1903, the old Gaiety closed, and a new Gaiety was opened in London with *The Orchid*, in which, as always, the chorus quickly became famous for its beauty. But by then, we no longer needed to import all the principal Gaiety productions, though *The Orchid* was given in America in 1907. Our own musical comedy was firmly and permanently established. We were beginning to have our own librettists, our own composers (most of them, to be sure, still European-born), our own interests; and American musical comedy had started off blithely down the highway that led to *Show Boat* and *Of Thee I Sing*, *Pal Joey*, and *Oklahoma!*

When *A Gaiety Girl* reached New York, the critic of the acerb *Dramatic Mirror* was not gifted with prescience as to the historic role the piece was to play in the development of the American musical theatre. For him, it was "really an indefinable musical and dramatic mélange," containing "sentimental ballads, comic songs, skirt-dancing, Gaiety Girls, society girls, life guards, burlesque, and a quota of melodrama." Not much, in all truth, could be said for the plot, though it was adequately functional. Blanche Massey appeared as the particular Gaiety Girl of the title. She was accused of stealing a diamond comb, but was ultimately able to clear her character and marry a handsome young life guard. The rage for skirt-dancing, initiated by Loie Fuller several years earlier, remained unabated, and Cissy Fitzgerald won acclaim for a dance tantalizingly described as "somewhat sensational."

Both the veteran Edward E. Rice and the somewhat younger Augustin Daly were quick to profit from the example of *A Gaiety Girl*, and to bring forward productions marked by the same light, sophisticated tone and style. In 1896, Daly staged a musical comedy entitled *The Geisha*, which, despite its Oriental title, was topical in content. In the latter part of its run it employed the services of Isadora Duncan, who had not yet discovered ancient Greece and Beethoven's Seventh Symphony. The music was by Lionel Monckton and Sydney Jones.

Rice followed with *The Girl from Paris*, for which he imported a company of British players. As a variant on the skirt-dance theme, now becoming a bit frayed around the edges, he presented Mabel Clark in a novelty, a "toe dance in long skirts." *The Girl from Paris* served to initiate the American reputation of Ivan Caryll, who became one of the popular composers of musical comedy in this country for upwards of three decades.

Daly tried to duplicate the success of *The Girl from Paris* in 1897 with *The Circus Girl*, another London production from the Gaiety, with a score by Caryll and the equally gifted Monckton. Daly made a move in the right direction by using an American cast instead of importing British performers, but the essentially English genre of the piece rather thwarted the American players. The prize comic scene was not written by the librettist, James T. Tanner, but was interpolated by James T. Powers, who convulsed the audience with his sketch of a man trying to see around, above, or under the enormous women's hats that were in fashion.

Another Daly production brought over from the Gaiety was *A Runaway Girl* (1898), also by Caryll and Monckton. Though the materials were slender, the expertness of Daly's staging made it a go. Even more than Rice—who had carried on with such British pieces as *The French Maid* and *Monte Carlo*—Daly was able to capture the light touch, the brisk direction, and the eye for a pretty chorus line that were the Gaiety's chief enduring gifts to the American musical-comedy stage. Rice was never really sure of himself in the new genre, and kept revising his productions after they had opened, in the hope of sharpening them up and extending their runs. Daly possessed the outlook of a modern producer and made sure that all was well before the curtain went up on opening night.

Actually, burlesque was more Rice's métier than the new musical comedy. None of his efforts in the new field matched the success of his final burlesque, *Little Christopher Columbus*, which he offered to the public in 1894, less than a month after the arrival of the Gaiety Girls. Even this attraction indicated Rice's new preoccupation with things British, however, for unlike his earlier burlesques, *Little Christopher Columbus* was not of his own devising. It was a London product, with a score by Caryll, to which Rice added, for New York consumption, some items by Gustave Kerker. The *Dramatic Mirror* gave a thumbnail sketch of Rice's mode of production:

"It is characteristic of Mr. Rice's methods throughout. There are gorgeous costumes and sumptuous scenery. There are pretty girls and shapely limbs in the chorus. There is an abundance of action and tableaux, and everybody bursts out in song and in dance on the slightest provocation." Not much, in fact, of the original London format seems to have remained in *Little Christopher Columbus* after Rice had indulged his predilection for revising and tinkering.

With comic operas, extravaganzas, and burlesques all bursting at the seams from their eagerness to cram in the variety entertainment that the public liked, it was inevitable that some producer should hit on a formula that would entitle him to bring variety to Broadway without the traditional encumbrance of a plot. Neither in the 1890s nor since has the theatregoing public been willing to concede (except in a few rare cases like the wartime *Priorities of 1942*) that outright vaudeville or music-hall bills warrant first-class theatrical status or first-line prices. A replica of one of Tony Pastor's variety shows, however engaging it might have been in its proper setting, did not belong in a legitimate house. Variety was variety and theatre was theatre. Yet the musical-comedy public, with sublime illogic, demanded a dressed-up, thinly disguised variant of the very entertainment it would not accept as top-grade without the dressing-up and the disguise.

The magic name of Paris came to the rescue. A vogue had set in there for topical entertainments called "revues," containing satires upon the fashionable life of the city, with specialty acts and choruses of pretty girls interlarded. Would the same device work in New York, as a framework for a diversified show without a plot? That remained to be seen: The Paris audience was more sure of itself, more formed in its tastes, closer and tighter and more specialized in its gossip. The entire audience could be expected to react more or less alike—to laugh at the same things, and to be scandalized by the same things. The New York audience was less attuned to subtleties, and infinitely less uniform in its tastes and attitudes. Moreover, the principle Broadway attractions had already begun to depend heavily on the trade of out-of-town visitors. Could a tourist from Syracuse or Cincinnati be expected to enjoy sketches and jokes lampooning a city he did not live in, whose ways were strange to him? The fate of a French-style review (the English spelling was used at first) obviously lay in the hands of the gods; but it was a gamble worth taking.

And so, on May 12, 1894, the Moorish interior of the Casino Theatre—diagonally across Broadway from the southeast corner of the Metropolitan Opera House—sheltered an elegant and knowing audience which had come to see *The Passing Show*, the first American example of the kind of show that later came to be known as a revue. Good talent went into the production, which had a score by the capable Ludwig Englander, now on the swift upgrade as a theatre composer, a book by the experienced Sydney Rosenfeld, and a cast including Adele Ritchie, Johnny Henshaw, and Paul Arthur. It was a long, loose, poorly organized affair, but it succeeded with its audience on the timeworn, and sometimes risky, principle of providing a little of everything, so that nobody could fail to like something in it. There were imitations of well-known actors, ribs of contemporary plays, and jibes at a nameless prima donna, "whose repertoire will be *Faust, Faust,* and after which *Faust*." (This was the period in which Gounod's opera was so popular that the Metropolitan was known as the "Faustspielhaus.") Lucy Daly and "a dozen colored youths" submitted "a plantation dance like that in *Princess Nicotine*" (a comic opera of the moment); Gus Pixley demonstrated "his original manner of walking with his head near his heels"; Mabel Stephenson told "her familiar stories about Jonah, Daniel, and the bear." Comedy was furnished by the Tamale Boys; muscular empathy was excited by the Acrobatic Burlesques of the Amazons; and the usual response, presumably, was stirred by Living Pictures and by a "Divertissement on L'Enfant Prodigue," a brush with art which was made palatable by the Parisian—i.e., risqué—attire of the dancers.

New York took all this to be something out of the ordinary, though the same diversions, in a somewhat less costly frame and without the Parisian reference, could be found wherever vaudeville (as it was coming to be called) and burlesque sketches were the order of the evening. The Casino thrived on its first review, and offered another one, The Merry World (this time anachronistically billed as a burlesque) in 1895. The formula was the same, and the performance had the help of Dan Daly and David Warfield, both able players, but the piece lasted only a month. The third attempt at the Casino, In Gay New York (1896), succeeded in spanning the summer, with Warfield, Virginia Earl, and several other veterans of The Merry World. Gustave Kerker wrote the music for In Gay New York, and performed the same service for the fourth Casino summer review, All of the Town, which had a four-month run in 1897. This last piece was hung on a thread of plot involving the theft of a mermaid from the Aquarium, and it leaned heavily upon caricatures of familiar figures about town. The 1898 review was known as Yankee Doodle Dandy, and for the third time Kerker provided the music. The company of The Merry World had remained something of a fixture until now; Edna Wallace Hopper and Thomas Q. Seabrook, however, were new faces in Yankee Doodle Dandy.

All of the Casino reviews were devised as hot-weather entertainment, and the house reverted to standard comic-opera and musical-comedy attractions throughout the rest of the year. It was many years before the association between revues (as the word was spelled after the first few years) and hot weather ceased to be taken as inevitable. Years later, the Ziegfeld Follies, the Shubert Passing Show, George White's Scandals, and the Earl Carroll Vanities continued to be launched in the late spring and early summer, on the apparent assumption that resistance to such frivolities was at its lowest ebb in that season.

In 1898, an autumn review, In Gotham, was staged after the pattern of the Casino shows, by Coster and Byles. They were, however, second-rate producers, and their offering was a poor man's Passing Show, with an old-fashioned burlesque-show olio bringing all the performers on at the end, one by one, and with the encumbrance of a stupid bit of farce-comedy plot alleging that Rip Van Winkle had come to life in 1899, and was moving all over town, accompanied by an Irish lawyer, in the attempt to prove his identity. Obviously Coster and Byles missed the point of the true review, and were merely trying to pass off old burlesque and farce-comedy routines in a new guise. Neither In Gotham nor its successor of 1899, Round New York in Eighty Minutes (which was notable only for the participation of James J. Corbett in a prize-fight scene), contributed to the progress of the review. Meanwhile, the Casino, running out of either ideas or patronage, did not continue its series past the turn of the century. It was a good start, but an abortive one. Not until the Winter Garden opened in 1911 did the review come back to life. For more than a decade it was kept from sight by the more adroit and homelier burlesque-extravaganzas of Weber and Fields, by the growing number of musical comedies, and by the renewed enthusiasm for Viennese comic opera initiated by *The Merry Widow*.

The great new institution of the late 1890s was Weber and Field's Music Hall, opened by the comedians in 1895. Joe Weber and Lew Fields had grown up together. As boys of eight they had already worked out their first routine, an Irish-comedy act. They were all of sixteen when they obtained their first professional job, in 1884, with the Ada Richmond burlesque company at Miner's Bowery Theatre. Though the boys at that time preferred Irish comedy, they were hired for a Dutch knockabout act—low comedy and horseplay, with a German-English dialect thick enough to cut with a knife. Fields was tall and fairly thin; Weber was short, and as time went on he became exceedingly fat. From their first engagement in burlesque they remained faithful to their Dutch-comedy characters, and it was in this guise that they appeared a decade later in their own productions at their own Music Hall.

Like Tony Pastor thirty years before, Weber and Fields wanted their enterprise to attract the steady patronage and long-term support of the family trade. Though their sketches and dialogue were rough-and-ready, they were never dirty; and the girls of the Music Hall Beauty Chorus, which was thought to live up to its name, refrained from displaying themselves in a prurient manner. Lew Fields, in reminiscences quoted by Bernard Sobel in his entertaining book *Burlycue*, maintained that "we never went back to burlesque"; but the Music Hall shows were in very fact burlesques with the features eliminated that might displease the good folk whom the partners sought to attract to their theatre.

"The Weber and the Fields Music Hall shows had girls, but we always avoided dirty material," Fields said. "We had a regular book that was legitimate burlesque of some New York hit such as *The Christian, Heart of Maryland*, or *The Messenger Boy from Mars*. Our first acts were originally written by Edgar Smith and Joseph W. Herbert, and once we were started on travesties we never went back to burlesque. Our company, as everyone knows, included such stars as Lillian Russell and Fay Templeton. Our shows were clean enough for women."

Fields has hinted at the format of his travesties, which was partly borrowed from the structure of the burlesques on which he frowned. The first half of the evening was given over to the travesty itself, more frequently based on a nonmusical play than on a current musical hit. The bills changed frequently, and the meaningless titles along with them, but the plan was unchanging. The second half of the performance amounted to an old-fashioned olio, with the performers coming out singly and in combination to offer their song, dance, and comedy specialties, and with a finale involving the girls and the whole company. It was not until Miss Russell appeared at the Music Hall for the first time, in *Whirl-I-Gig* (1899), that the olio was abandoned, in deference to the status her presence conferred upon the bill. While the appearance of Miss Russell was a credit to Weber and Fields, it seems to have been less of one for her, inasmuch as she suffered "a let-down in her style." Be that as it may, from the time of her association with their company, Weber and Fields allowed their shows to rest on their intrinsic merits, without an old-fashioned pendant of scattered variety acts.

The career of the Music Hall under their joint management lasted only nine years, for in 1904 Weber and Fields separated. They renewed their association on the Broadway stage in 1911, when, in a brief flash of their former glory, they achieved a run of 108 performances with their "jubilee revival" of the old type of extravaganza, an entertainment called *Hokey-Pokey and Bunty Bulls and Strings*. (The second half of the title was a parody of Graham Moffat's current comedy hit, *Bunty Pulls the Strings*.) Lillian Russell came back for the occasion, and William Collier was also in the cast. The next year they tempted fate with a less successful sequel, *Roly-Poly and Without the Law*. Their last association in a musical piece, after a lapse of six years, took place in Philadelphia in 1918, in *Back Again*, which they did not bring into New York.

Though they lived to see their project outmoded by changing times and tastes, Weber and Fields made an endearing contribution to the popular musical stage. After the death of Lew Fields in 1941, the New York *Times* carried an affectionate and nostalgic editorial, which must have been written by someone who remembered them in their day of glory:

"Lew was long and Joe Weber was short. They grew up together as if by agreement and for comic effect. Lew and Joe may be said to have learned to act before they felt steady on their legs. Their fun was simpler and heartier than ours.

"You would be bored to read the book of their once famous game of pool or burlesque bank—one finds in some of their scenes such properties as a cigar in the mouth of a bust, and a pig in a canary's cage—those derby hats, like shallow little shells, that tuft of chin beard, those checked suits audible afar were irresistible.

"In their burlesque plays they did finer work and may be said to have anticipated the revue. In the town of their time, their theatre—was it our first little theatre?—was an institution, a temple of drollery, a place where it was 'right' to go, a sight and sound of New York. 'Weber and Fields' was a landmark."

A few footnotes need to be added to the account of the 1890s. There was *The Belle of New York*, Gustave Kerker's first resounding success, a rather conventional cross between comic opera and musical comedy, which for some reason enjoyed greater success in London than here, and was subject to repeated British revivals until as recently as 1940. Apparently the topical allusions to New York life never became dated in London, and retained a flavor as characteristic and exotic as that of a gangster moving picture.

There was also an otherwise obscure musical comedy, in 1897, called *The Good Mr. Beth*, in which "a cinematograph played an active part in the last act." Had the producers been able to gaze into the future, they might have suppressed the satanic invention, which was one day to threaten the entire theatre business, and to rob it of nearly all the road, leaving New York an island of the legitimate theatre in a sea of motion-picture palaces.

The year 1899 also saw the last nail driven into the coffin of musical farce-comedy. Though *My Innocent Boy* was judged to be "one of the best farce-comedies in a long time" (there had been fewer and fewer of them, ever since 1890), it was able to stay open for only a week. Thereafter, nobody was tempted to call a musical piece a farce-comedy, and the genre was officially dead, after twenty years of useful service.

Negro performers finally made the big time, though rather tentatively, in two musical comedies in 1898. *A Trip to Coontown* and *Clorindy, the Origin of the Cakewalk*. The first of these was a short-lived and unimpressive piece. *Clorindy*, however, brought Will Marion Cook before the public as a composer, and might have brought Paul Laurence Dunbar into prominence as a librettist if nearly the entire libretto had not been eliminated before the show was finally produced. It was Edward E. Rice who finally, rather to his surprise and somewhat against his will, found himself sponsoring *Clorindy* on the Casino Roof.

In an excerpt from his autobiography published in *Theatre Arts*, Cook gave a vivid account of the tribulations and ultimate triimph of *Clorindy*:

"I went to see Ed Rice, and I saw him every day for a month. Regularly, after interviewing a room full of people, he would say to me (I was always the last): 'Who are you, and what do you want?' On the thirty-first day—and by now I am so discouraged that this is my last try—I heard him tell a knockabout act: "Come up next Monday to rehearsal, do a show, and if you make good, I'll keep you on all week.'

"I was desperate. . . . On leaving Rice's office, I went at once to the Greasy Front, a Negro club run by Charlie Moore, with a restaurant in the basement managed by Mrs. Moore. There I was sure to find a few members of my ensemble. I told them a most wonderful and welcome story: we were booked at the Casino Roof! . . . That was probably the most beautiful lie I ever told.

"On Monday morning, every man and woman, boy and girl that I had taught to sing my music was at the Casino Roof. . . . Luckily for us, John Braham, the English conductor of the Casino orchestra, was a brick. And, still more luckily for us, Ed Rice did not appear at rehearsal until very late that morning. . . . By this time my singers were grouped on the stage and I started the opening chorus, an orchestral and choral development of *Darktown Is Out Tonight*. I had twenty-six of the finest Negro voices in America. . . . Like a mighty anthem in rhythm, these voices rang out. . . ."

At the opening, "Rice's manager made the simple announcement that the Negro operetta, *Clorindy, the Origin of the Cakewalk*, would now be produced for the first time on any stage. Immediately I struck up the introduction and opening chorus. When I entered the orchestra pit, there were only about fifty people on the Roof. When we finished the opening chorus, the house was packed to suffocation. What had happened was that the show downstairs in the Casino Theatre was just letting out. The big audience heard those heavenly Negro voices and took to the elevators. . . .

"The Darktown finale was of complicated rhythm and bold harmonies, and very taxing on the voice. My chorus sang like Russians, dancing meanwhile like Negroes, and cakewalking like angels, black angels! When the last note was sounded, the audience stood and cheered for at least ten minutes. . . .

"Maybe, when the pearly gates open wide and a multitude of hosts march in, shouting, laughing, singing, emoting, there will be a happiness which slightly resembles that of *Clorindy's* twenty-six participants. I was so delirious that I drank a glass of water, thought it wine and got gloriously drunk. Negroes were at last on Broadway, and there to stay. Gone was the uff-dah of the minstrel! Gone the Massa Linkum stuff! We were artists and we were going a long, long way. We had the world on a string tied to a runnin' red-geared wagon on a downhill pull. Nothing could stop us, and nothing did for a decade."

XI. The Turn of the Century

FASCINATING FLORA is just another musical comedy built along the same lines as scores of its predecessors. Nothing but the expected happens: choruses sing, dance, stand in line, smile, wear colored clothes; principals get into trouble and out of it, burst into song at intervals commensurate with their importance, make jokes about New York, do specialties of more or less cleverness; the curtain falls to divide the evening into two parts; the orchestra plays the air that the promoter hopes will be popular. The whole thing is done according to formula as accurately as a prescription is compounded in a drug store. And the audience, strictly ritualistic as a musical comedy audience always is, is pleased."

Fascinating Flora, the object of the *Dramatic Mirror's* cynicism in this

review, appeared above the Broadway horizon in 1907. Although nobody—least
of all the producers—knew it then, the next few months were to bring two
pieces, the *Follies of 1907* and *The Merry Widow*, that warranted an abandonment of the ritualistic approach on the part of the audience. But in the
spring of 1907, the achievements of the New York musical stage, with
remarkably few exceptions to prove the rule, constituted a dreary retrospect
as far back as the turn of the century.

Instead of bringing fresh life to the popular musical theatre, the twentieth
century—let us agree, to circumvent the ancient argument, that the new
century began on January 1, 1900—seemed to offer almost no fresh impetus
at all. The polite and piquant tradition of the London Gaiety Theatre tapered
off in a series of reputable and often successful but unfailingly unoriginal
importations from that theatre and others in Britain; the most prosperous
and most neatly tailored of these usually had been composed by Monckton
and Caryll or Paul Rubens. Gustav Luders and Ludwig Englander provided
a series of watered-down replicas of middle-European operetta music, to
books garnished by their American adapters with appropriate bits of slang,
Tenderloin talk, and references to local people and institutions. Gustave
Kerker placed third in a desultory race with Luders and Englander.

The more formal comic operas, few in number, were uniformly poor in
quality; and, moreover, it was becoming hard to tell a comic opera from a
musical comedy, since most musical comedies were no more than vulgari-
zations of the comic-opera formula. Except for an occasional piece, once or
twice a year, that developed more than the usual momentum, and for the
springy, youthful stride of George M. Cohan, the musical theatre was content to bide its time. For the most part nobody made any serious complaint.
Times were good, and production costs and salaries were low. Producers
ran no risk in flooding the theatres with routine attractions—often sumptuously staged, it is true—when a run of fifty performances or less was
sufficient to pay off the initial costs.

Ivan Caryll, who kept the channel of communication with Britain open
by sending over one or two well-mannered musical comedies each year,
divided with Lionel Monckton the claim of being the successor, in his day,
to Sir Arthur Sullivan. This is not to say that Caryll's musical ideas were a
tenth as good as Sullivan's. But by his general competence and his ability
to turn out workmanlike scores on schedule, he attained a high position in
the British musical theatre. Since he worked with a variety of librettists,
most of whom were largely devoid of a sense of humor, he never had an
opportunity to show what he might have been able to achieve with the
stimulus of so inspired an author and lyricist as W. S. Gilbert. Until *The
Pink Lady*, more than a decade on into the century, Caryll never provided
the American theatre with a major hit, but nearly all his pieces were successful enough, in terms of the modest expectations of the day, to make his
name on a score a valuable talking point.

Caryll was not English by birth. He was born in Liège, Belgium, in 1861, and his real name was Felix Tilkins. His musical education was thoroughgoing, if conventional, for in Liége he studied with the celebrated violinist Eugène Ysaÿe and in Paris, a little later, with Camille Saint-Saëns. After a fling at the French stage he moved to London, where he became conductor at the Gaiety Theatre, and soon tried his hand at writing the sort of music the purposes of that theatre required. Until 1911 he remained in England, commuting across the Atlantic to share in the preparation of his musical comedies here after they were safely established in London. He took out American citizenship papers in 1911, and remained here during the last decade of his life. In its obituary of Caryll in 1921, the New York *Herald* provided a moderate and essentially just estimate of the composer, whose works had been almost as identical with one another as the peas in a pod: "Caryll's music combined freshness and lightness with careful workmanship, a knowledge of his medium that is uncommon among musical comedy composers today, and that enabled him to turn out musical hits of enduring merit."

Of the merit of Caryll's *The Ladies' Paradise* (1901), in which Queenie Vassar appeared as Marie Antoinette, there is room for doubt. It deserves to be recorded as a phenomenon, however, for it was the first musical comedy ever produced at the Metropolitan Opera House. Naturally it failed, without operatic voices to fill the vast spaces, at the end of three weeks.

Thereafter Caryll's contributions, in which he often shared musical responsibilities with Monckton (who did not move to the United States) were confined to more seemly surroundings. *The Toreador* (1902) required Francis Wilson to impersonate a footman inpersonating a bullfighter, a device already exploited by De Wolf Hopper in *Panjandrum*. It also required pretty Christie MacDonald to impersonate a boy; the Gaiety Theatre tradition retained a bit of this custom from the days of the 1880s when the house was devoted to burlesque.

Caryll and Monckton's biggest success of the decade, *The Girl from Kay's* (1903), abandoned a good deal of the typical Gaiety texture in favor of the low comedy of Sam Bernard and Hattie Williams, who attracted a popular audience that normally stayed away from better-bred English works. Part of the evening was given over to such vaudeville repartee as the following passage between Bernard, with his Dutch-comedy dialect, and Miss Williams:

"Vot iss id has two feet, has fedders all ofer id, und barks like a dog?"
"I give it up."
"A chicgen."
"Why, a chicken doesn't bark like a dog!"
"I know id; I chust pud id in to make id difficult."

In *The Girl from Kay's*, Bernard created the character of Mr. Hoggenheimer, an overbearing, uneducated comic Jew who was rotten with money.

This characterization, which he carried on in a subsequent musical comedy, *The Rich Mr. Hoggenheimer*, was considered by some to be the apogee of low humor, and gave him his most successful role until the later, nonmusical, period of *Potash and Perlmutter*.

The fatuous nature of the plots of the Caryll-Monckton musical comedies was epitomized in *The Orchid* (1907), whose American cast contained Eddie Foy, Trixie Friganza, and Irene Franklin. The action, which was forgotten altogether whenever it became a nuisance, centered upon the quest of a rich American for a $2,000 Peruvian orchid, to be sent, for obscure reasons, to Nice. When foul play kept the orchid from reaching its destination, the stunning discovery was made that a comparable orchid was growing in the garden kept by Eddie Foy, alias Artie Choke. This plot is not cited here as a chamber-of-horrors example, but as a characteristic phenomenon among early twentieth-century musical-comedy books. The opportunities it afforded Artie Choke enabled Foy to captivate his first Broadway audience, and to make a curtain speech in which he asserted that "you can go a long way in this world if you have a weak chin and a sunny disposition."

The musical comedies with scores by Gustav Luders and books by Frank Pixley were, if anything, even more uninviting in content. An academically trained Bremen musician, Luders came to Chicago in 1885, at the age of twenty, to conduct the orchestra in popular concerts given at the Schiller Theatre. After a few years spent in conducting and in composing such orchestral thrillers as *The Cavalry Charge*, he wrote a musical comedy called *The Burgomaster* (1900), which received enough praise to encourage him to continue in the field. *King Dodo*, produced in Chicago in 1901 and brought to New York in 1902, is memorable today only because it allowed Raymond Hitchcock, as the King of Dodo Land, to "jump into the front rank of comic opera comedians." The plot represented Hitchcock as an aging monarch with a yen for youth. He ordered the calender set back thirty years, with rejuvenating results, only to fall in love with a queen who had an exclusive penchant for old men.

By virtue of its success on the road rather than its 143 performances in New York, Luders' *The Prince of Pilsen* (1903) has come to be regarded as one of the historic items of the American musical stage. This celebrity is not justified by its thin, conventional score; nor, certainly, is it borne out by the plot (a Cincinnati brewer is mistaken for a prince when he lands at Nice), of which one observer wrote, "The story is worked out—if it is worked out at all—in the wings." Like half the pieces in the wake of *Florodora* (with which we shall concern ourselves in due season), it pinned part of its hopes on a sextette, patriotically entitled "The American Girl."

May we skip *The Sho-Gun* (1904), with its setting on the imaginary island of Ka-Choo, even if the book about the attempt of an American salesman to popularize chewing gum among the natives was the first attempt at libretto writing by the Midwestern humorist George Ade? And may we also skip

The Grand Mogul (1907)? From our point of vantage, it is difficult to tell them apart.

Ludwig Englander, like Caryll, had received schooling in the techniques of the Gaiety Threatre, but his musical style was more conspicuously Teutonic, sounding like memories of the restaurants in his native Vienna. With *The Jewel of Asia* (1903), Englander was taken to task by the *Dramatic Mirror* reviewer for a score that was completely stereotyped, even though "he has the fertile adjunct of Orientalism to assist him in his creations, and the tinkling cymbal and peculiar style and tempo of this sort of music are almost always provocative of successful work." Depending on the impulse of his librettists, Englander's books ranged from such straight comic-opera conceits as this to attempts at the vernacular like *A Madcap Princess* (1904), a musical treatment of Charles Major's novel *When Knighthood Was in Flower*, improved for the times by Harry B. Smith, who required Mary Tudor to speak in Coney Island slang. Only one libretto set by Englander, that of *The Wild Rose* (1902)—in which Smith also had a hand—appears to have commanded respect for its "coherent, consistent plot in these days of tommyrotical libretti."

The contributions of Westphalian-born Gustave Kerker were no more distinguished than those of Luders and Englander. Having climbed up the Broadway ladder from his first assignment as Edward E. Rice's conductor at the Casino Theatre in the 1880s to the triumph of *The Belle of New York* in the 1890s, Kerker's main interest lay in pieces about American situations; and to this extent his output was more homespun than the exotic, royalty-ridden, mistaken-identity pieces his colleagues so often set to music. He was even able to be inspired to a song by a lead-off line (in *The Billionaire*, in 1902) that went, "I will now sing a song written expressly for me by an expressman." On occasion, however, he could ally himself with the lovers of never-never-land as heartily as the next man. *Winsome Winnie* (1903) offered as its heroine a snake charmer in Montenegro, and *The Tourists* (1906) took place in Hindustan. The vernacular tone of most of Kerker's pieces may be illustrated by a further reference to *Fascinating Flora*, from the review quoted at the head of this chapter:

"Some of the novel features are a duet between Winnie Wiggles (a girl who has taken vocal culture from a correspondence school) and Caruso (represented by a phonograph record); a Subway Express song, with the chorus impersonating passengers in a subway car; a ballooning episode; and a dancing number by a dozen girls dressed as messenger boys."

Not one of the productions of the best-known light composers of the decade attained the fame and longevity of *Florodora*, which began its American run, exactly a year after its première in London, on November 11, 1900, and continued for 505 performances. It covered the entire nation on the road in the years following, and was successfully revived in New York in 1902, in 1905, and in 1920. It was one of the supreme hits of Broadway's history, and, with the oversimplification wrought by the passage of time, it has come to be remembered as the epitome of all that was delightful about the musical stage at the turn of the century.

For its early prosperity and its abiding fame alike, *Florodora* could thank one number: the famous sextette. Broadway reverberated with excitement after the first appearance of the six Florodora Girls—each one weighing 130 pounds to an ounce, five feet four inches tall, long-waisted, willowy, and either brunette or redheaded. "Tell me, pretty maiden, are there any more at home like you?" inquired their partners, the six Gentle Strangers. "There are a few," confessed the dainty maidens. Nobody believed them, however. How could any other girls match this perfect selection of six—Marie Wilson, Agnes Wayburn, Marjorie Relyea, Vaughn Texsmith (really Miss Smith from Texas), Daisy Green, and Margaret Walker?

The Florodora Girls were publicized as girls never were again until Florenz Ziegfeld, Jr., began to trade in "the most beautiful girls in the world." They were beset by admirers and besieged with suitors, and three of them set the fashion, not altogether accepted heretofore, of marrying men of wealth and position.

Take the sextette away from *Florodora* and what remained was disillusioning. Neither Leslie Stuart's music nor the book by Owen Hall and Frank Pixley departed from the routine manner of the English stage, whence *Florodora* came, with no outstanding record of success back home. The action took place on an island in the Philippines called Florodora, where Cyrus W. Gilfain, a wealthy American (played by R. H. Graham), manufactured a perfume named after the island. The six Florodora Girls were there to serve as typists ("typewriter girls," they called them then). Gilfain, it transpired, had stolen the island from the deceased father of one Dolores (Fannie Johnston), who now was reduced to working in the factory. A phrenologist, Anthony Tweedlepunch (Willie Edouin) became interested in restoring the island to its proper heiress. In the second act, in Wales of all places, Tweedlepunch invoked a ghost who frightened Gilfain into confessing, and paved the way for the marriage of Dolores to Abercoed (Sydney Deane), who had been around, in supernumerary fashion, all the time. It was a tough-minded audience that could put up with this story, scarcely lightened by its leaden English jokes, for love of the beguiling sextette. Without the droll facial contortions of the veteran Willie Edouin as the phrenologist, and the handsome presence of Edna Wallace Hopper in the peripheral role of Lady Holyrood, the tale might have been unbearably bleak.

But it is necessary to look at the rest of the Broadway scene to realize how grateful the audience felt for that sextette in the fall of 1900. Another English piece, *A Million Dollars*, had just opened at the New York Theatre and been dismissed as "a specific for insomnia." Peter Daly and Christie MacDonald were appearing at the Madison Square Theatre in *Hodge Podge*

& Co., the chief characters of which were named Ledger d'Main (he was a bookkeeper), Rudolph Roastemsum, Minnie Rausmittem, and Ainshee Grayt. *San Toy*, a mediocre though popular English musical comedy set in China, and a labored vaudevillian musical farce, *The Belle of Bridgeport*, with May Irwin and Raymond Hitchcock, were the other principal musical offerings of the moment. Against such a field, *Florodora* could scarcely fail to impress the town.

Not until 1903 was another musical comedy able to jar Broadway out of the doldrums. The magnificent new Majestic Theatre on Columbus Circle opened with *The Wizard of Oz*, adapted from L. Frank Baum's novel. This musical fantasy had been imported from Chicago, where the slipper of its heroine, the lovely Anna Fitzhugh (later, when she sang at the Chicago Opera, Anna Fitziu, and now, in her vocal studio, Anna Fitzu), was likely to be filled with champagne at after-theatre parties. Miss Fitzhugh came to New York with the production, the most celebrated musical comedy ever staged initially in Chicago. So did Fred A. Stone and David C. Montgomery, a pair of comics whose work was not known in legitimate theatres in the East.

The plot, kept alive in our day by the novel and the film version, told, as everyone must know, how Dorothy Gale (and, in the play, her pet cow, Imogene) were blown by a cyclone to the region called Oz, where they consorted with such remarkable folk as the Scarecrow and the Tin Woodman. Five elaborate scenes were required for the first act. The opening spectacle revealed a Kansas town in the grip of a cyclone. Through the use of stereopticon effects a transformation was managed, with a rainstorm on a gauze screen, to the Country of the Munchkins. Subsequent scenes showed a road in the woods, a poppy field with chorus girls in large hats representing the poppies, and, after another transformation, the poppy field in winter, with the poor girl-poppies dead in the snow. Act II was set in the lavish courtyard of the Wizard's palace, and Act III revealed a lovely grove, "with wisteria vines clambering over everything." The investiture, everyone felt, was rich enough to supply two or three ordinary musical comedies.

The music by Paul Tietjens and A. Baldwin Sloane was something short of memorable. But Julian Mitchell, drawn away from Weber and Fields to demonstrate even more fully in *The Wizard of Oz* how completely he was master of his craft, handled the staging with an ease and security that had seldom been equaled in recent times. And, beyond all else, there were those ingratiating people, Fred Stone, "apparently as boneless as an India-rubber doll," as the Scarecrow, and Dave Montgomery as the Tin Woodman, beginning a career that was to keep their names at the top of the list until Montgomery's death separated them. *The Wizard of Oz* was a joy for children, a delight for adults, a happy thing for everybody.

The Casino Theatre, impressed by the need for keeping its prestige high, brought forward a $75,000 production, *The Runaways*, to compete with *The*

Wizard of Oz. Though it was not, technically speaking, a revue, *The Run-aways* was a loosely constructed piece thrown together for gasps and laughs. It lacked universal appeal, however, and was intended for those who enjoyed "the conversational style affected by street gamins and loafers." The *Dramatic Mirror* observed bitterly: "To properly estimate it requires the talents of an appraiser rather than those of a dramatic critic. The Casino, which has always been more or less a temple of art, has now become a show room for the exhibition of $75,000 worth of costumes and accessories." The Casino's precipitate fall from grace is made vivid by the following lyric in *The Runaways*:

> "I'm going home, home, home,
> Down to the old plantation where I used to roam, roam, roam;
> With those my coming will be news to, home, home, home.
> To leave the folks again I will refuse to.
> Yes, I'm going back again to fair Dixieland."

Closer to the level of *The Wizard of Oz* was the extravaganza *Mother Goose*, presented by Klaw and Erlanger, a rapidly rising theatrical syndicate, in 1903. This spectacle could not be considered a direct imitation of the successful Chicago importation, for in 1901 Klaw and Erlanger had already offered *The Sleeping Beauty and the Beast*. Moreover, *Mother Goose* was an old-fashioned piece brought over from London, and built along the lines of the London pantomimes, though it involved no harlequinade—nor, in view of the Tenderloinish cast of its dialogue, was it aimed at the juvenile audience. The following year Klaw and Erlanger evoked memories of George L. Fox with *Humpty Dumpty*.

The Wizard of Oz was also reflected in *Piff! Paff!! Pouf!!!* (1904)—at least to the extent that Eddie Foy played a role evidently designed to resemble that of the Scarecrow as closely as possible. The force of this influential production was also evident in Victor Herbert's *Babes in Toyland*, one of the great successes of 1903.

Unadulterated comic operas, in contrast to musical comedies and extravaganzas, were relatively rare in the first years of the century, and they were uniformly unsuccessful. The public had lost its taste for French opéra-bouffe (the gifted Claude Terrasse never became known in this country) and for Viennese comic opera of the Millöcker and Strauss variety; they were out-of-date in their external conventions, much as *The Chocolate Soldier* is out-of-date today. English comic opera without admixtures of popular burlesque and musical-comedy elements was all but dead.

The list of comic operas given on Broadway in the first seven years of the twentieth century is pathetic. Sir Arthur Sullivan's last contribution, *The Rose of Persia* (1900), with a book by Captain Basil Hood, closed after twenty-five performances. Johann Strauss's *Vienna Life* (1901), lasted thirty-

1. The celebrated pas de démons in the last act of *The Black Crook*.

2. Salsbury's Troubadours, the first American farce-comedy troupe.

3. Two showmen: Tony Pastor (left) and Edward Harrigan.

4. Joe Weber, Marie Dressler, and Harry Morris at the Music Hall.

5. Anna Held, the first Ziegfeld beauty.

6. Charles Winninger greets the river-boat audience in *Show Boat*.

7. Walter Huston in *Knickerbocker Holiday*.

8. Bill Robinson in the title role of *The Hot Mikado*.

five, with a cast that held Raymond Hitchcock and Ethel Jackson, who was to remain practically unknown for six years more, until the part of Sonia in *The Merry Widow* fell her way. A contemporary objection to the solemnity of Strauss's treatment of the music in *Vienna Life* pointed out that "in modern works of the same class the song numbers are chiefly, if not entirely, incidental, recitatives are eliminated, and wearisome solo pieces are left out." Ernestine Schumann-Heink, in her only Broadway appearance, kept *Love's Lottery* (1904), a feeble British piece by Julian Edwards, open for fifty performances. Two opéra-comiques composed by André Messager, *Véronique* (1905) and *The Little Michus* (1907), failed to achieve long runs. Times had changed since the heyday of foreign comic opera ten and twenty years earlier. There seemed to be no audience left for pieces that were not colloquialized, at least to some degree.

The most colloquial amusement on the upper-class musical stage was still purveyed by Joe Weber and Lew Fields at their own Music Hall. Even if their yearly extravaganzas were sometimes, as Alan Dale said, "pitchforked publicward without rhyme or reason," Weber and Fields' hearty humor and generous provision of stars, combined with the expensive productions they were now able to afford, made their first nights as brilliant as any in New York. The ladies in the audience strove to outdress Lillian Russell with their Paris gowns and expensive jewels, and the floral offerings to the performers after the final curtain were staggering.

After *Whoop-Dee-Do*, their 1903-4 extravaganza, Weber and Fields determined to follow separate courses. Fields embarked upon a successful career as a producer of musical comedies. Weber, reluctant to change his field of operations, kept the music hall open, calling it Weber's Music Hall. For *Higgledy-Piggledy*, his first solo undertaking—in the fall of 1904—he was shrewd enough to make Flo Ziegfeld the co-producer, for the sake of obtaining the services of Anna Held, then Ziegfeld's wife. The still youthful Marie Dressler also belonged to Weber's first company, enhancing her popularity by her bubbling comedy. Weber continued to operate the music hall, with diminishing prosperity, until 1907, when he called it quits after *Hip! Hip! Hooray!* lasted only sixty-four performances. Leaving the extravaganza field wide open for Ziegfeld, whose first *Follies* had already demonstrated the potentialties of a fresh formula, Weber followed Fields into musical-comedy production.

One of the sincerest tributes of flattery was the persistence of Gus and Max Rogers, from 1898 to 1907, in imitating the Weber and Fields, or Weber, shows with poor man's vaudeville extravaganzas centering upon their own Dutch onslaughts upon the English language. Each year they exploited a new locale—Central Park, Mo. (the joke hung upon the Rogers Brothers' belief that they had bought a tract of land in Central Park, New York), Washington, Harvard, London, Paris, Ireland, Panama. The fact that they could return year after year is testimony to the inordinate popularity of Dutch-dialect comedy. Theirs was the *reductio ad absurdum*, or perhaps *ad nauseam*, of the Dutch-comedy routine; but their "assaults upon ethics" were an inescapable part of the Broadway scene until 1907.

The historic Hippodrome, which housed a sequence of spectacles for more than thirty years, was opened with great fanfare on April 12, 1905. More than a year in construction, the house cost $1,750,000, and was advertised as "the largest, safest and costliest playhouse in the world." For once, an opening-night audience forced Weber and Fields to take second honors, for the array of the spectators "would have made Solomon hide his diminished head. The sight on the stage was no less stunning, as a complete circus was transferred from the earth to Mars by airship." This opening transformation scene prompted the title *A Yankee Circus on Mars*. Productions in subsequent years ran a considerable gamut of subject matter. There was a double bill of *Pioneer Days* (replete with cowboys, Mexicans, half-breeds, United States troops, and Sioux Indians in war paint) and *Neptune's Daughter* (including a ballet, "Under the Sea," in which the girls simulated colored fish); there were *The Auto Race*, with a sight-seeing bus driving right onto the stage to bring on the chorus girls, *Sporting Days*, *A Trip to Japan*, and a triple bill of *The International Cup*, *Ballet of Niagara*, and *The Earthquake*. Each production could be counted on for a year's business, like the ice shows at the Center Theatre in more recent times. A trip to the Hippodrome was as essential an item in the sightseer's itinerary in New York as a visit to the Radio City Music Hall is today.

The Hippodrome was the only new institution founded in the first few years of the century. Two important individual figures in the realm of musical comedy, however, rose to prominence. They could hardly have been more diametrically opposed in every way—the Irish-born, English-bred, German-trained, cosmopolitan Victor Herbert, seeking to compose the American equivalent of the bést European comic operas, and succeeding in writing a great many pretty tunes without in any way changing the main course of events; and the Rhode Island-born, New York-bred vaudeville hoofer, George M. Cohan, winning a new audience by refusing to accept the sacredness of European taste and usages.

Before the turn of the century, Herbert had already indicated his gifts in *The Serenade* (1897), which encouraged devotees of a well-turned tune to believe that the bromides of Reginald de Koven need not always continue to set the standard for home-composed scores. Herbert had allowed himself to assimilate American life and tastes so thoroughly that he was generally considered an American composer from the beginning of his Broadway career. Since his entire contribution to the musical-comedy field was made in this country, there was no more reason to harp upon his foreign birth than there is today upon Gian-Carlo Menotti's.

After a few years of silence following the production of *The Serenade*, Herbert reintroduced himself to his audience with *Babes in Toyland* in

1903. This extravaganza was a frank attempt to repeat the success of *The Wizard of Oz* by paralleling it as closely as possible. But despite the resemblance of Toyland to Oz, the Herbert score, with its "March of the Toys" and its adroit use of connecting and incidental music, gave *Babes in Toyland* a musical lift *The Wizard of Oz* had sorely needed.

Now that he was back in harness, Herbert turned out musical comedies at a good clip. Some of them, like *Babette* (1903), which served Fritzi Scheff—fresh from the Metropolitan—for her debut in comic opera, may well be forgotten. In 1905, Herbert gave a helping hand to Lew Fields by writing the music for *It Happened in Nordland*, Fields's first independent producing venture. But until *Mlle. Modiste* opened on Christmas night, 1905, Herbert did not repeat the success of *Babes in Toyland*. With Fritzi Scheff to sing "Kiss Me Again" and to "assault the snare drum" as the Mascot of the Troups, Herbert's music was in good hands. This time, moreover, Henry Blossom, author of the book and lyrics, had provided him with the rarest of advantages by writing dialogue and text that were direct, crisp, fluent, and literate.

Of the plot, set in one of the Parisian shops (a hat shop this time) that were such popular working places for musical-comedy heroines, less that is pleasant can be said. But at least *Mlle. Modiste* more nearly gave the lie to a sweeping condemnation in the *Dramatic Mirror* than any of the contemporaneous pieces. "No one can long go the rounds of the New York theatres," the reviewer complained, "without becoming a student of theatrical kleptomania. Given from two to five acts which must be filled with material, and having no material scruples as to where or how it may be obtained, once he had discovered the emptiness of his own imagination, the ambitious author naturally takes to intellectual burglary and excuses himself on the time-worn plea of unconscious imitations and coincidences. This is said neither with particular reference to Henry Blossom nor to Victor Herbert, who conscientiously extracts principally from his own earlier works."

In the music for *Mlle. Modiste*, Herbert showed a growing ability to command a variety of styles. There was, of course, the usual sentimental waltz in "Kiss Me Again," but elsewhere in the evening he provided an ultra-Parisian touch in two songs devoted to local color, and was also able to turn with gusto to the task of composing a character song about the Keokuk Culture Club. Even so, most of the music was in his characteristic vein, accurately described by Amy Leslie in the Chicago *Daily News* as nearer Flotow than Audran, Humperdinck than Millöcker. In the countless waltzes he composed in *Mlle. Modiste* and other works, Herbert never captured the Viennese lilt of Strauss or Lehár; his waltzes plod conscientiously through all three beats of the measure, and never seem to get off the ground. His quickstep numbers, for all their dash and their frequently charming melodies, are factual and labored in comparison with those of Offenbach and Audran. But there is no use in thinking of these things. On a relative scale of judgment, Herbert was a marked improvement over Luders and Kerker; and, more important, the American public accepted him as its own composer.

The Red Mill (1906) was one of the gayest and most amusing of the earlier Herbert products. Fred Stone as "Con" Kidder and Dave Montgomery as "Kid" Conner (the quotation marks appear to be integral to their names) appeared as American tourists stranded at an inn in Holland. They were able, by luck, to uncover a plot involving the abduction of the petite Dutch heroine, and to effect her rescue in a scene in which they hung precariously from the arms of a big red windmill as they spirited her through the window. The production was a handsome one, with a Delft-blue setting in the second act that was in more restrained taste than usual.

After seven lesser efforts, Herbert next offered *Naughty Marietta*, under the aegis of Oscar Hammerstein, in 1910. One of the hardiest and most frequently performed of all the Herbert works in the years since its première, *Naughty Marietta* was no more than a mild success at first, attaining a run of only 136 performances. Once again, an operatic singer—Emma Trentini of Hammerstein's Manhattan Opera Company—was engaged as the soprano lead, to impersonate a French countess who ran off to New Orleans, presumably in order to institute enough complications for an operetta plot. One would think, in view of their longevity and continuing popularity, that the "Italian Street Song" and "I'm Falling in Love with Someone" would have been hailed as single achievements, but their superiority to other songs of the moment was not fully recognized. The most celebrated tune in *Naughty Marietta*, "Ah, Sweet Mystery of Life," was not a song at all in the original production, but an instrumental entr'acte, which recurred in the finale. The familar words were set to the melody later on, at the instigation of the leading tenor, Orville Harrold, also a member of the Metropolitan Opera.

By 1910, Herbert was just reaching the crest of the wave. By 1910, George M. Cohan was all but finished with his early career as author, composer, producer, director, actor, singer, and dancer of and in musical comedies, and about to begin a second career that kept him either on the speaking stage or writing for it, or both, the larger part of the time until his memorable return in 1937 as President Roosevelt in *I'd Rather Be Right*.

Born in Providence, Rhode Island, not on July 4, as was always said, but on July 3, 1878 (Ward Morehouse examined the city archives), Cohan never knew a life that was not associated with the stage. His father, Jerry J. Cohan, and his mother, Helen F., were itinerant vaudeville performers. As a small child, George learned to help them in their act, and he made his first professional solo appearance at the age of nine. For his own specialty he developed proficiency in the buck-and-wing dancing that was the turn-of-the-century precursor of present-day tap dancing.

As George and his sister Josephine became old enough to take share and share alike, their vaudeville act was billed as "The Four Cohans." In 1899, in an expanded version of one of their vaudeville sketches, the family made a modest bow on Broadway, without exciting much attention. *The Governor's Son*, also an elaboration of a vaudeville playlet, was their first musical comedy, in 1901.

Though no sizable public yet took them to heart, the Cohans began to climb up the ladder. George, in particular, was praised as a "grotesquely agile dancer," and as an actor who could "make the most ordinary lines seem unusually funny, and without a change of facial expression." From the beginning, George M. Cohan would have no traffic with the old-fashioned mugging that, ever since the days of George L. Fox and Willie Edouin and Francis Wilson, had served as a device of prime value in eliciting laughs from the naïve. He was the apostle of breeziness, of up-to-dateness, of Broadway brashness and slang. Straining for effect had no place in the modernized technique he sought to exploit. Speed, directness, and "ginger" were the chief ingredients of his musical plays.

By 1903, when *Running for Office* returned the Four Cohans to New York, their name had begun to spread around, and their opening stimulated a floral offering hardly less suffocating than those at Weber and Fields'. Three generations were represented in the theatre that night, for the daughter of George and his wife, Ethel Levy (who was also a member of the company), watched her parents and grandparents from a box.

George M. Cohan became a star in *Little Johnny Jones*, in 1904. The Four Cohans were no more, for Josephine had left to accept independent engagements. Contemporary observers felt that Cohan had given himself a poor role compared to that of Donald Brian, the future Prince Danilo of *The Merry Widow*. But he had an opportunity to introduce a characteristic Cohan song, "Yankee Doodle Boy," and to recite a sententious sermonette entitled "Life's a Funny Proposition," with which he perhaps justified the snobbish description of him as "the idol of middle-class playgoers." For the first time he was able to afford a production that compared favorably with those of longer-established managers, and to engage his own set of Girls and Boys, à la Florodora, to sing a double sextette. " 'Op in the 'Ansom." (The plot, it should be explained, took Cohan to England as an American jockey riding in the Derby.)

Patriotism and local color having paid off so far, Cohan located his next piece, *Forty-Five Minutes from Broadway* (1906), in New Rochelle, New York. The production was still not expensive; the $10,000 it cost was paid off within a few days after the opening. For the first time, Cohan himself stayed out of the cast, awarding the role of Kid Burns, who spotted and captured the two villains, to a young, tough comedian named Victor Moore, who had not yet evolved the plaintive, slow underplaying with which modern audiences associate his name. Donald Brian appeared as a dapper, rich young man, and the popular Fay Templeton was given the chance to appear in her "first clean play," after twenty years of burlesque and travesty. The play was peopled with two antithetical groups, the native yokels of New Rochelle and the wise guys from Forty-second Street. To the Milwaukee *Press*, "all the froth, the humor, the fatalism, the philosophy, compounded of epicureanism, cynicism, and opportunism, characteristic of the futile little rialto world are perfectly reflected by Mr. Cohan in his songs and slang dialogues." Broadway, in other words, now had a spokesman.

With *George Washington, Jr.*, (1906)—subtitled "an American musical play"—Cohan began to wave the flag in earnest, with the aid of a song entitled "The Grand Old Flag." The plot hinged upon the conflict between an Anglo-maniac father and a son so intensely patriotic that he renounced his own name and took that of the Father of Our Country. Cohan's conception of the ideal American youth was by no means universally admired. The dissenting view was strongly put by James S. Metcalfe, critic of the old *Life*:

". . . [He is] a vulgar, cheap, blatant, ill-mannered, flashily-dressed, insolent, smart Aleck, who, for some reason unexplainable on any basis of common sense, good taste, or even ordinary decency, appeals to the imagination and apparent approval of large American audiences. As a living character in any American town or village, it is hardly to be conceived that he would not be driven out as a public nuisance and a pernicious example to the youth of the community. The rounds of applause which greet the efforts of this offensive personality must convey to the minds of ignorant boys a depraving ideal for their inspirations and imitation."

The *Dramatic Mirror*, while baffled by the Cohan phenomenon, took a quieter view:

"Precisely why these Cohan concoctions are so popular with the New York public is a mystery the critic has never succeeded in solving to his personal satisfaction. They are clean; they are spirited; they are inspired with a variety of slang patriotism which may not be the less serious because it is not of superior elevation. Yet, after the last argument has been summarized, they must be classed, so to speak, as high-grade second-grade productions. Perhaps the true secret of Mr. Cohan's unprecedented success, too permanent for mere theatrical luck, consists of his admirable stagecraft. In the art of presenting musical comedy, Mr. Cohan is apparently without a peer."

Against which, almost as though in riposte, *Life* submitted an opposing judgment:

"These combinations of music are curious things, consisting mainly of several bars of well-known patriotic or sentimental songs strung together with connecting links of lively and more or less original musical trash. The words fitted to these curious contraptions are the kind of unmetrical stuff that children compose and call poetry, and are for the most part mawkish appeals to the cheapest kind of patriotism."

Whatever the merits of their content, Cohan's musical comedies introduced a wholly new conception of delivery, tempo, and subject matter into a form of entertainment that was rapidly dying for want of new ideas of any kind. Brushing aside the artifical elegances and the formal developments of the musical comedies based on English and German models, he reproduced successfully the hardness, the compensating sentimentality, the impulsive vulgarity, and the swift movement of New York life, which, except for surface sophistications, has not changed much between then and now. Though the plays might seem dreadful if they were revived today, it is impossible not to grant them validity as interpretations of the whole spirit and tone of life in and around the Broadway sector. "At times," wrote a reviewer in 1907 of *The Honeymooners* (a revision of *Running for Office*), "it goes so fast that it almost bewilders and gives the impression of a great machine shooting out characters, choruses, songs, dances with rapid-fire quickness and precision."

If he had been able to match his ability as a stage director with fresh materials, Cohan need never have temporarily deserted the musical-comedy field. But his plays came more and more to be rehashes—sometimes, as with *The Honeymooners* and *The Man Who Owns Broadway* (1909), reprises of pieces whose initial success had not satisfied him; sometimes, as with *Fifty Miles from Boston* (1908) and *The American Idea* (1908), applications of old recipes to different (yet always the same) characters and circumstances.

XII. The Merry Widow and the Ziegfield Follies

PUBLIC INTEREST in Viennese comic opera had declined to so low an ebb in the early years of the twentieth century that Henry W. Savage watched the inordinate success of *The Merry Widow* in Vienna and Berlin and London for two years before risking an American production of it, even though he had obtained the rights many months before. There was, after all, no reason to be sure that this piece with a score by an unknown young Hungarian named Franz Lehár would succeed with a public that had recently spurned so established a master as Johann Strauss. Savage had seen *The Merry Widow* in Hamburg and Vienna, and had been enchanted by what he called its "essence of youthfulness"; but perhaps it would look and sound different in English, on the other side of the Atlantic.

On October 21, 1907, he finally presented the operetta in New York. Adrian Ross had already provided idiomatic English lyrics for the London production; George Marion, whose youthfulness matched that of the score itself, undertook the stage direction. For the romantic leads, Savage engaged

Donald Brian, who had received his chief schooling thus far from George M. Cohan, and Ethel Jackson, a comic-opera soprano so little known that Savage pretended to a gullible press that he had discovered her—though those with good memories could recall her performances on Broadway in *Little Miss Nobody* and *The Runaway Girl*, and on the road in *Miss Bob White*, which never reached New York.

To those who were at the New Amsterdam Theatre on that opening night, the enraptured close of the second act has always remained a supreme recollection. The "Merry Widow Waltz" appeared first in hints by the orchestra; Brian and then Miss Jackson began to hum it; tentatively and experimentally at first, then with a crescendo of fervor, the couple moved into the waltz. As their dance continued, they became faster and lighter, until it seemed that their feet scarcely touched the stage at all. With this single dance, this single tune, the aging musical theatre recaptured its youth. The audience was transfixed as it watched the scene. At the end the tumult of applause forced an encore, and another encore, and still another.

For fifty-two weeks, *The Merry Widow* lifted its New York audiences into a heaven of romantic ardor. Ethel Jackson's laughter, which "sounded like water bubbling out of a small bottle," her lovely gowns and fashionable sailor hats, her exquisite singing of the "Vilia" melody; Brian's debonair gallantry and nimble movement; the sauciness of the girls at Maxim's; even the intrigue of the Marsovian plot—all these were delights as fresh and gay as the lilting waltz.

Chicago also saw *The Merry Widow* for the first time on the same evening, with a duplicate production equally lavishly staged and costumed, and with Lina Abarbanell—whom some connoisseurs preferred to Miss Jackson—as Sonia, and George Damarel as Prince Danilo. Other *Merry Widow* companies were organized to take the good news everywhere. *Merry Widow* hats, dresses, and drinks were a reigning fashion. Soon after the New York première, the statement was made—for which, at this late date, there is neither proof nor disproof—that more than a hundred *Merry Widow* companies were performing concurrently on the face of the globe.

Granting that the music of *The Merry Widow* was a considerable cut above most of that of Victor Herbert, and an incalculable improvement upon that of most of his contemporaries, it was not primarily its music that made *The Merry Widow* so transcendent a hit. Nor, certainly, was it the humor, since there was almost none to be discovered. It was the dancing, the animation of the waltz presented in the intimate, gallant terms of the ballroom rather than the formal figurations prescribed by established conventions. In *The Merry Widow* the ballroom dance was glorified as a symbol of romantic love and placed in the focus of attention. The "Merry Widow Waltz" did in fact start a new era, as the *Dramatic Mirror* hoped it would. It dealt a death blow to the marches, drills, and empty convolutions that had punctuated musical-comedy performances until then. It opened the way for Vernon and Irene Castle, the tango, the turkey-trot, and the fox-trot. It humanized dancing, and made it warm, immediate, and personal.

And so, thanks to Lehár and Savage and Brian and Miss Jackson, comic opera leapt back into favor. A rival to Lehár, Oskar Straus—no relation to the great Strausses with a double "s"—had also set up shop in Vienna, and his *A Waltz Dream* was brought over in 1908 to compete with *The Merry Widow*. A sprightly piece with a good score and an ample supply of humor, *A Waltz Dream* made its way nicely without dislodging its predecessor. Among the performers, the one who received the most generous praise was a young Canadian church and oratorio tenor, Edward Johnson, who made his first stage appearance as the romantic hero. "His voice," one review reported, "is a clear tenor of wide range, and he sings without any apparent effort, even the difficult finale of the last act. His stage presence is good and his acting is natural." *A Waltz Dream* was Johnson's first and last light-opera assignment. At the close of its run he went to Italy, changed his name to Edoardo di Giovanni, returned to the United States, changed his name back to Edward Johnson, sang at the Chicago Opera and then at the Metropolitan, and in 1935 began his fifteen-year tenure as general manager of the Metropolitan Opera Association.

Two more Viennese comic operas attained prosperity in 1909 and 1910. Leo Fall's *The Dollar Princess*, a somewhat bromidic piece about the complications aroused by the attempt of an American millionaire's daughter to purchase the affection of a young Englishman, brought Donald Brian back with "evident consciousness of his own merit." The only remarkable feature of *The Dollar Princess*, apart from an attractive score, was the final curtain, which left the romantic couple alone on the stage—"alone, yes, alone; no swaying chorus around them, no farewell jingle and patter—the lovers find awakening, and a golden curtain, like 'amber-glowing flood of light,' enshrouds them in its love mysteries."

The Chocolate Soldier (1909), by Oskar Straus, offered no amber love finale, but it was provided with something better—a book, not too greatly watered down, drawn from George Bernard Shaw's *Arms and the Man*. It also rejoiced in the first Viennese waltz that offered competition to the "Merry Widow Waltz," the long-lined, slow-mounting "My Hero." Though its first engagement lasted for only 296 performances, as against *The Merry Widow*'s 416, *The Chocolate Soldier* has since proved to be almost as durable an object of public affection.

When all was said and done, however, the Viennese-waltz operas were an exotic importation, a borrowed rapture. The chief really American contribution—apart from Cohan's—to the renewed vigor of the musical stage in this period was made by Florenz Ziegfeld, Jr. The son of a dignified, old-school German musician who became president of the Chicago Musical College, Flo Ziegfeld kicked over the traces while he was still a very young man, and served for a time as the manager of Sandow, the strong man whose muscles Chicago society dowagers liked to feel at the World's Columbian Exposition in 1893. His entry into theatrical production was provoked by his interest in Anna Held, whom he met in London in the late 1890s, placed under contract, and featured in a series of musical comedies, meanwhile marrying her to make the tie doubly binding. Anna Held's daintiness, her delicate accent, her flashing come-hither eyes ("I Just Can't Make My Eyes Behave") carried her to success in De Koven's *The Little Duchess* (1901), Luders' *Mam'selle Napoleon* (1903) ("a transplanted rose that turned out to be a particularly large and offensive cabbage"), and *The Parisian Model* (1906), with music by Max Hoffman and various collaborators. Only the last of these fully displayed the exactions of style and rich displays of feminine beauty which were henceforth to be the marks of every Ziegfeld production. While the chorus sang "A Gown for Each Hour of the Day," Miss Held appeared, disappeared, and reappeared in six costly gowns. In "I'd Like to See a Little More of You" a trick effect made the chorus appear to be nude, when in reality it was merely décolleté. A "pony ballet" of sixteen girls wore bells on their fingers, their toes, and "elsewhere."

In Paris in the summer of 1906, Ziegfeld was seized with the notion of furnishing America with a revue discreetly modeled after the Folies Bergère. He could not appropriate the lascivious features of the French revue, he knew; but he was sure that he could, without half trying, make a group of girls look more beautiful. His plan took tangible shape on July 8, 1907, when he presented an entertainment entitled *Follies of 1907* on the New York Theatre Roof, which he renamed the Jardin de Paris.

Let no dreamer imagine that the original *Follies* was planned with the luxury Ziegfeld promulgated in later years. He was still a struggling, impecunious producer, with only a few moderate successes to his credit, and without a large bank account or ready access to the bank accounts of angels. The whole production cost of the *Follies of 1907* was $13,000, and the entire weekly payroll amounted to $1,800. The cast included no important names, though Helen Broderick's became so later on. The music was picked up here and there, and the production was mounted like a high-class vaudeville show. It was reviewed in the *Dramatic Mirror*, in fact, not among legitimate attractions, but on the inconspicuous page headed "New Vaudeville Acts."

"A musical review of the New York sensations of the past season," and "a succession of incidents and specialties," the *Follies of 1907* was decorated by a large chorus of "girls who had appeared with Anna Held last season," who soon came to be called by the more economical name of Anna Held Girls. Their striking scene was a "motion-picture effect" in which the girls seemed to be splashing in the waves. At the end, twenty-four drummer girls paraded out into the theatre and back. Before then, Mlle. Dazie had offered her sensational Salome dance; Dave Lewis had sung "I Think I Oughtn't Auto Any More"; and George Bickel and Harry Watson, Jr., had given their already well-known band-leading specialty.

The public supported the *Follies of 1907* so willingly throughout the summer that Ziegfeld decided to move it to the street level, in the Liberty Theatre, for the fall season. The takings immediately dropped to $1,500 in the first week after the move. With great misgivings, the producer packed the show off to Washington, where, although it was housed in a legitimate theatre and not on a roof, it played to land-office business. So did it on the rest of a tour that took it as far as Chicago. The road was even more profitable than the Jardin de Paris for the first *Follies*.

During the winter—on January 28, 1908—Ziegfeld returned to musical-comedy production with *The Soul Kiss*, which he built around the Danish ballerina Adeline Genée, who made her first visit to the United States to appear in it. To the *Dramatic Mirror*, "Genée is a thing apart; a spirit untouched by her all too earthly surroundings; an elf, an angel, a bird, an incarnation of Terpsichore, indescribable in words, impossible of analysis, as intangible as sunbeams, as vapory as moonlight." Four dances were contributed by this lovely paragon, ranging from *ballet blanc* and an aristocratic piece in Empire gown and dancing slippers to a hunting dance in riding habit and boots and—Ziegfeld's *pièce de résistance*—a dance in which she wore a lace-trimmed negligee and very high-heeled slippers.

From the *Follies of 1907* and *The Soul Kiss* Ziegfeld earned enough to enable him to plan the *Follies of 1908* on a somewhat more elaborate, though still decidedly moderate, scale. Nora Bayes and Mae Murray were new luminaries in a revue designed to cast a glance at the entire history of society, politics, and the stage from the time of the Garden of Eden to New York in the summer of 1908. The girls were more pulchritudinous than ever, even when they paraded across the stage representing taxicabs.

Between summers, Ziegfeld again produced a musical comedy, *Miss Innocence*, for the benefit of Anna Held this time; it was his last musical comedy until *Sally* more than a decade later. The score was by Ludwig Englander.

But the *Follies of 1909* were in his mind all the while, and when they were revealed at the Jardin de Paris, they initiated the tradition of lavishness to which Ziegfeld was to remain faithful until the very end of his career. Dearest to the producer's heart in the 1909 edition was the exquisite Lillian Lorraine, for whom Ziegfeld always felt the warmest admiration and genuine affection. Miss Lorraine made her *Follies* debut in a sea of soap bubbles. Later on, she clambered into a flying machine and scattered flowers as she sang "Up, Up, Up, in My Aeroplane." As a foil for her serene beauty, Bessie Clayton, a pert and diverting comedienne, burlesqued a typical London Gaiety dancer, with silk hat, stick, tails, and a nether costume that was part masculine and part feminine.

A ponderable share of the *Follies of 1909* was given over to a rowdy representation of President Theodore Roosevelt on an African hunting trip. Harry Kelly impersonated Roosevelt, teeth, glasses, and all. A two-man elephant made friendly overtures to the hunters, and the chorus girls found diverse occupations as tigers, giraffes, and ostriches. An amiable lion allowed

the President to shoot at him, accommodatingly holding a large target between his paws. The President, dissatisfied with such easy game, insisted
upon shooting an apple off the lion's head. This done, the scene changed,
and Ziegfeld's patriotism was affirmed when the show girls appeared with
headdresses shaped like battleships. The background showed a harbor variously interpreted as New York and Hampton Roads; whichever it was, the
stage lights were dimmed, the girls turned on lights in their headdresses,
and the "greatest navy in the world" was seen riding at anchor. The giddy
evening ended with a baseball game among the chorus girls, into which they
swept the members of the audience as the curtain fell. Despite all these
inventions, however, the audience elected to be most impressed by the
Nell Brinkley Bathing Girls.

By the time the *Follies of 1910* took over the Jardin de Paris in June of
that year, Miss Lorraine had earned an assured place as a reigning beauty.
Never hesitant to make imposing claims when nobody could prove them
false, Ziegfeld was quoted in an interview as saying, "It was no unusual
thing for her to receive flowers night after night over the footlights, and
then upon taking the bouquets to pieces afterwards, to find a diamond ring
or a pin fastened to a cluster of American beauties." Obviously it paid to
take bouquets apart in those days.

In the *Follies of 1910*, Ziegfeld introduced one of his greatest future
stars—Fannie Brice, whom he saw at the Columbia Theatre, a cheap burlesque house, and engaged for an initial salary of $18 a week to sing a
character song, "Good-bye, Becky Cohen." Bert Williams, a graduate of
such successful Negro musical comedies as *In Dahomey* (1903), *Abyssinia*
(1906), and *Mr. Lode of Koal* (1909), made the first of many appearances
in the *Follies*. For spectacle, the show girls symbolized various schools in
the first-act finale, "Our American Colleges"; and Miss Lorraine brought
the second act to a climax by swinging out over the audience as she sang
to the accompaniment of eight girls, also in swings, ringing Swiss bells.

The *Follies of 1910* was conceived on a more massive scale than any of
its predecessors. Although three more years were to pass before Ziegfeld
abandoned the roof as the home of his revues, the pattern was set, and the
Follies had "come to be looked upon as the biggest thing of their kind of
the season." But the proof of Ziegfeld's triumph, and the triumph of the
glorified girls and of the revue idea, had already been vouchsafed in 1908,
when the Shuberts sought to parallel the *Follies* with a well-staged extravaganza entitled *The Mimic World*. Ziegfeld almost sued the Shubert brothers
when he claimed to have seen a score of the overture to *The Mimic World*
which appropriated the subtitle *Follies of 1908*. The *Follies* were his own
invention, and even the word "follies" in the title remained his sole property
until 1919, when the *Greenwich Village Follies* successfully appropriated
it.

XIII. Before and During the First World War

WHATEVER ITS FAULTS may be, the American musical theatre has never remained static for long. The peak popularity of each new fashion has inevitably been short and the turnover of modes and ideas rapid. Weber and Fields' Music Hall, which seemed as permanent as the Rock of Gibraltar in the late 1890s, disappeared as an institution in 1904, only nine years after it was established; by 1912, when the partners staged their "jubilee revival," their art was already a matter for nostalgia and sadness over the passing of the good old days. The Gaiety Girls, the models of feminine vivacity and attractiveness in 1894, were pushed into a back seat by our own native-born Florodora Girls in 1900. George M. Cohan's swift and brash musical farces of the New York scene were top attractions for less than a decade; the freshness of Cohan's inspiration had deserted him by 1911, when *The Little Millionaire* elicited the comment "If Cohan's reputation rested on this piece, he would never have come to own his own theatre on Broadway." The inordinate popularity of *The Merry Widow* was quite as much a threat as an encouragement to subsequent waltz operas, and Lehár's own *Gypsy Love*, in 1912, was coolly received.

At the beginning of the second decade of this century, the musical stage had again encountered the doldrums. New hits seemed like repetition of old ones. Upper-crust patrons who had been devoted to the most artistic comic operas and the best musical comedies found the intense and much-publicized rivalry between Hammerstein's Manhattan Opera and Otto Kahn's Metropolitan Opera far more exciting than any stimulus the lighter musical stage could offer. A gap had opened between the carriage trade and the mass audience, which adored its whirly-girly shows and wanted no traffic with art. During the next few years Broadway kept only an attenuated hold upon its audience of cultivated patrons. In 1913 and 1914 show business fell upon the most evil days it was to experience until the Depression of the 1930s. But it is always darkest just before dawn, and from 1915 on American musical comedy began to discover and realize its manifest destiny as a native and genuinely popular expression. A new generation flocked to the theatres, and what with wartime excitement and postwar prosperity, the industry entered upon fifteen years of high flying.

In 1911 and 1912, the beginning of the great four-year decline, there was still some life in the old formulas. *The Quaker Girl*, an importation of the Gaiety species from George Edwardes' Adelphi Theatre in London, cut off the usual bolt of goods and provided with an urbane and easy-flowing score by Lionel Monckton, ran for 240 performances in 1911-12. The older generation and the younger one met in the cast. May Vokes, of the once famous Vokes family, and Nellie McHenry, leading lady of Salsbury's Troubadours in the 1870s, shared assignments with Olga Petrova, soon to become an emotional star of the silent screen, and a young lady named Ina Claire, fresh from her first Broadway assignment in *Jumping Jupiter*, who sang in a small, clear voice, and danced in a manner that "entitles her to more than ordinary consideration." The Quaker girl of the title quickly "shed her sectarian prejudices but not her principles," for at the beginning of the second act she had found employment in a dressmaking establishment on the Rue de la Paix. The piece was the politest and most soothing pastime London had yet vouchsafed, and was undisturbed by the slightest tinge of novelty, beyond the fact that the "gentlemen of the chorus" did not all dress alike.

The Gaiety Theatre itself made an equally conventional contribution in *The Sunshine Girl*, presented by Charles Frohman in 1913. It was all about soap and a soap works, and Julia Sanderson was elevated to stardom in these spotless surroundings. The score (and most of the book) was by Paul A. Rubens, but the show-stopping tune, delivered with enormous aplomb by Joseph Cawthorn, called "You Can't Play Every Instrument in the Band," had music by Raymond Hubbell and lyrics by John Golden, who later dreamed up "Poor Butterfly" before moving into a long and successful career as a producer of nonmusical plays.

The Sunshine Girl employed as its featured dancers Vernon and Irene Castle. Castle had already appeared on Broadway in *The Hen Pecks* (1911), but this was the first musical-comedy appearance of the husband-and-wife team. The evolutions of the couple left the audience breathless, as they exhibited "the last note in the turkey-trot world." To the *Dramatic Mirror*, "Castle is an acquired taste; but once acquired, his fantastic distortions and India-rubber gyrations exert a decided fascination, while, moreover, he has grown artistically." It was a taste the audience acquired cheerfully and quickly. Castle's turkey-trot with his wife (a new dance, suggesting both wings of a turkey) and his tango with Julia Sanderson presaged a new era in which the waltz would be supplanted by dances from the Western hemisphere. By including the Castles in one of its productions, the Gaiety all but committed suicide in America. The contrast between old and new was too striking, and it was obvious that the audience preferred the new.

Franz Lehár's *The Merry Widow*, the supreme hit of the first decade of the century, had tallied up 416 performances in its first run in New York, in 1907-8, and a great many more than that on the road. Two years later, Oskar Straus's *The Chocolate Soldier* ran for 296 performances, and Leo

Fall's *The Dollar Princess* for 288. These were phenomenal records at a time when 100 performances constituted a highly profitable New York engagement. Naturally central European comic opera came to be highly esteemed by producers, and in the next five years the Shuberts, Klaw and Erlanger, Henry W. Savage, Charles Frohman, and even A. H. Woods, the bedroom-farce king, placed a number of their chips on it.

But it stubbornly failed to pay off. Lehár's *Gypsy Love*, in 1911, survived for Woods for only 31 performances. Lehár had overreached himself, and the score was thought to be too close to grand opera, "too portentous and heavy." Frohman's production of Fall's *The Siren* in the same year did better, and rated technically as a success, since it played 136 times. But Harry B. Smith's adaptation of the German lyrics, according to one critic, "bustled with unsingable words that ill accord with Fall's exquisite melodies," and only the combined talents of Donald Brian (the unforgotten Prince Danilo), Frank Moulan, and the gracious Julia Sanderson kept the piece in favor—along with "costumes that would cause women to leave the theatre with their heads crammed full of sartorial inspirations." Lehár's *The Count of Luxembourg*, presented by Klaw and Erlanger in 1912, achieved 120 performances, thanks partly to Frank Moulan's dry, cutting delivery of his comic lines and lyrics, and the skilled hand of Julian Mitchell as director of the dances and production numbers.

The next three Lehár pieces, presented consecutively by Klaw and Erlanger, the Shuberts, and Savage, all failed to make the mark. *Eva* (1912) was too advanced for its time. The book "resorted to the psychological problems of high drama," and in the score, "Eva says 'Yes' in the first act to discords that Schönberg might be proud to have written." (The New York *Times* drama critic evidently had already heard of *Pierrot Lunaire* in 1912). *The Man with Three Wives* (1913) went to the opposite extreme, being witless and superficial. Charlotte Greenwood, the future long-legged Letty, carried the burden of the evening, kicking into enjoyment an audience that found little other entertainment. *The Maid of Athens* (1914) was stripped of much of its Lehár score, allotted a poor English adaptation by Carolyn Wells, and provided with a finale, "amazingly realistic," on the gun deck of an American dreadnought. In 1915, the Shuberts finally hit pay dirt with Lehár's *Alone at Last*, which was conducted by Gaetano Merola, today and for the past quarter century the director of the San Francisco Opera Association. The cast included Roy Atwell, Marguerite Namara, and John Charles Thomas, fresh out of revue for his first operetta assignment. With a score more inventive than that of *The Merry Widow* and suave singing from Mr. Thomas, *Alone at Last* enjoyed a pseudo-operatic success, although the *Dramatic Mirror* complained that "Miss Namara never suggested a maiden." Thereafter, Lehár's sun went into an eclipse. Anti-German sentiment, as war approached, kept his pieces off the American stage, along with nearly all other German and Austrian items. In 1917, the Shuberts made the misstep of presenting Thomas in Lehár's *The Star Gazer*. Although the score was a good one, the temper of the time was shown by the fact that the operetta was forced to close at the end of the first week. No more Viennese operettas were heard in America until well after the end of the war.

A little earlier, however, three items from Central Europe by composers other than Lehár enjoyed respectable successes. Johann Strauss's *Die Fledermaus* finally came to notice, under the aegis of the Shuberts, in 1912, who offered it as a "London novelty" under the title *The Merry Countess*. The chief novelty appears to have been Gladys Unger's distortion of the book into the Winter Garden idiom, and the "sacrifice" of Strauss to the Dolly Sisters. In the same year, Bruno Granichstädten's *The Rose Maid*, with a book adapted by the unflagging Harry B. Smith, was similarly metamorphosed into a vehicle for Edward Gallagher and Al Shean, who kept it alive for 176 performances.

Henry Savage's production of *Sari*, in 1914, fortified the reputation of the Hungarian composer, Emmerich Kalman. As early as 1909, when he was only twenty, Kalman had introduced himself with *The Gay Hussars*, but *Sari* was his first hit. The motto of the operetta was "Victorious Ever Is Youth." Both the bubbling score and the high spirits of the performers bore the slogan out. For the title role, Savage brought from Hungary a diminutive singing actress named Mitzi Hajos (who later called herself plain Mitzi). Abandoning the conventional French heels, corsets, satin bodices, and multitudinous petticoats of the comic-opera heroine, Mitzi wore her plain hair in two straight braids down her back, and bounced and rollicked through the evening with capricious and disarming naturalness. Among her accomplishments was a grotesque dance, "Hu-za-za," in which she won applause for her "comical birdlike hoppings." Though its waltzes—notable among them "Love's Own Sweet Song"—offered "no solace for the tangoist and the turkey-trotter," Kalman succeeded in translating Viennese operetta into lively American terms. He remained active in this country, to share the field of sentimental operetta with Victor Herbert, Rudolf Friml, and Sigmund Romberg.

Sari was an oasis in a desert. On October 14, 1914, the *Dramatic Mirror* mourned, "Never before in recent history has there been such a dearth of musical plays." At that moment, the entire list in New York consisted of *The Girl from Utah, Pretty Mrs. Smith,* and a revue at the Winter Garden. "With the exception of Victor Herbert, there is no one in this country who seems to understand musical comedy requirements. Foreign composers and librettists are fighting for their colors. Will the war uncover native composers and librettists with works of merit?"

It soon did, but in the meantime Victor Herbert was obviously doing his best to merit the faith the *Dramatic Mirror* placed in him. Between 1911 and 1917 Herbert turned out five musical comedies (or operettas, or comic operas, or musical plays, or musical entertainments) of smash-hit proportions. In addition, he wrote eight pieces that achieved runs of from 12 to 71 performances. His services were in demand by nearly every producer in town, and his thirteen musical comedies in this period were staged under ten different auspices, ranging from Joe Weber to the Shuberts and the partnership of Ziegfeld and Dillingham.

With *The Lady of the Slipper,* a variant on the Cinderella story presented by Dillingham in 1912, Herbert gave Montgomery and Stone their most satisfactory vehicle since *The Wizard of Oz.* This "musical play" was mounted in the best Dillingham style, with the capable R. H. Burnside in the pit, and Elsie Janis, Vernon Castle, and Peggy Wood sharing billing with Montgomery and Stone. The production was in every way refined and in good taste, and was considered "as artistic as any ever seen on Broadway." Castle, as Prince Charming, and Elsie Janis, as Cinderella, danced a waltz. Fred Stone, as the Straw Man, sang and danced and contorted himself in an acrobatic feature known as the "Punch Bowl Glide." Elsie Janis delighted the audience with her imitations. And, to top things off, there was a Russian ballet with Lydia Lopokova as *première danseuse.* It was as lovely a show as could be found; and though the score is not one of his best, the production was one of the high points in Herbert's career.

Though *Sweethearts,* a Cinderella sequel to *The Lady of the Slipper,* was a lesser success when it was produced in 1913, its music proved to have more longevity, and is still subject to revival in outdoor summer-operetta theatres. The relative standing in their own day of these two allied pieces again shows the difficulty of distinguishing content from presentation, in looking back upon historical events in the theatre. What is done with a musical show can often be more important to its success than the intrinsic qualities of book, score, and lyrics. Had Werba and Luescher possessed Dillingham's professional skill, they might have given *Sweethearts* at the outset the standing it attained only over the years.

Herbert's other hits in this period were *The Only Girl* (1914), *The Princess Pat* (1915), and *The Century Girl* (1916). Surprisingly enough, Joe Weber's production of *Eileen,* with which Herbert realized his dream of composing an operetta of Ireland, ran up only 64 performances. To this day *Eileen* is not as popular as it should be; its music surpasses that of *Naughty Marietta* and *Mlle. Modiste,* and is perhaps the warmest of all Herbert's scores.

It was perhaps an oversight of the *Dramatic Mirror's* editorial writer not to link the name of Ivan Caryll with that of Herbert. For it was in the years from 1911 to 1914 that the Belgian-born, German-trained, English-veneered, American-adopted composer reached the height of his career. Only six days after the editorial appeared, in fact, Caryll achieved one of his most resounding successes with *Chin-Chin.* And both *The Pink Lady* and *Oh! Oh! Delphine* should still have been fairly fresh in the writer's memory.

The Pink Lady, which opened under Klaw and Erlanger's management on March 13, 1911, broke all records for receipts and attendance at the New Amsterdam Theatre in the course of its 320-performance run. In Baltimore, on tour, it broke all records in that city's history except that of *Ben Hur.* Its whole tour was a triumph—especially in Columbus, where it opened the Hartman Theatre, today the sole remaining legitimate house in the Ohio capital.

The Pink Lady was the *Oklahoma!* or *South Pacific* of its day. Everybody, the country over, had heard of it, and everybody wanted to see it. Earl Derr Biggers, then a drama critic in Boston, said that "everyone should see *The Pink Lady* to discover what a musical comedy should be." Philip Hale, of the Boston *Herald,* wrote: "Here we have, then, an amusing book, pleasing music, a rare combination. Here we have a musical comedy that does not depend upon the antics of an acrobatic comedian, on clowning or the independent display of brazen-faced show girls."

Pink became the rage in women's fashions. On the stage, Hazel Dawn, a Utah girl who had risen to stardom in London, wore a "princess effect, with a *chapeau directoire* of coral Milan straw, trimmed with a soft willow plume drooping softly over the left side of the head." Helen Taft pink supplanted Alice blue.

Audiences swooned pleasurably when Hazel Dawn played the dreamy waltz, "Beautiful Lady," on her violin. They gazed with awe upon the spectacular double stairway in the second act, on which the entire cast ranged itself for the chorus of the catchy comic song, "Donny Did, Donny Didn't," and they swayed with the "Ball of the Nymphs and Satyrs" in the third. It was all very striking, very wholesome and clean. But there was not a thing new about *The Pink Lady:* The Satyr Café in Paris was a lineal descendant of Maxim's in *The Merry Widow;* the pink coloring was a recollection of *Erminie.* Yet nobody had the right to say that Caryll could not write a musical comedy that was pleasing to the American audience—and certainly nobody said that Julian Mitchell did not know how to stage some of the most sumptuous production numbers on the New York stage.

For his next success, Caryll and his librettist, C. M. S. McLellan, turned to the naughty-but-nice school, working an obscure French farce into *Oh! Oh! Delphine,* which gave the first of 248 performances in the Knickerbocker Theatre on September 30, 1912. The basis of the plot was so dismal that it deserves to be told: It concerned the search of an artist for a model for the left shoulder of Venus. At the opening, the management instituted the unprecedented rule that nobody should be seated after 8:10. Diamond Jim Brady was forced to wait for an hour at the back of the house. Octavia Brosker, as Bimboula, a carpet-seller from Persia, wore "gorgeous flimsy garments and Turkish trouserettes," and sang the hit song, "The Venus Waltz." Frank McIntyre sang "Everything's at Home Except Your Wife." A parrot cried "Oh! Oh! Delphine" at regular intervals. At the beginning of the second act, the chorus sang:

> *"Now take them all up to the blue room,*
> *Or rather the bill and coo room."*

Another of McLellan's lyrics employed these inspired rhymes:

> *"Oo-la!*
> *Bimboula!*
> *Of my heart you are the ruler.*
> *When you are nigh,*
> *I only gaze and sigh.*
> *Oo-la!*
> *Bimboula!"*

After such lesser undertakings as *The Little Café* (1913), which had a "rarely beautiful garden scene, with the Venus familiar as a truss-maker's trade-mark," and *The Belle of Bond Street* (1914), in which Gaby Deslys wore garish gowns and sang "Who Paid the Rent for Mrs. Rip Van Winkle?," Caryll got down to business with *Chin-Chin, or A Modern Aladdin*. Produced by Charles Dillingham as a vehicle for Montgomery and Stone, this Oriental "musical fantasy" opened at the Globe Theatre on October 20, 1914, ran for 295 times, and made an extensive junket across the country. True to its subtitle, *Chin-Chin* had a modernized Aladdin plot, but Montgomery and Stone, in coolie costumes, with little round caps and pigtails reaching to the back of their knees, kept interfering with its natural progress. Montgomery was his usual amiable, nimble self. Stone appeared as a ventriloquist, a lady bareback rider, an eccentric dancer. As Paderewski, he left a mechanical piano going while he danced with Violet Zell.

Almost nothing was left out of *Chin-Chin*, which reverted in shameless fashion to the technique of suspending as heavy a weight of entertainment as possible from as tenuous a plot-thread as possible. The advertisement offered "caravans of pretty girls; carloads of novelties; tingling-jingling numbers; gorgeous costumes; wonderful scenes; startling situations; quaint Toy Bazaar; teddy bear dances; the Wishing Lamp; the Rain of Gold; the Inimitable 'Paderiski'; the Flight of the Pagoda; the Flight of the Airship; the Marvelous Ventriloquist; the Clown Band; Mademoiselle Falloffski, etc. etc." To top it all, the beauteous Marion Davies put in her appearance; and Fred Stone sang "Good-bye Girls, I'm Through."

In *Jack O'Lantern* (1917), Caryll wrote the score for an almost equally popular extravaganza, in which Fred Stone appeared in partnership not with Montgomery but with Oscar ("Rags") Ragland, the king of burlesque comics, who on this occasion made one of his few ventures into the presence of a legitimate-theatre audience. The following year Caryll wrote a musical comedy in collaboration with Guy Bolton and P. G. Wodehouse, *The Girl Behind the Gun*, in which Donald Brian and Wilda Bennett poked fun at "the godmother craze among French soldiers and the godson craze among French girls."

Among the composers of the older generation, Reginald de Koven had become by now something of a myth. A living myth, to be sure, for he kept right on feeling the impulse to compose. From the eagerness with which producers—even canny ones, like the Shuberts—seized at each new De Koven comic opera over more than twenty years, one would think that *Robin Hood* had been more of an earth-shaking work than it was. In point of fact, the chief use of *Robin Hood,* after its first far from immoderate run, was as a standard repertory piece for the Bostonians, who throve on the presentation of well-cast, smoothly staged comic operas of traditional stripe, from Gilbert and Sullivan to von Suppé's *Fatinitza.* In the later years of his career, De Koven disappointed producers and audiences who hoped for another "O Promise Me" or "Brown October Ale." Christine Nielson and Dorothy Jardon sang in *Her Wedding Trip* (1911), and Mitzi Hajos and Mae Murray lent their vivacious personalities to *Her Little Highness* (1913), to no avail. *Robin Hood* and *Rob Roy* were revived in 1912 and 1913, and *The Highwayman*, with Bianca Saroya, John Charles Thomas, and Jefferson de Angelis, in 1917; but the pavement was worn down by the footsteps of those who passed by the theatre without pausing to buy tickets.

Two more titles complete this end-of-an-era obituary. Gustav Luders was represented for the last time in 1913, by *Somewhere Else*, which was so harshly criticized that a rumor spread to the effect that Luders' subsequent suicide was caused by its bad reception. Ludwig Englander did not commit suicide after the nine performances of his last comic opera, *Madam Moselle* (1914), but it was obvious that he could no longer win the public that had supported his efforts a decade earlier.

When *The Firefly* opened at the Lyric Theatre, under Arthur Hammerstein's management, in 1912, it was apparent that the son of the former director of the Manhattan Opera had discovered an important new talent in Rudolph Friml, its composer. A young American who had started out as a piano virtuoso, Friml possessed a spontaneous gift for writing operetta tunes with a little more substance than the ordinary musical-comedy song. His sensitive feeling for the voice made his tunes grateful to singers, without taxing their resources. The score of *The Firefly* enabled Emma Trentini to make a good display of her large soprano voice in the role of an Italian street singer who, for love of a yachtsman, made her way to Bermuda as a cabin boy, and ultimately became a famous prima donna. Despite her voice, comic opera proved not to be Mme. Trentini's forte, for she lacked charm of presence, and she "acted like a jumping-jack and talked like a parrot. . .in bastard English." Other leading ladies, in revivals of *The Firefly*, have supplied qualities Mme. Trentini did not display; and, thanks partly to the "Donkey Serenade," the piece has found a haven in the outdoor operetta stadia.

With the collaboration of Otto Hauerbach, one of the most assured authors of books and lyrics, Friml turned out a succession of money-makers, not all of which matched *The Firefly* in intrinsic merit. *High Jinks* (1913) was more vaudevillian in the tone of its score and performance. But *Katinka* (1915) again justified Hammerstein's faith in the Friml-Hauerbach combination. If anything could revive comic opera in an age of ragtime, *Katinka* could; it ran for 220 performances, offering its customers a feast of exotic scenes—a villa on the Black Sea, Stamboul and its harems, the inevitable café in old Vienna. In the third act the great vaudeville performer A. Robbins was invited to demonstrate the act upon which he subsisted his whole life long, which entailed pulling an endless variety of incredible objects, large and small, out of his baggy trousers. Just why he should be an entertainer in a Viennese café was not clear then, and is not now, but nobody who ever saw A. Robbins will doubt that he supplied the funniest moments of the evening.

But comic opera had already become an anachronism. *Katinka* was "not a 1916 model." It was, as Heywood Broun wrote, "the sort of a play in which when a character wishes to sing a song she exclaims, 'What shall I do?' Fortunately, the leader of the orchestra was there to inform her." Broun's observation was typical of the thinking of the time. A split had now taken place in the ranks of the theatregoing public, a split that has remained to our own day. The larger part of the audience preferred to keep up with the times. But there remained a homey, melody-loving public, attuned to less exigeant matters than those of foreign-language grand opera, which had become fixated upon the easy delights of comic opera. For the next two generations, there was no exhausting the loyalty of this audience. Novelty was no longer a requisite of comic opera. The critics and the sophisticated public were seldom going to approve of it anyhow, and its own patient, special audience would continue to adore it—especially when it was given in the open on a hot summer night.

One Friml opera of the period, however, did break through the conventions—not because Friml intended it to, but because a man by the name of Ed Wynn would not let it alone. *Sometime* was what the piece produced by Hammerstein in 1918 was called, but any other title would have done as well. "When Mr. Wynn was on the stage the audience forgot *Sometime*," reported *Theatre* magazine. "In fact, time never occurred to them. But when he was not on the stage things dragged dreadfully. For instance, there was a hectic, pink young thing. She was supposed to be the leading lady—whatever that means nowadays—and did her best to make one forget Mr. Wynn, but, thanks to Mr. Wynn's genuine humor, one managed to live through the periods when the pink young thing was on the stage." The pink young thing, unhappy to relate, was Francine Larrimore. Another member of the cast was not even singled out for mention in *Theatre*. Her name was Mae West.

A rival to Friml soon appeared in Sigmund Romberg, who was responsible a little later on for the two hardiest comic operas of the post-World

War I repertory, *Blossom Time* and *The Student Prince*. European-born and educated, Romberg was a more thoroughly trained composer than Friml, and in consequence a more versatile one. Coming to this country in his youth, he found himself a job as staff composer at the Winter Garden, which for four years required his whole energy as a tunesmith for the spicy *Passing Show* and other revues. In 1916, for the Shuberts, he ventured into the comic-opera field for the first time, with *The Girl from Brazil*, which was not much of a success. In the same year he tried an out-and-out musical comedy, *Follow Me*, in which Anna Held, covered with diamonds and still retaining her figure, returned after several years' absence to sing "I Want to be Good but My Eyes Won't Let Me" in milk-white tights. Finally, with *Maytime*, produced by the Shuberts in 1917, Romberg hit upon the vein of refined and warmly spontaneous lyricism for which he is still held in affection. He could turn on the tin-pan-alley style at will, to write music for the Winter Garden or for *Over the Top* (1917), but it is in the style of *Maytime* that he has written his most enduring tunes, which he still plays for audiences of thousands on his annual tours with his orchestra.

XIV. A New Era

ON JANUARY 16, 1912, Winthrop Ames, an ardent young producer with a passion for the betterment of the theatre, entered the New York arena by bringing to the Casino Theatre the complete company of the Deutsches Theater in Berlin. There was no language difficulty, for their "play in nine tableaux" contained not a single spoken word. The accompanying music was composed by Victor Holländer, and the book—or scenario—was by Friedrich Freska. The piece was *Sumurun*, and it was a long and complicated Oriental fantasy.

Sumurun was by all odds the most challenging theatrical event of the twentieth century so far. It introduced America to Max Reinhardt, a stage director whose creative imagination was gradually to revolutionize much of the craft of theatrical production on the American stage, as it had already begun to in Europe.

Some of the critics were so busy expressing official distaste at the frankly erotic aspects of the pantomime in *Sumurun* that they almost overlooked its epoch-making qualities as sheer theatrical spectacle. The *Dramatic Mirror* observed that "the verb *amare* is conjugated in every form, and especially in the imperative." The *Globe* found it "the last word in erotology." The *Times* reported on "a scene of Oriental wooing which would come as near justifying the ringing down of the asbestos curtain as anything which has been disclosed."

But erotology comes cheap, and can be found almost anywhere one wants to look for it. It was in the practical application of Reinhardt's theories of the unity of all the elements of a lyric-theatre performance that *Sumurun* stood apart from and well above every contemporaneous production—so far, indeed, that only the intellectuals were attracted by it, and the run closed after only 62 performances, which were by no means enough to reimburse Ames for the immense cost of bringing the company over and equipping the Casino Theatre.

The stage settings fell oddly upon the consciousness of playgoers used to fussy, gaudy mélanges that were expensive-looking, cluttered-up, and full of color at every cost. Ernest Stern's scenery for *Sumurun* did not compete with the actors and did not swear at the costumes. It was marked by flat, plain-toned surfaces against which the acting and dancing, closely related to each other, could always be discerned without loss of focus. It was, moreover, scenery devised to permit—no, to require—the illusion of skillful lighting. Design, color, and lighting all conspired to enhance the moods of the fantasy, and to compel attention upon the central action. *Sumurun* was the archetype of all we now take for granted as desirable in modern unified design and presentation.

"The lines are straight," explained the *Dramatic Mirror*, "and crude colors are massed in broad, flat expanses. The closing scene of the first half exemplifies the style most strikingly, for it consists of three colors—a frieze of pure white, with the black, shadowy palace, behind it, against a dark but brilliant blue sky. The fantastic characters cross the stage before this white background like animated decorations on Keats's famous Grecian urn. The yellow harem, with its spiral staircase running up to the two corridor balconies, one above the other, is another example of the same poster style. The sheik's chamber was executed by utilizing light in an identical fashion. A huge lantern, hung from the centre of the ceiling, shed its glow slantingly down filmy white draperies leading from it to the bed. The guidance of the light and the eye left the remainder of the stage in obscurity."

The *Times* rounded out the picture with a description of the first scene, in an Oriental bazaar, "represented in a simple, flat elevation of a creamy color, punctuated here and there by oval windows with lattice work in a peculiar shade of blue, and a general effect both restful and unusual."

It was the *Tribune*, though, which came closest to understanding the point, even if its observation was meant to be grouchy: "The scenery is of the plainest. It suggests rather than illustrates."

In its love for gauche overdisplay and romantic realism, the American theatre had entirely forgotten how to "suggest rather than illustrate." For Reinhardt, the suggestion of a whole mood or concept was a more desirable achievement than the literal illustration of part of one. Instead of conforming to the limitations of the stage as they were then understood, he triumphed over them by violating them. He dared to "break the proscenium" by building a stage apron in front of the usual footlight trough and bringing his actors out onto the apron, in closer contact with the audience. He even instructed one actor to lie down right next to the footlights. Most startling of all, he constructed a runway from the front of the theatre to the orchestra pit, over the orchestra chairs, illuminated it with a blue light, and carried the action out into the house, above the heads of the spectators.

Such unabashed functionalism, so complete a challenge to the established canons of staging, was considerably in advance of its time. During the next decade Reinhardt's innovations were slowly incorporated, one by one—frequently in misunderstood or trivialized fashion—into American productions. It was considerably longer, however, before the basic principles of unity that guided Reinhardt's work were thoroughly apprehended and absorbed by American directors and producers; many, of course, have not apprehended them yet. The most immediate influence of *Sumurun* stemmed from its outward accidents rather than its inward essence.

The aspect of exotic Oriental splendor in *Sumurun* led, in due season, to such splashy displays as *Chu Chin Chow* and *Mecca*. For these evocations of the other side of the globe, however, *Sumurun* was by no means wholly responsible. Orientalism, whether in round-the-world extravaganzas or in such comic operas as *The Mikado, Wang,* and *The Geisha,* had long been considered a sure-fire device, if not used too often. And by way of fresh impetus, a new cult of the exotic was derived from Russia in 1911, the year before *Sumurun*. In that year, Klaw and Erlanger imported a Russian balalaika orchestra to make sounds such as had not been heard before. A few months later Gertrude Hoffman, having made due arrangements with Diaghileff, presented her Russian Ballet at the new Winter Garden, dancing the role of Zobéide in *Scheherazade,* with a décor devised after that of Léon Bakst, and engaging Lydia Lopokova and Alexandre Volinine to appear in *Cléopâtre* and *Les Sylphides*.

At the Winter Garden the art of ballet and the old commerce of pleasing the tired businessman learned to live together on congenial terms again for the first time since the decline of French ballet in the 1870s. Opened in 1911, the luxurious theatre, which still stands on the former site of the Horse Exchange, was dedicated to revues and extravaganzas. In the summer, the roof was used for the presentation of smaller midnight entertainments, with accompanying food and drink in the cabaret fashion that was at its height then and for a decade afterward.

The first entertainment at the Winter Garden, produced on March 20, 1911, by the Shuberts, who have been its sole owners since the beginning, was a double bill. The first half, *Bow Sing,* was devoted to art. The second half, *La Belle Paree,* concentrated upon frivolity, though the inclusion of the operatic soprano, Dorothy Jardon, who had been engaged mainly for *Bow Sing,* might be termed a concession to art. The new institution was thought to represent "a great outlay of money, energy, and brains," and the first bill left the audience "limp from the exhaustive spectacle and from

laughter." Once *Bow Sing*, a Chinese opera in three acts with a score by
Manuel Klein and a book by Carroll Fleming, had run its dutiful, and no
doubt beautiful, course, the audience was free to enjoy *La Belle Paree*.
Described in the program as "a Cook's tour through vaudeville, with a
Parisian landscape," the revue was studded with talent on all sides. Jerome
Kern and Frank Tours shared responsibility for the music; Edgar Smith, a
master of the discreetly dirty phrase and situation, contributed the book and
sketches. Melville Ellis, a leading designer of harmonious and fashionable
costumes for the musical stage, and Arthur Voegtlin, a scenic designer whose
father had devised the visual effects of *The Black Crook*, collaborated in the
decorative features. The pert Mitzi Hajos and young Al Jolson, whose days
of great popularity still lay ahead, were in the cast. The ballet offered not
only the classic graces of Mlle. Dazie and Signor Bonfiglio, but also the
more elemental divertissements of Tortajada and sixteen Moorish dancing
girls. It is worthy of note that *La Belle Paree* endured for 104 performances,
while *Bow Sing* was eliminated after 32.

Success breeds imitation. On April 27, at the Folies Bergère, Henry B.
Harris and Jesse L. Lasky launched an entertainment modeled after that of
the Winter Garden. The Folies Bergère was a restaurant-theatre, however,
and its shows, given at midnight, were shorter than those of the Winter
Garden, though hardly less elaborate in conception. The first attraction was
a triple bill. It began with a "profane burlesque," *Hell*. Elizabeth Goodall,
as the Statue of Liberty, got tired of standing on a pedestal, and decided
to go to Hades, "about the only free place nowadays." The Devil and Mrs.
Devil introduced her to a variety of people—a Pittsburgh trust magnate
looking for a "hot time," Phoebe Snow, a blasé first-nighter. Liberty soon
decided that Hell was no better than New York, and returned to her pedestal. The cynicism of *Hell* was counterbalanced by a one-act ballet, *Temptation*, in which Mlle. Britta and Signor Borghini were assigned the
choreographic task of showing "how pure love overcame earthly pleasure."
One critic complained that the constant manipulation of colored lights distracted from the dancing. The evening was rounded off by *Gaby*, a "satirical
revuette," which was again in a riot of color, ending with a "kaleidoscopic
assembly of tints."

The Winter Garden, unruffled by the borrowing of its formula, offered
two more entertainments in its first year. *The Revue of Revues* was a collection of three "musical satires." This time the order of things was reversed,
and the most popular material came first, with *In the Limelight*, in which
grace was sacrificed to grotesquerie in "dancing of the energetic, whirligig
kind." *Nel Giappone*, a Japanese pantomime ballet, followed. The order of
the program was finally explained by the third piece, a French "comedietta"
called *Les Débuts de Chichine*; for Gaby Deslys, making her first American
appearance in this, was expected to provide the climax of the evening. She
did not create quite the sensation the Shuberts must have hoped for, since,

though she was lovely to look upon, she was not much of a singer or dancer. Moreover, the sincerity and directness of Frank Tinney in his humorous monologues, and his quick gift for etching characters, made an impression that tended to obscure the claims of Mlle. Deslys.

Al Jolson came back in *Vera Violetta*, an entertainment that still retained shreds of a German libretto by Leo Stein. His popularity was now decidedly on the upgrade, as was that of Mlle. Deslys, who had begun to be intelligible in English. Mae West, always doomed to receive little notice at this early stage of her career, was also among those present. As a curtain raiser, a version of *Undine* was written and composed by Manuel Klein and provided with a setting reproducing what was described as a "Claude Manet landscape." Annette Kellerman, bereft of a tank, was able to demonstrate that "her dancing was as marvellous as her diving."

By the end of its first year, the Winter Garden had become an assured operation. The bill on March 5, 1912, started off with *A Night with the Pierrots*, in which the participants in the harlequinade were Al Jolson, Barney Bernard, and a bright young hoofer named George White. This time the art item in the middle was frankly played for laughs. Called *Sesostra*, it was a burlesque of the newly arrived *Sumurun*, in which the seemingly bizarre eccentricities of Reinhardt's staging were given a hearty ribbing. Actually, it was to the main piece of the evening, *The Whirl of Society*, that *Sumurun* made its real contribution. Envisaging uses for it of which Reinhardt had not dreamed, the management built a runway across the pit and out into the house. The hoydenish Blossom Seeley used it in a marathon around the aisles of the theatre. But more than this, the girls of the chorus came out on the runway, where the audience could see them much, much better.

With the coming of summer the Shuberts—now incorporated for this special purpose as the Winter Garden Company—revived a great name from the past, and, with the obvious intention of making it an annual affair like the *Ziegfeld Follies*, presented *The Passing Show of 1912*. For the new venture they engaged, or retained from previous assignments, what was to be a fairly permanent production personnel. Ned Wayburn, one of the slickest masters of show-dance routines, became the dance director (nobody called them choreographers in those days). Melville Ellis remained as costume designer. Harold L. Atteridge wrote the lyrics for George Bronson Howard's book; in subsequent editions Atteridge took care of both book and lyrics. Louis A. Hirsch, who did not stay on to do another one, wrote the score.

The chief performers in *The Passing Show* were all new to the Winter Garden, except Jobyna Howland, who had added to the good looks of *The Whirl of Society*. The book was nominally concerned with take-offs on such current theatrical hits as *The Quaker Girl* and *Bunty Pulls the Strings*, for to this extent *The Passing Show of 1912* was conceived in the image of its

predecessor of 1894. But the people in it were more important than its
material. The eighty artfully chosen girls—by whom, according to *Variety*,
"the *Sumurun* runway was again fully tested to its limit"—answered to three
specialized classifications, "show girls" (the tall, statuesque ones), "medi-
ums," and "ponies." Longer-legged than the show girls was the future Letty,
Charlotte Greenwood, who swung her legs about and tangled them up in
her usual fashion. Eugene and Willie Howard graduated from vaudeville
into a partnership that retained its hold upon popular affections for thirty
years. And the first act contained a song, "Ragtime Jockey Man," by a young
rehearsal pianist named Irving Berlin.

Once the enterprise was under way, the *Passing Show* arrived like clockwork every year—sometimes as early as April, sometimes as late as July,
depending on other bookings at the Winter Garden—and never failed to
run for from fifteen to twenty weeks before setting out on the road.

The second edition, *The Passing Show of 1913*, retained the runway and
Charlotte Greenwood, and introduced John Charles Thomas, in his first
Broadway engagement. Ned Wayburn provided every variant on the tango
and the turkey-trot, and revived the "almost forgotten" cakewalk of the
previous decade. The finale, the most imposing spectacle Voegtlin had yet
conceived for the Winter Garden, showed the steps of the Capitol in Washington, reaching "from the front of the stage to seventh heaven."

The Passing Show of 1914 was probably never surpassed in the history
of the institution. The two earlier editions had leaned quite heavily on their
stars—the Howards and Charlotte Greenwood. But the third *Passing Show*
was in every way a rounded, balanced, and lavish entertainment. To be
sure, it introduced (for the first time outside vaudeville) Marilynn Miller,
who was to become within a decade the highest-paid star the American
musical theatre had known. But now she was merely an unknown youngster,
though she made an instantaneous hit with her capable dancing and her
sprightly imitations of popular actresses.

But the third *Passing Show* went down in history primarily as the moment
of final triumph for the slender, modern chorus girl. Gone forever now were
the gigantic chorus ladies with their Amazonian marches and drills. "When
a Kiralfy show was announced," one old-timer recalled, "managers were
wont to look after the bracings under the stage. In the earlier days a chorus
person was not considered much of a charmer unless she possessed limbs
like barrels, and with a spear in hand, waddled about the stage."

This contrast is, of course, somewhat overdrawn, for fashions do not
change overnight, and the choral Amazon had been on the way out for some
years. But with *The Passing Show of 1914* the metamorphosis was complete.
It signalized the edging out of the baldheads from the front row, and the
usurpation of their places by "unwhipped cubs, the silken sons of dalliance
nursed in pleasure's flowery lap." For the benefit of the unwhipped cubs,
the girls' legs, which had been emerging from their tights inch by inch for

several seasons, were now presented unadorned and *au naturel*, underneath "torsos screened by glittering spangles." Skirts were short and arms were bare, and at one point the glittering spangles were dispensed with, revealing bare midriffs on the upper-class New York stage for the first time. The "winsome witches" gave a new and piquant meaning to the runway; and when they returned to the stage they revealed unwonted energy and talent by engaging in thoroughly professional tap dancing. In the midst of this "uproarious upheaval of lingerie and laughter," demure little Marilynn Miller (who had not yet cropped the final "n" from her first name) appeared as a Dresden Doll. Nor were the purely spectacular elements overlooked in this carnival of undress. Voegtlin provided a panoramic view of the San Francisco World's Fair and a scene representing the transatlantic flight of an airship; and art—not wholly forgotten—was solemnized in a "Beautiful Persian Garden Scene," in the style of Maxfield Parrish.

There is no need to recall subsequent *Passing Shows* in detail, for the pattern was now set. Marilynn Miller, with her adorable smile and happy dancing, was back in 1915, along with the Howards, to grant surcease from a "realistic invasion of London by Zeppelins." The *Globe* commented acidly that bare knees had "ceased to be a *sauce piquante*." But everybody loved Marilynn Miller when she appeared as First Love, opposite John Charles Thomas as Youth.

The 1915 edition showed a falling-off in wit and imagination, though Ed Wynn carried his end of the show, and there were novelties in the form of revivals of clogging and buck-and-wing dancing, an "Olympian ballet" suggesting *Scheherazade*, and a memorable tune by Sigmund Romberg called "Pretty Baby." In 1916, Ed Wynn sought to repair an inner tube with a saw and a hammer in a sketch entitled "A Modern Garage." The humor generally, however, was on the level of cracks about Philadelphia and the Ford car and fighting with one's wife; and the girls who still did boys' parts in the chorus were coming to seem old-fashioned. By 1917 *The Passing Show* had become hardly more than an expensive annual obeisance—this time with De Wolf Hopper and Jefferson de Angelis as veteran comics, and a "disappointingly overdressed" chorus. The 1918 edition had a brighter topical book, with sketches about War Savings Stamps and the new fad of having supper at Childs, and a burlesque showing Salome with the head of the Kaiser. The Howard brothers were back, and the cast also included such newcomers as Fred and Adele Astaire, Sammy White, Marion Stafford, Charles Ruggles, Frank Fay, and Nita Naldi.

In the months when *The Passing Show* was away, the Winter Garden housed other attractions of similar format and appeal. Of one of these, *The Whirl of the World* in 1914, Alan Dale of the New York *American*, describing the "sort of peninsula which separated the stage from the auditorium so that the girls could be touched," wrote pleadingly, "Oh, parents . . . keep tender boys at home. . . . . Keep them—aye, keep them from the Winter Garden. It is very, awfully, dangerous." To which Charles Darnton of the *World* added that the Winter Garden was "no place for a man with a weak heart." Plainly people did not come to *The Whirl of the World* with the primary object of seeing Lydia Kyasht and Serge Litavkin in "Harlequin and the Bluebird." A similar situation obtained with *Dancing Around,* later the same year, when the audience had no eyes for Clifton Webb and Eileen Molyneux, an English ballerina, in the "Shepherd Gavotte" and "Silhouette Ballet."

Let the Winter Garden itself provide an evocative finish for our consideration of its early years. How would the late Commissioner Paul Moss have reacted to this throwaway of *A World of Pleasure,* in 1915?

"PERFECT FROM THE PINKY OF THE CUTEST LITTLE PONY TO THE MAJESTIC BATTLESHIP, WHICH, FIRST HEADING TOWARDS THE AUDIENCE, TURNS COMPLETELY ABOUT AND PLOUGHS FORWARD IN THE OPPOSITE DIRECTION. . . . [*A World of Pleasure*] goes to extremes of undress—almost to actual nudity—that would have astounded the unsophisticated audience of five years ago. Unless a girdle of beads be considered a costume, there are scenes in which the chorus may truthfully be described as wearing no clothes at all. Stockings are as obsolete at the Winter Garden as the steel armor of a mediaeval soldier. A dress not cut to the waist line at the back is a curiosity—an impudent attempt at unwelcome modesty."

At the time the Winter Garden opened, Flo Ziegfeld indirectly gave aid and comfort to the project by letting his *Follies* decline in quality. The *Follies of 1911* depended chiefly upon the eccentric behavior of the Dolly Sisters, the weak ankle of Leon Errol, and the dancing of Bessie McCoy, "an attractive young woman in a defiant pose, as if of virtue, able to defend itself, on the aggressively defensive, with the wind or the movement tossing the skirts above the shapely ankles." A sketch, "New Year's Eve on the Barbary Coast," contained an Apache dance, and an elaborate production number required stacks of wheat in a field to turn into a dancing chorus. But some of the magic was missing. More still was missing in the following year's edition, for which Raymond Hubbell wrote music "that went in one ear and out the other," and Harry B. Smith performed one of his least inspired jobs of book- and lyric-writing. The women were now barelegged, though, and in "A Palace of Beauty," Ziegfeld introduced the device of having the show girls parade—to the tune of "Beautiful, Beautiful Girl"—one by one, in a spotlight, to their respective stations.

The fortunes of the *Follies* began to pick up in 1913. Julian Mitchell surpassed himself in the big picturesque numbers, beginning the show with an illusive tableau of Hawkeye and a group of fellow redskins gazing down on New York, and ending it with a depiction of the opening of the Panama Canal and the raising of a warship in the locks. Ann Pennington had now arrived on the scene, happily at a time when it was permissible for her to reveal her dimpled knees; Frank Tinney was the soul of amiability; and Leon Errol capsized the audience with an eccentric dance, "Turkish Trottishness," in which he left the turkey-trot without a leg to stand on.

Julian Mitchell had not spent the larger part of his sixty years in the theatre for nothing, and in 1914—the peak year of *The Passing Show*—he brought the *Follies* ensembles to a high level of disciplined sumptuousness. This time the most striking spectacle revealed the corner of Fifth Avenue and Forty-second Street after a severe snowstorm. Leon Errol—who directed the book as well as appearing in the show—chose the tango for his lampoon, and the graceful, lithe convolutions of Ann Pennington became the talk of the town.

Channing Pollock, Rennold Wolf, and Gene Buck, skilled hands all, took hold of the book, sketches and lyrics in 1915, and gave them more zest. But the greatest improvement of all was Ziegfeld's engagement of Joseph Urban as his designer. A student of the methods of Gordon Craig and Reinhardt, Urban gave the décors of his first *Follies* some of the look of *Sumurun*, making astute use of the flat colors American designers still disdained, and producing a total of twenty-one different scenes marked by an imaginativeness and ingenuity of design and color that neither *The Passing Show* nor any other spectacle could rival. Against Urban's flat surfaces and plain colors, Ziegfeld's curved beauties developed a fresh appeal, especially when they appeared in the Elysian Fields.

Urban remained Ziegfeld's designer thereafter, though not exclusively, for he was in great demand by other producers as well. His designs and Ziegfeld's unerring eye for the points of a girl remained the constants of subsequent editions of the *Follies*. The performing talent did not remain fixed, though Ziegfeld was wise enough to keep his most popular entertainers for as long as he could. One of these returned to his ranks in 1916—Fannie Brice, who had been in the *Follies of 1910,* and who now appeared as Theda Bara and in a burlesque of a burlesque dancer. Others in the same year were the adroit juggler W. C. Fields and the handsome, self-collected, clothes-horse Lilyan Tashman. Ina Claire, Marion Davies, and Justine Johnstone were in the 1916 edition, too, along with Ziegfeld's droll standby, Bert Williams, and a pert young hoofer, Carl Randall. In 1917, Ina Claire and Marion Davies and Justine Johnstone were gone, but Lilyan Tashman was back, along with Fannie Brice, Fields, and Williams. Peggy Hopkins (not yet Joyce) made one of her intermittent appearances. Eddie Cantor moved from Ziegfeld's cabaret show on the roof down to the street level for the first time. Will Rogers twirled his lariat as he drawled homespun Oklahoma philosophies. In 1918, to secure his permanent triumph over *The Passing Show,* Ziegfeld won Marilynn Miller away from the Shuberts, discovered a tall, dark, lanquid beauty with the single name of Dolores, and put them both against the luxurious background of Urban's settings, in the company of Eddie Cantor, W. C. Fields, Will Rogers, Ann Pennington, and the Fairbanks Twins.

George M. Cohan was quick to make capital of the new enthusiasm for elaborate revues. After the lukewarm reception of *The Little Millionaire*

(1911), he realized that the time for a change had come. Allying himself with Sam H. Harris in the producing firm of Cohan and Harris, he brought to the Astor Theatre in 1914 a "musical crazy quilt" (Billy Rose appropriated the term for the title of a revue in the 1930s), *Hello Broadway*. With William Collier as his partner, Cohan built his first revue more on the pattern of Weber and Fields than of *The Passing Show*, filling it with broad travesties of current plays and players, studding it with his own song-and-dance routines, and brightening it with the presence of Peggy Wood, Louise Dresser, Roszika (but not Yancsi) Dolly, and Florence Moore, one of the most hard-working and generally-liked comediennes of the decade.

Not until Cohan eliminated himself from the cast in favor of Charles Winninger, in *The Cohan Revue of 1916*, did the substance of the Cohan and Harris revues tend to become modernized, and even here the *Dramatic Mirror* observed that the décors were "not of the new art so much in evidence this season." There was one more Cohan revue, in 1918, before the managers determined to leave the field to Ziegfeld and the Shuberts. Irving Berlin provided some of the songs and Cohan the rest, and Nora Bayes was Winninger's vis-à-vis.

A few other revues cropped up under other managements, but not as many as might have been expected from the consistent prosperity of the established annuals. Klaw and Erlanger seized Joseph Urban immediately after the triumph of his first *Follies*, and had him design *Around the Map* (1915). Louise Groody, who still had several years to wait for *No, No, Nanette*, was the ingenue, but the cast was otherwise undistinguished, compared to those of Ziegfeld and the Shuberts. But the production itself outdid the *Follies of 1915*, amounting to "a gorgeous fashion show which moves in steady procession across three and a half hours." A prescient touch of modernity could be discovered in the chorus girls' dresses in the cabaret scene, which consisted of hoops of empty frames trimmed with fur at the bottom.

Of the rest of the miscellany, none is worth recalling, except perhaps Jack Norworth's "chummy" revue, *Odds and Ends of 1917*, of which Burns Mantle remarked, "The scenery is by someone who plays the Joseph Urban harmonies by ear, and is more or less tone deaf."

As is always the case when innovations come along, the new fashions did not immediately obliterate the old ones. Of Joe Weber's series of burlesques, and of the return of Weber and Fields in 1911, we have already taken cognizance. The two final Weber and Fields items do, however, deserve a bit more attention, because it was in them, despite their generally outmoded aspect, that the pre-*Tugboat Annie* Marie Dressler gave perhaps the fullest account of her gifts. "In one scene," Alan Dale recounted of *Roly-Poly* (1912), "she appeared in bright green satin, trimmed with a fur rug! She told me she made it herself in the hopes that she would be a laughing stock in it. That hope did not materialize." Her great triumph in *Roly-Poly* was a Spanish gypsy dance, in which "her evolutions caused tremendous laughter." The audience also laughed—the Lord forgive it—at her line, "Father, you are the one thing in Mother's life I can never forgive." A few months later, in 1913, Weber and Fields offered *Marie Dressler's All-Star Gambol*, which included, among a diversity of things, a one-act play by George Arliss. Miss Dressler and Jefferson de Angelis offered a burlesque of *Camille*. They also addressed themselves to "The Evolution of Dancing," in which they were joined by the rest of the company in Ancient Greek Dancing, Old-Fashioned Step Dancing, Original Spanish Dancing (something of a novelty; the first Spanish revue, *The Land of Joy*, did not reach New York until 1917), Classic Toe Dancing, Lightning Turkey Trot, Soft Shoe Dance, Wooden Shoe Dance, Russian Dances, and, to cap the climax, a "classic dance" by Miss Dressler and De Angelis.

Another series of essentially old-fashioned revues was inaugurated by Raymond Hitchcock with *Hitchy-Koo* (1917), to which Cohan and Harris devoted their managerial energies in between the two *Cohan Revues*. Surrounded by Irene Bordoni, Leon Errol, and Florenz Ames, Hitchcock used the revue format to serve the purposes of his informal, friendly style, greeting the arriving customers out front before the curtain went up, and engaging in confidential impromptu remarks throughout the evening. The same players, with the addition of Ray Dooley, came back the following year in *Hitchy-Koo of 1918*, of which Hitchcock himself was producer and Errol stage director.

Through thick and thin, through fair weather and foul, the mammoth Hippodrome pursued its own special, spectacular course, still attracting a year's business with each new production—except in the single case of *Wars of the World* in 1914, which ran only half the year and caused the Shuberts to relinquish the house to Charles Dillingham.

Since the site of the Hippodrome, at Forty-fourth Street and Sixth Avenue, is now no more than a large level scar on which automobiles are parked, its glories can best be called to mind by the excited prose of the 1912 souvenir program:

"After passing through the marble lobby, with its circles of box-offices and staircases leading to the mezzanine floor and balconies, the visitor reaches the spacious promenade half encircling the great auditorium. Lined with mirrors on the outer side, between supports of marble, and on the inner side, opening to the promenade boxes, it offers a sight of superb splendor and magnificence.

"The chief ornamentation consists of great and golden elephant heads, with silvered trappings, and these are studded with electric lights, of which there are just a few less than 8,000 from the entrance to the lobby to the dome. On either side of the stage are boxes of various seating capacities, some of them holding forty persons, and arranged for parties. Above is the wide sweeping balcony, the front of which is lined with loges, where smoking is permitted. A second balcony stretches out from above. On one mezzanine floor are attractive lounging rooms known as 'The Jungles,' where between scenes and during performances visitors find the comfort and attraction of lounging chairs and cozy corners for a chat, a rest, and refreshments."

The seating capacity at that time was given as 5,200, though in 1917 it was said to be 5,697. Two regulation-size circus rings could be installed on the stage apron. Under the apron was a tank, fourteen feet deep. The stage was 110 feet deep from footlights to back wall, and 200 feet wide, and could be moved up and down on a hydraulic elevator. The dressing rooms accommodated 1,000.

The Hippodrome shows took the whole world and all history as their province, and the mechanical skill of Arthur Voegtlin knew no limitations of time and place. *Around the World* (1911) carried spectators from New York out into mid-ocean, then to England, Switzerland, Constantinople, Egypt, and the Sahara Desert. "The effects in scenery, in distance, depth and height, and light and shade, clouds and storm and other effects impossible to the ordinary theatre, enable the Hippodrome to occupy a field all its own. Mere bigness of spectacle would soon tire the public, so that the success of the venture must be attributed to personal and artistic qualities."

Be that as it may, the "personal and artistic qualities" were bent toward essentially the same ends every year. The thirteen scenes of *Under Many Flags* (1912) included the sight of the White House lawn, the Naval Academy at Annapolis, a fishing village in Brittany, and views of Moscow, Scotland, Berlin, Peking, and Arizona. The Arizona scene included a herd of deer and a tornado that leveled the town. Not unnaturally, it was felt that "none but a magician can eclipse the genius of Voegtlin in creating illusions such as these." And at Annapolis, Alan Dale reported, "you saw the cadets. These were not chorus girls in a vulgarity of tights, but men—and the baldheads were routed." It was hard going for the baldheads everywhere in these years.

In 1913, with *America*, Voegtlin decided to remain in the Western hemisphere. He did not lack materials, however, for in the very opening scene he spanned American history from the landing of Columbus to the rush hour at the newly completed Grand Central Terminal. Later his audience visited a New England farm, the levee at New Orleans, the Alamo Plaza in San Antonio, the East Side of New York, where type characters helped the fire department fight a conflagration, and the Panama Canal, a popular and timely subject for spectacular treatment. At the end, the audience and the hundreds on the stage sang "America."

Wars of the World (1914) was the one halfway success of the series, and the last spectacle presented by the Shuberts. It offered a curious array of conflicts—Robin Hood, the "Holy War," the French Revolution, the Civil War, the Taking of Vera Cruz, and the "War of Sport." In one scene soldiers raced down the aisles and were catapulted over the pit onto the stage. The list of the subsequent Hippodrome spectacles becomes redundant. John

Philip Sousa and his band played in *Hip-Hip-Hooray,* in 1915. Emanuel List, later the Metropolitan Opera's Baron Ochs in Strauss's *Der Rosen-kavalier,* made his first major American appearance in 1917 in *Cheer Up,* which was also egregious because of the freight train, full-size, which chugged up to a rural station at the beginning of the second act. In 1918, for a show patriotically supplied with music by Sousa and Irving Berlin and lyrics by John Golden, Dillingham finally hit upon the ideal title for a Hippodrome spectacle—*Everything.*

XV. New Art and Old Formulas

THE LUSH "new art" movement, engendered in various ways by Reinhardt, the Ballets Russes, and Urban, was sumptuously represented on November 6, 1916, by *The Century Girl,* produced jointly by Dillingham and Ziegfeld to open the handsome new Century Theatre, up above Columbus Circle. Part musical comedy and part revue, *The Century Girl* subsisted on typical Urban-Ziegfeld effects, such as the Celestial Staircase, which Hazel Dawn descended; the Crystal Palace, with a "Procession of the Laces of the World"; and, for spice, a scene in the Garden of a Modern Girls' School. Victor Herbert and Irving Berlin provided the music; Leon Errol and Edward Royce directed; and Ned Wayburn staged the dances and musical numbers. Errol also displayed his comic ankle; Elsie Janis did her bit; Lillian (not Lilyan this time) Tashman offered her sophisticated beauty as a foil for Hazel Dawn's fresh innocence; and comic chores were allotted to Sam Bernard, the classic Dutch comic, Frank Tinney, and—in their first of several ventures out of vaudeville under Ziegfeld's aegis—Gus Van and Joe Schenck, the song pluggers.

The Century Girl was such a triumph that Ziegfeld and Dillingham spared no expense, even according to their expensive lights, in preparing its successor the following autumn, *Miss 1917.* Herbert and Jerome Kern, now two of the top names in the business, wrote the score, and Guy Bolton and P. G. Wodehouse, lately established as the brightest littérateurs in the light theatre, devised the book and lyrics. Urban, of course, did the sets, and Wayburn staged the production numbers. Lady Duff Gordon was engaged to design the costumes; and, since there was ballet as well as popular dancing, Adolph Bolm was assigned to the creation of a "choreographic poem, 'Falling Leaves.' " The rehearsal pianist was the teen-age George Gershwin. The cast was nothing short of incredible. Miss Tashman and Van and Schenck were carried over from *The Century Girl.* Lew Fields replaced Sam Bernard as the apparently indispensable Dutch comic. Young Vivienne Segal sang in her pretty, high lyric-soprano voice. Irene Castle, Ann Pennington, George White, and Bolm all danced. Marion Davies and Peggy Hopkins contributed their beauty. Bert Savoy and Jay Brennan camped. Scarcely an entertainment of the decade was so studded with magic names. But, alas, Ziegfeld and Dillingham quickly discovered what too many cooks can do, and *Miss 1917* perished ignominiously after 48 performances.

One other lavish escapist piece lightened the first fall of the war. Morris Gest, William Elliott, and F. Ray Comstock brought the splendor of Bagdad to the Manhattan Opera House on October 22, 1917, in a "musical tale of the East" called *Chu Chin Chow*. A sort of pageant, with elements of pantomime, ballet, musical comedy, grand opera, and fantasy, *Chu Chin Chow* was the first serious attempt to recapture the approach of Reinhardt in *Sumurun*. If it partially failed in its intention, the incompatibility of Reinhardt principles with those of Ziegfeld can be blamed. With Tyrone Power (Senior, of course), Florence Reed, and George Rasely taking care of the chief acting and musical assignments, the central roles were in good hands. Miss Reed, just beginning the important phase of her career, was singled out for a performance "in the right key from the beginning, that never deviated, and was vivid, pulsing, and vital."

But the production was more commanding than any of the individual contributions to it. The senses were "wooed, delighted, ravished, and astounded" by the settings, designed in a manner to "out-Bakst Bakst" by Joseph and Phil Harker of London, who earlier had designed Henry Irving's productions. The lighting employed Reinhardt techniques, which were still being overlooked elsewhere in the American musical theatre: "Only the slave market, which baked under the midday sun and the steel blue sky, was diffused with light. In the other acts the concentrated illumination fell directly on the moving character in the picture." To this illusion the music by Frederick Norton also contributed, for while "original it is not, it has a widely varied lilt, a salient trick in characterization, and unflagging vigor." An unwonted device of stagecraft—an application of moving-picture practices to the Reinhardt device of lighting only part of the stage—was manifested in the use of "close-ups," or little vignettes, during the changes of the big scenes. For this purpose the Harkers provided a single Moorish window set in a black curtain.

In this remarkable production, only Oscar Asche's book, with its pretentious poetry, was out of key in its own time, as can readily be discerned from "The Love Chant of the Wild Women of the Desert":

> *"Oh, ye who in walled cities dwell,*
>   *What do ye know of life?*
> *Oh, ye who strive to buy and sell,*
>   *What taste have ye of strife?*
> *Oh, ye who breathe but reek and dust,*
> *Who hoard your wealth for moth and rust,*
> *Whose veins are clogged with lazy lust,*
> *What can YE feel of Passion's gust?"*

These big-budget attractions—*The Passing Show*, the annual *Follies*, *Chu Chin Chow*, the Century shows, and the Hippodrome extravaganzas—presented no threat to the continuing existence of the bread-and-butter musical productions, the normal-sized musical comedies and operettas. The second decade of the twentieth century may, for purposes of convenient cataloguing, be divided—in oversimplified fashion, to be sure—into two periods. The first period, up to 1915, witnessed constantly diminishing returns from pieces whose style was a hangover from conventions of the previous fifteen years. The second, beginning in 1915, saw the rapid sprouting of new ideas and the appearance of fresh young talents, and laid the groundwork for much that has happened in the musical theatre ever since that time.

The old order, with relatively little admixture of anything novel, was perpetuated by Lew Fields in the three musical comedies he offered in quick succession in 1911. The first of these, *The Hen Pecks*, detailed the trip of the Peck family from Cranberry Cove to New York, where Fields (his Dutch-comedy dialect intact) and Blossom Seeley encountered the debonair Vernon Castle, who sang but did not dance, along with an assortment of chorus girls decked out now in canary yellow, white, and black, now in purple, violet, lavender, and brown against a light green background. The color effects were considered "astonishing," and there can be no doubt that they were.

The Never Homes, Fields's second piece of this busy year, had to get along without its producer's presence in the cast. It might, indeed, readily be forgotten for all eternity, if Helen Hayes, a "talented little girl" of twelve—already a veteran of two previous Fields musical comedies, *Old Dutch* and *The Summer Widowers*—had not raised a singing voice that was never to be heard again until 1946, in *Happy Birthday*. Her principal number was a duet, "There's a Girl in Havana," with "little Will Archie," who was actually twenty-five years old.

The Never Homes was burdened by a plot satirizing woman suffrage. In the election, women won all the offices in the town of Lilydale. Patricia Flynn, the mayor (impersonated by the fat George W. Monroe), ran things with a high hand. In the middle of a conversation with Mrs. Daly Bunn and Mrs. Talkington Louder, the telephone rang. "Girls, what do you think?" said Patricia, toying with her hair. "There's a fire!" Then, into the telephone: "Is it a little one or a big one? If it isn't a very big one we'll come around tomorrow, as it's sort of damp out today, and it wouldn't be good for the horses to go out." Finally the apparatus left, with all the girls but Patricia clinging to the sides. "Gee!" exclaimed Patricia. "The fools have gone to the fire, and I'm the only one who knows the address." This rudimentary comedy took place against settings by Voegtlin, who gave full rein to his usual elaborate taste, using costumes of massed colors in "blazing combinations of red and black or bright green and white" and creating a new effect with "shimmering strips of silvered cloth lighted with various colors." After two more productions, both short-lived—*The Wife Hunters* (1911) and *Hanky Panky* (1912)—Fields withdrew from musical-comedy production.

The low estate of musical comedy in 1911 was further revealed by *Jumping Jupiter*, whose score by Karl Hoschna, one ruthless observer said, "hadn't even a tune to keep it going." Edna Wallace Hopper, "in monkey-hat and accents strained," was "self-conscious and chorus-girly." It was a ragtime show, with the "Mississippi Dip" and the "Possum Rag." Like *The Never Homes, Jumping Jupiter*'s interest for posterity resides in its cast, which included Jeanne Eagels, Helen Broderick, and, for the first time out of vaudeville, Ina Claire.

The Red Rose, another memento of 1911, was a window display for the overdressed Valeska Suratt, who designed her own innumerable costumes, the most overpowering of which were a Spanish affair in canary yellow and black (the fashionable color scheme of the year) and a flaming harem skirt with the effect of a "perpendicular rainbow." Everybody on the stage wore a red rose from start to finish—in their buttonholes, on their hats, on their dresses, or between their lips. Rose-adorned girls handed out roses to first-nighters at the door. In addition to wearing clothes, Miss Suratt danced, with "sweeping freedom of movements." When she opened her mouth, however, her French and English had "a Chicago accent."

Julian Eltinge, the one human being who could successfully outdress Valeska Suratt, paid her the compliment, a few weeks after the opening of *The Red Rose,* of imitating her in *The Fascinating Widow,* a tale in which this most decorous and ladylike of female impersonators inhabited a college girls' dormitory. The fad for Eltinge's performances, which continued long after he could successfully impersonate only matrons and dowagers, is an extraordinary chapter in the history of American taste. The confusion of the sexes was, of course, a standard feature of earlier burlesques, but in these the male transvestites were always comic characters, while the girls pretended to be boys in order to show off their limbs within a code that frowned on short skirts. About Eltinge's impersonations, however, there was a serious quality that was unique. He avoided all off-color suggestion, and traded exclusively upon his grace, charm, and good manners. He endeavored to wear beautiful and modish clothes with the breeding and lack of self-conscious exhibitionism of a well-groomed woman. He never stepped out of character and never drew upon the double entendre used by rougher impersonators of the Savoy and Brennan school. Whole families came to see his eminently decent shows, and the women studied his costumes with all the detached interest they showed toward Valeska Suratt. No other female impersonator has ever equaled Eltinge's quiet dignity about his profession, or gained the same unqualified acceptance from the family trade.

The exposure of feminine anatomy and the exploitation of an unbridled use of color, usually without much taste or restraining sense of color harmony, were aims that in large measure took precedence over all else in the run-of-the-mill musical successes of 1911 and 1912. *Little Boy Blue* (1911) used Gainsborough's painting as a model for the costume of Gertrude Bryan in the title role. Boy Blue was turned into a barmaid from Paris, who found herself—the locale of the plot being Scotland—among a bevy of kilted, bare-kneed chorus girls. The operetta (for so it was designated) added a page to the superstitious lore of the theatre by disposing of its Boy Blues in rapid order. By 1913, when the piece was out on the road, the Detroit *News Tribune* pointed out that the current incumbent, Katherine Clifford, was the sixth in the line, and accounted—I cannot say how reliably—for the disappearance of the first five. Miss Bryan resigned in a dudgeon, because she was refused a raise. Katherine Stevenson was impelled to give the part up because her fiancé, a clergyman, objected to his betrothed's public revelation of her uncovered knees. Eva Fallon fell into the bass drum and had to pay for it, and left in anger. Lottie Engle "ran away with an automobile demonstrator, thinking the machine he drove so gracefully was his own." Florence Martin became increasingly afflicted with "stage fright over seeing the ghosts of her predecessors."

In *The Balkan Princess* (1911) Alice Brady, making her first New York appearance under the stage name of Marie Rose, was not required to make any improper exposure. This task was allotted to Vida Whitmore, who "wore stockings that were black up to about the ankle and then commenced to grow pink all the way to the waist." Miss Whitmore's stockings, which signalized the final phase of indecorum before the ladies began leaving their stockings off altogether, were celebrated by a rash of excited articles in the newspapers and magazines. One writer felt that she was "clad in a manner sensational enough to attract the attention of St. Anthony himself." Nor were all the sensations provided by Miss Whitmore, for Melville Ellis, the costumer, and the unnamed scenic designer went the whole way to make the production a "chromatic Gehenna" of purples, greens, and scarlets.

Flo Ziegfeld, whose taste was always a notch ahead of most other producers', began to bring order out of chaos in *A Winsome Widow* (1912). A modernization of the Charles H. Hoyt hit of the 1890s, *A Trip to Chinatown*, *A Winsome Widow*, having cast an eye at *Sumurun*, employed "bright colors in plain expanses without the aimless kaleidoscopic futility so often found." Leon Errol, Frank Tinney, and the Dolly Sisters provided the entertainment, and business was undoubtedly given a fillip (it ran for 172 performances) by Anna Held's divorce action against Ziegfeld. Nine days after the opening, according to *Variety*, "Mae West, a 'rag' singer in the *Widow*, abruptly left the cast and prepared to return to vaudeville."

American musical comedy, obviously in sore need of new themes, discovered the pioneer country of the West in 1912, when *The Red Petticoat* opened at Daly's Theatre, under the wing of the Shuberts. Neither Oklahoma nor Texas was first honored by Broadway's attention. Lone River,

Nevada, was the scene of *The Red Petticoat*, an outpost that, to the *Dramatic Mirror,* "would seem the last place in the world to furnish local color for a musical play." Rough miners with beards replaced the customary dandified chorus boys, and the girls found their way into the plot of this "comic-opera *Girl of the Golden West*" by becoming manicure girls in the shop of a lady barber. The score was written by Jerome Kern, who had now been performing occasional rather insignificant chores on Broadway for eight years. Even yet, Kern had not really found his stride, though the *Dramatic Mirror* found his tunes "sometimes catchy when they are reminiscent."

The West was also inspected through the jaundiced eyes of a pair of German librettists (rendered into English by Gladys Unger) in Victor Jacobi's "musical play," *The Marriage Market* (1913). Obviously conceived in Vienna and made over along the pattern of the London Gaiety, *The Marriage Market* caused Donald Brian, a tailor-made cowboy, to attend a marriage market in distant San Francisco. Only the first act took place in California, however, among the cowboys and native Spanish girls. The second act occurred on a yacht, in a manner suggesting *H.M.S. Pinafore,* and the third managed to get everyone back to the usual gilded palace.

The motion pictures, just coming into their first real popularity—with *The Birth of a Nation* just around the corner—provided matter for two satiric musical comedies at this time. It is significant that both pieces originated in central Europe. Apparently the activities of Hollywood had not yet struck any American authors as worth attention. The first, *The Girl on the Film*, was brought from England by the Shuberts at the end of 1913, with a predominantly British cast. The leading comedian was George Grossmith, whose recollections of the Gaiety Theatre we have already encountered. A "capital" technician, Grossmith "brought down the house in a little mimetic scene, when he attempts to make himself understood to the signora and uses the sign language of the cinematograph art to describe a dissolving scene." For the most part, however, *The Girl on the Film* would not strike the modern observer as being very pointed, since it devoted most of its energy to routine entertainment for "the tired business man, his ennuied wife, and blasé children"—loud and lively, with a whirlwind tango by Oy-Ra and Dorma Leigh. A fortnight later, on January 12, 1914, *The Queen of the Movies* touched upon the same subject matter with about the same pungency, and impressed its audience less because of its humor than because of its eight little "powder puff girls."

Nevada gave way to the Mormons of its neighbor state to the east in *The Girl from Utah* (1914). Jerome Kern again had a hand in the music, though most of it was by Paul Rubens and Sydney Jones. Utah was a British discovery, for Ina Claire and Isobel Elsom had played in the musical comedy in London before it was made known here with Julia Sanderson, Donald Brian, and Joseph Cawthorn as the featured performers. The title, while technically accurate, was misleading, for the action took place not in Utah but in London; the heroine, Una Trance, was a Mormon girl who had fled to London to avoid marrying the man to whom she had been "sealed." As the climax of her experiences in the British capital, the sugar-sweet Miss Sanderson, as Una Trance, attended an "arts ball" at which, amid an overload of Moorish settings and trappings, the old-fashioned, buxom girls of the chorus modeled fashionable Oriental styles. All this happened, in the creakiest manner of ancient musical comedy (ancient even then), after Miss Sanderson had wistfully sung, "I'd like to wander with Alice in Wonderland."

A momentary and abortive flirtation with more serious aesthetic concerns was initiated by *The Red Canary* (1914), which ran for only sixteen fainting performances. Its claim to documentary permanence—if not to an audience at the time—lay in its attempt to apply a theory of the effects of color upon the emotions and actions of the characters: blue indicated jealousy, red rage, and so on. The notion was not conclusive, and it buried the story under its abruptly shifting colors. But at least it is pleasant to pay obeisance to a show that recognized how greatly something needed to be done about the color schemes of the usual musical comedies.

Anticipating the various great doings that were to make 1915 and 1916 the years of the rebirth of the musical stage, Charles Dillingham ushered in an absolutely new era at the New Amsterdam Theatre on December 8, 1914. On this memorable evening the "syncopated musical show," *Watch Your Step,* equipped with music and lyrics by Irving Berlin and a book by Harry B. Smith, gave the American audience a foretaste of the ragtime and jazz delights that lay ahead in the musical theatre in the next decade or more. In this "ragtime riot and dancing delirium," the Castles took possession of the stage with their tangos, fox-trots (the fox had devoured the turkey), and one-steps. As a relief from the brash, nervous Berlin music and the lightning grace of the Castles, Frank Tinney provided periods of quiet hilarity with his confidential, *"entre nous"* patter, which made him the prototype of the modern master of ceremonies. Nothing was sacred to Berlin, who embraced a fashion that still continues when he provided a "rag" version of the *Rigoletto* quartet.

To be sure, one observer found Berlin's music "a little emaciated," and not the equal of his "Alexander's Ragtime Band," and remarked that the lyrics "have the same relation to poetry as limericks in a prize contest." But, he continued, "Mr. Berlin knows how to put the 'go' in tango. *Watch Your Step* has all the allurements of the craze [dancing] that has kept a majority of the populace high stepping in ballrooms and restaurants for the last two or three years. If there were ever a doubt that the tango and the fox-trot would resist becoming a musical-comedy theme it was dispelled by Mr. Dillingham's stroke of genius in making the Castles his two stars." *Theatre* magazine said, "Berlin is now part of America."

Ragtime and fox-trotting held no fascination for the more sedate young Jerome Kern, whose *90 in the Shade,* presented the following month (January 1915), evoked the Philippine Islands, and remained faithful to "the school of musical comedy which flourished some years ago, which always contained for background a picturesque and romantic country, for its characters bibulous Americans traveling for adventure; and which depended for its action on intrigue and mistaken identities." An important augury for the future—though it offered no aid to the present offering, which was poorly patronized—was the linking of Kern's name for the first time with that of Guy Bolton, who contributed the book. In less than a year, Bolton was again to collaborate with Kern in a full-scale hit. In the meantime Kern had to be satisfied with public commendation not for the score of *90 in the Shade*, but for his earlier services "as chief aid to anemic music" in pieces originally composed by others.

Kern spent a busy year in 1915, writing music for four shows. *Nobody Home* was the second one, smartly outfitted by Elsie de Wolfe (later Lady Mendl), given a book by Bolton and Paul Rubens, and presented on a small scale in the tiny Princess Theatre. It was a mild success, which was more than could be said of Kern's third 1915 production, *Miss Information*. Guy Bolton had no hand in this satire of the craze for publicity among society women; the book was not well written, and the combined labors of Elsie Janis and Irene Bordoni could not save it.

The generally agreeable reaction of the public to *Nobody Home* led F. Ray Comstock, its producer, to realize that a musical comedy in a small theatre could be given a special and friendly character that was not possible in a larger house. Joining with Elizabeth Marbury in the Marbury-Comstock Company, he commissioned Kern to prepare a second "intimate" musical comedy, in the light of his experience with the first. Bolton again prepared the book, which he derived from Philip Bartholomae's farce, *Over Night*. Elsie de Wolfe was shifted to the scenic department; Melville Ellis devised the costumes; and Schuyler Green wrote the lyrics. The finished product, called *Very Good Eddie*, opened on December 23, 1915, continued for 341 performances, and spanned a second year on the road.

Every feature of *Very Good Eddie* was scaled to the size of the house and the proximity of the entire audience to the stage. Everything was handled with a light touch, and the tempo of the performance was rapid and zestful. The plot, requiring only two scenes, recounted the contretemps of two honeymooning couples separated on a Hudson River steamboat, each man with the other's wife seeking shelter for the night and searching for his own bride. Elsie de Wolfe's settings were smartly simple and plain, though the hotel scene had "the inevitable symmetrical double staircase" at the back. There were only a dozen chorus girls. Though they were advertised as a "swagger fashion chorus," Ellis designed their clothes with a simplicity of line that accorded with the settings and the general tone of the performance. Their skirts reached down to the top of their high shoes, a style that led Heywood Broun to rejoice that "one is not called upon to gaze at the

knees of the world and weep." It was, moreover, an "individualized" chorus.
"Each girl has a dress of her own," Broun explained. "No; that's not exactly
what we mean. What we intend to convey is that each girl is costumed
differently, as suits her style."

Under Edward Royce's direction, the performers pitched their speaking,
singing, and acting in an informal low key. Oscar Shaw, said the *World,*
"sings just as he might in your own home after dinner." So did Ernest Truex,
though nobody thought much of his voice. His bright, clean humor and
ingenuous lisp carried the day for him, as the bridegroom of Helen Raymond,
a young woman of proportions about twice those of the frail Truex. The
second couple presented an opposite contrast, with John Willard big and
burly, and Alice Dovey petite and demure. Kern's score, in the main, was
"refined ragtime," with a sophisticated reference to Strauss's recent opera,
Der Rosenkavalier, in a celesta obbligato in the final waltz.

With little or no space separating the players from the audience, *Very
Good Eddie* depended upon the ease and credibility of the acting and characterization. Scarcely any previous musical comedy had been favored with
a plot and dialogue so coherent, so nearly related to those of well-written
nonmusical plays; "unlike most musical comedies it has a connected story
with laughable situations following one another in rapid succession." Dancing was kept to a minimum. There was only enough "to satisfy the audience
and incidentally recognize that the 'dancing craze,' as it is now reminiscently
called, is a thing of the past."

A few critics, spoiled by the louder and gaudier displays to which they
were conditioned, cast aspersive phrases at *Very Good Eddie*. One called
it a "kitchenette production," and another characterized it as "pleasing parlor
entertainment that has found its way to the stage." But the body of playgoers
found its principle acceptable, and the "intimate" musical comedy became
established as a suitable and successful genre.

The next partnership of Kern and Bolton was on a larger scale, in *Have
a Heart* (1917). P. G. Wodehouse, one of the brightest of all lyric writers,
joined the Kern-Bolton combination for the first time. *Have a Heart* was
possibly a little ahead of its time, at least as an attraction in one of the larger-
sized theatres. In its integration of music, book, and lyrics, it was an improvement over *Very Good Eddie*. Slapstick comedians were eliminated
(John E. Hazzard had perpetuated this tradition, as the clerk of the Rip Van
Winkle Inn, in *Very Good Eddie*), as were "obvious music cues, irritatingly
insipid lyrics, and inane characters."

The Kern-Bolton-Wodehouse triumvirate returned to the Princess, with
Oh, Boy, on February 20, 1917, to confirm the viability of the "intimate"
formula. Discovering that youth can often be a substitute for expensive
names, William Elliott and F. Ray Comstock, the co-producers, employed
such less-known players as Marion Davies, Justine Johnstone, Tom Powers,
and Edna May Oliver. The last-named of these, who was to reach her full

Broadway stature in a later Kern musical comedy, *Show Boat*, was cast as "the drunk lady without which no modern musical show could reach a second performance." A sensual pleasure of a different order was vouchsafed by Anna Wheaton, "one of the thousand and one victims of the pajama contagion which is now sweeping our theatres. Judging from recent examples, true artistic distinction in musical comedy can best be achieved by a pair of satin bedroom slippers, a shower of hair, à la Pickford, a pair of blue (or pink) silk pajamas, a smothered yawn, and a lighted candle, à la Lady Macbeth."

But it was not drunk ladies or pajamas and showers of hair that gave artistic distinction to *Oh, Boy* in the minds of those who had collaborated upon it. In the *Dramatic Mirror*, Bolton sought to explain how the Bolton-Wodehouse-Kern musical comedies differed from "those which have had their day on Broadway." The public now demanded realism in musical comedy, Bolton said. The new Princess musicals depended "as much on plot and character development for success as on the music." They also dealt with subjects near to the experience of the audience. "Americans laugh more naturally at a funny hotel clerk or janitor than a crudely drawn cannibal princess," he maintained.

In the outmoded type of musical comedy, he continued, "a prince from some neo-Balkan country, disguised, is in love with a poor maiden. She does not know he is a prince; he does not know she is the daughter of an Albanian Croesus. . . . There is one situation in each act; the rest is gaps. Comedians filled these gaps—with gun scenes, time-table scenes, soda-fountain scenes. . . ." In *Nobody Home*, upon which Wodehouse did not work, Bolton began to overthrow this standard conception. In *Very Good Eddie* "it was easy to have real plot and characters, but difficult to get altogether away from irrelevant scenes, of which there were still two." *Oh, Boy* contained nothing irrelevant. It was a "straight, consistent comedy with the addition of music. Every song and lyric contributed to the action. The humor was based on situation, not interjected by the comedians."

The Princess housed two more intimate "Oh" shows before the project was outmoded by postwar developments. *Oh, Lady, Lady* (1918) involved Constance Binney, Vivienne Segal, Margaret Dale, and Carl Randall in complications in Greenwich Village—a locale that was soon to be subject to wholesale exploitation on Broadway. *Oh, My Dear!* (1918), for which Louis A. Hirsch supplanted Kern as composer, was less adequately supplied with ideas, and fell back upon the "reliable formula of mistaken identity," with Roy Atwell, Joseph Allen, Joseph Santley, and Ivy Sawyer to help in the process.

Meanwhile Kern, who could apparently turn out a whole score as fast as the ordinary man can write his name, also busied himself with musical comedies of ordinary proportions. Bolton and Wodehouse were involved in only one of these, an adaptation of George Ade's *The College Widow* (1917), presented under the title *Leave It to Jane*. This was one of two or three pieces that discovered the American college campus at about the same time, and rigged it up with specialized slang, stalwart halfbacks, and co-eds who looked and behaved remarkably like chorus girls. Of the miscellany of other Kern pieces at this stage of his prolific career there is no need to take cognizance, since none of them offered anything new. It is impossible, though, to resist a sample of the literary style of the criticism that appeared in the *Dramatic Mirror* in connection with the performance of Mitzi (originally Mitzi Hajos) in *Head Over Heels* (1918): "Mitzi usually makes a hitzi in whatever bitzi she undertakes."

Under the stimulus of new ideas and wartime prosperity, the theatres were glutted with musical shows in 1916, 1917, and 1918. Only a few more warrant a momentary backward glance. For fifteen performances, beginning on March 28, 1916, at the Maxine Elliott Theatre, *See America First* ran its wobbly course. The music and—with the aid of T. Lawrason Riggs, the book and lyrics—were by a young unknown from Indianapolis, Cole Porter. A story about a "back-to-nature" debutante and a cowboy-duke underlay Porter's attempt to "combine Gilbert and Sullivan wit with college musical spirit," and the music was held to have "sought inspiration in George M. Cohan." Most of Porter's later shows were considerably more durable, and none of them imitated George M. Cohan.

Among other manifestations of the time, *So Long Letty* (1916) established the gangling Charlotte Greenwood in the character she kept alive for twenty-five years. *Canary Cottage* (1917) had a finale in which the girls tossed oranges at the audience, and employed "futurist" scenery. *Girl o' Mine* (1918), by Frank Tours and Philip Bartholomae, showed how easily an "intimate" musical comedy could fail when Kern, Bolton, and Wodehouse were not around. *Oh, Look!* (1918) opened the Vanderbilt Theatre, and introduced the song, "I'm Always Chasing Rainbows." Jazz took over in *The Rainbow Girl* (1918), in Florence Ware's dance, "The Alimony Blues."

As the war continued, Irving Berlin was inducted into the Army. He returned to Broadway for a month's stay at the Century Theater, beginning on August 19, 1918, in a soldier show for which he concocted the tunes and lyrics. It was known as *Yip, Yip, Yaphank*, "a musical mess cooked up by the boys of Camp Upton." Sergeant Berlin, in a thin, piping voice, came out alone on the stage to sing "Oh, How I Hate to Get Up in the Morning." Four months later the soldiers of Aberdeen Proving Ground, Maryland, followed suit, at the Lexington Opera House, with *Attaboy*. Their cast included Captain Frank Tinney, and they offered a skirted chorus rivaling that of *Yip, Yip, Yaphank*.

XVI. The Postwar Revue

AFTER THE ARMISTICE in 1918, the pleasure-seeking, prohibition-despising, boom-rich American public enabled the musical theatre to revel in a decade of luxury and wastefulness and irresponsibility such as it had never known before, and will probably never know again in our time. Money was available to produce anything with the slightest prospect of success, and audiences were lenient, easily amused, and generous with their patronage. Despite the H. C. L., as the high cost of living was affectionately called, people were making money faster than they could spend it. In the theatre, production costs had not yet risen in ratio to the increased national income. For one mad, magical decade, the Broadway theatre could afford to produce as many musical shows as it wanted to, and to market them at box-office prices that the audience could pay without feeling any pinch.

People wanted their pleasures to be easy-come-easy-go, swift, and full of kicks, like jazz music and bathtub gin. For theatregoers in a generation too overstimulated to want quieter and sweeter diversions, the revue, as it had been developed by Ziegfeld and at the Winter Garden, was the ideal format for an evening's gaiety. In attending a revue, the purest hedonist made no commitment that need deflect him from his course. And so, although a procession of musical comedies also shared the theatre sector, the revue was the archetype of postwar jazz-and-prohibition entertainment.

Beyond taking care to keep their visual appeal up-to-date, Ziegfeld did not tamper with the character of his *Follies*. Joseph Urban remained his collaborator, designing the scenery for all the successive annual editions, and in 1919 the costumes as well. Ziegfeld's stable of composers included, at one time or another, Irving Berlin, Victor Herbert, Harry Tierney, Rudolf Friml, Gene Buck, and divers lesser lights. Marilynn Miller appeared again (for the last time in the *Follies*) in 1919, as also did Eddie Cantor, who carried more than his share of the show, Bert Williams (for the last time before his death), and Eddie Dowling. And, of course, the "most beautiful girls in the world" passed before the footlights of the New Amsterdam Theatre. Fannie Brice, W. C. Fields, Charles Winninger, Ray Dooley, Van and Schenck, and Carl Randall came back for the 1920 *Follies*. All except Winninger and Randall stayed on in the 1921 edition, for which Raymond Hitchcock signed a contract with Ziegfeld, abandoning his endeavor to produce his own revues. Urban provided "masterly perspectives of limitless vastness," and a smaller but "more select" chorus wore "ventilated cobweb costumes" by James Reynolds and arranged themselves in living pictures under Ben Ali Haggin's direction. Miss Brice sang "Oy, I'm an Indian!"

The *Ziegfeld Follies of 1922* returned Will Rogers and his lariat to public notice, gave Gilda Gray an opportunity to shimmy, and caused Ed Gallagher and Al Shean to immortalize themselves with their "Mr. Gallagher and Mr. Shean" number, one of the most insinuating question-and-answer duos in the memory of the oldest playgoer. The unending Ziegfeld series continued without essential change in style or format, whether the production numbers were staged by Gertrude Hoffman, by Ned Wayburn, or by Julian Mitchell, and whether the roster included Bert Wheeler or Will Rogers, Gilda Gray or Ann Pennington, Fannie Brice or Lina Basquette, Paul Whiteman's band or George Olsen's. In the 1924 edition, a device later to become a favorite was inaugurated when the lights blacked out and the Tiller girls jumped rope with luminous ropes.

Through these lush times, the Shubert *Passing Show* at the Winter Garden continued to give the *Follies* their stiffest competition. Always more daring and risqué than the *Follies*, the postwar *Passing Show* pushed undress constantly nearer to absolute nudity; but if clothing was not abundant at the Winter Garden, it was always expensive. *The Passing Show of 1922* provided a striking indication of what righteous people thought to be the decline of moral standards in the early 1920s. A ballet was danced "in the manner of the Marquis de Sade." Francis Renault, whose female impersonations had not the decorum of Julian Eltinge's, swished about as the Diamond Girl. In a parody of Eugene O'Neill's *The Hairy Ape*, the chorus girls dressed like stokers and swore without shame.

As had long been their custom, the Shuberts provided miscellaneously titled collations of froth to fill the months when *The Passing Show* was away from the Winter Garden. One of these, *Make It Snappy* (1922), found a new use for the runway—of which the audience was beginning to tire—when the girls tossed ice-cream bricks to the orchestra patrons. *Innocent Eyes* (1924) brought the eternal Mistinguette from Paris to the Winter Garden, and, after 31 unsuccessful performances, sent her back to her adoring Parisian following, humiliated by notices that claimed that her voice lacked freshness and that her artistry "seldom rose above the level of mediocrity."

It was with a new annual series called *Artists and Models*, begun in 1923 and usually given in other theatres than the Winter Garden, that the Shuberts made their first unqualified, all-out appeal to what might be termed the baser nature of the public. "Never before," wrote one startled critic, "in an American revue has a similar degree of nudity been obtained." Before what *Variety* called a "75% stag audience," "women with naked breasts promenaded about the stage. . . . A burlesque on *Rain* was the rawest, smuttiest, most shameless misdemeanor ever committed." With content of this kind, it was not necessary for the Shuberts to proffer an expensive cast of principals. The girls were the thing; such comic duties as there were devolved primarily upon Frank Fay. In the 1924 edition—presented, by exception, at the Winter Garden—the beauties revealed their reflections in a lily pool. The runway was abandoned in favor of steps leading directly down into the orchestra. Chorus girls ran down the aisles handing the men in the end seats cords which, when pulled, uncovered examples of living statuary. The 1925 version was even more elaborate. The audience had a wonderful time with noisemakers—metal strips with little clappers on each side. In "The Rotisserie," the Gertrude Hoffman girls impersonated broilers turning on spits above the fire. Name performers, for a change, were numerous. Jay Brennan and Stanley Rogers carried on in the Savoy and Brennan routine, with Rogers taking over the character of the Dame created by Savoy, who had been killed by lightning. Phil Baker was a new and personable master of ceremonies; Aline MacMahon was a fresh young comic; and the future motion-picture star Jack Oakie was a member of the chorus.

Even Charles Dillingham's ponderous shows at the Hippodrome developed a fresh postwar aspect, though obviously the huge house was not the place to make the most of the contours of the female body. Abandoning the spectacular travelogues of earlier years, Dillingham transformed his extravaganzas into mammoth vaudeville revues, with circus elements as an added attraction. The old-fashioned flag-waving, geographical titles were supplanted by ones that promised a livelier evening—*Good Times, Get Together,* and *Better Times. Get Together* (1921) depended heavily on elephants and on clowns (who made their first entrance by stepping from posters on the wall), ice skating (in two scenes billed as "The Red Shoes"), and a ballet, "The Thunder Bird," with Michel Fokine and Vera Fokina. In the course of the evening a moving-picture comedy from the Fox studios, Clyde Cook in *The Toreador,* was shown. *Better Times* (1922) offered a Ladies' Jazz Band, more kinds of animals than ever before, including crows, an old-fashioned "shadowgraph" that threw moving shadows on a screen, and Mark Lawson's spectacle "The Story of a Fan," which evolved "from a fan to fans, to floods of fans, to an electrically lighted fan holding twelve girls in its panels and perched aloft of the whole."

As if it were not enough to have the theatres inundated with revues and extravaganzas between 8:30 and 11:15, the various roof-garden restaurant-theatres did a tremendous after-midnight business. On the Century Roof and the New Amsterdam Roof, in particular, the bright stars of revue and musical comedy foregathered to give the unsated patrons another hour or two of more intimate contact with their charms and talents. The *Morris Gest Midnight Whirl,* which opened, with Urban décors on the Century Roof in time for New Year's Eve business in 1919, gave employment to two youngsters—George Gershwin for the music, and Buddy de Sylva for the lyrics. One of their song titles will serve to suggest their callowness at this early stage of their careers. It was called "Cutie, Cut Your Cuticle." The *Midnight Whirl* kept memories of the war green by dressing chorus girls in Salvation

Army costumes and sending them out to distribute doughnuts to the customers.

The most expensive array of midnight cabaret talent was usually to be
found in Ziegfeld's *Midnight Frolic*, a dine-and-drink corollary to the *Follies*
on the New Amsterdam Roof. Fannie Brice and W. C. Fields were standbys.
Urban was the designer, and Ned Wayburn staged the dances. The girls
were chosen to stand even closer scrutiny than those of the *Follies*; in 1921
the producer's slogan was "See New York and Ziegfeld's girls and die." But
even with so generous a provider as Ziegfeld, the vogue for roof entertainment was short. In the early 1920s even the best floor shows began to
descend to the street and basement levels, and the night club largely supplanted the more formal roof-garden cabaret.

Some of the favorite performers of war and prewar days found it possible,
in the first flush of the revue craze, to promulgate loosely constructed
entertainments built around their special stellar abilities. Elsie Janis, who
made herself a national celebrity by her unflagging efforts to sustain morale
among the soldiers, made periodic appearances billed as *Elsie Janis and Her
Gang* (in 1919 her "gang" included Eva Le Gallienne). She last appeared
under Dillingham's management in 1925 in *Puzzles of 1925*, which contained
nothing more cryptic than Elsie's imitations of John Barrymore, Lenore
Ulric, and—to be up to the moment—Beatrice Lillie, who had recently
insinuated herself into the American consciousness in the first *Charlot's
Revue*.

Raymond Hitchcock produced for himself two more *Hitchy-Koo* revues,
in 1919 and 1920, before hiring himself out to Ziegfeld and other producers.
The 1919 edition was "Hitchier than ever in its fun, more Kooey than ever
before in its music." For the Kooeyness, Cole Porter, now beginning to pull
his lyric and satiric gifts into salable shape, was responsible. Jerome Kern
wrote the music for the 1920 edition. A fortnight before the opening of
Hitchy-Koo of 1920, another one-man-show entertainer, Fred Stone, was
given free rein in Dillingham's production, *Tip Top*. When Stone was off
the stage, Anna Ludmila, soon to become the partner of Adolph Bolm,
pirouetted and arabesqued, and the new sister act of Vivian and Rosetta
Duncan also appeared.

Al Jolson was the sole reason for the long run, in 1921, of the Shuberts'
Bombo. Though Sigmund Romberg was the official composer of *Bombo*,
many patrons came primarily to hear Jolson deal with "April Showers," an
interpolated song by Lew Silvers. Stirred by the public response to "April
Showers," Jolson announced that he would retire from the musical stage
after *Bombo*, to devote his whole time to "concert work." Needless to say,
he did not, but all his subsequent appearances were in musical comedies
rather than in revues.

For Ed Wynn, with his zany carnival of elaborate nonsense, the revue
provided a perfect frame. The *Ed Wynn Carnival*, in 1920, took him one

rung farther up the ladder of popularity. But it was in *The Perfect Fool*, a title he later appropriated as a description of himself, that he established himself, in 1921, upon a comic eminence from which the public has never been willing to allow him to descend. With constant changes of grotesque costume, Wynn devoted himself mainly to the demonstration of various labor-saving devices. Dragging a toy wagon onto the stage, he extracted from it a safety device for noiseless soup, a coffee cup with a hole in the bottom (to save the labor of pouring the coffee from the cup into the saucer), and a gadget to hold an ear of corn so that the ears would not get covered with butter. In a novelty scene for the chorus, a typewriter took up the larger part of the stage, with the girls' legs as stems for the keys. The commercial plug was now becoming known, for the typewriter was prominently labeled a Corona.

Three years later, in *The Grab Bag*, Wynn integrated his own performance more completely with that of the rest of the company, whose idiocies were the mirror of his own. He summoned forth a "Russian octette" to sing a Cossack folk song called "He Eats French Dressing Every Night So He Can Wake Up Oily in the Morning," and a lament entitled "She Might Have Been a School Teacher, But She Hadn't Any Class." Throughout the evening, music was provided by Spanish singers who plainly were not Spanish, Scottish singers who were not Scottish, and Russian singers who were not Russian. The Wynn touch pervaded the whole show, making *The Grab Bag* in many ways the most successful revue yet built around the idiosyncracies of a single performer.

George White, who had begun his career in the theatre as a musical-comedy juvenile and hoofer, turned entrepreneur in 1919, issuing on June 2 of that year a revue patently modeled after the *Ziegfeld Follies*, and called *Scandals of 1919*. With Ann Pennington as the leading Jazz Baby, dancing, "from the ancient toe whirling of grandpa's time to the shimmie," dominated the first *Scandals*. The score by Richard Whiting was workable if undistinguished; the book, on which White and Arthur Jackson collaborated, was less than that. "Where there was so much money to be spent," one reviewer complained, "Mr. White might have set aside a few dollars for a good scenario writer."

Having established his claim to a share of the takings from the revue-mad public, White continued with annual editions of the *Scandals*, each more fashionable and lavish than the last. George Gershwin became the *Scandals'* composer in 1920, and remained with the project through 1924, though it did not call forth the songs for which he is best remembered today. White himself was a member of the cast for the first four years, after which he withdrew into the producer's office. By 1921, his name meant enough in connection with the *Scandals* to merit incorporation into the title, and from then on the successive versions were always known as *George White's Scandals*. Essentially imitative of ideas and vogues already exploited by more inventive producers, the *Scandals* added nothing new to the over-all theatrical scene, though the elaborate stage pictures, appetizing girls, and generally competent routining of the shows guaranteed them a dependable following.

A fresher note was sounded by the *Greenwich Village Follies*, which began life in the Greenwich Village Theatre on July 15, 1919, remained there for a second edition in 1920, and moved uptown in 1921, where annual versions appeared with diminishing distinction until 1928. The *Greenwich Village Follies* were the brainchild of John Murray Anderson, one of the few designers of his day whose gifts could stand comparison with those of Joseph Urban. Even though the scale of the first edition was restricted by the small dimensions of the theatre, the investiture gave an impression of open-handedness, controlled by a degree of taste and an appeal to cultivated sensibilities which were not part of the basic assumption of the *Ziegfeld Follies* or *George White's Scandals*.

From the first, the *Greenwich Village Follies* were intended to be "sophisticated," which meant that the members of the audience could enter the theatre without checking their brains at the cloakroom. The plays, people, and foibles chosen for lampooning were matters of interest primarily to the intelligentsia. From the first, Anderson understood that the intelligentsia enjoyed a bit of dirt quite as heartily as the commoner folk, as long as it was handled in terms that were not too direct.

In the two years the *Greenwich Village Follies* productions remained in the Village, they faithfully sought to evoke the Village atmosphere—as in the cabaret scene of the 1920 edition, where the characters represented various well-known hotels, restaurants, and haunts of the locality. The move uptown to the Shubert Theatre in 1921 inevitably led to the abandonment of much of the local color, for the larger and more general audience of a Forty-fourth Street theatre could not be expected to understand or react to the fine points of neighborhood satire. Richard Watts found this first uptown *Follies* "as uneven and uncertain as life in Greenwich Village itself, with here a dull stretch and there a spot that gleams like unexpectedly successful homebrew." But Anderson still provided staging that was artistically and technically in advance of all the other revues in New York, and the tone of the production continued, on the whole, to appeal to the intelligent audience, even if it was "dirty without flowers and smeary with smut." At the opening, an unintentional thrill was provided when Bird Millman fell off a tightrope; but she was not seriously injured, and immediately tried again with success.

By 1922, this "most sophisticated of revues" was marked by a heaviness and coarseness that had been the very qualities its Village-inspired predecessor had avoided. The camping of Savoy and Brennan replaced more delicate humors, and there was a broad burlesque of Nikita Balieff, recently arrived as master of ceremonies of the *Chauve-Souris*. An emotional ballad told of a gold digger who wanted $5,000 not for a mink coat but to pay for an operation for her baby. Still, the members of the audience who were *au courant* were not wholly forgotten. The Swedish Ballet, the rage of the moment in Paris, was subjected to a burlesque; Eugene O'Neill was travestied; Oscar Wilde's "The Nightingale and the Rose" was made the subject of a ballet; and a *cantatrice* (nobody had yet invented the peculiar American locution, "chanteuse") named Yvonne George introduced "Mon Homme."

The *Greenwich Village Follies of 1923* has gone down in history as the one in which Martha Graham danced—not in the radically personal style she later evolved, but in her most girlish, pretty-pretty classical and interpretative manner. Among her fellow-performers were Sammy White and Eva Puck, whose great day came in *Show Boat* a few seasons later on; the Flying Cansinos, the parents of Rita Hayworth; and Joe E. Brown, who fell downstairs and injured himself in the opening performance. The première must have been jinxed, for later on in the evening, one of the show girls let the metal-cloth fringe of a net cloak trail into the footlight trough, where it caught fire.

Cole Porter composed the score for the 1924 edition. With the inclusion of the Dolly Sisters and Moran and Mack—the "Two Black Crows"—in the cast, the character of the *Greenwich Village Follies* was now strictly popular. By 1925, when Hassard Short replaced Anderson as the director, it had become largely indistinguishable from all the competing revues. The wit had gone out of the skits, and the heaviest play for laughs was made by a travesty on *Hamlet*, in which Florence Moore, as Ophelia, was determined to drown herself at the Fleischman Baths, but could not, because it was not ladies' day.

The introduction of Ted Lewis and his noisy band, devoted to "Jazz-What-Am," in the 1925 *Greenwich Village Follies* indicated the popularizing treatment to which the project was now being subjected. From this point on, the institution slid steadily downhill—from the point of view of the sophisticated audience for which it was initially conceived—until in its last manifestation in 1928, it was no more than another rough-and-ready, commonplace revue designed to furnish a springtime tenant for the Shuberts' Winter Garden. Its chief performers were funny enough and talented enough in their own right, but the *Greenwich Village Follies* was hardly the place one would have expected to encounter such mass-appeal entertainers as Doctor Rockwell, Blossom Seeley, and Benny Fields. Having become meaningless, the title was now no longer provocative, and it was allowed to drop into limbo.

A couple of efforts to present revues on an intimate scale at the Princess had failed swiftly in 1919 and 1920, because the seating capacity was not sufficient to finance productions more elaborate than the "Oh" musical comedies of the war and prewar years. But the idea of smaller-scale production, as exemplified by the first two *Greenwich Village Follies* before that entertainment moved uptown, continued to be a tempting one. As an experiment of in-between size, the Music Box Theatre was built by Irving Berlin in 1921. The first *Music Box Revue,* opening on September 22 of that year, was dedicated to the bright, sophisticated, fast-paced entertainment the *Greenwich Village Follies* was about to abandon. The Music Box itself was a tasteful structure with an interior attractively devoid of gewgaws and overdecoration. The first revue in the new house was far from economical, but it was neither vulgar nor naked. For their performers, Berlin and Sam H. Harris, who produced it together, relied largely on such tried-and-true personalities as William Collier, Sam Bernard, Joseph Santley and Ivy Sawyer, Florence Moore, and Wilda Bennett. Though there was little real novelty about either the players or the material, the *Music Box Revue,* by running for 313 performances, showed that an audience existed for a show that relied more on ideas and less on mere displays of the flesh than the *Follies* and *The Passing Show.* It also gave Irving Berlin a showcase for his lively new tunes, among which "Everybody Step" was outstanding.

The second *Music Box Revue,* in 1922, turned to younger talent. Ruth Page, fresh from her first success in Chicago in John Alden Carpenter's ballet, *The Birthday of the Infanta,* was a ravishing *prima ballerina.* Bobby Clark and Paul McCullough started down the path toward comic fame, and so did William Gaxton. One of the spectacle scenes made use for the first time of the effect in which a line of girls seemed to be dancing in front of mirrors, until it was revealed that the images were actually a second line of girls.

Grace Moore appeared in the *Music Box Revue* of 1923, along with Florence Moore, to whom she was not related. Grace was a member of an operatic sextet which delivered "Yes, We Have No Bananas," in the course of which incandescent oranges glowed on the stage and orange-blossom perfume suffused the theatre. Florence paid tribute to the Denishawn Dancers, then at the height of their popularity, by appearing as Flo O'Denishawn in a pantomime that required her to impersonate a starfish.

The fourth and last *Music Box Revue,* in 1924, suggested that the original formula must be wearing thin, for it was loaded with name performers, old and young; and John Murray Anderson took over the direction from Hassard Short. Irving Berlin, of course, continued to provide the music. Tamiris, who today, as Helen Tamiris, is a major musical-comedy choreographer, was the leading dancer. Grace Moore was again the prima donna. Fannie Brice, as a bewildered Russian immigrant, and Bobby Clark, as a prize fighter, led the comic contingent, and such folk as Oscar Shaw, Carl Randall, and Hal Sherman were men-of-all-work in the sketches, songs, and dances. Despite its hardworking personnel, the fourth *Music Box Revue* ran only half as long as the first, and the project was abandoned.

Earl Carroll was the next to initiate a series of revues. The *Earl Carroll Vanities,* begun in 1923, were a little more low-brow than the *Scandals,* and more completely dependent upon sumptuous girls, overdone scenic effects, and standard comic routines. Though the *Vanities* lasted, with interruptions, clear through the 1930s, they never developed a genuinely distinctive character. Carroll always seemed merely to elaborate needlessly upon themes already more than adequately taken care of in the *Follies, The Passing Show*, and the *Scandals*. But the *Vanities* were just the dish for the weary 1924 seeker after beauty who could be satisfied by a finale in which 108 Vanities Girls stood on a revolving staircase and revolved.

A particular joy to the intellectual audience from its first appearance in 1922 was the *Grand Street Follies*. Produced in a family manner on the little stage of the Neighborhood Playhouse down on the East Side, the *Grand Street Follies* remained, on a far more inexpensive scale, what the *Greenwich Village Follies* started out to be: a conceit in which ideas were more important than surfaces. The first edition was labeled on the program "A Low-Brow Show for High-Grade Morons; Music by the Great Composers, mostly arranged by Lily M. Hyland; Book by Everybody." Since elaborate production numbers were out of the question for the small company, satire—usually with sharp fangs—provided the whole substance of the bill. From a beginning laid in the home of the first dramatic critic, Adam Stale (with Aline MacMahon as Eve), the first *Grand Street Follies* proceeded to a satire on Walt Whitman's poetry; a series of dance travesties, "The Royal Damn Fango, or All Change Places," in which Albert Carroll impersonated a Lady with Fan; and burlesques of the inevitable Balieff, John Barrymore, Pavlova, Elsie Janis, Anna Duncan, Irene Castle, Feodor Chaliapin, and Maria Jeritza. Carroll, with his economical, sharply etched style and his facility for wearing either male or female attire, immediately became the kingpin of the *Grand Street Follies*, and remained indispensable to it all the way to the end, in 1929.

The next year, Dorothy Sands, as pointed and witty an imitator of acting styles as the American stage has known, joined the *Grand Street* entourage, and stayed with it through the rest of its eight-season history. In 1924, she made light of the manners of a recitalist at the newly opened Town Hall. Aline Bernstein became costume designer for this third edition, revealing her bright mind and powers of observation in her conceits for "The South Sea Islands According to Broadway."

For two more seasons, the *Grand Street Follies* continued its *succès d'estime* at the Neighborhood Playhouse. Among satires too numerous to detail, there were—in the 1925 edition—"The Wild Duck of the 18th Century (as Ibsen would have treated the theme had he really been born before his time)," and a gala performance of the opera "L'Irlandesa Rosa dell' Abie." In 1926, two composers of future distinction, Randall Thompson and Arthur Schwartz, contributed some of the music.

In 1927, the *Grand Street Follies* moved uptown to the Little Theatre, after giving a few preliminary performances in the Neighborhood Playhouse.

The 1928 and 1929 *Follies* were tenants of the Booth Theatre (with James Cagney a tap dancer in the latter one). While the sodden story of the *Greenwich Village Follies* was not repeated, since no essential change in style occurred, the undertaking was unable to thrive as a Broadway production. By the spring of 1930, the effects of the Wall Street crash the previous October were beginning to be felt all through the theatre, and there was no possibility of continuing. But throughout the noisy, nervous, coarse boom days of the 1920s, the *Grand Street Follies* had quietly and modestly served the valuable function of reminding the theatre audience that everything did not have to be big and costly and vulgar in order to be genuinely amusing. As the most persistent counterirritant to the prevailing diseases of megalomania and big noise, the enterprise had a significance that far exceeded the slender, and sometimes precious, values of its materials.

Moved by the example of the Neighborhood Playhouse, a group of youngsters in the Theatre Guild put together in 1925 their own intimate revue, which they styled the *Garrick Gaieties*. With Philip Loeb and Sterling Holloway among its leading lights, the first edition won an affectionate reception for its naïve high spirits, although, as Percy Hammond remarked, "It seemed to be saying, 'Ain't I cute, I'm only six.' " The second edition, in 1926, retained the same "bizarre ambition to please," but this time Hammond found "the Theatre Guild's precious bambino . . . a wise and flippant ingenue." Loeb appeared as a Broadway mortician, embalming such Theatre Guild "failures" as Shaw's *Arms and the Man* and *Androcles and the Lion*. Everyone from O'Neill to Gilbert and Sullivan was subjected to a ribbing, with *The Dybbuk* and *Lulu Belle* singled out for special treatment. The frayed conventions of musical comedy were ruthlessly exposed in "The Rose of Arizona," a richly devised sketch put together from all the current clichés. In this, a bevy of nasal chorus girls appeared dressed as flowers—each a different one. The heroine was introduced by a chorus girl, who observed, in the intonation of a shopgirl, "Why, here comes Rose now, with her horse." After a romantic duet to end all romantic duets, the cast marched off to war singing, "Hurrah for Pershing and Coolidge! To hell with Mexico!" Not only "The Rose of Arizona," but both editions of the *Garrick Gaieties in toto*, were decked out with the bright tunes and lyrics of Richard Rodgers and Lorenz Hart.

After four years, in 1930, the Theatre Guild offered a third set of *Garrick Gaieties*. But the time for it was past. The youngsters were not so young any more, and failed to recapture their earlier insouciance; and moreover *The Little Show* had now come along to show how to do the job better. Even Marc Blitzstein's "Triple Sec," a hilarious parody of the Frederick Lonsdale school of drawing-room comedy, and contributions by Aaron Copland and Vernon Duke were not enough to keep the revue alive in New York. The Guild salvaged it, however, by putting together a touring *Garrick Gaieties*, fabricated from snippets of all three editions, with the addition of a few items purchased from *The Little Show*.

After *Mr. Lode of Koal,* the last of the Williams and Walker shows before the war, all-Negro attractions were entirely absent from Broadway until Noble Sissle and Eubie Blake brought *Shuffle Along* down from Harlem to the Sixty-third Street Music Hall in 1921. Sissle's musical score was full of vim and vitality, and the choral arrangements were spectacular. The dancing was as swift and tricky as any to be seen in the standard houses. Yet *Shuffle Along,* which had already exhausted some of its potential business by luring patrons up to Harlem, lasted for only 27 performances. This is an important statistic, for the misconception still exists that Harlem-bred Negro shows have frequently enjoyed success on Broadway. Actually, all-Negro musicals have not often succeeded at all, and the Negro has found his rightful place on the New York musical stage—with only a few exceptions—in mixed-cast productions, from *Show Boat* to *Finian's Rainbow.* The venture of taking *Shuffle Along* downtown stimulated several other unrewarded efforts, but it was not until Lew Leslie presented Florence Mills and Hamtree Harrington in *Dixie to Broadway* (1924) that a Negro revue kept open long enough (77 performances) to pay back its cost.

England made its first major contribution to the gaiety of Broadway since the original Gaiety days when Arch Selwyn brought over *André Charlot's Revue* in 1924. It was a small revue, by current American standards, but its three leading performers burst out of its frame in all directions. They were Beatrice Lillie, Gertrude Lawrence, and Jack Buchanan. The music and lyrics were predominantly the work of Noel Coward. The songs and sketches glorified "not the English girl þut the English joke"—if the Coward twist may be considered typical of the English joke in general. The whole entertainment was given, most economically, in front of a single set that was hardly more than a white drop upon which lights could play. But nobody looked for settings—or for undraped girls—when Beatrice Lillie undertook to give a song recital, with all the manners of the concert platform but a voice that went back on her, or impersonated with dry brutality a tea-shop waitress or a faded ingenue; or when Gertrude Lawrence gave her characteristic pathetic turn to a sentimental ballad, or showed that she could be equally believable as a Chinese girl in Limehouse and as a super-smart Cowardesque Mayfair wife. Jack Buchanan was a trifle overlooked in the overwhelming experience of making the acquaintance of both Miss Lillie and Miss Lawrence on the same night; but he should not have been, for a suaver song-and-dance man has never existed, and he partnered both ladies with complete technical versatility. Two years later a second edition of *Charlot's Revue* arrived, with the same principals, Miss Lillie being provided with a travesty on ballet dancing in which she was supported by an invisible wire. Buchanan was not to pursue an American career further, though he returned in 1929 in *Wake Up and Dream.* Miss Lillie and Miss Lawrence found unmistakably that they could appear here whenever they wished, and from now on—to the continual benefit of the musical stage—they often did.

XVII. Musical Comedy from 1919 to 1925

THE ART MOVEMENT, which invaded the revue field in the *Greenwich Village Follies* and the Joseph Urban décors for the *Ziegfeld Follies*, was also expensively manifest in several pretentious and serious-minded exotic spectacles. F. Ray Comstock and Morris Gest made a contribution in the way of Oriental pageantry in *Aphrodite*, which occupied the Century Theatre for 148 performances in 1919–20. Henri Février, composer of *Monna Vanna*, an opera that gave Mary Garden one of her most scarlet roles, wrote part of the music, along with Anselm Goetzl. Michel Fokine devised the choreography, and Léon Bakst had a hand in designing the costumes. A "drama of profane love," *Aphrodite* displayed a gorgeous exterior, but was hollow inside. It reached its climax in a bacchanalian ballet, to Moussorgsky music, danced on a floor of rose leaves. *Mecca* (1920), staged by the same producers shortly after the closing of *Aphrodite*, had even less impressive music by Percy Fletcher, but the touch of Fokine and Bakst was again in evidence. Considered the most stunning extravaganza of its time, *Mecca* exploited Egypt and the Arabian Nights terrain. As a "blaze of color," nothing like it had been seen on the American stage since *Scheherazade*.

On a smaller scale, but no less exciting to the eye, was the Gest-Comstock production of *The Rose of China* (1919), set by Joseph Urban and provided with music by Armand Vecsey, lyrics by P. G. Wodehouse, and book by Guy Bolton. Straying far from their earlier element, Wodehouse and Bolton created a variant of the *Madama Butterfly* theme, recounting the poignant tale of a Chinese girl who lost caste by letting herself be kissed in public. The kiss took place in a singularly luxuriant Chinese garden.

One or two other musical plays of the day also sought to make use of advanced artistic materials. John Murray Anderson found time, in the midst of his preoccupation with the *Greenwich Village Follies*, to produce and direct a musical comedy, *What's in a Name* (1920), in which he used the classic Greek device of an inner and an outer stage, and decorated the scenes with draperies and screens in the manner of Gordon Craig and Reinhardt. He experimented extensively with overhead and side lighting, reducing the use of footlights to a minimum; but many observers found the production too dark. Lee Shubert paid obeisance to modern staging in *The Rose Girl*, an otherwise undistinguished musical comedy in which Lydia Lopokova and the ballet were carried up and down in elevators. More resourceful was the Selwyns' production of *Johannes Kreisler* (1922), a "fantastic melodrama" from German sources. The plot and music were thin enough; but the staging required forty-one changes of scene. Quick shifts were made possible partly by the artful use of lighting, and partly by using different segments and levels of the stage, and wagons on which rooms rolled out toward the audience.

Norman Bel Geddes entered the Broadway arena as director and co-producer with Richard Herndon of *Arabesque* (1925). The action took place on a single unit setting with three strata. Sometimes all three levels were brought into use at once. The book suffered from the vacuity that afflicted those of *Aphrodite* and *Mecca*. Bela Lugosi appeared as a sheik (pronounced "sheck"). The role may not have been too unpalatable at the moment when "a Bedouin girl, dressed down to the utmost finesse of nakedness, straddles a sheik, who lies full-length on a cloak on the floor of a savage tent at midnight, alone with her."

Conservative theatregoers by the thousands spurned these empty essays in beauty and contemporary stagecraft, and persisted in preferring the conventional, sentimental operettas and musical comedies whose charm, however attenuated, did not require so great an outlay of cultural energy. In the first half of the 1920s, old-fashioned operettas and musical comedies that were pretty and tuneful and entirely orthodox continued to attract a large following. Such pieces as Fritz Kreisler's *Apple Blossoms* (1919), the Cinderella story called *Irene* (1919), *Always You* (1920), *Mary* (1920), *Tangerine* (1921), *The Gingham Girl* (1922), *Sally, Irene and Mary* (1922), *The Lady in Ermine* (1922), and *Poppy* (1923)—all great successes—deserve mention here only because someone might look at the index and object to their omission. All were presented in tasteful, high-class fashion. All were supplied with music that rippled along lyrically, and plots that employed the expected clichés at the right time. None rose above the humor typified by Oscar Hammerstein 2d's book for *Always You*: "What," says the *jeune premier*, "do you say to a tramp in the park?" And the ingenue retorts, "I never speak to one." *Mary*, staged by George M. Cohan, was brisker than most of its old-fashioned contemporaries, and contained an especially well-favored ditty called "The Love Nest."

A number of musical comedies were frankly designed to serve as vehicles for popular performers. The Duncan Sisters, Rosetta and Vivian, enjoyed their moment of glory in *Topsy and Eva* (1924), a musical version of *Uncle Tom's Cabin*, including a good many incidents by Catherine Chisholm Cushing that could not be found in Mrs. Stowe's original, and a tearful song by Topsy (Rosetta), "I Never Had a Mammy." *Kid Boots* (1923) was a tribute by Flo Ziegfeld to Eddie Cantor, who dominated the production when George Olsen's band was not plugging its unusual jazz arrangements. The piece was the result of one of Ziegfeld's recurrent decisions—always revoked until toward the end of the decade—not to produce another *Follies*. The Shuberts made *Big Boy* (1925) a similar vehicle for Al Jolson.

Meanwhile the inexhaustible Victor Herbert continued to turn out scores, from *The Velvet Lady* (1919), in which young Eddie Dowling was featured, to his last work, *The Dream Girl* (1924), a romance of fifteenth-century England, with Fay Bainter and Walter Woolf as principals. But Herbert's great days were past, and much of his energy was being drained off into workaday songs for the revues. He never again produced another *Mlle. Modiste* or *Naughty Marietta*.

Rudolf Friml, however, was approaching the brief zenith at which he could be taken for a latter-day Herbert. In 1919 he was not yet able to write his own ticket, and in *Tumble In*, an adaptation of a farce by Avery Hopwood and Mary Roberts Rinehart, he was called upon to supply the score for "a 'chicken' song, a pajama scene, a fashion parade, and a number in which appeals and promises are somewhat embarrassingly made to the most centrally situated bald man in Row A." Friml's temperament was not suited to this sort of modishness, and it must have been with relief that he settled back into the saccharine requirements of *The Little Whopper* later in the same year, secure in the knowledge that Vivienne Segal would sing his melodies as prettily as anyone could. *The Blue Kitten* (1924), taken from a French farce, sent him back to accompanying shimmies and "blue" lines. But this was only a momentary aberration.

With *Rose Marie*, presented by Arthur Hammerstein in 1924, Friml finally reached the promised land of every sentimental operetta composer, for his tunes—particularly the "Indian Love Call," with its wordless mating-call—became part of the corpus of enduring light music. The plot, with its manly members of the Canadian Mounted Police, was no more refreshing than those of comparable pieces, but nobody cared, when Dennis King and Mary Ellis were on hand to sing the tunes. A better dramaturgical effort was *The Vagabond King* (1925). As full of tunes as *Rose Marie*, this adaptation of Justin Huntly McCarthy's *If I Were King* (in which E. H. Sothern had acted) gave Dennis King one of the best swashbuckling, romantic roles of his ardent career.

The peak of Sigmund Romberg's success coincided with that of Friml. After a couple of mildly successful tries—*The Magic Melody* (1919) and *Love Birds* (1921)—he delved into the music of Franz Schubert in an alleged biography of the composer, *Blossom Time*. The operetta was first given in central Europe under the title *Lilac Time*, but to avoid confusion with Jane Cowl's earlier play, the name was changed for the American première, under Shubert (Lee and J. J., not Franz) sponsorship, in 1921. The New York run of 295 performances did not begin to tell the whole story of *Blossom Time*. Bertram Peacock took his lachrymose impersonation of the near-sighted, bumbling composer out on the road, and, with his colleagues—Olga Cook, Howard Marsh, William Danforth, and Roy Cropper—created an audience that retains its fealty to this day. The "Song of Love," in which a theme from the Unfinished Symphony is turned into a singularly banal waltz, and the overwrought treatment of "Ave Maria" have become treasured staples of the American repertory of light music.

Blossom Time, with its phenomenal power to withstand bargain-counter casting, is probably one of the two most valuable musical properties the Shubert organization possesses. The other is *The Student Prince* (1924), for which Romberg was also responsible, this time without aid from Franz Schubert. *The Student Prince in Heidelberg* (to give its cumbersome original title) was a work of far greater integrity than *Blossom Time*. Homogeneous in musical style, reasonably well plotted and characterized, and free from the appalling mawkishness to which Schubert's airy melodies were subjected, *The Student Prince*, unlike its predecessor, has deserved the permanent acceptance it has gained. Musically it is one of the strongest compositions of its kind, both in the intrinsic merit of the songs themselves and in the highly professional handling of the solo voices and the ubiquitous chorus of male students. Nor is the general tone of the university capers nearly as repellent as it might be—or, indeed, as it has been in a good many musical pieces laid on American college campuses. Not until *Best Foot Forward* and *Too Many Girls* was school life again presented as agreeably.

Meanwhile a tunesmith with friendlier and more vernacular gifts, Jerome Kern, was busily consolidating and improving upon his past experience, although his best days were still five and ten years ahead. Because the pieces whose scores he contributed occupied a twilight zone between the older sentimental musical comedies and the up-to-date jazz ones, Kern's métier for some time remained somewhat ambiguous. For this reason, perhaps, his producers seldom supplied him with singers of a caliber equal to that of the best participants in the Friml, Herbert, and Romberg operettas. This deficiency was cause for complaint when Joseph Santley and Ivy Sawyer appeared in *She's A Good Fellow* in 1919: "As everybody knows, musical comedy has practically dispensed with the singing voice as an essential, most of the singers nowadays being engaged according to their ability to dance."

This objection could also have been leveled with justice at the otherwise enchanting Marilyn Miller, who became a star in Florenz Ziegfeld's sumptuous production of *Sally* in 1920. Victor Herbert and Jerome Kern collaborated on the score, but it was Kern who gave Miss Miller "Look for the Silver Lining." Her performance of the song provided an instance of the extent to which the public hears what it wants to, when it is enamored of a performer. Miss Miller possessed a wiry little voice, sometimes hardly audible, except for a single enormous tone on F (the climactic note of "Look for the Silver Lining"), which threw the whole song out of scale. But the little Ohio girl who had worked her way up through the *Follies* was gifted with a personality "like a burst of sunshine," with blue eyes and blond hair and a lovely, friendly face, and with exquisite airiness as a dancer. The stage of the New Amsterdam Theatre was raised above the footlights so that everyone could see her twinkling toes; singer or no singer, she was every inch a star. With *Sally*, Marilyn Miller became the dearest love of the musical-comedy audience of the 1920s. When Ziegfeld put her in its sequel, *Sunny* (1925), he paid her the highest salary—reported to be $3,000 a week—ever known in American musical comedy until Gertrude Lawrence signed her contract for *Lady in the Dark*.

In his book of memoirs, *G. G.*, George Grossmith preserved his recollections of the composer of *Sally*:

"*Sally* has been conceived, written and produced almost entirely by English brains. Guy Bolton and Clifford Grey made the story and lyrics and Edward Royce (son of the old Gaiety comedian . . .) had made the most gorgeous presentation of the play. [This was the English production, which antedated Ziegfeld's.] He it was who staged the long series of Daly's successes, beginning with *The Merry Widow*. And the music of *Sally!* . . .

"Somewhere between the years 1905–1910 there was a penniless little song writer who hailed from America, but made his home in London. I knew him as Jerry Kern and liked him immensely. He often came to my house and played to us. He played divinely like nearly all of his kind, with a tremendous gift of 'tune.' He was the only one I could detect in a barren field likely to fill the shoes of Monckton, Paul Rubens, and Leslie Stuart. In my dressing-room at the Gaiety was a tiny yacht piano on which Rubens had composed his first song that was sung in a London theatre—'Trixie from the Town of Upper Tooting.'

" 'Give me a lyric,' one night asked Jerry, 'and let me try what I can do on the same instrument'; and together we wrote and composed 'Rosalie,' which I sang in, I think, *The Spring Chicken*. . . .

"Kern wrote several things for George Edwardes, but had no outstanding success until his return to America a year or two before the War, when he married a little English bride."

After *Sally*, Kern attached himself principally to the office of Charles B. Dillingham, whose productions, while less plushy than those of Ziegfeld, were consistently as handsome as any Broadway had to offer. Kern's major status was thus assured, since everything he wrote was presented with discretion and technical mastery. *Stepping Stones* (1923), a Little Red Riding Hood piece, provided volatile and likable music for three dancing Stones—Fred and his daughters Dorothy and Allene. Except for *Sunny*, whose value was enhanced more by the bounding Jack Donahue and the Tiller Girls (billed as Eight Marilyn Miller Cocktails) than by any superior qualities in the score, the Kern pieces of this era are now all obscured by the more impressive quality of his later output.

The composers of rowdier character were kept busy by the demands of revue producers. Irving Berlin did not return to musical comedy until 1925, when he wrote a run-of-the-mill score for the Marx Brothers—who were easily able to demolish anybody's music—in *The Cocoanuts* (1925), which might as well have been a revue, for all the plot meant by the time the unbridled brothers and the stately Margaret Dumont got through with it.

Vincent Youmans, whose achievements would have warranted comparison with those of the best musicians in the field if his career had not been cut short by illness, first made his mark with *Wildflower* (1923), a colorful and richly orchestrated score. His chef d'oeuvre, however, was *No! No! Nanette,* in which Louise Groody and Charles Winninger appeared in 1925. Entirely conventional in scope, *No! No! Nanette* rode to popularity with two deft and refreshing tunes, "Tea for Two" and "I Want to Be Happy."

Almost indistinguishable in title from *No! No! Nanette* was George Gershwin's first musical comedy, *La! La! Lucille,* presented six years earlier, on May 26, 1919, at Henry Miller's Theatre. It was an unassuming little bedroom farce, full of people opening the wrong door at the wrong time. The music, described by one critic as "tinkly and sentimental as Kern at his best" scarcely identified the future composer of *Of Thee I Sing* and *Porgy and Bess.* Gershwin was new in show business, and had received almost no instruction beyond the mechanics he had been able to pick up in backstage jobs. He learned his craft in the full public gaze, making some mistakes as he went along, but adding to his own stature consistently, as his technique came to approach his talent. Probably no first-rank composer of musical comedies ever began with less preparation. A part of the idolizing attachment of his audiences probably sprang from their feeling that Gershwin had no secrets from them, that he was a local boy making good before their very eyes.

Gershwin kept so busy earning his living at the piano and making incidental contributions to revues that four and a half years passed before he composed his next musical comedy, *Sweet Little Devil* (1924). He still had not defined his own formula. But in *Lady, Be Good,* later in the same year, his rhythmic ebullience and lighthearted, unorthodox word scansion began to make their point. With Fred and Adele Astaire to translate the music into visual movement, its freshness and verve were doubly apparent. And now Gershwin had found a lyricist able to support and encourage his most spontaneous qualities—his brother Ira, who from now on had a hand in almost every Gershwin piece, through the final grand-opera phase of *Porgy and Bess.*

In Gershwin's *Tell Me More* (1925), Lou Holtz's low comedy and the unwonted sophistication of the music and lyrics canceled each other out. Holtz deserves to be forgiven, though, in view of his definition of pantomime, as observed in a Russian ballet—"pantomime, from the Greek *pantomimus: panto,* meaning pants, and *mimus,* without." Gershwin's *Tip-Toes* (1925) likewise failed to create a stir, though Jeannette MacDonald adorned the cast. The same year, in a strange assignment, Gershwin collaborated with Herbert Stothart in the music for an operetta, *Song of the Flame,* for which Arthur Hammerstein imported the Russian Art Chorus. But this was merely a passing chore for Gershwin, who was to ride a skyrocket for the next decade.

Another celebrated musical artisan, Richard Rodgers, made his modest entry into the field on July 27, 1920, with *The Poor Little Ritz Girl,* for which Sigmund Romberg also wrote some of the music. Lorenz Hart wrote Rodgers' lyrics, and Alex Gerber wrote Romberg's. Though the piece had a piffling plot, it was an unusually successful first try, for it lasted through 119 performances. After a five-year lapse, Rodgers and Hart resumed their partnership to begin work in earnest in an American Revolution item known as *Dearest Enemy,* and also the Theatre Guild's first *Garrick Gaieties.* But as with Gershwin, their day was still in the future.

PART THREE
1925–50

Beatrice Lillie as a traveler in *At Home Abroad*.

XVIII. The Revue Becomes Civilized

THE EASY MONEY of the middle 1920s was not an unmixed blessing. With an angel in every speakeasy and an almost inexhaustible supply of box-office patrons, Broadway's stages were uncritically hospitable to almost anyone who thought he could produce a revue and knew he could finance its production. From the distance of a quarter century, it seems incredible that 104 audiences would have been willing to attend something called *Bunk of 1926*; but they did, and applauded Gene Lockhart as an American variant of Balieff in a piece that offered little else in the way of humor or invention. *Bad Habits of 1926* fared less well, reaching only nineteen showings, with Robert Montgomery in the cast; its title should have been more appealing, signifying as it did that its patrons could expect to see bare bodies and hear dirty jokes. A similar orientation was evidenced by *Great Temptations* (1926), produced by the Shuberts, of which the *World* said, "There are probably more chorus girls, more pink feathers, more high notes on the cornet, and more sets of steps than in any two shows ever given." The *Herald Tribune* noted the presence in the cast of a newcomer, Jack Benny, "a pleasant imitation of Phil Baker."

Why go on through *Bare Facts of 1926*, *Nic Nax of 1926*, *Padlocks of 1927* (with Texas Guinan galloping onto the stage on a white horse), and *Delmar's Revels* (1927)? These were the manifestations of a jaded mood, the soiled playthings of people tired of the very diversions they thought they wanted most. Since there was no more dramatic way of ending the revue craze, it was allowed to die by inches, of inanition.

By the end of 1927, the revue was all but dead. Fly-by-night producers no longer found support for their sleazy smut fests. The only survivors in the once glutted field were the masters of the craft, who had fairly consistently given value received when the others were merely trying to make quick money. George White was able to maintain his annual *Scandals*, Earl Carroll his *Vanities*, and the Shuberts their variously titled extravaganzas. Probably White never offered a better *Scandals* than that of 1926, when it was still important for him to reiterate the difference between his productions and those of his parvenu competitors. On opening night he charged $50 for a seat in the first seven rows of the orchestra. He offered his $27,000 audience the ebullient Harry Richman as singer, master of ceremonies, and general liaison officer. Ann Pennington danced the "Black Bottom," the name of which, for the sake of decorum, was said to come from the black mud of the Mississippi River delta. Willie Howard—a perennial fixture of the *Scandals*, along with his brother Eugene—ran the gamut from a portrait of a feuding southern mountaineer to a prediction of the effete behavior of the hero of a "drama of tomorrow." The production was in every way attractive to look at; the chorus girls "gave the impression of wearing less than usual," relying mainly on brassières that were "not opaque." Subsequent *Scandals*, after 1926, while not unfailingly as well supplied with ideas as this one, never slipped far below its level of presentable material and zestful performance. Between 1927 and 1931, when Ziegfeld temporarily abandoned the *Follies* in favor of musical comedies, the *Scandals* were without a peer among the expensive revues.

The *Earl Carroll Vanities* were seldom as strikingly studded with performing talent as the *Scandals*. They were aimed at an audience that was entirely satisfied by extensive and sleek revelations of female skin. Seeking a touch of variety in 1927, Carroll called his *Vanities* an "international edition," and incorporated features from André Charlot's current London revue, bringing over Jessie Matthews as leading lady. The result was an odd mixture, for Moran and Mack, the Two Black Crows, were hardly at home in a Mayfair environment. Carroll, moreover, made the mistake of experimenting with a show in which there was no nudity. He did not make the same mistake twice. In 1928, he returned to his usual predilection, and threw in W. C. Fields, the knockabout team of Barto and Mann, and Vincent Lopez's band for good measure. Reinstated in the favor of the patrons with whose tastes he had tampered, he was able in 1929 to cut down his salary list again, and to rely on the one formula he had been able to bring to perfection. This time, for some reason, he abandoned the name *Vanities*, and called his show *Earl Carroll's Sketch Book*. In 1930, he returned to his trademark, and never again relinquished it until he abandoned Broadway for his modernistic theatre-restaurant in Hollywood.

Apparently finding it easier to rent the Winter Garden to other producers than to produce shows for it themselves, the Shuberts had given up *The Passing Show*. The stock title of *Artists and Models*, however, they applied to two more revues of their own, in 1927 and 1930. To justify the title, the chorus boys were dressed as artists, in smocks and other appropriate vestments of that calling. The girls posed no costume problem whatever when they impersonated models.

In 1926, 1927, and 1929, the Shuberts also offered a triumvirate of exotica, *A Night in Paris*, *A Night in Spain*, and *A Night in Venice*. Yvonne George, who had sung "Mon Homme" in the *Greenwich Village Follies*, provided almost the only perceptible Parisian note in *A Night in Paris*, with imitations of Mistinguette and Raquel Meller. Jack Pearl, with his guttural German dialect, was hardly a typical exponent of Gallic style. Phil Baker, Ted Healy, Helen Kane (the Boop-Boop-a-Doop girl), and Rogers and Brennan were the featured Spaniards in the second revue of the series, which had the fastest and best dancing and the least nakedness of the three. The Venetian evocation, the biggest and most expensive of all, reverted to nakedness as its central article of faith.

Meanwhile the old master, Flo Ziegfeld, was largely distracted by his multiple interests as a producer of musical comedies. The *Ziegfeld Follies of 1927* was followed by a four-year gap before he returned to the revue field. Engaging Eddie Cantor as the top player in the 1927 *Follies*, he made much of the fact that the enterprise, having reached its twenty-first edition, had now come of age. The program carried the slogan "He who glorifies beauty glorifies truth," inadvertently placed immediately ahead of Cantor's name. Crammed full of Albertina Rasch Girls, show girls, and Ziegfeld Dancing Girls who performed more complicated steps than before, the last *Follies* of the prosperity era lived up to the reputation of its twenty predecessors. As Brooks Atkinson observed, "In the art of handling groups of chorus girls on the stage amid whirls of dancing and costuming all through an evening, Mr. Ziegfeld has no equal." Percy Hammond thought the finale "the best of the thousands of revue finales" he had seen, as the chorus girls danced complex patterns and played on such diverse instruments as the banjo, the flute, the xylophone, the piccolo, the trombone, the cornet, and the snare drum.

One of the gayest revues of the late 1920s was a hands-across-the-sea affair, *This Year of Grace* (1928), in which the author and composer, Noel Coward, appeared in the company of his irresistible compatriot, Beatrice Lillie. Two years earlier Miss Lillie had saved a witless revue, *Oh, Please!* by her inspired clowning. So far, she had not found materials comparable to those of the two *Charlot's Revues* in which she had first appeared here. In *This Year of Grace* she was supplied with them. Covered with grease, she emerged from the water as a triumphant channel swimmer, and disrupted the welcoming crowd by her predatory attempts to require everyone to accept her autograph. She caroled songs with such refrains as "Whoops, girls, up and at 'em" and "A-ding, a-ding-a-dong." She sat pathetically on a bookkeeper's stool and ate her heart out in a song called "World Weary." As La Flamme, the Queen of Bohemia, in a *boîte* called La Chatte Vierge, she told of her acquaintance with an American named "Mr. Higginderrière." But Miss Lillie did not have to carry *This Year of Grace* alone. Mr. Coward was able to turn from an urbane ditty to the macabre "Dance, Little Lady," as bitter a satiric comment on the jazz age as the musical stage ever vouchsafed. This was, said the *Journal*, "a taut and jazz-strained piece, itched to a frenzy of saxophones as Mr. Coward chants out a deathly song to a girl almost tranced in the vacancy of the hypnotic music. As the rhythm leaps, a group of shiny mannequins shuffles onto the stage, with faces twisted into vapid masks, and presently the girl emerges with them, and becomes, with them, a dummy, treading out the crazy measure in the empty movement of automatons."

The British touch was also manifest in Charles B. Cochran's revue *Wake Up and Dream* (1929), for which the American-born Cole Porter had been commissioned to write the music. Arch Selwyn brought the London production over lock, stock, and barrel, with Jessie Matthews, Jack Buchanan, and Tilly Losch as featured performers. The piece had taste, refinement, and intelligence, but too little material. The sensation of the evening was Miss Losch in "Arabesque," to Ravel music—"a dance of the hands," wrote Arthur Pollock in the Brooklyn *Eagle*, "which she does fascinatingly while crouched in plain black silk on a black dais, her fingers and hands and wrists and arms only moving, her body occasionally in response to them." John Mason Brown was an unbeliever in Miss Losch and in the revue as a whole, for the best thing he could find to say in the *Post* was that "Pogo, the performing horse of the Griffiths Brothers, was the drollest and most convulsing human horse that has capered on any stage within or before recent memory."

Another transatlantic gesture, Lew Leslie's *The International Review* (1930), was markedly less successful. Leslie made the mistake of trying to crowd too much into a supervariety entertainment; and he also erred in picking so mismated a batch of foreign folk as Gertrude Lawrence, Argentinita, Anton Dolin, Viola Dobos of the Budapest Opera Ballet, and Robert Conche, a Parisian child prodigy, who played the violin and the concertina, conducted the orchestra, and then disappeared from sight forever. Dolin made his mark sufficiently in an Apache dance, "The Pet of Montmartre," but Argentinita, whose modest Spanish folk dancing required special care, was so badly stage-managed that she was unable to win an American audience for several years afterward. The show ended at 12:15, with six numbers omitted, and with "exhaustion on the part of all concerned."

Leslie's inept planning was only partly responsible for the failure of *The International Review*. It was badly timed, for only a few months earlier—on April 30, 1929, at the Music Box—the whole course of the revue had been remapped by *The Little Show*, produced jointly by William A. Brady, Jr., Dwight Deere Wiman, and Tom Weatherly. From the first measures of a paean to the celebrated hardware store that ran "Hammacher Schlemmer, I love you," it was evident that *The Little Show* cherished a purpose far removed from that of the various *Follies, Scandals,* and *Vanities*. In it, the viewpoint of the *Grand Street Follies* was elevated to the highest Broadway level, and a piece for an audience with a reasonable I.Q. was given the advantage of the skilled presentation usually reserved for revues of less aristocratic pretensions. *The Little Show* offered no "dream appearances of all the lovely ladies of antiquity," nor did it employ more of a chorus than it needed for a sketch purporting to show the home life of the Tiller Girls. It was a fast show, but it also knew the value of slow tempo and quiet tone, as was demonstrated by a beautifully underplayed scene showing, as Richard Lockridge described it in the *Sun*, two bums sitting on a park bench, "singing of the market reports and welcoming a street sweeper and a policeman, who stop to assist them in assuring the listening world that 'money is easier today.' " Fred Allen's monologues before the curtain held the audience transfixed, especially one about a little boy who shot both parents in order to be entitled to go to the orphans' picnic. Clifton Webb was fleet of foot and tongue, and superbly sartorial. Libby Holman penetrated deep under the hide of a tough first-night audience with her dusky, throaty, throbbing delivery of "Moanin' Low." The grace and wit of Jo Mielziner's settings marked the beginning of a post-Urban, and from the modern point of a view a super-Urban, conception of stage design.

Naturally the first *Little Show* was not the last. But it takes more than a general conception to keep an idea alive from one edition of a revue to the next; and except for the new Mielziner scenery and the artless delivery of Ruth Tester in "Sing Something Simple," a protest against the tricky rhyme schemes that had come into vogue, the *Second Little Show* (1930) gave its audience less to remember. By the time the *Third Little Show* came along in 1931, Wiman and Weatherly—now its sole producers—were tempted to make it less intimate, and to rely heavily on the overpowering personality of Beatrice Lillie. It was no longer a real *Little Show*, but thanks to Miss Lillie, everyone had a fine time. Seated in a rickshaw, she intoned Noel Coward's charge that only mad dogs and Englishmen go out in the midday sun. She dealt ruthlessly with the behavior of a late comer at the theatre—a theme Iva Kitchell, whether consciously or unconsciously imitative, has treated in a similar vein in recent years. She introduced a parody of Ruth Draper's "Railway Station on the Western Plains" by telling the audience, "In this little sketch, ladies and gentlemen, I want you to imagine far too much." For the benefit of what has sometimes euphemistically been called the "intellectual audience," she exhumed and reinterpreted a ballad of the 1890s by Liza Lehmann, entitled "There are Fairies at the Bottom of Our Garden."

The true successor to the first *Little Show* was Max Gordon's production, *Three's a Crowd* (1930). Even more assured in every department than its predecessor, it ran for 272 performances, whereas the first *Little Show*, in spite of a warmly favorable critical reception, closed after 55. Fred Allen, Portland Hoffa, Clifton Webb, and Libby Holman moved directly into *Three's a Crowd*, in which they were joined by Tamara Geva, Fred MacMurray, and Allan Jones. This revue, wrote Arthur Pollock, "has beauty and grace without effort, and high polish and a civilized sophistication and a little good, clean-cut, gentlemanly dirt unmarred by vulgarity or exhibitionism." It was a grown-up revue, entirely free from banality and largely free from routine usages; the first act, for instance, "ended so quietly you'd hardly know it was over." The Allen monologues, the Webb feet, and the Arthur Schwartz-Howard Dietz songs were major assets, and Libby Holman sang Johnny Green's torch song "Body and Soul," to which she gave an intensity of inward emotion that is rare on the light musical stage—or, for that matter, on any stage at all.

The reputation of *Three's a Crowd* was eclipsed, however, by Max Gordon's *The Band Wagon*, which arrived at the New Amsterdam Theatre on June 3, 1931. Twenty years later, unless memory bears exceedingly false testimony, it is still possible to believe that *The Band Wagon* was one of the most perfect revues in the history of Broadway. Schwartz and Dietz were again composer and lyricist, and Dietz collaborated with George S. Kaufman on the book. Hassard Short directed, and Albertina Rasch staged the group dances. The personnel on the stage was entirely different, however, from that of *Three's a Crowd*. Fred and Adele Astaire were the romantic singing and dancing leads. Tilly Losch contributed her individual compositions, which were as modern as Broadway could then tolerate. The major comedy assignments went to Frank Morgan, drawn away from the nonmusical stage for the first time; Philip Loeb, experienced from the *Garrick Gaieties*; and the dry, tough, economical Helen Broderick.

A part of the delight of *The Band Wagon* lay in its transmutation of stage machinery into something approaching lyric poetry. The first American revue to take full cognizance of the revolving stage, it had two of them, and used them in all sorts of imaginative ways as an integral part of the bright Albert Johnson settings and the action and business devised by Short. The Astaires danced on them as they revolved; in the first-act finale the turntables turned in opposite directions as the entire cast waved from a merry-go-round. The sketches, bearing the imprint of Kaufman's typewriter, were wonderfully malicious. In a manner far more telling than that of the *Garrick Gaieties*, a travesty of the set pieces of formula shows revealed in their true light the moonlight serenade, the waltz sequence, the uninspired dance routine, the close harmony of a male quartet, and the overworked device of the blackout. The last of these was handled memorably in a sketch, "Pour le Bain," portraying Miss Broderick as a Westchester matron in search of bathroom appliances in an especially cultivated sales salon. Having satisfied her interest in washbowls and bathtubs, she intimated that no mention of another type of fixture had passed between them. The salesman, who obviously always had a line from Keats on the tip of his tongue, replied, "Heard melodies are sweet, but those unheard are sweeter." Blackout. Elsewhere in the evening, Frank Morgan appeared as a southern colonel in "The Pride of the Claghornes," in which the Claghorne daughter was thrown out of the house because she had violated southern canons by never going wrong. The chorus girls were "not made of wood," and their comely freshness enabled Percy Hammond to bring out one of his most frequently repeated lines: "They look, as Miss Laurette Taylor used to say, as if they all had mothers."

The prescient Brooks Atkinson, of the *Times*, recognized that *The Band Wagon* had established a new era. "After the appearance of *The Band Wagon*," he predicted, "it will be difficult for the old-time musical show to hold up its head. George S. Kaufman and Howard Dietz have put the stigmata on stupid display by creating a thoroughly modern revue. It is both funny and lovely; it has wit, gaiety, and splendor."

The ascendancy of the intimate revue posed a challenge to Flo Ziegfeld. In 1931, he determined to revive the *Follies*, even though production money was hard to get and the public pocketbook had shrunk to a fraction of its pre-1929 thickness. On July 1, 1931, accordingly, he opened the *Ziegfeld Follies of 1931* at his own Ziegfeld Theatre, assigning the chief tasks to such experts as Harry Richman, Jack Pearl, Albert Carroll, and Helen Morgan, and exerting his special spell of glorification upon the beautiful Gladys Glad. Though the public supported him, Ziegfeld's triumph was a questionable one. Without Joseph Urban, the décors were less consistent, and the performance seemed to move sluggishly because it lacked the crispness and brisk projection of the more up-to-date revues. Ziegfeld would have done well to let the 1927 edition be his last, instead of indulging in this anachronistic effort.

Ziegfeld's continuing belief in the big, or nonintimate, revue was shared by a young producer, Billy Rose, who threw his hat in the ring with *Sweet and Low* (1930). A wholehearted believer in "belly laughs," and also the lucky possessor of a wife named Fannie Brice, Rose already manifested, in his first Broadway endeavor, a gift for assembling a low-comedy revue in a fashion that concealed a keen analytic intelligence. With Moss and Fontana to give the proceedings a ballroom lift, and with George Jessel, James Barton (with his perennial drunk act), and Arthur Treacher to share the comic chores with Miss Brice, *Sweet and Low* attained the very solid early-Depression figure of 184 performances in New York. In 1931, Rose devised *Billy Rose's Crazy Quilt* as a further vehicle for his wife, whom he placed in the company of Phil Baker, Ted Healy, and their assorted stooges. The long run and extensive tour of *Crazy Quilt* effectively established Rose as a new major producer, though his output in subsequent years was never large.

During these years a continuing procession of all-Negro revues made its way from Harlem to Broadway, though few of them were ever really assimilated in the Broadway scene. The most successful producer of Negro revues was Lew Leslie, whose series of *Blackbirds*, beginning in 1928, established a pattern of high-pressure delivery, musical pandemonium, and incessant tap dancing. Bill Robinson came to Broadway in *Blackbirds of 1928*; and Ethel Waters, having previously appeared in Earl Dancer's revue *Africana* in 1927, was the undebated star of *Blackbirds of 1930*. With *Rhapsody in Black* (1931), Leslie tried to take a more elevated view of the potentialities of a Negro show, and fell into the abyss of cultural pretense. Miss Waters, the Cecil Mack Choir, and the Berry Brothers carried the burden of a show in which dancing was minimal and "symphonic" montages predominated. "A sort of Harlem *Chauve-Souris*," wrote Howard Barnes in the *Herald Tribune*, "it dispenses with choruses and in large measure with the ecstatic shuffling that has marked sepia offerings in the past." When a Negro choir began singing Jewish and Russian music, the racial reason for presenting the show evaporated; and it was not until *Porgy and Bess* that the all-Negro show was restored to a position of importance. Meanwhile Miss Waters moved on to *As Thousands Cheer* and *At Home Abroad,* to conquer new provinces.

XIX. Musical Comedy Discovers Contemporary Life

As THE REVUE wore out its welcome, musical comedy moved back into a dominating position on Broadway. But these were still the mad 1920s, and an exclusive diet of moonlight-and-honeysuckle themes was not to the liking of an increasingly hysterical generation. Obviously musical comedy, which had been gradually catching up with the times for a decade or so, would have to complete the process if it hoped to recapture the attention of the audience that had been kept up to the minute by the satiric sketches of the revues. After all, there was no binding reason for avoiding current topics and fads as subject matter for musical comedies, merely because most (though, as we have seen, not quite all) past examples of the form had dealt chiefly in romantic intrigues. Accordingly, the topical musical comedy became one of the standard types of the late 1920s, and as time went on it tended to become the ruling type.

For sheer efficiency in handling a topical book in a manner that was intelligible and diverting to a large public, no team surpassed the trio of De Sylva, Brown, and Henderson. Beginning with *Good News* (1927), their names were listed together so inextricably that it was difficult to tell who did what. In point of fact, Ray Henderson wrote the music, Lew Brown and B. G. de Sylva worked together on the lyrics, and De Sylva took care of the book, sometimes alone and sometimes with the aid of a collaborator. In six years, from 1927 to 1932, they turned out an unbroken series of six hits, and they could probably have continued longer if the Depression and Hollywood contracts had not disrupted their team.

Good News (1927) was a college comedy. In those days, as Chancellor Robert M. Hutchins of the University of Chicago has pointed out, the colleges confused themselves with country clubs. Since any resemblance between De Sylva's imaginary Tait College and any real college was largely accidental, *Good News* was two steps removed from everything we associate with the seats of higher learning today. The orchestra began the evening with a cheer, "Rah! Rah! Rah!", before launching into the overture, and the ushers in the theatre wore dirty old jerseys. At Tait, college rhymed with knowledge, but bore no further relation to it. With George Olsen's band to play the "Varsity Drag," the collegians had a hot time of it, and to hell with studies.

Perhaps the most perplexed member of the first-night audience was Alexander Woollcott, whose reaction was a study in kid-glove detachment from the whole rowdy antic:

"I confess that I had not precisely expected to attend this season a musical comedy of which the plot would turn on whether Tom Marlowe would pass his astronomy exam, and so be able to go into the big game on Saturday and win for dear old Tait. I had not expected to hear a theatre hushed by Tom's big, manly resolve not to cheat in the exam, but to play fair and square. I certainly had not expected to see a cluster of chorus girls, led by a fair and writhing maiden with implausible hair, lift their approximately assembled voices in soprano fealty to Pi Beta Phi."

After taking time out to work on *Manhattan Mary* (1927), a "vast, bewildered, gorgeous extravaganza" produced by George White (in which he himself returned to the stage), the De Sylva, Brown, and Henderson triumvirate returned to more mundane interests with *Hold Everything* (1928), a fast and funny saga of the prize-fight ring. Bert Lahr, hailed as the best addition to the roster of comics since the advent of Ed Wynn, played the role of a pug who usually wound up on the floor. A high moment occurred when Nina Olivette, his vis-à-vis, said angrily, "For two cents I'd knock you out." "You're mercenary! You're mercenary!" howled Lahr.

Having disposed of prize fighting, De Sylva, Brown, and Henderson turned to golf in *Follow Thru* (1929). Eleanor Powell offered some of her cleanest and fleetest tap dancing to "Button Up Your Overcoat," one of Henderson's most felicitous and easy-moving songs. Jack Haley invaded a swanky country club, and commented to one of the golfers, "The trouble with your game is that you stand too close to the ball—after you hit it."

By refraining from digging very deep into the subjects they treated, the trio managed to avoid alienating any of their patrons. They had their formula down pat by now; it was easy to deal with aviation successfully in *Flying High* (1930), with the aid of Bert Lahr as an addled pilot. *Hot-Cha*, written for Flo Ziegfeld in 1932, enabled Lahr to be a fake matador in Mexico.

In 1932, De Sylva left his partners to team up with Vincent Youmans in *Take a Chance*. A somewhat nondescript show that had failed on the road as *Humpty Dumpty, Take a Chance* made history principally by adding luster to the reputation of Ethel Merman, who had emerged from the night clubs two years earlier in *Girl Crazy*. Youmans gave her two of the best songs anyone ever wrote for an American musical comedy—"Eadie Was a Lady" ("though her past was shady"), an evocation of preprohibition New

Orleans; and a rousing pseudo-revivalist hymn, "Rise and Shine," which brought the first-act curtain down in the midst of pandemonium. It would have taken no more than these two songs to establish, if *Girl Crazy* had not already done so, that Miss Merman was one performer the Broadway stage could not do without. Until now, happily, it has not had to. While *Take a Chance* was making its mark, Ray Henderson worked with Lew Brown and Mack Gordon on a vehicle for Jimmy Durante, *Strike Me Pink* (1933).

Take a Chance was the last Broadway score to which Youmans contributed before illness struck him. His loss was a deprivation for the musical stage, for in his time he alone deserved to be ranked with Gershwin, Porter, Rodgers, and Kern. Another of his notable achievements was the naval musical comedy, *Hit the Deck* (1927), which contained one of the unforgotten classics of the 1920s, "Hallelujah." *Great Day* (1929) included "Without a Song"; but the show deferred its opening so many times that in the end it did not become a success. Youmans' only other musical comedies of the 1930s were *Smiles* (1930), a Ziegfeld production in which Marilyn Miller and the Astaires appeared, and *Through the Years* (1932).

As a result of *Oh, Kay* (1926), George Gershwin finally enjoyed the pleasure of hearing himself called "the premier music-maker." Never before had he coordinated his powers so well, or joined the staff of so inviting a production as this one, mounted by the "freshman impresarios," Alex Aarons and Vinton Freedley (whose partnership is symbolized today by the name of the Alvin Theatre, made out of the first syllables of their first names). *Oh, Kay* dealt with the most overworked subject of the day, bootlegging; but the collaboration of first-class experts in every department lifted the treatment high above the ordinary. Gertrude Lawrence returned from England to play the role of the sister of a titled British bootlegger. Guy Bolton worked out a tight, amusing book; P. G. Wodehouse, the lyricist, was also credited with such high-voltage lines as "Never criticize a bootlegger's English if his Scotch is all right." Miss Lawrence displayed even more versatility as a mimic than the *Charlot's Revues* had led her audience to expect, and she "wrung the withers" of Percy Hammond's heart with her throbbing performance of "Someone to Watch over Me." The score, which also included "Clap Yo' Hands," "Fidgety Feet," and "Do-Do-Do Like You Done-Done-Done Before," reinforced Gershwin's reputation as a composer ready and able to deal with a wide range of situations, moods, and sentiments.

In *Funny Face* (1927), Gershwin returned to partnership with his brother Ira, who fitted out Victor Moore with the lyrics of " 'S Wonderful." The next year (1928), Ziegfeld lured both Gershwins away from Aarons and Freedley, to cooperate with Sigmund Romberg and P. G. Wodehouse in *Rosalie*, the most richly caparisoned piece the master ever produced for Marilyn Miller. With glowing Urban sets representing West Point, conveniently turned co-educational for the occasion, and the usual outlay of glorified girls, *Rosalie* buried the Gershwin music deep under its visual appeals. But at least the collaboration of Gershwin and Romberg was an amusing and unlikely idea, which made Woollcott "think we shall soon have a novel written by Harold Bell Wright and Ernest Hemingway." Woollcott's account of Miss Miller's entrée is too savorous to pass by:

"There comes a time once in every two or three years when the vast stage of that playhouse [the New Amsterdam Theatre] begins to show signs of a deep and familiar agitation. Down in the orchestra pit the violins chitter with excitement and the brasses blare. The spotlight turns white with exception. Fifty beautiful girls in simple peasant costumes of satin and chiffon rush pellmell onto the stage, all squealing simple peasant outcries of "Here she comes!" Fifty hussars in fatigue uniform of ivory white and tomato bisque march on in column of fours and kneel to express an emotion too strong for words. The lights swing to the gateway at the back and settle there. The house holds its breath. And on walks Marilyn Miller."

Ziegfeld and the exploitation of Marilyn Miller were not up Gershwin's alley. After writing two minor items for other producers—*Treasure Girl* (1928) and *Show Girl* (1929)—George and Ira Gershwin, with the help of Morrie Ryskind, turned their energies to the preparation of the most uncompromising musical comedy the American stage had yet tolerated. After *Strike Up the Band* opened in 1930, William Bolitho wrote in the *World*: "I don't remember ever before in a musical comedy having noticed or understood what it was all about. Here all is not only clear but really startling. Of all things in the world, here is a bitter, rather good, satirical attack on war, genuine propaganda at times, sung and danced on Broadway, to standing room only."

Not only war, but the Babbittry that had complacently led the country into a parlous financial and political situation, were the targets of Ryskind's book. Cushioning his story by telling it within a dream context, Ryskind detailed the events in a mock war between the United States and Switzerland over the high tariff on chocolate. Victor Moore, already recognized as ideally suited to political satire, was "the man behind the President," engaged in fixing up a peace treaty that involved the illegitimate annexing of territory, renaming Baluchistan Jugo-Slavia, and partitioning Russia. The miracle of *Strike Up the Band* was its ability to present its argument without losing its good nature, and without sacrificing opportunities for such ebullient Gershwin tunes as "Strike Up the Band" and "Mademoiselle from New Rochelle." *Strike Up the Band* was the precursor of the musical satires of the Depression period, most notably of *Of Thee I Sing*. It was the first real token of liberalism and a social conscience in the American musical theatre.

Gershwin did not, however, immediately pursue the implications of *Strike Up the Band*. In *Girl Crazy*, his other product of 1930, he reverted to a light-minded plot, provided by Guy Bolton and John McGowan, which told of the adventures in Custerville, Arizona, of a girl-crazy eastern youth who had been sent there to keep out of trouble. The theme apparently inspired little tenderness in Gershwin, for although *Girl Crazy* was one of his most inventive scores, it was also one of his coldest. There was softness, it is true, about "Embraceable You," and there was a melting languor in the ministrations of a male quartet, the Foursome, who covered the scene changes by returning again and again to sing in close harmony, "I'm bidin' my time; That's the kinda guy I'm." But for Ethel Merman, fresh from the night clubs, Gershwin wrote two of his hardest-hitting songs, the kinetic fury called "I Got Rhythm" and the western dance-hall torch song, "Sam and Delilah," a Barbary Coast satire on the Frankie and Johnny ballad. With its stern humors, *Girl Crazy* more than ever marked its composer a man of strong personal idiosyncrasy, with nothing but contempt for the tired clichés of his trade.

It would be unjust to imply that Cole Porter was less willing than Gershwin to deal satirically with social and political issues. His method, however, was different from the outset. He made use of satirically oriented books, but preferred to employ as his weapon the barbed shaft of an individual line or song. Moreover, he developed his technique of acid comment only slowly, contenting himself at first with a special urbanity of manner that was the reflex of one intent upon forgetting his Hoosier origins.

Fifty Million Frenchmen (1929) concentrated its attention in both music and lyrics (Porter, as always thereafter, wrote both) upon one matter—sex—somewhat to the discomfiture of Richard Watts, who complained, "The lyrics he devised for the new musical comedy once more discussed learnedly and wittily the sex habits of the beaver, oyster, armadillo, gnu, aardvark and kindred exhibits in zoölogy and proved again that their author is the most definitely individual and completely brilliant deviser of song words, but it also made some of us wish that Mr. Porter wouldn't pound at one theme so constantly." In William Gaxton, Porter found an abettor so engaging that Robert Littell of the *World* thought it would be all right to "take nearly all other musical comedy heroes and throw them into the Seine." Since the story provided by Herbert Fields was laid in Paris, Norman Bel Geddes was called upon for handsome sets of the proper places—the Ritz Bar, the American Express, the Café de la Paix, the races. It was all very chic, very brittle, and without much trace of the warmth of sentiment which middle age was to bring to its composer later on.

Porter claimed that *The New Yorkers* (1930) was a "sociological musical satire," but this phrase may have been no more than an obeisance to *Strike Up the Band*. At any rate, *The New Yorkers* offered no profounder social revelation than the sight of Hope Williams as a resident of Park Avenue, "the street where bad women walk with good dogs." Such satiric impact as the piece might have had was effactually shattered by Jimmy Durante, who was appearing in his first musical comedy, in the company of the irrepressible Lou Clayton and Eddie Jackson. Durante won the hearts of his sophisticated audience with an engagingly crude song entitled "The Hot Potata"; and at the close of the first act proceeded to an anthem in praise of wood and its place in American history, illustrating his meaning with exhibits in the form of miscellaneous trees, boxes, violins, and express wagons. In his comic play with Clayton and Jackson, wrote Brooks Atkinson, "Jimmy the superman burns his way across the stage, splintering the English language, assaulting his companions, hurling hats into the orchestra pit, whirling around to confront an imagined adversary, bursting with undisciplined energy." Porter lost this round to Durante.

Richard Rodgers and Lorenz Hart first adventured into the realm of satire by indirection. In 1927, Herbert Fields—son of Lew Fields—supplied them with a book inspired by Mark Twain, and on November 3 of that year, A Connecticut Yankee lifted the reputation of its collaborators to the top of the profession. Fields brought Mark Twain up to date with a host of 1927 references and slogans and slang expressions, and Hart followed suit with the lyrics of "Thou Swell." In the second act, as King Arthur's courtiers began to find their way around in the language of their American visitors, they could be heard remarking, "Methinks yon damsel is a lovely broad," or "I would fain walk a furlong for a Camel." A whole evening of this became a bit taxing, but the insouciant and unexpected rhymes of Hart's lyrics and the lift of such melodies as "On a Desert Isle" and "My Heart Stood Still," along with the tireless affability of William Gaxton as the Yankee, kept the interest of the audience from flagging. During the intermission the spirit of the occasion was kept intact by a curtain decorated by Robert Benchley's wondrous map of Camelot and its environs. The sentimental hit song, "My Heart Stood Still," incidentally, was not written for or first used in A Connecticut Yankee. Rodgers had composed it for a Cochran revue in London, One Damned Thing After Another. Flo Ziegfeld wanted to buy the song for the Follies, but Rodgers and Hart, having their own use for it, would not sell it.

Having entered the field of topical humor through the back gate, Rodgers and Hart, and Fields along with them, remained in it for Present Arms (1928). A patent imitation of Hit the Deck and Good News, it was a vehement and blary depiction of the behavior of the Marines in the Hawaiian Islands, made especially salable by the elaborate tableaux and evolutions dreamed up by Busby Berkeley. Hart's lyrics assumed even more of the cast that set them apart from all others, with such personalized end rhymes as "Egypt" with "he gypped" and "Scotland" with "what land."

Neither Present Arms nor the other musical comedy Rodgers and Hart wrote early in 1928 represented Rodgers at his most inspired. Beatrice Lillie and Clifton Webb took the spotlight away from both the composer and the lyricist in She's My Baby, though Rodgers and Hart were no less responsible than Miss Lillie for the supernal bathos of the song that ran, "You can have another friend, another lover; A baby's best friend is its mother." The shopworn book by Bert Kalmar and Harry Ruby required the combined genius of Miss Lillie and Webb to make anything out of such repartee as this:

WEBB: "Let us ensconce ourselves upon the sofa."

LILLIE: "No, I prefer to sit down."

Still relatively young practitioners of their craft, Rodgers and Hart spent most of the 1920s searching for their best métier, without quite finding it. Until they returned to Broadway with *Jumbo* in 1935, after a four-year absence, they remained hardly more than bright and fluent workmen, able to turn out attractive and moderately successful work without again tapping the rich lode they had momentarily uncovered in *A Connecticut Yankee*. They moved from one assignment to another, with no special conviction as to the direction in which their best usefulness might lie. There were moments of real distinction, it is true, in Rodgers' score for *Spring Is Here*—especially in the song bearing the title of the show. But *Heads Up* (1929), a spoof of life on a yacht, and *America's Sweetheart* (1931), a poorly aimed attempt to repeat the Hollywood satire of George S. Kaufman's *Once in a Lifetime*, were swiftly forgotten; and so would Ziegfeld's production of *Simple Simon* (1930) have been without Ed Wynn. In his familiar horn-rimmed spectacles, with his omnipresent lisp and giggle, Wynn ventured on a picnic. Admiring the canvas trees, he exclaimed, "I love the woods! Ah, how I love the woods!" Whereupon the woods, including a huge green frog which was one of the residents, proceeded to show Wynn that his sentiment was not reciprocated.

While Rodgers and Hart were engaging upon these early and inconclusive endeavors, the older and more experienced Jerome Kern came into the fullness of his powers. Although he supplied the music in 1927 for Charles Dillingham's musical-comedy-revue, *Lucky*, in which Paul Whiteman's band interpreted the score in the latest jazz arrangements, Kern appeared to realize that his real gift lay in the direction of sentimental and nostalgic evocations bordering upon the province of operetta.

Everything that was most persuasive and endearing about Kern as a melodist was summoned forth by Flo Ziegfeld's commission to write the score for Oscar Hammerstein 2d's dramatization of Edna Ferber's novel *Show Boat*. The production, presented at the Ziegfeld Theatre on December 27, 1927, proved to be one of those rare convocations of talent in which everyone concerned—authors, directors, and performers—was protected by a lucky star. Hammerstein suddenly found himself in possession of gracious and expert powers as a lyricist at which his earlier verses had only hinted. His easy, natural handling of dialogue gave life and credibility to a book that would have seemed in less skillful hands to be too slow-moving in the first half, and too rambling in the thirty-four-year span covered by the second half. Charles Winninger as the bluff and merry Cap'n Andy; the starchy Edna May Oliver as Parthy Ann; Helen Morgan, with her brave little sob, as the half-caste Julie; Howard Marsh as a dashing Ravenal; Norma

Terris as a fresh and pretty Magnolia—these were among the truest people the musical stage had ever represented. Filled with period devices as it now seems, *Show Boat* in its day was perhaps the only musical comedy to achieve a dramatic verisimilitude that seemed comparable to that of the speaking stage.

Because the play itself was so honest, the Kern-Hammerstein songs took on a double force. But in their own right they formed an astonishing procession—"Old Man River," "Only Make Believe," "Can't Help Lovin' That Man," "Why Do I Love You?", "Bill" (with words by P. G. Wodehouse). No other American piece of its vintage left so large a permanent musical legacy, and certainly no other surpassed it in quality.

Since masterpieces seldom come in quick succession, Kern slipped somewhat below the level of *Show Boat* in the succeeding *Sweet Adeline* (1929), perhaps partly because he was too intent on continuing the *Leitmotiv* plan of providing each character with his own theme, with which he had experimented unobtrusively in the earlier score. For *The Cat and the Fiddle* (1931) he again conceived a rich and lovely score (including "The Night Was Made for Love" and "She Didn't Say Yes"), but the effect of the piece as a whole was lessened by Otto Harbach's inordinately dull book about the love affair between musicians of disparate tastes—a sophomoric composer of serious intentions and an American girl devoted to popular music.

The plot of *Music in the Air* (1932)—dealing with a four-way intrigue absorbing two members of a Bavarian choral society, a prima donna, and a famous playwright—was scarcely more invigorating, but the smooth touch of Oscar Hammerstein 2d took some of the curse off. It followed the way pointed by *Show Boat*, moreover, in seeking to achieve honorable characterization and dramaturgy. Whether or not the story was worth attending to, the treatment of it was made significant by Hammerstein's exorcising of the precision dancing, the knock-about comics, and the overelaborate staging and costuming that had still related *Show Boat* to the conventions of its time. In everything except its plot materials, *Music in the Air* was thoroughly modern in conception. The integrity of its form required the music to be so intimately related to the circumstances of the book that even so charming a song as "Egern on the Tegern See" did not mean enough outside its context to become especially popular in its own right.

Though its composer is less celebrated than Rodgers or Kern, one other Ziegfeld musical cannot be left out of this chronicle. On February 2, 1927, *Rio Rita,* with a book by Guy Bolton and music by Fred Thompson, opened the producer's new "cathedral," the Ziegfeld Theatre. Today the proud possession of Billy Rose, the Joseph Urban façade and interior may still be inspected, in their original stage, at the corner of Fifty-fourth Street and Sixth Avenue. *Rio Rita* was an extremely ordinary affair with a villain and a tenor and an ingenue. To match it to the occasion it celebrated, Ziegfeld borrowed the beauteous Gladys Glad from the *Follies,* and gave Urban an even more than usually free hand to design a bewildering array of vermilion and black and turquoise costumes for the hundred girls who adorned the stage. Bert Wheeler and Robert Woolsey were the comics, and much of the dancing was allotted to the Albertina Rasch Girls, then a new ensemble, addicted to unison bending and swaying of a sleek and stylish kind.

Despite the rapid rise to favor of the younger practitioners, the composers of old-hat operetta also retained their hold over a portion of the Broadway public. Sigmund Romberg still had two robust and tuneful romances to offer—*The Desert Song* (1926) and *The New Moon* (1928)—as well as the more modestly successful *Nina Rosa* (1930). After this he lapsed into a fifteen years' silence which he broke only twice, with *May Wine* (1935) and *Sunny River* (1941), before writing *Up in Central Park* (1947). Emmerich Kalman made his best impression with *Countess Maritza* (1926), in which Odette Myrtil fiddled "Play, Gypsies, Dance, Gypsies" whenever she was permitted to. *The Circus Princess* (1927), a weaker story and score, was aided at the box office by the great clown Poodles Hanneford and a variety of equestrians and aerialists. Rudolf Friml composed his last hit in *The Three Musketeers* (1928), produced with splendor by Ziegfeld. Alexander Woollcott confessed that he "did greatly enjoy the first few years of Act I."

Viennese operetta, which has a way of coming back to life precisely when it looks deadest, put in a reappearance in 1929, when the Shuberts staged a sumptuous revival of Johann Strauss's *Die Fledermaus*, under the title *A Wonderful Night*. They stole a march on Max Gordon and *The Band Wagon* by making extensive use of a revolving stage. In its whole tone, the production was elegant, graceful, and faithful to the period. The libretto was much too faithful, for its "wormy" text was a source of universal ennui. The leading man was a young British actor named Archie Leach. In view of his later celebrity in the motion pictures as Cary Grant, Arthur Pollock's impression of his callow American debut is worth repeating: "Archie Leach, who feels that acting in something by Johann Strauss calls for distinction, is somewhat at a loss as to how to achieve it. The result is a mixture of John Barrymore and Cockney. He makes a handsome hero, though."

Largely neglected by American producers in the first few decades of its history, *Die Fledermaus* now came to be regarded as the most dependable of all Viennese products. As *Champagne Sec* (1933), Dwight Deere Wiman provided it with an attractively modernized book by Robert A. Simon, and Monty Woolley's direction taught the actors to treat their assignments in gay, posturing, period-satire fashion. As *Rosalinda* (1942), the New Opera Company offered a version that was both beautiful and modish, with Felix Brentano adapting Max Reinhardt's direction to Broadway needs, and with George Balanchine as choreographer, Oliver Smith as scene designer, and Ladislas Czettel as costume designer. In 1950, *Die Fledermaus* was awarded the ultimate accolade by being welcomed into the repertory of the Metropolitan Opera.

A *Wonderful Night* cannot be said, however, to have initiated a trend toward the general restoration of Viennese operetta to the American stage. The only other Broadway manifestation of it at this time was a production of Karl Millöcker's *The DuBarry*, undertaken in order to win Grace Moore away from the Metropolitan for a season. Otherwise Viennese music was still neglected except at that august house, where on January 2, 1931, von Suppé's *Boccaccio* was mounted for Maria Jeritza, who "cut a fine figure" in it.

The record of transatlantic curiosa can be completed with two more items. *The Wonder Bar,* a cabaret drama imported from Berlin, was unsuccessfully broached in 1931, with Al Jolson as its continental star. Noel Coward's delicately tasteful *Bitter Sweet,* a memento of the sixty-year incursion of British musical attractions, was the last musical importation from Britain, except the D'Oyly Carte Company, to reach Broadway for a decade—until Coward's *Set to Music* arrived in 1939, with Beatrice Lillie on hand to sing "Mad about the Boy," and a withering sketch, "The Stately Homes of England," to put the decaying upper classes in their place.

XX. The Depression Decade

A QUICKSTEP MARCH TUNE sounded from the orchestra pit. The curtain rose upon a crowded stage of excitedly moving people. "The marchers, with their torchlights and banners, move against a shadowy background of skyscrapers, churches, and—almost certainly—speakeasies. Across this background is thrown a huge election banner on which are gargantuan reproductions of the faces of the party's candidates. Highlit and prominent is the party's battlecry: 'FOR PRESIDENT, JOHN P. WINTERGREEN.' The name of the vice-presidential candidate, however, is lost in shadow. As for the countenances of the candidates, it is a little hard to pick them out in the general blur, and the chances are that that's a break for the party."

In this fashion, as the authors described it, musical comedy entered politics on the opening night of *Of Thee I Sing,* at the Music Box Theatre, on December 26, 1931. The election that lost the Republicans their lease on the White House was still almost a year in the future. But two years had passed since the great stock-market crash of 1929; and how many chickens were there in every pot now, and how many cars in every garage?

George S. Kaufman and Morrie Ryskind, and also George and Ira Gershwin, took a look at the calamitous state of affairs. They did not like what they saw, and they thought it would be good to do something about it.

American musical comedy had never fully learned from Gilbert and Sullivan the art of arguing about public issues by means of laughter. With another election—and a crucial one—just around the corner, it was time, they felt for Broadway to develop a sense of political responsibility.

Kaufman and Ryskind had made a start in this direction with *Strike Up the Band*, and the Gershwins had borne out their intentions with hardy, straight-punching tunes and lyrics. But *Strike Up the Band*, in retrospect, was hardly more than a tentative foreshadowing of the relentless yet incomparably funny unfrocking of American politics accomplished by *Of Thee I Sing*.

Kaufman and Ryskind hung their plot on two central pegs. The President was an unqualified nonentity, elected merely because the voters were stampeded by the party's platform of Love; and the Vice-President was a pathetic figure, a man nobody cared about and everybody forgot. Throughout the evening Victor Moore, a melancholy little bundle of sadness as Alexander Throttlebottom, the Vice-President, tried without much success to discover what he was supposed to do in order to fill his office. William Gaxton as President John P. Wintergreen talked glibly and constantly out of both sides of his face at once, and nearly plunged the country into war with France by refusing to marry the winner of a beauty contest held to select a bride for him; she was, it transpired, "the illegitimate daughter of the illegitimate son of the illegitimate nephew of Napoleon," and the French ambassador considered Wintergreen's attitude an insult to the French nation. Congress was likewise overwrought, and after some months of deliberation came to the brink of impeachment proceedings. But by this time Wintergreen was able to extricate himself. The girl of his heart, whom he had meanwhile married, was now in an interesting condition. As Vice-President Throttlebottom pointed out, shortly before the final curtain, "the United States has never impeached an expectant President."

Upon this improbable complication of incidents, worthy of the contrapuntal imagination of W. S. Gilbert, the authors festooned a profusion of colorful jests about national affairs and the behavior of politicians. By the end of the evening neither political party was left with a leg to stand on. But at least Love still reigned, as Wintergreen joined with the rest in the reprise of his love song to Mary, who now carried a twin on each arm:

> "Of thee I sing, baby,
> Summer, autumn, winter, spring, baby—
> Shining star and inspiration,
> Worthy of a mighty nation,
> Of thee I sing!"

In the spring of 1932, the Pulitzer Prize, for the first time in its history, was awarded to the authors of a musical play—for "the original American play performed in New York which shall best represent the educational value and power of the stage." If there had been a way to do so, the committee should have included George Gershwin in the citation. The songs and the accompanimental music were much more than the frosting on the cake: To a degree hitherto unknown in the musical-comedy theatre, the mood, pace, and placing of the musical numbers was an integral part of the construction of the play as a whole. If the music were removed, the structure would collapse. In its loud and raw way, *Of Thee I Sing* was a genuine music drama.

The creators of *Of Thee I Sing* were persuaded by Sam H. Harris, its producer, to go to work on a sequel. Nearly two more Depression years had idled by before *Let 'Em Eat Cake* was ready to be offered to the public, on October 21, 1933. Life had certainly become no more amusing, and Kaufman and Ryskind made the mistake of letting their bitterness find too plain an expression. "Their hatreds have triumphed over their sense of humor," wrote Brooks Atkinson. Then, too, Gershwin had begun to picture himself as a serious composer, and the score of *Let 'Em Eat Cake* was self-consciously modern and somewhat lacking in the spontaneity that had been the priceless asset of his music for *Of Thee I Sing*.

In between the two satires, George and Ira Gershwin picked up a bit of money by writing, with Herbert Fields, what turned out to be a routine and old-fashioned musical comedy, *Pardon My English* (1933). Gershwin's mind was now beginning to focus itself upon a distant goal, and except for *Let 'Em Eat Cake* this was his last musical comedy. He was determined to write an opera, and he had selected *Porgy*, DuBose and Dorothy Heyward's play of Catfish Row in Charleston, as his subject. Knowing that his technique was inadequate to the requirements of serious composition, he concentrated upon the disciplines of counterpoint and orchestration. The result of his labors, the "American folk opera," *Porgy and Bess*, was staged by the Theatre Guild, who had also presented the play in its original form—it was the Guild's first musical production, except for the *Garrick Gaieties* and *Parade*—at the Alvin Theatre on October 10, 1935. Rouben Mamoulian staged it, and Sergei Soudeikine designed the settings. The cast, which seems notable today largely because their participation in *Porgy and Bess* lifted so many of its members to prominence, included Abbie Mitchell (a veteran from the early Broadway days of Will Marion Cook, her husband), Todd Duncan (as Porgy), Ann Wiggins Brown, later known as Anne Brown (as Bess), Ruby Elzy, Georgette Harvey, Edward Matthews, Warren Coleman, J. Rosamond Johnson, and the dancers Buck and Bubbles. Eva Jessye directed the onorous choral ensembles. Mamoulian's staging was resourceful and reasonably appropriate, though it ran more to trick effects than Robert Ross's direction of Cheryl Crawford's revival in 1942, which was in many ways superior to the earlier version.

Porgy and Bess has been so thoroughly assimilated into our folkways that discussion of it is hazardous. Certainly it has become the best-loved American opera—if it is, indeed, an opera. But with due regard for its appealing features, it is a blemished masterpiece. More a Singspiel than an opera, it does not maintain a consistent tone or treatment. It lurches abruptly into vaudevillian clichés of the popular stage, and deserts them with equal suddenness when the time to be serious seems to have arrived. Musically most of the most expressive sections of the score are those allotted to the chorus; and the most felicitous instances of musical characterization are attached not to the central characters, but to Sportin' Life and Serena. Such pieces as Bess's "Summertime" and Porgy's "I Got Plenty o' Nuttin' " and "Bess, You Is My Woman Now" are decorative operetta divertissements, pure and simple, and serve little or no valuable end in advancing the plot or clarifying the characters.

The musical idiom of *Porgy and Bess* is a curious and unique amalgam of Broadway parlance and figures suggested by Hebraic and Oriental chants, with a surface sprinkling of Negro or pseudo-Negro jazz, religious, and minstrel-show elements. Because Gershwin's sincerity was so apparent, and because the context was so engrossing, audiences from the beginning have always been willing to suspend disbelief, and to accept *Porgy and Bess* as an authentic example of Negro music. As a result, its musical vocabulary has tended to become the official idiom of Negro music in the theatre, much as Aaron Copland's highly personal style in *Rodeo* and *Billy the Kid* has become the official way of suggesting the plains.

These considerations, however, are pertinent only if one chooses to regard *Porgy and Bess* as a full-fledged opera, and to subject it to the rigorous tests of excellence and consistency which that branch of art imposes. If it is viewed—as perhaps it should be—as an upreach of the light lyric stage, both its integrity and the viability of its songs entitle it to a high position. Its qualities serve to emphasize the width of the gap separating opera from music of lighter genre. As an opera, Gershwin's last work is an interesting but inconclusive first try by a stranger to the métier. As a Broadway musical play, it is one of the important mileposts in the developing craft of light musical composition.

Having poked its finger into politics and pulled out a plum, the musical theatre could not stay away from the savory mess. Irving Berlin and Moss Hart were the next to survey the current lot of man, with *Face the Music* (1932), of which Sam H. Harris was again producer. Hart was not satisfied with a Gilbertian contrivance of plot; he was intent upon coming closer to names, dates, and places. The Seabury investigation had just revealed evidence of corruption among the New York police. Hart therefore made the police force the target of his fiercest satire—with Hugh O'Connell as the chief of police, and Mary Boland as his wife. The Depression in general and the sorry state of show business in particular also received his attention.

A less sustained piece of work than *Of Thee I Sing, Face the Music,* by its references to actual people and events—in the manner of a revue—aimed its punches closer to the belt line. The opening sketch portrayed a group of Wall Street captains at the Automat, eating the regular five-cent dinner and singing at the finish, "Let's Have Another Cup of Coffee." Times were really bad: The Roxy was offering four films and a room and bath for ten cents; the Palace had become a nickelodeon, with a bill including Dr. Einstein, Ethel Barrymore, Aimee Semple McPherson, Eddie Cantor, Al Jolson, and a free lunch. Nobody had any money to invest in the production of a musical show—except the police, who, embarrassed by the bulging contents of their "tin boxes," rose enthusiastically to the proposal that they should be angels for a piece called *The Rhinestone Girl*. The first-act finale of *Face the Music* revealed the splendors of that production, which included a mirror dance (there proved, of course, to be no mirrors, but a second row of dancing girls reversing the movements of those in the first row) and a pretty production number, "Dear Old Crinoline Days," in which the hoop skirts were only a façade, as the audience discovered when the girls turned around.

In the second act, some of the offending police were brought to trial and convicted for ten years—Miss Boland with them. At this tense moment somebody offered her an immortal word of consolation: "Never mind, Mary; when you get out, the Lux soap people will still think you are thirty-nine." In due season she did get out, in time to bring down the final curtain by riding onto the stage upon a genuine, full-sized elephant.

Berlin's music possessed the right journalistic touch to carry off the hocus-pocus of *Face the Music*. When he and Harris and Hart contemplated a successor to it, they determined to abandon all attempt at a consecutive plot, and to incorporate their satire within the more flexible format of a revue. The result was *As Thousands Cheer* (1933), a topical revue that has never since been surpassed in hilarity, vitality, or the encompassing talent of all those involved. Except for *The Band Wagon*, no musical piece of its period received such unqualified approval; Brooks Atkinson wrote that he could "only give meek approval to every item on the program."

Curtains with newspaper headlines introduced the various numbers. Most startling of all was the sketch headed "Franklin D. Roosevelt Inaugurated Tomorrow." Never before had the White House been exposed to shafts of such pointedness. The action occurred on the last night of the Hoovers' tenancy, with Helen Broderick, as Mrs. Hoover, putting the final touches on their preparations for moving out, and commenting acidly to her family and the servants about the Roosevelts and their entourage.

"World's Wealthiest Man Celebrates 94th Birthday" showed John D. Rockefeller, Jr., endeavoring vainly to press Radio City upon his father as a birthday gift, and fleeing for his bodily safety at the end. Clifton Webb demonstrated unsuspected gifts of impersonation as the older Rockefeller, and, elsewhere in the evening, as Mahatma Gandhi. "Metropolitan Opera

Opens in Old-Time Splendor" depicted the way in which, allegedly, the new radio sponsor stole the show from the boxholders of the Diamond Horseshoe. "Heat Wave Strikes New York" enabled Ethel Waters, in the most notable assignment of her career thus far, to deliver the couplet that ran "She started a heat wave, By making her seat wave." Later on, Miss Waters struck a deeper note with an affecting song, "Supper Time," in which her man did not come to share her supper because a lynching had taken place. "Noel Coward, Noted Playwright, Returns to England" reported the effect of the Mayfair author's stay in New York upon the behavior and diction of the employees of the hotel in which he had lived.

The cast was scarcely less than a miracle. Webb plunged a sharp-edged rapier home in every scene. Marilyn Miller, in her last appearance on Broadway, was still all effulgence and humor and sweet loveliness, but she also showed a new aptitude for mimicry in her pat and hilarious imitation of Joan Crawford. Helen Broderick "never missed a chance to put poison in the soup," whether as Mrs. Hoover, as Aimee Semple McPherson (whose "foursquare gospel" was attaining its first notoriety), or as an acidulous Statue of Liberty. Charles Weidman's dancers—José Limón, Letitia Ide, and Bill Matons among them—employed choreography that made genuinely pertinent comment, and Albert Johnson's costumes had "meaning as well as beauty." Throughout the evening everyone behaved with wit and gaiety and grace, refusing to be tempted to the anger that had ruined a short-lived revue of similar intentions, *Americana*, the year before. Even unadulterated sentiment was not ruled out, for the first act closed with a colorful Easter parade on Fifth Avenue, to the strains of Berlin's nostalgic "Easter Parade." After so transcendent an achievement as *As Thousands Cheer*, Berlin felt justified in listening to the call of Hollywood, and his services were lost to Broadway until he returned for *Louisiana Purchase* in 1940.

As the national economy sank deeper and deeper into the miasma of the Depression, the theatre was increasingly preempted by authors and producers who wanted to use it as a means of protest. With a few notable exceptions, however, it cannot be said that the musical branch of the Broadway stage covered itself with great glory as an agent of propaganda—unless such a play as *Johnny Johnson*, which employed incidental music by Kurt Weill, is forced into a musical category. After Gershwin's espousal of operatic and symphonic composition and Berlin's departure for Hollywood, there was no commercially produced sequel to *Of Thee I Sing* and *As Thousands Cheer* until *I'd Rather Be Right*, in 1937.

On a smaller scale, the Theatre Guild endeavored to prove its social consciousness with *Parade* (1935), a "satirical revue" equipped with music by Jerome Moross and literary components by George Sklar, Paul Peters, and several others. Philip Loeb, erstwhile director of the *Garrick Gaieties*, staged the revue, and Robert Alton, later one of Broadway's breeziest choreographers, directed the dances. But Sklar and Peters tended to view the objects of their derision more as enemies than as humorous figures, and like *Americana* three years earlier, *Parade* died of a bad temper, in spite of Jimmy Savo's attempt to save it with his funny and touching pantomime.

Two seasons later, on November 27, 1937, the one truly memorable revue of the late Depression, *Pins and Needles*, was presented by a cast composed entirely of members of the singing, acting, and dancing classes of the International Ladies Garment Workers' Union. Conceived in the first place primarily as an entertainment for the union membership, *Pins and Needles*, thanks to the expertness and freshness of Harold Rome's music and lyrics and the high intelligence quotient revealed in the satiric sketches, quickly became one of the ruling successes of Broadway. Naturally, its point of view was what we should call "leftist"—though certainly not Red—today. Its burden was indicated by the opening number, "Sing Us a Song of Social Significance." The most celebrated, and the most violent, comment in the entire evening was made in a sketch, "Four Little Angels of Peace," which showed Chamberlain, Mussolini, Hitler, and an undesignated Japanese statesman in a highly unflattering light. Taking a leaf from the book of *As Thousands Cheer*, Rome did not forget to provide a touch of quiet sentiment as a foil for the prevailing tone of vehemence. Paralleling the "Easter Parade" finale of the Irving Berlin revue, *Pins and Needles* ended its first half with a genre scene, "Sunday in the Park," staged by Charles Friedman with exquisite reticence.

Pins and Needles became a quasi-permanent fixture, replacing old ideas with new ones when the timeliness wore off, and revising its title from time to time to *Pins and Needles 1939* and *New Pins and Needles*. The 1939 version introduced "The Red Mikado," in which the Russian Lord High Executioner chopped off the heads of the Three Little Maids, who then went into a dance while Gilbert and Sullivan rose in consternation from their graves. The skit was intended, it must be explained to readers in this remote age, as a double-barreled jibe at Russian dictatorship and at the pair of jazzed-up versions of *The Mikado (The Hot Mikado* and *The Swing Mikado)* that had recently swept Broadway off its feet. Elsewhere in *Pins and Needles 1939* the international scene was dealt with in a biting number called "Britannia Waives the Rules," while union interests were mirrored in a portrayal of the home life of Papa Lewis and Mama Green, and capitalistic promotion was given its comeuppance in "Cream of Mush," a burlesque of radio commercials. By now, the acting members of the ILGWU had forgotten how to operate their machines; and with the time occupied by the tour of *New Pins and Needles* they were kept away from the dressmaking business for three years. Many of them, having developed thoroughgoing professional competence, remained in show business.

Spurred by the surprise success of *Pins and Needles*, Max Gordon, George S. Kaufman, and Moss Hart joined together in producing a similar revue, *Sing Out the News*, in 1938. Full of comments about prominent people and expositions of New Deal philosophy, *Sing Out the News* amounted to "*Pins and Needles* in a Broadway tailor's dress suit." Harold Rome was its composer, turning out such well-wrought songs as "Just an Ordinary Guy" and "Franklin D. Roosevelt Jones." Jo Mielziner's fanciful scenery certainly did not hurt the chances of the show; but it did not help them, either. The point of view was no longer quite as fresh as it had been with the ILGWU, nor was it altogether consonant with an expensive production. The revue attained only a moderate run—105 performances.

The other side of the picture, the upper-class, rightist attitude, was set forth in 1939 by an expensive and beautiful little revue, *One for the Money*. For those who had approved of the liberal orientation of *Pins and Needles*, the piece, devised with a kind of superamateur gaiety by Nancy Hamilton and supplied with naïvely fresh tunes by Morgan Lewis, was a "sleek and glossy vacuum," an "orchid and patent-leather bore." Actually it was more than this, and probably would have been better appreciated in post-Depression years for the smartness of Raoul Pène du Bois' Parisian Park Avenue sets, Robert Alton's blithe choreography, and John Murray Anderson's smart staging. Presented without a chorus, its youthful cast of twelve included several performers who later made names for themselves—Alfred Drake, Gene Kelly, Nadine Gae, Brenda Forbes, Ruth Matteson, Philip Bourneuf, Don Loper, Keenan Wynn, and William Archibald.

The Title of *One for the Money* indicated that Nancy Hamilton had a succession of revues in mind. In 1940, *Two for the Show* duly came along, with Eve Arden and the inexhaustible Betty Hutton as new members of the company. Less well stocked with bright ideas, but closer to the Broadway pulse, it prospered somewhat better. Its success was not sufficient, however, for Miss Hamilton to obtain support for *Three to Make Ready* until six years later (1946). This third edition turned out to be a larger, more conventional show, dominated by the dancing of Ray Bolger and Harold Lang, neither of whom was given opportunities commensurate with his gifts. The whole original point of the series was lost, and to this day no word has been heard of plans for *Four to Go*.

Less pretentious than *One for the Money*, but similarly dedicated to the exploitation of youth, had been Charles Dillingham's *New Faces*, presented five years earlier, in 1934. Assembled by Leonard Sillman, a company including Imogene Coca, O. Z. Whitehead, and Henry Fonda modeled their performance on what was still remembered of the *Garrick Gaieties*, of which Miss Coca had been a charter member. Sergei Soudeikine designed cute little miniature sets. Nancy Hamilton tried out her literary hand with a sketch purporting to reveal Katharine Hepburn working herself into the appropriate mood for *Little Women*.

Sillman himself produced a second edition, *New Faces of 1936*, introducing Van Johnson and Helen Craig, and retaining the ever-present Miss Coca, whom one reviewer described as "A new face from a fairish way back."

After a seven-year lapse, Sillman brought out *New Faces of 1943* (actually on December 22, 1942), without adding as much as before to the sum total of human merriment.

In the meantime, Miss Coca had moved into *The Straw Hat Revue* (1939), picked up by Harry Kaufman and the Shuberts on the summer theatre circuit and brought into Broadway for a fall engagement. In this breezy enterprise, the rapid-fire delivery of Danny Kaye fell on Broadway ears for the first time, preparing the way for his rise to the top of the profession in *Lady in the Dark*. Alfred Drake was also in it, certainly not dreaming of the prestige that *Oklahoma!* was to bring him three and a half years later. Otherwise the emphasis was on dancing, with a roster including Jerome Andrews (the choreographer of the show), Jerome Robbins, Ruthanna Boris, William Bales, and Richard Reed.

The cycle of intimate revues designed to give unknown youngsters a chance was closed for the time by the most successful one of all, *Meet the People*, which pitted itself against a Broadway opening-night audience on Christmas night, 1940, after a year and a half in Hollywood and San Francisco. The first Hollywood musical production to make its way to New York, *Meet the People* was not particularly modish. But it was warm, informal, and friendly, and Jay Gorney had given it a spate of likable, if sometimes rather sprawling and poorly organized, tunes. A vivacious little girl named Nanette Fabares, who later phoneticized her name to Fabray, charmed the audience no end; and Marion Colby set a brief fashion by intoning emotion-charged torch songs with deadpan colorlessness and unyielding metricality.

During the years of the Depression, the United States was too preoccupied with its own ills to care much about Europe and its theatrical products; and, moreover, nobody had any money to risk upon steamship passage for foreign players. A single exception was *Continental Varieties* (1934), actually a sophisticated vaudeville show employing Nikita Balieff as master of ceremonies, and Lucienne Boyer, the exponent of "Parlez-moi d'Amour," and Vicente Escudero, the greatest of Spanish male dancers, as its headliners. No further European touch was to be discerned on the revue stage until 1939, when a group of indigent refugees offered their specialties in a pathetically ineffectual collation called *From Vienna*, and were sufficiently encouraged by the response of a sympathetic public to continue with *Reunion in New York* the following year.

The Federal Theatre Project of the WPA might have been expected to make some arresting contribution to the musical stage, since it occasionally did so in other areas. But the record of the New York unit was wholly undistinguished. A Negro revue, *Swing It* (1937), added nothing to what had already been offered earlier by Lew Leslie's companies. *A Hero Is Born* (1937), an extravaganza with music by Lehman Engel and a book by Theresa Helburn, went above, or around, the heads of the audience. *Sing for Your Supper* (1939), an elaborate revue that took a year and a half in preparation, succeeded in inverse ratio to the time spent on it.

The one historic production of the musical branch of the New York WPA Theatre was rejected by government officials before it opened. Marc Blitzstein's musical drama *The Cradle Will Rock*, a social-consciousness document written at white heat to expose the mistreatment of the honorable Larry Foreman by the capitalist big shot Mister Mister, with subsequent repercussions throughout the entire social structure, was scheduled to open under Federal Theatre auspices on the evening of January 3, 1938. That day word came through that Washington disapproved of the ultraliberal tone of the piece, and would not permit its presentation. Hastily the directors of Orson Welles's Mercury Theatre scurried to find a theatre that would be available that night. As the members of the audience assembled at the Venice Theatre, they were told the circumstances and asked to troop up to the Windsor Theatre. Once there, they saw a unique presentation. Neither Actors' Equity nor the Federation of Musicians, in view of the controversial nature of the situation, would allow its members to go through with their share in the performance. Blitzstein sat alone on the stage at a piano, playing the score and singing some of the songs. The more daring members of the cast sang their parts from the orchestra pit or from seats in the house, while some of the instrumentalists tootled from scattered seats in the balcony. Later on, *The Cradle Will Rock* was given in more orthodox fashion, but a little of the first excitement was inevitably missing.

In *The Cradle Will Rock* and its subsequent companion piece, *No for an Answer* (1941), Blitzstein (who wrote music, book, and lyrics) created another of those in-between pieces which, like *Porgy and Bess*, defies pigeonholing. The materials—songs, ensembles, and dialogue—were essentially those of any lighthearted musical comedy. But the composer's treatment of them was wholly serious, employing advanced devices of dissonance and instrumentation to give them a sardonic edge. These two works moved one step farther in the direction of a conciliation between Broadway and the soberer reaches of the lyric theatre.

The only other noteworthy accomplishment of the WPA in the musical theatre originated not in New York but in Chicago, in the fall of 1938. On March 1, 1939, the New York audience finally saw *The Swing Mikado*, in which Harry Minturn and Sammy Dyer had turned Gilbert and Sullivan's opera into a fiesta of fast trucking and hot vocalizing. John Pratt decked out the singing, dancing actors in Caribbean outfits of unbridled flamboyance. The opposing polarities of Gilbert's lines, most of which were kept intact, and the tropical brilliance of the production constituted a cosmic accident that could never be repeated.

By comparison, Michael Todd's production entitled *The Hot Mikado*, mounted in competition three weeks later, seemed effete and calculated, even with Nat Karson's blinding costumes and sets and the incomparable tapping of Bill Robinson as an adornment for the title role. But Todd's attempt to Harlemize a classic was not the last. Later in 1939, Erik Charell presented at the Center Theatre, at vast expense, one of the most confused failures of all time, a "musical variation" of Shakespeare's *A Midsummer Night's Dream* called *Swingin' the Dream*. A mixed-cast production, this abortive piece of nonsense enlisted the services of Dorothy McGuire, Ruth Ford, Butterfly McQueen, Maxine Sullivan, Bill Bailey, Benny Goodman, Louis Armstrong, Eddie Condon, and a variety of other jazz celebrities. Agnes de Mille created the statelier features of the choreography, and Herbert White directed the jitterbugs. The settings were designed after Walt Disney cartoons by Herbert Andrews and Walter Jageman. Never were so many unrelated people and ideas crammed into a single show. It closed after the thirteenth performance.

XXI. The New Audience

THE STANDARD Broadway musical stage, as opposed to these aberrant efforts, pursued an increasingly cautious course as the Depression deepened and lengthened. The theatre industry had received not one body blow but two at the end of the 1920s. Precisely when abundant free money for production all but disappeared, the motion-picture screen developed a voice. By the beginning of the 1930s it was clear that the flesh-and-blood theatre would henceforth occupy a far more restricted corner of the entertainment field than it had in the past. The musical stage was especially hard hit by the perfection of the rival medium, for the first all-talking picture, Al Jolson in *The Jazz Singer*, made use of music; and the host of cinema musical comedies and extravaganzas that followed this first experiment took away from the living musical stage a large audience that never came back.

The audience that remained faithful to the musical stage and was able to continue supporting it was relatively aristocratic in its tastes. Those who sought no more than a rowdy good time and a chance to hear some lively songs and see some splashy production numbers were now quite content with Hollywood provender. Broadway producers quickly learned that they might as well spare their energy and save the money of their backers if their shows were not equipped to outwit the motion pictures with more intelligent and fresher ideas, more pungent or subtle wit, better casting and direction, and superior taste in costumes and stage designs. *The Band Wagon* established a new level of discrimination. Along with the Gershwin and Berlin satires, it was fully attuned to the new, small, and demanding audience of the 1930s. Henceforth, the successful Broadway musical productions paid ever greater attention to art as well as to craft. The ascendancy of the stage designer, the costumer, and the choreographer was at hand. Generally speaking, only the most gifted composers were able to continue at their jobs; book-writers were no longer permitted to commit the indiscretion of being dull, and lyricists were expected to find some other rhyme for "June" than "moon."

Max Gordon fully understood the change that had come over the musical branch of show business when he commissioned Arthur Schwartz and Howard Dietz to write the music and lyrics for the revue, *Flying Colors* (1932). But business was so bad that he was afraid to risk another intimate and restricted piece like *The Band Wagon*. For the sake of success—which he achieved in reasonable degree—he decided to make *Flying Colors* a bigger affair, spectacular in mounting yet stylish and "modernistic," as they used to say, in treatment. Charles Butterworth, the melancholy dancer Tamara Geva, the hoofing Buddy and Vilma Ebsen, and Clifton Webb were the leading entertainers. In the face of Webb's subsequent transformation in the moving pictures, it is well to recall, in Percy Hammond's words, the qualities that made and kept him one of the most favored revue performers in this earlier period:

"Mr. Clifton Webb is the Town's pet dancer, tragedian, buffoon, vocalist and dude. The fastidious Mr. Webb, clad in garments now somber, then oriant, but always form-fitting and scrupulously in the mood of the moment, dominated the ceremonies by the rhythm of his movements, the music of his voice, the sadness of his pathos and the fun of his burlesque. Little or no scenery is needed by any play in which Mr. Webb appears, for he is his own production, combining in his appearance all the eleven arts of Joseph Urban and Norman Bel Geddes." (Geddes was the creator of the splendors of *Flying High*.)

Parting company with Gordon, Schwartz and Dietz attempted in 1934 to create for Arch Selwyn and Harold B. Franklin a modern parallel of *The Three-Cornered Hat*, the Spanish short story by Pedro Alarcón which Manuel de Falla, Léonide Massine, and Pablo Picasso had earlier turned into one of the rarest of ballets. *Revenge with Music*, as the paraphrase was called, turned out to be neither flesh nor fowl. In an unmistakably Broadway show, the book seemed tepid, and the whole undertaking is now memorable chiefly because it gave Libby Holman and Georges Metaxa one of the finest and sultriest of the Schwartz-Dietz songs, "You and the Night and the Music."

Closer to the focus of their original success was the revue, *At Home Abroad* (1935), written by Schwartz and Dietz and produced by the Shuberts as a co-starring vehicle for Beatrice Lillie and Ethel Waters. For Miss Waters, in her first Broadway appearance since *As Thousands Cheer*, they provided the sizzling, shouting "Hottentot Potentate." Hung on the around-the-world formula familiar in extravaganzas ever since the Kiralfys' version of Jules Verne's *Around the World in Eighty Days* in the 1870s, *At Home Abroad* gave Miss Lillie scope for action against a variety of exotic settings, freshly and gaily devised by the new young designer of the moment, Vincente Minnelli. It was in *At Home Abroad* that Miss Lillie twisted her tongue in endeavoring to order "two dozen double damask dinner napkins," impersonated Mitzi of Old Vienna and a Russian ballerina who could not "face the mujik," exploited to the hilt the Parisian grisette's motto, "L'amour the merrier," and popped out of the second line of a chorus of geisha girls to cry, "It's better with your shoes off."

The Show Is On (1936), another revue for Miss Lillie, also enlisted Schwartz and Dietz, though in this case the Shuberts, wanting to be sure that enough authors were involved, also obtained contributions from Richard Rodgers, Lorenz Hart, Vernon Duke, Moss Hart, and others. Minnelli both designed and directed the show. A crane carried Miss Lillie out over the heads of the audience on a property moon, whence she tossed garters (many more than two) to men in the front rows. The comedienne's supremacy was challenged by Bert Lahr, who rendered—there is no other word—the "Song of a Woodchopper," complete with a small fir tree, a property ax, chips flying into the air from an unseen hand in the wings, and, on the chopper's rotund head, a toupee which "took on a new personality every time it shifted to a new angle."

The last Schwartz-Dietz collaboration until *Inside U.S.A.* (1948) was *Between the Devil* (1937), in which Jack Buchanan again returned from England, this time in the company of Evelyn Laye. For *Stars in Your Eyes* (1939), a sumptuous outlay sponsored by Dwight Deere Wiman, Schwartz wrote tunes to lyrics by Dorothy Fields and music for the extensive ballets choreographed by Carl Randall. A name-heavy cast included Ethel Merman, Walter Cassel, Mildred Natwick, and Jimmy Durante in singing and speaking parts, and a roster of dancers headed by Tamara Toumanova, Alicia Alonso, Nora Kaye, Maria Karniloff, Jerome Robbins, Fernando Alonso, Dwight Godwin, and Richard Reed. Jo Mielziner was given a free hand, and—since the action took place on a Hollywood sound stage—had a field day, making use of moving cameras, a treadmill across the front of the stage, and shifting scenery that never required the curtain to be run down. There was also a dream ballet—not the first of its kind, since George Balanchine had already used the idea in Wiman's production of Rodgers and Hart's *I Married an Angel*. After this expensive failure, Schwartz remained away from Broadway until 1946, when he and Ira Gershwin wrote *Park Avenue*, another failure, smaller but scarcely less expensive. Dietz was represented in the ill-fated *Sadie Thompson* (1944), a musical version of Somerset Maugham's story, for which Vernon Duke wrote the music. More recently he made an English adaptation of the lyrics of *Die Fledermaus* for the Metropolitan Opera.

Though satire and smartness and modernity were the order of the day in the 1930s, Jerome Kern remained true to his essentially lyric temperament. His last triumph on Broadway, before he assigned his talents to the motion pictures, was *Roberta* (1933). Nobody cared a fig about the book, based on Alice Duer Miller's story of a young fullback who inherited his aunt's stylish dressmaking establishment. But when Tamara (not to be confused with the dancer Tamara Geva) sang "Smoke Gets in Your Eyes" and joined with William Hain in "The Touch of Your Hand," the audience felt, and rightly, that it was hearing some of the most enchanting music of make-believe since *Show Boat*. Some of the drama critics thought the music not up to Kern's standard, but time has proved them wrong, since the passing years have awarded its songs an undebatable second place in the long Kern list. In the first scene, the veteran Fay Templeton, come out of retirement to play the brief role of the aunt, was called upon to sing "Yesterday," and quietly expire in her chair.

Only once more were Jerome Kern's melodies heard in a new Broadway musical comedy, in *Very Warm for May* (1939), a quietly charming piece, with book and lyrics by Oscar Hammerstein 2d, which never quite caught the public fancy. *Show Boat* was appropriately honored in 1946 by a revival produced without thought of cost by Hammerstein. With Carol Bruce in the Helen Morgan role of Julie and Kenneth Spencer taking over "Old Man River," sung originally by Jules Bledsoe and later by Paul Robeson, the revival ran a full year. In future seasons it is reasonable to imagine that other Kern musical comedies may be restored to the stage, for his tunefulness was true and sweet, and his sentiment still speaks to the present generation.

Richard Rodgers and Lorenz Hart renewed their association in 1935 with *Jumbo*—"a sane and exciting compound of opera, animal show, folk drama, harlequinade, carnival, circus, extravaganza and spectacle," Percy Hammond called it—devised by Billy Rose for the Hippodrome. In the following year Rodgers and Hart turned out, with George Abbott as author of the book, a less gaudy but historically more significant work, *On Your Toes*. As he returned to the producing field, Dwight Deere Wiman felt that the American musical theatre had reached a point of maturity that permitted the introduction of more serious dancing than it had known in the past. Within a plot of backstage ballet life, in itself a new subject on the American stage, he incorporated two major ballets, in addition to the expected incidental dances. From the Ballet Russe he engaged George (then Georges) Balanchine to create his first musical-comedy dances. Balanchine's "Scheherazade" ballet was perhaps an inevitable concession to a public not yet used to extensive dance compositions in a light entertainment. But with "Slaughter on Tenth Avenue," in which Ray Bolger and Tamara Geva gave a sardonic, vivid portrayal of an unmistakably American subject, Balanchine achieved a serious, tautly organized, forcefully projected work of art. For the first time, the dance department of a musical comedy took the center of the stage with claims to attention at least as irresistible as those of such superior Rodgers and Hart songs as "It's Got to Be Love" and "There's a Small Hotel."

Rodgers and Hart turned to a celebration of youth in *Babes in Arms* (1937), whose cast was composed largely of performers in their teens and early twenties. With two sixteen-year-olds, Wynn Murray and Mitzi Green, as his leading ladies, Robert Sinclair, who directed, sought to suffuse with un-Broadway innocence a cheerful tale about the children of touring vaudeville performers, spending the summer in a camp at Seaport, Long Island. George Balanchine exploited the talent of Duke McHale in "Peter's Dream," one of the earliest musical-comedy dream ballets, and Rodgers and Hart were at the top of their bent in the uninhibited song called "Johnny One-Note." The settings of Raymond Sovey and the costumes of Helene Pons caught the fancy of John Anderson, who wrote in the *Journal* of the dream ballet: "There were cardboard skyscrapers, swirling seas of blue-cloth ocean and the tropical enchantment of paper palm trees and cellophantasy mermaids."

The Boys from Syracuse (1938), for which George Abbott was producer as well as author of the book and stage director, was the lineal antecedent of *Kiss Me, Kate*. It was based on Shakespeare's *A Comedy of Errors*, but Abbott had the good sense to employ Shakespeare's web of double-identity situations without appropriating his lines. Ronald Graham and Eddie Albert appeared as the two Antipholuses, of Ephesus and Syracuse, and Teddy Hart (the brother of Lorenz) and Jimmy Savo as the two Dromios. The score and lyrics were fabulously brilliant in their unfailing wit and their variety of texture and expression.

Until now, Rodgers and Hart had been too busy trying to cure the aches and pains of the Depression with merriment and romance to give much thought to the soberer expression of satire. With *I'd Rather Be Right* (1937), written in collaboration with George S. Kaufman and Moss Hart, they made a bold gesture in the direction of political protest. In *As Thousands Cheer*, the audience had peeked inside the White House and seen the departure of the Hoovers. Now Franklin Delano Roosevelt was put on the stage—a tap-dancing Roosevelt, played to the life by George M. Cohan, equipped with the requisite pince-nez and Hyde Park-Groton inflection of speech. Only Cohan, or an actor of his standing and his delicately adjusted control of his effects, could have portrayed the popular President without giving offense. One reporter remarked that Cohan's performance, and the piece as a whole, resembled an entertainment given by the Washington newspaper men of the Gridiron Club, except that it was not given in private. The book poked ridicule at the innumerable alphabetical agencies of the New Deal; dealt summarily with Roosevelt's recent attempt to pack the Supreme Court, and sent the bearded judges into a lively jig; represented the defeated Republican candidate, Alf Landon, as a White House butler; worried over the budget, which could never be brought under control; and put into the President's mouth the confession "The trouble with the country is that I don't know what the trouble with the country is." At the finish, a White

House Jamboree was arranged to persuade the nation of the need for a third term. *Of Thee I Sing* and *As Thousands Cheer* were roundabout by comparison; *I'd Rather Be Right* not only named names, but pursued its controversial themes to the bitter end.

Though their score and lyrics were admirably keyed to the tone of the Kaufman and Hart play, the participation of Rodgers and Hart in *I'd Rather Be Right* was in a measure an act of self-abnegation. The fine points of their work tended to be lost in the shuffle, and the piece was more Kaufman and Hart than Rodgers and Hart.

Their virtue was rewarded the following spring, however, for Dwight Deere Wiman's production of *I Married an Angel* (1938) inspired them to one of their most notable accomplishments. As perfect in every detail of conception and execution as *The Band Wagon* a few seasons back, *I Married an Angel* still remains one of Broadway's high memories. As a permanent fixture of its scenery, Jo Mielziner worked out a combination of curtains and panels providing a stage within a stage, and Joshua Logan's direction—his first musical assignment—took advantage of the possibility of presenting the action on a variety of interesting planes. As in *Stars in Your Eyes* the following year, the furnishings were whisked on and off by means of a treadmill, which also played a novel part in Balanchine's choreography.

The plot, derived from a Hungarian play by Janos Vaszary, told, in a vein half fantastic and half farcical, of Dennis King's infatuation for a genuine angel, in the form of Vera Zorina, who flew into his study after he had sworn that he would never marry a woman unless he could be certain that she was an angel. A former member of the Ballet Russe de Monte Carlo, Miss Zorina captured utterly the essence of her part, and danced enchantingly. A geographical sequence of dances representing the honeymoon reached an illusory and beautiful climax in a blizzard in the Eskimo country. The sophisticated worldliness of Vivienne Segal and the brisk energy of Audrey Christie were excellent foils for Miss Zorina's fragility. In their songs for *I Married an Angel*, perhaps even more than at any time before, Rodgers and Hart achieved the complete identity of purpose that was the hallmark of their mature output. Without thwarting his melodic feeling or his knack for a subtle harmonic twist, Rodgers was able completely to respect Hart's words. He never distorted their accent or inflection, and he manipulated his musical ideas in a way that kept the lyrics uppermost in the attention of the audience.

In *Too Many Girls* (1939), Rodgers and Hart dealt with college life, as put onto the stage by the ebullient George Abbott. Such engaging youngsters as Desi Arnaz, Eddie Bracken, Hal Le Roy, Marcy Wescott, and Mary Jane Walsh kept matters in a pleasant ferment, and the songs—notably "Love Never Went to College" and "I'd Like to Recognize the Tune"—were among the most delectable the pair ever turned out. From this they turned to Wiman's unsuccessful but handsome *Higher and Higher* (1940), in which

a group of jitterbug dancers trained by Robert Alton and a highly cultivated
seal named Sharkey managed to steal rather too much of the show from Jack
Haley and Marta Eggert.

The summit of the Rodgers and Hart partnership was reached with *Pal
Joey* on December 25, 1940. *Pal Joey* was an enlargement by the author
himself of a series of sharp, slangy sketches contributed by John O'Hara to
The New Yorker. O'Hara managed not only to write one of the most continuously witty books any musical comedy ever had, but also to create
unwontedly lifelike characters. He recounted a gusty tale of a young heel
who made and unmade himself by capturing and losing the fancy of a bored
society woman.

A low-grade Chicago night club, said to be on Cottage Grove Avenue,
was the chief locale. Robert Alton seized upon the opportunity afforded by
a floor show to devise a superb variety of dances satirizing everything that
was wrong and out-of-date in that field of entertainment. A song and dance
depicted "The Flower Garden of My Heart," and another employed lights
of changing colors corresponding to a series of colors specified in the lyrics.
The girls were overdressed in feathers and frills and engaged in shockingly
bromidic dance routines. As Joey, Gene Kelly, fresh from *One for the
Money*, managed to present a character as lovable as it was despicable, and
he danced with superb ease and bravado. Vivienne Segal, as the infatuated
society woman, delivered "Bewitched, Bothered and Bewildered" and "In
Our Little Den of Iniquity" with a cool literalness calculated to make the
most of their rhyming innuendoes, and June Havoc, as Gladys Bumps,
wrung the last drop of amusement from her portrait of an entertainer whose
intellectual ceiling was appallingly low. One of her songs ended with these
lines:

> "I'm a red hot mamma, but you're white and cold;
> Don't you know your mamma has a heart of gold;
> Though we're in those gray clouds, some day you'll spy
> That terrific rainbow over you and I."

But of all the satiric verses of *Pal Joey*, perhaps the most imperishable are
those of the horticultural ballet:

> "In the flower garden of my heart,
> I've got violets blue as your eyes;
> I've got dainty narcissus
> As sweet as my missus,
> And lilies pure as the skies.
> In the flower garden of my heart,
> I've got roses as red as your mouth;
> Just to keep our love holy
> I've got gladioli,
> And sunflowers fresh from the south.

But you are the artist,
And love is the art,
In the flower garden of my heart."

Only one more musical comedy, *By Jupiter* (1942), appeared before the
partners were separated by a personal disagreement. Hart based the book
and lyrics on *The Warrior's Husband*, by Julian F. Thompson, a play revealing the rule of the Amazons. Inversion of secondary sexual characteristics
was the running gag of *By Jupiter*, and Ray Bolger acted and danced his
way through the role of the pantywaist hero with consummate taste. Though
it was an amusing *jeu d'espirt*, *By Jupiter* by no means repeated the achievement of *Pal Joey*, which was one of the great escapades of the American
musical-comedy stage.

Rodgers and Hart were essentially an unaffected tunesmith and a quick-
trigger versifier, who developed only gradually the sophisticated artifices
and the taste for a drop of vitriol manifested by *I'd Rather Be Right* and *Pal
Joey*. At heart they were rather simple, often even sentimental, artisans,
ready to take at face value any workable book that came their way, and to
do their best to add a special touch to it. Cole Porter, on the other hand,
appears never to have been simple, never artless. Even in his early contributions to *Paris* and his first complete score, *Fifty Million Frenchmen*,
he took a detached, wry, and often incredulous attitude toward the characters
and contexts that were supplied him. A *mot* or a turn of phrase always meant
more to him than anything else about his work; give him a choice between
sacrificing the integrity of a character and sacrificing a rhyme, and he would
unhesitatingly sacrifice the character. He always was, and still is, primarily
a littérateur and genteel pornographer. Some of his songs have not had
much heart to them, but none has ever lacked a glittering surface. By
combining the functions of lyricist and composer, he has been able to keep
a remarkable uniformity of texture in his verse-and-song conceits; but lacking
a spontaneous sympathy for the homely traits of people, he has tended to
become categorical—to supply each new show with songs of several standardized types. Yet his inexhaustible urbanity and his easy flow of stylized
language and equally stylized music have made him the most reliable performer among American musical-comedy composers. No composer or lyricist
has achieved a larger proportion of hits, and not even Rodgers and Hart
have written a larger number of brilliant songs. Nor does he have only one
string to his bow; he functions with equal felicity in a topical patter song
like "You're the Top," an outright gag song like "Friendship," a pert exchange of amatory amenities like "I Get a Kick Out of You," and a broodingly
erotic ballad like "Night and Day."

It was in *Gay Divorce* (1932) that the world first became acquainted with
"Night and Day," which many consider if not the best, at least the archetypal,
example of Porter's gift for extending a long-lined, dusky melody far beyond
the usual confines of the standard thirty-two-bar structure. Porter showed

the expertness and individuality of his musical style in its bittersweet harmonies and well-prepared climax, and his impatience with convention in
such lines of the text as "I've an O such a hungry feeling under the hide of
me." Apart from "Night and Day" and one or two other songs, however,
Gay Divorce was all exterior and "bedroom fiddle-faddle," and is not one
of the noteworthy entries in the chronicle of its composer's career.

For several years in the middle 1930s, Porter maintained an extraordinary momentum. After *Gay Divorce*, each new piece was freshly triumphant. *Anything Goes* (1934) revealed an acuteness of perception and
calculation he has never surpassed. A shipboard piece, *Anything Goes* presented Victor Moore as an unseemly character for the first time; carrying
a machine gun and wearing the habiliments of a parson, he was in reality
a gangster pigeonholed as Public Enemy No. 1. This whimpering menace
was aided and abetted by William Gaxton, a man-about-town whose main
business was to capture the affections of the strident, trumpet-voiced Ethel
Merman. Between these two passed the compliments of "You're the Top,"
and Miss Merman was enabled to pull out all the stops in "Blow, Gabriel,
Blow." The handsome settings introduced a new and important designer to
musical comedy in Donald Oenslager. In its outlines, *Anything Goes* was
actually a conventional affair, but, as John Mason Brown said, "if it stays for
the most part within the time-honored limits of these conventions, it does
so only to make clear why it is that time has honored them."

Experiments in dramaturgy never interested Porter, then or later. The
usual shape and ordering of musical comedy, as these were handed down
from the 1920s, have always been adequate to his purposes, since he needs
no more than a reasonable excuse for songs and for the presence of capable
performers to give the songs their due. His conception of the relation of
music to a play has always been marked rather by a consummate mastery
of the usual practices than by any search for strikingly new devices.

On a trip around the world, Porter and Moss Hart wrote *Jubilee* (1935),
a merry dig at the British royal family that managed to find room for the
insinuating "Begin the Beguine," a song that was not nearly as popular when
Jubilee was at the Imperial Theatre as it became five or ten years later. *Red,
Hot and Blue* (1936), a loud piece about a lost girl who could be readily
identified because she once sat down on a red-hot waffle iron, pitted Miss
Merman's lungs (in "Ridin' High") against Jimmy Durante's nose, and for
good measure threw in the slapstick ballroom dancing of Paul and Grace
Hartman and the life-of-the-party personality of Bob Hope, with whom Miss
Merman shared the lyrics of "It's De-Lovely." In a sage comment to the
press, Vinton Freedley, the producer, pointed to a change of fashion in
chorus girls, a change that has persisted to our own day: "The hard type is
out, and so is the languid show girl of a few years ago, the stately peacock
who strutted downstage and flashed one little smile—at the orchestra conductor. Men nowadays like fresh, sweet girls—peppy and talented, yes, but
untheatrical."

In *Leave It to Me* (1938), Victor Moore, as the gift of Topeka, Kansas, to the diplomatic service, grappled piteously with foreign policy in the capacity of American ambassador to Russia. He shared top billing with Sophie Tucker, as a dominating ambassador's wife, and William Gaxton, as an omnipresent nuisance of a newspaper man. Moore was a lovable, henpecked simpleton, dreaming of the day he would be allowed to go back home, to order a double banana split at the corner drugstore and wash it down with sarsaparilla. In a scene in the Siberian vastness, an unknown singer, Mary Martin, performed a discreet striptease as she sang "My Heart Belongs to Daddy." After the opening night she was unknown no more.

Mistaken judgment caused Porter, in 1938, to ally himself with a small-scale musical comedy, *You Never Know*, derived from the play *Candlelight*, by Siegfried Geyer. Libby Holman made her last musical-comedy appearance in a role that gave her next to nothing to do, and Clifton Webb, Lupe Velez, and Rex O'Malley were among the other unhappy ones present. The following year (1939) Porter redeemed himself with *Du Barry Was a Lady*, in which Bert Lahr, as a washroom attendant, dreamed that he was Louis XV and that Ethel Merman was the lady of the title. Lahr gave one of the most remarkable performances of his career, a two-strata characterization in which words issued from the lips of the mincing, dandified king that he could only have heard in the washroom of the opening scene. The production, by Raoul Pène du Bois, was French and beautiful; Betty Grable acquainted the Broadway public with her legs; the chorus girls were lovely and animated. But under its veneer, B. G. de Sylva, its producer, intended *Du Barry Was a Lady* as a high-class modern low-brow smut show.

Panama Hattie (1940), with which De Sylva induced Porter to follow *Du Barry Was a Lady*, flung its dirt with a somewhat smaller pitchfork, but it again indicated that De Sylva was intent on recapturing the subintellectual audience for which he and Brown and Henderson had written in their days as musical-comedy authors. The sketches, blackouts, and dialogue of *Panama Hattie* ran to corn decidedly less green than that with which Ethel Barrymore was concerned that year; burlesque blue and the black of common dirt were the prevailing colors of the book—counterbalanced by the harmonious and gay pastel palette of Du Bois, again De Sylva's scenic designer. But smoking-room humor was balanced by sentimentality of purest ray serene when Miss Merman, as a Panamanian siren of dubious virtue, was called upon to lavish affection upon a small girl who strayed defenselessly into her life. Porter revealed an unwonted vein of bathos in her song, "What Say, Let's Be Buddies," but elsewhere spiked the score with many a piquant harmonic surprise and many a neat twist of sophisticated verse.

While these metropolitan revels thrived (though in infinitely smaller numbers than in the pre-Depression years), operetta showed its customary unwillingness to perish. The opening of the Center Theatre at Rockefeller Center, in 1932, posed a problem to the owners: With the big Radio City Music Hall a block up the street, there was no call for a second motion-picture house in the new development. After two unsatisfying years of devotion to the cinema, the Center Theatre was turned into a legitimate playhouse on September 22, 1934. The first attraction was *The Great Waltz,* Max Gordon's potpourri of waltzes by Johann Strauss, father and son, strung on a libretto alleged to have something to do with the facts of Strauss's life. Moss Hart made what passed for a book out of German sources, Marion Claire and Guy Robertson sang in it, Albertina Rasch worked out the sinuous group dances, Albert Johnson designed the settings, and Hassard Short directed. Good names, all of them; and everyone did all he could. As a result, *The Great Waltz,* in the inviting setting of the new theatre, prospered well, though nobody ever called it a work of art. The Center Theatre continued, after *The Great Waltz,* with similar items, such as *White Horse Inn* (1936) and *Virginia* (1937). But in time even the management tired of trying to find suitable spectacular operettas. In 1940, the house was turned over to an ice show, *It Happens on Ice,* and for a decade, until the habit was broken in 1950, almost nothing but skating was ever seen there.

Huge spectacles were for the most part impractical in the 1930s, since no money was available to finance them. The magic name of Max Reinhardt, however, was enough to obtain the $600,000 necessary to stage *The Eternal Road,* a pageant of Jewish history, at the Manhattan Opera House, with music by Kurt Weill and a book translated from the German of Franz Werfel. It was bigger, but not better, than *The Miracle,* with which, in 1924, Reinhardt's staging was shown to an American audience for the first time since *Sumurun.* The entire proscenium arch of the opera house was removed, and massive constructions of concrete were installed. As a result, the auditorium, made famous by Oscar Hammerstein's Manhattan Opera Company, has never been of any use theatrically since then, for its out-of-the-way location on West Thirty-fourth Street has made its restoration a questionable investment. Despite its 1,772 costumes, or perhaps because of them, *The Eternal Road* was as crushing a bore as New York theatre patrons ever saw.

Throughout the 1930s, old-fashioned girl-studded revues put in their appearance only at widely spaced intervals. George White sought to make a comeback in hard times by reducing his conception, in 1932, to the modest size implied by the title *George White's Music Hall Varieties.* He ventured a full-sized *Scandals,* with Bert Lahr, Rudy Vallee, and Willie and Eugene Howard, in 1935, and another, still with the Howard brothers, in 1939. Earl Carroll's activities were even more vestigial; he presented an economical *Sketch Book* in 1935, and made a final, wholly unsuccessful stab at the *Vanities* in 1940. The old names and the old ideas were quite played out.

After the death of Ziegfeld, the *Ziegfeld Follies* disappeared from the scene until 1934, when a new edition was offered under the nominal patronage of Mrs. Florenz Ziegfeld (Billie Burke), with Shubert backing. Fannie Brice was back, in her old form, with a revivalist sketch, "Soul-Saving Sadie," a travesty on a fan dance at Minsky's, and the first of her fruitful

Baby Snooks playlets. The production, however, lacked the intangible Ziegfeld touch. While it was competently put together, and undeniably furnished a good money's worth, it had more the scattered character of a Shubert *Passing Show* than the homogeneous texture of the old-time *Follies*. In 1936, the Shuberts produced another *Follies*, this time under their own name, retaining Fannie Brice, making an ill-starred attempt to win an American audience for Paris' admired Josephine Baker, and prettying things up with Minnelli settings that were the *dernier cri*—and, incidentally, Minnelli's last work for Broadway before he left to continue his meteoric career in Hollywood. After a seven-year lapse, the *Ziegfeld Follies* were once more revived, in 1943, under the three-way sponsorship of Alfred Bloomingdale, Lou Walters, and the Shuberts. Though the show was handsome in a conventional way, with Watson Barratt décors, not even Robert Alton's exciting dances could counterbalance the fact that Milton Berle, Arthur Treacher, Ilona Massey, and Sue Ryan were all too far removed from the classic days of the *Follies* to know what it meant to be in them.

A more appropriate Shubert revue, because it geared present-day performers to present-day humors, was *The Streets of Paris* (1939). The last revue produced by the Shuberts, except for the *Ziegfeld Follies of 1943*, *The Streets of Paris* was so heavily loaded with talent that bargain-counter settings and a helter-skelter mode of presentation did not reduce its merriment. Bobby Clark sang "I'm Robert the Roué, of Reading P-a." Bud Abbott and Lou Costello emerged from limbo to become first-line comics overnight. Carmen Miranda came from South America, and, flanked by six suave Brazilians, wore headdresses of flowers and fruit, and cackled apparently sly little songs in Portuguese. Jean Sablon purred his café song, "Le Fiacre," with appropriate hoofbeats in the orchestra. Ramón Vinay, later a leading tenor at the Metropolitan Opera, had an inconspicuous assignment. Ben Dova performed his immortal drunk act, performing feats bordering on levitation as he hung perilously from a bending lamppost.

Even cheaper in outlay than *The Streets of Paris* was *Hellzapoppin*, a frank compendium of vaudeville acts over which the slapstick comedians Ole Olsen and Chic Johnson presided, and to which they gave countless foot pounds of personal energy. No attraction for thinking people, *Hellzapoppin* drew a huge popular audience, and kept its originators in work for three years, after which it was easy enough for them to assemble *Sons o' Fun* (1941) and *Laffing Room Only* (1944) without changing the formula an iota. The quick money that came rolling in for *Hellzapoppin* at the Forty-sixth Street Theatre box office led other producers to hope that a vaudeville bill disguised by a revue title would bring similar riches to them. Ed Wynn did well with *Boys and Girls Together* (1940), and so did the sponsors of other mixed bills called *Priorities of 1942* (with Lou Holtz, Willie Howard, Phil Baker, Paul Draper, and Hazel Scott), *Top-Notchers* (1942) (with Argentinita, Federico Rey, Pilar Lopez, Walter O'Keefe, Gracie Fields, and

A. Robbins), *Show Time* (1942) (with George Jessel, Jack Haley, Ella Logan, and the De Marcos), and *Laugh Time* (1943) (with Ethel Waters, Frank Fay, Bert Wheeler, Buck and Bubbles, and the incredible dog act known as The Bricklayers). The public soon found, however, that these tiresome titles were attached to equally tiresome exhumations of ancient acts and songs, and the vaudeville revival ceased as abruptly as it had begun.

XXII. War and Postwar Years

THE SECOND WORLD WAR gave Broadway fresh impetus. Prosperity, or something that passed for it, was back again, and a big new audience, composed partly of servicemen, had discovered the legitimate theatre. At the Stage Door Canteen and in their tours of army camps here and abroad, theatre folk had discovered that their gifts as entertainers were valuable to morale. A fresh ardor pervaded Broadway, and each new musical show seemed to be more exciting than it actually was.

Cole Porter was one of the first to react to the mood of the times, with *Let's Face It* (1941), a musical version of *Cradle Snatchers*, a farce written in 1927 by Russell Medcraft and Norma Mitchell. Herbert and Dorothy Fields brought the book up to the minute by involving three ladies at a rest camp in complications with Danny Kaye and Benny Baker, who appeared as inductees in the Army. A scene detailing the tribulations of the soldiers drafted under the new universal conscription law was inserted for topical laughs, and Kaye was a tireless, rapid-fire corporal. The wittiest song, however, had nothing to do with military affairs; it was a diatribe against rural life entitled "Farming."

Let's Face It barely scratched the surface of wartime subject matter, for the United States did not enter the war until more than a month after it opened. Porter's *Something for the Boys* (1943), genuinely a wartime diversion, was placed in and near an army camp, with Ethel Merman as a girl who could receive radio messages through the fillings in her teeth. Jack Cole's dances were a stroke of genius. Without being mere drills, they were built out of military formations, except for a big party scene, which maintained a similar regularity of design by employing square-dance figures. Toward the end of the evening, with little or no excuse for it in the plot, Ethel Merman amazed her audience by abandoning her characteristic ramrod stance, donning moccasins and a long, black, stringy Indian wig, and intoning duet-wise with Paula Laurence one of Porter's most convulsing trick-rhyme songs, "By the Mis-sis-si-ni-wa"—or, as the music actually went, "By the Mis-sis-sis-sis-sis-sis-sis-sis-sin-i-wa," which rhymed terminally with "since you've been awa'."

After getting a decidedly second-class inspiration, *Mexican Hayride*, out of the way as a piece for Bobby Clark, Porter turned his thoughts to Billy Rose's new brainchild, the revue *Seven Lively Arts*, which opened at the Ziegfeld Theatre on December 7, 1944. *Seven Lively Arts* was devised by Billy Rose as a costly token of his proprietorship of the handsome Joseph Urban-designed theatre, into the possession of which he had only recently, and very proudly, come. As though the musical contributions of Porter were not sufficient ornament for so monumental a landmark in Broadway history, Rose engaged Igor Stravinsky to compose a score for a *ballet blanc* choreographed by Anton Dolin, in which Dolin and Alicia Markova were the leading dancers. This piece, known subsequently as *Scènes de Ballet*, and now a feature of the Sadler's Wells repertory, was less to the liking of a majority of the customers than Porter's songs and Jack Donahue's typical musical-comedy dance routines.

Rose spent a fair share of the $350,000 production money of *Seven Lively Arts* upon the hire of a stable of big names, but unhappily he was not able to require his authors to supply top-drawer ideas, nor could he receive full value from performers supplied with second-class material. Beatrice Lillie carried much of the show on her shoulders, with Bert Lahr helping out as effectively as circumstances would allow. Ben Hecht wrote comments for Doctor Rockwell to deliver. Moss Hart, George S. Kaufman, and several other schooled practitioners wrote sketches, which were directed by Philip Loeb. Norman Bel Geddes devised the settings and Mary Shaw and Valentina the costumes. Robert Shaw trained the chorus, and Maurice Abravanel conducted the orchestra. Hassard Short took care of the lighting and staged the ensemble numbers. Opening-night customers paid $24 for orchestra seats and were served champagne in the intermission. Perhaps there were too many expensive chefs. At any rate, *Seven Lively Arts* failed to jell, and it is still spoken of nostalgically as something that might have been wonderful, but wasn't.

In his next assignment, *Around the World* (1946), Porter's songs were again obliterated by too elaborate a superstructure. In attempting to return the Jules Verne romance to the Broadway musical stage, Orson Welles—who was author, director, and one of the principal actors—simply had too many ideas. The production, wrote Howard Barnes in the *Herald Tribune*, "combines silent movies, Hoboken melodramatic satire, a magic show and Olsen and Johnson japes in a singular potpourri." Robert Davison provided a resourceful stage setting equipped with panels at right and left, in which miniature scenes were enacted while the bigger ones among the thirty-two different settings were prepared on the main stage—which, in turn, was so planned that the front and back halves could be used either separately or together. *Around the World* had everything from an elaborate circus at Yokohama (with acrobats and tightrope walkers) to a breathtaking pint-size reproduction of a western railroad train falling through a trestle. Welles himself overacted in classic fashion as the Copper's Knark, and Arthur Mar-

getson gave a drily self-contained, and very British, performance as Phileas
Fogg. But there was too much staging; the script was laborious and weak,
despite Welles's efforts to gag and trick it up; and Nelson Barclift's choreography was as feeble as Porter's songs, which were about the poorest he
ever wrote.

These two disasters—*Seven Lively Arts* and *Around the World*—cast a
long and depressing shadow over Porter's reputation in the theatrical world.
He was finished, people said; never would we hear more of the inventive
rhymes and the well-pointed tunes that brought his fame. *Kiss Me, Kate*
(1948) routed the prophets of gloom, and proved, if anything, that Porter
was at the peak of his powers, and needed only the help of a good book to
bring forward a spate of songs as exhilarating as any he had supplied since
Anything Goes.

For their libretto, Bella and Samuel Spewack used the play-within-a-
play device, striking a parallel between the real-life conduct of an acting
couple—divorced but still in love—and the behavior of Katharine and Petruchio in a road-company performance of Shakespeare's *The Taming of the
Shrew* in Baltimore. *Kiss Me, Kate* was one of those well-favored musical
comedies that got off on the right foot, apparently, from the first planning
stages, and never got off it. It was superlatively handled in every department,
and each contribution was perfectly geared to the others. Hanya Holm's
choreography, wider in range than the work of most of her more celebrated
contemporaries, covered a gamut, as *Variety* put it, "from ballet to hot
hoofing," and always seemed to come up with the proper ideas at the proper
time. Lemuel Ayers' designs for the scenes and the costumes and John C.
Wilson's perceptive and expressive stage direction added the final polish to
the performances of a personable cast headed by Alfred Drake as Petruchio
and Patricia Morison as Katharine. And what a brilliant and diversified set
of seventeen songs the rejuvenated Cole Porter turned out! *Kiss Me, Kate*
was perhaps the only Porter score in which not a single song was weak or
careless. The musical literature of Broadway was perceptibly enriched by
such deft pieces as "I Hate Men," "Wunderbar" (with its vicious parody of
Viennese operetta music), "So in Love Am I," and the extroverted "I've
Come to Wive It Wealthily in Padua," in which the name of the city rhymed
with "what a cad you are" and "how mad you are." Obviously Cole Porter
belongs to the future of the musical stage as well as to the past.

No sooner had Pearl Harbor been attacked than Irving Berlin began to
talk about reviving and expanding *Yip, Yip, Yaphank*, the revue he wrote
and appeared in during the First World War. Until this war began, however,
he remained faithful to escapist materials. Returning from Hollywood, he
contributed the music and lyrics of *Louisiana Purchase* (1940), a piece
vaguely satirizing the Huey Long régime, which was less engaging for its
materials than for the knowing performances of Victor Moore, William Gaxton, Irene Bordoni, and Vera Zorina, and for the fresh impression given by
Carol Bruce's youthful singing.

Berlin then contracted to provide some of the songs for Michael Todd's revue, *Star and Garter* (1942), along with Harold Rome and Harold Arlen. Todd's revue was based on the assumption that since the Minsky burlesque houses had been closed by legal action, it was a logical move to bring burlesque into the big time at a $4.80 top. He spared no cost with Harry Horner's tasteful settings and Irene Sharaff's equally attractive costumes, and he entrusted the direction to a wise showman, Hassard Short. As a result, even Gypsy Rose Lee's lyric and classical stripping and Carrie Finnell's flamboyant exhibition of mammalian control did not keep *Star and Garter* from seeming much like any other well-mounted revue lucky enough to boast Bobby Clark as its star. In *Peep Show* (1950) Todd again sought to dress up burlesque for the carriage trade, this time with Bobby Clark as stage director.

Only ten days after the opening of *Star and Garter*, Berlin took part in the première of *This Is the Army*, at the Broadway Theatre, on the carefully chosen date of July 4. *This Is the Army* was the show Berlin had in mind when he talked of reviving *Yip, Yip, Yaphank*. In the course of preparation it took on a wholly different character, and about the only resemblance it bore to its predecessor lay in its all-soldier cast, and the reminiscent voice of Berlin singing "Oh, How I Hate to Get Up in the Morning."

Under the stress of patriotic wartime emotion, *This Is the Army* provided an incomparable experience. The three hundred military participants had been drilled and rehearsed to the last degree of precision. More important, they had been given good material to work with, and Sergeant Ezra Stone's direction was on the same high level as Berlin's vivacious score. A scene representing the Stage Door Canteen, with soldier impersonators of such luminaries as Jane Cowl, Lynn Fontanne, and Gypsy Rose Lee, attained instant fame, though other more masculine features of the show were equally worthy of praise for their entirely professional pace and presentation. In the last analysis, the most stirring moments were the massed scenes in which purely military formations and drills were turned into genuine choreography, under the direction of Private Robert Sidney and Corporal Nelson Barclift. The effectiveness of the spectacle was enhanced in September by the addition of a new finale, in which the entire stage was triumphantly filled by uniformed men with upraised and crossed bayonets, ready to go to war.

Returning to civilian considerations at the end of the war, Berlin turned out, with the expert literary cooperation of Herbert and Dorothy Fields, the biggest popular success of his Broadway career in *Annie Get Your Gun* (1946). Ethel Merman spanned two New York seasons in the title role of Annie Oakley, the Ohio girl who could outshoot the best shots in Buffalo Bill's Wild West show. Mary Martin headed a "national company" in 1947. Duplications were presented, with immense éclat, in London and in Australia, and a Parisian version, with Lily Fayol as a gunwoman of Montmartre stripe, triumphed under the title *Annie du Far-West*.

Annie Get Your Gun was completely devoid of novelty or aesthetic risks. It was a thoroughly standardized product, produced by Richard Rodgers and Oscar Hammerstein 2d with unerring comprehension of all the ingredients and proportions of the recipe for success, handsomely designed by Jo Mielziner, and staged by Joshua Logan with rare common sense. The Fields duo had learned by now, perhaps better than anyone else in the book-writing business, how to tell a story without wasting a word; and Berlin, on a high wave of inventiveness, dotted the score with such superlatively efficacious songs as "Doin' What Comes Naturally," "Show Business," "You Can't Get a Man with a Gun," and "They Say It's Wonderful." Helen Tamiris reverted to high, wide, and handsome devices of traditional musical-comedy choreography in a ballet depicting the induction of Annie Oakley into the Sioux tribe, and offered a counterargument to those who had been led by some of Agnes de Mille's ballets to believe that musical-comedy dancing should wear its art on its sleeve. Neither Miss Merman nor Ray Middleton, as her heart interest Frank Butler, let the authors or the composer down for a minute. As Robert Garland observed in the *Journal-American*: "She's no longer Miss Merman acting like Ethel Merman. She's Miss Merman acting like Annie Oakley."

In the summer of 1941, George Abbott, contemplating plans for autumn production, gave thought to the probable effects of universal army conscription upon male actors of draft age. Why go to the expense of putting together a potential hit show, he reasoned, only to see its cast and chorus progressively depleted by the inexorable action of the selective service boards? Why not produce a show with a cast well below the minimum draft age, and thus guarantee the permanence of its personnel? The cast and book of *Best Foot Forward* (1941) were the result of this consideration. John Cecil Holm, author of *Three Men on a Horse*, a farce Abbott had directed with conspicuous success (transformed in 1941 into a musical comedy, *Banjo Eyes*, for Eddie Cantor), put together a serviceable libretto about a Hollywood siren who put in her disruptive appearance at an innocent prep-school prom. Abbott held countrywide auditions for new talent, and discovered, among others, the rough-and-ready Nancy Walker and an appealing little colleen named Maureen Cannon. Rosemary Lane—later supplanted by Joy Hodges—was the visiting motion-picture queen. Ralph Martin, who had supplied vocal arrangements for *Pal Joey*, *Louisiana Purchase*, and several other prominent musical comedies, composed a first score so copious that *Best Foot Forward* sometimes tended to turn into a cantata. But the piece was quite winning, for the youngsters carried out their tasks in a candid and unassuming way, and raised the roof with their rousing football song, "Buckle Down, Winsocki, Buckle Down."

In *Beat the Band* (1942), his next musical production, Abbott turned to the glorification of jive, jitterbugging, and hepcat interests. A fierce and noisy postadolescent revel composed by Johnny Green, who had once supplied Libby Holman with "Body and Soul," *Beat the Band* relied chiefly upon its two orchestras, on the stage and in the pit, reaching its climax midway in the second act with the hot trumpet licks of Leonard Sues in "Steam Is on the Beam." Some of the songs sounded to Brooks Atkinson "less like music than the clearing of a throat," and often seemed to have "no notes at all." But there were stunning sets by Samuel Leve and costumes by Freddy Wittop (known as Federico Rey when he engages in Spanish dancing), energetic dancing by Doris York and Marc Platt (Marc Platoff of the Ballet Russe de Monte Carlo, who dropped the Russian suffix and restored his original Seattle patronymic when he went into show business), and passable choreography by David Lichine, in his Broadway bow. The run of *Beat the Band* was constricted, however, by its specialized appeal, and by a threadbare book detailing the romance of Jack Whiting, as a band leader, and Susan Miller, as a Caribbean actress.

In contrast to *Beat the Band*, whose stridency only a confirmed jive addict could love, *On the Town* (1944) was a youthful fancy nearly everyone loved. Produced by the new team of Oliver Smith and Paul Feigay, themselves not yet out of their twenties, *On the Town* was an extension and amplification of a ballet, *Fancy Free*, which Leonard Bernstein, as composer, and Jerome Robbins, as choreographer, had conceived for Ballet Theatre. Since a full-length musical comedy, unlike a ballet, needed a book, one was provided by Betty Comden and Adolph Green, fresh and unspoiled humorists who had climbed to attention through their informal performances in a Greenwich Village basement café.

Though its central characters were three sailors and the girls they met on shore leave, *On the Town* was in every way one of the most literate works Broadway had yet produced. While the audience was not aware of it (so spontaneous were the antics of the youngsters), the carefree story was firmly controlled by an exceptional amount of strictly formal planning of the music and the choreography. Bernstein was eager to demonstrate that all manner of structural subtleties could be concealed under the happy-go-lucky rhythmic exterior of the Broadway tunes, and when the extended ballet episodes came along he was ready to cope with them with a musical command such as only Kurt Weill had hitherto been able to call upon. Robbins' dance designs were equally seriously conceived, and the dances and the music were born together, through painstaking daily colloquy between composer and choreographer. At its best *On the Town* was supremely imaginative, with Oliver Smith's settings and Alvin Colt's costumes conspiring with the music, the dances, the earthy comedy of Nancy Walker, and the fleet grace of Sono Osato to give a lively yet poetic panorama of "New York, New York." Manhattan has not been so buoyantly treated by its own theatre people since that time.

In *Billion Dollar Baby* (1945), their second and last joint production, Feigay and Smith undertook a satire of the 1920s, a decade now become—to the bewilderment of those who felt they had quite recently lived through it—an object of derision to the younger generation. Betty Comden and Adolph Green upheld their standard of *On the Town* in the lyrics and book, George Abbott's direction was blunt and funny, and Oliver Smith's settings were broadly to the point. But Jerome Robbins, though he had investigated the Charleston and other manifestations of the era in question, lacked a firsthand feeling for the requirements of the dancing, and only those who could not actually remember the 1920s felt that he had quite equaled his accomplishment in *On the Town*. For *High Button Shoes* (1947), on the other hand, Robbins dreamed up a parody of Mack Sennett's Keystone Cops and bathing beauties which was a convulsing interlude in an otherwise bromidic musical-comedy flashback to the year 1913.

The cessation of hostilities quickly returned a great many actors to civilian life. To celebrate their demobilization, and also to earn a little money, a group of veterans got together for a revue, *Call Me Mister* (1946), containing mementoes of military life and impressions of the nonmilitary existence seen from the ex-fighting-man's perspective. Harold Rome wrote songs and lyrics more innocuous and less tinged with social protest than those of *Pins and Needles*, setting the tone for a show that was pleasant enough, but devoid of distinction. The timeliness of *Call Me Mister* earned it a profitable run.

The first revue since the *Ziegfeld Follies of 1943*, *Call Me Mister* encouraged new faith in nonbook shows, especially when prepared in terms of a restricted budget. Several subsequent revues were launched, of which *Lend an Ear* (1948) and *Small Wonder* (1948) were much the cleverest. Dating back several years to an informal revue first given at Carnegie Institute of Technology in Pittsburgh, and later in a summer theatre at Cohasset, Massachusetts, *Lend an Ear* brought back from Hollywood a former Carnegie Tech student, William Eythe, who had been seen by film scouts for the first time at Cohasset. It also focused attention upon Carol Channing, who in 1949 triumphantly appeared as Lorelei Lee in the musical version of Anita Loos's *Gentlemen Prefer Blondes*. *Small Wonder* employed nineteen performers, one of whom was Tom Ewell as the Normal Neurotic, to present its skeptical and critically oriented sketches and its slick dancing, choreographed by Gower Champion. The adroit lyrics, if anything too sophisticated, were by Phyllis McGinley and Billings Brown, another name for Burt Shevelove, who was also director and co-producer.

One of the indirect effects of the war was a renewed enthusiasm for that perennial escapist form of entertainment, the operetta. The best-considered efforts in this field were those of Yolanda Merö-Irion's New Opera Company. Along with more serious endeavors along the lines of grand opera, the company, with Lodewick Vroom, produced *Rosalinda* (1942), the brilliant Max Reinhardt version of Strauss's *Die Fledermaus*. The gracious Jarmila Novotna of the Metropolitan Opera sang the title role in *Helen Goes to Troy* (1944), a rather ruthlessly modernized variant of Offenbach's *La Belle*

Hélène. The production was superbly mounted, with settings and lighting by Robert Edmond Jones, in one of his rare concessions to light entertainment; with choreography by Léonide Massine, stage direction by Herbert Graf of the Metropolitan, and gleaming costumes by Ladislas Czettel; and with Erich Wolfgang Korngold, himself a composer of reputation, as conductor. In the same year, Felix Brentano directed for the New Opera Company a handsome revival of *The Merry Widow*, with the delectable Marta Eggert as the Widow, and her husband, Jan Kiepura, every inch an operatic tenor in the part of Prince Danilo. George Balanchine choreographed the waltz and the attendant divertissements with charm and taste; Howard Bay designed the settings, and Walter Florell the costumes. A luxuriant opéra-bouffe revival of Offenbach's *La Vie Parisienne* was also accomplished, in 1945, before the New Opera Company fell short of funds. Massine again supplied the choreography and Czettel the costumes. Ralph Herbert directed, and Richard Rychtarik created the settings. All these New Opera Company productions, like its concomitant staging of Verdi's *Macbeth*, were enormously admired, but only *Rosalinda* prospered.

Balanchine was responsible for much of the success of *Song of Norway* (1944), a pastiche of rearranged Grieg music and bogus biography brought from the Pacific Coast by Edwin Lester. Because the plot, fortunately, was too spare to fill the whole evening, Balanchine tacked on at the end a long, elaborate, and cleanly composed ballet, also entitled "Song of Norway," in which, for three weeks at the start, Alexandra Danilova and Frederic Franklin of the Ballet Russe de Monte Carlo participated. A full year of prosperity for *Song of Norway* induced Lester to bring *Gypsy Love* eastward in 1946. A crude coalition of Victor Herbert's *The Fortune Teller* and *The Serenade*, it was a hopeless botch from the first.

Meanwhile Kiepura and Miss Eggert, finished with touring in *The Merry Widow*, dedicated themselves to *Polonaise* (1945), a wallow of sentiment and Polish nationalism in which a great deal of Chopin music was mired. The Ballet Russe suffered one more depredation in the engagement of Tatiana Riabouchinska as *prima ballerina*.

Richard Tauber, another celebrated tenor, followed Kiepura's example, making his first, last, and only Broadway appearance—subject to constant absences caused by the illness that led to his death the next year—in Lehár's *Yours Is My Heart* (1946). In 1947, Bobby Clark did his best to reanimate Herbert's *Sweethearts* by injecting into it his special prescription of horseplay. In the same year, Oskar Straus's *The Chocolate Soldier* failed to make much headway, despite fashionable settings by Jo Mielziner and extensive choreography by Balanchine. A still more disastrous box-office calamity was *Music in My Heart* (1947), an attempt to prove, by means of snippets of Tchaikovsky's music and half a dozen really handsome ballets choreographed by Ruth Page, that the true secret of the Russian composer's melancholia was his unrequited love for a French singer named Desirée Artot. *Mag-*

dalena, staged on the West Coast by Homer Curran in the summer of 1948 and brought to New York that fall, misrepresented life in South America, to a musical score of loudly orchestrated rag-bag leavings by Heitor Villa-Lobos. Since that time it cannot be said that traditional operetta has enjoyed a favorable standing on Broadway, though one of its perennial resuscitations may always occur on a moment's notice.

Bordering on operetta were two period musical comedies offered to the wartime escapist audience. *Bloomer Girl* (1944) evoked the militant feminism of Dolly Bloomer, with artful costumes by Miles White, lilting music by Harold Arlen, and an Agnes de Mille ballet that viewed the Civil War in gloomy terms. *Up in Central Park* (1945) returned Sigmund Romberg to the theatre as the composer for Herbert and Dorothy Fields' quiet and agreeable memento of Tammany's heyday. An ice-skating ballet, devised by Helen Tamiris in the manner of Frederik Ashton's *Les Patineurs*, was especially felicitous.

The Theatre Guild contributed to the prevailing mood of nostalgia by asking Elie Siegmeister to arrange a "salute to American folk and popular music," *Sing Out, Sweet Land* (1944). A rather bloodless compendium of Americana, its best features were the ballad singing of the jovial Burl Ives and the neatly patterned dances devised by Doris Humphrey and Charles Weidman, for whom this was the last joint undertaking. Events of still less moment in the early 1940s were Hoagy Carmichael's debut as a musical-comedy song writer in an abortive nonsense starring Kitty Carlisle, *Walk with Music* (1940), and Al Jolson's momentary return to the stage, with Martha Raye, in *Hold On to Your Hats*, an attractively produced show with music by Burton Lane and lyrics by E. Y. Harburg—the pair who later cooperated in *Finian's Rainbow*.

Fantasy had returned to the musical theatre with *I Married an Angel*. The trend was carried further by *Cabin in the Sky* (1940), an imaginative exposition of the Negro folk outlook upon life, death, and immortality. While *Cabin in the Sky* awakened overtones of the classic Negro fantasy *The Green Pastures*, its presentation was more sophisticated, at the same time that its plot and characterization retained no less connection with the realities of everyday life. The action presented the struggle between Lucifer, Jr., and the Lawd's General for the soul of Little Joe, who had a hard time remembering to be good. Petunia, with her deep faith in prayer, assisted the Lawd's General, while the worldly Georgia Brown did her best to add force to the devil's overtures. Ethel Waters, as Petunia, and Katherine Dunham, as Georgia Brown, were perfectly cast and ideally contrasted in style. Todd Duncan, the Porgy of *Porgy and Bess*, sang admirably as the Lawd's General, and Dooley Wilson portrayed the pathetic Little Joe with an instinct that was infallible. George Balanchine and Miss Dunham both had a hand in the choreography, which was as wide in range and as brilliant in execution as any the Broadway stage has seen to this day. Vernon Duke (whose alter ego is Vladimir Dukelsky, the symphonic composer) composed his one genuinely distinguished light score, and John La Touche made his first reputation with the happily turned lyrics.

After *Cabin in the Sky*, Miss Dunham and her company struck out on their own, returning intermittently to Broadway in fast-paced revues compounded of Caribbean folk and American jazz evocations. Her most elaborate production, *Carib Song* (1945), bogged down under the weight of Baldwin Bergerson's music and William Archibald's book; and Mary Hunter's direction was not able to save it. Miss Dunham and her company have always, since *Cabin in the Sky*, succeeded best in their most informal endeavors.

Miss Dunham once undertook the choreography for a musical play in which she and her company did not appear. *Windy City* (1946), which opened at the Shubert Great Northern Theatre in Chicago and never came to New York, brushed within an inch of success, but somehow its picture of life on the South Side of Chicago, decorated by some of Jo Mielziner's most striking settings, never quite jelled. Perhaps the chief trouble was Walter Jurman's watery imitation-Rachmaninoff music; for Philip Yordan's book was cogently put together. Miss Dunham has never created a more breathtaking dance than one that was performed up, down, and around the steel pillars of an elevated railroad structure.

Windy City was potentially a better conceived venture than *Beggar's Holiday* (1946), which borrowed from it the opening scene of the blank wall of a building, with a high catwalk upon which various people scurried about. John La Touche planned his book as a modern interpretation of John Gay's *The Beggar's Opera*, and in a measure it was successful. But his love of verbiage got the better of him in the lyrics, and Duke Ellington, drafted into the musical-comedy field for the first time, revealed an almost complete inability to relate his musical compositions to dramatic situations. Oliver Smith and Walter Florell accomplished spectacular results with the settings and costumes; and Valerie Bettis revealed glimmerings of her powerful talent despite the amorphousness of her first choreographic contributions to Broadway. As an object lesson in democracy, a mixed cast of Negro and white performers—headed by Alfred Drake, Zero Mostel, Avon Long, Bernice Parks, and Mildred Smith—was employed, and for the first time Broadway saw a white man make love to a Negro girl in simple, natural terms. Everyone wanted *Beggar's Holiday* to succeed, but it could not, for it was too chaotic.

Far happier as a demonstration of the gifts of Negro artists had been Billy Rose's production of *Carmen Jones* (1943). In the hope of giving immediacy to the Carmen story, Rose engaged Oscar Hammerstein 2d to rewrite the libretto. Hammerstein changed the locale to North Carolina, where a tobacco factory is quite as normal a phenomenon as the original cigarette-manufacturing establishment in Seville. Retaining the main features of the Meilhac and Halévy libretto, Hammerstein performed the seemingly impossible feat of transferring its people and incidents into entirely different ethnic surroundings. Since a large part of Bizet's music was re- tained, somewhat caponized at times by Robert Russell Bennett's editing and reorchestration, Hammerstein applied his phenomenal skill to the task of writing lyrics that were appropriate and believable in diction, faithful to the meaning of the original, and equipped with satisfactory vowel sounds.

With Muriel Smith and Muriel Rahn alternating in the title role, *Carmen Jones* aroused 231 audiences to enthusiasm by the directness and force with which the dramatic action made its points. Charles Friedman, who staged the book, taught his actors economy and well-pointed ensemble playing. Eugene Loring, abandoning his dancing functions with Ballet Theatre, was alive with choreographic ideas, and the dancing of his severely trained group proved to be perhaps the most telling single feature of the staging, upon which Hassard Short kept a supervisory eye. Howard Bay's settings—so elaborate that they occupied more than their fair share of the floor space—employed a unique device of color. Each scene was a monochrome. Both scenes of the first act (outside the factory, and by a roadside) were yellow. The scene in the café "run by my friend Billy Pastor" was purple. The country club which replaced Bizet's smugglers' scene in the mountains was blue. The final scene, not technically a monochrome, was done in red, black, and white. Raoul Pène du Bois designed the costumes for each scene either in obedience to the ruling color or in subtle counterpoints to it.

Less persuasive as a spectacle, because it was overelaborate, was Robert Edmond Jones's treatment of the settings and costumes for Michael Myer- berg's well-intended production of *Lute Song* (1946), an adaptation by Sidney Howard and Will Irwin of a Chinese classic, *Pi-Pa-Ki*. Nearly everything was misconceived about *Lute Song*. The story, concerned with two women in love with the same man, was thrown out of focus when Mary Martin was engaged for the cast. An established star since *One Touch of Venus*, Miss Martin dominated the stage to a degree that was not warranted, and ap- parently nobody was able to persuade her that a touch of Broadway song- plugging was out of place in the hollow songs Raymond Scott wrote for her. When Dolly Haas replaced Miss Martin as partner to Yul Brynner on the tour, a better balance was established, but it was too late.

In a mixed vein of fantasy and realism, *The Day Before Spring* (1945) investigated—not without overtones of *Lady in the Dark*—the psychic life of a married woman who, at a college reunion, met the man she did not marry, and came within an inch of running off with him—an act which would have spoiled everything for her, since she really loved her husband all the time. This tale, supplied with ineffectual dream ballets choreographed by Antony Tudor (in his introduction to Broadway) and danced by Mary Ellen Moylan and Hugh Laing, was woven into a musical comedy of smooth texture, in which the songs and dances grew naturally out of the contexts of the action. The piece enjoyed no more than a *succès d'estime*, for it was rather pale, and became uncomfortable in a scene in which Irene Manning, as the wife, listened to advice from Plato, Freud, and Voltaire. To the composer, Frederick Loewe, and the author of the book and lyrics, Alan Jay Lerner (previously represented only by *What's Up* in 1943), it provided an opportunity to sharpen the talents they were soon to call upon in *Brigadoon*.

Fantasy took full possession of the affections of the New York public in *Finian's Rainbow* (1947), which added the Irish town of Glocca Morra to the map of Broadway's never-never-land. Finian McLonergan, accompanied by his irresistible daughter Sharon, had come from Ireland to the United States in order to bury in the Rainbow Valley in Missitucky a pot of gold Finian had stolen from the leprechauns. Og, a lithe and indefatigable leprechaun, had followed them in the hope of getting it back. The conventional features of the plot hinged upon the pot-of-gold situation; but much of the energy of the librettist was devoted to the task of giving Senator Billboard Rawlings of Missitucky, an ardent advocate of white supremacy, a satisfactory dressing-down. With remarkable adroitness, *Finian's Rainbow* slid back and forth between the imaginary realm of the leprechauns and the uncomfortably real world of race prejudice. Michael Kidd's flexible choreography, in which it was difficult to tell when action was ending and dance was beginning, served as the chief emollient in a play whose opposing elements ought normally to have engendered a great deal of friction. Equal credit for the believable realization of the conceit was due to Bretaigne Windust, who left the nonmusical field of *Life with Father* and other plays to apply his directorial skill to *Finian's Rainbow*.

The main parts of the two McLonergans, the leprechaun, and the girl who made him renounce leprechaunship in favor of a human existence, were all characterized and presented with unusual felicity. Albert Sharpe, imported from Ireland, was pricelessly right as Finian. Ella Logan, as Sharon, knew how to make the audience lose its heart both to her and to Glocca Morra with the first phrase of her singing. David Wayne accomplished the unlikely trick of imbuing a leprechaun with manly proclivities. Anita Alvarez, whose role compelled her to remain mute through most of the evening, conversed fluently with her dancing. In every regard *Finian's Rainbow* bordered upon first-class lyric drama, except that most of it, when one took it home and thought it over, was not as distinctive in artistic substance as it had seemed to be in the theatre.

Fantasy without social preachment was the métier of *Brigadoon* (1947). The plot, a variant on the *Connecticut Yankee* device, told of the encounter of two disillusioned Americans with the inhabitants of a mysterious Scots village which appeared from nowhere once every hundred years, and where the archaic folkways never changed. A piece that might easily have turned into a commonplace, milk-and-water operetta was made captivating by the perceptive direction of Robert Lewis, who knows better how to make a fantasy credible than most of our régisseurs, and by the strong dances choreographed by Agnes de Mille.

In several earlier musical comedies—*Oklahoma!*, *Carousel*, and *Bloomer
Girl* among them—Miss de Mille had demonstrated that the choreography
of a Broadway show could be a reasonable extension and amplification of
the plot. *Brigadoon*, however, was her chef d'oeuvre, and she has not had
occasion to equal her work in it since. Not only did the dances originate
spontaneously in the plot, but Miss de Mille explored an artistic dimension
beyond that of the materials she had used before. The impressive funeral
ceremonial, accompanied only by the snarling wail of bagpipes, would not
have seemed out of place in the most serious ballet, nor would the traditional
sword dance which James Mitchell performed with superb élan during the
wedding ceremony.

The score by Frederick Loewe amounted to less than the dancing. He
was too ready to abandon the vein of Scotch folk music, which brought him
his most attractive results toward the beginning, in favor of desultory love
songs, whose routine aspect was enhanced by some of Alan Jay Lerner's
lyrics.

The death of Kurt Weill in April 1950 removed from the American
musical theatre its most accomplished craftsman. In Germany, before the
Hitler régime forced him out, Weill attained an immense reputation for a
series of stage pieces that reflected the confusion and moral unrest of the
post-war period. The most famous of these, his paraphrase of Gay's *The
Beggar's Opera* entitled *Die Dreigroschen-Oper*, was presented in New
York in 1933, with a cast unable to handle either its pithy style or its
intellectual outlook, under the title *The Three-Penny Opera*. Its innuendo
and sardonic manner were beyond the grasp of an American audience that
felt no need for that particular form of expression, and one of the most
remarkable satiric efforts of the twentieth century withered after twelve
performances. Later on, those who attended French motion pictures were
given a second chance to admire the work, in René Clair's *L'Opéra de Quat'
Sous*.

Weill came to the United States to live soon afterward, and in 1936
wrote the pungent incidental music for the Group Theatre's memorable
production of Paul Green's play *Johnny Johnson*. His second American
assignment, in 1937, was *The Eternal Road*. In 1938 he formed what looked
at first glance like an unlikely partnership with Maxwell Anderson, to write
Knickerbocker Holiday, a musical comedy about New York in the days of
Dutch rule in the seventeenth century. Peter Stuyvesant, with his historic
silver peg leg, was impersonated by Walter Huston. The list of characters
was studded with such well-known names as Vanderbilt, Van Rensselaer,
De Puyster, and Roosevelt. Since the idea of writing *Knickerbocker Holiday*
was suggested to Maxwell Anderson by Washington Irving's *Father Knickerbocker's History of New York*, Irving appeared anachronistically in the

show, in the shape of Ray Middleton. In one of his happiest achievements, Anderson suffused the lines and lyrics with the glow of life and beauty, and at the same time presented an eloquent argument for the democratic conception of government. Weill's music was mixed in quality. At its worst it was both more sophisticated and more banal, in the continental jazz manner, than the run-of-the-mill products of Broadway. On the other hand, Weill was a full partner with Anderson and Walter Huston in the triumph of the moment when Huston, in a voice hardly more than a confidential whisper, posed the problems of advancing age in the "September Song."

Weill's best gift to the American stage, beyond all debate, was the refined and sensitive score for *Lady in the Dark*, which opened, with Gertrude Lawrence in the central role, on January 23, 1941. In *Knickerbocker Holiday*, Weill had worked with an author who was, in effect, a gifted amateur in the musical branch of the theatre. In *Lady in the Dark* he was associated with two of the most assured artisans of the trade—Moss Hart, who wrote the book, and Ira Gershwin, who wrote the lyrics.

By no stretch of the imagination could *Lady in the Dark* be described as a simon-pure musical comedy. It was a serious drama, with dream interludes of song and dance expertly integrated in the basic structure. The chronicle of a successful but troubled magazine editor who found her true self through the aid of psychoanalysis, *Lady in the Dark* derived its format from the contrast between the actual world and the world of fantasy brought to consciousness by the device of the psychoanalytic couch. The action moved back and forth between Liza Elliott's office and the doctor's consulting room, which evaporated in the imaginings and recollections of Liza's subconscious—fortunately an exceedingly vivid and colorful one. The contrast of the tailored modernity of the office and the clipped dialogue that took place in it with the riotous decorations and unpredictable free associations of the dream scenes made these musical episodes doubly effective. Like the pieces of a jigsaw puzzle, the dream passages fitted into the surrounding narrative with constantly increasing intelligibility; at the end, but only then, it was possible to see the dexterity with which action, spectacle, lines, lyrics, and music had been put together with uncommon lucidity of purpose.

Miss Lawrence's performance—for which she is said to have received $3,500 a week, a percentage of the gross receipts, and the guarantee of a three-month summer holiday—was one of the supreme virtuoso feats of the modern theatre. From her everyday character she moved, within a split second, and with no possibility of the external aid of changed makeup, into a variety of startlingly different phases. She became the schoolgirl selected at graduation time as the most popular member of her class, not, as she privately wished, the most beautiful. In the gaily colorful circus scene, over which Danny Kaye cracked the whip as ringmaster, she sang of Jenny, who always made up her mind (Kurt Weill's contribution to sultry music of the "Eadie Was a Lady" school). As the central figure of the New York Chapter of Liza Elliott Admirers, she lived up to the terms of the admirers' apostrophe:

> "Oh, Fabulous One in your ivory tower—
> Your radiance I fain would see!
> What Mélisande was to Pelléas
> Are you to me."

Mary Garden's Mélisande sang no more affectingly than this Liza Elliott, in such simple and melodious lyrics as "My Ship" and "The Princess of Pure Delight." It was a many-sided performance, in which each new facet was as arresting as the last.

Although Miss Lawrence quite properly dominated the evening, the men in her life were able to hold their own—Danny Kaye, as an effeminate photographer; Victor Mature, as a "hunk of man"; and Macdonald Carey, as the explosive, solid, straightforward managing editor Liza finally found she loved. Harry Horner's settings, derived largely from German functionalist techniques of the 1930s, made use of two revolving stages in a manner that expedited the shifting of scenes without calling attention to the machinery for its own sake. Irene Sharaff designed the costumes for the fantasies and Hattie Carnegie those for the office; Albertina Rasch contributed her last significant choreography; and at the conductor's stand Maurice Abravanel, formerly of the Paris Opéra and the Metropolitan, brought out the fresh and interesting timbres of Weill's masterly instrumentation without overbalancing Miss Lawrence's slender voice.

Such opportunities as those afforded by *Lady in the Dark* come seldom, and Weill's later Broadway pieces were not its equal. *One Touch of Venus* (1943), in which Mary Martin brilliantly impersonated a statue of Venus which came to life, was bright and entertaining in lighter vein, and contained one particularly expressive song, to Ogden Nash's text, "Speak Low." *The Firebrand of Florence* (1945), with Earl Wrightson as Benvenuto Cellini, failed to create a stir. *Street Scene* (1947), was more an opera than a light entertainment. *A Flag Is Born* (1946) and *Love Life* (1948) are better forgotten. *Lost in the Stars* (1949), a musical version of Alan Paton's South African novel, *Cry the Beloved Country,* reunited Weill and Anderson, but the product of their labors was maladroit in its failure to contain the music naturally within the story; and—unhappily, since this was Weill's last work—the score was at no point worthy of comparison with his best earlier music for Broadway.

Weill's operatic experiment with his setting of Elmer Rice's *Street Scene* added a page to the chapter contributed by serious opera to the history of the Broadway theatre. Though some wishful thinkers have professed to discover a steady progress on the part of the bored public toward the acceptance of opera as an amusing evening's diversion, the facts do not wholly bear them out. Serious musical endeavors have never been unwelcome on Broadway, if someone wanted to pay their costs. *Cavalleria Rusticana* has been presented on Broadway, and so have Verdi's *Macbeth* and Douglas Moore's *The Devil and Daniel Webster*. *Everywoman* had a musical score by George Whitfield Chadwick, who was anything but a light composer, and Engelbert Humperdinck, who wrote *Hansel and Gretel* and *Königskinder*, composed the incidental music for *The Miracle*.

None of these belong within the scope of a book intentionally limited to the lighter phases of the New York stage, for they pose problems of value judgment requiring the entirely different, and perhaps more unrelenting, aesthetic standards that are customarily applied to works conceived unequivocally as art objects, and only secondarily as entertainments. For the same reason, Virgil Thomson's *Four Saints in Three Acts*, Benjamin Britten's *The Rape of Lucretia*, Marc Blitzstein's *Regina*, and Gian-Carlo Menotti's *The Telephone*, *The Medium*, and *The Consul*, along with Weill's *Street Scene*, require treatment not here but in some other book whose critical assumptions are appropriate to the discussion of opera. Perhaps the operatic repertory of Broadway will grow rapidly from this point forward, thanks to the relative success of *The Consul*; but even if it does, *Kiss Me, Kate* will still be separated from operas like those of Menotti (for all their command of contemporary trick stagecraft) by a gulf as wide as that between *The Merry Widow* and *Der Rosenkavalier*. And up to now, the Menotti operas have been the only ones to make a dent at the box-office.

The two greatest popular successes of the 1940s, *Oklahoma!* and *South Pacific*, resulted from the coalition of Richard Rodgers' talents with those of Oscar Hammerstein 2d. Rodgers had scarcely terminated his association with Lorenz Hart before word circulated that he and Hammerstein had agreed to work together, under the auspices of the Theatre Guild, on a musical adaptation of Lynn Riggs's folk play, *Green Grow the Lilacs*, in which Franchot Tone and June Walker had appeared for the Guild in 1931. In March 1943, a tryout audience in New Haven saw the new piece, which then bore the noncommittal title, *Away We Go*. Midway in the Boston engagement the name was changed to *Oklahoma!*, and *Oklahoma!* it remained when what was to be the longest run of any musical piece of Broadway's history began, amid tumult and cheering, at the St. James Theatre in New York on March 31, 1943.

Any first-year dramatic student can readily prove that *Green Grow the Lilacs* was more tightly constructed than *Oklahoma!* The Rodgers and Hammerstein musical comedy was sprawling in outline, ready to stop on a moment's notice for a song or a dance, and less authentic musically than the cowboy songs of Riggs's play. But its gangling good nature proved to be its best asset. Though its pace was really swift, under Rouben Mamoulian's direction, it always seemed easygoing and possessed of plenty of time and space.

Rodgers and Hammerstein were ideally suited to each other, to so phenomenal a degree that there almost seemed in retrospect to have been a disparity—unnoticed at the time—between Rodgers' flowing lyricism and Hart's brittle, caustic wit. In any event, the sunny homeliness of Hammerstein's book and lyrics—which concealed, as in *Carmen Jones*, consummate craftsmanship—inspired in Rodgers an upwelling of friendly melodies whose inflections often suggested a folk feeling, even though they were not literally based upon folk idioms. Without quite knowing what had happened to him, perhaps, Rodgers took a long step away from Broadway toward a more universal and less insular type of light music. Without losing touch with his audience and their predilections, he made of *Oklahoma!* more of an operetta and less of an out-and-out musical comedy than any of his earlier works.

The union of two sympathetic temperaments created the first all-American, non-Broadway musical comedy (or operetta; call it what you will) independent of the manners or traditions of Viennese comic opera or French opéra-bouffe on the one hand, and Forty-fourth Street clichés and specifications on the other. *Oklahoma!* turned out to be a people's opera, unpretentious and perfectly modern, but of interest equally to audiences in New York and in Des Moines. Its longevity and sustained popular appeal are explained by the fact that it transcends the outlook of Broadway musical comedy without disturbingly violating the canons of presentation to which the musical-comedy public is conditioned.

The performance of the first cast—nearly everyone has appeared in *Oklahoma!* sooner or later—was admirably calculated to strengthen the good features and disguise the defects. Alfred Drake developed an appealing drawl as Curly, and sang "O What a Beautiful Mornin' " with artless ease. Celeste Holm, a newcomer from Chicago with less than a year's stage experience in *Papa Is All*, revealed scintillant comic gifts as the girl who couldn't say No; and everyone else was ebullient and natural.

Agnes de Mille's dances, numerous and elaborate, combined square dances and cowboy movements with balletic devices, to the unbounded delight of the audience. At the end of the first act she set a fashion, which quickly became a rubber stamp in later shows, by introducing a dream ballet purporting to act out the difficulty that Laurey, the heroine, had in making up her mind. (Between *Oklahoma!* and *Lady in the Dark* there was grave disagreement over the advantages of making up, or not making up, one's mind.) Miss de Mille's personal touch in the choreography consisted in the combining of pure dancing with pantomime in a way that related the dances clearly to the story. Though she has tended to repeat her tricks in subsequent musical comedies, she helped a great deal toward solving the problem of bringing ballets into the line of action.

The stage decorations of *Oklahoma!* were refreshing and entirely appropriate. Lemuel Ayers employed a poster style for the exterior scenes, in which unessential details were eliminated without sacrifice of color and virility. Miles White made a 1900 Sears-Roebuck catalogue his bible, and designed costumes that were fabulously gay without forcing themselves out of context.

In the same year (1943), Rodgers himself produced a revival of the Rodgers and Hart classic, A *Connecticut Yankee*. Time had not dimmed the best of the Hart lyrics:

> *"Thou swell! Thou witty! Thou sweet! Thou grand!*
> *Wouldst kiss me pretty? Wouldst hold my hand?"*

For Vivienne Segal, as Morgan Le Fay, there was a new song, in the double-entendre vein of *Pal Joey*, "To Keep My Love Alive."

Two years after *Oklahoma!*, the next Rodgers and Hammerstein collaboration, *Carousel* (1945), came along. The book was based on Ferenc Molnár's *Liliom*, shifted to a New England locale and equipped with a clambake. The evening started out marvelously, with a scene on a merry-go-round as giddy and beautiful as the one in *The Band Wagon*. In the course of events Rodgers proffered many winning tunes, especially the infectious "June is Bustin' Out All Over." But as the drama developed tension and mystical implications near the end, Rodgers displayed, as he had once before in his ballet score for *Ghost Town*, an inability to deal with musical problems that lie off the beaten track of show music. His attempt to write dramatic recitative was merely trashy, and *Carousel* ended in an abrupt downward plunge. For a time, however, it challenged the popularity of the older *Oklahoma!*

In *Allegro* (1947), ushered in by the longest and most persistent barrage of advance publicity any musical attraction had ever received, Rodgers and Hammerstein went arty. The enterprise brought expensive elaborations of music, dance, and stagecraft to a trivial life-chronicle of a young doctor who, at thirty-five, was forced to choose between a rich but empty practice in Chicago and a poor but honorable career of humanitarian service as his aging father's associate in the town in which he was born. That he chose the nobler course amounted to the final affront in a story that all evening piled cliché upon bromide and stock character upon contrived situation.

The staging of *Allegro* consisted largely of gadgetry raised to the *n*th power. Recollecting some of the devices he used in *I Married an Angel* and *Stars in Your Eyes*, Jo Mielziner again equipped the stage with a treadmill upon which bits of setting, furniture, properties, and actors rode on and off stage, with tormentor curtains at each end which rose unobtrusively as they passed through. At the back of the stage the usual backdrop was supplanted by a large screen upon which singularly uninventive images (nothing more exciting than the balloons at a college dance) were now and again projected. Many interesting visual effects were achieved by exploiting the whole gamut between transparency and opacity upon the curtains that separated the front half from the back, as well as by various colors, angles, and intensities of lighting. The stage was frequently monopolized by a verbose speaking chorus, reenforced by a singing chorus ready to commit itself on any subject. These imperious groups served as a combined Super-ego and Id for the young doctor, leaving remarkably little for John Battles, who played the role, to do in his own behalf except respond in a chain of reflexes.

Allegro had been described in advance as an adventure into the domain of serious lyric theatre. Actually its heavy superstructure of external production rested upon an excessively weak substructure of ideas. After the first flurry, the public saw through its pretenses, and its patronage lasted less than a full season.

With *South Pacific* (1949) Rodgers and Hammerstein returned to a more normal field of operation. *South Pacific* actually made some of the advance in the direction of seriousness which *Allegro* claimed to be making. Excerpts from James Michener's *Tales of the South Pacific* provided Hammerstein with suitable materials for an attractive and believable romance between an island planter (Ezio Pinza) and a fresh and spirited nurse from Little Rock, Arkansas (Mary Martin). Both Hammerstein's book and Joshua Logan's clarifying direction made *South Pacific* more nearly a wholly satisfactory drama than any musical piece since *Lady in the Dark,* and Miss Martin and Pinza gave thoughtful, well-characterized, technically mature performances on a far higher level than that of most musical-comedy acting.

Though it has not the choreographic elaborations of the Moss Hart play, *South Pacific* resembles it in the exceptional extent to which the songs and ensembles develop spontaneously within the action, instead of being thrust upon it. The abandonment of formal choreography in favor of Logan's resourceful and beautifully fluid handling of the group scenes enabled the stage director to control the dramatic values at every point, and to see that even the minor actors never slipped out of character. Rodgers' score, filled with his most inviting outlay of tunes since *Oklahoma!*, was also expertly calculated, for even the set pieces and obvious hit tunes belong to the play and do not disturb its progress.

Though it was not an example of wingèd inspiration, *South Pacific* must be accounted the most useful and instructive musical entertainment of the immediate postwar period. The integrity of the writing and of the production as a whole will make it more difficult for dramatically implausible musical pieces to win acceptance in the future. Musical comedy and the allied forms of entertainment are still, in the last analysis, more dependent on craft than on art, and the craft displayed in *South Pacific* will stand as a model for a long time to come.

XXIII. The Past, the Present, and the Future

MUSICAL COMEDY has often been called the only unique American contribution to the theatre. This claim is not merely oversimplified; it is false, or partly false, in two opposite directions. That musical comedy is not the only unique American contribution can be seen by a moment's contemplation of the "living newspaper" technique of the 1930s, which may have originated in German expressionist devices, but possessed its own special manner of presentation; or the prose style and the whole conception of tempo and dynamics of such playwrights as Clifford Odets and Lillian Hellman, who capture a wholly American idiom and rhythm of expression; or the prose-poetry of Tennessee Williams, who has a completely American notion of what poetic values are and how they should function in the theatre; or the machinery of farce as revised by George S. Kaufman and Moss Hart, who devised for that métier an idiom as distinctly American as that of Odets and Miss Hellman in the serious drama.

That musical comedy, on the other hand, is something other than an all-American victory over European lethargy and conventionality has, I should hope, been sufficiently demonstrated by the findings of the preceding chapters. In its basic form, musical comedy is not specifically American even now. The theatrical form in which speaking and action are alternated with musical set pieces and usually with dances, with some sort of plot as the chief unifying factor, is the form of Singspiel, comic opera, operetta, opéra-bouffe, burlesque (in its historic aspect), and pantomime as well as of modern American musical comedy. It is, in short, the form of all musical works for the stage except revue, ballet, and through-composed opera.

American contributions to theatre-music form have taken the shape of surface improvements or alterations in the conventions of presentation. In such musical comedies as *Finian's Rainbow* and *South Pacific*, the machinery was better oiled than it had been before. The interpolated numbers emerged from plot and characterization more smoothly and spontaneously, and in one way or another created some illusion of helping to move the plot forward. But it all boils down to a matter of greater technical acumen in concealing the joints, rather than a revision of the single basic form that applies to all light pieces for the musical stage—except the revue, which is substantially a glorification of the variety show.

Perhaps the most noticeable job of concealing the joints was accomplished in *Lady in the Dark,* in which the psychiatrist's couch provided a flamboyantly effective instrumentality for breaking over from realistic action into song and dance. The very flamboyance of the device, however, made it a one-time affair, useless in general practice since it was just one more way of tempering the artificiality of the traditional alternating structure of musical comedy. *Allegro,* it is true, did reach after something new in the way of form by trying to graft the use of a narrator, radio fashion, onto the usual procedures of musical comedy. The experiment turned out to be pure hokum, for there was no need for a narrator when all the visual facilities for action were present; and the speaking choirs, projections, and tricks of staging were so crudely used that they amounted to no more than window dressing.

The plot materials of the Broadway musical stage today are American in varying degrees. Certainly the subject matter and viewpoint of contemporary musical pieces are drawn more largely from the American scene and from American experience than they were before the First World War. Since about 1915, when American subjects came to be the rule rather than the exception, there has been no fundamental change in this regard; and European materials have by no means been completely eliminated even yet. The plot of *Brigadoon* was a German romantic fantasy given American and Scotch trimmings. *Carousel* was a Hungarian play, moved uneasily to New England and given a clambake. *On the Town,* on the other hand, was pure urban American; and *Oklahoma!* was pure rural American. But the Harrigan and Hart farce-comedies in the 1870s and 1880s, and Charles Hoyt's *A Trip to Chinatown* in the 1890s, were pure urban American, too; and if there was no counterpart to *Oklahoma!* in those earlier days, it was because the West, having been only recently discovered, was not yet in need of rediscovery. *Kiss Me, Kate,* which collates a literary classic with a modern American plot, has its antecedents not only in *The Boys from Syracuse* but in such early burlesques as *Evangeline* and *Hiawatha*.

In general, the type characters of contemporary musical comedy continue to follow immemorial formulas of the light musical stage, though their outward attributes have been changed to conform with the times and with our national predilections. The routine love match between people of discrepant social stations and backgrounds is repeated in *South Pacific,* in which the amatory interest between the planter and the nurse attains its end despite obstacles no less formidable than those separating a nobleman from a peasant girl. The heavy villain in *Oklahoma!* speaks with a drawl and surrounds himself with dirty pictures in a smokehouse, but he is the same miscreant more naïve audiences used to hiss in the 1890s. The soubrette, with or without a heart of gold, and the regulation comics, both low and effete, are still with us a good deal of the time, though it is now unfashionable for the very best musical comedies to employ them without a great many refinements.

There is no denying, however, that the whole tone of American musical comedy over the past thirty years has reflected in striking fashion our national moods, attitudes, and interests. The cynicism of the 1920s was mirrored in the shows whose main concerns were raucous jazz, naked girls, and jibes at prohibition. The saddened 1930s, the years of the Depression, produced sharp social protests, expressions of nostalgia for better days, and idealistic hopes for the future. The late 1940s and early 1950s have plumped for Romantic escapism, whether into Scotland, the islands of the Pacific, or the United States in the mid-1920s.

The lyrics, choreography, and music of Broadway musical entertainments have made steady progress—particularly in the last thirty-five years—toward an unmistakably American character, and toward general artistic excellence as well. The lyric writers, perhaps, have done the best work of anybody. In the later decades of the nineteenth century, punning, pat rhymes, stereotyped imagery, doggerel structure, and high-sounding *thees* and *thous* were slowly nudged out of the way. Slang crept in the back door, through the burlesques and farce-comedies, and in the 1880s and 1890s became, rather self-consciously, an important feature of the best musical-comedy lyrics. In the era of Lorenz Hart, Ira Gershwin, B. G. de Sylva, and early Cole Porter, lyrics came to be written wholly in the American language, with no hangovers except satiric ones from the artful verse of comic opera. When talking pictures and the Depression forced Broadway to cater to a class instead of a mass audience, words of more than two syllables and increasingly erudite references became permissible in the lyrics of all but the most low-brow shows, and rhyme and rhythm schemes that were inventive rather than conventional became a requirement of the trade. An interesting example of the indigenous nature of present-day lyrics is the text of "There's No Business Like Show Business," which had to be equipped with new ideas for the Paris version of *Annie Get Your Gun*, since there are no French equivalents for its concepts.

Nationalism is a harder thing to define in the realm of music than in that of words. Perhaps the lumbering waltzes of the 1890s were American, since they certainly did not sound like Strauss or Offenbach. But it was ragtime, and later jazz, which first gave an indisputable national color to American musical-comedy music. Though Europe, and particularly Germany, tried to appropriate American jazz, it never sounded like the same thing. Even today, with the crest of the jazz wave many years in the past, the rhythm of Broadway musical comedies is suffused with syncopations and figures which became rooted in our national musical consciousness in the 1920s, and the melodies are constantly influenced by tin-pan-alley and folk elements, and by a prosody that faithfully represents characteristic American verbal inflections and speech habits. At the same time, musical-comedy music has displayed a constantly increasing urbanity and internationalism over the last two decades, as its composers have become better-educated musicians. Present-day scores have a wider vocabulary and expressive range than earlier ones, because the American elements which still give the music its special idiom have been absorbed into cosmopolitan techniques.

Choreography, as opposed to the dance routines of soloists and chorus girls, has scarcely more than a twenty-year history in musical comedy. The stylized convolutions of the Albertina Rasch girls and the pioneering efforts of Charles Weidman made way for the triumphal entry of George Balanchine onto Broadway; and the success of "Slaughter on Tenth Avenue" in *On Your Toes* admitted the ballet to a new partnership with the musical and literary elements in the productions of the later 1930s and the 1940s. Agnes de Mille's ability to integrate her ballets with action and characterization enhanced the reasonableness of extended dances in the eyes of the general public. Today, only a *South Pacific*, which has an equally cogent substitute to offer in Joshua Logan's handling of the concerted scenes, can afford to overlook the important function of the choreographer. Nor was progress confined to the field of ballet, for Robert Alton showed, before his departure for Hollywood, the extent to which popular materials could be given a comparable choreographic integrity.

If I have leaned over backward, in summarizing the status of musical comedy today, in the direction of minimizing its qualities of uniqueness or the magnitude of its development, I have done so for one main reason. There is a widespread belief today that musical comedy is becoming more and more serious in its artistic accomplishments, and that in a few more years it will grow right into American opera. This strikes me as a misinterpretation of the facts in the first place, and as an undesirable hope in the second. The American audience has become more experienced and more sophisticated over the years, and its entertainment naturally has moved onto an increasingly high plane of craftsmanship and literacy. But musical comedies and revues are still entertainments; if they are art at all, they are only incidentally so. A musical comedy does not exist for the same purpose as an opera, nor, essentially, does it employ comparable musical or plot materials.

It is not likely that opera can ever appeal to the wide musical-comedy public unless it makes as many popular concessions as *The Consul* did, in which case it becomes questionable as opera. I should hate to discover that I am wrong, and that *Finian's Rainbow* and *South Pacific* will one day be regarded as the prototypes of American opera. For if I am wrong, there will be no more chapters to add to this book.

Musical Comedy in America

From *The King and I* to *Sweeney Todd*

by GLENN LITTON

PART FOUR
The 1950s

Gertrude Lawrence and Yul Brynner in *The King and I*.

XXIV. The Book Musical Refined

AFTER THE INNOVATIVE mid-'40s and the jubilant late-'40s, American musical theatre coasted. It had the wherewithal—the momentum, talent, and money—to produce *Guys and Dolls, The King and I, The Pajama Game, My Fair Lady, The Most Happy Fella, The Golden Apple, Candide, The Music Man,* and *West Side Story*. But at the same time it began to languish. Imitation of Rodgers and Hammerstein was too universal, and their fresh inventions were inevitably reduced by their imitators to formula and hack work. Because it failed to renew itself, the American musical couldn't win new audiences. By the mid-'60s, its customers were the same romantics—or the same tired businessmen—who had first set foot in the theatre to see *Oklahoma!* in 1943. But time had diminished both their numbers and their love for musical comedy. Young people stayed away. And expenses rose. Musical theatre lost earning power and popularity. By the end of the 1960s it had the reputation of being senile. Even the last collaboration of Rodgers and Hammerstein, *The Sound of Music* (1960), gave off a faded, oppressive odor, something between lilac and camphor.

Everything in a Rodgers and Hammerstein musical—its melodies, lyrics, dialogue, instrumental arrangements, choreography, sets, costumes, and lighting—was meticulously harmonized so as not to disturb the illusion of a world vulnerable to romance. The Alps in *The Sound of Music* were alive with the promise of love, so were the street corners of San Francisco's Chinatown in *Flower Drum Song,* and the shadows where the secret lovers of *The King and I* met. Musical numbers, which either moved the plot ahead or allowed a character to release a pent-up emotion, dovetailed with a simple story always about love. It couldn't end the King's tyranny in *The King and I,* or the poverty of Cannery Row in *Pipe Dream,* or the advance of the Nazis in *The Sound of Music;* but love, glorified by Rodgers and Hammerstein's songs, was, they assured us, all we needed to make our dreams come true. That was the sentiment and the sentimentality of Rodgers and Hammerstein's musicals of the '50s, the naïve but understandable dream of a proud, postwar country that wanted to believe in an untroubled future.

When *The King and I* opened in 1951, *South Pacific* was still playing. The two shared not only their audiences but much of what attracted them: an exotic, romantic locale—the lianas and lagoons of Siam for *The King and I*—and a confrontation between a man and a woman from two very diverse cultures who find each other fascinating but puzzling. The odd and daring novelty of *The King and I* was that its principal characters were only dimly aware of their love. Even if they had been totally conscious of it, they could never have admitted it or acted on it.

Gertrude Lawrence played Anna, a Welsh governess hired in the 1860s by the King of Siam (Yul Brynner) to teach English to his sixty-seven children and numerous wives. Without the King's knowledge, Anna also indoctrinates her charges in the abolitionist philosophy of Abraham Lincoln, the humanistic principles of constitutional monarchy, and the Christian prohibition against polygamy. All of this is anathema to the King, who, when he learns of the heresy spreading in his court, first denounces Anna and then, as her popularity grows, tries to ignore her. But he is intrigued by her intelligence, her courage, and her odd, Western ideas. The beginnings of his appreciation for her first stir in his comic song "A Puzzlement."

Although Gertrude Lawrence and Yul Brynner were not trained singers, their forceful stage presences and intuitive musical abilities created two of the most vivid characterizations in the musical theatre of the '50s. Anna's charm radiated from her intelligence, her dignified humor, and her stubborn, often self-righteous, integrity. But the King's more volatile temperament and wild self-contradictions stole the show. Brynner played him as an imperious if often befuddled soul caught between the urge to banish Anna and the desire to win her as an ally and friend.

Hammerstein based his script on Margaret Landon's novel, itself adapted from the late nineteenth-century autobiography by Anna Leonowens, the governess of the title. Not only was his libretto a perfect vehicle for its principals, it offered just the kind of exotic locale and romantic suggestion that he and Richard Rodgers were geniuses at realizing in song. "Shall We Dance?," in which Anna gives the King his first coaching in Western terpsichore, became, under the Rodgers and Hammerstein imprint, a whirling invitation to romance. Their finest song was an evocation of past love, Anna's poignant "Hello, Young Lovers," in which she remembers her happiness with her young husband and, in spite of the pain caused by his death, wishes others a love like hers. With the help of Robert Russell Bennett's gently percussive orchestrations, Rodgers created a musical Siam that would have been unrecognizable to the Siamese; but to Americans brought up on Hollywood's musical ideas about the Orient the evocation worked perfectly. "The March of the Siamese Children" and "The Small House of Uncle Thomas" (the latter a danced interpretation by the Siamese of Harriet Beecher Stowe's pre-Civil War novel) were perfect musical complements to Irene Sharaff's silk and brocade costumes, Jo Mielziner's gilded temples, and Jerome Robbins' picturesque choreography. The illusion was persuasively sumptuous, a musical Shangri-la.

The King and I (which won a Tony for Best Musical) and *South Pacific* were still running when Rodgers and Hammerstein opened their sixth collaboration, *Me and Juliet* (1953). In a preproduction interview with the New York *Times*, Rodgers boasted that what distinguished their show from an old-fashioned musical was its realistic characters and their compelling hold on an audience. He hadn't looked too critically at Hammerstein's script, his first original since *Allegro* (1947). The intent was clear: an affectionate backstage plot that, instead of merely providing an excuse for a hodgepodge of unrelated show-within-a-show numbers, would involve audiences in the tensions and politicking of theatre life as well as its glamour. A chorus girl (Isabel Bigley) and an assistant stage manager (Bill Hayes) fall in love; their romance persists despite an attempt on their lives by one of the girl's rejected admirers (Mark Dawson). In the subplot, for comic relief, a dancer (Joan McCracken) chases a reluctant stage manager (Ray Walton).

The story's resemblance to *Oklahoma!* was increased by the casting of Bigley and McCracken, who had both appeared in the run of the earlier show. No one would have minded another variation on an old theme, if the variation rejuvenated the theme. But Rodgers and Hammerstein smothered their valentine to show business in verbose dialogue and crushed it with busy staging and heavy spectacle. Hammerstein hadn't found a middle course between drab understatement and shrill melodrama. Even Rodgers' melodic invention faltered. Only the "No Other Love" tango was distinctive enough to receive much play outside its setting in the show. It too was secondhand goods, originally composed to accompany tropical sequences in the television documentary *Victory at Sea*.

Me and Juliet played 358 performances, a disappointing run in comparison to its immediate predecessors, *South Pacific* (a record-setting 1,925 performances) and *The King and I* (1,246 performances). After *Me and Juliet* closed in the spring of 1954, Rodgers and Hammerstein were absent from Broadway until the winter of 1955, when *Pipe Dream* opened.

Three years before, New York newspapers reported that John Steinbeck might collaborate on a musical with Frank Loesser, the composer for *Where's Charley?* (1949) and *Guys and Dolls* (1950). But after a long struggle trying to write a script populated by some of the characters he had introduced in his novel *Cannery Row*, Steinbeck gave up and converted the work he had done to a new novel, *Sweet Thursday*. Cy Feuer and Ernest Martin, the producers who owned the theatrical rights to *Sweet Thursday*, then sold the project to Rodgers and Hammerstein.

Rodgers and Hammerstein's *Pipe Dream* drained most of the zest from Steinbeck's vision of skid-row life in Monterey, California. If life in Steinbeck's novel was lackadaisical, in *Pipe Dream* it was desultory. William Johnson played a marine biologist who sets up a research station on the beach near Cannery Row. In the bromidic style of the dedicated scientist, he scarcely notices Suzy (Judy Tyler), a drifter who is rooming—not working—

in a nearby bordello. This phlegmatic duo has to be coaxed into a romance by the colorful vagrants of Cannery Row and Madame Fauna (Helen Traubel), the proprietress of the brothel.

If the casting for *Me and Juliet* had been uninspired, the choice of Traubel, an opera singer, to play a madam was adventuresome—but miscalculated. She couldn't relax the stiff poses of a concert artist, and her formal dignity jarred with her bawdy throwaway lines. Even her voice was too large for Rodgers' leisurely, unforced melodies. Johnson and Tyler, also cast for their powerful voices, couldn't invigorate Rodgers' drowsy melodies, and around them the lazy flow of life in Cannery Row froze into postcard scenes in neat pastels. Only when the Cannery Row riffraff made their appearance was *Pipe Dream* animated by Steinbeck's warm humor. The show had the shortest run of any Rodgers and Hammerstein musical, 246 performances.

Hammerstein found his next source for a libretto in yet another novel, *Flower Drum Song* by the Chinese-American Chin Y. Lee. Hammerstein liked the book, he told a reporter, because it reminded him of a Chinese *Life with Father*. He failed to mention how similar the ingredients of Lee's novel were to *South Pacific* and *The King and I*. At the heart of the novel was the conflict between two cultures, only this time both factions were nominally American: the older versus the younger generation of naturalized Chinese-Americans living in San Francisco's Chinatown. The elders want to preserve their Chinese identity and customs, while the young want complete assimilation. Once again the East would meet West and in a locale that could be made to seem as romantic and exotic as Bali Ha'i or Siam. Once again Rodgers could evoke the East with lyrical, pseudo-Oriental melodies and the West with brash, jazzy showstoppers, while Hammerstein and colibrettist Joseph Fields naturally concentrated on the romantic implications.

Aside from the reputation of its authors, what drew audiences to *Flower Drum Song* was its physical beauty and its craftsmanlike song and dance. Oliver Smith's set featured a backdrop of the Golden Gate Bridge resembling a classical Chinese painting, and Irene Sharaff's costumes were equally evocative in their blending and contrasting of traditional Chinese and contemporary American styles. Her finest design was a gaudy, peek-a-boo outfit worn by the chorus girls from a dive called Sammy Fong's Celestial Bar. Gene Kelly's direction and Carol Haney's dances skillfully paced a graceful show, but one in which the peaceful moments given to the ancient Chinese culture were overwhelmed by the razzmatazz of the nightclub acts.

Rodgers and Hammerstein's songs disappointed because they were so closely derived from their earlier works, especially *South Pacific*. A jaunty celebration of femininity, "I Enjoy Being a Girl," didn't have the conviction of Nellie Forbush's "Cockeyed Optimist," and "A Hundred Million Miracles," charming as it was, lacked the enchantment of "Happy Talk" or "Bali Ha'i." The creative reserves of the Rodgers and Hammerstein collaboration had begun to diminish.

In November of 1959, while *Flower Drum Song* was still playing, Rodgers and Hammerstein opened their final show, *The Sound of Music*. On August 23, 1960, Hammerstein died of cancer.

The Sound of Music won a Tony for Best Musical and became the second longest-running production of Rodgers and Hammerstein's collaboration. Its marzipan sentimentality and exploitation of precious children made the critics queasy, but the public relished every morsel. This time Hammerstein concentrated on the lyrics, while Howard Lindsay and Russel Crouse wrote the libretto. Their story, based on fact, told how Maria, an ex-postulant, marries into a family of Austrian nobility, the Von Trapps, and how the family becomes a professional folk-singing act. It needed few excuses to introduce music in the folksy style of Rodgers and Hammerstein's best work. "Edelweiss," "My Favorite Things," "Sixteen Going on Seventeen," "Maria," "The Lonely Goatherd," "So Long, Farewell," and "Do-Re-Mi"—all were as disarming as they were plain and homey. Several of them were touched with just enough minor modality and chromaticism to link them with *lieder* and their Austrian setting. "The Sound of Music" and "Climb Ev'ry Mountain," which were less Tyrolean than Tin Pan Alley, huffed and puffed for their modest inspirational power.

The story of the Von Trapps, as reconstructed by Lindsay and Crouse, was an idyll darkened only momentarily by signs that the Austria of 1938 would soon be overrun by Nazis. Most of the stage action, until the concluding scenes, was given to Maria's loving care for the widowed Baron's seven children and, inevitably, to Maria and the Baron's romance and marriage. Without much attention to why the Von Trapps eventually fled their homeland, the show's concluding half hour had all the suspense of a Nelson Eddy-Jeanette MacDonald operetta.

Strengthening the impression that *The Sound of Music* was more operetta than musical comedy was the casting of Mary Martin, then in her late forties, as the young Maria. Miss Martin overcompensated in the direction of coyness, but whenever she sang one of Rodgers and Hammerstein's songs, audiences quite easily suspended their disbelief. Theodore Bikel, as the Baron, swelled with a convincing Prussian pomposity, which couldn't hide his vulnerability to Maria's charm.

The Sound of Music was the fourth Rodgers and Hammerstein musical to play over 1,200 performances. Of their nine shows written during seventeen years as partners, six ran for more than 600 performances. Little wonder, then, that enterprising producers began in the early '50s to revive musicals that Rodgers and Hammerstein had written with other partners before their collaboration. In 1951, Hammerstein directed a new edition of *Music in the Air*, which he had written with Jerome Kern in the early '30s. The unintentionally camp revival lasted only 56 performances. Rodgers and Hart's *On Your Toes* (1936) returned to Broadway for 64 performances in 1954. The 1952 version of *Pal Joey* (1940), another Rodgers and Hart show, was the only revival to outdo its original both in popularity (a 542-performance run versus a 374-performance run in 1940) and in critical acclaim.

In 1940, the critics hadn't realized what a coup Rodgers, Hart, and John O'Hara had pulled by converting to a musical the story of an amoral young man kept by a hedonistic older woman. Some even thought the story unsuitable for a musical. By 1952, they were less puritanical and more receptive. Walter Kerr described John O'Hara's libretto as ". . . one of the shrewdest, toughest, and in a way the most literate books ever written for musical comedy," and the New York Drama Critics Circle gave it their Award for Best Musical. Vivienne Segal's perfect diction, economy of style, and imposing presence made her interpretation of the playgirl even more convincing than it had been in the original production. Opposite Miss Segal was Harold Lang, who had begun his career in ballet and had first won recognition in musical comedy for his performance in Cole Porter's *Kiss Me, Kate*. He may not have had the roguish venality of Gene Kelly's original Joey, but he managed to hold the stage even in the company of the powerful Miss Segal. The show's brittle comedy was well served by choreographer Robert Alton, who avoided rarefied techniques from ballet and modern dance and instead based his dances on old-fashioned hoofing.

The new *Pal Joey* showed how narrowly Rodgers and Hammerstein had defined the expressive range of musical theatre. But most theatregoers were still content with shows that glossed American legend with spectacle and the optimism of bright melodies. The postwar economic boom and the residue of wartime patriotism had made the musical ballyhoo of America as popular as ever. And Rodgers and Hammerstein were hardly alone in trying to satisfy the public's craving. In 1946, Irving Berlin had glorified the Old West in *Annie Get Your Gun*. In 1949, he joined Robert E. Sherwood—playwright, historian, and film writer—on yet another musical set in American pseudo-history, *Miss Liberty*.

Sherwood had never written a musical, but he was the most successful of the '40s popularizers of American history. His play *Abe Lincoln in Illinois* had won the Pulitzer Prize; and his screenplay for *The Best Years of Our Lives*, about the return of discharged servicemen to their families after World War II, had won an Academy Award. Justifiably confident of his talents, Sherwood told the press, before *Miss Liberty* went for its out-of-town trials, that he didn't expect that much—if any—tinkering with the book would be necessary. Director Moss Hart didn't agree. After seeing that Boston audiences were—even for Boston audiences—unusually subdued, he brought in Garson Kanin to add jokes. The final version of the book was a mishmash of farce, nostalgia, and patriotism all encased in the very thin skin of a comic plot about a young Frenchwoman (Allyn McLerie) who, at the prompting of her grandmother (Ethel Griffies) and a reporter (Eddie Albert), fraudulently promotes herself as the model who posed for the Statue of Liberty. All was shenanigans until the final scene, when the show took an unexpectedly sober turn so that Berlin could make his pledge of allegiance, via a choral rendition of the inscription on the base of the Statue: "Give me your tired, your poor, your huddled masses yearning to breathe free. . ." The number was more suitable for a Veterans of Foreign Wars pageant than for a Broadway musical.

Berlin's next show, *Call Me Madam* (1950), starred Ethel Merman, the abrasive stage personality Howard Lindsay described as "the most American American" he had ever met. Inspired by Miss Merman's personality, Lindsay and his partner, Russel Crouse, wrote a patchwork vehicle about a loud-mouthed, yet amiable dynamo who won't take no for an answer, a combination of George M. Cohan and Perle Mesta. As Mrs. Sally Adams, the Washington partygiver who is appointed ambassadress to the mythical Alpine country of Lichtenburg, Merman did curb her gusto somewhat, if only to avoid looking ridiculous in the $11,000 worth of Mainbocher gowns she wore.

Berlin's score was as lighthearted—and as patriotic—as Lindsay and Crouse's very tolerant cracks about Yankee egotism. Instead of the blatant flag-waving of *Miss Liberty*, Berlin let the cheer in his melodies carry his optimism about America. Besides, every time Sally Adams, or Ethel Merman, was celebrated in song (as she was in "The Hostess with the Mostes' on the Ball"), Berlin was celebrating the Great American Go-Getter. If Berlin was bullish on America, he was just as bullish, in a most graceful and lighthearted way, on love. In "It's a Lovely Day Today," a meek young diplomat (Russell Nype) invited the Princess of Lichtenburg (Galina Talva) to share an afternoon that, if his song was any clue, would be as mild and playful as a zephyr. Even love sickness ("You're Just in Love") sounded like a very agreeable kind of malady.

Before *Call Me Madam*, Ethel Merman had told reporters that she wanted to perform in a nonmusical drama—implying that her stereotyped roles in the musical theatre no longer challenged her. But the next role she accepted after *Call Me Madam* bore a suspicious resemblance to Mrs. Sally Adams. In *Happy Hunting* (1956), another show tailored for her by Lindsay and Crouse, Merman played a Philadelphia socialite who visits Monaco at the time of the Prince Rainier and Grace Kelly nuptials. When she's not invited to the wedding, the proud American decides to retaliate by finding a prince for her own daughter (Virginia Gibson) and arranging a wedding to outshine the Rainier-Kelly festivities. She corrals an agreeable Spanish grandee a bit down on his luck (Fernando Lamas) but falls in love with him herself.

In spite of Merman's hard sell, the charm of Fernando Lamas, the fresh spirit of Virginia Gibson, and two hit songs by Harold Kerr and Matt Dubey ("Mutual Admiration Society" and "Two to Tango"), audiences realized they had seen and heard this all before. Both *Happy Hunting* and *Call Me Madam* were from a subgenre of musical comedy in oversupply during the

'50s: a light parody of American culture (or lack thereof) mixed with an equally good-natured satire of our politics. In the season before *Call Me Madam* opened, Anthony B. Farrell had brought to New York *Texas, Li'l Darlin'*, a busy show about Texans, political skullduggery, the power of the press (in particular the Luce publications), and that staple of all '50s musicals—romance. John Whedon and Sam Moore, two writers for the radio show "The Great Gildersleeve," were responsible for the libretto, and Johnny Mercer (the lyricist for such great standards as "Blues in the Night," "That Old Black Magic," and "Autumn Leaves") collaborated with the film composer Robert Emmett Dolan on the score.

Texas, Li'l Darlin' was patched together from a rag bag of sources. Its sets and production style looked like *Oklahoma!;* one of its best songs, "The Big Movie Show in the Sky," parodied the whip-cracking absurdities of Frankie Laine's "Ghost Riders in the Sky"; another song ("Affable, Balding Me") and a fair amount of dialogue mocked the political meddling and the odd verbal style of the Luce publications. All of this was thrown into a spoof of politics apparently derived from *Of Thee I Sing.* Even the casting of Kenny Delmar as an old Texas politico was a secondhand inspiration, for Delmar had played Senator Claghorn on Fred Allen's radio show.

During the same season (1949–50), Farrell and the Theatre Guild produced *Arms and the Girl*, an adaptation by Herbert and Dorothy Fields and Rouben Mamoulian of the 1933 comedy *The Pursuit of Happiness.* Nanette Fabray played a Colonial patriot who tries to abet General Washington's campaign against the Redcoats. But her efforts result in the defection of only one Hessian mercenary (Georges Guetary), whose switch of allegiance is motivated more by his infatuation with the would-be saboteuse than any dedication to the Revolutionaries' cause.

Fabray clowned her way through mock coquetry and slapstick bumbling, while Guetary, a star of French cabaret and musicals, made do with heroic poses and a singing voice that one critic described as "indestructible." Pearl Bailey played a runaway slave whose slight relevance to the plot was only emphasized by her domineering personality and her rendition of the show's best song, "There Must Be Something Better than Love." The rest of the score, by composer Morton Gould and lyricist Dorothy Fields, was unremarkable. What kept *Arms and the Girl* alive for its short run was a lavish production directed by Mamoulian and choreographed by Michael Kidd.

More popular with musical-comedy audiences than the Revolution was America during the 1890s, the setting for *A Tree Grows in Brooklyn* (1951) and *By the Beautiful Sea* (1954). Arthur Schwartz wrote the music for both, and Shirley Booth starred in both.

Betty Smith's novel, which she and George Abbott adapted for *A Tree Grows in Brooklyn*, detailed the sad childhood of Francie Nolan and her mother's attempts to reform a weak, alcoholic husband and to keep Francie's hopes alive. The musical shifted its attention to Francie's Aunt Cissy (played by Booth), an eccentric who, although she's never been married, has lived with five "husbands," each of whom she calls Harry. Booth's maternal warmth and Schwartz's florid score rendered every last tear and laugh from a vehicle that couldn't decide whether it was melodrama or comedy.

By the Beautiful Sea (libretto by Dorothy and Herbert Fields) was merely an excuse for some of Schwartz's most raucous and nostalgic music and for scenic and choreographic re-creations of Coney Island at the turn of the century. Choreographer Helen Tamiris, set designer Jo Mielziner, and costume designer Irene Sharaff exploited the Coney Island setting to its fullest. They conducted audiences on a tour of the amusement park from its Midway, through the Tunnel of Love (complete with luminous skeletons and monsters), into the Dreamland Casino, and finally, onto the stage of the Brighton Beach Vaudeville Theatre. When a production number like "Throw the Anchor Away" took over, the stage was mobbed by acrobats, sailors, beer-garden waiters, and a glut of obliging tourists ready to vocalize.

But Texas, Connecticut, Coney Island, and Brooklyn were outposts of the American dreamland in comparison with Times Square, the setting for Frank Loesser's *Guys and Dolls* (1950). This quintessentially American musical was based on stories by Damon Runyon, the "Boswell of Broadway," who had a gift for converting mere mortals into colorful archetypes. Runyon's heroes were knights of mid-Manhattan, tinhorns, touts, and small-time gangsters with names like Harry the Horse, Angie the Ox, Big Jule, Nicely-Nicely Johnson, and Benny Southstreet.

Guys and Dolls was Loesser's second musical comedy. With the encouragement of his friend Cy Feuer and the advice of veteran librettist and director George Abbott, Loesser had shifted from composing for films to composing for Broadway musicals in the late '40s. Abbott and Loesser collaborated on *Where's Charley?*, an adaptation of Brandon Thomas' Victorian farce, *Charley's Aunt*. Loesser had trouble molding his own musical language to Abbott's script, so instead of turning out a score with a consistent style of its own, he pasted together a sampler of musical-comedy standards. The best of them—a march, "The New Ashmoleon Marching Society and Student Conservatory Band"; a ballad, "My Darling, My Darling"; and a soft shoe, "Once in Love with Amy"—spread little more than a thin gloss over old formulas. By the time the show closed, after 800 performances, Ray Bolger had expanded "Once in Love with Amy" to a ten-minute solo of his loose-limbed, eccentric dancing, and the song had become a national hit. But Loesser, if he was really to show his stuff, needed a book with a spirit closer to home than Victorian England. He got the chance with *Guys and Dolls*.

The script from which Loesser worked had been written by Jo Swerling, the third writer to submit an adaptation to the producers Cy Feuer and Ernest Martin. Even after Loesser had finished his score, Feuer and Martin were still soliciting rewrites of the book. They tried seven more writers before Abe Burrows, who had plenty of radio and television but no musical-comedy credits, gave them the Runyonesque mix of worldliness and romance that Loesser's songs had captured. Burrows (and perhaps Swerling and the rest deserve some credit) imitated very closely the arcane magniloquence of Runyon's characters and kept the pace of action and dialogue at a rush-hour bustle. To blend fairy-tale glitter with urban soot he relied on a gimmick as old as Shakespeare: a double love story. The first, about the handsome gambler Sky Masterson and the beautiful Salvation Army worker Sarah Brown, was a variation on Prince Charming's search for his Princess, complicated somewhat by making the Prince a sinner and his future Princess a saint. To temper the sentimentality of that plot, Burrows introduced a laughable—and equally improbable—love affair between the tinhorn Nathan Detroit and the adenoidal chorus girl Adelaide.

Loesser's score mirrored the comic contradictions in Runyon's Manhattanites. "The Oldest-Established" rang with the solemn harmonies of a hymn, while its lyrics extolled the glories of Nathan's floating crap game. The mock Salvation Army hymn, "Follow the Fold," sounded, by contrast, tinny and comically pathetic. One of Loesser's subtlest musical jokes started the show: Three touts sang tips on the daily races in fugal counterpoint, a perfect analogue to the tangle of Times Square at rush hour. To Adelaide, Loesser gave three of his funniest novelty songs, always a Loesser speciality: "A Bushel and a Peck," "Adelaide's Lament," and "Take Back Your Mink." All capitalized on the nasality, little-girl inflections, and non sequiturs of the stereotypical chorus girl.

Perhaps because Burrows wrote his script after Loesser had written his songs, every one of the show's musical set pieces fits perfectly its dramatic moment. "Luck Be a Lady Tonight," sung by Masterson and his opponents just before their $1,000-a-bet crap game, charged the scene with a constantly rising, strongly punctuated melodic line. And for the scene in which the losers of the big bet have to attend the prayer meeting, Loesser wrote a mock-gospel number entitled "Sit Down, You're Rockin' the Boat," which sounded just like the kind of jazzy, mock-Hollywood tune that an all-white, New York-bred gang of tinhorns might extrapolate from big-band swing.

Another reason for the success of *Guys and Dolls* (it won both the Tony and Drama Critics' Circle Awards for Best Musical) was director George S. Kaufman's imaginative casting. For Sky Masterson he chose Robert Alda, whose previous experience included burlesque, vaudeville, radio, and film—but no musical comedy. Alda brought to the role just the right debonair toughness, including a limited vocal range and unrefined vocal quality that for once in a musical had some justification. Vivian Blaine, as Adelaide, also made her Broadway debut in *Guys and Dolls*. After considerable experience—but only slight recognition—as a singer and dancer in film musicals, she gave the best performance of her career doing a parody of her old self, the singing, dancing chorine. Isabel Bigley, who played Sarah Brown, had gained most of her musical-theatre experience as Laurie in the London production of *Oklahoma!* She made the change from Plains ingenue to Manhattan evangelist with ease. The only veteran of Broadway theatre among the four principals was Sam Levene, an obvious choice for Nathan Detroit. He had played Patsy, the racehorse tout in both the film and stage versions of *Three Men on a Horse* and would again play the same role in the musical-comedy adaptation, *Let It Ride* (1961). The featured roles of Nicely-Nicely Johnson and The Mission Head were taken by two ex-vaudevillians, Stubby Kaye and Pat Rooney, Sr. Rooney, seventy years old when *Guys and Dolls* opened, had toured in the original *Daughter of Rosie O'Grady*.

Well before *Guys and Dolls* closed (after 1,200 performances), Loesser had begun work on a new project that occupied him for four years and resulted in a bountiful score that has been described as "a Broadway opera." Loesser's own characterization for *The Most Happy Fella* was "a musical with music." Not only had he written enough songs in the traditional style to fill at least one conventional Broadway score, he had added arias, trios, quartets, a canon, instrumental interludes, and a folk hymn.

The source for Loesser's own libretto, the 1924 play *They Knew What They Wanted*, is set in California's Napa Valley, where the robust family-centered customs of Italian immigrants play boldly against the melancholic wanderlust of other pioneers. Tony (Robert Weede) is a vintner—middle-aged and longing for marriage. He proposes to Amy (Jo Sullivan), the young waitress he's been writing to, but he's afraid she'll reject him if she finds out his age and unromantic looks. So in answer to her request for his photo, he sends one of his young and handsome foreman, Joe (Art Lund). The trick brings Amy, whom Tony calls Rosabella, the last step to agreeing to marriage. Their eventual meeting—on Tony's farm—is a disaster. On his way to the train station, Tony crashes his truck, and Rosa is confronted with a fellow who's not only older and less handsome than she expected but one who's also incapacitated from the accident. Her pity for the man she knew from his letters compels her to go through with the marriage just before Tony is rushed to the hospital. The same night, out of loneliness and the need for solace, Rosa sleeps with Joe. As she helps nurse Tony through his recovery, she comes to love him, only to discover that she's pregnant with Joe's child. She confides in Tony, who at first rages but eventually responds with compassion and forgiveness. The story ends with their reunion.

Loesser sometimes obscured the finesse of his "serious" work and the wit of his musical parodies with Broadway rousers like "Standing on the Corner (Watching All the Girls Go By)" and "Big D." His songs also had to fight the distractions of Jo Mielziner's bulky sets, Dania Krupska's busy choreography, and some of the cast's overacting. Still, as Brooks Atkinson wrote, "Mr. Loesser has caught the anguish and the love [in his story] in some exalting music. Broadway is used to heart. It is not accustomed to evocations of the soul." *The Most Happy Fella* won the Drama Critics' Circle Award for Best Musical.

While Loesser was trying to push musical comedy into new territories, others found more profit in holding it back. In 1953, Edwin Lester, the general manager of the Los Angeles Civic Light Opera, exported to New York *Kismet*, a show with the same format that in 1944 had sold his first export, *The Song of Norway*. The score for *Song of Norway* had been adapted from the melodies of Edvard Grieg by Robert Wright and George Forrest; the same team adapted the melodies of Borodin for *Kismet*. And, while the sets for *The Song of Norway* had encompassed Norwegian vistas better proportioned to Hollywood sound stages than Broadway theatres, the sets for *Kismet* held enough burnished minarets and golden latticework for three Baghdads.

To the great extent that it capitalized on extravagant visions of old Baghdad, *Kismet* was an imitation of Rodgers and Hammerstein's *The King and I*, but with none of the dramatic nuances that had often made the spectacle in *The King and I* superfluous. Audiences came solely to ogle the sets and the harem girls and to luxuriate in Borodin's familiar melodies, most of them from *The Polovtsian Dances*. Persistent radio play, well before the show reached New York, had already made hits out of "Stranger in Paradise" and "Baubles, Bangles and Beads," and *Kismet's* publicity was further enhanced by a Tony Award for Best Musical.

To compete with the spectacle and the lush melodies, the cast had to play about five times bigger than life. Alfred Drake, as the poet Hajj, swaggered in the Douglas Fairbanks style he had mastered in *Kiss Me, Kate* and sang Borodin's melodies with the sensuous resonance they deserved. Richard Kiley, as the Caliph, could muster a romantic flair equal to Drake's, but his singing, although agreeable, was comparatively subdued. The contrast worked well, since the Caliph's affection for one of the young women in the evil Wazir's harem was far more tender than Hajj's lusty attentions to Lalume, the shapeliest of the Wazir's wives, played with self-mocking innuendo by Joan Diener.

Kismet wasn't the only ghost of musical-comedy past to materialize on Broadway in the early '50s. In 1950, Cole Porter, Arnold Saint Subber (producer), and Lemuel Ayers (producer and designer), the team that only two years before had given Broadway *Kiss Me, Kate*, threw themselves into reverse for *Out of this World*, in which they burlesqued the Amphitryon legend. In this version, Jupiter (George Jongeyans) fell in love with an American woman touring Greece (Priscilla Gillette) before Juno (Charlotte Greenwood) intervened and hauled him back to Olympus. Even with George Abbott's help during out-of-town tryouts, Agnes de Mille (director) and Hanya Holm (choreographer) couldn't bring the old sex farce to life. Lemuel Ayers' droll and elegant sets occasionally diverted audiences from the book, and likewise, Charlotte Greenwood kept the folks laughing with her grotesque dancing, in which she flailed her long legs as if they were dangling by a couple of strong threads. Porter had given the show the musical wings needed to carry it over the weak bridgework between numbers, but his best tune, "From This Moment On," was cut during the tryouts.

Porter's next show *Can-Can* (1953), for which Abe Burrows wrote the book and directed, was based on a minor scandal over can-can dancing in Montmartre, circa 1890, during which bluenoses took dance-hall proprietors to court on charges of obscenity. From newspaper reports of the cases Burrows fabricated a love story about a young judge (Peter Cookson) and the proprietress of a can-can establishment, played by the French chanteuse Lilo. The bulk of Porter's score wasn't as ingratiating as "C'est Magnifique," "I Love Paris," and "It's All Right With Me," but his less distinctive can-cans, hurdy-gurdy tunes, and pseudo-Parisian ballads all sustained the illusion of Montmartre in 1893. Jo Mielziner strengthened the effect with sets derived from the posters of Toulouse-Lautrec, and, quite appropriate to a musical about the can-can, Michael Kidd's choreography was its best feature. A comic Garden of Eden ballet featuring Gwen Verdon, several exhausting can-cans, a parody of an Apache dance, and a burlesque duel gave the show enough momentum to glide through a choppy second act.

Porter's last musical was *Silk Stockings* (1955), based on the Lubitsch film *Ninotchka*. George S. Kaufman and his wife, the actress Leueen MacGrath, adapted the screenplay. Kaufman had also been hired by Feuer and Martin to direct the show, but during tryouts he quarreled with the producers and, complaining of ill-health, quit. Abe Burrows subsequently rewrote most of the book, Cole Porter replaced discarded songs with new ones, and Cy Feuer directed.

As they had done with *Guys and Dolls*, Feuer, Martin, and Kaufman chose leads who were experienced performers but had never starred in a Broadway musical. Hildegarde Neff, in the role that Garbo had created in the film, was a German stage and film actress who had emigrated to Hollywood. Don Ameche, Ninotchka's Sir Galahad, had appeared in only one other stage play before *Silk Stockings* and had never sung in a show before. Making her Broadway debut in a featured role was Gretchen Wyler, as a talentless and temperamental Hollywood star similar to Jean Hagen's Lina Lamont in *Singin' in the Rain*. All three triumphed. Although handicapped by limited singing ability, Neff made convincing Ninotchka's transformation from a dour Leninist to a femme fatale. Wyler gave her stereotyped role enough humanity to make the imbecile charming. But Ameche was the director and producers' greatest find. Instead of the awkwardness one might expect from an actor making his first try at a musical, Ameche handled his songs in a seemingly artless, natural way. His style made male singers realize they didn't have to use hypermasculine bravura to seem virile.

Despite the fine performances of its leads, *Silk Stockings* proved inferior to its source. Its book was seldom funny, and several times in the second act it became overly serious about Soviet "dogmatism and tyranny." Cole Porter's score also disappointed; only "All of You" bubbled with the suggestive wit and debonair melody typical of his finest songs.

As Cole Porter had discovered, writing an "integrated" book musical was more strenuous and riskier than writing an old-fashioned evening of musical set pieces bundled in a make-do plot. The collaborators for an integrated book musical had to subordinate their egos to a production concept, sometimes suffering the tortures of discarding great inspirations that didn't conform to the dramatic vectors of their script. Rodgers and Hammerstein constantly worked to perfect the coordination of their talents, but even they suffered lapses, as with *Allegro, Me and Juliet*, and *Pipe Dream*. The longevity of their partnership—seventeen years—allowed for trial and error. Most teams didn't have the determination or the time to weld their talents and harmonize their fractious egos. The few who did find partners with whom they liked to work and with whom they worked well were often forced to separate long before their collaborations could mature.

E. Y. Harburg and Fred Saidy, the librettists and lyricists, had worked with Harold Arlen on *Bloomer Girl* (1944) and with Burton Lane on *Finian's Rainbow* (1947) before joining still another composer, Sammy Fain, for *Flahooley* (1951). Like *Finian's Rainbow, Flahooley* was a curious combination of fantasy and social satire. Harburg squeezed into a single plot a magic doll with the power to create universal happiness, a genie and an Arabian princess, a political witch hunt modeled after the McCarthy hearings, a satire on big business, and a romance between an inventor of toys and a typical musical-comedy ingenue. Audiences were confused; the show played only 40 performances.

In 1957, Harburg and Saidy again collaborated, this time on the book for *Jamaica*. Harold Arlen wrote the music, and Harburg wrote the lyrics. David Merrick, who produced, had originally sought Harry Belafonte and then Sidney Poitier to play the lead role of a poor Caribbean fisherman. When neither actor agreed to take the part, Merrick had Harburg and Saidy rewrite the script to feature Lena Horne. Their show now had three highly exploitable attractions: its star, its exotic setting, and calypso music. Miss Horne sang in eight of the show's musical numbers, her sensuous voice and seductive presence completely justifying the overtime. "Take it Slow, Joe," a suggestive blues, was her best. She, Arlen, and Jack Cole, the show's choreographer, draped a bland story in holiday colors and coaxed it to life.

Arlen was the logical choice to write the score for *Jamaica*. Only a few years before, he had composed the tunes for another show set in the Caribbean, *House of Flowers* (1954). His melodies for it were so self-effacing they hid their charms from audiences accustomed to the self-proclaiming clamor of most Broadway song. *House of Flowers* was Arlen's masterpiece, a wistful, quiet score perhaps best heard apart from the distractions of a Broadway production, but both the original edition and an Off-Broadway revival in 1958 failed at the box office. Truman Capote's fragile story of an innocent girl (Diahann Carroll) sheltered in a brothel was obscured by the spectacle of a West Indian Mardi Gras. The only moments in Capote's libretto that successfully competed with the hoopla were the comic insults hurled between two competing madams, Fleur (Pearl Bailey) and Tango (Juanita Hall). Bailey also got to project her raffish stage personality in "One Man Ain't Quite Enough," while Diahann Carroll, making her stage debut at the age of nineteen, sang the best of the show's delicate numbers, "I Never Has Seen Snow" and "A Sleepin' Bee." The most infectious of the show's songs was a devil-may-care calypso tune: "Two Ladies in De Shade of De Banana Tree."

In 1959, Arlen worked on *Saratoga* with yet another set of collaborators. Morton Da Costa, the film and stage director, adapted Edna Ferber's novel *Saratoga Trunk*, and Johnny Mercer, with whom Arlen had written the songs for *St. Louis Woman* (1946), again contributed lyrics. In spite of their experience and a cast headed by Howard Keel and Carol Lawrence (as two adventurers fortune-hunting at the upper New York resort), *Saratoga* ran only 80 performances. Da Costa, writing his first musical, hadn't been able to pare Ferber's novel to the sparse yet clear narrative demanded by the musical theatre.

Johnny Mercer had had better luck with other collaborators. His songs for *Top Banana* (1951) hit just the right hollow sentimentality and manufactured gaiety for Hy Kraft's trifle about an ex-vaudevillian now with his own television show. Book and songs were tailored to Phil Silvers' speciality: the frenetic egotist whose incompetence is equaled only by his dopey optimism. In addition to Silvers, the cast list read like a Who's Who of vaudeville and burlesque funnymen: Joey and Herbie Faye, Jack Albertson, Walter Dare Wahl, Bradford Hatton, Zachary Charles, Hal Loman, Eddie Hanley, and Johnny Trama. Their finale was a hilarious travesty of every classic gag, every pratfall and monkeyshine that had once been the glory of the old five-a-day.

Mercer's next show was *Li'l Abner* (1956), for which he wrote the lyrics and Gene de Paul wrote the music. The transfer of Al Capp's Dogpatch from comic strip to the musical stage had kept a succession of producers laboring for nine years before Norman Panama and Melvin Frank wrote a workable libretto and then joined with choreographer-director Michael Kidd to produce their own handiwork. Their show was a natural for the musical stage of the '50s, a double satire on politics and the war between the sexes in the tradition of *Call Me Madam, Texas, Li'l Darlin', Silk Stockings*, and *Flahooley*. Daisy Mae (Edith Adams) hotfooted it after Abner (Peter Palmer), while the Dogpatchians, under the leadership of Marryin' Sam (Stubby Kaye), had to decide whether or not to give the Feds the recipe for Mammy Yokum's magic elixir, Yokumberry Tonic. The tangle of complications began with the government's decision to use Dogpatch as an A-bomb test site, and then, in a spirit closer to Will Rogers' than Al Capp's, unwound through burlesques on the military-industrial complex, technology, conflict of interest, conformity, marriage, and sex. To get through all of this in one evening, Michael Kidd had to set a hell-bent pace, which Mercer and De Paul's ballads and gentle novelty songs ("If I Had My Druthers," "Namely You," "Unnecessary Town," and "Past My Prime") couldn't relieve. Although their tranquil songs weren't very compelling, their citified hillbilly tunes, especially "Jubilation T. Cornpone" and "The Country's in the Very Best of Hands," were irresistibly sunny.

In the same season (1951–52) that Mercer's *Top Banana* opened, Alan Jay Lerner and Frederick Loewe brought their fourth show, *Paint Your Wagon*, to Broadway. Like so many of the '50's librettists, Lerner was attracted to American folklore. His reading of Bret Harte and Mark Twain convinced him that tall tales about the California Gold Rush were prime material for musical comedy, and from a handful of them he built a vehicle for James Barton, a veteran song-and-dance man from burlesque, vaudeville, and the Shubert musicals. Barton played a prospector who strikes a rich vein of gold in northern California, builds a town, watches it prosper, and, after the lode is exhausted, moves on to the next strike with the rest of the miners. Lerner packed his libretto with eyewitness accounts of pioneer life in the far West: a prospector's trading for a wife from an overstocked Mormon polygamist; the arrival of the first woman in a mining camp of all males; a circuit court trial conducted in a saloon, the only hall in the frontier town large enough to hold all the curious spectators. The patchwork book never held together, but Agnes de Mille's can-cans for a troupe of dance-hall girls and Barton's diverting but totally incongruous soft shoe filled the gaps. Frederick Loewe, more at home in Old Vienna than the Old West, had trouble finding melodic complements for Lerner's story. Only a mock hymn sung by a Mormon and his two wives and "They Call the Wind Maria" sounded as if they might have come from any territory farther west than Lexington Avenue. "I Still See Eliza" and "I Talk to the Trees" got plenty of radio play.

Public enthusiasm for musicals built on American legend also convinced producers to revive two of George Gershwin's shows, *Of Thee I Sing* (1931) and *Porgy and Bess* (1935). George S. Kaufman revised his and Morrie Ryskind's book for *Of Thee I Sing*, but in spite of allusions to current political shenanigans and the excellent performances of Jack Carson as John P. Wintergreen and of Paul Hartman as Alexander Throttlebottom, the show played only 72 performances. The satire had lost its pungency.

The following season (1952–53), after a tour of the United States and Europe, a revival of *Porgy and Bess* (the fourth) arrived on Broadway. If the new *Of Thee I Sing* failed because it lacked vitality, the revival of *Porgy and Bess* erred in the opposite direction. Director Robert Breen magnified every accent in Gershwin's melodies by coordinating simple actions, like the closing of shutters, to orchestral and vocal cues. To make sure that his leads kept a high pitch of energy, he double-cast Leontyne Price and Urylee Leonardos in the role of Bess and triple-cast Le Vern Hutcherson, Leslie Scott, and Irving Barnes in the role of Porgy. None of them were subtle actors, but what they lacked in acting skill they more than compensated for in vocal bombast. Cab Calloway made Sportin' Life an extension of his waggish stage personality.

Porgy and Bess was one of the few Broadway shows, until the late '60s and early '70s, to depict black Americans. And although blacks were featured in a handful of '50's musicals—*Shuffle Along* (1952), *My Darlin' Aida* (1952), *House of Flowers* (1954), *Mr. Wonderful* (1956), *Shinbone Alley* (1957), and *Jamaica* (1957)—no producers tried to attract black audiences to Broadway or encourage black writers and composers to contribute to the musical stage.

The only musical written principally by blacks that was produced on Broadway during the '50s was the revival of the 1921 all-black revue, *Shuffle Along*. The new edition ran for only 4 performances. Flournoy Miller (one of the original librettists) and Paul Gerard Smith tried to give the old routines a dramatic framework by converting their revue into a book musical about black GIs and WACs at the end of World War II. But the plot was overly complicated; the humor, as one critic put it, was of the "Amos 'n' Andy School"; and the production suffered from low morale due in part to illnesses which had hospitalized some of the cast and a fire that had destroyed the original sets. In an attempt to rescue the severely crippled show, the original songwriters, Eubie Blake and Noble Sissle, sang a medley of their hits (including "I'm Just Wild About Harry" and "Love Will Find a Way") at the end of each performance.

In the 1952–53 season, Hassard Short and Charles Friedman tried to repeat the success of their *Carmen Jones* (1943) with an Americanized version of *Aida*, renamed *My Darlin' Aida*. Their strategy was the same as it had been for reworking Bizet's *Carmen*. They Americanized Antonio Ghislanzon's libretto by moving the plot's setting from the Egyptian Memphis to Memphis, Tennessee, and updated the period from several thousand years before the birth of Christ to the first years of the American Civil War. Radames became a young Confederate captain, and Aida became a mulatto slave. By transferring the action to the American South, the adapters did the best they could to find an American locale where grandiloquence wouldn't seem absurd. But Friedman, who served as lyricist, didn't have the experience to solve all the problems consequent to the shift. His lyrics vacillated between precise, formal English and self-conscious slang. Unlike *Carmen Jones, My Darlin' Aida* was stiff and inaccessible.

Although neither production concerned itself with black culture, *Mr. Wonderful* (1956) and *Shinbone Alley* (1957) starred black celebrities. The more successful of the two, *Mr. Wonderful*, ran on the popularity and talents of Sammy Davis, Jr. Joseph Stein and Will Glickman supplied a book that did little more than build to Davis' nightclub routine, while wasting the talents of Jack Carter, Chita Rivera, Pat Marshall, and Olga James. The score for the show, by Jerry Bock (music), Larry Holofcener, and George Weiss (lyrics), was eclipsed by the song standards that Davis performed in his nightclub finale. The exceptions were the title song and "Too Close for Comfort," a sizzler performed by—who else?—Sammy Davis, Jr.

Eartha Kitt, who, like Davis, had worked as a cabaret entertainer, played mehitabel, an amoral alley cat, in *Shinbone Alley*, derived from Don Marquis' newspaper columns about mehitabel and her confidant, archy the cockroach. Archy supposedly reported mehitabel's adventures to newspaper readers by jumping from key to key of Marquis' typewriter, his light weight the reason for the absence of upper-case letters, capricious margins, and the free verse look of the text. Some of archy's "verse" was first converted into song by lyricist Joe Darion and composer George Kleisinger for a record album subtitled "a back alley opera." Its success prompted a stage version written in collaboration with Mel Brooks. Their adaptation failed, although Eddie Bracken made archy warm and likable, especially for a cockroach, and Eartha Kitt, eschewing mehitabel's back-alley raunchiness, was all sleek sexiness and blissful indolence.

Marquis' stories needed a more unconventional production, one housed in a small theatre, where close rapport between actors and audience and the absence of distracting spectacle would have encouraged make-believe. In an intimate, Off-Broadway production, *Shinbone Alley* might have caught the sardonic spirit of what archy had to say about mehitabel's slumming. A case in point: Off Broadway's Theatre de Lys was the perfect size to amplify the odd combination of vivacity and depravity in the 1954 version of *The Threepenny Opera*, directed by Carmen Capalbo. It ran for an unprecedented 2,707 performances.

An earlier English version of the Brecht-Weill masterpiece, which had opened on Broadway in 1933, lasted only 12 performances. Almost twenty years later, Marc Blitzstein, who, like Kurt Weill, had turned from avantgarde, serious music to the popular theatre, began a translation of Brecht's words into colloquial English. The results were as racy and current as Loesser's lyrics for *Guys and Dolls*, but far more cantankerous about modern society. Blitzstein's words fit snugly over Weill's melodies and made the new version easier to sing than the German original, for which Brecht had intentionally written flinty, ill-fitting lyrics.

Carmen Capalbo chose a vivacious cast that performed with such enthusiasm that the decadent eroticism in Weill's score and the cynicism of Brecht's script seemed almost jolly. Capalbo's greatest coup was casting Lotte Lenya, Weill's widow, in the role of Jenny. But he also had an eye for other talent: The original cast included Charlotte Rae as Mrs. Peachum, Jo Sullivan as Polly, Beatrice Arthur as Lucy Brown, Gerald Price as The Streetsinger, and George Tyne as Tiger Brown. Among those who succeeded the original cast during the seven-year run were Jerry Orbach, Jo Wilder, Edward Asner, James Mitchell, and Jane Connell.

Just one night after the première of *The Threepenny Opera*, another precedent-setting musical opened Off Broadway. *The Golden Apple* (1954), the first book musical produced by the Phoenix Theatre, became the first Off-Broadway musical to be optioned for a production on Broadway, where it won the New York Drama Critics' Circle Award as the Best Musical of 1953–54.

The Golden Apple was also the first literate musical to make affectionate fun of American musical comedy and American culture. John Latouche (librettist and lyricist) parodied Broadway's current infatuation with American myth by transplanting episodes from the *Iliad* and *Odyssey* to the city of Rhododendron, in the state of Washington, U.S.A., and advancing the time to shortly after the Spanish-American War. Paris became a traveling salesman, who meets Helen, the wife of Rhododendron's tycoon, while on a business trip. Ulysses became a much-decorated hero of the Spanish-American War. The Trojan War was reduced to a boxing match, during which Ulysses knocks out Paris, wins back Helen, and restores the honor of Rhododendron. Composer Jerome Moross set this mock epic to a suitably wry score. Just as Latouche had miniaturized Greek myth, Moross dwarfed into one score a history of theatre music. From the crowding and reducing, things inevitably came out delightfully misproportioned. John Chapman of the New York *Daily News* described the effect as "off-beat, off-rhyme, [and] off-harmony." The jumble of "influences" was itself impressive, if disorienting: Gilbert and Sullivan next to Stephen Foster, calypso sharing the program with Appalachian folk song, and everything twisted out of shape by Moross' unusual harmonies. Many of the musical jokes were too subtle for the less erudite, but "By Goona Goona LaGoon" was obviously a very funny parody of "Bali Ha'i."

After playing 48 performances at the Phoenix Theatre, *The Golden Apple* moved to Broadway for another 125 performances and became an early *success d'estime* for the Off-Broadway musical.

The Phoenix Theatre's next two musicals, *Sandhog* (1954) and *Livin' the Life* (1957), didn't stir much interest; but in spite of the public's indifference—or maybe because of it—Norris Houghton and T. Edward Hambleton, founders of the company, gave their fourth try, *Once Upon a Mattress* (1959), an impressive mounting. George Abbott, in his first assignment Off Broadway, led a high-powered team, which included Joe Layton as choreographer and William and Jean Eckart as designers of the sets and costumes. The television comedienne Carol Burnett was cast in the lead, and Jack Gilford, from the theatre and vaudeville, was cast for the major supporting role.

Houghton and Hambleton had first seen *Once Upon a Mattress* at the Tamiment Playhouse (the Poconos boot camp for Broadway writers and performers), where, as a one-act, it was one of many short musicals designed for the resort's summer bill. Convinced of the show's potential, the producers asked Mary Rodgers (music), Jay Thompson, Marshall Barer, and Dean

Fuller (book and lyrics) for a full-length version. Their new version was still a daffy, transparently thin take-off on Hans Christian Andersen's "The Princess and the Pea," but now it had more clowning for Miss Burnett and a farce subplot about a Lady-Not-So-in-Waiting who is unmarried and very pregnant. Mary Rodgers' tunes were mostly simple and direct like those of her famous father, but she did try some irregular meters in "Sensitivity" with fine comic effect. The entire production remained as delightfully inconsequential as the original, and it played through the summer to sold-out houses.

Sales were still strong in the fall, but Hambleton and Houghton decided to close the show because they had booked their theatre for the new season. Led by Carol Burnett, the cast picketed until the producers relented and moved the show uptown. There, the vicissitudes of Broadway real estate forced the show into an orphan's wanderings: during the course of 406 performances it played the Alvin, Winter Garden, Cort, and St. James. A London production with Jane Connell, Max Wall, and Thelma Ruby was booed by its opening-night audience, but staggered through a month's run. Two companies that toured the United States lost about a quarter of a million dollars.

Because it hewed so closely to the Rodgers and Hammerstein model, *Once Upon a Mattress* had more of a chance outside New York and abroad than any other Off-Broadway product of the decade. The one thing it lacked was spectacle, that fetish of Broadway directors and producers, who often spent so much time and money on the design and logistics of a spectacular set that a neglected book and score would collapse. Such was the case with Harold Rome's first book musical, *Wish You Were Here* (1952), which he and Joshua Logan adapted from *Having a Wonderful Time*. The original had been a gentle, unassuming comedy about a Brooklyn secretary on vacation in the Catskills. Rome and Logan plowed under its quieter nuances—and with them much of its warmth and unpretentiousness—to build a monumental stage spectacle. Their new wonder featured a center-stage swimming pool and every other extravagance for which they could invent an excuse: a basketball game during which the baskets were scored to musical cues, a fire that seemed to burn down a recreation hall, and a rain storm that interrupted a picnic complete with glowing barbecue pits.

Neither the spectacle nor the performances of Sheila Bond and Jack Cassidy could warm what was left of the original comedy. On opening night the critics, even the dispassionate ones, growled their disgust. Weekly receipts soon slumped to a low of $25,000. To save the backers' investment in the swimming pool, Joshua Logan and Arthur Kober (the author of *Having a Wonderful Time*) revised the musical's book as the show continued to run. They restrained the Brooklyn girl's penchant for Yiddish-American malapropisms and brought in Jerome Robbins to restage many of the dances and add a new ballet. Harold Rome contributed a new song. Then they called back the critics—who were still not very enthusiastic. But all the scurrying about paid dividends at the box office: Weekly grosses climbed from $25,000 to $47,000 and *Wish You Were Here* endured for 597 performances.

Joshua Logan also directed (and coproduced with David Merrick) Harold Rome's next musical, *Fanny* (1954), an adaptation by Logan and S. N. Behrman of Marcel Pagnol's three plays, *Marius, Fanny,* and *César.* Although their show called for the large cast and heavy scenery expected by audiences of the '50s, it deviated in one essential from the Broadway formula. Two years before Frank Loesser's *The Most Happy Fella* would feature a balding, middle-aged romantic as its protagonist, Logan and Behrman put two aging and sedentary Frenchmen at the center of a musical.

César (Ezio Pinza), a widower who runs a dockside tavern in Marseilles, wants his son Marius (William Tabbert) to marry Fanny (Florence Henderson). The father plays hovering cupid to the young couple, but Marius, an incurable drifter, is soon off on another sea voyage of indefinite length and uncertain destination. After he's sailed, Fanny discovers she's pregnant. César's best friend Panisse (Walter Slezak) has been trying to convince Fanny—and everyone else—that she should marry him, even though he's far too old to interest her romantically. To give her son a father, she accepts. Panisse is overjoyed: Now he will have a son to inherit his business! The child thrives in Panisse and Fanny's care. Twelve years pass, and Fanny never loses the hope than someday she will be free to wed Marius. The dilemma is resolved in a bittersweet coda as Marius returns, and Panisse, knowing that he's about to die, anticipates with contentment the eventual happiness of the young couple.

A story with so many views of love inspired Rome to write a copious score of short, direct songs. The lighter, more humorous ones were given to Panisse and César, whose notions of love were moderated by their age and paternal concerns; the more impetuous songs were given to Fanny and Marius. Slezak and Pinza were especially adept at conveying the warmth and panache of Rome's score. Their final scene was a musical-comedy actor's dream: Panisse's death and the parting of two lifelong friends. The farewell ended with a reprise, by César, of "Welcome Home." "Close your eyes, close your eyes," he sang to his old friend, "And the world will settle down to size. . . ."

Logan and Behrman wisely heeded the advice of opening-night critics and continued to rewrite *Fanny* during the first three weeks of its run. Their efforts, the charm of the cast, and the masterful promotion of producer Merrick kept ticket sales healthy for a run of 888 performances.

Another of Merrick's hits, *La Plume de Ma Tante* (1958), depended on Gallic charm, but of a more direct sort. A revue written, directed, and choreographed by the husband and wife team of Robert Dhery and Colette Brosset, it had originated in Paris and played in London for two years before Merrick imported it. A cast of zanies, including Pierre Olaf who went on to

Carnival and other domestic shows, performed elaborate sight gags with such precise timing and mock diffidence that they transformed obvious humor into comic virtuosity. Their best invention was "Frères Jacques," in which a quartet of monks got carried away by their bell ringing and broke into swinging (literally and figuratively) jazz. *La Plume de Ma Tante* won the Drama Critics' Circle Award for Best Musical.

Merrick again employed Harold Rome in the last years of the decade to work on an adaptation of Max Brand's classic American Western, *Destry*. Its shy but courageous sheriff (first played by Tom Mix in 1932), heart-of-gold dancehall hostess, and villains in black hats had appeared in four versions of the novel filmed at Universal Studios and in countless films made by competitors. By 1955, television had also begun to capitalize on Western lore, when *Gunsmoke's* Mister Dillon first rode into the video version of Dodge City. Deciding it was high time for Broadway to cash in on the Western, Merrick hired Leonard Gershe to adapt *Destry* for a musical, Harold Rome to supply the songs, and Michael Kidd to direct and choreograph.

Their version, *Destry Rides Again* (1959), was half genial spoof and half poker-faced tribute. Andy Griffith played Destry, a lawman "mild as milk and friendly as a pup," until the villains back him to the wall, when he shows an ornery streak by finally drawing his six-shooter and miraculously blasting every lamp and bottle in the town's saloon. That cows the outlaws and wins the heart of the dance-hall hostess (Dolores Gray).

Rome's cleverest songs parodied the Western. His "Paradise Alley" was a mock alma mater to a bordello, sung by its girls and their clients, and "Are You Ready, Gyp Watson?" made fun of Bible-thumping revivalists. He also composed a menacing accompaniment for the show-stopping dance number in which the desperadoes intimidate the peace-loving townsfolk with a violent whip dance. Most of Kidd's staging was equally pictorial and vigorous. But the indefinite tone of its script, the lack of romance, and the low morale of the company (unnerved by a feud between Kidd and Dolores Gray) knocked the whoop and holler out of *Destry Rides Again*. Even Merrick's gift for promotion couldn't sustain a run for more than 473 performances.

By the late '40s, one of Harold Rome's contemporaries, Jule Styne, had already established himself as a composer of book musicals. In 1947, he collaborated with Sammy Cahn (lyrics) on *High Button Shoes* and in 1949 with Leo Robin (lyrics) on *Gentlemen Prefer Blondes*. In the early '50s, he began to work with Betty Comden and Adolph Green and in 1959 joined lyricist Stephen Sondheim and librettist Arthur Laurents for *Gypsy*, the gaudiest and truest love-hate tribute to stage mothers ever produced.

But Styne's first show of the decade, *Hazel Flagg* (1953), was less than a triumph. Ben Hecht adapted his own screenplay, *Nothing Sacred*, and, probably in deference to musical-comedy frivolity, erased most of his sardonic wisecracks. If any plot needed his bracing mockery it was one about publicity flacks and vulturous reporters trying to exploit a fake victim of radiation poisoning. Even Jule Styne's best songs, "How Do You Speak to an Angel?" and "Every Street's a Boulevard in Old New York," sauntered amiably and in the opposite direction from the satiric premises of Hecht's screenplay. Their misjudgments wasted the caustic ebullience of Helen Gallagher, who, as Hazel, played her first starring role.

In 1954, Styne rejoined Comden and Green on a new version of *Peter Pan*. Their team wrote half the songs, and Mark "Moose" Charlap and Carolyn Leigh wrote the other half. Their show first played Los Angeles and San Francisco with Mary Martin as Peter, after which Martin's husband, Richard Halliday, brought it and his wife to New York for a limited engagement.

Both teams of songwriters caught the spirit of Never-Never Land, where, if a boy doesn't want to, he doesn't have to grow up. The best of the Comden-Green and Styne songs was "Captain Hook's Waltz," a mock-macabre ditty in which an effete Captain, played with lisping panache by Cyril Ritchard, praised himself as "Mrs. Hook's baby boy," "the swiniest swine," and "the creepiest creep in the world." The Charlap-Leigh team contributed two of Peter's chirrupy boasts: "I Gotta Crow" (something he does regularly to blow off a little steam and trumpet his contentment) and "I Won't Grow Up" (his defiant stand against becoming an adult fuddy-duddy).

Whenever Tin Pan Alley bombast threatened the fantasy of J. M. Barrie's original, Jerome Robbins' staging came to the rescue. Peter and the Darling children flew above London's rooftops against a backdrop of winking stars; the invisible sprite Tinker Bell made small objects seem to float around the stage; Peter's shadow danced with him; trees instantaneously budded; and arrows, shot from invisible bows, twanged through the forests of Never-Never Land. But the visual effects never upstaged Mary Martin and Cyril Ritchard. Martin gave Peter her Texas bluster, while Ritchard played the Captain with the braggadocio of an obvious faker, whose impish foppery children immediately understood and loved.

The next Comden-Green and Styne collaboration, *Bells Are Ringing*, was produced by the Theatre Guild in 1956. Comden and Green wrote an ersatz—but amiable—vehicle for Judy Holliday, with whom they had worked as The Revuers, a satirical song-and-skit act. Holliday played her specialty, a slightly bubble-headed blonde with the faith of an innocent, the determination of a moralist, and the moonstruck sweetness of a romantic. The show's other assets were from Styne's pen: "The Party's Over" and "Just in Time," a couple of songs so durable that they didn't suffer at all from being dropped helter-skelter into a make-do romance about a telephone operator and a struggling playwright.

Comden and Green next signed to write the lyrics for Arthur Laurents' *Gypsy* (1959), the musical biography of Gypsy Rose Lee, but other commitments forced them to withdraw. David Merrick and Leland Hayward, who owned the rights to the book, then aproached the young composer-lyricist Stephen Sondheim, whose credits were the lyrics to *West Side Story* and the songs for a musical that had not reached Broadway because of its producer's death. When Ethel Merman, who was slated to play Gypsy Rose Lee's mother, balked at starring in a musical for which a neophyte would write the score, the producers hired Jule Styne to write the music for Sondheim's words.

Mama Rose, Gypsy's mother, was the centripetal force of Laurents' book. She was complex: a stage mother of paleolithic might and manners, but also a vulnerable ego who wants to succeed through her two daughters and who tries to win their love by hounding them toward stardom. June, the more talented of the two sisters, outgrows both her kiddie routine and Rose's domination; she deserts for marriage and her own career. In panic, Mama tries to replace June with Louise, but Louise is awkward and shy. No one wants to see a gawky kid stumbling through a tatty old vaudeville routine. Audiences want the bawdy jokes and striptease of burlesque. Almost by accident, Louise finds herself on stage faking a strip, and to her amazement she stays poised and loves teasing her audience. "Gypsy Rose Lee" is born. Mama finally has the celebrity she wanted only to discover that her "creation" has its own mind and a need for independence. Momentarily it looks as if Mama will have to bull ahead without Gypsy, but Louise relents and includes Rose in her new life.

Laurents' portrait of Mama wasn't flattering, and the garish colors and grotesque curlicues gave a tawdry vitality to his book. Styne worked the same way. A master of musical-comedy conventions, he transformed everything that was meretritious and raucous in the old vaudeville and burlesque music into dazzling caricature. Even the ballad "Small World" and the gentle, kidding love song "You'll Never Get Away From Me" hinted at vaudeville swagger. Styne's best material—"Some People," "Everything's Coming Up Roses," "I Had a Dream," and "Rose's Turn"—barreled ahead with all of Mama's indefatigable bravura.

Sondheim's lyrics were sometimes more self-conscious than Styne's tunes, but more often than not they deepened a moment or a characterization without drawing undue attention to themselves. His words to "Some People," for example, not only made clear Mama Rose's yearning for the good life but also uncovered her less attractive and pungent disdain for the simpler ambitions and narrower horizons of, in Rose's words, "some humdrum people." His vaudeville parodies captured, with off accents and intentional mispronunciations, the tacky, make-do approach of an earlier, artless form of musical theatre.

The script and score for *Gypsy* gave Ethel Merman the challenge she had long wanted. Her role could easily have become monstrous, a vain harridan who exploits her children to appease her own hunger for fame. Merman—with the help of director-choreographer Jerome Robbins—found the key to making Mama Rose sympathetic: the concern that Mama will not admit to herself, the worry that one day her offspring will desert her. Behind her zest, her plans, and her wrangling was always a hint of that maternal fear; it was enough to add warmth and a touch of pathos to the role.

In 1974, *Gypsy* was revived for a London run, followed by a tour of the United States and a limited engagement on Broadway. Arthur Laurents directed a production that, except for skimpier sets, looked much the same as the original. Angela Lansbury, as Mama Rose, brought greater vulnerability and self-kidding to the role than Ethel Merman had, but in the process lost Rose's awesome vulgarity. Even though Lansbury's performance was merely mortal and the touring sets looked a bit shabby, *Gypsy*'s book and score hadn't lost a carat of their gaudy splendor. The show was now a classic.

Jule Styne had begun his musical life as a child prodigy, who, by the age of nine, was a piano soloist with the Chicago Symphony. But his early training in the classics had little influence on the style of his songwriting. As a composer of show music he seemed to have been cradled in Tin Pan Alley. That wasn't the case with Leonard Bernstein, whose first musical comedy, *On the Town* (1944), opened only three years before Styne's first show, *High Button Shoes* (1947). Bernstein never divorced his "serious" composing and conducting from his work in musical theatre, and whenever the resources of popular music seemed too limited to give him the effects he wanted, he fused popular-music idioms with the style and techniques of his concert music.

Bernstein's second musical was *Wonderful Town* (1953), written in collaboration with Comden and Green (lyricists), Joseph Fields and Jerome Chodorov (librettists). Beginning in 1948, at least four veteran producers (Leland Hayward, Richard Krakeur, Fred Finklehoffe, and Max Gordon) had considered musical versions of Fields and Chodorov's play, *My Sister Eileen*, itself adapted from Ruth McKinney's stories. Robert Fryer eventually signed Leroy Anderson to write the music and Arnold Horwitt to write the lyrics, but they withdrew from the project late in 1952 because of a disagreement with Fryer over "the emphasis to be placed on the songs in relation to the story." Bernstein, Comden, and Green were brought in, and the score of fourteen musical numbers was finished in five weeks. George Abbott directed, and Raoul Pène du Bois designed scenery and costumes.

Wonderful Town, like *On the Town*, was a love song to New York City, but this time not as manic as one sung and danced by three sailors on a twenty-four-hour shore leave. This time the city was reflected in the bedazzled eyes of two Ohioans, the Sherwood sisters, who in 1935 set out from a bohemian apartment in Greenwich Village to conquer New York. Ruth (Rosalind Russell), the elder, is a waspish skeptic who wants to succeed as a writer; Eileen (Edith Adams) is an aspiring actress so open and unpretentious that she charms a platoon of battle-weary New Yorkers into helping her through the city's initiation rites. After an act and a half of comic disasters, Ruth sells her first story and Eileen lands a job in a night club. New York isn't exactly at their feet, but it has turned its smile on them.

Bernstein and his collaborators had to be versatile to keep up with the newcomers' rapidly changing perspectives: bright and bold strokes for romantic enthusiasm or the joys of making new friends and discovering new places; quiet, lyrical colors for homesickness or lovesickness; mordant caricature for dealing with pretentious phonies; and witty but tolerant parody for New York's eccentrics and their odd rituals. For "Christopher Street" Bernstein composed a melody that suggested the jive patois and bustle of Greenwich Village in the '30s. His "Ohio" closely imitated gushy tributes to home states, while "Pass the Football," rasped out the bogus academic career of a gridiron hero, who, after four years in college, still thinks Da Vinci was a halfback for Notre Dame. But the tunes that gave *Wonderful Town* a blast of ozone and set it vibrating in resonance with the mad heartbeat of New York were its dances: "Conga!," "Swing!" (whose exclamation points were well deserved), and "Wrong Note Rag" (complete with quarter-tone dissonances).

Rosalind Russell had interrupted her eighteen-year career in films to play the older sister, the role she had originated in the 1942 film version of Fields and Chodorov's play. Although she was neither an impressive singer (one critic described her voice as "an amiable croak") nor a graceful dancer, Russell could work all the comic variations on Ruth's conversion from a standoffish mother hen to a big-city hedonist who charms half of the Braziliam Navy. Edith Adams' comedy was less flexible, but her fresh-scrubbed sexiness and sweet, full voice fitted hand in glove with Russell's gruffer, less musical Ruth.

Wonderful Town received both the Tony and the Critics' Circle Award for Best Musical.

Bernstein next accepted the challenge of adapting Voltaire's eighteenth-century satire *Candide* for the musical stage. His solution was to write a mock operetta perfectly in tune with Voltaire's corrosive ridicule of button-eyed optimists. Bernstein's score for *Candide* (1956) parodied, with great affection, the popular set pieces of nineteenth- and early twentieth-century operetta: the coloratura extravaganza ("Glitter and Be Gay"), the grand waltz ("What's the Use?"), the nationalistic dance ("Mazurka" and "Gavotte"), the effervescent choral salute ("Bon Voyage"), rapturous duets ("Oh Happy We" and "You Were Dead, You Know"), and the contest of vocal power always prompted by quartets ("Quartet Finale to Act I"). The hilarity of these florid, posturing numbers was doubled by their popping up in the middle of earthquake, inquisition, torture, slavery, rape, drowning, and a colorful variety of other degradations visited upon Candide and Cunegonde. But not all of Bernstein's songs were as nasty as Voltaire might have liked. Candide sang "Eldorado," a wistful, lilting apostrophe to the legendary Utopia, and the entire cast joined in the anthemlike finale, "Make Our Garden Grow."

Bernstein's collaborators failed to match the grace and wit of his music. Without benefit of a detached narrator who could spin laughter from catastrophe and life from caricature, Lillian Hellman's script was little more than an ever-repeating shaggy-dog story. And Tyrone Guthrie's staging, which depended too often on the static pageantry of operetta, was as inflexible as Doctor Pangloss' aphorism that "All is for the best in this best of all possible worlds."

Bernstein's magnificent score couldn't rescue *Candide,* which after opening with a flourish on December 1, 1956, closed after a short run of only 73 performances.

Candide had delayed another project with which Bernstein had been toying since 1949, when Jerome Robbins telephoned him to suggest their working with Arthur Laurents on a contemporary version of *Romeo and Juliet.* Robbins' initial idea was to make Juliet Jewish and Romeo Catholic and to set the action in the lower East Side of New York during the concurrent holidays of Passover and Easter. The final script eventually set the action in the slums of mid-Manhattan's West Side and made Juliet a Puerto Rican immigrant, Maria, and Romeo a second-generation American, Tony. Like their Shakespearean counterparts, Maria and Tony were tragic victims of their romantic idealism in conflict with the violent reality of their families' hatred.

Tension was everywhere—in the dialogue, the choreography, and the score—of *West Side Story.* "The Prologue" introduced the Jets, Tony's ex-gang, and the Sharks, led by Maria's brother, Bernardo. To a skittish rhythm of false bravado the rival factions taunted one another, the teasing intensified, switchblades appeared, gang members lashed out at one another, a police whistle blew, and the kids scattered. Not a word of dialogue had been spoken, the entire scene was danced and pantomimed. Even the comic set pieces and love songs were shadowed by tragedy. In "Gee, Officer Krupke," the Jets's vaudeville turns only half hid the gang's bitterness about their pathetic home lives. When Tony and Maria sang "Tonight," the melody glided—but not far above—an agitated rhythm suggesting the reckless haste and danger of their love. Purely melodic associations between violence and romance were subtly made by repeating the same opening intervals in songs as disparate in style as the taut jazz of "Cool" and the exuberant romance of "Maria."

Because the play was the thing, Robbins cast unknowns, on whose youth and anonymity he could imprint his production concept: the frightening beauty of Shakespeare's tragedy converted to romantic song and dance. Larry Kert, a former Hollywood stuntman, won the role of Tony; Carol Lawrence, who had made her debut in *New Faces of 1952,* played Maria; and the featured roles of Tony's friend Riff and Maria's confidante Anita went to Mickey Calin and Chita Rivera. Robbins encouraged his cast to maintain their gang rivalries between rehearsals as well as during them, and soon the actress playing a tomboy rejected by both gangs found herself taking breaks and walking home alone. Robbins' strategy worked just as well with audiences, who were shocked by the intense conflict between the gangs.

No previous musical had depended so heavily on dance, and few other Broadway choreographers would have tried for such convincing brutality. As indispensable as the rumbles and as faultlessly conceived were "The Dance at the Gym" and "Ballet Sequence." "The Dance at the Gym" took place on "neutral turf," where, instead of attacking each other with tire chains and switchblades, the gangs competed in a dance contest, while a comically inept social worker, intimidated by the violent undercurrents of the contest, stood helplessly by. The "Ballet Sequence" was Tony and Maria's dream of peace which, after a naïve vision of brotherhood between the gangs, quickly gave way to a premonition of vicious death.

Stephen Sondheim, the only member of the production team who hadn't been through the rites of a Broadway opening, proved himself the equal of more experienced lyricists. His finest song was "Gee, Officer Krupke," that without condescension and without falsifying their argot, showed the street toughs relieving their pain with mockery and play acting. He blundered seriously only once, in the lyrics for Maria's "I Feel Pretty," which, with a filigree of internal rhymes (pretty/witty/pity; charming/alarming; entrancing/dancing), made a teen-age Puerto Rican sound like Mrs. Miniver.

West Side Story may not seem all that daring today, and some of what was taut, slangy, and poignant in 1957 now sounds self-consciously preachy and histrionic. That in no way diminishes it as a precedent. Bernstein, Robbins, and Laurents proved that the conventions of musical comedy were much more flexible and expressive than the public, producers, and most critics had thought—that a "musical tragedy" derived from "musical comedy" was possible. On opening night, no one bolted into the street proclaiming a new golden age for the musical. But after the great success of the film version (1961) of *West Side Story*, producers had to take notice, and slowly, very slowly, the musical theatre began to diversify.

West Side Story was only the fourth venture for its producers Harold Prince and Robert Griffith. Their third musical, *New Girl in Town* (produced in association with Frederick Brisson, as were their earlier shows), had opened in the spring of 1957. The second, *Damn Yankees*, was just ending its run of 1,022 performances as *West Side Story* opened. And *The Pajama Game*, their debut as producers, had amassed 1,063 performances before it closed in 1956. The tally for Griffith and Prince productions: three hits in four years.

Prince and Griffith were both stage-managing Abbott's *Wonderful Town* when they persuaded their boss to collaborate with Richard Bissell on an adaptation of Bissell's novel, *7 1/2 Cents*. Then the fledgling producers tried to find a composer and lyricist, but not one of the composers and lyricists then writing musicals could see a libretto about a strike in a garment factory and its effects on a romance between the female union representative and her male counterpart in management. Frank Loesser eventually took pity on the would-be producers and introduced them to Jerry Ross and Richard Adler, writers of pop songs ("Rags to Riches") and contributors to the 1953 edition of *John Murray Anderson's Almanac*. Writing the songs went easier than finding backers. Large investors refrained, so Griffith and Prince had to collect their $250,000 in driblets from 164 backers, chorus boys and girls, seamstresses, family, and friends.

George Abbott agreed to direct (with some help from Jerome Robbins on the musical numbers). Bob Fosse, who had been working in Hollywood, was chosen as choreographer, and Fosse convinced Griffith and Prince to take a chance on another unknown, the dancer Carol Haney, with whom he had worked in the film version of *Kiss Me, Kate*. Eddie Foy, Jr., the veteran song-and-dance man, played Hines, a double-threat neurotic, totally compulsive about his job as a time-study expert and insanely jealous of his girl friend (Haney). John Raitt represented management and Janis Paige labor.

Under Abbott's quicksilver direction, *The Pajama Game* never hesitated, never scowled, never tried to say something significant. Instead, it gave every featured performer the chance to do what he or she could do best. John Raitt got a custom-made love song, "Hey There," all velvet curves and crooner sincerity. Eddie Foy, Jr., exploited his vaudeville specialties, a laconic delivery and lazy soft shoe, which he absurdly played against Hines's jitters and manic fits of jealousy. Carol Haney got "Steam Heat," a dance number disguised as a morale booster for the strikers that had more to do with Haney's impish sexuality than union solidarity. And Janis Paige got "I'm Not at All in Love," a brassy protest (in the tradition of "I'm Gonna Wash That Man Right Outa My Hair") that meant she'd be eating her words by intermission.

In fourteen weeks *The Pajama Game* had paid back its investors, and it later won a Tony for Best Musical. Griffith and Prince, who, to keep their hands in, had stage-managed its opening, immediately started on their next project, *Damn Yankees*.

Although based on the Faust legend, *Damn Yankees* proved just as frolicsome and unpretentious as *The Pajama Game*. George Abbott and Douglass Wallop (with the uncredited help of Richard Bissell) adapted the book from Wallop's novel, *The Year the Yankees Lost the Pennant*; Adler and Ross composed the songs; and Fosse choreographed. In this version of the Faust story, a rabid Washington Senators' fan, Joe Boyd (Robert Shafer), accepts the help of a mysterious Mr. Applegate (Ray Walton), who transforms the middle-aged Boyd into the baseball superhero Joe Hardy (Stephen Douglass), so that Joe can spirit the Senators to the pennant. The catch in the deal is that Boyd has to forfeit his soul if he doesn't return to his wife by the end of a year. Applegate brings in Lola (Gwen Verdon), a spirit so seductive that with just a quarter swivel of her hips she can disintegrate a man's will power. But it's Lola who falls in love with Boyd and helps him outwit Applegate. Her punishment is to revert to her former self, "the ugliest girl in Providence, Rhode Island." Joe returns to his wife and quiet domesticity.

In spite of extensive rewriting and the elimination of more than one third of the original songs while the show was out of town, Ross and Adler's score—with the exception of "Whatever Lola Wants" and "Heart"—proved only serviceable, and the book quickly exhausted its small stock of wit in the first act. But Gwen Verdon generated enough mock sensuality to power a vehicle far more decrepit than *Damn Yankees*. With hips gyrating in over-drive and feathery eyelashes fluttering in synch, she outvamped (and out-camped) the most delirious of male sex fantasies.

Damn Yankees, which won a Tony for Best Musical, was the last show for which Adler and Ross collaborated. In 1955, Jerry Ross died from a chronic respiratory ailment.

Griffith and Prince made their only miscalculation with *New Girl in Town*, a project set in motion when they met Bob Merrill, the composer of several novelty hits, including "How Much Is That Doggie in the Window?" and "If I Knew You Were Coming, I'd Have Baked a Cake." Merrill had written a score for a film version of Eugene O'Neill's *Anna Christie*, but Metro-Goldwyn-Mayer had scrapped plans for the film, which was to have updated the story from the nineteenth century to the mid-twentieth. Griffith and Prince admired Merrill's film score and asked him to write music and lyrics for a stage version.

Their eagerness might have been primed by the success of *My Fair Lady*, which Lerner and Loewe had adapted from G. B. Shaw's *Pygmalion*. If Shaw on the musical stage, why not O'Neill? Besides, New York was in the middle of an O'Neill renaissance. *The Iceman Cometh, Long Day's Journey into Night*, and *A Moon for the Misbegotten* were all playing in the season that *New Girl in Town* opened.

George Abbott wrote the book for *New Girl in Town* and directed; Bob Fosse choreographed; and Gwen Verdon played Anna. Preparations, which are always hectic for a musical, were more than routinely exhausting. Abbott rejected modernizing the story, so Merrill was obliged to throw out most of the score he had written for the film version and substitute nineteen new musical numbers. His new score of rousing ensembles and sentimental ballads was thoroughly professional, yet decidedly in a commercial style that dimmed the gaslight glow of Abbott's book. Verdon took acting and singing lessons to prepare for her role, but when it became obvious in rehearsal and tryouts that much of the show needed bolstering, she got less and less dialogue and more and more dancing. As her lines dwindled, the unique spirit of O'Neill's original faded. The best to be said for *New Girl in Town* was, as Elliot Norton wrote for the Boston *Daily Record*, that it had "the brassy brightness and high professional gloss of a first-rater." But as an adaptation of *Anna Christie*, it paid only slight courtesy to its source and consequently lost its gamble for distinction.

Gwen Verdon and Bob Fosse were soon loaning their talents to yet another period piece, *Redhead* (1959), whose artisitic ambitions were far from O'Neill. *Redhead* was in the tradition of melodramas based on the Sherlock Holmes and Jack the Ripper legends. Its heroine, played by Verdon, was a sculptress working in a London wax museum, circa 1900, who, through mysterious psychic powers, fashions a close likeness of an unidentified murderer. From then on, *Redhead's* problem was how to sustain an evening of cat and mouse between the sculptress and the murderer. Rouben Ter-Arutinian's sets provided the right mix of Gothic and gaudiness. Bob Fosse's production numbers, especially "The Uncle Sam Rag," in which American ragtime was interpreted in English music-hall style, were diverting. Richard Kiley played a music-hall strongman and amateur Sherlock Holmes with his usual command. And Gwen Verdon, as pert and graceful as ever, danced her way through one close call after another, climaxing in a Keystone Kops chase and the capture of the murderer. But none of them could awaken Arthur Hague's melodies, nor could they give forward thrust to a script that Dorothy and Herbert Fields had been writing at Herbert's death and which was then passed to Sidney Sheldon and David Shaw (the authors of the source) to finish as best they could. *Redhead* lasted about a year and won a Tony Award for Best Musical.

Redhead and *New Girl in Town*, both adaptations, might have profited from the example of *My Fair Lady*. While retaining long stretches of Shaw's *Pygmalion*, Lerner and Loewe gave their musical a romantic gloss quite foreign to the original. Henry Higgins remained the self-satisfied bachelor and renowned phonologist who, on a bet, teaches the flower seller Eliza Doolittle to speak and act like a lady. But calculating that musical-comedy audiences would grow disgruntled with a totally unresponsive Higgins, the authors had him admit in his sung soliloquy, "I've Grown Accustomed to Her Face," that Eliza has become a comforting, even desirable, part of his life.

Lerner and Loewe (and director Moss Hart) were fairly discreet in their romanticizing of *Pygmalion*. Eliza's love for Higgins was only one third infatuation ("I Could Have Danced All Night"), the other two thirds perturbation ("Just You Wait" and "Without You"), while Higgins staunchly held to his chauvinism ("I'm an Ordinary Man," "You Did It," and "A Hymn to Him"). Even the concluding scene, a total counterfeit, avoided all the usual demonstrations of musical-comedy love. As Higgins finished "I've Grown Accustomed to Her Face," Eliza appeared on the threshold of his darkened study. Without turning around, Higgins greeted her with a curmudgeonly but affectionate "Eliza, where the devil are my slippers?" and the curtain fell as Eliza smiled a tolerant, somewhat patronizing smile.

Lerner and Loewe also expanded the part of Alfred P. Doolittle, Eliza's delinquent father and the "common dustman" whose scorn for middle-class morality unexpectedly drops him into the ultra-bourgeois life of a popular lecturer on moral philosophy. Doolittle was a natural for musical comedy—a roistering boozer and philanderer with a gift for musical speech. Lerner wrote two new scenes for him, and Loewe gave him two bumptious, music-hall tunes, "With a Little Bit of Luck" and "Get Me to the Church on Time," which Hanya Holm choreographed with all the cheer of a pub at closing time.

My Fair Lady was the '50's musical raised to its highest art. Cecil Beaton's pre-World War I costumes and Oliver Smith's sets made both peers and commoners fanciful. Their opening day at Ascot was, among a bounty of elegant scenes, the most sumptuous. The canopied boxes were pink and white to set off the lords and ladies in brilliant black and white, lustrous gray, and all shades of purple from lilac to plum. To the fastidious strains of "The Ascot Gavotte" the men paraded in frock coats and striped pants, while the women, balancing fantastic wide-brimmed hats and ostrich plumes, circa 1912, minced about in hobbled gowns. The parade stopped only once, while everyone took a precarious high-fashion pose for the beginning of the race.

For Rex Harrison, the nonsinging actor who played Higgins, Loewe composed melodies that could be half-spoken in Higgins' dry, petulant tone. For Julie Andrews, who possessed a healthy range, bright tone, and clear diction, Loewe wrote supple melodies in an emotional range from delicate daydream to vituperation. And although restrained by Shaw's plot from writing any conventional love songs for Eliza and Higgins, Loewe did manage one of the most bracing of romantic melodies for Eliza's stalwart suitor, Freddy Eynsford-Hill: "On the Street Where You Live."

Even Shaw, whose executors were reluctant to allow any tinkering with *Pygmalion*, would have applauded the casting for *My Fair Lady*. Rex Harrison, all suave dignity and cool sex appeal, was a perfect Higgins. Julie Andrews, just twenty when she was cast as Eliza, had appeared only once before on Broadway, as Polly in the British import *The Boy Friend* (1954), a spoof of '20's musicals that demanded none of the virtuosity required by Shaw. But after quite a struggle, Andrews mastered the more demanding role. Her Eliza has never been surpassed.

The role of Alfred P. Doolittle went to the veteran character actor Stanley Holloway, whose apprentice days were spent in British music halls and whose acting career had taken him from stage classics to movie comedies. He wasn't a stranger for long to American audiences, who immediately warmed to his avuncular wit, gingerly footwork, and rumpled grandeur.

My Fair Lady opened in the 1955–56 Broadway season and played 2,717 performances, at that time the longest run for any musical. It won almost every prize, including the Tony and Critics' Circle Awards for Best Musical. The original-cast album, produced for Columbia by Goddard Lieberson, be-

came the highest-selling recording of a Broadway musical, and a second edition, in stereophonic sound, was recorded with most of the original cast—
and all of its stars—during the London run. By 1970, national and
international companies had grossed over $80 million. A ponderous film ver-
sion, starring Rex Harrison and Audrey Hepburn and directed by George
Cukor, was released by Warner Brothers in 1964.

The trend of converting literary classics into musicals continued in the
late '50s with three other shows: *Juno* (from O'Casey's *Juno and the Paycock*,
with a sophisticated, if far too understated score by Marc Blitzstein), *First
Impressions* (from Jane Austen's *Pride and Prejudice*), and *Take Me Along*
(from O'Neill's nostalgic comedy, *Ah, Wilderness!*). Only the latter ran long
enough, 448 performances, to qualify as a modest success.

The producer of *Take Me Along* (1959), David Merrick, was not the kind
of showman to grapple with O'Neill for the prestige of it all. To draw the
crowds, he cast the television comedian Jackie Gleason as Uncle Sid, and
Walter Pidgeon, a veteran of over seventy Hollywood films, most of them in
the '30s and '40s, as Nat Miller.

Gleason played an alcoholic newspaper writer well into middle age who,
for as long as anyone in Centerville, Connecticut, can remember, has
courted the spinster schoolmarm Lily (Eileen Herlie). Their hopeless romance, as O'Neill had written it, was silly but poignant. Gleason did sup-
press his mugging, but still played Uncle Sid with all the assurance of a
vaudevillian instead of the introversion of a writer. Pidgeon was also miscast.
He fell in and out of character, almost always too blasé for a small-town
patriarch, yet just right fumbling his way through a paternal lecture on the
facts of life. The supporting roles were far better cast. Eileen Herlie, playing
opposite Gleason, managed to temper their scenes with a turn-of-the-century gentility that was always in danger of being squelched by musical-comedy bravado. And, although in his late twenties, Robert Morse was well cast
as a teen-age romantic whose reading of great literature fuels his escapist
fantasies. One of them was staged by Onna White as a ballet. In it the soused
dreamer is pursued by Salome, Camille, and other femmes fatales costumed
by Miles White in serpentine extravagances reminiscent of Aubrey
Beardsley. The dream ballet was the one episode in *Take Me Along* that
found common ground between Broadway, 1959, and Centerville, Connecticut, 1910. The remainder of Joseph Stein and Robert Russell's libretto and
Bob Merrill's score suggested only fitfully O'Neill's tender affection for an
innocent period in America's coming of age.

Take Me Along was evidence that in 1959 audiences still couldn't get
enough of musical Americana, especially the lucrative myth promoted by
Broadway that to find America's heart you had to tramp into the country.

In 1955, *Plain and Fancy* got just about as far afield as any musical has
ever gone without leaving the continental United States: the fictional Amish
village of Bird in the Hand, Pennsylvania. Joseph Stein and Will Glickman

had fun, not without its ironies, writing about two New York sophisticates (Shirl Conway and Richard Derr) who disrupt a quiet, tradition-bound community. To make something theatrical out of an agrarian culture that discourages any type of exhibitionism, the librettists and their collaborators (lyricist Arnold B. Horwitt, composer Albert Hague, director Morton Da Costa, choreographer Helen Tamiris, and designer Raoul Pène du Bois) heaped more color and calamity on Bird in the Hand than it would have seen in a millenium: a barn fire, the communal raising of a new one, and the eccentric Amish customs of betrothal and "shunning" (ostracizing one who has disgraced himself). But the illusion of authenticity—and the spell it cast—dissolved when, in the second act, a young Amish lad was debauched by a drunken spree at a carnival and *Plain and Fancy* reverted to Broadway's oldest clichés about drunkenness, sex, and the gypsy life.

The musical of the late '50s most adept at satisfying our nostalgia for a rural past was Meredith Willson's *The Music Man*, which, between 1957 and 1961, ran for 1,375 performances and won both Tony and Critics' Circle Awards for Best Musical. His Midwest in the early 1900s was a cloudless Fourth of July in River City, Iowa, its Main Street draped in red, white, and blue and packed with Tom Sawyers and Becky Thatchers. Into this idyll prances Harold Hill (Robert Preston), traveling salesman, part-time Casanova, and full-time charlatan. His modus operandi is to fast-talk the rubes into ordering band instruments and uniforms in expectation that "Professor Hill" will stay around to teach the kids how to play. But he's always gone the day after the goods arrive and the cash is in his pocket. This time he falls in love, and, conservatory training or no conservatory training, he'll lead the band and marry River City's librarian and piano teacher, Marion Paroo (Barbara Cook).

The Music Man has been the only musical to date that without apology or subterfuge could bring a barbershop quartet onstage to croon a number ("Lida Rose") in close harmony. The rest of Willson's score was just as corny, but it never dawdled and it never took itself seriously. Hill flirted with Miss Paroo to "Marion the Librarian," an old soft shoe rejuvenated with a raffish melody, and when the town gossips started clucking about a man in Marion's life, their scandalized henpeckings were delightfully transformed into the staccato bantering of "Pickalittle." Willson's River City, 1912, was the kind of fantasy land where even a steam locomotive made music, as Hill and a carload of traveling salesmen, without melody or rhyme, chanted the acceleration of their train out of the station and its rattling flight through Iowa farmlands ("Rock Island"). At the same clip but to a skeletal melody, Hill delivered his pitch, "Trouble," to the townsfolk of River City, only this time the buoyant rhythms were geared to the evangelical rhetoric of the cure-all peddler.

When "The Wells Fargo Wagon" carrying the band instruments and uniforms popped over the horizon, all of River City turned out to cheer it on. Of course, we never saw the wagon; we didn't need to, because Willson's song, with its galloping and neck-craning melody, painted one brighter and jouncier than anything that might have come from the scene shop. But nowhere was Willson's command of his audience stronger than with "Seventy-Six Trombones," the irresistible march in which Hill, prancing about like a pied piper, envisioned for the children their own band, ten times bigger than Sousa's and a thousand times sprightlier.

The entire production of *The Music Man* (sets by Howard Bay, costumes by Raoul Pène du Bois, direction by Morton Da Costa, choreography by Onna White) was swift, light, and bigger than life. Robert Preston, a stage and film star who had never sung or danced in a musical, commanded the stage with dash and roguish charm. Barbara Cook was a captivating archetype of Midwestern sex appeal, a mix of propriety and unself-conscious allure.

The only kind of '50's Americana to outnumber the pastoral was the show that glorified New York City, a genre that went back at least as far as the 1870s to Harrigan and Hart's musical plays about New York's East Side and skyrocketed in the early 1900s with George M. Cohan and his brazen disdain for any place farther than two blocks from Herald Square. The musicals of the 1950s were less chauvinistic, but New York still looked very romantic in *Guys and Dolls, A Tree Grows in Brooklyn, Wonderful Town, By the Beautiful Sea, West Side Story,* and *Fiorello!*.

The last of these to open, the Griffith-Prince production of *Fiorello!* (1959), evoked a time never to come again when, singlehandedly, a feisty, charismatic mayor seemed capable of surmounting the problems of New York City. From the beginning of World War I to the mid-1930s, Fiorello La Guardia had fought the Tammany Hall machine. His determination, his scrappiness, his amiable impertinence, his cheek—in short, the virtues of an archetypal New Yorker at his best—were the substance of George Abbott and Jerome Weidman's book and the spirit of Jerry Bock and Sheldon Harnick's best songs: "Politics and Poker," "Little Tin Box," and "On the Side of the Angels."

What distinguished *Fiorello!* from past musical biographies was its authors' candor about their subject's personality. Except for some unnecessary—and undramatic—puffing of La Guardia's love life (a concession to the Rodgers and Hammerstein school), it stuck to the man's politicking and his image. The tally wasn't always flattering: in the positive column Fiorello's zeal for social reform, his theatrics (including a childlike identification with firefighters), his aggressive charm, and his sympathy for the poor; in the other column his obstinancy, fierce temper, and imperious disregard for the feelings of his subordinates. But the most uncanny of all contributions to the portrait was the performance of Tom Bosley, a thirty-two-year old unknown. Not only was Bosley about the same height and heft as La Guardia, he had learned, by watching old newsreels (some of which were shown during the musical on an overhead screen) all of the mayor's idiosyncracies—the spring-like wagging of his head, his staccato walk, and his sudden bursts of nervous fidgeting. Bosley's Little Flower was more reincarnation than performance.

He was helped by the plan of Bock and Harnick's score. They gave their lead only one major song, "The Name's La Guardia," which he sang as he campaigned in ethnic neighborhoods throughout New York. It was all he needed. The zesty musical theme and the campaigner's orotund speech-making were so close in sound and spirit that Bosley could break into song and convincingly remain the hard-edged politico. The rest of the songs about La Guardia were sung by his vivacious public, the ward heelers and bosses, the suffragettes, the cops on their beat, and the ethnics who gave detail to a bright, nostalgic portrait of a leader who symbolized everything that was vital about New York in a trying but inspiring time.

In spite of an Actors' Equity strike—the first since 1919—that forced thirteen musicals to shut down, *Fiorello!* ran for 796 performances. Along the way, it amassed an impressive collection of prizes. It shared, with *The Sound of Music*, the Antoinette Perry (Tony) Award as Best Musical of the Season. The New York Drama Critics gave it their top honor. And the Pulitzer Prize Committee awarded it the third Pulitzer Prize given to a musical, which put it in the company of Gershwin's *Of Thee I Sing* and Rodgers and Hammerstein's *South Pacific*. *Fiorello!* became Prince and Griffith's most prestigious venture of the '50s.

One clamorous and very contemporary aspect of the American scene was totally ignored by musical comedy until the last Broadway season of the '50s, when composer Charles Strouse and lyricist Lee Adams joined one of Sid Caesar's writers, Michael Stewart, to write *Bye Bye Birdie* (1960). It was the first musical about a mysterious power that had enraptured teen-agers and galled their parents since the middle of the decade: rock 'n' roll.

To adults, rock 'n' roll laments about pubescent love sounded like the Chinese water torture gone electric, the tedious repetition of four chords twanged out on amplified, out-of-tune guitars competing with a twitching, suggestive rhythm. To producers of musical comedies, rock 'n' roll was worse: a dubious investment. When The King of Rock, Elvis Presley, fell from grace—due either to old age (defined by teens as any point between thirty and death) or to a switch in allegiance by his fickle fans—the rock phenomenon would evaporate, so the argument went. But when Elvis was drafted into the Army in 1958, the doubters were proved wrong. Instead of disappearing, his music thrived, and millions of fans kept the faith until he returned.

Inspired by Elvis' leave-taking, the authors of *Bye Bye Birdie* began their show with the Army's announcement that it was drafting Conrad Birdie (Dick Gautier), a caricature of the torso-twisting, hip-thrusting Elvis. Conrad's manager, an ex-schoolteacher named Albert Peterson (Dick Van Dyke), concocts a publicity stunt as a send-off before the induction: On a television variety show Conrad will sing "One Last Kiss" to a teen-age girl representing all the singer's fans. But the appearance doesn't go quite as planned when the girl's father (Paul Lynde), intoxicated with the idea of appearing on network television, interrupts the ceremony and tries to mug his way to instant celebritydom. This is the kind of silliness that has made Albert rich but miserable, and it fuels the campaign of his fiancée, Rose (Chita Rivera), to get him back into teaching. The only obstacle is Albert's zany mother (Kay Medford), a virtuoso of self-pity, who fears the loss of her son and his money to another woman. But Peterson triumphs over momism, marries Rose, and gives up the rock 'n' roll business for the classroom.

Bye Bye Birdie, which won a Tony for Best Musical, was Broadway's death wish for rock 'n' roll. It appealed not to rock fans but to everyone who wanted to be done with the whole inexplicable craze (and that included most producers, writers, and composers of musicals, all of whom had no idea of how to adapt rock for the stage). Only Birdie's adenoidal laments "Honestly Sincere" and "One Last Kiss" came within shouting distance of real rock. Dick Gautier, shaded by a lion's mane of pomaded black wig and stuffed into a gold lamé jumpsuit, groaned the songs to such ludicrous bumps and grinds that the slight tunes were pulverized by his gyrations. The point of his imitation, the leitmotif of *Bye Bye Birdie*, was that rock idols were latter-day Mesmers and their music the fabrication of venal businessmen eager to snatch the pennies out of the hands of America's teen-agers.

Apart from their lampoons of rock 'n' roll, Strouse and Adams wrote in the standard Broadway idiom. For "Put on a Happy Face" and "A Lot of Livin' to Do" they followed the conventions to the letter, and their diligence won a large audience—but not among rock fans, the future audience for musical comedy. This is not to make scapegoats of Strouse and Adams for Broadway's timidity. No one can argue that in the late '50s rock looked as if it could add a jot to the expressiveness of a musical score. But if musical theatre had been more tolerant and curious about rock in the late '50s, by the mid-'60s, Broadway might have attracted the young, ethnically diverse audience that instead it alienated.

In aspects other than its musical style, *Bye Bye Birdie* was a daring gamble. Not only was its songwriting team unknown, but its producer, Edward Padula, a former stage manager, had never produced a show. Michael Stewart, the librettist, had previously written a concert version of *Candide* and had contributed material to revues, but he had never written a complete, original script for a book musical. The director and choreographer Gower Champion, although a veteran of film and the stage, had limited his musical-comedy directing to two revues, *Lend an Ear* (1948) and *3 for Tonight* (1955). And many in the cast, including Paul Lynde, Susan Watson, Dick Gautier, and Dick Van Dyke had never been featured in a book musical.

What the production lacked in well-known, bankable talent, it compensated for in eagerness—and ability—to please. Champion's staging was the primary asset, especially the opening number, which showed a giant honeycomb filled with teen-agers chatting by phone. He also staged a wild dance number for Chita Rivera in which she stupefied a den of libidinous Shriners. The performances Champion elicited were uniformly broad and hilarious. Kay Medford, one of the few veterans in the cast, played Albert's mother with waspish truculence. Paul Lynde burlesqued all suffering parents of rock fans and mugged outrageously as his character was overwhelmed with the urge for overnight stardom. And Dick Van Dyke projected such affability that his appearance in *Bye Bye Birdie* initiated a lucrative career in television.

Rock 'n' roll was only the latest musical outbreak of American paganism. In the '20s it had been jazz and jazz dances, especially the Charleston. But from the perspective of the mid-'50s, the decade of the flapper, the shimmy, and hot rhythms from, of all things, the banjo, seemed too improbable to take seriously. Where the inanities of the '20s were concerned, brash parody had long since given way to affectionate mockery. Sandy Wilson, a young Englishman, capitalized on that nostalgic view of the '20s, when, in the early '50s, he wrote the book and songs for *The Boy Friend* (1954).

Imported from London, *The Boy Friend* played, in its first Broadway version, for 483 performances. An Off-Broadway production, which opened in 1958, lasted for 761 performances, and another Broadway edition, starring Sandy Duncan and Judy Carne, played 119 performances in 1970.

In its London version *The Boy Friend*'s satire of the music and musical comedy of the '20s was very polite, no more than a giggle and a blush. Vida Hope, who directed, described her conception as "a nostalgic period piece of 1926. It's not a parody but an evocation. We went to a great deal of trouble to keep all the details authentic."

Feuer and Martin, who imported the show, decided that for American audiences the satire would have to be broadened and production values augmented. One of their first moves was to expand the small jazz combo that had accompanied the London production to a large band capable of filling a Broadway theatre with sound. The arrangements were reorchestrated by two Americans, Ted Royale and Charles L. Cook, to imitate the sound of a 1922 band called the California Ramblers. The producers also pressured Hope and Wilson to accelerate the pace and broaden the humor. Hope and Wilson balked. Finally, during the last weeks of rehearsal, the producers barred the recalcitrant author and director from the theatre. Wilson and Hope returned to London, and Cy Feuer assumed the directorship.

In spite of the producers' changes, the New York version of *The Boy Friend* lost few of the charms that had attracted London audiences to over 2,000 performances. Wilson's book still endeared to his audiences the poor-little-rich-girl Polly, whose greatest concern is whether or not she'll have an escort for the carnival ball. Julie Andrews, an eighteen-year-old from England, made her American debut as Polly, and although she burlesqued the cloying innocence of Polly, Andrews' hesitant gestures and wistful face made her lovesickness almost heartrending. Polly's romance with Tony, Lord Brockhurst's son working incognito as a delivery boy, had all the clichés of '20's musicals but also a perishable, flowerlike sweetness. Around Polly and Tony swarmed a company of well-known and equally evanescent types: the French maid; the giggling girl friends whose ebullience borders on frenzy; the John Held boy friends; the lecherous, philandering husband matched with a shrewish wife; the coquettish matron and her long-lost lover.

Wilson's score, like his book, was a meticulously embroidered pastiche of '20's clichés. Most of its melodies were contoured to popular dance rhythms of the era and matched with lyrics designed to announce a simplehearted sentiment, then evaporate: "I could be happy with you/If you could be happy with me." In spite of their predictable features, the best of Wilson's songs ("Won't You Charleston with Me?," "The Boy Friend," "I Could Be Happy with You," and "A Room in Bloomsbury") shimmered with the radiance of an era that, at least as it's viewed in the popular imagination, lived only for the moment. And every so often, as with "Fancy Forgetting," a duet of two reunited lovers past their prime, and "Poor Little Pierrette," in which Polly and her mentor, Mme. Dubonnet, lament the disappointments of young love, the ironies of parody gave way to sad whimsy. The tinkling melodies and evanescent lyrics floated on short-lived abandon and perishable infatuations.

The Boy Friend was the first of three productions of the late '50s to capitalize on the novelty, nostalgia, and good-natured mockery that unavoidably came with any return to early musical comedy. Audiences laughed at the inanities and improbabilities of earlier musical theatre, but, consciously or not, they indulged themselves in its carefree, affirmative fantasy.

Rick Besoyan's *Little Mary Sunshine* (1959) was the American counterpart to *The Boy Friend,* with its affectionate ridicule aimed at Rudolf Friml's *Rose Marie* (1924) and other similar operettas. At the center of an absurdly convoluted plot was the romance between Little Mary (Eileen Brennan), the adopted daughter of the Kadota Indians (whose tribe has shrunk to three members in good standing), and Captain Big Jim Warington of the Mounties (William Graham). When those two weren't trilling ecstatically, the stage was occupied with one after another of all the pasteboard stereotypes from the musical melodramas of the Teens and Twenties: a giggling housemaid, a taciturn Indian chief, a pompous diva, a bewildered Indian guide, a Casanova, and a skulking villain, among others. The outcome of their shenanigans was never in doubt. As Louis Calta, a reviewer for the New York *Times,* put it, *Little Mary Sunshine* evoked an era when " 'justice always triumphed,' when 'good meant good' and 'bad meant bad.' "

Director Ray Harrison, Besoyan, and their cast spoofed the fastidious gentility of operetta without sneering at its pretensions. Eileen Brennan was especially adroit with posturings that were just on the far side of credibility.

"Her cloying characterization," Brooks Atkinson wrote, "her gestures that are just a bit too florid, her impregnable self-assurance, and her maddening belief in the mawkish things she says are both radiant and comic." William Graham matched her with a humorless, stolid Mountie, devoted to righting all wrongs without rumpling his uniform or scuffing his boots.

Besoyan, a voice coach, had apprenticed with the Savoy Light Opera Company, producers of the Gilbert and Sullivan repertory. He not only wrote the music, lyrics, vocal arrangements, and book for *Little Mary Sunshine* but also directed his own dialogue. Beneath every bombastic vocal ornament, every overacted line, and every incredible twist in the plot's denouement was Besoyan's finesse. *Little Mary Sunshine* played Off Broadway for 1,143 performances. In 1962, a London company, reciprocating for *The Boy Friend*, opened in the West End. On opening night the cast received ten curtain calls.

Leave It to Jane (1959) was the genuine article: a vintage musical from 1917 given a loving new Off-Broadway production that neither spoofed nor sentimentalized itself. Written by Kern, Bolton, and Wodehouse in the style of their Princess musicals (but not one of them because it was never performed in the Princess Theatre), *Leave It to Jane* had been one of the earliest shows to glorify—very quietly—the old college days of raccoon coats, Stutz Bearcats, serenades, and, above all, football. As Donald Malcolm wrote in *The New Yorker*, it evoked a "time when bamboo canes beat time to a soft-shoe shuffle, when professors wore cutaways, and romantic men in striped blazers courted fair young things to the strum of a banjo." Kern's translucent melodies, especially "The Siren's Song," "Sir Galahad" and the title song, still glowed like a string of Chinese lanterns illuminating a twilight garden party. On their delicate charm alone *Leave It to Jane* could have played its 928 performances.

The Fantasticks, which opened late in the 1959–60 Off-Broadway season, also asked its audiences to imagine the past when, according to its first song, "life was young and, oh, so tender." But this wasn't the evocation of a past style of musical comedy; it was simply the remembrance of a time when maturity and disillusionment had not yet weakened the spell of romance. To dispose their audience to this kind of time travel, Tom Jones (book and lyrics) and Harvey Schmidt (music) depended on suggestion. A ladder became a wall or a tree. Confetti, scattered from the top of the ladder, somehow turned to star dust as it fell. A cardboard disc painted yellow was the sun; another, painted white, was the moon. Duels (and what's a romantic story without duels?) were fought with broom handles and yardsticks. The inhabitants of this make-believe land were just as fanciful as their props: an ingenue and her gallant young man; their apparently bumbling—but truly wise—fathers; a pair of scalawags like Mark Twain's Duke and Dauphin; the story-teller, who doubles as a dashing abductor for hire; and a mime, as supernumerary and Ariel-like stage manager.

The first half of *The Fantasticks* takes place in the moonlight. The Boy (Kenneth Nelson) and the Girl (Rita Gardner), convinced that their fathers oppose their romance, meet secretly at the wall that divides their lands. The fathers (William Larsen and Hugh Thomas) are only pretending to disapprove, but they know that young lovers are fickle unless their pledges of love are sealed by sweet defiance of their parents. To further intensify the lovers' longing, the fathers arrange with a troubadour (Jerry Orbach) to fake The Girl's abduction. All goes according to plan: The Boy rescues The Girl, The Girl loves him all the more, and he loves himself all the more. The fathers give their blessings to the romance. End of Act I.

The second half takes place in the sunlight. As the fathers had feared, the young love that thrived on misfortune now, without opposition, withers. The Boy and The Girl whine and snap at each other. Inevitably, they part, The Boy to seek adventure, The Girl to dally with other men. But fate, time, and true adversity play Cupid. After The Boy is beaten and robbed and The Girl becomes disenchanted with playing at love, the cycle of their romance begins again. The fathers rejoice. Finale.

As they did with their staging, Jones and Schmidt kept their tunes and lyrics simple enough to seem improvised and light enough to buoy a heavy load of cuteness. "Try to Remember" beckoned—it didn't collar—audiences into reminiscing about those times when "love was an ember about to billow." "Metaphor" was The Boy's search for words to blazon his love, and, of course, he couldn't find any. "Soon It's Gonna Rain" promised that the lovers would always shelter each other from all storms, literal and figurative, but its delicate, untroubled melody was predicting only a few sprinkles. Although Jones and Schmidt's comedy songs weren't as unforced or evocative as their ballads, two of them put a light—and refreshing—sting into a dangerously coy entertainment. "Rape Song" paired an idiotically grinning tango with a catalogue of rapes offered by the troubadour El Gallo. And "Plant a Radish" was a treatise by the two disgruntled fathers, who compare raising children to cultivating vegetables and decide that only the vegetables are worth the trouble.

In 1979, *The Fantasticks* began its twentieth year at the 150-seat Sullivan Street Playhouse in New York's Greenwich Village, which proves that the most seductive illusions need only a gentle invitation and a few trappings to prime an audience's imagination. But in the '50s that was anathema to Broadway. Audiences expected and producers were willing to give them spectacle, too often in place of imaginative musical drama. Postwar confidence was dimming, and American musical comedy was beginning to reflect the confusions that would lead to the Vietnam War and Watergate. When, as happened too frequently in the late '50s, expenditures on sets and costumes rather than strong dramatic and musical ideas propped up decrepit shows, American musical theatre either stood still or regressed. With the exception of those few productions willing to take artistic risks, the musical theatre of the 1950s was almost identical with the musical theatre of the 1940s. The domination of Broadway by the spirit of Rodgers and Hammerstein hadn't weakened since 1943. Refinement of the "integrated" book show produced some of the finest musicals ever, but it did not renew the form. The '50s may have been a golden age for American musical comedy, but the decade's legacy was the inevitable decline of the 1960s.

PART FIVE
The 1960s

"If I Were a Rich Man" sings Tevye (Zero Mostel) in *Fiddler on the Roof.*

XXV. Trouble

CAMELOT. COSTALOT. CUTALOT. That was director Moss Hart's call to arms during the out-of-town tryouts for Lerner and Loewe's first show of the 1960s, a gorgeous, lumbering fantasy based on T. H. White's *The Once and Future King*. The preopening assaults on its bulk were quite literally battles—and ones that claimed victims. Moss Hart suffered a heart attack from which he never fully recovered; Frederick Loewe had to take time off for rest and recuperation on doctor's orders; and Alan Jay Lerner, who assumed Hart's duties in additon to his own as lyricist-librettist, eventually was bundled off to the hospital with a bleeding ulcer.

Lerner thought that he could do the same thing that T. H. White had done in his novel: retell, from a contemporary point of view, the glory of King Arthur's Camelot and its decline, beginning with the love affair between Queen Guenevere and Lancelot. Lerner told reporters he wanted to dramatize White's "wit and irony, his tenderness, his extravagant use of anachronism, his mockery."

For about its first half hour *Camelot* did just that. It introduced King Arthur (Richard Burton) and Guenevere (Julie Andrews) on the eve of their wedding. Not having met, they're both terrified. To bolster his courage Arthur sings the perky "I Wonder What the King Is Doing Tonight?" in which he reminds himself of how his subjects see him—merry, stouthearted, fearless, composed. But when Guenevere trespasses on his hiding place, he literally climbs a tree, where he listens to her sing "Where Are the Simple Joys of Maidenhood?," a wistful farewell to the joys of youth. Her song charms Arthur out of his tree and into song: In "Camelot" he describes to the beautiful stranger a kingdom so ideal, where rain never falls unless it's wanted and where winter is forbidden until December, that Guenevere is instantly smitten.

But just as quickly as it had come to life, *Camelot* reverted to an ornate mechanical toy, a Macy's window at Christmastime. Lancelot and Guenevere's romance slowed everything to a stiff pavane accompanied by Arthur's hurt looks, pompous aphorisms, and, when those didn't work, bellowing. Around them—and in spite of them—the decor and pageantry won out. Gilbert Adrian and Tony Duquette (costumes), Feder (lighting), and Oliver Smith (sets) had found the right proportions of bombast, fantasy, affection, and insouciance. Their coronation scene was all gold, crimson, and royal blue—no one could have asked for weightier, more spectacular pageantry. And when they had to create an enchanted forest for Guenevere's May outing, their lacework canopy of birches was as delicate as it was fanciful.

Frederick Loewe's melodies and Lerner's lyrics had charm, but their sentiment was out of focus, as if, after the opening scene, the authors had lost their fix on Camelot. Their talky songs for King Arthur diverted attention from Burton's limited vocal range, faulty intonation, and sandpaper timbre—with one exception, "How to Handle a Woman," in which the king tries to come to terms with the news that Guenevere and Lancelot are lovers. For once Burton had to stop jabbering and really sing. If his vocal quality was any clue to the state of his heart, Arthur's was broken. Still, the song became one of the two most popular numbers in the show. The other, "If Ever I Would Leave You," was sung by Robert Goulet, whose performance as Lancelot was limited to heroic poses but whose voice was so rich and expressive that it more than compensated for his waxen presence. The only principal who didn't get a set piece worthy of her talents was Julie Andrews. Her love songs, "Before I Gaze at You Again" and "I Loved You Once in Silence," merely repeated a few plaintive, unconvincing phrases over and over, and her lighter numbers, "The Simple Joys of Maidenhood," "The Lusty Month of May," and "What Do the Simple Folk Do?" (the latter with Burton), tried gamely for old English quaintness but fell consistently into preciousness.

Camelot had as much, sometimes more glamour than *My Fair Lady* but much less wit and elegance. Where *My Fair Lady* had spontaneously danced and even soared, *Camelot* fussed and postured; *My Fair Lady* had the sparkle of the Cinderella story; *Camelot* had the stiff dignity and beauty of an illuminated manuscript. *My Fair Lady* was musical drama and fantasy; *Camelot* was an attempt at fantasy and musical drama that, whenever it fell short, settled for melodrama and operettalike extravagance. Whatever their relative merits, the two Lerner-Loewe hits reigned in tandem over Broadway in the early '60s and inspired plenty of imitations, shows that aimed for wit and elegance but were quite willing to settle for glamour, at least the kind that could be bought for upward of a half million dollars.

Tovarich (1963), for one, tried to sustain itself on the opulence of its Parisian decor and the considerable charm of its leads, Vivien Leigh and Jean Pierre Aumont. Aristocratic elegance was their forte, and they were glamorous and thoroughly convincing as a Romanoff princess and her escort. But neither could sing, and Leigh's dancing was, as one critic diplomatically phrased it, "a triumph of poise over proficiency." Even musical-comedy veterans would not have been able to make something of David Shaw's bland script, and Lee Pockriss and Anne Croswell's pastiche of song styles of the '20s.

Ben Franklin in Paris (1964) offered Paris during the reign of Louis XVI and a novel romance between the sexy, young Comtesse de Vobrillac and seventy-year-old Franklin. But Ulla Sallert, the Swedish star of musical comedy who played the Comtesse, was too tentative to be convincing as an aristocrat, Oliver Smith's sets were surprisingly gauche, and a subsidiary romance between Ben's son (Franklin Kiser) and a poor Parisienne (Susan Watson) was too clichéd to bother with. The score (by Mark Sandrich, Jr., and Sidney Michaels) showed signs of life only twice, both of them drinking songs, as if wine and spirits were the only reasons for the gaiety of eighteenth-century Paris. The whole thing should have been converted to a vehicle for Robert Preston, whose Ben, complete with the hobbles, creaks, and catarrhs of old age, was so full of life he could easily have seduced a beautiful woman half his age, while between times attending to diplomatic chores.

The foggy streets of Victorian London and the sleuthing of Sherlock Holmes might also have inspired an elegant musical, but they didn't. Jerome Coopersmith's book for *Baker Street* (1965)—or a production concept dictated by producer Alexander Cohen—obscured the icy grace of Holmes (Fritz Weaver), who almost disappeared in all the show's smoke, fog, and tomfoolery. Blond zombies crept out of sewers blazing with the fires of hell; young women seemed to float on the thick smoke of an opium den; murderers reached out of dense fog to garrote their victims. And in the show's most ingenious scene—as well as its greatest distraction—Victoria's Diamond Jubilee parade was staged with puppets to give the illusion that the audience was watching from a rooftop.

The fascination of Conan Doyle's mysteries could have been preserved if *Baker Street* hadn't knuckled under to conventions of the '50s and reduced poor Holmes to a mere mortal who tolerates a singing, dancing gang of juvenile apprentices, The Baker Street Irregulars, and who, in complete abdication of his superman status, warms to Irene Adler. Ironically, Inga Swenson's Adler was one of the most intriguing of *Baker Street*'s characters, an intelligent and dignified beauty whose affectionate mockery often gets the better of Holmes. As Holmes, Fritz Weaver negotiated the obvious contradictions by adopting a bemused surprise at his own softheartedness.

Even with his new romantic streak, Holmes would have looked silly breaking into rapturous, full-throated melody, and so Marion Grudeff and Raymond Jessel wrote his songs in the *sprech-stimme* that had worked so well for Rex Harrison in *My Fair Lady*. But their lyrics were just too prosaic for Holmes's prodigious intelligence, and their melodies were more insipid than their lyrics. *Baker Street* was a musical that really wanted to be a play, and as a play it would have made a fine vehicle for its poorly served actors.

In October of 1965, as *Baker Street* trudged into its last fogbound month, Alan Jay Lerner, now in partnership with composer Burton Lane, opened his latest show, *On a Clear Day You Can See Forever*. Richard Rodgers had supplied the original idea for a musical about a young woman with ESP, but he didn't like either of the two drafts Lerner submitted to him and he backed out of the project before writing any songs. As it finally appeared on Broadway, *On a Clear Day* owed more to recycled plot lines from Lerner's previous libretti than to any fresh ideas about extrasensory perception. Daisy Gamble (Barbara Harris), the show's heroine, is hypnotized by a psychiatrist to cure her compulsive smoking, and the hypnosis sends her back through the cycle of reincarnation to a previous life as Melinda, an Englishwoman in the late eighteenth century. Like Tommy and Fiona in *Brigadoon*, Daisy and her psychiatrist, Mark Bruckner (John Cullum), are first trapped on opposite sides of a time warp, as Mark falls in love with Daisy's other self, the unobtainable Melinda. But his fixation eventually reverts to the flesh-and-blood woman before him, just as Henry Higgins' pride in his diction-perfect "princess" turns to affection for the real Eliza.

Burton Lane's melodies deserved a fresher book and better lyrics. Like Daisy/Melinda, his period numbers, ranging from the pastoral "Tosy and Cosh" to the robust "Don't Tamper with My Sister," had a betwixt-and-between charm, half eighteenth-century refinement, half twentieth-century jazziness. The best of his contemporary tunes were Daisy's "What Did I Have That I Don't Have?" a light, bluesy shuffle, and the title song, a forthright, almost inspirational tribute to the powers of the human mind.

Back in 1961, the fashion designer Gabrielle ("Coco") Chanel had awarded Lerner the exclusive rights to adapt her biography as a musical, and Frederick Brisson was to have produced the show as a vehicle for his wife, Rosalind Russell. After two delays and Russell's exit, *Coco* finally made it to Broadway in 1969, a vacant, money-gorged colossus led on a golden chain by its star, Katharine Hepburn. To the accompaniment of André Previn's featureless score and surrounded by haute couture mannequins in Chanel designs, Hepburn played virtuoso variations on Hepburn—the growls and purrs, the brittle gestures, and especially the suggestion of tears beneath a chipper smile. But neither she, nor Cecil Beaton's 253 costumes, nor Michael Bennett's graceful staging of fashion parades, nor production expenditures totaling more than $900,000 could transform Lerner's script, a patchwork of Chanel's best-known quips, into anything like drama. *Coco* ran only 333 performances, two months beyond Hepburn's departure.

Lerner wasn't the only veteran of musical theatre whose shows in the '60s pretended to elegance and wit but had to make do with spectacle. For *The Gay Life* (1963), Arthur Schwartz and Howard Dietz composed songs with all the lilt and debonair romance of Vienna at the turn of the century, but the show's galumphing book, adapted by Fay and Michael Kanin from Arthur Schnitzler's bedroom farce *The Affairs of Anatol*, made its absurd confusions look more like wrestling than deft comedy. It wasn't the first time during the '60s, nor would it be the last, that Oliver Smith's sets, which flew in and out, revolved, and glided without missing a beat, showed more personality and grace than the actors in a musical.

The Gay Life was vintage Schwartz and Dietz, rich melody and effortless lyrics; but their last score, for *Jennie* (1963), although it managed a couple of novelty numbers ("Waitin' for the Evening Train" and "Lonely Nights") brimming with the naïve gaiety of America in 1906, never found even the mildest passion for its love songs. The show wasted its time on Jennie's wretched marriage to a philandering drunk and her anemic romance with a milquetoast playwright. The only compensations for having to sit through the indifferent backstage scenes of this fictionalized biography of Laurette Taylor were its parodies of the early twentieth-century melodramas. These potboilers were the ancestors of movie serials like *The Perils of Pauline*, and stage directors were just as inventively sadistic as their movie counterparts in devising hairbreadth escapes for their heroines. But of course the scenic limitations of stage shows, in which a trickle of water over a papier-mâché boulder had to make do for Niagara Falls, made the cliff hanging preposterous. Director Vincent J. Donehue and scenic designer George Jenkins gleefully exploited every bogus sentiment, cheap thrill, and scenic fraud in the old set pieces. *Jennie* never topped its opening scene, in which Mary Martin, as Jennie, had to dangle over a pathetic canvas and lathe waterfall, as a moth-eaten grizzly bear menaced her—from a safe distance.

Fred Saidy and E. Y. Harburg, who hadn't written for Broadway since *Flahooley* in 1951, also gave it one more try in the '60s. Someone had the quirky notion of pairing Aristophanes' antiwar comedy *Lysistrata* with Offenbach's frothy melodies. Neither the ancient Greek satirist nor the Parisian boulevardier were well served by *The Happiest Girl in the World* (1961), an olio of moldy one-liners, some impressive dancing by Janice Rule, and frantic camping by its director-star Cyril Ritchard. Only Jean Eckart's sets suggested the fun that might have been, when her antique cloud machine creaked its way from the flies to the stage floor and deposited with a shudder and thud all the gods of Olympus.

Of all the veteran writers who, during the '60s, ended their musical-comedy careers with whimpers instead of bangs, Noel Coward was the most accomplished, the wittiest, and the most elegant. Ironically, the last show for which he wrote words and music was little more than a counterfeit of someone else's idea of elegance, *My Fair Lady*. The heroine of *The Girl Who Came to Supper* may have been more glamorous and worldly than Eliza Doolittle, but she was still a commoner (this time an American show girl) who, Cinderella-like, plays the princess for an evening, this time on the arm of the Prince Regent of Carpathia as he visits London for the coronation of George V. The show even had its female counterpart to Stanley Holloway in Tessie O'Shea, who played a fish 'n' chips monger along the parade route and who sang "London Is a Bit of All Right," a ditty with more than a chance echo of "With a Little Bit of Luck." But the most endearing of Coward's musical numbers owed nothing to *My Fair Lady*; it was an impromptu concert version of *The Coconut Girl*, a fictional show in the style of the Princess musicals, performed by the show girl at the command of Carpathian royalty. The rest of Coward's score fell far short of the pastiche from *The Coconut Girl* and never equaled the inspiration of Loewe's tunes from *My Fair Lady*.

Coward had been in better form early in the decade with *Sail Away* (1961), an evening of bristly sketches disguised unconvincingly as a book musical about shipboard romance. Elaine Stritch played a cynical social director whose idea of fun is to egg her charges on to making fools of themselves; and the funniest, most Cowardian of the show's songs were filled with similar jaundiced mockery: "Why Do the Wrong People Travel?," "The Passenger's Always Right," "The Little One's ABC," and "You're a Long Way from America."

Coward's last assignment in musical theatre was as director for *High Spirits* (1964), an adaptation of his popular comedy, the adult ghost story *Blithe Spirit*. But only Noel Coward could have written songs equal to the bizarre fantasy, mordant wit, and fastidious romance of his play. Instead, Timothy Gray and Hugh Martin, perhaps sensing they were over their heads, produced a handful of innocuous, highly commercial tunes that seldom got in the way of Coward's dialogue, which the master and his cast had polished to its full brilliance. Tammy Grimes, as the ghost Elvira, was half seductress, half Peter Pan as she flew about her husband's estate and plotted to lure him across the pale so they might share immortal bliss as ectoplasms. Her reedy voice and changeling's face were disturbingly other worldly, the equipment of someone—or something—quite capable of plotting murder for the sake of future romance above the ether. And as Madame Arcati, the meddling medium who conjures Elvira and then can't get rid of her, Beatrice Lillie played the zany with hilarious sobriety, as if mediumship were a kind of secular sainthood. She would mug, then admonish the laughers with a double whammy of a stare, then she'd mug some more. She gave the same crazy dignity to her wardrobe, a running gag of harem blouse and pantaloons, a mandarin's robe, a Valkyrie's horned headgear, hats overrun with moldy plumes, endless coils of phony pearls, and boots that looked like surplus from an intergalactic mission, all of which she wore with the panache of a high-fashion model gone to seed. *Blithe Spirit* was still an actor's gem, and the best things about its reincarnation as a musical were the grace and wit of Coward's dialogue, his intelligent direction, and the talents of Beatrice Lillie and Tammy Grimes.

If Noel Coward was the quintessential spirit of British songwriting from the second decade of the twentieth century onward, then Irving Berlin was his American counterpart. But after *Call Me Madam* in 1950, he didn't write for the musical stage until the early '60s, the apogee of the Kennedy era and what looked like a rebirth of patriotism or at least of glamour in Washington. Berlin returned to Broadway with a tribute to J.F.K., a musical about a President who looked like a matinee idol (and was played by a movie star, Robert Ryan). The only trouble with *Mr. President* (1962) was that Lindsay

and Crouse's book made presidential politics, international diplomacy, and
the private life of the first family so immaculate, so devoid of anything but
the best intentions that the show would have made Frank Capra blush.
Berlin tried some neoflagwaving in the lyrics to "This Is a Great Country,"
but the line "If this is flag waving, flag waving / Do you know of a better flag
to wave?" was curiously defensive for a man who had needed no excuses for
the past fifty years. His patriotic pipings for *Mr. President* were of uncertain
vintage and unconvincing zeal.

The country had changed radically since *Call Me Madam*. The baby
boom after World War II had reversed a rise in the median age of Americans, and the young, because they had a lot of money and few compunctions
about spending it on something new, became the trend setters for the popular arts. They wanted novelty, not professionalism, and manufacturers of
mass-produced pop art—record albums, paperback books, television shows,
even motion pictures—changed their product almost overnight to conform
to the latest shift in public taste. But not musical comedy. Book, songs, and
orchestrations took months, sometimes years, to write; unless a show was a
smash hit, it could only play eight times a week in one theatre; and the
expense of mounting a show—by 1965, a half million dollars and up—made
producers and directors reluctant to hurry their work beyond the hectic pace
of the usual rehearsal and tryout period. The one component quickly inter-
changeable in musical theatre was the talent that appeared on stage, and so
the one mass-marketed novelty that musical comedy could offer a fickle public was the performer who may have apprenticed, even starred, for long
years in the theatre but whose fame did not come until national exposure
through television or movies. The trend had begun in the '50s but it peaked
during the '60s and the master composer of star vehicles of the '60s was Jule
Styne.

Two of his shows of the '60s were conceived as vehicles for established
stars: *Do Re Mi* (1960) for Phil Silvers and *Fade Out—Fade In* (1964) for
Carol Burnett. Two others were tailored for emerging celebrities: *Hallelujah, Baby!* (1967) for Leslie Uggams and *Funny Girl* (1964) for Barbra
Streisand. Comden and Green wrote the lyrics and Garson Kanin adapted
his own novelette as the script for *Do Re Mi*. Comden and Green wrote both
the lyrics and the book for *Fade Out—Fade In*, and they also provided the
lyrics for *Hallelujah, Baby!*, while Arthur Laurents contributed the book.
Bob Merrill wrote the lyrics and Isobel Lennart the book for *Funny Girl*.

In *Do Re Mi* Silvers played Hubert Cram, a loud-mouthed frantic hustler
who tries to muscle in on the juke-box racket in New York and ends up in
front of a U.S. Senate subcommittee investigating the underworld. The
downward spiral of Cram's fortunes kept the pace of the show at a dizzying
blur, and, with a few exceptions, Styne's score passed similarly, with brasses
screeching and percussion held at full throttle. Only when the hurly-burly
calmed, so that Silvers could catch his breath, did the songwriters get a

chance to show their talents. Their "Cry Like the Wind," in the style of a coffeehouse folk song, imprinted its wraithlike melody with a hypnotic rhythm; "Make Someone Happy" rose above its trite lyrics on Styne's eiderdown melody; and "All of My Life," in which Hubert came to terms with being a loser, gave Silvers the rare opportunity to play the vulnerable soul beneath his comic mask.

Between *Do Re Mi* and *Funny Girl*, Styne, Comden and Green wrote their only musical of the '60s that wasn't a showcase for a star or star-to-be, although *Subways Are for Sleeping* (1961) did have its plum roles: a southern beauty queen who fights eviction from her New York apartment by refusing to wear any clothes in hope that her super wouldn't dare throw a naked lady into the street, and her equally eccentric boy friend whose fantasies about his mate run to speculations about how she might look fully dressed. Phyllis Newman played the beauty queen and got one of the show's two best songs, "A Shoo-In," the comic history of her triumphs back in Mississippi, including interpretive readings from *Gone With the Wind* interspersed with Stephen Foster, coloratura flourishes, toe dancing, and hooting. All this had won her the titles of "Miss Watermelon," "Miss Blossom," and "Miss Southern Comfort." Orson Bean played the boy friend and got the show's other comic treasure, "I Just Can't Wait," a swooping tango in anticipation of seeing the woman he loves with her clothes on. Unfortunately, these two zanies were the secondary roles in *Subways Are for Sleeping*, and the leads, Sydney Chaplin and Carol Lawrence, had to make do with a predictable romance and a handful of slick, uninspired melodies.

Funny Girl, Styne's next show, was the vehicle on which Barbra Streisand rode to fame. She had begun her career as a chanteuse in a lower Manhattan night club, progressed to a role in the Off-Broadway revue *Another Evening with Harry Stoones*, and then caught the public's attention as the sad-sack working girl Miss Marmelstein in *I Can Get It for You Wholesale* (1962). In a decade of bogus musical-comedy stars, some of whom could act but not sing, some of whom could sing but not act, Barbra Streisand was the real thing: a singing actress who could belt with the focus, if not the volume, of Ethel Merman and who could clown in a style made half of self-caricature and half of devilish charm. She was the perfect choice to play Fanny Brice in a musical biography of the *Ziegfeld Follies* headliner.

But *Funny Girl* had more to offer than Barbra Streisand; it had Jule Styne's best score since *Gypsy*. As the story followed Brice from 1910, through vaudeville, World War I, and eventually to stardom in the *Ziegfeld Follies*, Styne got the chance to spoof the old ricky-ticky styles of the two-a-day as well as the musical excesses of the Broadway extravaganza in its heyday. The best of his show-within-a-show numbers were "Rat-a-Tat-Tat," inspired by the tap-dance drills of chorus girls armed with silver-painted balsa carbines, and "His Love Makes Me Beautiful," a resplendent Ziegfeld tribute to matrimony, which Fanny unhinged by appearing at its climax dressed in full bridal regalia and padded around the midsection to make her look eight months' pregnant. But the songs that sold the show and sold Barbra Streisand to the public were "People" and "Don't Rain on My Parade," both of which arose from Fanny's unhappy liaison with the n'er-do-well gambler Nick Arnstein (Sydney Chaplin). "People," which became Streisand's musical signature, got more play than "Don't Rain on My Parade," but the latter has finer lyrics and a hell-bent melody. "People" was pure self-indulgence for Streisand, an unashamed mix of narcissistic vocal pyrotechnics and maudlin lyrics ("People who need people are the luckiest people in the world").

Funny Girl, which had to delay its opening five times before its directors (three of them) felt it was ready to face the critics, seemed a poor bet in comparison with *Fade Out—Fade In,* the next Styne, Comden and Green opus, which, during its first week at the Mark Hellinger Theatre, set a record for the largest weekly gross ever taken in at that box office. As its star it had America's première television comedienne, Carol Burnett, and as its director, the dean of American musical-comedy directors (his tally of shows was then 103), George Abbott. To anyone who didn't know how disappointed Miss Burnett was with her vehicle the prospects for *Fade Out— Fade In* seemed limitless.

But Miss Burnett—and the opening-night critics—knew that *Fade Out—Fade In* was a decrepit and remarkably unfunny pastiche of old jokes about Hollywood's Golden Age. The gags hadn't worked in two other Broadway shows on the same subject, *The Vamp* (1955) and *Goldilocks* (1958), and wouldn't work in 1964 without gigantic expenditures of energy from Burnett and the supporting actors Jack Cassidy and Lou Jacobi. Early in the run, she began to miss performances—twenty-six in the first twenty-five weeks. Then, in November, six months after the opening and while the accounts were still $400,000 in the red, she left the show entirely for treatment of neck and back injuries sustained, she told reporters, when a taxi she was riding in suddenly braked. Producers Lester Osterman and Jule Styne filed several legal actions in which they alleged that their star was malingering, then entered into negotiations with her, and closed their show. Meanwhile, Comden and Green tried to improve their libretto, Styne wrote several new songs, and Jack Cassidy dropped out and was replaced by Dick Shawn. For thirteen weeks the idle company collected their paychecks until the show reopened at an additional cost of $100,000. But it lasted for only 72 more performances. The *coup de grâce* was Burnett's announcement that she was pregnant. If a star could pilot a vehicle, she could also sabotage it.

Comden, Green, and Styne went back to work on their songs for an ambitious libretto by Arthur Laurents, whose success with *West Side Story* had persuaded him to write another musical with a social conscience. *Hallelujah, Baby!* (1967) was no less than a history, from 1907 to 1967, of black America's struggle for equality. Laurents had cleverly unified and condensed his story by putting at its center two young blacks, Georgina (Leslie

Uggams) and Clem (Robert Hooks) who, as the century ages, never grow older. She begins as a housemaid and he as a railroad porter; at the halfway point she is a singer-dancer in all-black Harlem nightclubs, and he is a member of the Communist Party; by the '60s, she is a show-business headliner performing wherever she wants, and he is organizing demonstrations for a civil rights campaign. Laurents' idealized version of history made the black struggle for equality unambiguous and invigorating, but not very meaningful, and the show's faith that blacks would inevitably succeed was especially naïve to audiences who had recently watched television newscasts of Watts burning. Styne's melodies kept percolating, whether the times were good or bad, while Comden and Green's lyrics cherished their liberal clichés as if they were gospel. The submerged rage and open, raw despair of blues, jazz, gospel, and spirituals were missing from a score that was strictly Tin Pan Alley, an idiom not alien to black performers but far removed from most blacks' struggle for freedom. Despite its oversimplified history, *Hallelujah, Baby!* won a Tony Award for Best Musical.

The last of Jule Styne's '60's musicals, *Darling of the Day* (1968), played only 31 performances. The show's admirers blamed its dismal reception on a disparaging first-night review by the second-string critic for the New York *Times*, Dan Sullivan. Perhaps Sullivan did unjustly slight Patricia Routledge's ripe voice and heartfelt acting, and perhaps he lacked the musical sophistication to recognize the gentle virtues of Styne and E. Y. Harburg's score. But he was dead right about the uncredited libretto and Vincent Price's acting. In combination they flattened all the nuances of the musical's source, Arnold Bennett's novel *Buried Alive*. In the novel Priam Farll was an eccentric, totally captivating genius, a famous Victorian painter and militant nonconformist who tries to escape his fame by faking his own death and, while "buried alive," marrying an equally unpretentious and lovable soul, Allice Challice. Vincent Price reduced Farll to an unctuous wooden Indian, who sang in a pinched-nosed quaver that missed the pitch as often as it landed on it and who danced, as Martin Gottfried of *Women's Wear Daily* described it, "in movie monster style."

Price wasn't the only show-business celebrity wounded by the critics' brickbats and worn down by Broadway's eight-shows-a-week endurance test. In 1960, Lucille Ball survived only 172 performances of *Wildcat*, a show she had supposedly commissioned. N. Richard Nash, the librettist, had designed a role for her that matched her screen image as an indomitable, loony battler. Wildcat Jackson was a superwoman of the Wild West, a combination John D. Rockefeller and Annie Oakley, who finagles the deed to a Texas oil well and fast-talks a crew into working the well until they bring in a gusher and she ropes into matrimony the foreman. But for all her guile, Wildcat was about as animated as a cactus. In compensation, Cy Coleman and Carolyn Leigh's score whipped by, leaving behind only "Hey Look Me Over" to refresh the bored audiences.

Coleman and Leigh didn't give up on the star vehicle; their next one was *Little Me* (1962), written in collaboration with Neil Simon for Sid Caesar. Without forcing, their songs managed a big-city sassiness that often equaled Caesar's absurdity ("Boom, Boom"), macabre cheerfulness ("Goodbye"), and daffy satire ("I love you, as much as I am able/Considering I'm wealthy, considering you're poor"). Their underrated score also offered the crowd-pleasers "I've Got Your Number" and "Real Live Girl." But Caesar's clown-ing was what audiences came for, and Simon's libretto gave him the opportu-nity to run through his entire repertory. He played six characters, all the men in the life of Belle Poitrine (Virginia Martin), gold digger *extraordinaire* who, in flashback, relives the escapades that made her a very rich widow. Caesar was Noble Eggleston, graduate of Harvard and Yale, doctor and law-yer, and intimate of Dun & Bradstreet; Noble's son, Noble Eggleston, Jr.; Mr. Pinchley, a doddering, lecherous old coot of a banker; Val Du Val, a continental cabaret singer; Otto Schnitzler, a dictatorial, Germanic film di-rector; Prince Cherney of Rosensweig, ruler of "the only country ever de-feated by Luxembourg"; and Fred Poitrine, a penniless World War I dough-boy and Belle's one true love. Caesar's versatility and stamina always met the strenuous tests of Simon's book: he sprinted from one character to the next without losing his poise or comic timing, and whether he was a stiff-necked Prussian or a winsome adolescent, the details were true and hilar-ious. His only limitations as a musical-comedy performer were an untrained voice and a tendency to play too small, as if he was still performing before the telescopic eye of the television camera.

Of all the clowns to hold the musical-comedy stage during the '60s the greatest was Bert Lahr, whose vehicle *Foxy* (1964) was a much softened and sweetened version of Ben Jonson's satire *Volpone*. To exploit Lahr's most famous image, his Cowardly Lion from the 1937 film *The Wizard of Oz*, authors Ian McLellan Hunter and Ring Lardner, Jr., made their title charac-ter a crafty—but entirely lovable—old geezer who strikes gold in the Klon-dike, circa 1900. But Lahr wanted to do more than play his old self: He wanted to orchestrate *Foxy* as a grand accompaniment to his own concerto of favorite monkeyshines. As early as its two-month tryout in Dawson City, Yukon Territory, where the show played as a tourist attraction, the battle lines were drawn: on one side the star; on the other, the writers (including composer Robert Emmett Dolan and lyricist Johnny Mercer), the produc-tion staff, and Lahr's co-star Larry Blyden. Lahr knew that without him there wouldn't be a *Foxy*, so, despite the odds, he stood his ground. By the time *Foxy* reached Broadway it was in shambles, a teetering lean-to of mug-ging and slapstick built on the ruins of what had originally been an odd but sturdy composite of musical ideas ranging from the seventeenth century, the period of its source, to Broadway in the mid '60s. Despite—or because of—Lahr's frantic bits (he went as far as scaling the proscenium to get a laugh), *Foxy* collapsed after 172 performances.

An egotistic or insecure star would often become the *de facto* producer of his vehicle, and his perfectionism—expressed in threats, sulking, temper tantrums, and nit-picking—would keep designers awake around the clock, directors in perpetual anxiety, and librettists, composers, and lyricists in Boston or New Haven hotel rooms trying to come up with songs or dialogue that would make every word or sound uttered by the star a showstopper.

Sammy Davis, Jr., wanted no less for his first serious role in a musical, Joe Wellington in Strouse and Adams' *Golden Boy* (1964). But his demands and the turmoil they caused were only the second-act catastrophe in a long, behind-the-scenes drama that had begun with Clifford Odets' decision to attempt a musical version of his play of the same name. It was hardly the kind of plot that immediately suggested song and dance. Its fated hero was a young ghetto Italian who has to choose how he's going to use his hands: as a prize fighter or as a concert violinist. He chooses the more immediate and material rewards of prize fighting, but fighting mangles his hands, he can't play the violin any more, and his depression over that turns to despair when he unintentionally kills one of his opponents. His torment ends with an automobile accident in which he and the woman he loves are killed.

For his musical version Odets made the young Italian a young black who has to decide between medical school and prize fighting. His white girl friend leaves him for another man. If anything, the musical had the potential to be more realistic and more depressing than Odets' original play. In the middle of rewrites, Odets died, and William Gibson, author of *The Miracle Worker* and *Two for the Seesaw*, finished the adaptation by revising most of Odets' work in—according to show-business legend—five days. Gibson transposed the action from the '30s to the '60s and added references to current racial troubles in Harlem and Mississippi. When he joined the production team out of town for what would normally be the final polish, the show was still in complete flux and would be for four months, during which the original director, Peter Coe, was fired or quit after Davis took a swipe at him; Arthur Penn entered as director; and the original costumes, orchestrations, underscoring, and even advertising were all replaced. Charles Strouse and Lee Adams threw out many of their original songs, revised those they retained, and wrote new ones, including two that eventually became permanent.

When the show finally opened on Broadway, whatever doubts Davis still held were kept well in check while he was onstage. Although a bit of the nightclub performer still lingered in Joe Wellington's barely controlled nervous energy, he was not Davis the song and dance man. Davis played him as a serious, preoccupied young man devoted to the woman he loves and disillusioned with the good life. He even underplayed many of his songs with the ironic result that they weakened the dramatic tensions built by the dialogue. One exception was "Don't Forget 127th Street," in which Joe, now a rich prize fighter, returns to his old neighborhood and sings a sardonic alma mater accompanied by the street people he left behind. The rest of Strouse and Adams' score, perhaps to balance the melodrama of Odets' plot, didn't bear down very hard, except for "This Is the Life," Joe's half-sung, half-spoken dream of glory, and "No More," a pseudogospel with a Gershwin-like melody. The show's real excitement was generated by Donald McKayle's choreography: the opening number, in which fighters trained to rhythmic accompaniment, and the fatal boxing match, in which every punch thrown by Davis and Jaime Rogers was coordinated to musical cues.

Despite episodes brought low by the weariness of both the performers and their material, *Golden Boy* was a unique and impressive musical for the early '60s. It took audiences into Joe's sweaty, unglamorous training gym and faced them with the pain of being a talented black in a bigoted society; it presented his interracial love affair with understated honesty; but even more to its credit, it found music in Joe's life, not great stores of it, but enough to place it well beyond most of the other star vehicles of the decade and qualify it as a true musical drama.

Golden Rainbow (1968), the vehicle for Steve Lawrence and Eydie Gorme, never pretended to be serious theatre nor more than a spectacular variation on the singers' nightclub act. To make their stars as comfortable as possible, Michael Stewart and Ernest Kinoy even shifted the locale of their source, *A Hole in the Head*, from Miami to Las Vegas and added a couple of production numbers (the only numbers in which Lawrence and Gorme didn't sing) that in gaudy feathers, sequins per square inch, and gleaming female shanks out-Vegased Las Vegas. The only musical payoffs for all the hoopla were "For Once in Your Life" and "I've Got to Be Me," tailored by composer Walter Marks in the throat-clutching style expected by Lawrence and Gorme's fans. The two hits weren't enough to keep *Golden Rainbow* in business for more than a year, an impressive record for a club act but a financial failure on Broadway.

Illya Darling (1967) was less than a good nightclub act, but it did have Greek movie star Melina Mercouri, of lithe body and leonine face, in her American musical-comedy debut. She played the same role, now with a little droning and a few hesitant dance steps, that had briefly made her the reigning sex goddess in 1960: the whore with the heart of gold in Jules Dassin's film, *Never on Sunday*. Dassin adapted his screenplay and directed the musical; and Manos Hadjidakis, who had written the film score, tried to parlay the film's hit title song into a full musical comedy, but Stephen Sondheim had to be brought in out of town to intersperse the overly repetitious, bouzouki-inflected numbers with some variety. With only a very slight musical evocation of the Greek islands and without the film's loving photography, the stage version unintentionally revealed Dassin's story for what it really was: a commonplace male fantasy about an innocent provincial who has to be seduced into enjoying life.

George M! (1968) was packaged for those who wanted the domestic brand of celebrity and show-business legend. Its legend was a very flattering biography of George M. Cohan, and its celebrity was Joel Grey, whose vampirish master of ceremonies in *Cabaret* had recently made him a star. Star and legend were well matched. Grey had the same cold and cocksure salesmanship with which Cohan had sold himself and his shows, while Joe Layton's production numbers and Philip J. Lang's arrangements were stampedes of Cohan's rousing tunes played so fast and loud that the younger members of the audience must have thought Cohan had written only one song, something called "If You Get Over There, Yankee Doodle Dandy, Give My Regards to the Grand Old Flag."

The dialogue portions of *George M!* devoted to the private life of Cohan were at best perfunctory, at worst fraudulent. But the spirit of the whole enterprise, especially musical numbers so bullish that one would often begin before the previous one finished, was doubtless Cohan's. Hoofing, swaggering, and bellowing, Grey had all of them perfected, and the boys and girls of the chorus were drilled to sing and dance with laserlike precision and force; they had to be, for each was responsible for more than one role, often as many as four. Their energies and a trunkload of Cohan's songs, over forty-five in two hours, sustained *George M!* for 435 performances, which bested the record of any of the eighty shows that the real George M. had directed, written, or produced.

The George M. Cohan of *George M!* was a favorite archetype of American popular theatre and popular literature: the never-say-die opportunist who proves that Yankee ingenuity and perseverance guarantee success in the land of the free. Molly Brown, of Meredith Willson's *The Unsinkable Molly Brown* (1960) was George M.'s second cousin and sister to Willson's previous Yankee go-getter, Harold Hill of *The Music Man*. As played by Tammy Grimes, Molly was her own creation, the nouveau riche wife of a gold miner, self-proclaimed debutante, and prototypical social climber. After failing to buy her way into Denver society of the late 1800s, she retreats to Europe, salves her wounds, then makes a second attempt at coming out, which is unintentionally spoiled by the brawling friends of her husband Johnny (Harve Presnell). She again retreats to Europe, where a ragtag of minor aristocracy, charmed by her simplicity, adopts her as its own. But Johnny longs for his old friends and the mountains of Colorado, and he soon returns home followed by Molly, who books passage aboard the *Titanic*. But not even the sinking of an unsinkable liner can stop her: She takes command of a lifeboat and survives.

Aside from Miss Grimes, the liveliest attraction was Willson's score, which on two occasions, "Belly Up to the Bar, Boys" and "I Ain't Down Yet," exploded with the same Fourth-of-July crackle as "Seventy-Six Trombones." But the gentler delights of *The Music Man,* songs like "Goodnight My Someone" and "Lida Rose" that evoked spring nights dreamed away in a porch swing, were missing from *The Unsinkable Molly Brown*.

Willson based his next show on a film, George Seaton's Yuletide perennial, *Miracle on 34th Street*. In plain black and white and against background footage shot on location in New York City, Seaton's 1946 film made believable the story of a portly old gentleman with full white beard who claims to be the real Kris Kringle. Where *Miracle on 34th Street* had been understated, *Here's Love* (1963) was a bombardment of exclamation points destroying any chance that the show might duplicate the fantasy of its source. Willson's songs were spot-welded together from melodic scraps, unfinished or truncated musical ideas.

Borrowing screenplays as sources for musicals was only the most recent development in the sixty years of commerce between Broadway and Hollywood. Since the birth of the movies, the two capitals had been exchanging technicians, designers, writers, directors, and actors; and, since the late 1920s, when the movies learned to talk and sing, lyricists and composers had been meeting themselves coming and going between the coasts. Two of those peripatetic souls were Sammy Cahn (lyricist) and Jimmy Van Heusen (composer). When they returned to theatre work in the mid-60s, Cahn had been away from Broadway for about twenty years (since *High Button Shoes*, in 1947), Van Heusen for about ten (*Carnival in Flanders*, in 1953); in the meantime their songs for movies had won them three Academy Awards. At the bidding of Cy Feuer and Ernest Martin they cranked out two musicals back to back: *Skyscraper* (1965) and *Walking Happy* (1966), but their speed and productivity had more to do with craft than inspiration. Their scores were, in keeping with the shows for which they were written, die-cast products of the assembly line.

For *Skyscraper* Michael Kidd (choreographer) and Peter Stone (librettist) chrome-plated the sentiment in Elmer Rice's *Dream Girl* and obliterated its quiet fantasy with sleek production numbers. The show—tailored for Julie Harris—had all the relaxed warmth of a movie chase, for which Cahn and Van Heusen set the pace with their blandly ticking songs. The score for *Walking Happy* tootled just as innocuously and without any hint of its dramatic milieu, a village in Lancashire, circa 1880. Of all the production staff and cast only Norman Wisdom, the English comedian whom Feuer and Martin imported to play Will Mossop, understood the nuances of *Hobson's Choice*, from which *Walking Happy* had been adapted.

Younger songwriters than Cahn and Van Heusen tried in the '60s to rework formulas long overdue for retirement. Charles Strouse and Lee Adams joined librettist Mel Brooks to write *All American* (1962), which was supposed to be a satire on the old collegiate musical, but Brooks ran wild with burlesques on collegiate football, Madison Avenue, American egotism and greed, and nostalgia for good ol' college days. The result was a mangy, slightly daft musical, which liked to chase its own tail and roll over and play dead at inopportune times.

Strouse and Adams' next two shows, *Golden Boy* (1964) and *It's a Bird . . . It's a Plane . . . It's Superman*, (1966) dared far more than *All American. It's a Bird . . . It's a Plane . . . It's Superman* introduced a flesh-and-blood Superman as guileless and preposterous as his pen-and-ink alter ego. To any compliment the musical-comedy man of steel would respond with a straight-faced "Yes" and bristle only when his arch-rival sniggered at his red cape and blue tights. But aside from a masterful parody of Superman, librettists David Newman and Robert Benton didn't find much inspiration for comedy in the streets of Metropolis or the newsroom at the *Daily Planet*. Their chief villain, played by Jack Cassidy, was almost as blank as their Superman, which left Cassidy to fill the dead space with vaudeville turns and camping. Neither were Strouse and Adams' songs of much help. They smiled with enough insipidity to complement the cartoon style of Bob Holiday's performance as Superman, but they lacked the wit to save the rest of the evening's weak comedy. Without finding the pop-art rakishness it so obviously longed for, the show closed after 129 performances.

Strouse and Adams retreated to the star vehicle and the oldest of musical-comedy conventions, the backstage plot. Their librettists Betty Comden and Adolph Green transformed the screenplay *All About Eve* into *Applause* (1970), a vehicle for Lauren Bacall, whose middle-aged agelessness, mellowed veneer of glamour, cultivated snarl, and affected but charming diffidence were ready-made for the role of Margo Channing. Even Miss Bacall's unsure singing voice and hesitant dancing fit the personality of an insecure, ex-glamour queen who competes—for both roles and men—with her young and unprincipled protegée, Eve Harrington (Penny Fuller).

Strouse and Adams wrote an icy score. "Backstage Babble," "But Alive," "Fasten Your Seat Belts," and "Welcome to the Theater" paired clipped phrases with lopsided, insistent rhythms, which lunged, fell back, flashed a compulsive smile, and plunged onward. The only question left unanswered by such jittery encounters—and even by Strouse and Adams' ballads—was why Margo Channing and Eve Harrington would fight to keep their memberships in such a driven profession. That question was partly answered by the show's title song, a classic set piece for Ron Field's choreography and a walloping paean to show business. As explanation for Eve Harrington's treachery and Margo Channing's determination to stand and fight, it couldn't possibly replace the pages of dialogue and the close study of faces in the film *All About Eve*. And so, in *Applause* the ego war between the two women was reduced to a few skirmishes over territory that seemed to have little spiritual or practical value, but the unnerving sparkle of theatre make-believe gone cold was still there in almost every one of Strouse and Adams' songs. Their show won a Tony Award for Best Musical.

The conversion of screenplays to musical comedies accelerated in the 1960s. In addition to *Applause, Illya Darling,* and *Here's Love,* there were, among others, *Sweet Charity* (from Fellini's *Nights of Cabiria*), *Promises, Promises* (from Wilder's *The Apartment*), *Do I Hear a Waltz?* (from *Summertime,* itself an adaptation of Arthur Laurents' play *The Time of the Cuckoo*), *Buried Alive* (from *Holy Matrimony*), *110 in the Shade* (from *The Rainmaker,* another play-then-movie), *La Strada* (from Fellini's movie), *She Loves Me* (from the play *Parfumerie,* then the film *The Shop Around the Corner*), *Look to the Lilies* (from *Lilies of the Field*), *A Time for Singing* (from the novel and film *How Green Was My Valley*), *Zorba* (from the book and movie of the same name), *Carnival!* (from *Lili*), *Henry, Sweet Henry* (from *The World of Henry Orient*), *Cabaret* (from *I Am a Camera,* the film version of both a play and series of short stories), and *Dames at Sea* (a spoof of the Busby Berkeley spectaculars).

That producers were willing to risk duplicating on the stage the power of well-known and well-loved movies is some indication of how desperate musical theatre was for scripts. The greatest obstacle to the success of the adaptations was that most movies depended on realism (or at least realistic detail, as in the case of *Miracle on 34th Street*) to spellbind their audiences, while musicals depended on broad strokes and, perhaps even more, an audience eager (and nurtured by years of theatregoing or innate talent for make-believe) to participate with a director and cast in building a fantasy world from very unrealistic, even abstract, parts. Most of the adapters couldn't find ways of translating realistic detail into the language of musical theatre, so most of the adaptations failed. But *Carnival!,* which won the Drama Critics Circle Award for Best Musical, was one of the few happy exceptions.

Each component of *Carnival!* was fragile. Bob Merrill's score, for instance, had only one song, "Love Makes the World Go 'Round," that eventually led a life of its own as a pop hit. Even it needed frequent reprising throughout the musical and a close resemblance to Bronislau Kaper's "Hi-Lili, Hi-Lo" from the film score to attract and hold the public's attention. The rest of Merrill's score, especially "Mira," Lili's farewell to her home, was equally poignant and evocative but unable to stand on its own. With so little distinctive melody to feature, director Gower Champion wisely did away with the traditional overture and began with the wheezings of a sad accordion and a bare stage dimly lit. He had the circus performers stroll one by one down the aisles, climb onto the stage, and begin to put together a skeletal set (designed by Will Steven Armstrong), only the suggestion of a tent. Each performer was accompanied by a musical motif, and as the setup became a confusing, happy bustle, the overlapping, now cacophonous motifs strengthened the illusion of a small city rebuilding itself at its latest stop. From that moment on, Champion had his audiences playing along with him so that Michael Stewart's almost nonexistent story line was transformed into a counterpoint of Lili's delicate adolescent fantasies against the hard glitter and artificiality of the carny folk and their acts. The docile performances of Anna Maria Alberghetti, as Lili, and Jerry Orbach, as a crippled puppeteer, were played against roustabout interludes of sword swallowing, fire-eating, belly dancing, and juggling. *Carnival!* was one of the few of musicals of the '60s to succeed on the principle of less is more.

The champions of "less is more" in musical theatre of the '50s had been Tom Jones and Harvey Schmidt, the authors of *The Fantasticks*. But, in the early '60s, when David Merrick tempted them with an offer to try a big Broadway show, they accepted. He wanted a musical version of N. Richard Nash's *The Rainmaker*, which had already survived three incarnations, first as a television drama, then a play, and, most recently, a film. Miraculously, none of the recastings had disturbed its tissue of fantasy, and the story seemed ideal for Jones and Schmidt's gentle, romantic style: A mysterious stranger named Starbuck wanders into a parched Texas outpost and promises that for a handsome fee he will conjure up a cloudburst or two. The skeptical but desperate town hires him, and he sets to work with a wagonload of crazy gadgetry. But the drought persists. Starbuck buys time with outlandish mumbo-jumbo and fast-talking, while he also romances Lizzie, the painfully timid daughter of one of the local patriarchs. Responding to his attentions and his stubborn certainty that anything is possible if you believe in it, Lizzie blossoms. The clouds gather and thunder rolls as Starbuck leaves for the next town.

In the musical *110 in the Shade* (1963) the story lost its spell. The first mistake was the casting of Robert Horton, the star of a popular television Western, as Starbuck. His tentative acting convinced no one, and the show's chief mystery became not how Starbuck persuaded Lizzie of her own worth but how he managed to con the townsfolk into hiring him in the first place. In contrast to Horton's Starbuck, Inga Swenson's Lizzie seemed almost brazen, too strong a personality and singer and too beautiful a woman to be a wallflower. Neither Agnes de Mille's choreography, which looked suspiciously like *The Return of Oklahoma!*, nor Jones and Schmidt's modest songs, which were lost in a full-size theatre, could compensate for the missing spirit. *110 in the Shade* was neither a success nor a fiasco; it played 330 performances on Broadway, closed $120,000 in debt, but recouped that from a national tour.

Jones and Schmidt went back to the small show but stayed on Broadway. *I Do! I Do!* (1966) had only two characters, Agnes and Michael. David Merrick again produced and hired as his director Gower Champion, fresh from Merrick's latest hit, *Hello, Dolly!* (1964). Knowing that a two-character musical on Broadway would require thorough professionals with the drawing power of celebrities, Merrick and Champion cast Mary Martin and Robert Preston. Their assignment was grueling: In the course of the show they had to progress from young marrieds in the 1890s to grandparents in the 1950s, stopping along the way to depict the major satisfactions and minor reverses of Agnes and Michael's sixty years together.

I Do! I Do! was a sentimentalized version of Jan de Hartog's comedy, *The Fourposter*, which had served, in the early '50s, as a vehicle for Hume Cronyn and Jessica Tandy. In the musical, all crises, including two extramarital affairs, were navigated without disturbing the show's placid and idealized sketch of married life. But, as he had done with *Carnival!*, Champion managed to prevent the show's turning mawkish. Every theatrical moment, even the onstage changes of makeup and costumes, was played with a flourish, which encouraged Martin and Preston to wage an ongoing contest for one-upmanship. What their calculated antics lost of the newlyweds' innocence and vulnerability they more than redeemed by muting the show's inherent sentimentality.

Jones and Schmidt wrote very folksy, four-square songs, the best of which was "My Cup Runneth Over with Love." Although its style was unassuming, the score was the most ambitious of their career. Agnes and Michael sang almost as much as they spoke. In the prologue alone they sang three duets before uttering a word of dialogue, and throughout the rest of the show, each had seven solos in addition to four duets. Because of the exhausting vocal demands, Carol Lawrence and Gordon MacRae took over the matinee performances not long after the show opened and the following year played the full schedule while Martin and Preston toured twenty-seven cities. *I Do! I Do!*, although far more elaborate than *The Fantasticks*, proved that a relatively small show could work in a Broadway theatre.

Since the early '60s, whenever they could steal time from their other work, Jones and Schmidt had been writing a show in a "ritualistic, nonnaturalistic" style (Jones's words) that fit more closely their conception of musical comedy. The show was *Celebration*, which opened at Broadway's Ambassador Theatre in January of 1969 and closed four months later. As Clive Barnes of the New York *Times* put it, *Celebration* was "pretentiously unpretentious." Its flimsy scaffolding was an allegory: Rich (Ted Thurston) tries to seduce Angel (Susan Watson) and cheat Orphan (Michael Glenn-Smith) out of his patrimony. To tell this simple story Jones and Schmidt patched together a very complicated and jumbled evening of mime, dance, song, ritual, and choric comment. The only relief from all the arch posturing was the sardonic and lecherous humor—the *esprit de Groucho*—of Potemkin (Keith Charles), the show's hobo interlocutor.

In spite of the failure of *Celebration*, Jones and Schmidt went right on experimenting. They financed a small theatre workshop on West 47th Street, where, under the aegis of Portfolio Productions, they began, in the early '70s, to sponsor a series of miniature musicals, all designed to do without the trumpery of Broadway.

Most young songwriters still thought of their Off-Broadway work as an apprenticeship and moreover a showcase of their talents for scouts from Broadway; they looked uptown and dreamed of an opening night when their songs would be boomed to the last seat in the second balcony by a cast of fifty and a full orchestra. Jerry Herman was one of the few who in the '60s realized that ambition. He started, while still in college, by writing the songs for the revue *I Feel Wonderful*, which, in 1954, was produced Off Broadway. Then, after two other revues, *Nightcap* in 1958 and *Parade* in 1960, he joined librettist Don Appell to write his first show for Broadway: *Milk and Honey* (1961).

Milk and Honey started as a nonmusical play about two middle-aged Jews who meet and fall in love at a resort. But when Don Appell showed his outline to potential backers, they told him to come back with a musical about Israel. He obliged with a change of locale and an additional story line about a young Sabra caught between his allegiance to Israel and love for his American wife, who longs to settle in the United States. To link the young marrieds with the middle-aged couple, Appell put the older woman (Mimi Benzell) into a flock of American widows touring Israel and brought the older man (Robert Weede) on the scene by making him the father-in-law of the Sabra. Everything was neatly balanced until Molly Picon, as one of the widows determined to find a new husband, stole the show with her buck and wing, high kicks, and spry acrobatics.

Jerry Herman borrowed rhythms from Ukranian and Polish folk dances and inflected his tunes with Middle-European modalities and Arabic wailing. But too frequently he ladled out weak Broadway stock seasoned with jaunty, two-step rhythms. Whenever Herman's score failed to be evocative, Howard Bay's understated sets and Albert Marre's staging filled in with a sight-seeing tour through Israel, from a narrow alley in Jerusalem, to a sidewalk café in Tel Aviv, to a kibbutz in the desert, to a triple Yeminite wedding performed by candlelight. The pageantry and travel brochure rhetoric slowed the show, but at the same time relieved the sameness of Herman's music.

Milk and Honey ran for 543 performances, not enough to recoup its initial investment but more than enough to create a demand for Jerry Herman, who was summoned by David Merrick to compose the songs for *Hello, Dolly!* Merrick had gathered a cadre of talent whose experience guaranteed that *Hello, Dolly!* (1964) would be the slickest and most ebullient musical of the '60s. (It would win "Best Musical" Awards from the American Theatre Wing (Tony) and the Drama Critics' Circle.) He chose Michael Stewart to adapt the book from Thorton Wilder's *The Matchmaker*, Gower Champion to direct and choreograph, Freddy Wittop to design the costumes, Jean Rosenthal to design the lighting, and Oliver Smith to design the sets. Carol Channing was to play Dolly Levi, the widow and matchmaker out to find a new husband for herself. Merrick coordinated their work with the intention of making *Hello, Dolly!* a candy store of a musical: No one was to worry about nourishment or cavities; the idea was to make indulgence irresistible.

His staff gave him what he wanted. Herman, Stewart, and Champion anchored the show to two gigantic production numbers, which operated on the principle of the topper, the climax no one believes can be surpassed until the next wonder—the next topper—leaves the audience cheering and the performers gasping for breath. Neither "Hello, Dolly!" nor "Put on Your Sunday Clothes" was essential to the book; they were grand diversions, thrills. In the first, Dolly returns to one of her old haunts, a red-flocked and gilt Victorian restaurant called the Harmonia Gardens. The anticipation of her visit so excites a platoon of waiters that they begin a gallop which progresses to a series of acrobatic challenges, all dispatched while they dash back and forth from the tables to the kitchen. At the climax of their romp, Dolly appears—a vision of platinum curls, crimson feathers, and dazzling beadwork—at the top of the central staircase; the waiters line up at attention; and while they and the entire restaurant give forth with a strutting chorus of "Hello, Dolly!," she descends on the downbeats. Champion's staging, Wittop's costumes, and Smith's sets made each succeeding stage picture more intricate and flamboyant than the preceding. For "Put on Your Sunday Clothes" they topped a slow, steady augmentation of lateral movement—a parade of Sunday strollers—with the arrival of a fantastic steam locomotive.

Hello, Dolly!, nominally an integrated book musical, was streamlined for Carol Channing and seamlessly welded to a highly nostalgic evocation of New York City in the 1880s. Oliver Smith's sets looked like pen-and-ink drawings from the rotogravure section of an antique newspaper. Freddy Wittop's costumes were all flounces, frills, ribbons, hyperbolic haberdashery, waistcoats, and white ties. And Herman's score never lost its smile. Like their counterparts in the Teens and Twenties, Herman's melodies were so simple in their architecture that they could expand and contract without losing their identities. "Hello, Dolly!" and "Put on Your Sunday Clothes" were played and sung in almost every tempo from *maestoso* to *presto,* and with each change a different, highly polished facet would glint.

Because the woman playing Dolly Levi was as much a part of the show's nostalgia as its sets and costumes, Merrick hired a succession of veterans, some of them masterful comediennes, most of them ageless wonders, to replace Carol Channing after her twenty-month stint. Ginger Rogers, Martha Raye, Betty Grable, Phyllis Diller, Ethel Merman, and Pearl Bailey (in an all-black version with Cab Calloway) kept *Hello, Dolly!* running for over five years beyond Channing's departure. Their reign set a trend that lasted through the second half of the '60s and well into the '70s: the musical of rosy and energetic nostalgia presided over by a veteran from the heyday of Broadway and Hollywood.

9. *Porgy and Bess*, with Todd Duncan as Porgy.

10. A shop window, Gene Kelly, and Leila Ernst in *Pal Joey*.

11. Ethel Merman and Bert Lahr in *Du Barry Was a Lady*.

12. Ezio Pinza, Mary Martin, brandy, and romance in *South Pacific*.

13. Julie Andrews produces a "musical mixture of sounds" for Rex Harrison in *My Fair Lady*.

14. Scenes from *Oklahoma!* (above) and *On the Town*.

15. Above, set design by Oliver Smith and lighting design by Jean Rosenthal for *West Side Story*. Below, an uplifting moment from *How to Succeed in Business Without Really Trying*.

16. The lion dance from *Pacific Overtures*. Set design by Boris Aronson.

In Herman's next show, nostalgia of stock vintage—the '20s, '30s and '40s—was again served up by yet another female wonder, Angela Lansbury. *Mame* (1966), an adaptation by Jerome Lawrence and Robert E. Lee of Patrick Dennis' novel, *Auntie Mame*, was another celebration of female bravura, in which an eccentric Park Avenue matron introduces her orphaned nephew, Patrick, to the wonders of her sybaritic life-style. The only hint of something approaching dramatic conflict came at the very end of the show when Patrick, now college age, seems about to go against his aunt's wishes—and her entire philosophy of life—by marrying a priggish Connecticut debutante.

Mame was the obvious successor to *Hello, Dolly!* The period from 1928 to 1946 was fastidiously reconstructed. Onna White's choreography dutifully imitated the tango, the Charleston, the Lindy, and the jitterbug, but the show's most startling visual moment was a diagonal line of horsemen in riding pinks who closed ranks to welcome Mame to the Burnside family manse in Georgia. Jerry Herman seemed to have written the scores for *Hello, Dolly!* and *Mame* at the same sitting. *Mame*'s title song, another "Hello, Dolly!," progressed from a whisper accompanied by one distant banjo, to a raucous gallop, to a Wagnerian hymn. The rest of Herman's songs were just as familiar. "Open a New Window," "It's Today," "We Need a Little Christmas," and "That's How Young I Feel" bounced along. "Bosom Buddies," "Gooch's Song," and "The Man in the Moon Is a Lady" proved that, as long as Jerry Herman continued writing, the comic insult, the patter, and the burlesque song were still alive. Only one number, "If He Walked into My Life," did the unexpected by combining Mame's doubts about herself as a surrogate mother with an appropriately unmotherly torch melody. Its dark passion had nothing to do with the love between aunt and nephew, but it sold the tune on the pop market.

Mame ran for more than 1,500 performances. Herman next tried a musical adaptation (again with Lawrence and Lee) of the Giraudoux-Valency fantasy, *The Madwoman of Chaillot*. He muted his style, accommodating it to the daft and mystical fantasy of the play, but a good jingle divested of its few unexpected twists and stripped of its aggressive orchestration could not suggest the eccentric and romantic personality of the play's heroine, the Countess Aurelia, a waggish old crone who presides over a decaying corner of Paris. Without musical support, Angela Lansbury, as the Countess, resorted to camping. Only Oliver Smith's scenery captured the absurdity—both humorous and sad—of Aurelia's love for Paris and its street people. *Dear World* (1969), after 57 previews, ran for only 132 performances.

While Herman was fabricating his diesel-powered imitations of the '50's musical, its master, Richard Rodgers, was preparing his first show since the death of Oscar Hammerstein. Rodgers wasn't content to do things the way he'd done them before, so this time out he was both composer *and* lyricist for *No Strings* (1962), a show written for the beautiful singer Diahann Carroll. The production itself was mildly innovative; it had to be in order to freshen Samuel Taylor's boy-meets-girl-boy-loses-girl story. Rodgers and director Joe Layton played against racial stereotypes by casting Miss Carroll as a worldly fashion model residing in Paris, but their greatest coup was the way they evoked the favorite haunts of the Parisian chic. They used sixteen chorus girls dressed and coiffed as haute couture models to shift a set composed mainly of bright, abstract panels. At times the girls danced, at other times they posed and paraded like mannequins as if in a showroom or designer's atelier. Layton and Rodgers also moved their orchestra backstage, reduced its size ("no strings" had its literal as well as figurative meaning), and occasionally brought some of the musicians onstage during the songs to join the action as they accompanied it.

At their best Rodgers' lyrics were craftsmanlike, at their worst hackneyed. But his melodies, although far less expansive than those he had written to Oscar Hammerstein's lyrics, occasionally struck a moodiness or a sassiness that recalled Rodgers' best work with Lorenz Hart. The lyrics for "The Sweetest Sounds" spoke in conventional terms of an ideal love not yet realized ("The sweetest sounds I've ever heard/Are still within my head"), while the melody stepped downward in minor intervals suggesting something unhealthy about the obsession. In a completely different direction, "Loads of Lovely Love" was a wonderfully hardheaded cheer for gold digging.

The short run of *No Strings*, seventeen months, may have convinced Rodgers he could use the give and take of working with a lyricist on his next show, so he agreed to join Stephen Sondheim for *Do I Hear a Waltz?*, which Arthur Laurents had adapted from his play *The Time of the Cuckoo* and its subsequent film version *Summertime*. It was a somber play about an American spinster who, while touring Venice, briefly overcomes her timidity and has an affair with a married man. As the spinster, Elizabeth Allen got little help from Laurents' elliptical script and even less from Rodgers' stock tunes and Sondheim's uninspired lyrics. They hadn't found musical expression for Leona Samish's bewilderment—her joy, her guilt, her disappointment, in short, her essence. As her lover, Sergio Franchi had the advantage of several lush melodies that persuasively argued his character's talent for seizing the day. But Franchi's acting was more stoic than dionysian, and when not singing he, like so much of the production, faded into the bronze shadows of Beni Montresor's sets. *Do I Hear a Waltz?* lasted for 220 performances.

Frank Loesser, another veteran of the musical theatre of the '50s, also had his troubles in the '60s. His *Greenwillow* (1960) closed after 95 performances, and his *Pleasures and Palaces* (1965) closed out of town. But between those two came *How to Succeed in Business Without Really Trying* (1961), which won a Pulitzer Prize, Tony and Drama Critics' Circle Awards, and ran for 1,417 performances.

How to Succeed in Business Without Really Trying was a smiling presage of the new decade's cynicism. Not since *Candide* (1956) had a musical been so gaily poisonous. Robert Morse, all gap-toothed smile and lap-dog eagerness, played J. Pierrepont Finch, window washer and mail clerk for the World Wide Wicket Corporation, who covets a seat at the head of the company's board of directors and for whom no connivance, no fraud, no felony, no venal or mortal sin is too awesome in its possible consequences to discourage his climb. A combination Faust, Machiavelli, and Jiminy Cricket, he butchers his competition without blinking and loves himself unashamedly. In spite of ourselves, we love him too. That was the genius of the show. Everything—the book (by Jack Weinstock, Willie Gilbert, and Abe Burrows, who also directed), the performances, and the music—was lovably nasty.

As Finch decapitated his opposition, Loesser's tunes skipped around the guillotine and threw flowers. The frolic was so guileless, so wide-eyed that the devastation, like the car wrecks of the Keystone Kops, didn't seem to hurt. Finch and the head of the mailroom hymned the glories of "The Company Way"—in blissful celebration of compromise and conformity. The office manager and chorus, assuring themselves "A Secretary Is Not a Toy," proved just the opposite. Finch sang "I Believe in You" not to his fiancée (Bonnie Scott) but to himself, which had to be Broadway's first love song for the narcissist by the narcissist. But Loesser saved his best effort for the "Brotherhood of Man," which bounced like India rubber and grinned like a lunatic. In short, it was the quintessential musical-comedy production number sung by a platoon of paper pushers whose true notion of brotherhood was closer to the Cosa Nostra's than to the Quaker's.

How to Succeed in Business Without Really Trying was the first of five '60's musicals to satirize the red-toothed, red-clawed competition in big business. Its successors were tougher and more cynical, and their antiheroes were far less attractive than J. Pierrepont Finch—some evidence that the Broadway musical was growing up. Whether crafty or dumb, strong-willed or pliable, righteous or corrupt, these boobs never really conquered the metropolis or the omnipotent corporation. They lost more often than they won, and if they did win, they had little cause to brag: Luck, not talent, saved them, and as winners they weren't any happier than they had been as losers. About twenty years after Joey Evans set the precedent in *Pal Joey*, the central figure of a Broadway musical comedy no longer had to be a hero, and New York or Hollywood was no longer the Promised Land: *I Can Get It for You Wholesale* (1962), *What Makes Sammy Run?* (1964), *How Now, Dow Jones* (1967), and *Promises, Promises* (1968) were Broadway's belated commentary on the man in the gray flannel suit.

Jerome Weidman adapted his 1937 novel and Harold Rome wrote the songs for the Merrick production of *I Can Get It for You Wholesale*, whose antihero Harry Bogen was played by Elliott Gould (fresh out of the *Irma la Douce* ensemble). Harry's Byzantine double-talk and double-dealing were worth a couple of Harvard Business School dissertations, but his roguery wasn't always persuasive. Rome's score didn't help. Like Harry, it pushed hard but without conviction. Rome inflected it with bits of Jewish folksong, which were supposed to evoke the soulfulness of the garment district, but the effect was strained and lackluster in comparison with *Pins and Needles*, the composer's revue, which in the '30s had celebrated unionization in the same industry. Rome's best song, "Miss Marmelstein," went to a secondary character played by Barbra Streisand, then an unknown, whose doleful recitation about the tribulations of an unloved and unliberated working girl always stole the show. One masterful song and the skillful performances of Streisand, Bambi Linn, Lillian Roth, Harold Lang, and Sheree North couldn't keep *I Can Get It for You Wholesale* running beyond 301 performances.

Steve Lawrence gave his first musical-comedy performance in *What Makes Sammy Run?*, an adaptation of Bud Schulberg's novel and television drama. Lawrence was very credible as a ruthless egotist who hacks his way from newspaper copy boy to head of a motion-picture studio, then finds himself alone and without the solace of knowing why he fought to get where he is. The musical was as tough as—and to some critics tougher than—the novel and television adaptation. Abe Burrows, who had directed *How to Succeed* and who was brought in to direct *What Makes Sammy Run?* during its out-of-town tryouts, said that whenever he saw Sammy Glick abandoned, he put him back in, and whenever Glick looked soft, he toughened him. Sammy became the most unregenerate of musical-comedy louses since Joey Evans of *Pal Joey*, and audiences responded appreciatively by giving the show a run of 504 performances.

American musical comedy usually sidestepped the practical complications of romance. But in *How Now, Dow Jones*, a show with a Wall-Street ambience, a finicky and sentimentalized view of sex would have seemed incongruous. And so, when Kate (Marilyn Mason) bedded with Charley (Anthony Roberts), she got pregnant, and when Charley found out he was soon to be a father, he ran away. After that, the musical compromised its honesty: Charley returned, and the godfather of stockbrokers (Hiram Sherman) singlehandedly saved Charley from financial disaster and Kate from marriage to the boring dolt to whom, in her panic, she had become engaged.

How Now, Dow Jones was another of David Merrick's productions, as was *Promises, Promises*. Neil Simon adapted the latter from Billy Wilder and I. A. L. Diamond's screenplay for *The Apartment* (1960). The pop composer Burt Bacharach and his librettist partner Hal David wrote the songs.

Merrick's enlistment of Simon, Bacharach, and David was a coup. Not since the heyday of George S. Kaufman and Moss Hart had stage comedies been as popular as Simon's work. His nonmusical shows—*Come Blow Your*

Horn, Barefoot in the Park, and *The Odd Couple*—had played long and lucrative engagements and had also done healthy business as films. Less spectacular but still impressive were the records of Simon's musicals: *Little Me,* 257 performances, and *Sweet Charity,* 608 performances. Bacharach and David were equally popular in their own field as the originators of a sophisticated and intricate song style driven either throughout or at climactic phrases by staccato lyrics and asymmetrical rhythms. Bacharach's instrumental arrangements featured strings and muted brass, which surrounded his tunes with a cool, chic exterior belied by the rapid and irregular heartbeat of his rhythms.

Bacharach and David's style was potentially an ideal complement to Simon's libretto, which, although it lacked the mordancy of Wilder and Diamond's film script, hadn't destroyed its flippant, wisecracking tone. Chuck Baxter, still a quite likable *schlemiel,* is trapped by his ambitions and his timidity into surrendering his apartment keys to his bosses for their extramarital noontime and afternoon affairs. When Fran, one of the executives' mistresses and a secretary in the corporation, tries to commit suicide in the apartment, Baxter rescues her and they fall in love, which is treason not only to Fran's boss but also to Baxter's ambitions. From then on the lovers maneuver quite clumsily and hilariously like amateur spies in enemy territory.

Bacharach and David failed their promise. Their songs too often dribbled along, one indistinguishable from the other. Only their title number came close to the comic tensions of Chuck and Fran's romance, but the song's lyrics were almost incomprehensible at a presto tempo and against fortissimo brass. The real charmer in the score was the leisurely, wistful "What Do You Get When You Fall in Love?" which Fran sang—quite intelligibly—to a simple guitar accompaniment.

In spite of Bacharach and David's second-place showing, *Promises, Promises* was a first-rate show. Jerry Orbach's portrayal of Chuck Baxter, although lacking the original character's bewilderment, so charmed audiences that they had to wonder why Chuck stooped to loaning out his keys to get ahead. Jill O'Hara was pert and sympathetically vulnerable as Fran Kubelik, and the rest of the principals, Edward Winter as the boss, A. Larry Haines as Dr. Dreyfuss, and Marian Mercer as Marge MacDougall, kept faith in Simon's masterful script and did not soften its wit with irrelevant clowning. The choreography, always jittery and always exciting, was designed by Michael Bennett, who was just beginning the career that, in the mid-'70s, would lead him to *A Chorus Line.* The striking orchestrations were by Jonathan Tunick. For the first time in the history of musical comedy, he scored extensively for electronic instruments and for an amplified quartet of women's voices to supplement the orchestra, which gave the show a distinctly contemporary, urban sound. *Promises, Promises* might not have been the toughest of the tough shows to follow *How to Succeed,* but it was the most popular. It ran for 1,218 performances.

The tough style of *I Can Get It for You Wholesale, How Now, Dow Jones*, and *Promises, Promises* may have said something about David Merrick's tactics as a businessman, producer, and promoter, but their consistency was likely a fluke. A full list of Merrick's musicals from 1954 to 1968 reveals only that during those years he was the man who came the closest to owning Broadway: *Fanny* (1954), *Jamaica* (1957), *La Plume de Ma Tante* (1958), *Gypsy* (1959), *Destry Rides Again* (1959), *Take Me Along* (1959), *Do Re Mi* (1960), *Irma la Douce* (1960), *Carnival* (1961), *Subways Are For Sleeping* (1961), *Stop the World—I Want to Get Off* (1962), *I Can Get It For You Wholesale* (1962), *Oliver!* (1963), *110 in the Shade* (1963), *Hello, Dolly!* (1964), *Foxy* (1964), *Oh, What a Lovely War* (1964), *The Roar of the Greasepaint—the Smell of the Crowd* (1965), *Pickwick* (1965), *Holly Golightly* (1966), *I Do! I Do!* (1966), *How Now, Dow Jones* (1967), *The Happy Time* (1968), and *Promises, Promises* (1968).

Merrick's loyalty to domestic products wasn't unstinting. From 1960 to 1965 he sponsored six American versions of shows that had originated in London. His judgment was so accurate that only one of his imports, *Pickwick* (1965), failed entirely. Although *Oh, What a Lovely War* (1964) played only 125 performances, it encouraged the few writers and producers who wanted to experiment. In particular, it helped confirm one of Hal Prince's beliefs: that a lively, entertaining musical could take up a brutal subject like war without prettifying it. *Oh, What a Lovely War* would be one of the inspirations for Prince's *Cabaret* (1966). The rest of Merrick's imports had little or no influence on American musical theatre except to encourage other producers to begin their own importing.

Merrick's first import, *Irma la Douce* (1960), should have been as influential as *Oh, What a Lovely War*. It was as innovative and far more popular (over 500 performances), but it came to America when *My Fair Lady, Camelot, The Music Man, Gypsy, The Sound of Music, Bye, Bye Birdie*, and *Do, Re, Mi* were the order of the day.

Elizabeth Seal, the only woman in a cast of sixteen, played the title role, a Parisian prostitute in love with a poor law student, Nestor Le Frippe (Keith Michell). Irma wants to finance Nestor's schooling from her earnings, but Nestor, an uncompromising gallant, will hear nothing of it and insists that Irma quit her work. When she refuses, he borrows enough money to rent her for a full twenty-four hours and disguises himself as a wealthy roué interested only in companionship. Irma is delighted; she takes the money and gives it to Nestor; Nestor, disguised as "Monsieur Oscar," gives the money back to Irma; Irma gives the money to Nestor; Nestor, disguised as Oscar, gives the money back to Irma. *Et voilà! Le mouvement perpétuel!*

But romance and sex in *Irma la Douce* were not merely farcical. The bistro owner, the judge, and the convict (all played by Clive Revill) felt obliged—as Frenchmen and lovers—to reflect philosophically and nostalgically on Nestor's first romance, then, with a shrug, to venture that passion, whatever its form and however silly, must be tolerated—what else can a civilized man do? That was the predominant spirit of *Irma la Douce*, especially in its music. The show's songs, written by Marguerite Monnot, didn't blast from the stage and orchestra pit—they expanded, like a gentle perfume, to the accompaniment of accordion, xylophone, and trombone. Because it never leered and seldom spoke above a *mezzo piano*, *Irma la Douce* could be frank and very funny about sex. Its loud American cousins had much to learn.

Leslie Bricusse and Anthony Newley's *Stop the World—I Want to Get Off*, imported by Merrick from London in 1962, was as irreverent as *Irma* but not as subtle. It looked as if inspired by Tessie O'Shea, Marcel Marceau, Aristophanes, Shakespeare, and Rube Goldberg. Newley played an Everyman figure, Littlechap, who stumbles from one adulterous affair to another in search of love. (He also directed and, with Bricusse, wrote the libretto and songs.) The star's makeup and his miming recalled Marcel Marceau's "The Seven Ages of Man," but *Stop the World* wasn't stolen goods. It was a half-serious, half-zany contraption into which Newley had tried to cram every piece of theatre he had ever loved: slapstick, puns, references to classical and Elizabethan theatre, night-club set pieces, shaggy-dog stories, burlesque, *commedia dell'arte*, and music-hall routines. Holding all this together was Newley's presence, itself a strange synthesis of baggy-pants comedian, harlequin, crooner, melancholic, major domo, and bumpkin. His eccentricities asserted themselves most forcefully during his songs. Different wills seemed to control the twistings and untwistings of his fingers, hands, and arms. With eyes clenched and mouth busy in weird contortions he looked deep in some kind of pained ecstasy or Voodoo trance.

Bricusse and Newley's lyrics frequently slipped into doggerel, and their melodies pushed too hard, but their adolescent, stage-struck enthusiasm was—despite Newley's grimaces—compelling. "What Kind of Fool Am I?" made self-flagellation seem almost heroic; "Once in a Lifetime," another lapel grabber, was Littlechap recovered from self-pity and determined to make something of himself; and "Gonna Build a Mountain," the most ingratiating and least compulsive of Littlechap-Newley's odes to himself, was a jolly, unpretentious mix of hillbilly stomp and Maypole dance.

The Roar of the Greasepaint—The Smell of the Crowd (1965), Bricusse and Newley's next brainstorm, almost shook apart from its contrary motions. Before admitting defeat, one reviewer identified snippets from *Tristan and Isolde*, *My Fair Lady*, *Waiting for Godot*, *Hamlet*, Chaplin's films, burlesque, vaudeville, religious ritual, and musical quotations from Mendelssohn, Gershwin, Tschaikovsky, and early Bricusse and Newley. The cement for all this was supposed to be an allegory about the proletarian underling, represented by Cocky (Newley), versus the Establishment, represented by Sir (Cyril Ritchard). Costumed as hobo clowns and striking absurd poses on a giant gameboard in the middle of a circus arena, Newley and Ritchard played like zanies with Shakespearean pretensions, their grotesque bathos both funny and touching. But neither their eccentric overacting nor a bundle of attractive songs—"Who Can I Turn To?," "A Wonderful Day Like Today," "The Joker," and "This Dream"—could convince playgoers that *The Roar of the Greasepaint—The Smell of the Crowd* was more than leftovers from *Stop the World—I Want to Get Off*; it played for less than 250 performances.

Merrick's most successful import of the '60s was *Oliver!*, an adaptation of Dickens' *Oliver Twist*. Lionel Bart, who wrote both songs and libretto, condensed the novel to the events we all remember from high school English: Bumble sold Oliver to the undertaker Sowerberry, Fagin drilled his boys in the art of light-fingered pickpocketing, and Bill Sikes killed Nancy. The novel's sentimentality was left intact, but its macabre humor, its anti-Semitism, and its preoccupation with grotesques were filtered out.

Despite its antiseptic rendering of Dickens, *Oliver!* ran for almost 800 performances. Its saving graces were a talented cast and a collection of jingle-like songs that got extensive play in America long before the show arrived. Bruce Prochnik was a sweet and innocent Oliver, whose piping, doleful rendition of the tearjerker "Where Is Love?" came close to Dickens' more maudlin excesses. As Nancy, Georgia Brown sang "As Long as He Needs Me," a masochistic pledge of loyalty that was no more than several limp phrases repeated over and over; still, she was able to give them surprising variety and intensity. But whenever Bart's score and book tried to be anything but sentimental, they usually came up with a mood more akin to Disney than Dickens. Fagin (Clive Revill) may have looked like a warlock, but he treated his boys with all the bluster and fuss of a lovable uncle. And his young pickpockets, children toiling at crime in a grim underworld, sang only the most chirrupy of songs: "Consider Yourself at Home" and "I'd Do Anything."

Other producers were quick to compete with Merrick in the importing business. In 1965, Stevens Productions, with Allen-Hodgson and Harry Rigby, brought *Half a Sixpence* from London's West End. Its librettist Beverly Cross and its songwriter David Heneker had also written the London version of *Irma la Douce*, but *Half a Sixpence*, before Americanized, was as placid and proper as *Irma* had been frisky and sloe-eyed. By American standards (or the standards of the slam-bang '60s) *Half a Sixpence* was positively Victorian, a very respectful rendition of *Kipps*, H. G. Wells's genteel romance about a penniless clerk who, after inheriting a fortune, momentarily deserts his working-class fiancée to chase after a society girl. The original production was also a vehicle for Tommy Steele, twenty-seven when the show opened and a rock 'n' roll idol in England (soon to be eclipsed by John, Paul, George, and Ringo) since 1956, when he recorded a Lionel Bart tune called "The Caveman Rock." But Steele wasn't the typical rocker, if Elvis

Presley is your prototype. Blond, curly-haired, with a smile as wide as a billboard and bright as a kleig light, he resembled a British Andy Hardy.

Steele kept his grin turned on throughout the American run, but on Broadway he was upstaged by Onna White's dances, newly added for restless Americans impatient with a staid Victorian romance. Her work made every production number effervescent, and the best of her concoctions had Steele, who hadn't danced in the London production, hoofing and plunking on a banjo. Still, *Half a Sixpence* was remarkably restrained by American musical-comedy standards of the mid-'60s: a tea dance under Chinese lanterns, a midsummer night at the seashore, a brief kiss and giggles in the dark.

Of all the imports from England, *Oh, What a Lovely War,* which Merrick sponsored in 1964, deviated the farthest from what American audiences expected from a musical. The eighteen members of its cast were almost anonymous in their black-and-white Pierrot and Pierrette costumes, and each played a variety of roles in scenes unrelated by plot but tightly bound by time, 1914–18, and by theme: the folly of war. *Oh, What a Lovely War* mocked that folly, but its mockery, even when slapstick, was rueful; as it jested, it grieved.

Its bare, unlocalized set, by John Bury, stressed the universality of the show's theme and its disturbing ironies. Toward the back of the stage hung an electrical sign that, as it periodically spelled out statistics about the First World War, seemed to advertise proudly the numbers of men missing in action, wounded, and killed. Every song, even the maudlin "Keep the Home Fires Burning," was converted to an antiwar testament by the impassive unreeling of the electrical tickertape. But the most bitterly ironic of the scenic touches were the giant projections of battlefield photographs that, against the clowning and the patriotic jingles, played a dissonant counterpoint of haggard faces and mangled bodies.

The show had been put together in Stratford's Theatre Workshop, where the original cast, directed by Joan Littlewood, had improvised scenes from ideas and bits of dialogue supplied by several writers. Many of their characters and speeches were historical, and all of the songs had been favorites in England and at the front during the war. Against the inanities of "I'll Make a Man Out of You" or "Over There," the pontification and sword rattling of Von Moltke, John French, Henry Wilson, and Douglas Haig sounded doubly absurd. The lampooning, played in a blithe, music-hall style, spared no one: the stiff-necked, bawling drill sergeant, the compromised clergyman, the cowardly rich who bought their way out of military service. The only gentle sketch in the show was a Christmas celebration during which the German and English troops, emerging hesitantly from their trenches, exchanged greetings and gifts; but even that episode—in the context of the rest of the show—wasn't a release.

One of the greatest admirers of *Oh, What a Lovely War* was Harold Prince, who believed it had " . . . fractured the musical [comedy] form into something resembling a revue, discarding central characters, a story line." Here was a form that freed the musical from the rigid prescriptions of the integrated book, particularly the rule that all the songs in a musical must grow out of its dialogue, that they must help tell its story. The countless alternatives suggested by *Oh, What a Lovely War* were especially inspiring to a producer-director who, since *West Side Story*, had been trying to renovate rather than replace the book musical but who had become increasingly frustrated by his efforts.

In 1960, Hal Prince had produced and George Abbott had directed *Tenderloin*. The show, which tried to wink at its own moralizing, was as self-conscious as a tipsy Puritan. Abbott and colibrettist Jerome Weidman had wanted to depict how much fun debauchery was during the gay '90s in one of New York City's busiest red-light districts, but they had also felt compelled to laud their central character, a fanatical spoilsport dedicated to closing the brothels. Try as they might, they couldn't make the bluenose, played by Maurice Evans, as attractive as a rakehell reporter, played by Ron Husmann, who moonlights by singing in one of the bordellos. Jerry Bock and Sheldon Harnick further glamorized the reporter by giving him their best song, an ersatz, turn-of-the-century lip-trembler, "Artificial Flowers."

In 1963, at a time when the likes of *Hello, Dolly!* ruled, Prince dared to make his debut as a producer-director with a very quiet show featuring a small cast, an orchestra composed mostly of strings, no production numbers, and only two perfunctory dances. Of course, *She Loves Me* lost money. But its grace and its playful, shy romance showed that Prince was an adroit and uncompromising director.

She Loves Me was adapted by Joe Masteroff from the Hungarian play *Parfumerie*. In Ernst Lubitsch's film version, *The Shop Around the Corner*, James Stewart and Margaret Sullavan had more than compensated for the unglamorous lives of the two shopkeepers they played. In the Broadway version the necessary glow came from Bock and Harnick's flirtatious score, a copious twenty-three songs in all, somehow schmaltzy without pretension. Its understatement perfectly complemented the show's gentle crisis, when the two bewildered shop assistants (Barbara Cook and Daniel Massey) realized their hatred for each other was only love turned inside out.

The challenge of Prince's next show, *Fiddler on the Roof* (1964), was how to add music and dance to Joseph Stein's book without prettying or sentimentalizing it. Granted, Stein had already pared some of the bitterness and brutality from his source, the stories of Sholom Aleichem, but he hadn't made Tevye, his protagonist, into a hero, nor had he changed Tevye's stubbornness into indignant melodrama or inspirational slush. The poor Jewish peasant, who lives in Russia at the turn of the century, survives a pogrom not because he is wily or brave—the thought of merely contradicting his wife,

Golde, terrifies him—but because traditions are more important to him than his meager plot of land. He knows that resistence to his persecutors will be suicide, and so he loads a small cart with his family's belongings and trudges off to start again in a friendlier country, perhaps America.

Prince knew that if anyone could make Tevye's story dance, Jerome Robbins could. After reluctantly agreeing to direct and choreograph the show, Robbins fashioned it to his own vision of life in a *shtetl*; he strengthened the ties between Tevye's family and the other Jews of their village and crystallized the antisemitism of the Czarists. His brilliant opening number, "Tradition," was a simple hora but a rich symbol of the Jews' unity, of their reverence for the past, of their good will—even among quarreling factions—and of their isolation from political power, hence their fragility. The small Jewish population of Anatevka joined hands in a circle and rotated slowly as Tevye introduced the community's "special types," Yente the matchmaker, Reb Nahum the beggar, and their revered Rabbi; but the gentiles—his Honor the Constable, his Honor the Priest, and their lieutenants—avoided the circle, stalking quickly across the stage and nodding perfunctorily in the direction of the Jews. The most solemn and joyous meeting of Anatevka's Jews was at the wedding of Tevye's oldest daughter, Tzeitel, and the tailor Motel. The scene built from a dulcet candlelight ceremony to an uproarious czardas, which was suddenly disrupted by the local constabulary who, under orders from their superiors, come to vandalize the Jews' homes. Robbins' final image of Anatevka was of small groups of refugees slowly dispersing toward all points of the compass.

Boris Aronson's sets were like the fiddler on the roof, who, from his precarious perch, scratched out a thin but happy melody. Tevye's ramshackle hovel stood very forlorn on a large, barren stage, but across the backdrop, in a style that recalled Marc Chagall's gravity-defying fantasies, Aronson had suspended a zigzag of shanties that seemed to dance their way into the heavens. Just as joyful—in an austere way—were the costumes by Patricia Zipprodt. Every piece of clothing looked authentically bedraggled, and yet, the rough textures and the dull earth colors of the peasants' working garb, at times overlaid with the greenish blacks of Sabbath coats, seemed richer, deeper, and more varied than the fantasies of bright color invented for most musicals.

Jerry Bock and Sheldon Harnick's score, while spirited, was never thunderous, always in scale with the quiet but joyful life of Anatevka. Even when Tevye fabricated for Golde a visitation from Grandma Tzeitel's ghost, the squeaky ditty sung by the fake poltergeist was less horrific than homespun. But the modesty of Bock and Harnick's score was also its greatest fault. It never ascended to the anguish of Tevye and his friends, who, although powerless, were not weaklings. Whenever their strength needed musical expression, Bock and Harnick resorted to melancholic underscoring instead of the words and music that would have crystallized the passions of their very articulate and sensitive characters. Their other mistake was to lapse, if only for three songs—"Matchmaker, Matchmaker," "Miracle of Miracles," and "Now I Have Everything"—into a jingling style that could have come from any musical currently on Broadway. The rest of their score—particularly "Tradition," "If I Were a Rich Man," "To Life," "Sunrise, Sunset," "Do You Love Me?," and "Anatevka"—had the simplicity and the soul of folk music.

But most of the soul in *Fiddler on the Roof* came from Tevye, who, less from humility than convivial indignation, pleads with his God, "Would it spoil some vast, eternal plan/If I were a wealthy man?" He knows the answer, but asking makes him feel better. Besides, life is too difficult to further encumber it with hatred, so he holds no grudge.

Zero Mostel, who originated the role, played Tevye as a cross between a would-be patriarch and a rotund, capricious sprite who every time he's thwarted, which is just about always, turns upward a beseeching look of half prayer and half why-me? shrug. But the role wasn't a vehicle unaccommodating to other performers, seven of whom succeeded Mostel during the show's record-breaking run of 3,242 performances. Harry Goz, whose Tevye was far warmer and more docile, starred for 928 performances. Herschel Bernardi, Luther Adler, Jan Peerce, Jerry Jarrett, Paul Lipson, and Topol also inherited the role and made it their own.

By 1973, *Fiddler on the Roof* had received over thirty international productions, including one by East Germany's Komishe Opera, which staged it after taming the constabulary's viciousness and cutting any mention by the refugees of their destinations in America. Eighteen original-cast recordings were made in English, Dutch, German, Spanish, Norwegian, Swedish, French, Hebrew, Yiddish, and even Japanese. Perhaps the greatest testimony to the show's universality—or its adaptability—was a remark made by a Japanese theatregoer to librettist Joseph Stein. He couldn't understand, he told Stein, how the show could have appealed to New York audiences. In spirit it was just too Japanese.

Fiddler on the Roof won the Tony and the Drama Critics' Circle Awards for Best Musical.

Bock and Harnick next teamed with producer Stuart Ostrow and ex-comedian Mike Nichols, who was directing his first musical. The most novel feature of their show, *The Apple Tree* (1966), was its offering of not one but three short musicals, each a variation on the vainglorious male subdued by the irresistible, cunning female. As a bow to the antiquity of their theme, the authors (Harnick, Ostrow, and Jerome Coopersmith) began their show with "The Diary of Adam and Eve," adapted from Mark Twain's short story. Their treatment was simple, in the tradition of *Our Town*. No fig leaves, no wax apples, no flora and fauna from the scene shop. Adam (Alan Alda) wore denim pants and a workshirt, Eve (Barbara Harris) wore a smock, and the snake (Larry Blyden) a tuxedo. Bock and Harnick kept their songs close to the style of a lullaby, and that in combination with the unforced, wry style of the book made "The Diary of Adam and Eve" a most promising beginning for *The Apple Tree*.

But the next two stories failed the promise. Barbara Harris had to exhaust herself to make them work, while Alda and Blyden, whose talents could have eased Harris' burden and strengthened the show, spent most of their time on the sidelines. The second fable was a miniature spectacle written and staged as a parody of Hollywood's Babylonian epics. But the feather fans, the papier-mâché breastplates, the cootch dancers, the wailing, the bombast from the tympani and French horns, and the unending parades with Princess Barbára (Harris) toted back and forth on a litter stretched the plot contrivances of Frank R. Stockton's "The Lady or the Tiger?" beyond comedy and well into tedium.

The final musical of the evening redeemed some of what was lost in "The Lady or the Tiger?" In a turnabout of the Cinderella story Harris played a chimney sweep who dreams of becoming a sex goddess complete with bust line, platinum coif, and smile of Cinemascope proportions. When her wish is granted and as Passionella she finally meets her Prince Charming/Rock 'n' Roll Idol (Alda), he says he likes her better as a chimney sweep. The tale, originally written by Jules Feiffer, was both preposterous and sardonic, and Tony Walton, the production designer for the musical version, styled his sets and costumes to match. But Bock and Harnick couldn't find a complementary musical style. They copied the unctuous blatherings of television and film scoring but didn't go far enough. Passionella and her Prince Charming were never as funny or as fatuous when they sang as when they clowned.

Meanwhile, Harold Prince, who was not yet convinced that he should always direct his own productions, hired his old mentor, George Abbott, to direct *Flora, the Red Menace* (1965). The show was intended as a nostalgic satire on the idealistic American Communists of the '30s, but Abbott had little sympathy for the subject. His communists were, in the words of his disappointed producer, ". . . cartoon characters, some of them farcical, others evil." *Flora, the Red Menace* played only 87 performances. But Prince had introduced Liza Minnelli, as Flora, to Broadway audiences, and he had met and worked with the songwriters Fred Ebb and John Kander. Their next collaboration would be *Cabaret*, one of the most unique and influential musicals that Broadway had seen in the last twenty years, a show that did more than any previous American musical to loosen the constraining hold of the integrated book musical.

Prince worked closely with Joe Masteroff on the book, an adaptation of John van Druten's play *I Am a Camera*, itself an adaptation of Christopher Isherwood's *Berlin Stories*. Isherwood's stories told of a young writer from England who, while living in Berlin during the rise of Nazism, crosses the path of Sally Bowles, a creature of the times, a personification of prewar Berlin. Aimless but for a vague ambition to act in movies, she revels in her "divine decadence," boasts of her sexual conquests, and seems entirely incapable of caring for others or thinking about the future. Her lair is a seedy nightclub, where she sings and meets the men who buy her for a night or two.

Masteroff and Prince weren't ready to abandon all the romantic conventions of the musical of the '50s, so they plotted a brief affair for the writer and Sally, and added a secondary romance between the aging landlady of Sally's boardinghouse, Fraulein Schneider (Lotte Lenya), and one of her tenants, the Jewish widower Herr Schultz (Jack Gilford). But these were the only concessions to expected practice. As if to compensate for the stock romance, Masteroff gave it an abrupt, ugly end, Sally's decision to get an abortion and the writer's bewildered flight. Even the comic romance between Fraulein Schneider and Herr Schultz was lanced to expose the infection spreading through Germany, as Fraulein Schneider, threatened by Nazi sympathizers, reneges on her promise to marry.

In Isherwood's stories and Van Druten's play Sally's club was only mentioned; in the musical it replaced a character study of Sally as the controlling symbol of Berlin's decadence. Scenic designer Boris Aronson hung a giant mirror upstage center, where it could be tilted to reflect not only the acts at the Kit Kat Klub but also the audiences that came to watch *Cabaret*. Patricia Zipprodt's costumes for the chorines and the all-woman band were out of a misogynist's fantasies, garish and clumsy and as hard and meretricious as the girls' makeup, blotches of rouge and mascara around hollow cheeks and eyes. But more disturbing than the German Expressionist decor of the Klub and its ghastly loreleis were the musical numbers performed there.

Although some of the numbers had their place in the chronology of the narrative, most appeared without warning, as if shuffled haphazardly between the scenes in Sally's apartment. But their placement and design were anything but capricious. They were studies in decadence, musical-theatre sketches analogous to George Grosz's *Ecce Homo*, their bitterness and grotesque humor spreading throughout every scene of the show. A couple of examples: In "If You Could See Her Through My Eyes," the lecherous and epicene master of ceremonies, played by Joel Grey, made goo-goo eyes at a mincing gorilla in a tutu; they hugged, two-stepped, and tried a couple of waltz turns to a Kander and Ebb tune as silly and inane as the pantomine. All was fun until the closing line of the song, when, leaving his mate upstage, the m.c. padded down to the footlights, put hand to cheek, and confided in a stage whisper, "If you could see her through my eyes,/She wouldn't look Jewish at all." Or take "Two Ladies," another chipper, Disneyesque melody—complete with Diddlididdlidee's—only this time performed by the m.c. and two mädchen whose starched smiles and acrobatic tangles suggested the gropings of a very hectic *ménage à trois*.

The club acts and the two romantic plots resonated in phase with each other and amplified Prince's daring, frightening concept. As Sally (Jill Hayworth) and the writer (Bert Convy) progressed from infatuation, to passion, and finally, to disillusionment and recrimination, the acts coalesced in a harrowing vision of things to come, of jackboots marching on cobblestone and legions saluting the Führer. The Broadway musical had finally found its way back to Brecht and through him liberation.

Cabaret received "Best Musical" Awards from the American Theatre Wing (Tony) and the Drama Critics' Circle.

Kander and Ebb's next collaboration with Prince was *Zorba* (1968), a reworking of the popular novel and film about a poor fisherman who arms himself with a yea-saying, life-affirming philosophy against his harsh life on Crete. Joseph Stein, librettist for *Fiddler on the Roof*, retained every depressing episode from the film, the suicide of a youth rejected by a young widow, the murder of the widow by vengeful friends of the suicide, and the death—from natural causes this time—of Zorba's mistress. On the stage, these tragedies overwhelmed Herschel Bernardi's less-than-heroic portrayal of Zorba; Boris Aronson's sets and lighting glowered, as if at any moment a deluge might revive the withered crones and their decaying village—but the rains never came; the villagers wore black, for death and mourning; and even the all-male chorus, installed in a bouzouki parlor, where they pass the day singing, drinking, and swapping stories, wasn't meant to banish the gloom with their nervous bravado. Prince's vision was uncompromisingly bleak, but fascinating to those who long ago had grown tired of musicals about happy people with happy problems.

The bleakness of *Zorba* and the offstage bickering between its stars, Herschel Bernardi and Maria Karnilova, closed the show prematurely, after 305 performances. The time for compromise had come: Prince and his associates revised their show so that its tone was less austere and mounted a touring version starring John Raitt, for whom Kander and Ebb wrote the spry "Bouboulina." The plan was to route the show back to Broadway after its tour, but the reviews in Los Angeles and Toronto were less than ecstatic and the show never got a second chance at a Broadway run.

Hal Prince was working with the best of Broadway's young songwriters: Bock and Harnick, Kander and Ebb, and Stephen Sondheim. Their collaborations were the most innovative of the decade, and their belief in the musical as a popular art form was vindicated by the shows they wrote—*Fiorello!*, *Tenderloin, She Loves Me, Fiddler on the Roof, Cabaret, Zorba,* and *Company*—works that prompted a renaissance for the American musical. Although the slowest to come into his own, Sondheim eventually became the most influential of this coterie.

The Prince-Sondheim association dates from *West Side Story* (1957), for which Sondheim wrote the lyrics. Then, in 1962, Prince produced *A Funny Thing Happened on the Way to the Forum*, Sondheim's debut as both lyricist and composer. (An earlier Sondheim show, *Saturday Night*, was planned for a late 1959 or early 1960 opening on Broadway, but its producer Lemuel Ayers died before the project could mature.)

A Funny Thing was vaudeville in togas, a bedlam of one-liners and sight gags literally as old as Plautus, from whom Larry Gelbart and Burt Shevelove had appropriated most of their material. To make certain that every guffaw got its due, director George Abbott cast a bevy of master zanies— David Burns, Jack Gilford, John Carradine, Raymond Walburn, Ruth Kobart, and Zero Mostel, as Pseudolus, a slave who wants to be free. Their shenanigans and Abbott's breakneck pacing made *A Funny Thing* a headlong marathon of bawdry, slapstick, and every other kind of baggy-pants farce.

Sondheim wasn't convinced the show even needed songs until he realized that the audience could use some rest from all the belly laughing. So, he wrote a very neat, very dry score, almost cerebral in its humor, that every so often would do the unexpected and with perfect comic timing burst out in a few vaudeville antics of its own. "Everybody Ought to Have a Maid," for example, was a patter song whose deferential melody at first hid behind a cascade of innuendoes about employing a "working girl," a "lurking girl/To putter around the house," but as it swung into its coda, the melody suddenly roared into a strident, brassy applause beggar that ushered its singers on and off the stage for the traditional three bows. Or in "Pretty Little Picture," a limping bass line punctuated with woodblock, plucked strings, and squeaks from the woodwinds put a mince and a leer into Pseudolus' rapt fantasy of marital bliss.

A Funny Thing Happened on the Way to the Forum won an Antoinette Perry (Tony) Award for Best Musical.

Sondheim next collaborated with Arthur Laurents on *Anyone Can Whistle* (1964), the first musical with a theme borrowed from the Absurdists, the premise that it's a mad world and that distinguishing the sane from the insane isn't easy, if at all possible. But Laurents' try at being profound in comic guise made his script labored, and if the medium was the message, his script did the right thing: It split apart. But more discouraging to the casual theatregoer were Laurents' satire and Sondheim's music. There was little fun— and mostly bitterness—in Laurents' mockery of political corruption, gullibility, and the assumptions we make about who's normal and who's not. And Sondheim's score was so complex that it couldn't be assimilated in one sitting. The show closed after a week's run.

Goddard Lieberson, then president of Columbia Records, gave Sondheim's music a reprieve with an original-cast recording. In retrospect, Sondheim's monumental production numbers—"Simple" and "The Cookie Chase"—are too difficult, too self-consciously arty for their own good. They're a prodigious talent's proof that he's more than a tunesmith, he's a composer; and although they prove the point, they're overlong and overinsistent. In "Simple," J. Bowden Hapgood (Harry Guardino), a mental patient mistaken for a psychiatrist, tries to sift the crazies from a crowd of supposedly normal townspeople, but when he's finished, the confusion's greater than when he began. Sondheim's giddy music, a delirious tone poem instead of the usual strophic song, is suitably jagged and dissonant through-out, and as Hapgood's bewilderment spirals, the number degenerates into rhythmic shouting and finally self-destructs in a blast of circus fanfares. But long before that, its manic swats have lost their sting. Just as overblown but less strident is "The Cookie Chase," a roundup of escapees from the local asylum, set to elegant, erudite variations on a Romantic waltz theme—as if Von Weber, Brahms, and Tschaikovsky had been commissioned to write the underscoring for a silent movie chase.

Far more modest and more exciting are "Everybody" and "See What It Gets You," both breathless patter songs of urban anxiety, a Sondheim spe-ciality. And "Anyone Can Whistle" is a wistful, ingratiating ditty that at least for its duration brings Laurents' caricatures to life.

With *Company* (1970) Sondheim came of age as Broadway's most innova-tive and sophisticated composer of the '60s. The show was conceived when George Furth, actor-turned-playwright, showed eleven one-acts to Harold Prince. Prince suggested condensing them into a series of episodes about marriage to be linked by theme and by the presence of a thirty-five-year-old bachelor, Robert, whose ambivalence about marriage is fueled by what he sees when he visits his married friends, all upper middle-class New Yorkers. Sondheim was asked to join the collaboration, and Prince decided to direct as well as produce. Because it was a collage of loosely related vignettes, *Company* gave its creators the freedom to incorporate music, dance, and all the other components of musical theatre in ways dictated only by their imag-inations, not by the limits of the integrated book musical.

Furth's script isn't very encouraging about the institution of marriage: His five married couples enter two by two but seldom exit that way. Sarah and Harry brag about the cooperation that they claim makes their marriage work, but their handholding and mutual backslapping, if viewed closely, look more like arm wrestling and kidney punches. Susan and Peter are more intensely in love than ever—now that they have decided to divorce. Amy and Paul, after many years of living together, are about to get married—if only Amy can get up enough nerve to go through with the ceremony. Jenny and David keep the peace by trying not to say what they really think. And Larry and Joanne are the old pros: Each has been married and divorced so many times that Joanne has lost count, and changing partners has become such a habit that she can't stop auditioning new prospects. Everybody's old chum Robert, meanwhile, happily serves as handholder, confidant, media-tor, court jester, drinking buddy, baby-sitter, and godfather. But he's an engima to his married friends, who can't understand why, after they've in-troduced him to just about every beautiful and intelligent woman in Manhat-tan, he's still single. What they don't know is that he's as confused as they, that he wants to get married but fears the compromises that marriage obvi-ously demands. The only resolution to *Company* is Robert's admission that he does need someone.

Sondheim made his title song—and opening number—a recurring motif that both celebrates and taunts a compulsive search for companionship. His rhythms are exhilarating but driven, his lyrics are affectionate but often smothering. "Company" is fun, but "Company" is also crazy. Almost every other song in the show keeps a similar balance between warmth and cold, vivacity and cynicism. The title of "Sorry-Grateful" sums up the ambivalence of three men who, in a song that is tender but not one whit sentimental, try to explain why they stay married. "Another Hundred People," a peculiar lament by a young woman for all the young hopefuls on whom the city feeds, rushes along with all the high expectancy of those just getting off the buses, planes, and trains, but the message to and from them is anguished: "It's a city of strangers." "The Ladies Who Lunch," is Joanne's bitchy, bluesy sa- lute to the matrons who have found a tolerable routine in their luncheons, club dates, hairstyling appointments, and theatre parties, the ladies, who, from Joanne's tipsy and cynical perspective, are lonely, bored, and afraid of death's slow approach. The song is Sondheim at his best. The one disap- pointment in his score, "Being Alive," was intended as its climax. In it, Robert admits to what has slowly been surfacing: his desire to commit him- self to another person. After all the complex emotions of the previous num- bers, this straightforward, unambiguous sentiment fails to convince. And Sondheim's repetitious melody, which depends for power on regular shifts upward in the song's tonality, rather than an interesting melodic line, is no more persuasive than the song's lyrics.

To stress the compulsiveness of life in Manhattan's Upper East Side, Prince and choreographer Michael Bennett staged their small cast of four- teen amid the confines of chrome, plexiglas, and skeletal steel platforms designed by Boris Aronson. Their production numbers made little pretense of supporting a plot line or of locating the action at a spot other than some- where in the cold vaults of Manhattan's fashionable apartment buildings. Just as Furth's book and Sondheim's songs had converted the oldest and dearest of musical comedy's traditions, its sentimental view of romance, into a skeptical, often disturbing review of contemporary marriage, Prince and Bennett turned the old staging conventions inside out. In "Side by Side," for example, when Robert lines up with all of his friends to strut and kick in celebration of companionship, he finds himself at the end of a chorus line with only an empty space to gesture toward.

In one respect *Company*, which won the Drama Critics' Circle Award and a Tony for Best Musical, was a typical show of the late '60s: Its style had been determined as much by its director and choreographer as by its libret- tist and composer. Since the death of Oscar Hammerstein and at about the same time the dissolution of other long-standing partnerships, the style of musicals had been increasingly dictated by their directors, choreographers and director-choreographers, the most active and influential of whom were

Jerome Robbins, Michael Kidd, Joe Layton, Gower Champion, Michael Bennett, and the greatest success of the late '60s, Bob Fosse.

A dancer since his early teens, Fosse began to work on the other side of the footlights in the early '50s after returning to New York from a stint in Hollywood as a performer-choreographer. From 1954 to 1961, he choreographed five shows for George Abbott. In 1959, he directed his first show, *Redhead,* and followed it with *Little Me* (1962) and *Pleasures and Palaces* (1965). But he didn't catch the attention of the theatregoing public until he rescued *Sweet Charity* in 1966.

Neil Simon, who took on the scripting of *Sweet Charity* after Fosse had given it a try, faced the impossible task of Americanizing *The Nights of Cabiria,* Federico Fellini's inimitable film classic about a waiflike and none too seductive prostitute—a role tailor-made for Fellini's wife, Giulietta Masina—who dreams of a faithful lover but never finds one. For the musical, Cabiria became Charity, a New York taxi dancer played by Gwen Verdon doing her specialty as a delightfully brash, hip-swiveling con artist and vulnerable, lovelorn little girl. But the poignancy of the film was lost, and after two acts of Verdon's jigging and jiving and Fosse's twitchy dances, the show flip-flopped into a self-consciously unhappy ending.

Along the way Fosse pushed everything at such a clip that the book's contradictions and empty spaces washed away behind his vivid, sinuous production numbers, the best of which were "Big Spender" and "There's Gotta Be Something Better Than This." For the former he had Charity and her coworkers at the Fan-Dango Ballroom lined up at the footlights and draped along a railing, their ischia grinding in a slow, wicked torque to growls from the brass; for the latter he staged the girls' disdain for their grubby work in a mock-haughty flamenco, complete with heel stomping, chin thrusting, back arching, castanet pounding, and nostril flaring. Cy Coleman (music) and Dorothy Fields (lyrics) supplied him with one musical set piece after another: a mock gospel for "The Rhythm of Life," a march for "I'm a Brass Band," and slick ballads for "Too Many Tomorrows" and "Sweet Charity." Like Charity, the numbers brimmed with an old-fashioned, untempered eagerness to please that kept the show running for 608 performances.

In additon to the work of Bob Fosse, Hal Prince, and Stephen Sondheim, there were other encouraging signs for musical theatre during the bleak years at the end of the decade: with *1776* (1969), the musical based on American legend made a comeback, and with *Purlie* (1970), the black musical, for the first time ever, attracted to Broadway a substantial black audience.

1776 was a fictionalized chronicle of the trying, steamy months in Philadelphia when the Declaration of Independence was debated, written, ratified, and signed. Peter Stone's libretto, half history and half flimflam, stuck tenaciously and claustrophobically to events inside the chambers of the First Congress and introduced only two women, Jefferson's new bride and, in an imagined exchange with her husband, Abigail Adams. Most of the fun, which depended on masterful ensemble work, came from watching intrigue, compromise, and delay tie themselves into a neat inevitability as July 4th approached: the signers' waffling and final capitulation to the proslavery faction ("Molasses to Rum"), the delegates' refusal to listen to John Adams, the one idealist among them ("Sit Down, John"), news of death from the battlefield ("Momma, Look Sharp"), and, once the Declaration was ready for ratification, uncertainty about whether or not the legislatures would support it ("Is Anybody There?"). Sherman Edwards' score made wry, amiable music out of the political dialectics, and somehow Eddie Sauter's arrangements managed a suggestion of lace collars and buckle shoes from a battery of electronic keyboard instruments. In complementary style, Onna White's choreography for the all-male ensemble was a set of very decorous variations on the minuet. By the usual Broadway standards 1776 was understated, even austere, but by avoiding extraneous production numbers, a flip tone, and irrelevant romance its authors produced a taut musical drama, which won the Tony and Drama Critics' Circle Awards for Best Musical.

Purlie was the only Broadway show of the decade with a convincing black sound, a volatile mix of rock, gospel, soul, and blues that catapulted Ossie Davis' sputtering libretto into jubilant flight. Composer Gary Geld, lyricist Peter Udell, and choreographer Louis Johnson couldn't surpass the fireworks of their curtain raiser, the gospel shout "Walk Him Up the Stairs," but exploiting the vocal talents of Melba Moore, Cleavon Little, and a preternatural ensemble brought them close at least three other times: "I Got Love," a spiraling squealer that carried Miss Moore upward to the bounds of audible sound, "New Fangled Preacher Man," a down-home pledge of black pride sung by Cleavon Little to jew's harp and harmonica accompaniment, and "First Thing Monday Morning," a muscular work song that pounded out the black man's determination to be free.

The conduit by which black music usually reached white audiences was rock 'n' roll, a musical form at least thrice removed from the full-powered spirit of the blues, early jazz, spirituals, and gospel. But rock—even the docile strain bred in the mid-'60s for consumption by middle-aged theatregoers—hadn't completely forgotten its roots. It still swaggered, it still throbbed with some of the insolence, the frustration converted to musical expression, that made black music so potent. Rock brought to Off Broadway—and eventually to Broadway—some of the excitement that had waned as musical theatre sifted over and over the phrasings, rhythms, orchestrations, and sentiments that by the mid-'60s were more than thirty years old. With rock came the extraterrestrial scats, riffs, and rills of electronic music, high-decibel amplification, Indian ragas, the cult of the rock superstar, and worship of the '60s Youth Culture, including its holy orders—the Hippies, the Yipees, the War Protesters, the Love Generation—and their bumper-sticker catechism: "Turn On, Tune In, Drop Out," "Do Your Own Thing," "Let It All Hang Out," "Make Love—Not War."

The rock musical of the decade was *Hair* (1967), an innocent orgy and occasional Bronx cheer made suitable for dancing by ingratiating, jingle-like tunes that, at least for the legions of suburbia, could pass for rock. Now, without guilt and without violating the musical dictates of his peers, a kid could take the train in from Paramus to see a Broadway show. His parents would sneak in later. The authors of *Hair*—Gerome Ragni and James Rado (book and lyrics), Galt MacDermot (composer), and Tom O'Horgan (director)—weren't above titillating the tired businessman and his bored wife. Their show's celebration of hippie life, as it made its way from the Public Theater, to a discotheque, and then Broadway, got more profane, more obscene, and more outrageous as it moved closer to high rents and big profits. In went more sloganeering against the Vietnam War, in went more singing, pantomiming, and talking about sex, and in went a brief, dimly lit, and completely gratuitous nude scene. *Hair* became a vision of the under thirties' life-style as fantasized by the over thirties.

Everything about *Hair*, its antibook, its disposable songs, and its free-form dances, was designed to feel spontaneous, the antithesis of the la-quered smiles, drill-team formations, rehearsed whoops and hollers of other latter-day musicals. And the accomplishment of *Hair* was that it sustained its illusion of spontaneous fun, of joyous anarchy, without really becoming formless, without too many lapses into self-indulgent maundering. Its snatches of dialogue made about as much sense—close to nil, if not there—as the catch phrases that passed for social philosophy with the adolescents of the '60s. But its spirit of sweet rebelliousness, a force field borne aloft by O'Horgan's staging and Ragni, Rado, and MacDermot's songs, was clear and reverberant and strong enough to keep *Hair* from disintegrating. A series of chain reactions, close to thirty musical numbers in all, few of them lasting more than two or three minutes, propelled the show through its love-ins, be-ins, antiwar protests, send-ups of the Establishment, and parodies of pop song. The best numbers —"I Got Life," "Be-In," "Walking in Space," "Good Morning Starshine," "Let the Sunshine In," and "Aquarius"—limned the glories of a euphoric new age as revealed by the LSD hallucinations of *Hair*'s collective protagonists, a hirsute "tribe" of dropouts. Their tunes' un-flagging spirits and short, endlessly repeated phrases riding on a gentle rock beat made them the nursery rhymes for a new generation.

Michael Butler, the young producer of *Hair*, quickly capitalized on a Broadway run that looked as if it would never end. Rather than outfit na-tional touring companies and incur exorbitant costs for travel and shipping, he opened as many regional companies as possible and cast them with local talent. (This may have been the reason for a briefer New York run than expected: 1,670 performances.) His international companies also used local talent sometimes abetted by professionals imported from the United States. Within a few years after *Hair*'s Broadway opening, thirty-five troupes performing in fourteen languages had played in twenty-two countries. As of May 1972, it had grossed $65 million, which did not include collateral income from the rights to amateur production, souvenir programs, and record albums. The original-cast album became RCA's highest selling musical-comedy recording to date.

Although its spectacular success encouraged the trend away from the book musical, *Hair* did not initiate the trend. Nor was its rock 'n' roll very authentic; the current arbiter of rock, *Rolling Stone* magazine, called it "the music of a toothpaste commercial." But some of the raunchy and raucous vitality of rock 'n' roll did manage to cling to MacDermot's score, just enough to entice the youngest crowd that any musical had enjoyed in two decades and enough to show that musical theatre could mine rock 'n' roll for enormous profits.

If *Hair* was rock puréed, then *Your Own Thing* (1968) was rock pasteurized—rock with all its funk, grit, and musk boiled away, the residue filling the cracks in a prefab update of Shakespeare's *Twelfth Night*. Antisepsis and inoffensiveness were its virtues, come-ons for the tourist trade, whose curiosity about the '60's counterculture and anti-Establishment protest were satisfied by unisex costumes, some mild grousing about the Vietnam War, here and there a titter about sexual polymorphism, and a "multimedia" set with hundreds of rear projections accompanied by snatches of dialogue on tape. The seductive packaging of *Your Own Thing* as a "rock" musical worked: It played 937 performances Off Broadway, toured extensively, and won the Drama Critics' Circle Award for Best Musical.

Few of the rock musicals of the '60s were as commercial and none was as successful as *Your Own Thing*. Their importance lies elsewhere, in their gropings to find production styles compatible with their varieties—often adulterations—of rock. Most of them, like the modestly successful *Salvation* (1967), opted for variations on a rock concert given loose continuity by nose thumbing at the Establishment. But rock's rhetoric was less instrumental in shaping these new musicals than the rock medium itself, in particular its abrasive intimacy, its wrap-around, claw-at-your-nerves, shout-in-your-ear omnipresence. To find a theatrical analogue to the rock medium, the creators of rock musicals had to move performer and audience closer together, if not physically, then spiritually. And so the rock musical became autobiographical, sometimes communal, a sharing between performers and audience of the performers' experience and their reactions to it. In 1969, a commune of young Texans actually lived in Joseph Papp's Public Theater while they revised their show, *Stomp*, for its New York première. During the performances they invited audience participation in their rambling history—really a confessional—about their disenchantment with life back home and their rebellion, by now an old story of experimenting with drugs and sex and disdaining everything their parents held dear.

Just as autobiographical was Ron Steward's *Sambo,* which also opened at the Public in 1969. Steward wrote its lyrics, collaborated on its music with Neal Tate, and played its central character, a black who rejects the "opportunities" offered him by white society because he fears he'll have to pay for assimilation with his black pride and black identity. Ironically, the show's score was Exhibit A of the hero's fears realized: Its highly commercial "soul music," a redi-mix of swing, jazz, blues, and rock, ran straight and flat.

Also under the sponsorship of the Public Theater, Myrna Lamb, an activist in the feminist movement, wrote her musical indictment of exploitative males and willingly subjugated females. *Mod Donna* was a case study of a *ménage à trois* that began as farce, slogged through melodrama, and concluded with a murder. Like the other Public Theater-sponsored musicals, it was a personal show, a self-indulgent show, but a praiseworthy departure from the creations that had become the standard for uptown musical theatre. Six years later, from Papp's workshop, would come the greatest of its autobiographical shows, *A Chorus Line.*

The doyen of Off-Broadway songwriters was Al Carmines, minister and director of the arts program for the Judson Memorial Church, a Greenwich Village congregation, many of whom are theatre professionals. The arrangement spurred Carmines' theatre ambitions; and between 1961 and 1972 he wrote over sixty shows, four of which were produced during the '60s Off Broadway: *Home Movies* (1964), *In Circles* (1968), *Peace* (1969), and *Promenade* (1969).

The only thing consistent about Carmines' shows was their capriciousness, their unwillingness to be fettered by anybody's definition of musical theatre. And yet they didn't take themselves seriously; if anything, they too frequently parodied themselves, smothering beneath heavy camp what might have been piquant satire—for instance, the Ionesco-like romance between a lonely girl and her television set in *Home Movies.* Sometimes, though, the supercilious approach was just right, as with *In Circles,* an evening of Gertrude Stein's verse set to pantomime and music; a line like "Papa dozes/Mama blows her noses," when set by Carmines to a Pucciniesque tune, was galvanized with a new zaniness. Whatever the libretto, Carmines supplied a prodigiously eclectic score refined from styles as varied as opera, operetta, ragtime, barbershop quartet, Kurt Weill, spirituals, jazz, and '50's pop. His encyclopedic command of song styles and the Dadaist fantasy of his shows were signs that musical theatre was liberated from romantic realism while holding on to the best of our pop music heritage.

Of course the longest-running Off-Broadway musicals of the '60s were hardly as provocative as Carmines' experiments. In the tradition of *The Boy Friend* and *Little Mary Sunshine, Dames at Sea* (1968) again spoofed old musicals. On a stage with almost no depth and with a cast of six and orchestra of three, it pretended to be a Busby Berkeley film extravaganza of the '30s. Its Tom Thumb scale and junk-shop ambiance made absurd fun of Hollywood glamour, but its book (by George Haimsohn and Robin Miller) and its tunes (by Jim Wise)—right out of the Harry Warren-Al Dubin mold—never sniggered, just smiled affectionately, at the classic fairy tale of the anonymous chorus girl who gets her big break when the star falls ill. As Ruby, the chorus girl from Centerville, Utah, Bernadette Peters was the dewy-eyed reincarnation of the Depression-era heroine.

Man of La Mancha (1965)—the greatest Off-Broadway hit of the '60s—was also a throwback, a return to those romanticized adaptations of literary masterpieces that in the '50s had culminated in *My Fair Lady* and *West Side Story*. The strategy for adapting Cervantes' *Don Quixote* to the musical stage was to shrink it to a parable: Don Quixote became an eccentric idealist, a combination of Santa Claus, Henry David Thoreau, and Elwood P. Dowd, who battles—more in his imagination than on the fields of sixteenth-century Spain—for the privilege of being a dreamer of impossible dreams in a cynical and selfish world. By boiling off Cervantes' mockery of his demented knight errant, Dale Wasserman (librettist), Mitch Leigh (composer), and Joe Darion (lyricist) left behind enough concentrated sentimentality to stock an Off-Broadway and Broadway run of 2,329 performances and win the Tony and Drama Critics' Circle Awards for Best Musical.

Wasserman located his opening scene in a Seville prison, where Cervantes (Richard Kiley), jailed for his debts, acted out for the prisoners of the Inquisition his novel about a man who cherishes his illusions and finds his nobility in them. By applying greasepaint and false whiskers, Cervantes became Don Quixote; his man servant (Irving Jacobson) took the part of Sancho Panza; and the guards, inquisitors, and other prisoners played all the supporting roles. Without ever leaving the confines of Howard Bay's stylized prison, the show gracefully—thanks to Albert Marre's direction and Jack Cole's choreography—swept in and out of Don Quixote's chivalric fantasies. Toward the back of the set a gangplank hung in midair until a new prisoner or officer of the Inquisition would enter, and then the stairway, poised like a heavy blade, would slowly descend to the clatter of pulleys and chains as the prisoners cowered in the shadows. But when Cervantes began his storytelling, the shadows softened and the menacing dungeon was transformed into an enchanted arena in which anything could happen. The staging was a brilliant illustration of the show's theme, the miraculous power of illusion.

But Marre and Cole's virtuosity and the compelling performances of their cast were too often compromised by Mitch Leigh's score. Based on nineteenth-century transcriptions of Spanish folk music, especially flamenco, his tunes suffered from a melodic and rhythmic predictability that discouraged imagination instead of firing it. They traded away inspiration for the kind of melodic needling that implants commercial jingles permanently in the brain. A persistent two-bar phrase, lyrics surpassing "You'll Never Walk Alone" in soggy homiletics, and a hypnotic bolero rhythm made "The Impossible Dream" the most persistent—and most popular—number in a score replete with instantly recognizable and easily assimilated tunes.

Commercial bonanzas like *Man of La Mancha, Hello, Dolly!, Fiddler on the Roof,* and *Hair* kept Broadway alive while only five out of fourteen new musicals opening in 1969–70 survived beyond 85 performances. American musical theatre had become a victim of its own timidity and business-as-usual mentality, but it was also the victim of history, of change over which it had no control.

Young people commandeered the popular arts in the '60s. Their music was rock, their medium television, and to them live musical theatre looked and sounded archaic. But the popularity of rock music and the boycott of theatregoing by those under thirty do not explain why even the older fans, the diehards, stayed away. Of course one reason was the product: They weren't making them like they used to. Broadway had its greats in the '60s— Hal Prince, Kander and Ebb, Bock and Harnick, Gower Champion, Bob Fosse, and Stephen Sondheim. But it didn't have the stable of lesser but prolific talents who could have sparked a renaissance of the small show or the show with no pretensions. Musical theatre didn't have the time, money, or the apprenticeship system for nurturing young writing talent.

That's assuming producers would have been willing to take their chances with talented newcomers. But with average production costs between $300,000 and $850,000, few investors were willing to risk their dollars on untried composers and librettists. Inflation was also a deterrent to the health of musical theatre; it squeezed from both ends: Fewer shows got produced, and those that made it to Broadway had to fight entertainments that cost the public less—television, movies, and recordings. The shows that survived ran longer and made more money than any previous musicals in history. But their triumph had its negative side. With *Hello, Dolly!, Mame, Camelot, How to Succeed in Business Without Really Trying,* and *Carnival* determining the magic formula for success, Broadway was not about to make giant strides toward a more innovative and diverse musical theatre.

Musical theatre was also the victim of the cultural upheavals of the '60s, when the most gripping, most immediate theatre was, quite literally, in the streets—which meant on the television screens of middle-class Americans. The assassinations of John F. Kennedy, Martin Luther King, Malcolm X, and Robert Kennedy, the Vietnam War protests, the police riots of the 1968 Democratic Convention, the Newark and Watts riots mesmerized us and left us stunned and cynical. Musical theatre didn't have too much to say about a very unfanciful, unromantic, unsentimental world. For many it seemed too trivial—even as a diversion.

And finally, musical theatre was the victim of urban decay and the sexual revolution. By the late '60s, the New York theatre district was surrounded

by porn shops, X-rated movie theatres, massage parlors, and their accompanying effluvia, commercial and human. Muggings, theft, and all sorts of
imaginative con games proliferated in the Times Square area, and the good
burghers from the suburbs, the stalwarts of musical theatre, decided that the
long drive in from Fair Lawn to risk life and limb getting from the parking lot
to the Winter Garden Theatre just wasn't worth a couple hours of live entertainment. Marquees were dark, lobbies empty. The theatre district was for-
bidding, dangerous territory.

PART SIX
The 1970s

Len Cariou and Angela Lansbury contemplate the barber's "friend" in *Sweeney Todd*.

XXVI. An Uncertain Comeback

THE NEW DECADE started with a thud. In the 1970–71 Broadway season, only forty-six productions opened—the puniest record in the history of American theatre. Only two of that season's seventeen new musicals—a revival of *No, No, Nanette* and *Godspell* (Off Broadway)—eventually paid their own way, and only one of the season's new offerings, *Follies*, affirmed unequivocally that the American musical theatre still had creative energy.

But producers didn't give up. As the decade gathered momentum, they and their writers and directors tried everything to win back their lost audiences and find new ones. They gave us the *Hair*-derived, rock-environmental musical, the hit-record-album-dramatized musical, the Jewish musical, the Jesus musical, the club-act-expanded-for-Broadway musical, the country and western musical, the bicentennial musical, the all-dancing musical, the sexual liberation musical, the new black musical, the history lesson musical, and the revival. By the end of the decade, Broadway, Off Broadway, and regional theatre had produced a tidy share of entertaining—and sometimes artistically noteworthy—musicals: *A Chorus Line, Pacific Overtures, Sweeney Todd,* a new *Threepenny Opera, Annie, The Wiz, Bubbling Brown Sugar,* and splendid revivals of, among others, *My Fair Lady, Guys and Dolls, Porgy and Bess,* and *The King and I.* The big moneymakers made healthy contributions to the incomes of Broadway and the road, incomes that, by the end of the decade, had never been higher. (*Variety* reported that the total box office take for the 1978–79 Broadway season was over $128 million, and that was exceeded by income from the road, which reached just under $149 million.) The popularity of these hits also showed up as increased paid attendance on Broadway: in the 1978–79 season, over nine million.

As regional theatre grew (by 1979 there were sixty-five large resident regional theatres in the United States), so the commissioning and production of musicals by those companies grew. *Annie, Shenandoah, Very Good Eddie,* and *Whoopee!* all came from only one of those regional theatres, The Goodspeed Opera House, and by the end of the decade, exports to Broadway from other centers had begun to accelerate.

But the signs that the American musical theatre was regaining its strength had to be qualified. Incomes from shows were swelled artificially by

inflation. The increased cost of doing business also discouraged some investment, even though Broadway angels have always been notorious gamblers,
quite willing to risk great sums on the most ephemeral of ventures. More
troubling than inflation was the large number of flops that demoralized and
financially drained the musical theatre toward the end of the decade. Where
was the new generation of writers, composers, and lyricists? Had they
turned to other forms of musical and theatrical expression during the antiwar and Nixon years, and had the necessary tradition of apprenticeship been
broken? Would the post-World War II generation, which during the late-
'60s and early '70s had shown little interest in musical theatre, develop into
an audience as it grew older?

While the history of musical theatre during the '70s can't answer those
questions with finality, the evidence is clear that Broadway, Off Broadway,
and regional theatre were offering more diversity than at any other time in
the past and that new talent, much of it unschooled and some of it chafing at
the restraints of the old conventions, was lining up. The permanence of the
musical's new health was in doubt, but its physique had been toughened and
its spirit brightened by its trials. And so the history of American musical
theatre in the '70s becomes a narrative—not without its absurdities—of the
crises in a long illness and, if not its cure, the early signs of new vitality that
give reason for at least cautious hope.

Behind *The Rothschilds*, the first musical of the 1970–71 season, was a
scramble for the theatregoers, many of them Jewish, who had made regular
pilgrimages to *Fiddler on the Roof*. Two other shows pursued the same
crowd: *Ari* (1970), which survived only thirty performances, managed to
convert the bestseller *Exodus* to a waxworks pageant; and *Two by Two*, the
latest by Richard Rodgers, was undermined by its own star.

Two by Two's librettist Peter Stone had transformed Clifford Odets' *The
Flowering Peach* into "Noah and the Flood As Told By Henny Youngman."
Quite logically Danny Kaye was cast as Noah. But not long after the show
opened, Kaye tore a ligament in a foot and had to maneuver in a wheel chair
and on crutches. The new props suggested new stage business, and soon
Kaye was playing with his Broadway musical like a kid playing with a new
toy, which only made the show's weaknesses all the more obvious. Richard
Rodgers' melodies, sedentary and reluctant to dare the heights without some
support and coaxing, lost all gumption in the bullying company of Kaye's
ad-libs, and *Two by Two* closed after 343 performances. *Variety* reported a
loss of $300,000, but Rodgers, who also produced the show, claimed a profit.

At a cost of $850,000, *The Rothschilds* kept all of its promises to audi-
ences who paid for opulence and Jewish lore. The story of Mayer Rothschild,
who by force of will and cunning became the richest patriarch in the history
of Western civilization, was ready-made for the oldest of musical plots, the
dream that comes true. So taken was librettist Sherman Yellen by Mayer
Rothschild's deeds—his climb out of the Frankfort ghetto, his founding of a

worldwide banking dynasty, his cornering of the London market, and his defiance of Metternich—that he forgot to dramatize the passions and genius driving his hero. The best that Yellen could do was to have Mayer Rothschild declaim over and over that, whatever the sacrifice, he would free his sons from the ghetto. Only the casting of Hal Linden humanized the role. His fatherly benevolence, benign smile, and warm singing voice of the John Raitt-Howard Keel school could have charmed a Metternich.

Sheldon Harnick and Jerry Bock, whose score for *Fiddler on the Roof* had been at its best when simple and folksy, wanted songs for *The Roths-childs* that would suggest the cosmopolitan Europe of the late eighteenth and early nineteenth centuries. And so they subordinated their Jewish-gypsy motifs to operetta pastiche, Broadway baroque, and resonant, male-dominated ensemble work. (Mayer Rothschild had five sons.) The result was an unrelenting, slightly formal amiability, which left the impression that all there was to the secret of the Rothschilds' success was a determined smile and graceful bow.

Later in the decade Sheldon Harnick and Sherman Yellen joined Richard Rodgers to write a show more grandiose than *The Rothschilds*. With a daring more foolhardy than courageous they musicalized, in a labored pageant called *Rex* (1976), the bloody reign of Henry VIII. Their Harry was a romantic, confused soul, who, having executed Anne Boleyn, realized she was the only woman dear to him. *Rex* was just as confused as its Henry. Rodgers mistook stodginess for majesty; Harnick, trying to imitate Oscar Hammerstein, wrote lyrics that were more often bland than tersely eloquent; and Yellen so overburdened and slowed his libretto that it was easy to sympathize with Henry's swift means of divorce.

Rodgers came back at the end of the decade with a show that had far more potential for the musical theatre. It was an adaptation of Kathryn Forbes's stories, which had been the source of John van Druten's play, *I Remember Mama* (produced on Broadway by Rodgers and Hammerstein), then an RKO film (1948), and, in the '50s, the very popular television series that starred Peggy Wood. Every version told of an Old World family constantly improvising in order to survive and find acceptance in America. At the center of the family and giving it her character and strength was Mama: warm, loving, firm in her Old World beliefs, and totally unself-conscious in her profound understanding of human nature. And so the wisdom of casting Swedish film star Liv Ullman for the musical *I Remember Mama* (1979), which without an actress of her skill, would have glowed very faintly. Her radiant presence gave distinction to a very professional enterprise—but hardly one that captured all of Mama's spirit. David Mitchell's turn-of-the-century sets and Theoni V. Aldredge's costumes were as evocative as sets and costumes could be. But Thomas Meehan's book and Martin Charnin and Raymond Jessel's lyrics never echoed Mama's simple profundity, nor did Rodgers' tunes, although occasionally aglow with real joy and sadness, match Ullman's performance.

If *I Remember Mama* proved that Richard Rodgers, seventy-six at its opening, was past the apex of his powers, it wasn't the only musical during the '70s to expose one or more veterans to the embarrassment and cost of expensive failures. *Prettybelle* (1971) with book and lyrics by Bob Merrill and music by Jule Styne closed in Boston during a tryout run. But within a year Merrill and Styne's next show, *Sugar*, had made the entire distance to Broadway—not without tribulation. The show's libretto, an adaptation of the film comedy *Some Like It Hot*, was finally written by Peter Stone (with help from Neil Simon), after earlier versions by Michael Stewart and George Axelrod had been discarded shortly before rehearsals began. Most of the film's comedy had come from chases and reaction shots, the grimaces of Jack Lemmon and Tony Curtis who escape Al Capone's henchmen by disguising themselves as females and joining an all-girl band. What the intimate eye of the film camera and perfect editing had made into deft comedy, *Sugar* recycled as burlesques on transvestitism. Director-choreographer Gower Champion's only inspired contribution was a tap-dancing mobster, and Styne and Merrill's score merely coated the proceedings with a patina of '20's musical clichés. Left to his own devices, the show's star, Robert Morse, tried every possible variation on the boy who, in spite of of himself, enjoys being a girl.

Two productions that opened in 1974 showed Jule Styne in better form; and both revived his earlier work. *Gypsy*, although playing only a limited run of 120 performances, stirred as much, if not more, enthusiasm as its first edition. Critics revised upward their original praise of Arthur Laurents' book and Styne and Sondheim's songs (one called the show a "masterpiece"). And, at the annual Tony Awards' presentation, Angela Lansbury, who played Mama Rose, won Best Actress in a Musical.

Lorelei, which preceded the touring *Gypsy* to Broadway by only eight months, had begun its out-of-town tryouts as a sequel to *Gentlemen Prefer Blondes* (1949). While retaining ten songs from the original (including "Little Rock," "Diamonds Are a Girl's Best Friend," and "Bye Bye, Baby"), Styne, with Betty Comden and Adolph Green, wrote five new numbers, which stayed in the ear only long enough to make one wish the whole original score had been saved. By the time *Lorelei* reached the Palace, it was less a sequel than a rehash of the original show and a spangled vehicle for Carol Channing. Her full-moon eyes, framed by a sunburst of platinum hair on top and a cosmic smile beneath, could still light an entire theatre, and her voice was, if anything, reaching deeper into subsonic levels than it had when she appeared in the 1949 version of the show. But she stood out the show's most exciting numbers—Lester O. Flatt's dances, including a ferocious tap number at the close of act one.

In 1971, Ron Field directed and choreographed a revival of another '40's musical, *On the Town*, for which Comden and Green had supplied the book and lyrics and Leonard Bernstein had composed the music. The original was a ballet converted to a musical comedy, and even in its Broadway metamorphosis it contained more than a half hour of Jerome Robbins' dances. Field's new choreography, in comparison with Robbins' legendary work, looked tentative and forced. The whole spirit of the revival was strained. Bernadette Peters, as Hildy the taxi driver, overacted more than Phyllis Newman and Donna McKechnie, but everyone (including the three sailors: Remak Ramsay, Ron Husmann, and Jess Richards) pushed far too hard. Their innocent love for New York, italicized by Bernstein's romantic, boogie-woogie score, was irritatingly at odds with the political and social realities of the early '70s. *On the Town* lasted only 65 performances.

After a stint on Broadway and on tour with their revue, *A Party with Comden and Green*, Betty Comden and Adolph Green went back to work on a new book musical with songwriter Cy Coleman. Their script was a second adaptation of an original play by Charles Bruce Milholland, first re-written by Ben Hecht and Charles MacArthur; but the most popular version of the story was the '30s film, which had starred John Barrymore and Carole Lombard.

Comden, Green, and Coleman geared their production style to match the over-sized egos of their two principals: Oscar Jaffee (John Cullum), a Broadway impresario running from the backers of his latest flop, and Lily Garland (Madeline Kahn), one of Oscar's discoveries and ex-loves who has since become a great star. Oscar's attempts to entice Lily into his next production are complicated not only by the couple's shared past but also by Lily's current involvement with a filmland juvenile (Kevin Kline). In anticipation of signing Lily, Oscar tries to get backing from a daffy matron (Imogene Coca), who thinks she's spreading the Gospel by plastering "Repent!" signs everywhere. The unique setting for this romantic farce is The Twentieth Century Limited as it makes one of its runs between New York and Chicago in the early 1930s.

Coleman's melodies (and Hershy Kay's arrangements) for *On the Twentieth Century* (1978) approached the extravagances of operetta—but without the effortlessness of the best old shows. His neat, attractive melodic ideas were puffed up to hideous dimensions, which may well have been the satirical intent, but it didn't make for the fun that book, music, and production were obviously attempting. Only the theme song and several interludes sung and danced by a quartet of Red Caps were agreeably proportioned.

Cullum stalked about in opera cape and fedora, gesticulating with the full sweep of the hammiest ham. His acting was of a piece with Coleman's score and just as uncomfortably bloated. In an early flashback, Madeline Kahn got to make full use of her comic talents as the not-so-ingenuous ingenue who sabotages another singer's audition to get her first break. But beyond that brilliant scene, she had only her mock-coloratura songs in which to show her stuff. Soon after the musical's opening, she extricated herself from the run. Imogene Coca also had to struggle against the limits of the show's book and music. Her specialty, perfected during the early days of television, was the kind of comedy dependent on double takes and other varieties of close-up mugging. Like Cullum, she seemed uncomfortable with the oversized style of playing that director Hal Prince demanded.

The only unqualified success Prince had in realizing the comic overstatement he wanted was in his collaboration with set designer Robin Wagner. *On the Twentieth Century*, but for an opening scene and a few flashbacks, took place entirely on a train, but that didn't limit Wagner's imagination. His sleek, Art Deco, chrome and smoked glass locomotive became the most stylish and clever of the show's characters. Its mauve and cream compartments glided around the stage, shuffling and reshuffling themselves, so that a few basic modules provided an intriguing variety of combinations. And, in consort with Prince, Wagner even dared take his audiences outside the train during a chase led by Imogene Coca, the high point of which came when she was at first seen riding the train's cow-catcher, then dangling from its caboose—all to musical accompaniment.

With so little attractiveness in its book and music, *On the Twentieth Century*, despite its flashiness, couldn't stay in business for long. Another, far more modest show, also with music by Cy Coleman, had already enjoyed almost a year's run when *On the Twentieth Century* was just opening. Coleman's *I Love My Wife* was one of a trio of musicals (the others: *Annie* and the revue *Side by Side by Sondheim* imported from London) that opened within five days of each other near the end of the 1976–77 Broadway year and thereby redeemed what had otherwise been an arid season. The publicity for the show made much of the titillating premise of Michael Stewart's book: the decision by two young couples from Trenton, New Jersey, to try wife-swapping (or, should that be spouse-swapping?). The show's title and its cheery spirit (summed up by the lyric, "Though it's sexy, it's a family show") belied any suspense about the outcome of the experiment, but no one could feel cheated when the foursome's plans for a mini-orgy broke apart on the rocks of marital fidelity. The fun came in watching the young people, all attractive and all wanting to be hip, talk themselves into sexual brinksmanship.

Although four in bed might be considered a crowd, the subject of *I Love My Wife* was still intimate, and director Gene Saks and his collaborators gave it just the right intimate staging. Aside from the couples (Lenny Baker, Ilene Graff, James Naughton, and Joanna Gleason), the only other performers sharing the stage were a quartet of musicians, who accompanied, occasionally sang, and, in general, played a scruffy and unpredictably zany Greek chorus. (They were more involved in the proceedings than the musicians who joined the cast of Richard Rodgers' *No Strings*, in 1962.)

The smallness of *I Love My Wife* seemed to be an inspiration for all concerned, especially Cy Coleman. His songs (lyrics by Michael Stewart) ingratiated themselves by being frank enough not to seem coy and bright enough not to seem lubricious. The best were "Hey There, Good Times," a barrelhouse interlude for the band, and the title number. The cast equalled the vivacity of Coleman and Stewart's songs. Its star clown was Lenny Baker, who, as a Trenton moving man and devoted husband, succumbs to the urgings of his quick-talking friend (James Naughton) but never gets completely with the spirit of the enterprise. His reluctance was hilariously realized in a *tour de force* of pantomime, when, as he made his preparations for the climactic bedding down, he found every excuse for delay, disrobed with the speed and zest of someone about to go before a firing squad, and, once he got into bed, puffed his pillow and made neat with such meticulousness that he looked more ready for a mother's goodnight kiss than heavy duty as a swinging lover. That was the spirit of *I Love My Wife*: clownish, adroit, and solidly behind the old virtues. It strongly enhanced the reputations of Michael Stewart and Cy Coleman.

In 1969, Leonard Bernstein had resigned from his post as musical director of the New York Philharmonic to rest and devote more of his time to composing, including work for the musical theatre. But neither of his two new compositions, the ecumenical *Mass*—one-third theatre piece, one-third ritual, and one-third oratorio—and a bicentennial musical, *1600 Pennsylvania Avenue* (1976), enhanced his reputation as much as a new version of *Candide* produced and directed in 1973 by Harold Prince. Even the latter did not do complete justice to Bernstein, for its busy, gimmicky staging and its abbreviated book necessitated the removal of several of his witty songs and the trimming of others.

1600 Pennsylvania Avenue subtracted from Bernstein's reputation and also from that of another veteran, Alan Jay Lerner, who wrote the book and lyrics. Lerner attempted a backstairs history of the White House from John Adam's term to that of Teddy Roosevelt. Not only that, Lerner introduced a pair of black servants (Gilbert Price and Emily Yancy) who symbolized the fretful course of white/black relationships during the one hundred years. Without any clear dramatic vectors to follow, Bernstein wandered back to some of his favorite musical ideas: the close, dissonant harmonies and anxious jazz rhythms of *West Side Story,* the long-lined melodies reminiscent of Copland, the operetta pastiche of *Candide.* His finest inventions for the new show were "A Duet for One," in which Julia Grant surrenders the Executive Mansion to a bewildered Lucy Hayes, and "Take Care of This House," a typical Bernstein anthem which gained its power from a very close convergence of ascending vocal and instrumental lines. Aside from those numbers, the score seemed to have been written under the same lethargy afflicting the entire one-million-dollar production. Only Patricia Routledge's portrayals of all the first ladies maintained a healthy vivacity. Ken Howard, as all of the Presidents, was just slightly more animated than the half-dozen wigs he was asked to wear; his lines, written in a style endemic to historical pageants, would have thwarted an Olivier. *1600 Pennsylvania Avenue* lived a mercifully short life of 7 performances on Broadway.

Lerner had to console himself with a reverent new edition of *My Fair Lady*. The revival came on the twentieth anniversary of the show, and its original producer, Herman Levin, was once again in charge. His intention was to duplicate, with as much fidelity as possible, the original production. Oliver Smith's set designs were only slightly modified to fit the smaller stage of the St. James Theatre, and Cecil Beaton's costumes, with a few improvements, were re-created. Jerry Adler, the production stage manager of the 1956 *Lady*, directed, and Crandall Diehl, the dance captain for the first production, followed Hanya Holm's original choreography.

But neither Rex Harrison nor Julie Andrews returned (although Robert Coote, the original Pickering, was on hand). Levin's new Eliza was twenty-four-year-old Christine Andreas, whose only Broadway credit of consequence was as a standby for the revue *Words and Music*. Higgins was played by Ian Richardson, a consummate Shakespearean actor and member of the Royal Shakespeare Company. He sang more than Harrison had, which made his lyrical outbursts hard to reconcile with Higgins' dry wit and reclusive life-style. Andreas was also an accomplished singer, just as vibrant as Julie Andrews. As if trying to match an outdated preconception of musical comedy style, both of the new leads played quite broadly, making their scenes blustery and obvious. But George Rose's expansiveness as Doolittle was just right, a snorting, lecherous, and very animated ladies' man, who'd definitely need a sobering-up to get him to the church on time.

Although a critical success, the new *My Fair Lady* lasted only a year on Broadway. It offered no new perspective on a musical capable of many interpretations; and, despite an energetic cast, it had the waxy smile of something embalmed. Still, it fared better than Lerner's other musicals of the '70s; *Lolita, My Love* (1971), based on Nabokov's novel and written in collaboration with the English composer John Barry, folded in Boston. *Gigi* (1973), an adaptation by Lerner and Loewe of their film musical, lasted only 103 performances. *Carmelina* (1979), for which Lerner (as author and lyricist) collaborated with Joseph Stein (book) and Burton Lane (music), opened and closed quickly on Broadway. Its story about the reunion of an Italian woman with three ex-G.I.'s, all of whom she had slept with toward the end of the World War II and one of whom—but which was in doubt—had fathered her daughter, should have inspired plenty of comic romance. Instead, *Carmelina* came to life only sporadically, when one of the three possible fathers was on stage and during a couple of the Lerner-Lane songs, "One More Walk Around the Garden" and "The Image of Me."

The first hit of the new decade was *No, No, Nanette* (1971). Originally produced in 1925, at the height of America's Jazz Age, it was all fluff wrapped in pink tissue paper and bound with tinsel ribbon. In the usual three acts a Bible-publishing philanderer, his suave attorney, their suspicious wives, and the publisher's girl friends tangled and untangled, while the

ingenue Nanette fell in love, out of love, then back in again. All the plot had
to do was to open holes for as much singing and hoofing as possible. And
Irving Caesar, Otto Harbach, and Vincent Youmans filled those gaps with
very danceable, very durable tunes, the classics "I Want to Be Happy" and
"Tea for Two" and plenty of lesser knowns that were just as spry.

The new *Nanette* kept all the songs from the original and added one
number ("I've Confessed to the Breeze") cut from the first production and
another ("Take a Little One Step") that had appeared only in the first London edition. The inclusion of the additional material was entirely in keeping
with the spirit of the Jazz Age musical: the more the merrier. Not that Harry
Rigby, who conceived the revival, or Cyma Rubin, who produced, or Burt
Shevelove, who adapted and directed the book, was concerned with authenticity. They wanted a new *Nanette* that would make fun of the old one without deflating its zest. And they wanted to make *Nanette* jazzier than it had
originally been to exploit the theatrical and musical technology unknown in
the '20s but expected in the '70s.

While the performances Shevelove drew from his first-rate principals
were not exactly camp, they did underline every old joke and contrivance.
He also made no attempt to motivate entrances for the singing and dancing
choruses; a cadre of John Held lounge lizards and their flapper girl friends
would, without any reason except the sound of the orchestra, stride from the
wings, in full voice and choreographic precision. The musical arrangements
(by Ralph Burns, Buster Davis, and Luther Henderson) were amalgams of
'20's pseudo jazz, '40's big-band instrumentation, and '50's movie-music
bombast. Amazingly, their concoctions were homogenous and effervescent.
Even the choreography was often anachronistic—but, somehow, it always
fit. Donald Saddler mixed hoofing routines as old as vaudeville with popular
dances from both the '20s and '30s: the Castle Walk, the Turkey Trot, the
polka, Bunny Hug, Peabody, Shimmy-Sham, Charleston, and the Black Bottom—among others! For one production number—"Peach on the Beach"—
Saddler borrowed from the Busby Berkeley film musicals of the '30s by asking his bathing beauties to enter and maneuver their way across the stage
while standing atop giant beachballs. (Berkeley was credited in all advertising as "Production Supervisor.") To give this three-ring circus some visual
continuity, Raoul Pène du Bois designed sets and costumes that married the
sophisticated geometries of Art Deco with the gaudy two-dimensional style
of '20s musical comedy.

Cyma Rubin pulled the decade's publicity coup by signing Ruby Keeler,
the star of the Busby Berkeley extravaganzas, to play the wife of the Bible
publisher (Jack Gilford). Berkeley's films were once again popular, and
Keeler, now sixty, had become a celebrity to a new generation. But she
contributed far more to the show than just a nostalgic personal appearance.
She could still hoof, and her vigor and vivacity hadn't dimmed one kilowatt
over the forty-one years she had been retired from show business. The rest

of the cast, which included Bobby Van, Susan Watson, Roger Rathburn, Patsy Kelly (returning to the stage after a thirty-eight-year hiatus), and Helen Gallagher matched Keeler's spunk and endurance. Gallagher, who played the soubrette, won a Tony Award as Best Actress in a Musical; and Kelly, as the wisecracking maid, won as Best Supporting Actress in a musical.

No, No, Nanette began a fad. Harry Rigby next mounted a hoked-up rivival of *Irene* (first produced in 1919). This version starred Debbie Reynolds, the '50s counterpart to Ruby Keeler. For one week in June of 1973, Reynolds drew the largest box-office gross—$144,620—to that date in the history of New York theatre, and the show ran for almost 600 performances, eventually with Jane Powell as Irene.

Rigby evidently thought the original score (by Harry Tierney and Joseph McCarthy) had not endured as well as that of *Nanette,* so he inserted "You Made Me Love You" from another Tierney-McCarthy show and hired Charles Gaynor and Otis Clements to add new songs. But none of their material was as memorable as the four songs remaining from the original, especially the title song and "Alice Blue Gown." While the show was out of town, Rigby had to replace John Gielgud, who had begun as director, with Gower Champion; Billy De Wolfe, one of the leads, withdrew; Joseph Stein was called in to doctor Hugh Wheeler's adaptation of the book; and Miss Reynolds proved occasionally disdainful of her audiences. Rigby got little consolation from the New York critics, many of whom damned his show as flagrantly commercial.

The cash flow into the box offices of *Irene* and *Nanette* inspired yet another nostalgia revival: *Good News* (first produced in 1927). After a pre-Broadway tour lasting almost a year and after 51 preview performances on Broadway, *Good News* opened just before Christmas 1974. All the touring and final revisions (Michael Kidd restaged Abe Burrows' direction and Donald Saddler's choreography in the few weeks before its New York debut) could not save it. Alice Faye—unlike John Payne who had left the show after its tryout tour—was dutifully present to lend what remained of her cinematic glamour. But thirty years after her heyday, she had grown too reserved and self-conscious for the shenanigans of De Sylva, Brown, and Henderson's first collegiate musical. The only solid virtue of *Good News* was the generous offering of De Sylva, Brown, and Henderson hits: "The Varsity Drag" and "The Best Things in Life Are Free" from the original show, plus "Button Up Your Overcoat," "Life Is Just a Bowl of Cherries," "You're the Cream in My Coffee," "Together," and "Keep Your Sunnyside Up"—all interpolated from other productions.

If audiences wanted classic popular songs embellished with dance, costumes, lights, and scenery—and never mind a coherent plot—why should producers have bothered tinkering with the anachronistic books and inconsistent scores of old shows? A few entrepreneurs saw the light and commissioned new shows either built around old hit songs or furnished with new songs written to sound like the old favorites.

In 1976, *Bubbling Brown Sugar* led its audiences on a tour of the great night spots of Harlem: from the clubs popular in the '20s and '30s—the Cotton Club, Small's Paradise, and Connie's Inn—to jitterbugging at the Savoy Ballroom in the '40s, and, finally, to rhythm and blues at the Apollo in the '50s and later. The score was a compendium from the greatest of black composer-performers (Eubie Blake and Noble Sissle, Duke Ellington, Billie Holiday, Andy Razaf, Cab Calloway, Earl (Fatha) Hines, W. C. Handy, and Fats Waller). Alexander Roberts and Bert Williams added a handful of new but, in such company, invisible continuity songs. Billy Wilson designed a seamless history of popular dance that caught each composer's distinctive rhythmic style and flattered his dancers. The major beneficiary of Wilson's art was Vivian Reed, a stunning singer and danseuse. Her rendition of "Sweet Georgia Brown" became the show's greatest crowd pleaser, and Miss Reed became a national celebrity.

Bubbling Brown Sugar only began to skim the great music from Harlem's Golden Age. *Ain't Misbehavin'* and *Eubie!*, revues which opened in 1978, went further by presenting, respectively, the music of Thomas "Fats" Waller and Eubie Blake. Blake, the son of former slaves, was ninety-five at the opening of *Eubie!*, and he was present to join the cast of twelve during the bows. He then sat down at the piano to reprise several of his greatest hits, including "I'm Just Wild about Harry" from *Shuffle Along*, the first black musical to make its way from Harlem to Broadway. His appearance that night transformed what was an otherwise conventional retrospective of black music into living history. But none of Blake's songs and rags were as memorable as the best of Fats Waller, and *Eubie!* never reached the excitement of *Ain't Misbehavin'*.

Waller, famous during the '20s, '30s, and early-'40s for his stride piano style of jazz, managed, during his brief life (he died in his late thirties), to influence not only jazz artists but also composers of popular and show music. Beyond Harlem he reached audiences through his recordings for RCA, his 1943 Broadway hit *Early to Bed*, his songs for revues (among them, *Hot Chocolates*), and his influence on George Gershwin, Paul Whiteman, and Irving Berlin. The essence of Waller's music was its humor, which came in many forms. Most often jovial, frequently rambunctious, it mirrored the spirit of its composer: full of life and full of the devil. And that was what made *Ain't Misbehavin'* far more than just a review of the work of a musical genius. It revived Waller's spirit and the spirit of his times, especially the rent parties, where only the clarion style of stride piano could be heard above the din of neighbors who had come to carouse and pass the hat for a friend threatened with eviction.

The show, which had been developed at Off Off Broadway's Manhattan Theatre Club, breezed along without much explanation of where it was going. It depended on the spunk of Waller's music, the vivacity of its cast, and the fresh evocativeness of Richard Maltby, Jr.'s direction to keep its audiences so strongly under a spell that signposts weren't needed. Most of the tunes were Waller's, others he had not composed but had made popular. The staging was simple, just a false proscenium, a curtain, which opened to reveal a six-piece jazz band, and out front a huge upright piano that, as an obligingly mobile prop, trundled back and forth across the stage and even rotated. Seated at the piano was "The Professor" in bowler hat, vest, and sleeve garters—a suggestion of Fats Waller, ever-present to keep the music—and the good times—rolling. The cast of three women and two men was far too young to have lived in the Harlem that Waller knew, but Richard Maltby, Jr. and choreographer Arthur Faria had shaped an ensemble whose every move and vocal inflection brought not only Waller's music but also his times alive. Each had at least one virtuoso solo turn, the most memorable of which were: Nell Carter's "Mean to Me," Ken Page's "Your Feet's Too Big," and Armelia McQueen's "Squeeze Me." When joined for ensemble numbers, their work kept all the nuances of solo performance, in numbers as diverse as "The Joint Is Jumpin' " and "Black and Blue," a rueful reflection on race and hard times ("What did I do to be so black and blue?"). Every tune of *Ain't Misbehavin'* was a new discovery for those who hadn't known Waller's music—and a cherished recollection for those who had lived through his times.

Ain't Misbehavin' received both the Tony Award and the Drama Critics' Circle Award for Best Musical.

Over Here! had already celebrated the '40s. Patti and Maxene Andrews, the surviving members of the most popular singing trio of the decade, had come out of retirement to star in the show and give it some authenticity. They were in fact its only genuine articles: Its producers, Kenneth Waissman and Maxine Fox, were barely walking, much less jitterbugging, in the mid-'40s, and the only way that most of the cast knew about swing, zoot suits, and USO canteens was by reading Will Holt's script. Even the score (by Richard and Robert Sherman), although it sounded like real big-band swing, had been manufactured in the '70s. But for the serious nostalgia buff—or for anyone whose musical tastes had been formed in the war years—the show's neoprene smile was easy to take, especially at the curtain call, when Patti and Maxene sang a medley of their greatest hits: "Bei Mir Bist Du Schoen," "Beer Barrel Polka," "Don't Sit Under the Apple Tree," and "Boogie Woogie Bugle Boy." *Over Here!* may have been ersatz from top to bottom, but that was all part of the dopey, cornball spirit of the young men and women who came home in the mid-'40s to begin their civilian lives again in a world free of global war.

Several years before they opened *Over Here!*, Waissman and Fox made their reputation as savvy producers by bringing to New York a curiosity that they had first seen in Chicago. Its name was *Grease*, a mocking tribute to the heavily pomaded, baroque hairstyles worn by teen-age street toughs back in the '50s. In Chicago the show had been little more than a revue of musical parodies on early rock 'n' roll, but in New York, with more dialogue and sharply stylized performances, it became a comedy of manners, a burlesque on all the rituals of '50's adolescence: going steady, staying awake all night at slumber parties, hanging out at a favorite hamburger joint, drinking and petting at the drive-in movies, and getting stood up for the junior prom. The charm of the show, which attracted such business Off Broadway that it eventually moved uptown, was its mindless evocation of the '50s, a time—at least according to *Grease*—when the problems of being a teen-ager came down to whether or not Dad would loan you the car for Saturday night or how you would get a date for the big dance.

What sold *Grease*—and all the nostalgia shows—was not substance but style, and so the critics' complaints that its songs were insipid didn't take into account what the show was trying to do. Its songs *were* insipid—but intentionally so. The pablum effect of early rock fit perfectly with the show's evocation of teen-agers in the throes of adolescent role playing: the James Dean rebel, the class Adlai Stevenson, the Sandra Dee romantic.

Grease became the longest-running musical in the history of the American theatre. It succeeded in attracting young people, both the teens of the '70s, who looked back affectionately at the '50s as the Golden Age of Rock, and those young adults who actually grew up in the '50s and had spent a good deal of their adolescence listening to the real thing—Elvis, Chuck Berry, Buddy Holly, and the rest. *Grease* used its own wry affection for the period to play on that nostalgia.

With *Mack and Mabel* (1974) Jerry Herman and his collaborators tried to do the same for the heyday of the silent movie comedy and its stars. But the show failed to stir any warmth and so its quick end after only 66 performances. Herman had written his usual score, including another "Hello, Dolly!"—this time called "When Mabel Comes into the Room." And Gower Champion, as he had with *Hello, Dolly!*, staged every number with all the expansive movement and spectacle that producer David Merrick could buy for $900,000. But *Mack and Mabel* was just not the "musical love story" its billing advertised. Its book, by Michael Stewart, was tongue-tied about the romance of Mack Sennett (Robert Preston), the king of silent movie comedies, and his star comedienne, Mabel Normand (Bernadette Peters). Neither came to life. Mack was all dictatorial bustle and obsession with success, while Mabel was all tender—and long-suffering—devotion.

Champion's idea of a loving re-creation of the two-reelers and their heyday was lots of gymnastic and mechanical wonders: Mack and Mabel sliding down ropes for one of their entrances, bathing beauties frolicking on a pastel slide, a camera crane swinging out over the audience, and a chase on horseback performed by immobile players in front of a rotating backdrop. When, after all the frenzy, the show had to confront Mabel's pathetic death at the age of thirty-four from an overdose of drugs, Champion waffled. His—and the script's—evasive handling of her death only underscored the show's cold professionalism.

The same fault undermined Stewart and Herman's second show of the '70s, *The Grand Tour* (1979). An adaptation of Franz Werfel's play (by way of S. N. Behrman's 1944 version) *Jacobowsky and the Colonel*, it began with the partnership-by-necessity of two vivid, prickly souls: S. L. Jacobowsky, played by Joel Grey, and Colonel Tadeusz Boleslav Stjerbinsky, played by Ron Holgate. The former, a Polish Jew fleeing from occupied France in 1940, finds himself in league with the Colonel, an anti-Semite. As they sojourn together, their mutual respect grows, and eventually it blossoms into affection, not without setbacks that threaten both the alliance and Jacobowsky's survival. Joel Grey had no trouble convincing his audiences of his character's feisty determination. ("I'll be here tomorrow," was his motto.) Beyond that, neither he nor Herman's score could engender much concern for the fellow's survival. The show was reduced to a series of set pieces, the principal one a Jewish wedding that showed off Grey's talents as a singer and dancer but abandoned the musical and dramatic development of its two unique refugees.

The most old-fashioned new musical of the decade was *Shenandoah* (1975). It seemed to have been written, directed, and choreographed by a crew living in the spirit of the musical's book, a period piece about a Virginia farmer and his family who, quite against their wills, are drawn into the Civil War. From then on their adventures become a McGuffey's Reader on the pioneer ideals of self-reliance, patriotism, clean-living, and Christian faith. Every scene was a set piece, and, accordingly, during the musical numbers the singers, especially John Cullum as the father, would plant themselves facing their audience and sing full voiced to the last row of the upper balcony. Unfortunately their songs, by Gary Geld and Peter Udell (late of *Purlie*), sounded like second-best Rodgers and Hammerstein. The dancers meanwhile were stuck with thigh slapping, whooping and hollering, and variations on the Virginia Reel. But the most anachronistic thing about *Shenandoah* was its spirit: It had little guile and no irony. Charlie Anderson's kneeling at his wife's graveside and communing with her spirit in the laconic way of the stock movie pioneer was played straight as was every other weepy or high-spirited moment. Perhaps because *Shenandoah* made no excuses for itself and perhaps because audiences wanted relief from the bitter humor of the post-Watergate era, the show lasted more than two years.

Another throwback was *Annie* (1977), which took its inspiration from Harold Gray's comic strip, "Little Orphan Annie." Martin Charnin, who nursed the show from conception to birth, wrote its lyrics, and directed it, borrowed three central characters from the cartoon—Annie, Oliver Warbucks, and the dog, Sandy—plus its naïve optimism. "The sun'll come up tomorrow. / Bet your bottom dollar / That tomorrow there'll be sun," everyone sings at one time or another. As Charnin had calculated, his story—and the show's libretto by Thomas Meehan—turned out to be one of pluck and good will. But the greater reason for the show's popularity was its appeal to a fantasy that every child has and that every adult cherishes: the wish to trade away an ordinary, sometimes dreary, family for new parents who want the kid without reservation, who never scold, nag, or spank him, and who are also rich enough (Warbucks is a multi*billionaire* and that's during the Great Depression) to give him everything he's ever wanted.

And so in *Annie* the little girl with the bright red hair (Andrea McCardle) runs away from the meanest—and funniest—of parent surrogates, the orphanage matron Miss Hannigan (played with bawdy sadism by Dorothy Loudon). As Annie searches New York City for her parents, she's joined by the mutt, Sandy, and fed by Hooverville-ites who live under the 59th Street Bridge. Eventually Oliver Warbucks (Reid Shelton) takes her in for the Christmas holidays and decides to adopt her. Of course there are obstacles to a happy ending, among them a plot by Miss Hannigan, her ex-con brother (Robert Fitch), and his floozey of a girl friend (Barbara Erwin) to impersonate Annie's lost parents and claim a reward. But Warbucks' allies include Franklin Delano Roosevelt, his Cabinet, and the FBI. So Annie gets plenty of protection and investigative help, which leads to the sad news that her real parents are dead but also to the good news that Oliver Warbucks is the greatest parent that a kid could want.

Annie was straight sentiment: little girls, an orphan wandering the streets of New York in the middle of winter, a forlorn mutt, the reunion of Warbucks and Annie beneath a giant Christmas tree, and repeated promises of a better world tomorrow. Charnin and his collaborators wisely decided not to camp, not to temper the sentiment with irony. *Annie* was a return to the kind of musical that made no bones about picturing a world as we'd like it, not as it is. Audiences could hiss Miss Hannigan—and love her at the same time. They could—and did—applaud the reunion of Annie and Sandy. They wept when Annie recognized Oliver Warbucks' love for her. For audiences who had endured a period in American history when nothing was as it appeared to be, their relief and gratitude for the simple pleasures of *Annie* made it the biggest Broadway hit since *A Chorus Line*.

Charles Strouse's score harked back to some of the purest of musical-comedy conventions, and, if it didn't entirely freshen them, it at least found enough life in the old dance rhythms and the melodic and harmonic gimmicks to invest *Annie* with the spirit of a younger Broadway, when every song was a toe-tapper or a heart-grabber. "Tomorrow," a hard-sell promise of better times ahead, immediately became a pop anthem. In the show Andrea McCardle belted it with a volume and resonance worthy of Ethel Merman. "Easy Street," sung and danced by Dorthy Loudon, Robert Fitch, and Barbara Erwin, had the throaty sensuality of slow ragtime mixed with New Orleans blues. "We'd Like to Thank You [Herbert Hoover]," sung by the

Hooverville-ites with irony so blatant that it became a direct statement, started with a snazzy introduction in the style of Brecht and Weill but then switched to an unfortunately insipid refrain. And the show had a couple of tearjerkers guaranteed to work: "Maybe," Annie's fantasies of what her natural parents might be like, and "Something Was Missing," Warbucks' pledge of love set to a gentle waltz. Although Charnin's lyrics could not have won any prizes for literateness or originality, they, like every other component of the show, were perfectly in tune with the simple, direct spirit of the enterprise.

Annie won the Drama Critics' Circle and Tony Awards for Best Musical.

Both Annie and Shenandoah had originally been staged at the Goodspeed Opera House in East Haddam, Connecticut. (Goodspeed's first contribution to New York musical theatre was Man of La Mancha in 1965.) By the early '70s, the Opera House was running a thirty-week season, during which it revived classics of the American musical and nonmusical theatre and produced one new musical each season. Its director, Michael Price, hunted the libraries for old musicals. By 1979, the Goodspeed Opera House had brought to Broadway, in addition to those named above, another new musical, Something's Afoot (billed as a musical whodunit) and three revivals, Otto Harbach and Louis Hirsch's Going Up (1917), a show about the infancy of aviation; Jerome Kern, Schuyler Greene, and Guy Bolton's Very Good Eddie (1915); and Gus Kahn and Walter Donaldson's Whoopee! (1928).

Very Good Eddie was a charmer. One of the Princess musicals and only the second of Kern's shows, it seemed wholly fashioned of lilac blossoms and the tinkling of amiable banjos. The score (with interpolations from later Kern shows) was equally simple and, in its pert and innocent way, very seductive. Although straining more than Very Good Eddie for its charm, Whoopee! brought back the old Eddie Cantor vehicle with full respect for its musical and choreographic potential. Director Frank Corsaro was criticized for exaggerating the show's dramatic style to something between silent movie hyperbole and operetta flounce, but only purists objected to his adding later Kahn/Donaldson songs to the score. From the original came "Makin' Whoopee," "Love Me or Leave Me," and "Bringing a Red, Red Rose." The interpolations were all gems: "My Baby Just Cares for Me," "Yes Sir, That's My Baby," "That Certain Party," and "You" (with lyrics by Harold Adamson).

The revival business remained strong through the mid-point of the decade, but its character changed. The earliest nostalgia shows—No, No, Nanette, Irene, and Good News—were dowagers in glad rags and heavy makeup, who, afraid of seeming pathetic, made fun of themselves. When, as with the latter two shows, their false bravado failed them, their cracked voices and arthritic gestures no longer seemed funny. Soon after them, another kind of revival stepped forward. Its intention was not to mock itself but to display, quite proudly, how fresh and young it had remained in spite of the passing years. The Goodspeed Opera House was the most daring pro-

ducer of this kind of show. Other producers ventured back only as far as the
'40s, '50s, and '60s.

A revival of *The Pajama Game* in 1973 made one significant change in the
original: The female lead was played by a black, Barbara McNair, the male
lead by a white, Hal Linden, and the rest of the cast was integrated. The
biracial approach was not a diversionary tactic to lead audiences away from
the book or songs. They had withstood time so well that, in comparison, the
performances of many of the supporting players and the direction of George
Abbott, then eighty-six, looked anemic. Not so with the all-black revival of
Guys and Dolls in 1976. Its entire cast had charisma and that, not the performers' race, made the production romantic and exotic. As Sister Sarah,
Ernestine Jackson used her precise enunciation and warm voice to portray
musically the salvationist prude doing battle with her romantic heart, and
James Randolph brought to Sky Masterson a supple, lush baritone and sei-
gnorial dignity befitting a princely gambler living in the graces of Lady Luck.
Adelaide and Nathan Detroit were just as well played by Norma Donaldson
and Robert Guillaume. But the young actor who stopped the show was Ken
Page, as Nicely-Nicely Johnson. Page and the entire cast rocked and rolled
through "Sit Down, You're Rocking the Boat," which every night got at least
two encores.

Guys and Dolls was not the first revival in the '70s of a Frank Loesser
musical. In 1974, Circle in the Square produced *Where's Charley?* Its small,
arena theatre at Circle in the Square necessitated a staging without proscenium arch and the reorchestrating of Loesser's score for a small ensemble.
Director Theodore Mann turned these limitations to his advantage by em-
phasizing the Victorian period of the farce: Four prep-school types in wing
collars and striped blazers shifted the scenery, while the orchestra, now a
refined sextet of strings and harpsichord, accompanied from a latticework
gazebo. For many the concept was too restrained, but it did serve to high-
light the performance of Raul Julia as Charley Wykeham. Julia, who had
made his musical-theatre debut as Proteus in Joseph Papp's *Two Gentlemen
of Verona* (1971), was fast becoming one of the most versatile and stylish of
New York's young actors. He compensated for an incongruous Puerto Rican
accent, limited vocal range, and graceless dancing with a mesmerizing stage
presence.

Theodore Mann next gambled that Edward Villella, premier dancer with
the New York City Ballet, would display an equal charm as Joey in the Circle
in the Square's 1976 revival of *Pal Joey*. But singing and acting frightened
Villella, and the kind of hoofing asked by choreographer Margo Sappington
was just as alien. Villella called in his mentors Jerome Robbins and George
Balanchine, but their help didn't allay his fears. A few days before the show
was to open, Villella withdrew; at that, Eleanor Parker, who was to have
played Vera, also left; and all the director could do was put in the under-
studies, Christopher Chadman and Joan Copeland. Copeland held her own,

but Chadman floundered. The Circle in the Square's *Pal Joey* became one of the decade's best publicized gaffes.

As the decade continued, the traffic in revivals didn't let up. *Fiddler on the Roof* returned with Zero Mostel. *The King and I* once again starred Yul Brynner, who now brought to the King's role a greater maturity that deepened the poignancy of his dilemmas and the comedy of his stubbornness. *The King and I* grossed twelve million dollars during the 1977–78 Broadway season and went on to do healthy business on the road. Two other revivals followed a similar pattern, beginning with runs in New York and then continuing with very successful tours. *Hello, Dolly!* featured the original Dolly Levi, Carol Channing; and *Man of La Mancha* put Richard Kiley back in the saddle as Don Quixote/Miguel de Cervantes. All of these productions duplicated quite assiduously their originals. The producers of *The King and I* went so far as to ask Jerome Robbins to check the re-creation of his dances by Yukiro, an alumna of the Martha Graham dancers and performer in the original. An attempt to bring back the spirit of the '60s with a new production of *Hair* drew praises from some critics for ensemble work that was tighter and more exciting than the original. But it was evidently too early for both the critics and the public to get nostalgic about the '60s, and this version of *Hair* (unlike Milos Foreman's film version) didn't find an audience. Two other revivals tried new variations on their sources. *Timbuktu!* was director/designer Geoffrey Holder's all-black version of *Kismet* transported from Baghdad to Mali, West Africa, circa 1360. Holder, who in 1975 had tricked out *The Wizard of Oz* for an outlandishly theatrical re-make, did essentially the same for *Kismet*. Despite all the glitter, it was still a trifle, merely an excuse for visual baubles and the lush tunes of Borodin. This version did boast the additional seductiveness of Eartha Kitt as Sahleem La-Lume, Joan Diener's old sexpot role. But the winner of the Why-did-they-bother? contest was the revival of Anthony Newley's *Stop the World—I Want to Get Off*. The new version—with an updated book—was a vehicle for Sammy Davis, Jr., who could have better pleased his fans by simply bringing his nightclub act to Broadway.

In a decade of revival mania, inevitably producers returned to the work of Bertolt Brecht and Kurt Weill. Carmen Capalbo, who in the '50s had staged the long-running Off-Broadway edition of *The Threepenny Opera*, directed an odd, multimedia version of Brecht and Weill's *The Rise and Fall of the City of Mahagonny*, which, when it opened Off Broadway in April of 1970, had been in rehearsal and previews since the first of the year. Some of the delay was caused by threats of court action from the composer's widow, Lotte Lenya, who objected to the producers' tinkering with the score. The original had been closer to opera than musical comedy and strongly influenced by Hindemith. Now it sounded like Mahler as interpreted by the Beatles. Barbara Harris and Frank Poretta negotiated the songs with ease, while their costar, Estelle Parsons, no matter how hard she struggled to project, always lost to the band. All three were upstaged by Capalbo's frantic attempts to revive the dead propaganda in Brecht's libretto. Despite closed-circuit televising of the actors, distracting rear projections, and a kitschy wardrobe that mixed periods from the '30s to the '70s, his busy *Mahagonny* had little excitement. Even less successful was the revival of *Johnny Johnson* (1971), which Weill had written in the mid-'30s with librettist Paul Green. José Quintero, the highly esteemed interpreter of O'Neill's plays, chose to cast singers in all the roles except that of Johnny. Not surprisingly, the production succeeded as a reverent performance of Weill's score; as a theatre piece, it only emphasized how badly the librettist had fumbled his imitation of Brecht.

But Brecht and Weill soon got their due with the new version of *The Threepenny Opera* produced in 1976 by the New York Shakespeare Festival at Lincoln Center. The cold heart of this fierce production was a new translation by Ralph Manheim and John Willett. While not denying the grace of Marc Blitzstein's 1954 version, the new translators took him to task for prettifying Brecht, carving out the scatology and blunting his anticapitalist, anti-imperialist diatribe. Manheim and Willett claimed that their translation was far more in the spirit of the original: bitter, at times obscene, and often so asymmetrical and prosaic that words and music went their separate ways.

This was *The Threepenny Opera* that Richard Foreman (director) and Stanley Silverman (musical director) had long wanted to stage. Foreman, the founder of the avant-garde Ontological-Hysteric Theatre, composed his staging as a surrealistic nightmare. The beggars, con men, thieves, and prostitutes of Macheath's London were too loose-limbed or too rigid, too hollow-eyed and chalk-faced to be human. Like a chorus line of zombies they entered from the cavernous depth of the Beaumont stage, walking stiffly in a straight line, staring straight ahead. The lighting (by Pat Collins) was as blank as their faces. Against this backdrop of damned souls, the lead actors performed in bold, grotesque movements. Raul Julia's fastidious Mack stepped first with his toe and then his heel, as if he couldn't break the murderer's habit of tiptoeing away from the scene of the crime. Ellen Greene, as Jenny, was the embodiment of sick sexuality: white breasts tortured in a Merry Widow corset, skeletal arms and hands that seemed involuntarily to wrap themselves around Mack's thighs, and a surprisingly husky, commanding voice that with "Pirate Jenny's Song" left no doubt about the blood lust in her dreams.

The previous hit musical produced in the '70s by Joseph Papp and the New York Shakespeare Festival couldn't have been further from the spirit of their *Threepenny Opera. Two Gentlemen of Verona*, adapted by John Guare and Mel Shapiro from Shakespeare's comedy and set to music by Galt Mac-Dermot, was pure romp. "With this one," Joseph Papp told an interviewer, "we want to out-Broadway Broadway." Beginning with a contrived plot that even Shakespeare had mocked, the librettist, cast, and director improvised a multiethnic, highly anachronistic farce. Exposure to MacDermot's score was like, as one critic put it, opening the window of a tenement on a still summer's night and hearing "all the neighbors play their radios one after the other—soul, calypso, pop, blues, even some old ditties." The crazy mix of musical and theatrical styles captured the fleeting gaiety, the volatility and sudden reversals of young love that Shakespeare had celebrated in the original. *Two Gentlemen of Verona* was named "Best Musical" by the American Theatre Wing (Tony Award) and the Drama Critics' Circle.

Joseph Papp's production of musicals increased as the '70s advanced and his New York Shakespeare Festival took over production of drama at Lincoln Center. By the 1976–77 Broadway season, when Papp finally withdrew from his frustrating involvement with the Center, he still remained one of the busiest and most influential producers in America since Ziegfeld and the Shuberts. His role in developing theatrical talent could be explained only partially by the millions of dollars at his disposal. He gave young writer-directors time and space away from distractions, away from the usual proddings of the commercial world (although, as with *Two Gentlemen* and, later, *A Chorus Line*, the result might be very commercial). In the Festival's workshops talented young people could shape their ideas through research and improvisation. The workshops were Papp's greatest contribution to the musical theatre of the '60s and '70s.

One of the most promising young composer-writer-directors to make good use of Papp's workshops was Elizabeth Swados. At the age of twenty-five, when her first Off Broadway musical, *Nightclub Cantata* (1977), opened at the Top of the Gate, Swados had already worked with Andrei Serban, Peter Brook and the La Mama Company. *Nightclub Cantata*, which she had worked on at the Lenox, Massachusetts, Art Center, was, in her own words, an attempt "to combine the seriousness of the cantata with the frivolousness of a nightclub." As the work of someone still learning and still trying on various musical styles (everything from rock to raga) it tended more toward the serious than the frivolous—which couldn't be avoided when many of the numbers were musical settings of poetry from such high-powered writers as Sylvia Plath, Frank O'Hara, Carson McCullers, Delmore Schwartz, and Pablo Neruda. After a modest run in New York, the show was produced regionally and for public television, but the most significant upshot of Swados' auspicious debut was the opportunity for her to work in one of Joe Papp's workshops.

Under the sponsorship of the New York Shakespeare Festival, Swados spent ten months developing a musical about runaways, the children who, usually because of a life at home they find intolerable, take to the road. The author interviewed runaways, visiting playgrounds, social agencies, schools, and community centers to pick up, in the kids' own words, the stories of their flights. Then, from over 2,000 potential cast members, she worked her way down to eighteen, who ranged from eleven to twenty-five years old.

Only three of them had ever had professional theatrical experience, and several had actually been in trouble with the law and had fled from home. During half-day improvisations at the workshop, Swados prompted her cast to contribute their experiences and their fantasies. From these she fashioned a collection of songs and monologues. One kid sang about his fantasies of being the forgotten or lost child of a celebrity like Judy Garland or Reggie Jackson. Another lamented—with obvious parallels—the loneliness of stray dogs that wander the streets of a big city. And another told of her encounter with the pimps who prey on runaway young women. Because the show came principally from the imaginations of young people, it struck hard at parents for their responsibility for intentionally or unintentionally driving kids out of the nest. But it took a more neutral stand on the value of running away. All of this commentary—a serious but sometimes playful reflection of our times—was bound together by a variety of music, most of which was derived from current pop styles—disco, soul, salsa, reggae, and rock. After playing at the cabaret in the Shakespeare Festival's downtown headquarters, *Runaways* (1978) moved to Broadway for a brief run. It was a novel show, even for a period of musical theatre that sought novelty. Angry, disturbing, and ultimately too prosaic for sustained musical flight, it was complete proof that Elizabeth Swados had new plans for the musical and that she had the talent to realize them.

Her next theme show, also under the sponsorship of Papp's New York Shakespeare Festival, tested even further the extent to which Swados could successfully mold a musical from intractable material. This time the material resisted, and *Dispatches* (1979) had to go on the record as a noble, if wrong-headed experiment. Swados called the show "a Rock-War musical," and found her text in journalist Michael Herr's account of his days in Vietnam, his book from which the show took its name. The specific inspiration for Swados' attempt was a passage from the book that equated the veterans of the Vietnam War with what Herr called "the rock and roll veterans." He wrote, "The Sixties had made so many casualties, its war and its music had run power off the same circuit for so long they didn't even have to fuse."

Whole chunks of Herr's book found their way into the show, and Swados was meticulous in her inclusion of musical styles that recalled the popular singing groups of the period. But Herr's observations were too unique to reveal their horrific beauty in the setting provided by Swados. *Dispatches* ran briefly at the New York Shakespeare Festival.

During the '70s, as many commercial sources of financial support, encouragement, and training for musical-comedy artists continued to weaken, those like Papp who still had faith in the musical theatre had to find new ways to nurture talented writers and performers. Ever since 1959, the veteran musical conductor Lehman Engel, under the sponsorship of Broadcast Music, Inc., had regularly conducted classes in the writing and production of musical theatre at workshops in New York and Los Angeles. (Edward Kleban, the lyricist for *A Chorus Line*, was an alumnus of Engel's workshops.) In the mid-'70s, Stuart Ostrow, the ex-musician who produced *Here's Love*, *The Apple Tree*, *1776*, and *Pippin*, opened his own Musical Theater Laboratory, where *The Robber Bridegroom* began its life.

Another unique and self-contained musical-theatre workshop was the Portfolio Studio, which in 1967 Tom Jones and Harvey Schmidt had financed with some of their earnings from *The Fantasticks*. (By 1979, *The Fantasticks* had played over 8,000 performances in New York.) At the Portfolio Studio, until its closing in 1977, Jones and Schmidt continued their experiments with the small, intimate musical. They produced, in 1975, a short repertory season of four shows, *Portfolio Revue*, *Celebration*, *The Bone Room* (a work in progress), and *Philemon*. When the latter sold out its 12 performances, another limited run of 48 performances was scheduled.

Unlike Jones and Schmidt's previous work, *Philemon* was not romantic comedy. If anything, its story of martyrdom approached tragedy. The authors took their plot from an incident that supposedly occurred in Antioch in A.D. 278, when Roman centurions pressed into service a street buffoon to spy on the Christian nonconformists. The clown—named Cockian in the musical—did infiltrate the sect posing as the spiritual leader Philemon but, once on the inside, refused to betray his new friends. Their love made him want to prove that he too could act selflessly.

Cockian's initial instinct for self-preservation and his bawdy joking rescued the early part of the show from its inclination toward Sunday-school platitude. In the second half, the unyielding residue of melodrama was disguised to some extent by the nimble grace of Jones and Schmidt's score and by a unique staging that transformed costumes into scenery. Some of the performers wore what appeared to be simple brown capes, but lining the capes were mosaics made of bright cloth. To indicate a change of scene, a player would doff his or her cloak, reverse it, and hang the mosaic across the entrance to the inner stage. This, a few props, and sculptural lighting gave a high theatricality—without bombast—to a modest chamber drama.

Theatre workshops and institutional production companies (the New York Shakespeare Festival, Circle in the Square, the Chelsea Theater Center of Brooklyn, as well as regional institutions such as the Goodspeed Opera House in Connecticut, the Lenox Art Center, the Musical Theater Lab in Washington, D.C., and the Houston Grand Opera Association) grew stronger in the '70s and produced more musicals than ever, while many independent producers, even those working Off Broadway and Off Off Broadway, went out of business because theatre had become too expensive and too risky. Under these conditions it's especially impressive that, in 1972 and 1973, three of Al Carmines' shows were optioned for commercial production Off Broadway: *Wanted*, *Joan*, and *The Faggott*.

Having survived the fickle '60s, Carmines still trundled back and forth over his favorite landscape, an odd composite of Oz and Alcatraz, of whimsy and concern for the misfit. His minstrelsy still encompassed almost every musical style from grand opera to pre-'60's rock 'n' roll, all in the service of a social conscience that refused to take itself completely seriously. Yet now, in the '70s, his meandering, camp shows were aimed more directly at specific social issues. *Wanted* (with book by David Epstein) satirized, in a frivolous, self-mocking way, the paranoia of J. Edgar Hoover while glorifying America's legendary outlaws—John Dillinger, Ma Baker, Billy the Kid, and Jesse James. In *Joan*, Lee Guilliatt played a revolutionary martyr radicalized by a vision from a mini-skirted Virgin Mary. And for his revue *The Faggott*, Carmines wrote a diverse collection of songs about homosexuality that were praised by some for their enlightened and enlightening openness about the gay life, while condemned by others for perpetuating stereotypes.

Although Off Broadway and Off Off Broadway continued to introduce new talent and avant-garde work, they were no longer the brave outposts of eccentric and experimental drama they had been in the '50s and '60s. Regional, or resident, theatre, institutional theatre, and even Broadway had eagerly, often desperately, absorbed both the innovations and much of the energy of what used to be the noncommercial theatre. Especially for musical theatre, the '70s was a decade of assimilation. Social protest, country and western music, environmental theatre, and rock 'n' roll increasingly found their way into Broadway shows.

In the early '70s, Gerome Ragni and James Rado, the librettists of *Hair*, Galt MacDermot, its composer, and Tom O'Horgan, its director, tried to bolster their reputations as supermen of the counterculture, rock musical. Ragni's *Dude* (1972) epitomized the desperation but also the euphoria and audacity of Broadway musical theatre during the late '60s and early '70s. The project would never have found sponsors had Ragni not been one of the golden boys of *Hair*. He never bothered to write a conventional script, although, since beginning to think about *Dude* in 1968, he had amassed a two thousand-page "manuscript" of scribblings. Adela Holzer, who with her husband produced the show, described what Ragni offered his cast in the way of a script as a "jumble" without, at the beginning of rehearsals, any dialogue and no second act. By the approach of opening night, after a desperate month of reworkings, Ragni was handing cast members scraps of paper with cryptic notations that only he could translate. To rescue themselves, cast members began to write their own dialogue. Ragni's brother helped the preview audiences by posting in the theatre lobby mimeographed explanations of the plot.

The general idea was to show a hippie St. George who grapples with the Establishment and stops its polluting of the environment. Most of the message was in the medium: Production designers Eugene and Franne Lee, with Roger Morgan, were hired to turn the Broadway Theatre into an Eden Come Again. They removed all the seats from the the orchestra level of the theatre and built a circular stage surrounded by ramps and overhung with sound equipment and circus rigging. On the stage they dumped carloads of what looked like earth. (At first it was earth. Ragni wanted real grass and real flowers to sprout. But that proved impractical. When watered, the seed bed turned to quagmire; when dry, it turned into a dust bowl.) The audience sat on reserved seats or bleachers surrounded by this "environment." Ragni wanted them to feel like participants in his drubbing of the Establishment, and the unconventional setting was to remind them of the production's sincere iconoclasm. And so the "environmental theatre" of avant-garde groups was dragooned for Broadway.

As they took their seats, preview audiences were awed by the novel setting, but once the production began, they turned nasty. Unable to hear the lyrics and annoyed by the awkward staging that required them to be constantly twisting around to catch the next bit of action, they booed and shouted "Ripoff!" Previews were suspended, Tom O'Horgan was called in to restage the mess, and sound engineers were summoned from M.I.T. to correct the amplification problems. But Ragni wasn't able to clarify his libretto. Neither cast nor audience could make much sense of the action. Even Galt MacDermot, who composed the score, admitted he had little idea of the show's meaning; and his score revealed his ignorance. Its melodies—about thirty-five in all—never made anything but little popping sounds.

Dude gave the lie to its own pretensions. By trying so ineptly—and so extravagantly—to rid itself of Broadwayisms, it returned full circle to flamboyant nonsense. It lasted only 16 performances and lost its full investment of $900,000.

Between directing *Hair* and trying to save *Dude*, Tom O'Horgan replaced Frank Corsaro as director of *Jesus Christ Superstar* (1971), which was the first full-scale Broadway musical to have originated as a record album of pop-rock songs.

In the late '60s, rock groups had begun recording albums of songs that were thematically related; one of the first and most celebrated was the Beatles' *Sgt. Pepper's Lonely Hearts Club Band*, a very sophisticated—at least by rock standards—collection of songs about two favortie themes of the '60s: anonymity and alienation. Then came the album *Tommy*, which its composers and performers, a group named the Who, had with tongue-in-cheek subtitled "a rock opera." Fans took the title seriously, and the Who began performing "concert versions" of the album; soon a very abstruse continuity of dance, pantomime, and lighting effects was patched together, and *Tommy*, in limited engagements, was touring as the first rock opera.

Taking the same strategy, the young, conservatory-trained composer Andrew Lloyd Webber and lyricist Tim Rice, both Englishmen, wrote and produced a two-record album based loosely on Christ's last seven days. Rice's lyrics were commonplace and Webber's score a hodgepodge of borrowings from Tschaikowsky through the Beatles. But *Jesus Christ Superstar* was undeniably unique—and shrewd. Rice and Webber had converted

Christ to a hero rock fans could easily understand: a poet-prophet, whose quasi-musical howls are cherished, if misinterpreted, by his followers and denounced as incendiary by the paranoid authorities.

O'Horgan, who took command about ten weeks before the show was scheduled to open, inflated its visual style to grotesque limits. Inspired by the audacious commercialism of Webber and Rice's songs, he asked costume designer Randy Barcelo, set designer Robin Wagner, and lighting designer Jules Fisher to synthesize a vision that had never been seen on the musical stage before. Christ (Jeff Fenolt) made his first appearance extruded like toothpaste from the mouth of a giant silver chalice. But his penultimate entrance, just before the crucifixion, topped that. It began with a giant cocoon billowing out of a trap at center stage; as the cocoon rose, dancers pulled sections away to reveal Christ's head and shoulders, and beneath them, a tentlike robe. The figure glided upward, while chorus members pulled at straps to unveil three more robes, until at the end of the lift-off, as Fenholt's head and shoulders stood fifteen feet above the stage floor, a final strap was pulled, revealing a conical gown made of one hundred yards of gold lamé and sequins. That was the most awesomely vulgar of the show's wonders but only a sample of its hyperbolic styles. Flats were painted and shaped to look as if Georgia O'Keeffe had turned to illustrating kidney dissections. The high priests and their flunkies were dressed in helmets and gowns that suggested insect larvae. Judas, played by Ben Vereen, descended from the flies on a butterfly with the wing span of a Piper Cub. And Herod, rouged and outfitted like a drag queen, camped his way through the taunting of Christ.

Only five months before *Jesus Christ Superstar* opened, another musical based on the Gospels quietly started an Off-Broadway run. It would remain Off Broadway for 2,000 performances, then transfer to Broadway in the summer of 1976 and continue strong for more than two years.

Godspell originated in the theatre department of Carnegie-Mellon University, where John-Michael Tebelak staged it as his Master of Arts thesis. Working with another student, composer-lyricist Stephen Schwartz, Tebelak and a cast of ten improvised a commentary on the Gospel According to St. Matthew, inspired by Christ's admonition to accept his words with the openness and innocence of children. The cast dressed in T-shirts, blue jeans, beanies, bright suspenders, striped knee socks—anything that suggested children. Many of them painted their faces with clown makeup, and everyone—with the exception of the actor playing Christ—assumed multiple roles, from Aquinas to John the Baptist. Their pantomime, speech, and song meandered through the evening with the apparent aimlessness of child's play. Jesus and John the Baptist danced a soft shoe while reciting parables. Jesus divided the sheep from the goats, as the rest of the cast, down on their hands and knees, nuzzled each other like a button-eyed flock in a Disney cartoon. And the disciples often lapsed into corny imitations of Jack Benny, Groucho Marx, Jimmy Durante, and television personalities. Their choice of when to sing seemed as arbitrary as their other play, and the score, an amalgam of original songs and old hymns (the most infectious a twelfth-century prayer adapted as "Day by Day") was as blandly homespun as the rest of the production.

Meanwhile, *Jesus Christ Superstar* was the only direct descendant of *Hair* to survive for very long. *Via Galactica* (1972), with songs by Galt MacDermot, and *Sgt. Pepper's Lonely Hearts Club Band on the Road*, directed by Tom O'Horgan, both flopped. *Via Galactica* tried to glamourize a very befuddled science-fiction story about a cosmic garbageman (Raul Julia) who becomes an intergalactic Adam. The only intriguing thing about Peter Hall's direction was a spectacular display of stage machinery: six trampolines hidden in the stage to simulate weightlessness, a pulsating spaceship rising in a burst of contrail, and special projectors (imported, with operators, from Italy) that brought the entire Milky Way into the Uris Theatre. *Sgt. Pepper's Lonely Hearts Club Band on the Road* was fashioned by the same team that had translated *Jesus Christ Superstar* from recording to stage: in addition to O'Horgan, Robin Wagner as scenic designer, Jules Fisher as lighting designer, and Randy Barcelo as costume designer. But Lennon and McCartney's songs did not need oversized props, giant puppets, and all the rest of O'Horgan's camp relics to stimulate the imaginations of their audiences.

Musical theatre had just begun to experiment with rock 'n' roll when, in the late '60s and early '70s, the popularity of rock was increasingly challenged by country and western ("c & w") music, which since the late '40s had been spreading to the cities. Its origins in country fiddling, cowboy laments, bluegrass, and hymn singing were still very evident, but country and western had also assimilated urban technology. It was now electrified, although it depended less on rock's high decibels than on electricity's endless current, over which c & w musicians could stretch and bend their notes into bluesy moans. And while rock lyrics were derived from the jack-hammer slogans in television ads, country and western lyrics evolved from the storytelling habits of folk song.

Until the mid-'70s, country and western music was not popular enough with Broadway audiences to keep a c & w show running for longer than a month. In 1954, *Hayride*, billed as a "Hillybilly Folk Musical," played 24 performances on Broadway. Starring our greatest banjo virtuosi, Lester Flatt and Earl Scruggs, *Hayride* was little more than a concert, and its life was limited to a brief mid-'50's fad for what the critics called "mountain music." Twelve years passed before Broadway saw its first country and western book musical, *A Joyful Noise* (1966); but its songs were obvious fakes and its plot the old melodrama about the show-business hopeful (this time a knockabout c & w singer) who, when he makes it big (a contract with the Grand Ole Opry), temporarily deserts the girl who loves him for a citified hussy. It ran for only 12 performances.

Experimenting with country and western musicals moved Off Broadway, where *Touch* (1970), improvised by a commune of young men and women from Pennsylvania, skipped along like a country boy gone fishin', while *Earl of Ruston* (1971), advertised as a "country rocker," dunned its audiences with pitiful anecdotes about a village idiot and deafened them with amplified music as loud as anything heard at a rock concert.

By 1975, country and western music was so popular with city folk that two c & w shows opened in Manhattan within nine months of each other. The Chelsea Theater Center brought to town *Diamond Studs*, a "saloon musical" performed by two country bands from Chapel Hill, North Carolina. They called their show a "saloon musical" because it was essentially a cabaret entertainment set in a classic Old West barroom, where the bands sang, fiddled, strummed, and kidded their way through a rambling folk history of Jesse James. *The Robber Bridegroom*, based on Eudora Welty's novella, was more in the book-musical tradition. And although composer Robert Waldman borrowed extensively from country music, his songs were anything but naïve; as one critic put it, the score sounded like country and country rock as interpreted by Igor Stravinsky, an appropriate hybrid for the strange mix of Gothic fairy tale and bawdy romp that librettist-lyricist Alfred Uhry had fashioned from Welty's novella.

The first country and western musical to pay its own way on Broadway didn't show up until the 1977–78 season. *The Best Little Whorehouse in Texas* (1978) began as an article in *Playboy* magazine, a report by Larry L. King about a brothel that for the past hundred years had been tolerated—actually subsidized—by the politicos of a small Texas town. The drama in King's report was the commotion stirred up by a local television muckraker, who made his demand for closing the house into a media campaign with himself as star. Peter Masterson, while acting in *That Championship Season*, read King's article, saw its potential for a musical, and talked King into a collaboration with himself as co-librettist and Carol Hall as songwriter. (All three, at one time or another, had lived in Texas.) After a workshop production at the Actor's Studio and a showcase at the Off-Broadway Entermedia Theater, they found backing for a Broadway production from Universal Pictures.

The musical version of King's report kept his amiable, tolerant view of sexual and political shenanigans. The whorehouse, its madam (Carlin Glynn), and her charges were, if not glamorized, romanticized, while the media type (Clint Allmon) and his political cronies were caricatured in the outrageous but toothless style of television burlesque. Caught between these adversaries was the local sheriff (Henderson Forsythe), a good ol' boy given to flights of baroque profanity who after trying gallantly to protect the ladies from imminent unemployment, has to surrender to the political power of television. His spirit—folksy, charming, eventually melancholy in the face of defeat—was the spirit of the show, which chronicled the fall of the house with a smile for all the good times it had provided and a tear for the end of its good, clean sinning.

What made *The Best Little Whorehouse in Texas* entertaining were the performances of its leads, several of choreographer Tommy Tune's inventions, and Carol Hall's songs, which were accompanied by a virtuoso on-stage group calling itself the Rio Grande Band. The funniest of Tune's numbers featured a chorus line of football cheerleaders, blond, blue-eyed beauties, only five of them flesh-and-blood girls; the others were life-sized puppets, who, vacant-eyed and voluptuous in their pneumatic way, jiggled in precision with the real dancers.

Sometimes it was hard to distinguish between the Broadway, pop music, and country and western strains in Carol Hall's songs. Part of the reason was her skill in combining the styles, and yet the principal cause was the intermingling of styles that had come about because of the emergence into the popular music market of country and western. What was anathema to the purists was of benefit to composers like Hall who wanted to exploit the potential of country music but also knew that a score of "pure" c & w would never be diverse enough to handle the variety of musical expression needed in a first-rate show.

Hall's score for *The Best Little Whorehouse in Texas* had that diversity plus the backwater spirit at the source of King and Masterson's book. "20 Fans," "Girl, You're a Woman Now," and "No Lies" approached the nearest to old-fashioned c & w, while "Twenty Four Hours of Lovin', " sung by Delores Hall, reached back still further to one of the ancestors of c & w: gospel or shout music. The lyric for "A Lil' Ole Bitty Pissant Country Place," which spelled out Madame Mona's rules for her "girls," was typical of both Hall's writing style and the show's treatment of sex. Frank, prosaic, and rough-hewn, it sometimes sounded amateurish but most of the time spontaneous, just the kind of thing that her characters might come out with. One song, "Good Old Girl," approached poetry. In it the sheriff complimented his long-time friend and ex-lover, Mona, with the kind of praise that reveals love even though the fellow delivering it wouldn't and couldn't admit to such feelings. Henderson Forsythe gave it a perfect interpretation—convincing in its warmth, yet far short of sentimentality. *The Best Little Whorehouse in Texas* only occasionally found such eloquence in its musical origins, but when it did, the dramatic strength of country and western music brought new vitality to our theatre.

Another trend, one more influential than country and western music in rejuvenating the musical theatre of the '70s, was the participation of blacks—as authors, directors, choreographers, performers, producers, and, most importantly, as audiences.

The voice of the new black musical was proud, mocking, passionate, self-assured—and occasionally belligerent, as it was in Melvin Van Peebles' *Ain't Supposed to Die a Natural Death* (1971). The jaws of Van Peebles' show were his songs—raspy, taunting verse, which was chanted, not sung, to compulsive riffs. Their threat was intensified by his angry, unblinking scenes of urban black life: a blind man gets up his courage to introduce himself to a girl, but she's really a he in drag; two lesbians swap news, the one standing in the street while the other shouts down from the Women's House of Detention; a girl is raped by two policemen. These and similar episodes built to a unique number in musical-theatre history: a confrontation between the all-black cast and its audiences. The song was "Put a Curse on You," and it indicted everyone, especially the exploitative white, for the sufferings of those in the black ghetto. Van Peebles didn't stop there. He ended his show with a ghetto riot.

Because it intimidated audiences, both black and white, *Ain't Supposed to Die a Natural Death* attracted comment from pop sociologists who debated whether or not it was helping the black pride movement. But the show's importance to the history of musical theatre came from Van Peebles' efforts, once his box-office receipts began to dwindle, to attract more blacks to Broadway. His promotions in the black communities in and around New York brought to the theatre many blacks who had never seen a musical. He had found a new audience for musicals, and he had helped begin a new trend of shows by and about blacks.

The decade's first black musical hit with a full-scale book came to New York from the Arena Stage in Washington, D.C. Along the way to Broadway it increased in size but without the addition of spectacle or musical bombast. From the beginning, *Raisin* (1973) had been unassuming. Its libretto, by Robert Nemiroff and Charlotte Zaltberg, lacked the quiet anger and urgency of its source, Lorraine Hansberry's *A Raisin in the Sun*. And its score, by Judd Wolin (composer) and Robert Brittan (lyricist), asserted itself only when encouraged by Donald McKayle's dances. In place of much excitement, *Raisin* offered a placid view of black family solidarity, which, in a period of disintegrating family life in America, had a strong appeal.

Virginia Capers, as a widow determined to move her family out of Chicago's South Side and to a white community in defiance of racist opposition, kept the production's bleakness away from the scenes she dominated. And eleven-year-old Ralph Carter, as her grandson, did his part to warm things up with an endearing rendition of "Sidewalk Tree," a kid's fantasies that turn his squalid neighborhood into an urban Disneyland. The only other times the show roused itself were three of Donald McKayle's production numbers: a Chicago street scene set to jazz, a scene in a pentecostal church with, of course, gospel and spiritual singing, and a fantasia of African dance brought on by the romance between one of the daughters and an exchange student from Africa. The producers wisely featured about thirty seconds of the African segment on a television commercial. (*Pippin* was the first musical to exploit television advertising, and its effect was immediately evident when audiences began to clap at the beginning of the dance that had been shown in the commercial.) With the help of this latest promotional gimmick, *Raisin* lasted for 847 performances. The American Theatre Wing honored it with an Award for Best Musical.

But the most popular black show of the decade was *The Wiz* (1975), an updating of Frank Baum's *The Wizard of Oz*. In the new version, Dorothy

(Stephanie Mills) is still a rural Kansan, but the Oz into which the tornado deposits her is a fantasy land that could only have been dreamed up by a very hip, very urban soul sister. Dorothy doesn't skip so much as boogie down the Yellow Brick Road, itself personified by four skinny dudes in wild orange plaid and giant yellow Afros. The tap-dancing tin man (Tiger Haynes) is riveted into a suit made from a garbage pail, giant beer cans, and a skillet; the wicked witch, now called Evillene (Mabel King), struts her stuff like the last of the red-hot mamas; and even demure Aunt Em (Tasha Thomas) sounds a bit like soul singer Aretha Franklin. Oz itself is an emerald and Art Deco discotheque presided over by a fey Wizard (Andre De Shields) decked out in a skin-tight white jumpsuit and a glitter Afro.

Costume designer Geoffrey Holder, who was also appointed director during out-of-town previews, took credit for the show's success. It may have been self-aggrandizing of Mr. Holder not to have given more credit to George Faison's disco-inspired choreography, Tom H. John's funk-fantasy sets, or William F. Brown's dialogue of sassy put-downs (Evillene to a new slave: "You *do* do windows, don't you?"), yet Holder's costumes were the most audacious part of a very audacious production. He also drove the show at a gyrating, full-tilt pace, as if all the action, once Dorothy landed in Oz, took place in the middle of a discotheque. Everyone, orchestra and cast, was amplified through a system that made Charlie Smalls's tunes sound like standard pop dilutions of soul and Latino music blasted through a mammoth transistor radio.

His music got better treatment from the producers of the original-cast recording who decided not to tape the score in an all-day session at a New York ballroom or concert hall, which was the usual practice. Instead, they recorded in a studio, where the engineer could better preserve—and exaggerate—the individual orchestral and vocal colors. The result was sound quality equal to the best of pop records. Teen-agers bought the album, and soon two of its songs, "Ease on Down the Road" and "Everybody Rejoice," were heard daily on television and radio. The latter, written by Luther Vandross, was even used as a commercial jingle to promote a Polaroid camera— and, less directly, *The Wiz*. (The show won a Tony Award for Best Musical.)

Encouraged by the popularity of the new black musical, the Houston Grand Opera shipped to Broadway its productions of Scott Joplin's *Treemonisha* (1975) and George Gershwin's *Porgy and Bess* (1976). The Houston company advertised their shows as operas, which they are in form, yet the decision to house them on Broadway among popular musicals made sense. *Treemonisha*, written in the first decade of this century, and *Porgy and Bess*, written in the early '30s, were the spiritual ancestors of the new black musicals. The respect for black culture, the sass, and the sentiment of the new black musical were everywhere in them.

Joplin did everything he could to dignify ragtime, but he couldn't completely tame its disreputable spirit, the spirit of vaudeville and bordello life.

Whenever it was absent from *Treemonisha*, the score sounded like almost any European light opera of the early 1900s. Whenever it was on the loose, whether in principal numbers ("We're Goin' Around," "Frolic of the Bears," "We Will Rest Awhile," "Aunt Dinah Has Blowed De Horn," and "A Real Slow Drag") or even in the accompaniments to recitatives, *Treemonisha* sounded like young America—ripe, proud, and fun-loving.

Joplin spent the last decade of his life (1907–17) and his last reserves of failing health trying to interest publishers and producers in his opera. But the white musical establishment was antagonized by his presumption; to them his commerical and social place was composing ragtime. No full-scale *Treemonisha* had ever been mounted until the Houston production. Gunther Schuller, who previously had arranged and conducted some of Joplin's rags for recordings, orchestrated the opera from Joplin's piano-vocal score and conducted the performances. Franco Colavecchia designed sets, masks, and costumes in a romantic, primitive style that joined the crude hovels and work clothes of antebellum southern field hands with brightly colored voodoo fantasies from Haiti. Frank Corsaro directed, and Louis Johnson choreographed with an eye to preserving the naïve, fairy-tale style of Joplin's libretto.

As Joplin had intended, this *Treemonisha* was gentle and earnest. Corsaro made no apologies for what today are considered racial stereotypes— the singing field hands, the mammies, the superstitious bumpkins. They were indelible parts of Joplin's vision of his own people, a race supposedly emancipated by Lincoln's Proclamation of 1863 but unable to exploit their new freedom because of superstition and ignorance. Through his story of an educated black girl who defeats a pair of backwoods conjurers Joplin wanted to preach the power of education in freeing his people. It was hardly a radical, or even a very dramatic theme, but Joplin's writing of the opera and his attempts to have it produced affirmed a new and quite daring faith in black music and black culture.

The Houston production of *Porgy and Bess*, by including all of the recitatives and principal numbers often cut, restored the musical integrity of Gershwin's masterpiece and along with it the passions and atmosphere of Catfish Row missing from productions that split the show into dialogue and musical set pieces. Director Jack O'Brien kept his three-hour production aloft by staging all shifts of scene openly, without pause, and by casting singers who could act. He kept his two leads fresh by triple casting. On opening night, Clamma Dale played Bess with a luscious sensuality that often upstaged Donnie Ray Albert's Porgy, but in their duets ("Bess, You Is My Woman" and "I Loves You, Porgy") their voices and acting embraced each other with equal rapture.

The revival of *Porgy and Bess* was a reminder that the most interesting works of our musical theatre have always stood at the intersection of entertainment and art, where show business caters to the public without condescending to it. Since the '50s, no producer/director had met that challenge more successfully than Hal Prince. In partnership with Stephen Sondheim he continued in the '70s to set the standard for artistic excellence in our musical theatre.

Always on the lookout for ways to renew musical theatre, Prince had been impressed with the idea—if not its first Broadway realization in *Dude* (1971)—of environmental theatre. He had been contemplating a revival of *Candide*, and an environmental setting for it inspired him to see the new production as an all-encompassing sideshow of Voltaire's freaks. But by the time Prince staged his new *Candide* at the Brooklyn Academy of Music (with the Chelsea Theater Company), he had softened the idea of sideshow grotesquerie to madcap farce occasionally darkened by hints of voyeurism.

He retained only a suggestion of the circus arena so that most of his audience sat on bleachers around three-quarters of the playing area and a few sat on stools in two pits that flanked a small central platform. Ramps, catwalks, drawbridges, and stairways connected nine other small playing areas, and the actors, by forging their way through the onlookers, could sing and dance on either the platforms or the bridgework connecting them. On the fourth side of the Chelsea loft was a small, shallow proscenium stage, where scenes requiring backdrops could be played. To design this combination treehouse and jungle gym, Prince hired Eugene and Franne Lee, who had done the set for *Dude*. Their advice proved especially valuable when, after a sold-out run in Brooklyn, Prince moved the show to the Broadway Theatre. As they had with *Dude*, the Lees removed all of the theatre's orchestra seats and replaced them with a labyrinth of scaffolding.

Even in Broadway's biggest house the new *Candide*, which won the Drama Critics' Circle Award for Best Musical, was a relatively intimate show: The capacity of the Broadway Theatre had been halved to about nine hundred; the twenty-piece orchestra was—with the help of an elaborate amplification and video-monitoring system—divided into four parts and scattered throughout the audience; and the running time of the production was held to under two hours. Prince kept his promise to involve his audience, although his staging made little attempt to encourage direct participation. Most of his business was hardly new, but the unfamiliar context of an environmental musical gave it dazzling novelty. When a Brazilian jungle was needed, a rain forest of green streamers fell to entangle both actors and audience. Candide took to sea aboard the center platform, which rocked and heaved to invisible waves and the rhythms of Bernstein's barcarole. The auto-da-fé became an ironic production number with a platoon of Carmen Mirandas shaking maracas and hips to "What a day, what a day for an auto-da-fé!" But the most surreal of Prince's inspirations was very modestly staged: Cunegonde stood behind a woman harpsichordist who was coiffed in an elaborate eighteenth-century wig festooned with ropes of pearls, brooches, pendants, and diamond stickpins. As the heroine sang her coloratura aria "Glitter and Be Gay," bemoaning the necessity of making the best of her ignominy as a courtesan, she eagerly plucked the baubles from the harpsichordist's wig and adorned herself with them.

A young and bouncy crew scampered about this *Candide*. Lewis J. Stadlen, by swapping wigs, frock coats, and vocal inflections while on the run, played both the narrator and Pangloss with the lubricity of Groucho Marx and the stamina of a welterweight prize fighter. As Cunegonde and Candide, Maureen Brennan and Mark Baker enthused their way through holocaust, inquisition, plague, and slavery without forfeiting a speck of moxie. In fact, the entire production looked a bit like a precocious kindergarten at playtime. Voltaire's nonchalant cruelty and Bernstein's sophisticated parodies were trivialized, the former reduced to snappy patter and sight gags by Hugh Wheeler's libretto, the latter drawn thin and raspy by deep cuts, an undernourished orchestra, and a cast whose voices were seldom equal to the demands of the score.

Candide was a conceptual musical, a term invented by journalists to characterize the unique style of theatre that since *Company* (some would claim, since *She Loves Me*) Prince had been producing and staging. The components of a conceptual musical were integrated by a theme instead of a narrative, although telling a story was not prohibited. Because the emphasis was on theme, the test of a conceptual musical was not how smoothly it moved between song, dance, and dialogue, but how successfully its style mirrored its concept. *Candide* failed as a conceptual musical because it wanted to be a musical satire on a par with Bernstein's score and Voltaire's work, but instead of stretching to its inspiration, it stooped to gimmickry and burlesque.

Prince and Stephen Sondheim had long wanted to create a romantic musical, a show that would update operetta by preserving its elegance while discarding its marionettelike characters and their clockwork love stories. True to their concept, they painstakingly transformed Ingmar Bergman's film *Smiles of a Summer Night* into the stylish and intelligent *A Little Night Music* (1973).

Set in turn-of-the-century Sweden, Bergman's comic movie blends fantasy with muted satire, farce with melancholy, and Victorian propriety with very contemporary psychology. Bergman's six lovers are elegantly prim, neatly contained in their wing collars and whalebone stays. But, like modern neurotics, everyone is frazzled, dissatisfied, and afraid of owning up to their misery. Only after drinking a magic potion supplied by an old courtesan do they summon the nerve to switch partners.

To capture in rhythm the anxieties and passions of the lovers, Sondheim wrote almost all of his songs in triple meters. Whether the song was a Viennese waltz, a mazurka, or a polonaise, it retained at least some of the seductiveness of three-quarter time. But that was only half of his strategy for creating a Late Romantic ambience. With the help of his orchestrator, Jonathan Tunick, he filled his score with allusions to Brahms (particularly the "Liebeslieder Waltzes"), Ravel, Rachmaninoff, Chopin, Mahler, and the Strausses, Johann Sr. and Jr., as well as Richard. His score was not, however, a pastiche; he distilled most of the sentimentality from the Romantic style and left behind a clear, slightly acrid liquor.

The soul of *A Little Night Music* was its lyrics—urbane, compact, and so true to the characters who sang them that the actors needed very little spoken dialogue. Almost every lyric was an inspired and very humane essay on love. In "Now," the middle-aged widower Frederick Egerman invents new ways to seduce his child bride. They've been married for eleven months and still haven't consummated the union. But Frederick discards all his schemes, either because they will make him look a fool or scandalize Anne. Exhausted from his mental efforts, he falls immediately asleep. In "Later," Frederick's son, a divinity student whose conscience has kept him an unwilling virgin, despairs that he'll never prove his manhood. In "Soon," the child-bride Anne delays lovemaking once again. And then, in brilliant counterpoint, the three blend their frustrations.

Mme. Armfeldt thinks all this anxiety about love is ridiculous. In her heyday as a courtesan, love was, as she sings in "Liaisons," a simple matter of *quid pro quo*—the exchange of her favors for ". . . some position/Plus a tiny Titian." The hussar Carl Magnus confuses love and ego: To him wife and mistress are valuable for what they reveal of his good taste ("In Praise of Women" and "It Would Have Been Wonderful"). His wife, Charlotte, has tried to adjust herself to sharing her husband with his mistress—but without much success; for Charlotte, love brings "Every Day a Little Death." The Egermans' maid Petra seems to agree, but she escapes with a romp in the hay ("The Miller's Son"). Desirée Armfeldt, Frederick's ex-mistress and the woman he has always loved, surveys all their confusions and comes up with the only possible solution. "Send in the clowns," she sings, but then adds, "Don't bother, they're here."

A Little Night Music (winner of the Drama Critics' Circle and Tony Awards for Best Musical) was Sondheim at his best. But its theatrical daring was surpassed considerably by two of his other collaborations with Hal Prince: *Pacific Overtures* (1976) and *Follies* (1971).

When John Weidman brought Prince a nonmusical drama about Admiral Perry's first visit to Japan in 1853, the producer-director asked for a rewrite and suggested that Weidman tell the same story as if he were a contemporary Japanese who had seen a few Broadway musicals. By the time *Pacific Overtures* was ready for production it had become a musical saga about the Westernizing of Japan. It still began in 1853, but it told its story through two Japanese prototypes: Kayama, initially a samurai of little consequence, and Manjiro, a poor fisherman. Because they're completely dispensable, the two are sent as pawns to appease the impatient American warrior. A treaty of absolutely no force is hastily concluded with Perry and, by strewing his way from ship to shore with rush mats, his "hosts" even manage to keep him from touching sacred Japanese soil. But the Americans—later joined by the British, Dutch, French, and Russians—will not go away, and Japan is eventually forced to honor its promises. Manjiro, now a full-fledged samurai, opposes the West's incursions, but Kayama, made rich by trading with his former enemies, wears his bowler hat proudly and carries a pocket watch. Nothing can stop the change, and a final production number jumps to the present, to a Japan that supplies the world with automobiles, digital watches, monosodium glutamate, and polyvinyl chloride—a Japan whose beaches on the Inland Sea are unfit for bathing and whose air is unfit to breathe.

If its script oversimplified the loss of Japan's feudal culture, *Pacific Overtures* was anything but a simple musical. Weidman (with the help of Hugh Wheeler), Prince, choreographer Patricia Birch, Boris Aronson, and Stephen Sondheim intertwined Oriental and Occidental theatrics so stylishly, recalling Brecht's historical epics, that the twain not only met but—with a few exceptions—fused. To one side of the stage sat a reciter (Mako). Dressed in the traditional silken robes and accompanied by a singer and a duo playing ancient instruments, he chanted in gutturals familiar to anyone who has ever seen a samurai movie—except, of course, he spoke in English. Behind him floated a versatile, ever-changing set of rice-paper screens, delicately painted trees, and houses that unfolded and folded like bright paper fans. Men played all the roles, until the final vision of modern Japan, when women made their first, very liberated appearance.

The borrowings from Noh and Kabuki were not merely decorative. They were metaphors, reflections of the grace and nobility—but also the insularity and inbreeding—of old Japan. The actors hobbled down a traditional runway, the *hanamichi*; they padded back and forth across the stage in Kabuki style to represent journeys; they pantomined a samurai duel and a poignant leavetaking between husband and wife; and, at the end of the first act, a solo dancer, his face painted in a ferocious mask to represent the invader Perry, performed an adaptation of the ancient Lion Dance.

Sondheim wrote with far more economy than he had for *A Little Night Music*. In several numbers he even imitated the Japanese *haiku*, a three-line poem of seventeen syllables. Sometimes he lapsed into pseudo-Orientalisms of the "Confucius-say" variety, but just as often he compressed a very touching image of a lost Japan into an elegantly sparse lyric. "Someone in a Tree" was the most eloquent, the most poignant—an object lesson in Japanese aesthetics, an eyewitness report of the negotiations with Perry, and a meditation, not without Buddhist mysticism, on history.

Pacific Overtures received the Drama Critics' Circle Award for Best Musical.

With the dazzling *Follies* (another winner of the Drama Critics' Circle Award), Sondheim turned inside out the features of the nostalgia musical. It boasted more spectacle, more celebrities from the heyday of theatre and film, and more period styles of theatre music than any of the revivals. But instead of competing with these, it commented on them by paying homage to the past while dramatizing the sad futility of trying to relive it. Although James Goldman's libretto about two unhappy marriages edged dangerously close to soap opera, it seldom detracted from the show's essence: a sonata of choreography, spectacle, and music.

Boris Aronson's set was the stage of a grand old theatre, where, from 1918 to 1941, *Weismann's Follies* had played. The act curtain was missing and much of the gilt and plaster had fallen away from the proscenium arch revealing here and there the skeleton of its superstructure. As the ghostly orchestral prelude began and lights onstage glimmered like images half remembered, the true locale of *Follies* was established: our memories, anywhere the past still commands the present, where ghosts walk, where the folly of confusing the past with the present overtakes us.

It's 1971, and a reunion is in progress. Past members of *Weismann's Follies* are gathering to renew friendships, perform some of their old routines, and take a last look at the theatre before it becomes a parking lot. Among the partygoers are two middle-aged couples who ran around together in the early '40s when the men were in law school together and the women were chorus girls in the *Follies*. Benjamin (John McMartin), Phyllis (Alexis Smith), Buddy (Gene Nelson), and Sally (Dorothy Collins) arrive, while behind them trail the ghosts of themselves as they were in their youth. Other ghosts, parading through the shadows, are specters of former show girls, magnificent in their extravagantly beaded gowns and feathered headdresses (the creations of costume designer Florence Klotz).

Amid the shadows, the ghosts of the couples act out their past and present entanglements. In the '40s, Sally and Ben had a brief affair, but Ben married Phyllis, and Sally married Buddy. Since then, Buddy and Sally have settled in Phoenix, where Sally keeps house and raises the kids while Buddy, now a traveling salesman, takes long business trips to be with his mistress. Ben has become a successful lawyer, writer, and diplomat. Although he's given Phyllis a glamorous life, his preoccupation with his work and with himself has emptied their marriage of its passion. During the course of the reunion, the couples turn their regrets into fantasies of how it all might have been, and *Follies* becomes a revue of follies.

Just as their recriminations and cries of pain climax, the shadowy stage is flooded with brilliant light. Lace and pastel archways, layer upon layer of them, descend to form a gigantic nineteenth-century valentine. It looks as if the past has won out over the present and that, once again, the couples' follies have become *The Follies*. To an unctuous melody, a parade of statuesque chorus girls, in Marie Antoinette wigs and outrageous farthingales, sashay through the center portal. The "Loveland" sequence has begun, not a flashback to the idyllic days of the couples' youth, but a theatrical metaphor for their romantic delusions—the naïve promises of happiness that inevitably brought disillusionment. A chorus of Dresden dolls and cavaliers sings "You're Gonna Love Tomorrow" and "Love Will See Us Through," followed by a vaudeville olio in which each number is a folly unmasked.

Buddy dons baggy pants and shuttles in a toy car between wife and mistress as he sings "The God-Why-Don't-You-Love-Me-Blues." Sally still dreams of thirty years ago and her brief romance with Ben. She wants to see herself as the sophisticate that Phyllis has become, and so she projects her thwarted dreams in a torch song, "Losing My Mind." Phyllis converts her plight into "The Story of Lucy and Jessie," an ironic novelty number in the style of Cole Porter about two ladies who want to be the opposite of who they are. The cold and dressy Phyllis—Jessie in the song—would rather be yielding and vivacious. The confusing sounds in Sondheim's lyrics echo the ladies' sad confusion about their identities:

> *"Lucy wants to be dressy,*
> *Jessie wants to be juicy.*
> *Lucy wants to be Jessie,*
> *And Jessie Lucy."*

Ben is no more content than the others, but he can't summon the courage to admit his guilt and fears. He begins his solo, "Live, Laugh, Love," in the debonair Fred Astaire style. He is even dressed in white tie and white tails. But soon the melody turns dissonant, the orchestra seems to be playing in two keys, the neat dance patterns break down, the chorus line splits apart, and, wandering in from the wings, come the partygoers, only now, amid the cacophony, they look like gargoyles, Ben's nightmare of his faults unmasked. The madness dissolves, and the scene reverts to the drab stage of Weismann's theatre. As if purged of their follies, Ben reunites with Phyllis and Buddy with Sally. They leave the theatre, while their ghosts still call to each other from the shadows.

To make their musical a true ghost sonata, Hal Prince and choreographer Michael Bennett staged their numbers contrapuntally. Downstage were the oldsters struggling through what they could remember of the old songs and dances, while upstage, in the gloom of Tharon Musser's eerie lighting, their chalk-faced doppelgängers, dressed in the full regalia of the *Follies*, executed the number perfectly. The most impressive of these time warps was "Who's That Woman?" in which Stella (Mary McCarty), an ex-headliner, was backed by a ghostly chorus line dressed in black velvet inlaid with mosaics of mirror. By the time the music broke into a time step, the ghost chorus had moved downstage to mingle with its flesh-and-blood counterpart, exploding the mirror dance into another metaphor.

Much of Sondheim's score was remarkable pastiche: imitations of Kern, Gershwin, Lehár, Rodgers, Schwartz and Dietz, Arlen, Porter, Ruby, not to mention a whole gallery of anonymous masters. Often Sondheim and his orchestrator Jonathan Tunick distorted their models into wry, mocking comments on Tin Pan Alley clichés about love. But the most powerful of Sondheim's songs were neither loving imitations nor parodies. Written in a distinct, proto-aria style undeniably Sondheim's, they were the bewildered thoughts and voices of the couples: "Don't Look at Me," the embarrassed reunion of dowdy Sally and glamorous Ben; "The Road You Didn't Take," Ben's admission that his wealth and prestige count for little; "Could I Leave You?," Phyllis' snarling attack—in waltz rhythm—on a husband who has forgotten her emotional needs; "The Right Girl," Buddy's confusions about his wife and his mistress; and "In Buddy's Eyes," Sally's sad attempt to content herself with the role of a cheated housewife. Sondheim dared write about love and marriage from perspectives never taken by musical-comedy songwriters, from inside the tired, confused, and disillusioned minds of his characters. *Follies* was a stream-of-consciousness musical.

The idea for the last Sondheim/Prince collaboration of the decade originated with Stephen Sondheim, who, while in London, had seen the melodrama *Sweeney Todd* and was intrigued by the challenge of converting it to a "musical thriller." The plot of the melodrama came from a popular old ballad, which told the grisly story of a crazed London barber who took to slitting the throats of his customers. It was a story so well known in Victorian England that parents would scare their children into obedience by telling them that if they didn't behave, "old Sweeney would get 'em." The version Sondheim had seen was a new reworking by Christopher Bond, which the Broadway producers Richard Barr and Charles Woodward had already planned to bring to New York when Sondheim persuaded them both to wait for a musical. It was five years later, in early 1979, that *Sweeney Todd, the Demon Barber of Fleet Street* opened at the Uris Theatre.

Sondheim and Prince went in several different, if related, directions with their source: Grand Guignol, a commentary on the social Darwinism of early industrial London, and a parody of Victorian romance and melodrama. The most impressive accomplishment of the production was its evocation of Sweeney's madness and its argument, à la Brecht, that Todd's insanity was linked to the cruelties of his times. But Sondheim and Prince's success in managing so much in two acts was also their undoing. *Sweeney Todd* frightened its audiences, amused them, even stimulated their thought, but it did none of these with enough concentration, with enough commitment to a single concept, to make people care about its unjustly wronged, half-crazed protagonist.

Theatregoers, even in the cynical times of the late-'70s, still went to a musical wanting the emotional highs that song can induce. *Sweeney Todd* played against that expectation. In place of real love songs, it offered Sweeney's lust for vengeance and a love song to the accomplices who didn't try to argue him out of his vicious preoccupation—his razors ("My Friends"). And

Todd's paean to "Pretty Women," sung with Judge Turpin, who had seduced and raped Todd's wife and then sent Todd to prison, was put in such a chilly, suspenseful context—as the barber prepared to slit the judge's throat—that the tender beauty of the song was perverted, quite intentionally, to an exposé of hypocrisy and blood lust. Even the show's romantic subplot, involving Todd's daughter Johanna and a young sailor, was too waxen, too much a caricature of Victorian sensibilities (at least as it was acted and sung by Sarah Rice and Victor Garber), to relieve the numbing misanthropy of Todd and the wickedness of those around him.

Of course an insanely murderous protagonist was hardly the kind to warm an audience's heart. And Len Cariou, under Prince's direction, played the character brilliantly for all his intense madness, as well as his more accessible humanity. Still, Sweeney was a ghoul, and although his murdering instinct was clearly a metaphor for the thoughtless malevolence of Victorian industrialism, that in no way diminished his horror.

All this might have worked better had the cruelties of *Sweeney Todd* been written and played with consistent glee. Its finest songs and staging did have a maniacal grin, and the cast member with the best intuition for this kind of comedy was Angela Lansbury, who played Mrs. Lovett, the baker who turns Sweeney's victims into meat pies. Her duet with Todd, "A Little Priest," was mad hilarity mixed with bitter truth ("The history of the world, my sweet,/Is who gets eaten and who gets to eat."). Whenever Mrs. Lovett held center stage, *Sweeney Todd* resounded with oddly dissonant overtones of comic madness that prevented its bitter melodrama and horror from drowning out its fun.

If Sweeney's despair left many theatregoers indifferent, the theatrical genius expended in telling his tale provoked awe and admiration. Sondheim's melodic powers had never been stronger, and his music flowed almost without interruption from curtain to curtain. He had written far more than a collection of songs; with the help of orchestrator Jonathan Tunick, he had spun a taut web of leitmotifs that intersected to produce their own musical ironies. "The Ballad of Sweeney Todd," which began the evening and returned now and then throughout its course, included a caricature of the "Dies Irae" from the Roman Catholic mass for the dead—both a lugubrious reminder that death would be the preoccupation of old Sweeney and also a black joke about revenge masquerading as righteous fury. This is not to make Sondheim's tunes and lyrics seem overly complex and inaccessible; at their best they shone with the clarity of the madman's gaze. But they weren't simple or easy. Sondheim had written a very demanding score, one that frequently called for solo and ensemble voices of operatic dimensions.

After "The Ballad of Sweeney Todd" had set the right tone of grim exultation for our protagonist, the rest of Sondheim's numbers were as carefully shaped to the more specific, weird contours of Sweeney's world. Johanna, Todd's daughter, sang a melancholic complaint ("Green Finch and Linnet

Bird") that rose just short of cheerfulness, then fell into despair. Mrs. Lovett, in "The Worst Pies in London," babbled of hard times, her breathless distraction both comic and ominous, especially when she admitted her admiration for a competitor who, given the rarity of good cheap meat, had depopulated the neighborhood of its cats. Sweeney, at first silent and seemingly in agreement with the young sailor's ode to London ("No Place Like London"), later turned the melody into a curse and demonic pledge ("Epiphany") to rid the earth of all its humanity.

Powerful and strange as Sondheim's songs were in their initial presentations, they gained even more dramatic effect when he repeated parts of them in ironic combinations: snatches of Todd's condemnation of London worked into the sailor's love song for Johanna; the melody used by a simpleton to hawk a phoney elixir sung by the same fellow to advertise Mrs. Lovett's pies; the sprightly waltz tune of "A Little Priest" bubbling up as Todd, at his most delirious, gave voice—and action—to his bloodiest intent.

The staging for all these unhinged doings, if not as rich and varied as Prince's work for *Follies* and *Pacific Overtures*, perfectly matched Sweeney's nightmarish vision. Eugene Lee's gargantuan set was a three-tiered factory chock full of sinister machinery—pulleys, belts, gauges, governors, scaffolds, and piping. At the rear hung an enormous corrugated iron wall that rose to reveal a backdrop painted to resemble a Victorian panorama of London's docks and harbor. Overhead the shadow of a crane passed menacingly up- and downstage, while below, Sweeney, enveloped in the red glow and greasy smoke of Mrs. Lovett's ovens, dispatched his victims to the squeals of a factory whistle. The murders were Prince's finest inventions, the best of them beginning with a long tease, during which Sweeney would tuck a pristine cover under the chin of his customer, lather his face, then poise an over-sized razor next to the fellow's throat. The tableau agonizingly prolonged the moment of truth, and, like most of Prince and Sondheim's work for *Sweeney Todd*, it was gloriously grim theatrics.

Sweeney Todd won both the Tony and Drama Critics' Circle Awards for Best Musical.

Theatre buffs raved about the Sondheim/Prince shows, but casual theatregoers found them cold and inaccessible. Musical subtleties, literate song lyrics, and brilliant theatrics—none could compensate most theatregoers for what Sondheim and Prince had intentionally denied them: the undemanding, unsubtle routines of classic musical comedy and consistently likable characters.

What better man to serve them than Bob Fosse, a director-choreographer who claimed to have been raised on vaudeville, cheap nightclub acts, burlesque, and striptease. Judging by *Pippin* (1972) and *Chicago* (1975), the spirit and marrow of Fosse's theatrics were the bump and grind. And yet, in *Dancin'* (1978) he proved that the vocabulary of popular dance was large and varied enough for a stylist of his talent to shape into visual poetry. But *Dancin'* wasn't really a musical; it was a dance recital sprinkled with a few perfunctory skits and an occasional song. It was for *Pippin* and *Chicago* that Fosse made musical drama out of the old burlesque and vaudeville routines and gave them novel meanings that, if not as complicated or graceful as Prince and Sondheim's theatrical metaphors, were far more suggestive and bitter than musical comedy usually dared. His work for those two shows never smiled without a superimposed leer, and often that leer completely obliterated the smile.

It was Fosse's idea to convert *Pippin*, initially a quiet allegory about a young man's search for his identity, into a carnival of show business razzle-dazzle. Its librettist Roger O. Hirson and songwriter Stephen Schwartz balked, but Fosse won out—and his intuition proved sound. By the time it closed, in June of 1977, *Pippin* had earned net profits of over $3.3 million.

Hirson's libretto and Schwartz's songs told the story of an eighth-century prince who, while on his way to becoming ruler of the Holy Roman Empire, tries almost everything—soldiering, politics, orgies, even patricide—to find out who he is. Fosse retold the story in a very anachronistic way by packing the show with every theatrical trick known to the musical stage, from *commedia dell'arte* farce to the rock 'n' roll dances of *Hair*. To string these bright remnants together, he invented a role not in the original libretto, The Leading Player; and in that role he cast Ben Vereen, a black singer-dancer of inexhaustible energy who had last been seen as Judas in *Jesus Christ Superstar*. The Leading Player, a combination of interlocutor, song-and-dance man, and Svengali, began the proceedings with the song "Magic to Do," a dedication, complete with legerdemain, to the joys of being fooled, of surrendering to illusion.

Whenever the script threatened to take itself seriously, Fosse undercut its adolescent sobriety with an irreverent flourish. If an antiwar statement was to be made, he would put the battleground upstage, complete with feudal knights in chain mail hacking away at each other with their broadswords, while downstage, vaudevillians in straw boaters danced a soft shoe ("Glory"); at the end of battle, the decapitated head of a warrior would open its eyes, smile sarcastically, and review the situation. *Pippin* was a theatrical caprice with more than a tinge of bitters, but Fosse so hypnotized his audiences with the old razzle-dazzle that the bitters were hardly noticed.

Ignoring them in *Chicago* was more difficult. Fosse called his second hit of the decade "a musical vaudeville," and true to his word he pieced together novelty acts, songs, and dances with scraps of dialogue. But this was not clowning for the sake of clowning. Its heroines, Roxie (Gwen Verdon) and Velma (Chita Rivera), were convicted murderesses, circa 1920, intent on parlaying their notoriety into vaudeville careers. Its hero was their crooked lawyer, Billy Flynn (Jerry Orbach). Together and separately they sang and danced through lust, murder, perjury, and a caseload of other sins and felonies. Their Chicago was a unit set of black lucite, chrome, and neon, designed by Tony Walton to project all the warmth of a slab at the Cook County Morgue. Chalk-faced dancers prowled the shadows like cat burglars from the other side of the pale, while Patricia Zipprodt's androgynous costumes made it hard to tell the chorus boys from the chorus girls. John Kander and Fred Ebb's songs—with the masterful help of arranger Ralph Burns—generated the lickerish torpor and frenzy of dances of the '20s, but after sparking mightily, most of them quickly shorted out. The entire production had a dazed, jittery look about it, which was certainly Fosse's intent. But *Chicago* seemed alive only from the waist down—it pumped flagrantly in the pelvis—its eyes blank and its vocal chords inflexible.

The strange sexiness of Fosse's choreography made *Chicago* and *Pippin* two of the biggest hits of the '70s, and his *Dancin'* rode high on the new popularity of dance. But the greatest magnet of the decade was yet another show ruled by its director-choreographer: Michael Bennett's *A Chorus Line* (1975).

Bennett had danced in plenty of chorus lines—after which he advanced to choreography and directing: *A Joyful Noise, Henry, Sweet Henry, Promises, Promises, Coco, Company, Follies,* and *Seesaw.* Having lived a dancer's life and endured the agonies of auditions from both sides of the footlights, he respected the gypsies and their absurd lives—the bone-wearying toil and the discipline of learning to dance and then keeping in shape, the overwhelming odds against getting into a show, the anonymity and unvarying regimen of chorus work, and the minuscule life-span of a dancing career.

A backstage musical was the oldest of ideas, but Bennett's approach was fresh. He wanted authenticity, and to get that was quite willing to do without a conventional plot and even without starring roles, for, after all, a chorus line's best feature is its anonymity. He began by taping interviews with dancers. He asked them what had attracted them to dancing, why they had got into such a crazy profession. Then he took his tapes and his idea for *A Chorus Line* to Joe Papp, who offered financial backing and rehearsal space at the Public Theater. Bennett chose a cast, and they began to improvise around the taped autobiographies. They were joined by James Kirkwood and Nicholas Dante, both ex-performers, who shaped the libretto; Marvin Hamlisch, an ex-rehearsal pianist, who wrote the music; and Edward Kleban, who wrote the lyrics.

A Chorus Line attracted standing-room-only business from its first day at the Public Theater in May, 1975, and that success continued after it moved to Broadway in the same year. It became *the* hit of the decade, and, along with multiple Tonys and Drama Critics' Circle Award, won the Pulitzer Prize.

A hit of such proportions can never be explained by formulas; it is always greater than the sum of its parts. But the parts, of themselves, are impressive. First, suspense. *A Chorus Line* is a dramatized audition, during the course of which, twenty attractive young hopefuls will be cut to eight—four girls and four boys. Their stories are intimate and surprisingly frank for a musical—even a musical of the '70s. Most of them are quietly funny but only because the teller would rather laugh at himself than cry in public, and every one of the stories makes its teller very human, deserving of our vote. We like them all, we want all of them to win. But we know that can't be, which produces a unique mood for a musical, a suspension between the joy of watching twenty singers and dancers execute flashy steps and sing perky songs and the melancholy of watching the heartless process of elimination.

In a black, empty space, save for a bank of rotating mirrors far upstage, the hopefuls gather. After a first elimination, the remaining twenty line up along a white stripe downstage. They occasionally spread out and roam the full space, but they always return to the lineup and to a vulnerable pose facing straight out, peering into the lights that hide the director Zach, whose presence is most often a disembodied voice. He asks each dancer to step forward and tell why he or she is a dancer. Most respond with a solo turn of one kind or another—a dance, monologue, or song. Marvin Hamlisch and Edward Kleban's songs seem improvised from every show tune that's ever been written. They itch to dance and blush with Broadway chauvinism. They offer the release into fantasy that makes the dancer's life bearable.

Mike in "I Can Do That" sings about his initiation into dance, of how he had to take his little sister to dancing school and began to pick up the steps just by observing the class. Three young women started dancing because they fantasized a happier life in ballet ("At the Ballet"). Kristine dances, because, as she and her husband, Al, explain in "Sing!," she never learned how to carry a tune. Diana at first wanted to be an actress and studied the Method at the High School for the Performing Arts. But she just couldn't see the sense in pretending to be a bobsled or a table or an ice-cream cone ("Nothing").

Other dancers tell about their careers. Val couldn't get a job until, with the help of a plastic surgeon, she filled out, in her words, her "orchestra and balcony" ("Dance: Ten; Looks: Three"). Cassie had once been a featured dancer on Broadway, and she and Zach had been lovers. When Zach left her, she went to Hollywood, where, after work in a few commercials, her career shriveled to nothing. After two years without work, she's ready to take a job in a chorus—anything so that she can keep dancing ("The Music and the Mirror"). Paul is too timid to open himself before the rest of those auditioning. Zach calls a break, and Paul, now alone on the dark stage, relives the humiliation of working as a female impersonator in a homosexual revue and the catastrophe when, unexpectedly, his parents showed up backstage.

Bennett's staging prevented the confessionals from turning mawkish. Whatever the frustrated ambitions, the self-pity, the desperation of the gypsies, their dancing took on a joyful meaning. And although the conformity of the dancers to one style made them anonymous, it also made them a single cooperative being. The audition tune and dance routine that Zach teaches them ("One") became a razzle-dazzle celebration of harmony, the perfect synchrony of the chorus line.

After *A Chorus Line*, Michael Bennett and Marvin Hamlisch went their separate ways. Hamlisch joined Neil Simon and lyricist Carole Bayer Sager to write *They're Playing Our Song* (1979), a small, tuneful show that did quite well. Bennett, at first with the New York Shakespeare Festival and eventually on his own, began work on an adaptation of the 1973 television drama, "The Queen of the Stardust Ballroom." *Ballroom* (1979), as the musical was titled, occupied more than a year of Bennett's time, cost him two million dollars of his own money to produce, then lasted only three months on Broadway.

The source for *Ballroom* was a fragile, personal drama about a middle-aged widow who finds companionship, a smidgen of glamour, and even love on regular visits to a Bronx dance hall. The unpretentious story, reworked by author Jerome Kass, remained almost intact, but around it Bennett and his collaborators had devised a striking visual metaphor about the powers of dance. Whenever the on-stage dance band struck up a tune, Tharon Musser's lighting transformed Robin Wagner's stately ballroom into a sculpture of shadow criss-crossed with dazzling light, and Bennett's cast of thirty-two would sweep into elegant variations on ballroom favorites—the samba, tango, cha-cha, Lindy, waltz, and the Latin Hustle. It was a vivid yet dignified spectacle. But it never came close to the power of *A Chorus Line*. Bennett's concept didn't get the support it needed from the score by Billy Goldenberg (music) and Marilyn and Alan Bergman (lyrics). Their songs were far too undramatic to bring audiences very close to the illusions and hopes that kept the regulars of the Stardust coming back, and so the dialogue portions of the show lacked a strong musical bridge to the vivid reveries Bennett wanted to evoke with his choreography. Despite Bennett's admirable work and the fine performances of Dorothy Loudon and Vincent Gardenia, *Ballroom* was one of the most expensive box office failures of the decade.

They're Playing Our Song was the kind of show that Broadway of the '70s needed more of—not because it carried the musical to new highs but simply because, without appearing to try too hard or at too great an expense, it entertained. It brought back to the musical theatre Neil Simon, Marvin Hamlisch, and the actor-comedian Robert Klein, and it introduced to Broadway the lyricist Carole Bayer Sager, who had established herself as a writer of popular songs, and Lucie Arnaz, who had apprenticed in stock and television.

Couples in the late '70s had, in the psychobabble of the period, "relationships" instead of love affairs. Women's lib, sexual freedom, the fashion of self-improvement, and the pressures and pleasures of an age that had discarded many old ideas about love without finding replacements certainly

complicated "relationships." But the dizziness, the pangs, and the follies of
love remained. The creators of *They're Playing Our Song* managed a style
that blended the old and new of love in an unsubtle but graceful way. Their
show was hip enough to reflect the skepticism of the new generation of
lovers, yet it was also romantic enough to radiate the warmth of their confused passions.

It was essentially a two-person show, augmented with an ensemble of
three women and three men, who appeared whenever a backup, à la pop
recordings, was needed or whenever Vernon and Sonia's thoughts needed
singing. Simon's book, supposedly a fictional version of Hamlisch and
Sager's "real life" romance, followed—at times in confusing detail—the ups
and downs of a songwriting partnership that turns into a "relationship." Its
tolerant humor, pointed by Simon's sharply perceptive one-liners, made fun
of two vulnerable egos who bring to their affair a lot of bruises from past
romances. Lucie Arnaz played a kooky lyricist who can't completely break
her ties with her dependent ex-boy friend, Leon, and Robert Klein was the
new man in her life who has to put up with Leon's midnight phone calls.
Klein and Arnaz played deftly, and if their voices weren't exactly operatic,
they were quite equal to the pop style of Sager and Hamlisch's score.

Hamlisch, as with *A Chorus Line*, again found the missing links between
the musical comedy styles of yesteryear and the trends of current pop. Most
of his tunes, built with short, catchy phrases, had a pushy charm, and yet he
could also write a reflective, even poignant melody, as with "Fill In the
Words," Vernon's tongue-tied love song. The show's title song was
Hamlisch's most hummable creation, with the rest of his score not far behind
in immediate appeal. Sager's lyrics, like most written for the pop market,
hovered dangerously close to cliché, but at their best they produced a very
convincing illusion of coming directly from the heart.

If only Broadway had had a few more shows in the late '70s like *They're
Playing Our Song*. What it did have, in overabundance, were disappoint-
ments and flops. In the 1976–77 season, *Hellzapoppin'*, the new version of
Olsen and Johnson's 1938 extravaganza, closed in Boston where its star Jerry
Lewis raised more hell off-stage than on by refusing to cooperate with his
co-star, Lynn Redgrave. *The Baker's Wife*, produced by David Merrick, and
Music Is, directed by George Abbott, both quickly folded. In combination
with *Hellzapoppin'*, they cost a total of three million dollars.

The 1977–78 season lost Bob Merrill's *The Prince of Grand Street* while
it was still trying out in Boston. Although Robert Preston starred as an aging
matinee idol of the Yiddish theatre, circa 1900, and Merrill completely rewrote the first act, their efforts couldn't save the show. Two counterculture
revivals, *Hair* and *Jesus Christ Superstar*, lasted only months, while *Angel*,
an adaptation of Ketti Frings's *Look Homeward, Angel*, sank out of sight
after five performances. It had been the first Broadway-bound show to save
on costs by trying out at a dinner theatre on Long Island.

Two other shows that made it to Broadway—and survived far longer than *Angel*—disappointed for more troubling reasons. *The Act* (1977) had an impressive roster of production personnel: George Furth (librettist), John Kander (composer), Fred Ebb (lyricist), Tony Walton (set designer), Tharon Musser (lighting designer), Halston (costume designer), Ron Lewis (choreographer), and Martin Scorsese, the filmmaker and director of *Taxi Driver* (director). All of this talent—and Gower Champion, who doctored the show before its Broadway run—was gathered in the service of a vehicle for Liza Minnelli. It was a great nightclub act. The star worked ferociously, Kander and Ebb's tunes fit her as becomingly as Halston's wardrobe, and the dancing, mostly variations on the Vegas style, gave everybody, cast and audience, a workout. But the book, a bit of piffle, should have been completely discarded so as not to detract from Liza Minnelli's performance as Liza Minnelli. The show's greatest distinction was the price of its tickets. The Shubert Organization, who produced, charged twenty-five dollars for the top seats, the highest ticket price in the history of Broadway. According to Bernard Jacobs of the Shuberts the reasons for the inflated price were rising labor costs, real estate taxes, security expenses, inflation in all of the economy, and Minnelli's salary. His excuse for mounting such an expensive yet hollow extravaganza had an ominous ring to it. The Broadway theatre, he said, in order to stay alive had to compete with other entertainment forms, principally television and movies, for talent. To do that, it had to pay the outrageous salaries that celebrities knew they could demand. *The Act* was for Liza Minnelli's fans, and they were willing to pay the high prices—not to see a musical—but to see their idol in the flesh.

The vehicle—and perhaps any "specialized " show—presents a dilemma. It's designed to appeal to a smaller audience than the classic blockbuster of the past, and in order to make a return on its investment, it must charge its smaller, special audience higher ticket prices. That doesn't mean that in an age of shows aimed at special audiences the total audience for musicals will necessarily shrink. The aggregate of shows appealing to disparate audiences may equal or exceed past numbers. At first. But once the decision has been made to appeal to smaller, perhaps more affluent, perhaps more sophisticated audiences, can musical comedy continue to be a popular entertainment? The floundering of the musical theatre in the late '70s was evidence that some producers had chosen narrower themes and smaller audiences, while some had tried to find the general audience (if such a thing still existed), and many—too many—couldn't make up their minds. The shows of the undecided were odd mutants, neither richly melodic, sentimental, and optimistic (like the revivals), nor hip, cynical, and complex (like the productions of Prince and Sondheim). The in-betweens tried to be a little—or a lot—of both, and the result was too often compromise and confusion.

A specific case was the failure of *Working* (1978), which was put together by Stephen Schwartz from Studs Terkel's book of interviews. Terkel spoke to

waitresses, firemen, a parking lot attendant, a newsboy, teachers, a professional hockey player, a call girl, a gas meter reader, and many others. Without glorifying the mundane, his book formed a composite portrait of the
American worker. It was always intriguing; and, sometimes, when its inter-
viewees were most candid about their hopes and frustrations, it reached far
beyond reportage to dramatic monologue.

The theme of America at work that held together Schwartz's production
was well in the tradition of musical Americana, and the grouping of "confessionals" around a theme was in the recent fashion popularized by *A Chorus
Line*. But patching together excerpts from the small, everyday experiences
of Americans on the job made it difficult to generate musical and dramatic
excitement. *Working* had too many flat spots, especially in its score, itself a
patchwork of songs by Schwartz, Craig Carnelia, Micki Grant, Mary
Rodgers, Susan Birkenhead, and James Taylor.

The confusion—and the failures—continued into the 1978–79 season.
Alice (1978), to date the most elaborate and expensive (over a million dollars)
of Vinnette Carroll's shows, failed in spite of the efforts of co-producer Mike
Nichols. In Philadelphia, where it closed, the critics panned its attempt to
fuse black hipness with the Victorian sensibilities of Lewis Carroll's *Alice in
Wonderland* and *Through the Looking Glass*. *Home Again, Home Again*
(1979), with music by Cy Coleman and book by New York *Times* columnist
Russell Baker, had gone through many transformations since Coleman had,
in 1972, initiated the idea of a musical adapted from Baker's writings. The
final version, billed as "a saga of three generations of a family in Illinois,"
closed in Toronto. *Platinum* (1978) tried to be everything to everybody. It
told of an aging movie star who tries to make a comeback in a new nightclub
act; she falls in love with the rock composer-performer who's brought in to
prepare the act; and they eventually part, but not until both have professionally and personally gained from the encounter. For rock fans the show had a
few tunes by Gary William Friedman and Will Holt that resembled, if none
too closely, the real thing. For nostalgia buffs it had Alexis Smith as the
movie queen. It also had disco music, '40s big band numbers, and settings in
both New York and Hollywood. What it didn't have was much continuity or
musical distinction. *King of Hearts* (1978), a very elaborate adaptation of the
'60s cult film starring Alan Bates and directed by Philippe de Broca, tried
mightily—too mightily—for the fragile allegory of its source. For *A Broadway Musical* (1978), Charles Strouse and Lee Adams couldn't figure out how
to write a good show about the pre-opening trials of a bad show. After a
single performance, *A Broadway Musical* was no longer a Broadway musical.

The malaise of the American musical at the end of the '70s was in many
ways a reflection of the country's uncertainties. America was tired, cynical,
aware that it had wastefully expended many of its finest resources—both
physical and spiritual—and confused about where to look for new strength.
The musical was also plagued by the troubles that had helped to unbalance

the country. One of them was inflation. Many of the shows that opened on Broadway now cost in the neighborhood of a million dollars. Out of town tryouts were becoming prohibitively expensive. And ticket prices rose steadily: in the 1975–76 season the top price broke fifteen dollars; in 1976–77 it broke twenty dollars; and in the same season, with *The Act*, it broke twenty-five dollars. Surprisingly, paid attendance for Broadway's 1978–79 season was the highest since *Variety* had been keeping track. And although small investors—and a good number of the bigger angels—found they could no longer afford to back musicals, new money arrived from film companies. From 1972 to 1979 major film companies paid some twenty-five million dollars for rights to Broadway shows (including nonmusicals) and backed Broadway production to the tune of three million dollars. Warner Communications even set up a special division for the financing of Broadway ventures.

The American musical was not about to expire, nor was it an endangered species. But it was a rarer creature—at least on Broadway—than in the past. In the decade of the '20s, 444 new musicals of one kind or another opened in New York City; in the '60s, the number was 144; and in the '70s, it was 132. No doubt about it, the '20s were, if only the quantity of production matters, the good old days. Yet, who would trade *Fiddler on the Roof*, or *Cabaret*, or even *Hello, Dolly!* for fifty of the also-rans from the bountiful '20s? Another consolation is that musical-theatre production has not shrunk in the last two decades. Live musicals may have a smaller audience than fifty years ago, but they're holding their own. And this doesn't take into consideration the film adaptations of musicals that play in theatres and on television to millions of Americans who didn't see the originals.

Another encouraging sign is the rise of regional theatre in this country. Since the early '60s, more and more first-rate, fully professional regional companies, which can operate more cheaply than Broadway, have begun to include musicals in their repertoire, and they have also begun to commission originals. *Cyrano* came to Broadway in the '60s from the Tyrone Guthrie Theatre in Minneapolis. *Grease* came from Chicago, *Raisin* from Washington, D.C. And *Man of La Mancha*, *Very Good Eddie*, *Whoopee!*, *Shenandoah*, and *Annie* from East Haddam, Connecticut. If we add to the regional companies the institutional theatres and workshops in musical theatre, the total of new musicals produced yearly throughout the country might well equal or surpass the statistics for any year in the '20s. And we haven't taken into consideration the new musicals produced by theatre departments in colleges and universities, many of which are beginning to introduce musical-theatre courses and curricula.

Another cause for guarded optimism: Touring business for musicals is growing. Creative promoters, starting with *Pippin*, have used television commercials to whet the appetites of audiences beyond New York. New performing-arts centers, like the Kennedy Center in Washington, D.C., have the facilities and the capacities to guarantee first-class productions and long runs. And a new breed of adventuresome and savvy local promoters has come of age. The result is that some cities—chief among them Boston and Chicago—that have always been receptive to touring or pre-Broadway shows now generate even greater interest—and larger box-office receipts— than before. Other towns that previously had been able to sustain only short runs now can plan on runs of at least a one-week duration. Los Angeles and Washington, D.C., are now on almost every show's itinerary. And a few cities, like Miami and San Diego, that had never been thought of as theatre towns are now regularly visited by at least truck-and-bus companies. At the end of the 1978–79 Broadway season, *Variety* reported that road grosses for that season were approximately $148.9 million, which was $19 million more than the season's Broadway grosses.

Just as encouraging are the revivals of past musical hits, again a national phenomenon but one quite visible on Broadway within the last decade. The revivals of *The Pajama Game, Gypsy, Guys and Dolls, Where's Charley?, Pal Joey, My Fair Lady, Very Good Eddie, No, No, Nanette, Fiddler on the Roof, The King and I, Kismet* (as *Timbuktu!*), and *Man of La Mancha* can, it is true, be seen pessimistically as evidence that Broadway is running out of new material, that it must scrounge among the tried and true to please the appetites of an older audience that longs for the heyday of Rodgers and Hammerstein. These shows do attract the older fans, but they also attract young people and people who have never been to a live musical. No less an expert than Gerald Schoenfeld, president of the Shubert Organization, told the New York *Times* in 1979 that, "Broadway audiences want musicals most of all." Producers and audiences are once again recognizing what a treasure of artful and entertaining musicals has been accumulating for more than a hundred years.

Index

Aarons, Alex, 153
Abarbanell, Lina, 88
Abbey, Henry, 27
Abbott, Bud, and Costello,
    Lou, 181
Abbott, George, 173, 174,
    175, 186–87, 188, 215,
    216, 219, 226, 232, 235,
    236–37, 242, 260, 282
    285, 288, 291, 316, 344
Abravanel, Maurice, 183, 196
Abyssinia, 92
Act, The, 345, 347
Adams, Edith, 222, 232–33
Adams, Lee, 243–44, 263–
    64, 266–67, 346
Adams, Maude, 37
Adamson, Harold, 315
Ade, George, 76, 123
Adler, Gerry, 307
Adler, Luther, 284
Adler, Richard, 236–37
Adonis, 23–25, 27, 37, 51
Adonis, Young, 15
Adrian, Gilbert, 252
Africana, 150
L'Afrique, 43
Ain't Misbehavin', 310
*Ain't Supposed to Die a
    Natural Death*, 327–28
Aladdin, Jr., 60
Alarcón, Pedro, 171
Alberghetti, Anna Maria, 269
Albert, Donnie Ray, 330
Albert, Eddie, 174, 213
Albertson, Jack, 222
Alda, Alan, 284–85
Alda, Robert, 217
Aldredge, Theoni V., 302
Alice, 346
All American, 266–67
All of the Town, 69

Allegro, 199–200, 202, 210,
    221
Allen, Elizabeth, 274
Allen, Fred, 148
Allen-Hodgson, 280
Allen, Joseph, 123
Allmon, Clint, 326
Alone at Last, 95
Alonso, Alicia, 172
Alonso, Fernando, 172
Alton, Robert, 165, 167, 176,
    181, 204, 213
Alvarez, Anita, 193
Always You, 137
Ameche, Don, 220
America, 113
American Idea, The, 87
Americana, 165–66
America's Sweetheart, 157
Ames, Florenz, 112
Ames, Winthrop, 102–3
Anderson, John, 174
Anderson, John Murray,
    130–31, 132, 136, 167
Anderson, Leroy, 232
Anderson, Maxwell, 194–95,
    196
Andreas, Christine, 307
Andrews, Herbert, 170
Andrews, Jerome, 168
Andrews, Julie, 239, 245–46,
    252–53, 307
Andrews, Maxene and Patti,
    311
Angel, 344–45
Annie, 300, 305, 313–15,
    347
Annie Get Your Gun, 185–
    86, 203, 213
Anyone Can Whistle, 288
Anything Goes, 178, 184
Aphrodite, 136–37

Apollo, 59
Appell, Don, 271
Applause, 267–68
Apple Blossoms, 137
Apple Tree, The, 284–85, 321
Apron Strings, 55
Arabesque, 137
Archibald, William, 167, 191
Archie, Will, 116
Arden, Eve, 167
Argentinita, 147, 181
Arlen, Harold, 185, 190,
    221–22, 336
Arliss, George, 112
Arms and the Girl, 215
Armstrong, Louis, 170
Armstrong, Will Steven, 268
Arnaz, Desi, 175
Arnaz, Lucie, 343
Aronson, Boris, 283, 286, 287,
    290, 334–35
Aronson, Rudolph, 52
Around the Map, 111
Around the World, 113,
    183–84
*Around the World in Eighty
    Days*, 28–29, 31, 42, 171
Arthur, Beatrice, 225
Arthur, Paul, 68
Artists and Models, 126,
    145
As Thousands Cheer, 151,
    164–66, 171, 174–75
Asche, Oscar, 115
Asner, Edward, 225
Astaire, Adele, 108, 141, 149,
    153
Astaire, Fred, 108, 141, 149,
    153
At Home Abroad, 151,
    171–72
Atherton, Alice, 24, 34

Atkinson, Brooks, 146, 149, 156, 162, 164, 187, 218, 247
Attaboy, 124
Atteridge, Harold L., 106
Atwell, Roy, 95, 123
Audran, Edmond, 22, 39, 42, 46, 47, 58, 83
Aumont, Jean Pierre, 253
Auto Race, The, 82
Axelrod, George, 303
Ayers, Lemuel, 184, 198, 219, 287

Babes in Arms, 174
Babes in Toyland, 80, 82–83
Babette, 83
Bacall, Lauren, 267
Bacharach, Burt, 276–77
Back Again, 71
Bad Habits of 1926, 144
Bailey, Bill, 170
Bailey, Pearl, 215, 222, 272
Bainter, Fay, 138
Baker, Benny, 182
Baker, Josephine, 181
Baker, Lenny, 305–6
Baker, Mark, 332
Baker, Phil, 127, 144, 145, 150, 181
Baker, Russell, 346
Baker Street, 254
Baker's Wife, 344
Bakst, Léon, 104, 115, 136
Balanchine, George, 159, 172–74, 175, 189, 204, 316
Bales, William, 168
Balieff, Nikita, 130, 133, 144, 168
Balkan Princess, The, 118
Ball, Lucille, 261
Ballet of Niagara, 82
Balloon Wedding, The, 6–7, 22
Ballroom, 343
Band Wagon, The, 149–50, 159, 164, 170–71, 175, 199
Banjo Eyes, 186
Barcelo, Randy, 324–25
Barclift, Nelson, 184, 185
Bare Facts of 1926, 144
Barer, Marshall, 226
Barnes, Clive, 270
Barnes, Howard, 150, 183
Barnes, Irving, 223
Barnett, R. A., 60

Barnett, W. A., 26
Barnum, P. T., 4, 9
Baronova, Irina, 10
Barr, Richard, 337
Barras, Charles M., 8–10
Barratt, Watson, 181
Barrett, Lawrence, 34
Barry, John, 307
Barrymore, Maurice, 30
Bart, Lionel, 280
Bartholomae, Philip, 121, 124
Barto and Mann, 145
Barton, James, 150, 231–33
Basquette, Lina, 126
Batchelor, W. F., 60
Battles, John, 200
Baum, L. Frank, 79
Bay, Howard, 189, 192, 242, 271, 296
Bayes, Nora, 91, 111
Bean, Orson, 259
Beat the Band, 186–87
Beatles, The, 323, 325
Beaton, Cecil, 239, 255, 307
Beggar's Holiday, 191
Begum, The, 43–44
Behrman, S. N., 228
Belafonte, Harry, 221
Belasco, David, 58
Bell, Digby, 43–44, 46
Belle Hélène, La, 47, 188–89
Belle of Bond Street, The, 99
Belle of Bridgeport, The, 79
Belle of New York, The, 53, 71–72, 77
Belle Paree, La, 104–5
Belles of the Kitchen, 32
Bells Are Ringing, 230
Ben Franklin in Paris, 254
Benchley, Robert, 156
Bennett, Michael, 255, 277, 290–91, 336, 341–43
Bennett, Robert Russell, 192, 209
Bennett, Wilda, 99, 132
Benny, Jack, 144
Benton, Robert, 267
Benzell, Mimi, 271
Bergerson, Baldwin, 191
Bergman, Marilyn and Alan, 343
Berkeley, Busby, 156, 308
Berle, Milton, 181
Berlin, Irving, 107, 111, 114, 120, 124, 125, 132, 140–41, 163, 165, 166, 170, 184–86, 213–14, 257–58, 310

Bernard, Barney, 106
Bernard, Sam, 55, 61, 75–76, 114, 132
Bernardi, Herschel, 284, 287
Bernstein, Aline, 133
Bernstein, Leonard, 187, 232–35, 303–4, 306, 331–32
Berry Brothers, 150
Bertram, Helen, 59
Besoyan, Rick, 246–47
Best Foot Forward, 139, 186–87
Best Little Whorehouse in Texas, The, 326
Better Times, 127
Bettis, Valerie, 191
Between the Devil, 172
Biche au Bois, La, 8, 11–12
Bickel, George, 90
Big Boy, 138
Big Pony, 27
Biggers, Earl Derr, 98
Bigley, Isabel, 210, 217
Bikel, Theodore, 212
Billee Taylor, 48
Billion Dollar Baby, 187
Billionaire, The, 77
Binney, Constance, 123
Birch, Patricia, 334
Birkenhead, Susan, 346
Birthday of the Infanta, The, 132
Bissell, Richard, 235–36
Bitter Sweet, 160
Bizet, Georges, 192
Black America, 33
Black Crook, The, 2–7, 7–12, 14, 15, 17–18, 19, 20–21, 24, 28, 29, 42, 59, 105
Black Hussar, The, 46
Black Sheep, A, 37
Blaine, Vivian, 217
Blake, Eubie, 135, 224, 310
Bledsoe, Jules, 173
Blitzstein, Marc, 135, 169, 197, 225, 240, 318
Bloomer Girl, 190, 194, 221
Bloomingdale, Alfred, 181
Blossom, Henry, 83
Blossom Time, 21, 102, 138–39
Blue Kitten, The, 138
Blyden, Larry, 262, 284–85
Boccaccio, 160
Bock, Jerry, 224, 242, 282, 283–85, 287, 297, 302
Bohemian Girl, The, 48

INDEX

351

Boland, Mary, 163–64
Bolger, Ray, 167, 173, 177, 216
Bolitho, William, 154
Bolm, Adolph, 114–15, 128
Bolton, Guy, 99, 114, 121–23, 124, 136, 140, 153, 154, 158, 247, 315
Bombo, 128
Bond, Sheila, 227
Bone Room, The, 321
Bonfanti, Marie, 10
Bonfiglio, Signor, 105
Booth, Shirley, 215–16
Bordoni, Irene, 112, 121, 184
Borghini, Signor, 105
Boris, Ruthanna, 168
Borodin, Alexander, 219, 317
Bosley, Tom, 242–43
Bottle of Ink, A, 54
Boucheron, Maxime, 58
Bourneuf, Philip, 167
Bow Sing, 104–5
Boy Friend, The, 239, 245–47, 295
Boyd, Hannah, 60
Boyer, Lucienne, 168
Boys and Girls Together, 181
Boys from Syracuse, The, 174, 202
Bracken, Eddie, 175, 225
Brady, Alice, 55, 118
Brady, William A., 54
Brady, William A., Jr., 147
Braham, Davis, 34, 35, 36
Braham, John J., 26, 72
Brass Monkey, A, 37
Brecht, Bertolt, 225, 317–18
Breen, Robert, 223
Brennan, Eileen, 246
Brennan, Jay, 115, 117, 127, 130, 145
Brennan, Maureen, 332
Brentano, Felix, 159, 189
Brian, Donald, 85, 88–89, 95, 99, 119
Brice, Fannie, 92, 110, 125–26, 128, 132, 150, 180–81, 259
Bricklayers, The, 182
Bricusse, Leslie, 279
Brigadoon, 193–94, 202, 255
Brinkley, Nell, 92
Brisson, Frederick, 235, 255
Britta, Mlle., 105
Brittan, Robert, 328
Britten, Benjamin, 197
Broadway Musical, A, 346

Broderick, Helen, 90, 117, 149, 164–65
Brook, The, 24, 31–34
Brooks, Mel, 225, 266
Brosker, Octavia, 98
Brosset, Colette, 228
Brougham, John, 6, 19, 24, 32
Broun Heywood, 101, 121–22
Brown, Anne, 162
Brown, Billings, 188
Brown, C. F., 28
Brown, Charles, 43
Brown, Georgia, 280
Brown, Joe E., 131
Brown, John Mason, 147, 178
Brown, Lew, 151–53, 179, 309
Brown, William F., 329
Bruce, Carol, 173, 184
Bryan, Gertrude, 118
Bryant's Minstrels, 3
Brynner, Yul, 192, 209, 317
Bubbling Brown Sugar, 300, 310
Buchanan, Jack, 65, 135, 147, 172
Buck and Bubbles, 162, 182
Buck, Dudley, 43
Buck, Gene, 110, 125
Bunch of Keys, A, 36
Bunk of 1926, 144
Bunty Bulls and Strings, 71
Burgomaster, The, 76
Burke, Billie, 180
Burke, J. J., 60
Burnett, Carol, 226, 258, 260
Burnham, Charles, 9
Burns, David, 288
Burns, Ralph, 308, 341
Burnside, R. H., 97
Burrows, Abe, 216–17, 220, 275, 276, 309
Burton, Richard, 252–53
Bury, John, 281
Butler, Michael, 293
Butterworth, Charles, 171
By Jupiter, 177
By the Beautiful Sea, 215–16, 242
Bye, Bye, Birdie, 278

Cabaret, 265, 285–87, 347
Cabin in the Sky, 190–91
Cadman, Charles Wakefield, 59
Caesar, Irving, 308
Caesar, Sid, 262
Cagney, James, 134

Cahn, Sammy, 229, 266
Calin, Mickey, 234
Call Me Madam, 214–15, 222, 257–58
Call Me Mister, 188
Calloway, Cab, 224, 272, 310
Calta, Louis, 246
Camelot, 252–53, 278, 297
Canary Cottage, 124
Can-Can, 220
Candide, 208, 233–34, 244, 275, 306, 331–32
Cannon, Maureen, 186
Cantor, Eddie, 110, 125, 137, 146, 164, 315
Capalbo, Carmen, 225, 317–18
Capote, Truman, 221
Capra, Frank, 258
Carey, Macdonald, 196
Carib Song, 191
Cariou, Len, 338
Carlisle, Kitty, 190
Carmelina, 307
Carmen Jones, 191–92, 198, 224
Carmen Up-to-Date, 65
Carmichael, Hoagy, 190
Carmines, Al, 295, 321–22
Carne, Judy, 245
Carnegie, Hattie, 196
Carnelia, Craig, 346
Carnival, 229, 268–69, 278, 297
Carnival in Flanders, 266
Carousel, 194, 199, 202
Carpenter, John Alden, 132
Carradine, John, 288
Carroll, Albert, 133
Carroll, Diahann, 221–22, 274
Carroll, Earl, 69, 132–33, 144–45, 180
Carroll, Vinette, 346
Carson, Jack, 223, 224
Carter, Mrs. Leslie, 58
Carter, Nell, 311
Carter, Ralph, 328
Caryll, Ivan, 26, 58, 67, 74–76, 77, 97–99
Cassel, Walter, 172
Casselli, Signor, 15
Cassidy, Jack, 227, 260, 267
Castle, Irene, 62, 89, 94, 114, 120, 133
Castle, Vernon, 62, 89, 94, 97, 116, 120
Castles in the Air, 53, 55
Cat and the Fiddle, The, 158

Cavalleria Rusticana, 59, 197
Cavalry Charge, The, 76
Cawthorn, Joseph, 94, 119
Celebration, 270, 321
Cellier, Alfred, 40, 50
Century Girl, The, 97, 114
Chabrier, Emmanuel, 58
Chadman, Christopher, 316
Chadwick, George Whitfield, 61, 197
Champagne Sec, 159
Champion, Gower, 188, 244–45, 268, 269–70, 271–72, 291, 297, 303, 309, 312–13, 345
Chanel, Gabrielle ("Coco"), 255
Chanfrau, Frank, 6
Channing, Carol, 188, 271–72, 303, 317
Chaplin, Sydney, 259–60
Chapman, John, 226
Charell, Erik, 169
Charlap, Mark "Moose," 230
Charles, Keith, 270
Charles, Zachary, 222
Charlot, André, 135, 145
Charlot's Revue, 128, 135, 146, 153
Charnin, Martin, 302, 313–15
Chassaigne, François, 47
Chauve-Souris, 130, 150
Cheer Up, 114
Chicago, 339–41
Childs, Nathaniel, 24
Chimes of Normandy, The, 34
Chin-Chin, 97, 99
Chocolate Soldier, The, 80, 89, 94, 189
Chodorov, Jerome, 232–33
Chopin, Frédéric, 189
Chorus Line, A, 277, 295, 300, 314, 319, 321, 341–44, 346
Christian, The, 70
Christie, Audrey, 175
Chu Chin Chow, 104, 115–16
Cigale, La, 58
Cinderella, 57
Cinderella at School, 56
Cinderella Up-Too-Late, 65
Circus Girl, The, 67
Circus Princess, The, 159
Claire, Ina, 94, 110, 117, 119
Claire, Marion, 180

Clark, Bobby, 52, 132, 181, 183, 185, 189
Clark, Mabel, 66
Claude Duval, 48
Clayton, Bessie, 91
Clayton, Lou, 155–56
Clements, Otis, 309
Clifford, Katherine, 118
Clorindy, 72–73
Coca, Imogene, 167–68, 304–5
Cochran, Charles B., 147, 156
Coco, 255, 341
Cocoanuts, The, 141
Coconut Girl, The, 256
Coe, Peter, 263
Cohan, George M., 35, 37, 74, 82, 84–87, 88, 89, 93, 110–11, 112, 124, 137, 174, 214, 242, 265
Cohan, Helen F., 84
Cohan, Jerry J., 84
Cohan, Josephine, 84–85
Cohan Revue, 111
Cohen, Alexander, 254
Colavecchia, Franco, 330
Colby, Marion, 168
Cole, Jack, 182, 221, 296
Coleman, Cy, 261–62, 291, 304–6, 346
Coleman, Warren, 162
College Widow, The, 123
Collier, William, 71, 111, 132
Collins, Dorothy, 335
Collins, Pat, 318
Colt, Alvin, 187
Comden, Betty, 187–88, 229–30, 232, 258–61, 267, 303–4
Company, 287, 289–90, 332, 341
Comstock, F. Ray, 115, 121, 122, 136
Conche, Robert, 147
Condon, Eddie, 170
Connecticut Yankee, A, 156, 193, 199
Connell, Jane, 225, 227
Conor, Harry, 37
Conried, Heinrich, 46, 54
Consul, The, 197, 204
Contented Woman, A, 37
Continental Varieties, 168
Convy, Bert, 286
Conway, Shirl, 241
Cook, Barbara, 241–42, 282
Cook, Charles L., 245
Cook, Clyde, 127

Cook, Olga, 138
Cook, Will Marion, 72, 162
Cookson, Peter, 220
Coopersmith, Jerome, 254, 284
Coote, Robert, 307
Copland, Aaron, 134, 163
Copeland, Joan, 316
Corbett, James J., 69
Cordelia's Aspirations, 35–36
Corsair, The, 26
Corsaro, Frank, 315, 323, 330
Costa, Signor, 11
Costello, Lou, 181
Coster and Byles, 69
Cottrelly, Mathilde, 44, 46
Count of Luxembourg, The, 95
Countess Maritza, 159
Coward, Noel, 135, 146, 148, 160, 165, 256–57
Cox and Box, 34
Cradle Will Rock, The, 169
Craig, Gordon, 110, 136
Craig, Helen, 167
Crawford, Cheryl, 162
Crazy Quilt, 111, 150
Croffut, W. A., 43
Cronyn, Hume, 270
Cropper, Roy, 138
Cross, Beverly, 280
Crossey, J. S., 43
Croswell, Anne, 253
Crouse, Russel, 25, 212, 258
Cukor, George, 240
Cullum, John, 255, 304–5, 313
Curran, Homer, 190
Cushing, Catherine Chisholm, 137
Cyrano, 347
Czettel, Ladislas, 159, 189

Daboll, William S., 52
DaCosta, Morton, 222, 241, 242
Dale, Alan, 81, 108, 111, 113
Dale, Clamma, 330
Dale, Margaret, 123
Daly, Augustin, 43, 45, 66–67
Daly, Dan, 69
Daly, Lucy, 68
Daly, Peter, 78
Damarel, George, 88
Dames at Sea, 268, 295–96
Damn Yankees, 235, 236–37
Danby, Charles, 65

Dancer, Earl, 150
Dancin', 339–41
Dancing Around, 109
Danforth, William, 54, 138
Danilova, Alexandra, 189
Dante, Nicholas, 341
Darion, Joe, 225, 296
Darling of the Day, 261
Darnton, Charles, 108–9
Dassin, Jules, 264
Daughter of Rosie O'Grady, 218
Daughter of the Revolution, A, 62
David, Hal, 276–77
Davies, Marion, 99, 110, 115, 122
Davis, Buster, 308
Davis, Ossie, 292
Davis, Sammy, Jr., 224–25, 263–64, 317
Davison, Robert, 183
Dawn, Hazel, 98, 114
Dawson, Mark, 210
Day Before Spring, The, 192
Dazie, Mlle., 90, 105
Deane, Sydney, 78
DeAngelis, Jefferson, 44, 54–55, 56, 100, 108, 112
Dear World, 273
Dearest Enemy, 142
DeKoven, Reginald, 44, 59, 61, 82, 90, 100
Delmar, Harry, 144
Delmar, Kenny, 215
Delmar's Revels, 144
DeMarco, Sally and Tony, 182
DeMille, Agnes, 11, 170, 186, 190, 194, 198, 204, 219, 223, 269
Denier, Tony, 16
Denishawn Dancers, 132
DePaul, Gene, 222
Derr, Richard, 241
Deseret, 43
Desert Song, The, 159
DeShields, Andre, 329
Deslys, Gaby, 99, 105–6
Destry Rides Again, 229, 278
DeSylva, B. G., 127, 151–52, 179, 203, 309
Devil and Daniel Webster, The, 197
DeWalden, Thomas, 6
DeWolfe, Billy, 309
DeWolfe, Elsie, 121
Dhery, Robert, 228

Diamond Studs, 326
Diehl, Crandall, 307
Diener, Joan, 219, 317
Dietz, Howard, 148–49, 150, 171–72, 255–56, 336
Diller, Phyllis, 272
Dillingham, Charles B., 97, 99, 112, 114–15, 120, 127–28, 140, 157, 167
Dispatches, 320
Dixey, Henry E., 22–26
Dixie to Broadway, 135
Do I Hear a Waltz?, 268, 274
Do Re Mi, 258–59, 278
Dobos, Viola, 147
Dockstader, Lew, 3
Dr. Syntax, 56, 57
Dog in the Manger, A, 37
Dolan, Robert Emmett, 215, 262
Dolin, Anton, 147, 183
Dollar Princess, The, 89, 95
Dolly, Roszika and Yanczi, 96, 109, 111, 118, 131
Dolores, 110
Donahue, Jack, 140, 183
Donaldson, Norma, 316
Donaldson, Walter, 315
Donehue, Vincent, 256
Dooley, Rae, 112, 125
Dorothy, 50
Douglass, Stephen, 236
Dova, Ben, 181
Dovey, Alice, 122
Dowling, Eddie, 125, 138
D'Oyly Carte, Rupert, 40–41, 48, 50–51
Drake, Alfred, 167, 168, 184, 191, 198, 219
Draper, Paul, 181
Dream Girl, The, 138
Dreams, 34, 36
Dresser, Louise, 111
Dressler, Marie, 59, 61, 81, 111–12
DuBarry, The, 160
DuBarry Was a Lady, 179
Dubey, Matt, 214
DuBois, Raoul Pène, 167, 179, 192, 232, 241, 242, 308
Dude, 322–23, 331
Duke, Vernon (Vladimir Dukelsky), 134, 172, 190–91
Dumont, Margaret, 141
Dunbar, Paul Laurence, 72
Duncan, Anna, 133

Duncan, Isadora, 66
Duncan, Rosetta and Vivian, 128, 137
Duncan, Sandy, 245
Duncan, Todd, 162, 190
Dunham, Katherine, 190–91
Dunn, Arthur, 26
Duquette, Tony, 252
Durante, Jimmy, 153, 155–56, 172, 178
Dybbuk, The, 134
Dyer, Sammy, 169
Dynamite, 11

Eagels, Jeanne, 117
Earl, Virginia, 69
Earl Carroll's Sketch Book, 145, 180
Earl Carroll's Vanities, 69, 132–33, 144–45, 147, 180
Earl of Ruston, 325–26
Early to Bed, 310
Earthquake, The, 82
Ebb, Fred, 285–87, 297, 341, 345
Ebsen, Buddy and Vilma, 171
Eckart, Jean, 226, 256
Eckart, William, 226
Ed Wynn Carnival, 128
Edouin, Willie, 24, 34, 36, 78, 85
Edwardes, George, 27, 64, 65–66, 94, 140
Edwards, Julian, 81
Edwards, Sherman, 292
Eggert, Marta, 176, 189
Eglantine, 11
Eileen, 97
El Capitan, 58
Elfins and Mermaids, 43
Ellington, Duke, 191, 310
Elliott, William, 115, 122
Ellis, Mary, 138
Ellis, Melville, 105, 106, 118, 121
Elsom, Isobel, 119
Eltinge, Julian, 117, 126
Elzy, Ruby, 162
Engel, Lehman, 168, 320–21
Englander, Ludwig, 61, 62, 68, 74, 77, 91, 100
Engle, Lottie, 118
Epstein, David, 322
Erlanger, Abraham Lincoln, 80, 95, 98, 104, 111
Erminie, 42, 51–53, 98

Errol, Leon, 109–10, 112, 114, 118
Erwin, Barbara, 314
Escudero, Vicente, 168
Eternal Road, The, 180, 194
Eubie, 310
Evangeline, 10, 12, 13, 19–27, 33, 34, 40, 41, 56, 60, 202
Evans and Hoey, 37
Evans, Maurice, 282
Everything, 114
Everywoman, 197
Ewell, Tom, 188
Excelsior, 26, 29–30
Excelsior, Jr., 25, 26
Eythe, William, 188

Fabray (Fabares), Nanette, 168, 215
Face the Music, 163–64
Fade Out–Fade In, 258, 260
Faggott, The, 321–22
Fain, Sammy, 221
Fairbanks Twins, 110
Faison, George, 329
Falka, 47
Fall, Leo, 58, 62, 89, 94–95
Fallon, Eva, 118
Fancy Free, 187
Fanny, 228, 278
Fantasticks, The, 247–48, 269–70, 321
Faria, Arthur, 311
Farnie, H. B., 47
Farrell, Anthony B., 215
Farren, Nellie, 65
Fascinating Flora, 73, 77
Fascinating Widow, The, 117
Fatinitza, 34, 40, 44, 100
Faust and Loose, 65
Faust Up to Date, 27
Faust-on-Toast, 65
Fay, Frank, 108, 127, 182
Faye, Alice, 309
Faye, Herbie and Joey, 222
Fayol, Lily, 185
Feder, 252
Feiffer, Jules, 285
Feigay, Paul, 187
Fencing Master, The, 59
Fenolt, Jeff, 324
Ferber, Edna, 157
Feuer, Cy, 210, 216, 245, 266
Février, Henri, 136
Fiddler on the Roof, 282–84, 287, 297, 301–2, 317, 347, 348

Field, Ron, 267, 303
Fields, Benny, 131
Fields, Dorothy, 172, 182, 185–86, 190, 215–16, 238, 291
Fields, Gracie, 65, 181
Fields, Herbert, 155, 156, 162, 182, 185–86, 190, 215, 238
Fields, Joseph, 211, 232–33
Fields, Lew, 27, 38, 49, 54, 61, 70–71, 79, 81–82, 83, 85, 93, 111–12, 114, 116–17, 156
Fields, W. C., 110, 125, 128, 145
Fifty Miles from Boston, 87
Fifty Million Frenchmen, 155, 177
Fille de Mme. Angot, La, 39
Finian's Rainbow, 135, 190, 193, 201, 204, 221
Finklehoffe, Fred, 232
Finnell, Carrie, 185
Fiorello!, 242–43, 287
Firebrand of Florence, The, 196
Firefly, The, 100–101
First Impressions, 240
First Life Guards at Brighton, The, 43
Fisher, Jules, 324–25
Fitch, Robert, 314
Fitzgerald, Cissy, 66
Fitzhugh (Fitziu, Fitzu), Anna, 79
Flag Is Born, A, 196
Flahooley, 221, 222, 256
Flatt, Lester O., 303, 325
Fledermaus, Die, 46, 59, 96, 159, 172, 188
Fleming, Carroll, 105
Fletcher, Percy, 136
Flora, the Red Menace, 285
Florell, Walter, 189, 191
Florodora, 64, 76, 77–79, 85, 93
Flotow, Friedrich von, 58, 83
Flower Drum Song, 208, 211–12
Flying Cansinos, 131
Flying Colors, 171
Flying High, 152
Fokina, Vera, 127
Fokine, Michel, 127, 136
Follies, 300, 333–37, 339, 341
Follow Me, 102
Follow Thru, 152

Fonda, Henry, 167
Forbes, Brenda, 167
Forbush, Nellie, 211
Ford, Ruth, 170
Foreman, Richard, 318
Forrest, George, 219
Forsythe, Henderson, 326–27
Fortesque, George K., 21–22, 24
Fortune Teller, The, 189
Forty Thieves, The, 19
Forty-Five Minutes from Broadway, 36, 85
Fosse, Bob, 236–38, 291, 297, 339–41
Four Saints in Three Acts, 197
1492, 60
1492 Up to Date, 26
Fox, Della, 44, 53, 54, 56, 57
Fox, George L., 5, 13–16, 24, 31, 52, 53, 80, 85
Fox, Maxine, 311
Foxy, 262, 278
Foy, Eddie, 76, 80
Foy, Eddie, Jr., 236
Franchi, Sergio, 274
Frank, Melvin, 222
Franklin, Frederic, 189
Franklin, Harold B., 171
Franklin, Irene, 76
Freedley, Vinton, 153, 178
French Maid, The, 67
Freska, Friedrich, 102
Friedman, Charles, 166, 192, 224
Friedman, Gary William, 346
Friganza, Trixie, 76
Friml, Rudolph, 96, 100–102, 125, 138–39, 159, 246
Frisky Cobbler, The, 13
Frohman, Charles, 94, 95
From Vienna, 168
Fryer, Robert, 232
Fuller, Dean, 226–27
Fuller, Loie, 27, 34, 37, 66
Fuller, Penny, 267
Funny Face, 153
Funny Girl, 258–60
Funny Thing Happened on the Way to the Forum, A, 287–88
Furth, George, 289, 345

Gaby, 105
Gae, Nadine, 167

Gaiety Girl, A, 64, 65 – 66
Gallagher, Edward, 96, 126
Gallagher, Helen, 309
Garber, Victor, 338
Garden, Mary, 136
Gardenia, Vincent, 343
Gardner, Rita, 248
Garland, Robert, 186
Garrick Gaieties, 134, 142, 149, 162, 165, 167
Gautier, Dick, 243 – 44
Gaxton, William, 132, 155, 156, 161, 178 – 79, 184
Gay, John, 191, 194
Gay Divorce, 177 – 78
Gay Hussars, The, 96
Gay Life, The, 255 – 56
Gaynor, Charles, 309
Geddes, Norman Bel, 137, 155, 171, 183
Geisha, The, 66, 104
Gelbart, Larry, 288
Geld, Gary, 292, 313
Genée, Adeline, 91
Genée, Richard, 45, 46, 47
Gentlemen Prefer Blondes, 188, 229, 303
George, Yvonne, 131, 145
George M!, 265
George Washington, Jr., 86
George White's Music Hall Varieties, 180
George White's Scandals, 69, 129 – 30, 132 – 33, 144 – 45, 147, 180
Gerber, Alex, 142
Gershe, Leonard, 229
Gershwin, George, 2, 114, 127, 129, 141 – 42, 153 – 55, 160 – 63, 165, 170, 223, 264, 310, 329 – 30, 336
Gershwin, Ira, 2, 141, 153 – 54, 160 – 62, 172, 195, 203
Gest, Morris, 115, 127, 136
Get Together, 127
Geva, Tamara, 148, 171, 173
Geyer, Siegfried, 179
Ghislanzon, Antonio, 224
Gibson, Virginia, 214
Gibson, William, 263
Gielgud, John, 309
Gigi, 307
Gilbert, W. S., 22, 39 – 42, 43, 46, 47 – 49, 50 – 51, 53, 56 – 57, 64, 74, 100, 124, 134, 161, 163, 166, 169
Gilbert, Willie, 275

Gilford, Jack, 226, 286, 288, 308
Gill, William, 25, 53
Gillette, Priscilla, 219
Gingham Girl, The, 137
Girl Behind the Gun, The, 99
Girl Crazy, 152 – 53, 154 – 55
Girl from Brazil, The, 102
Girl from Kay's, The, 75
Girl from Paris, The, 66 – 67
Girl from Utah, The, 96, 119
Girl o' Mine, 124
Girl of the Golden West, The, 119
Girl on the Film, The, 119
Girl Who Came to Supper, The, 256 – 57
Giroflé-Girofla, 39
Glad, Gladys, 150, 158
Gleason, Jackie, 240
Gleason, Joanna, 305
Glenn-Smith, Michael, 270
Glickman, Will, 224
Glover, W. F., 60
Glynn, Carlin, 326
Godspell, 300, 324
Godwin, Dwight, 172
Goetzl, Anselm, 136
Going Up, 315
Golden, John, 94, 114
Golden Apple, The, 208, 226
Golden Ax, The, 5, 13
Golden Boy, 263 – 64, 267
Golden Rainbow, 264
Goldenberg, Billy, 343
Goldilocks, 260
Goldman, James, 335
Gondoliers, The, 53
Good Mr. Beth, The, 72
Good News, 151 – 52, 156, 309, 315
Good Times, 127
Goodall, Elizabeth, 105
Goodman, Benny, 170
Goodwin, J. Cheever, 20 – 22, 23, 24, 56 – 57, 60, 62
Goodwin, Nat C., 27, 34
Gordon, Lady Duff, 114
Gordon, Mack, 153
Gordon, Max, 148 – 49, 159, 166, 171, 180, 232
Gorme, Eydie, 264
Gorney, Jay, 168
Gottfried, Martin, 261
Gould, Elliot, 276
Gould, Morton, 215
Goulet, Robert, 253
Governor's Son, The, 85

Goz, Harry, 284
Grab Bag, The, 129
Grable, Betty, 179, 272
Graf, Herbert, 189
Graff, Ilene, 305
Graham, Martha, 62, 131
Graham, R. H., 78
Graham, Ronald, 174
Graham, William, 246 – 47
Grand Mogul, The, 77
Grand Street Follies, 133 – 134, 147
Grand Tour, The, 313
Granichstaedten, Bruno, 96
Grant, Cary, 159
Grant, Micki, 346
Grau, Maurice, 27, 39
Gray, Dolores, 229
Gray, Gilda, 126
Gray, Timothy, 257
Grease, 311 – 12, 347
Great Day, 153
Great Temptations, 144
Great Waltz, The, 180
Green, Adolph, 187 – 88, 229 – 30, 232, 258 – 61, 267, 303 – 4
Green, Daisy, 78
Green, Johnny, 148, 186 – 87
Green, Mitzi, 174
Green, Paul, 194, 318
Green, Schuyler, 121, 315
Greene, Ellen, 318
Greenwich Village Follies, 92, 130 – 32, 133, 134, 136, 145
Greenwillow, 274
Greenwood, Charlotte, 95, 107, 124, 219
Grey, Clifford, 140
Grey, Joel, 265, 286, 313
Grieg, Edvard, 189, 219
Griffies, Ethel, 213
Griffith, Andy, 229
Griffith, Robert, 235 – 37, 242 – 43
Griffiths Brothers, 147
Grimes, Tammy, 257, 265
Groody, Louise, 111, 141
Grossmith, George, 65, 119, 140
Grudeff, Marion, 254
Guinan, Texas, 144
Guardino, Harry, 288
Guare, John, 318
Guetary, Georges, 215
Guillaume, Robert, 316
Guilliatt, Lee, 322

Guthrie, Tyrone, 234
Guys and Dolls, 208, 210,
    216–18, 220, 225, 242,
    300, 316, 348
Gypsy, 229, 230–32, 259,
    278, 303, 348
Gypsy Baron, The, 59
Gypsy Love, 93, 95, 189

H. M. S. Pinafore, 35, 39–42,
    45, 48, 50, 51, 53, 54, 119
Haas, Dolly, 192
Hadjidakis, Manos, 264
Hagen, Jean, 220
Haggin, Ben Ali, 126
Hague, Albert, 241
Hague, Arthur, 238
Haimsohn, George 296
Hain, William, 173
Haines, A. Larry, 277
Hair, 293–94, 297, 300, 317,
    322–23, 340, 344
Hajos, Mitzi, 96, 100, 105, 124
Hale, Philip, 55, 98
Haley, Jack, 152, 176, 182
Half a Sixpence, 280
Hall, Carol, 326–27
Hall, Delores, 327
Hall, Juanita, 222
Hall, Owen, 78
Hall, Pauline, 52
Hall, Peter, 325
Hallelujah, Baby!, 258,
    260–61
Halliday, Richard, 230
Halston, 345
Hambleton, T. Edward,
    226–27
Hamilton, Nancy, 167
Hamlet II, 62
Hamlisch, Marvin, 341–44
Hammerstein, Arthur, 100–
    101, 138, 142
Hammerstein, Oscar, 62, 84,
    93, 180
Hammerstein, Oscar 2nd,
    137, 157–58, 173, 186,
    191, 197–200, 208–13,
    219, 221, 227, 242, 243,
    249, 273–74, 290, 302,
    313, 348
Hammond, Percy, 134, 146,
    149, 153, 171, 173
Handy, W. C., 310
Haney, Carol, 211, 214, 236
Hanky Panky, 117
Hanley, Ed, 222
Hanlon Brothers, 6

Hanneford, Poodles, 159
Hanson, Howard, 59
*Happiest Girl in the World,
    The*, 256
Happy Birthday, 116
Happy Hunting, 214
Happy Time, The, 278
Harbach (Hauerbach), Otto,
    100–101, 159, 308, 315
Harburg, E. Y., 190, 221, 256,
    261
Harker, Joseph, 115
Harker, Philip, 115
Harnick, Sheldon, 242–43,
    282, 283–85, 287, 297,
    302
Harrigan, Edward, 34,
    35–37, 202, 242
Harrington, Hamtree, 135
Harris, Barbara, 284–85, 317
Harris, Henry B., 105
Harris, Julie, 266
Harris, Sam H., 111–12, 132,
    162, 163–64
Harrison, Louis, 61
Harrison, Rex, 239–40, 246,
    254, 307
Harrold, Orville, 84
Hart, Lorenz, 2, 134, 142,
    156–57, 172, 173–77,
    197–98, 199, 203, 212–
    13, 274
Hart, Moss, 163–64, 166, 172,
    174–75, 178, 180, 183,
    195, 200, 201, 213, 238,
    252, 276
Hart, Teddy, 174
Hart, Tony, 34, 35–37, 202,
    242
Hartman, Grace, 178
Hartman, Paul, 178, 223
Harvey, Georgette, 163
Hassan, 51
Hatton, Bradford, 222
Have a Heart, 122
Haverly, J. H., 34
Havoc, June, 176
Hayes, Bill, 210
Hayes, Helen, 116
Haynes, Tiger, 329
Hayride, 325
Hayward, Leland, 230, 232
Hayworth, Jill, 286
Hazel Flagg, 229
Hazzard, John E., 122
Head Over Heels, 124
Heads Up, 157
Healy, Ted, 145, 150

Heart of Maryland, The, 70
Hecht, Ben, 183, 229–30
Helburn, Theresa, 168
Held, Anna, 81, 90, 91, 102,
    118
Helen Goes to Troy, 188–89
Hell, 105
Hellman, Lillian, 201, 234
Hellmesberger, Joseph, Jr.,
    59
Hello Broadway, 111
Hello, Dolly!, 269, 271–73,
    278, 282, 297, 311, 317,
    347
Hellzapoppin', 21, 181, 344
Hen Pecks, The, 94, 116
Henderson, David, 60
Henderson, Florence, 228
Henderson, Luther, 308–9
Henderson, Ray, 151–53,
    179
Henderson, W. J., 50
Heneker, David, 280
Henry, Sweet Henry, 341
Henshaw, Johnny, 68
Hepburn, Audrey, 240
Hepburn, Katharine, 255
Her Little Highness, 100
Her Wedding Trip, 100
Herbert, Joseph W., 70
Herbert, Ralph, 189
Herbert, Victor, 80, 82–84,
    88, 96–97, 114, 125, 138,
    139, 189
Here's Love, 266, 268, 321
Herlie, Eileen, 240
Herman, Jerry, 271–73,
    312–13
Herndon, Richard, 137
Hero is Born, A, 168
Heyward, Dorothy and
    DuBose, 162
Hiawatha, 6, 24, 25, 34, 36,
    202
Hickory Dickory Dock, 15
Higgledy-Piggledy, 81
High Button Shoes, 188, 229,
    232, 266
High Jinks, 101
High Spirits, 257
Higher and Higher, 175
Highwayman, The, 100
Hines, Earl (Fatha), 310
Hip! Hip! Hooray!, 81
Hip-Hip-Hooray, 114
Hirsch, Louis, A., 106, 123,
    315
Hirson, Roger O., 340

Hit the Deck, 153, 156
Hitchcock, Raymond, 76, 79, 81, 112, 125, 128
Hitchy-Koo, 112, 128
Hobbies, 34
Hodge Podge and Co., 78–79
Hodges, Joy, 186
Hoffa, Portland, 148
Hoffman, Gertrude, 62, 104, 126, 127
Hoffman, Max, 90
Hokey-Pokey, 71
Hold Everything, 152
Hold on to Your Hats, 190
Holder, Geoffrey, 317, 329
Hole in the Ground, A, 37
Holgate, Ron, 313
Holiday, Billie, 310
Holiday, Bob, 267
Holländer, Victor, 102
Holliday, Judy, 230
Hollingshead, John, 64
Holloway, Stanley, 239, 256
Holloway, Sterling, 134
Holly Golightly, 278
Holm, Celeste, 198
Holm, Hanya, 184, 219, 239, 307
Holm, John Cecil, 186
Holman, Libby, 148, 171, 179, 187
Holofcener, Larry, 224
Holt, Will, 311, 346
Holtz, Lou, 141, 181
Holzer, Adela, 322
Home Again, Home Again, 346
Home Movies, 295
Honeymooners, The, 87
Hood, Basil, 80
Hooks, Robert, 261
Hope, Bob, 178
Hope, Vida, 245
Hopper, DeWolf, 44, 46, 53, 55–58, 75, 108
Hopper, Edna Wallace, 57, 69, 78, 117
Hopwood, Avery, 138
Horne, Lena, 221
Horner, Harry, 185, 196
Horton, Robert, 269
Horwitt, Arnold, 232, 241
Hoschna, Karl, 117
Hot Mikado, The, 166, 169
Hot-Cha, 152
Houghton, Norris, 226–27
House, E. F., 18
House of Flowers, 221, 224

How Now, Dow Jones, 275–76, 278
How to Succeed in Business Without Really Trying, 274–76, 297
Howard, Eugene, 107, 108, 145, 180
Howard, George Bronson, 106
Howard, Ken, 306
Howard, Sidney, 192
Howard, Willie, 107, 108, 145, 180, 181
Howland, Jobyna, 106
Hoyt, Charles, 36–38, 118, 202
Hubbell, Raymond, 94, 109
Hulbert, Jack, 65
Humming Bird, The, 33
Humperdinck, Engelbert, 83, 197
Humphrey, Doris, 190
Humpty Dumpty, 5, 13–16, 19, 20, 28, 30, 31, 40, 80, 152
Hunter, Ian McLellan, 262
Hunter, Mary, 191
Husband in Clover, 32
Husmann, Ron, 282, 304
Huston, Walter, 194–95
Hutcherson, LeVern, 223
Hutton, Betty, 167
Hyland, Lily M., 133
Hylton, Millie, 65

I Can Get It for You Wholesale, 259, 275–76, 278
I Do! I Do!, 269–70, 278
I Feel Wonderful, 271
I Love My Wife, 305–6
I Married an Angel, 172, 175, 190, 199
I Remember Mama, 302–3
I'd Rather Be Right, 84, 165, 174–75, 177
Ide, Letitia, 165
Illya Darling, 264, 268
In Circles, 295
In Dahomey, 36, 92
In Gay New York, 69
In Gotham, 69
In the Limelight, 105
In Town, 66
Innocent Eyes, 126
Inside U.S.A., 172
International Cup, The, 82
International Revue, The, 147

Iolanthe, 41
Irene, 137, 309, 315
Irma la Douce, 276, 278–79, 280
Irwin, May, 79
Irwin, Will, 192
It Happened in Nordland, 83
It Happens on Ice, 180
It's a Bird . . . It's a Plane . . . It's Superman, 267
Itzel, Adam, Jr., 59
Ives, Burl, 190
Ixion, 16–18

Jack and the Beanstalk, 14
Jack O'Lantern, 99
Jackson, Arthur, 129
Jackson, Eddie, 155–56
Jackson, Ernestine, 316
Jackson, Ethel, 81, 88–89
Jacobi, Lou, 260
Jacobi, Victor, 119
Jacobs, Bernard, 345
Jacobson, Irving, 296
Jacoby, Josephine, 55
Jageman, Walter, 170
Jakobowski, Edward, 51–53
Jamaica, 221, 224, 278
James, Olga, 224
Janis, Elsie, 97, 114, 121, 128, 133
Jardon, Dorothy, 100, 104
Jarrett, Henry C., 8, 11, 24
Jarrett, Jerry, 284
Jazz Singer, The, 170
Jenkins, George, 256
Jennie, 256
Jensen, Marie, 49
Jeritza, Maria, 133, 160
Jessel, George, 150, 182
Jessel, Raymond, 254, 302
Jessye, Eva, 162
Jesus Christ Superstar, 323–25, 344
Jewel of Asia, The, 77
Joan, 321–22
Johannes Kreisler, 137
John, Tom H., 329
Johnny Johnson, 165, 194, 318
Johnson, Albert, 149, 165, 180
Johnson, Edward, 89
Johnson, J. A., 15
Johnson, J. Rosamond, 162
Johnson, Louis, 292, 330
Johnson, Van, 167
Johnson, William, 210–11
Johnston, Fannie, 78

Johnstone, Justine, 110, 122
Jolson, Al, 105–6, 128, 138, 160, 164, 170, 190
Jomelli, Mme. Léon, 5, 6
Jones, Allan, 148
Jones, Robert Edmond, 189, 192
Jones, Sydney, 66, 119
Jones, Tom, 247–48, 269–70, 321
Jongeyans, George, 219
Joyce, Peggy Hopkins, 110, 115
Joyful Noise, A, 325, 341
Jubilee, 178
Julia, Raul, 316, 318, 325
Jumbo, 157, 173
Jumping Jupiter, 94, 117
Juno, 240
Jurman, Walter, 191

Kahn, Gus, 315
Kahn, Madeline, 304
Kalman, Emmerich, 58, 96, 159
Kalmar, Bert, 156
Kander, John, 285–87, 297, 341, 345
Kane, Helen, 145
Kanin, Fay, 255
Kanin, Garson, 213, 258
Kanin, Michael, 255
Kaper, Bronislau, 268
Karniloff, Maria, 172
Karnilova, Maria, 287
Karson, Nat, 169
Kass, Jerome, 343
Katinka, 101
Kaufman, George S., 149, 150, 157, 160–62, 166, 174–75, 183, 201, 217, 220, 223, 276
Kaufman, Harry, 168
Kay, Hershy, 304
Kaye, Danny, 168, 182, 195–96, 301
Kaye, Nora, 172
Kaye, Stubby, 218, 222
Keel, Howard, 222
Keeler, Ruby, 308–9
Kellermann, Annette, 106
Kelley, Edgar Stillman, 59
Kelly, Gene, 167, 176, 211, 213
Kelly, Harry, 91
Kelly, Patsy, 309
Kerker, Gustave, 26, 53, 54, 55, 61, 67, 69, 71, 74, 77, 84

Kern, Jerome, 23, 105, 114, 119, 120–24, 128, 139–40, 141, 153, 157–58, 172–73, 212, 247, 315
Kerr, Harold, 214
Kerr, Walter, 213
Kert, Larry, 234
Kid Boots, 137
Kidd, Michael, 193, 215, 220, 222, 229, 266, 291, 309
Kiepura, Jan, 189
Kiley, Richard, 219, 238, 296, 317
King, Dennis, 138, 175
King, Larry L., 326–27
King, Mabel, 329
King and I, The, 208–11, 219, 300, 317, 348
King Dodo, 76
King of Hearts, 346
Kinoy, Ernest, 264
Kiralfy, Arnold, Bolossy, and Imre, 12, 15, 28–30, 31, 59, 60, 107, 171
Kirkwood, James, 341
Kiser, Franklin, 254
Kismet, 219, 317, 348
Kiss Me, Kate, 174, 184, 197, 202, 213, 219, 236
Kitchell, Iva, 148
Kitt, Eartha, 225, 317
Klaw, Marc, 80, 95, 98, 104, 111
Kleban, Edward, 320–21, 341–42
Klein, Manuel, 105, 106
Klein, Robert, 343–44
Kleisinger, George, 225
Kline, Kevin, 304
Klotz, Florence, 335
Knickerbocker Holiday, 194–95
Knife and Falka, 65
Kobart, Ruth, 288
Kober, Arthur, 227
Korngold, Erich Wolfgang, 189
Kraft, Hy, 222
Krakeur, Richard, 232
Kreisler, Fritz, 137
Krupska, Dania, 218
Kyasht, Lydia, 109

La! La! Lucille, 141
Ladies' Paradise, The, 75
Lady Be Good, 141
Lady in Ermine, The, 137
Lady in the Dark, 140, 168,

192, 195–96, 198, 200, 202
Lady of the Slipper, The, 97
Lady or the Tiger, The, 44
Laffing Room Only, 181
Lagarde, 30
Lahr, Bert, 152, 172, 179, 180, 183, 262
Laing, Hugh, 193
Lamas, Fernando, 214
Lamb, Myrna, 295
Land of Joy, The, 112
Lane, Burton, 190, 254–55, 307
Lane, Rosemary, 186
Lange, Harold, 167, 213, 276
Lang, Philip J., 265
Lansbury, Angela, 232, 273, 303, 338
Lardner, Ring, Jr., 262
Larrimore, Francine, 101
Larsen, William, 248
Lasky, Jesse L., 105
LaTouche, John, 191
Laugh Time, 182
Laurence, Paula, 182
Laurents, Arthur, 229, 230–32, 234–35, 258, 260–61, 268, 274, 288–89, 303
Lawrence, Carol, 222, 234, 259, 270
Lawrence, Gertrude, 49, 135, 140, 147, 153, 195–96, 209
Lawrence, Jerome, 273
Lawrence, Steve, 264, 276
Lawson, Mark, 127
Laye, Evelyn, 172
Layton, Joe, 226, 265, 274, 291
Leach, Archie, 159
Leave It to Jane, 123, 247
Leave It to Me, 179
Lecocq, Alexandre-Charles, 39, 58
Lederer, George W., 61
Lee, Eugene, 322, 331, 339
Lee, Franne, 322, 331
Lee, Gypsy Rose, 185, 230–31
Lee, Robert E., 273
LeGallienne, Eva, 128
Lehár, Franz, 42, 58, 83, 87, 89, 93, 94–96, 189, 336
Leigh, Carolyn, 230, 261–62
Leigh, Dorma, 119
Leigh, Mitch, 296
Leigh, Vivien, 253
Lend an Ear, 188, 244

Lennart, Isobel, 258
Lenya, Lotte, 225, 286, 317
Leonardos, Urylee, 223
Lerner, Alan Jay, 193, 194,
    223, 237–39, 252–53,
    254–55, 306–7
LeRoy, Hal, 175
Leslie, Amy, 83
Leslie, Fred, 65
Leslie, Lew, 135, 147, 150,
    168
Lester, Edwin, 189, 219
Let 'Em Eat Cake, 162
Let It Ride, 218
Let's Face It, 182
Leve, Samuel, 187
Levene, Sam, 218
Levin, Herman, 307
Levy, Ethel, 85
Lew Dockstader's Minstrels,
    3
Lewis, Catherine, 45
Lewis, Dave, 90
Lewis, Jerry, 344
Lewis, Minard, 15
Lewis, Morgan, 167
Lewis, Robert, 193
Lewis, Ron, 345
Lewis, Ted, 131
Lichine, David, 187
Lieberson, Goddard, 239, 288
Lil Abner, 222
Lillie, Beatrice, 128, 135, 146,
    148, 156–57, 160, 171–
    72, 183, 257
Lilo, 220
Limón, José, 165
Linden, Hal, 302, 316
Lindsay, Howard, 25, 212,
    214, 257
Linn, Bambi, 276
Lion Tamer, The, 59
Lipson, Paul, 284
List, Emanuel, 114
Litavkin, Serge, 109
Littell, Robert, 155
Little, Cleavon, 292
Little Boy Blue, 118
Little Café, The, 99
*Little Christopher Colum-
    bus*, 26, 67
Little Don Caesar, 64
Little Duchess, The, 90
Little Jack Sheppard, 27, 65
Little Johnny Jones, 85
Little Mary Sunshine, 246–
    47, 295
Little Me, 262, 277, 291
Little Michus, The, 81

Little Millionaire, The, 93,
    110
Little Miss Nobody, 88
Little Night Music, A, 332–
    33, 334
Little Show, The, 134,
    147–48
Little Tycoon, The, 43, 54
Little Whopper, The, 138
Littlewood, Joan, 281
Livin' the Life, 226
Lockhart, Gene, 144
Lockridge, Richard, 147
Loeb, Philip, 134, 149, 165,
    183
Loesser, Frank, 210, 216–19,
    225, 228, 236, 274–75,
    316
Loewe, Frederick, 193, 194,
    223, 237–39, 252–53,
    257, 307
Logan, Ella, 182, 193
Logan Joshua, 175, 186, 200,
    204, 227–28
Lolita, My Love, 307
Loman, Hal, 222
Long, Avon, 191
Look to the Lilies, 268
Loos, Anita, 188
Loper, Don, 167
Lopez, Pilar, 181
Lopez, Vincent, 145
Lopokova, Lydia, 97, 104, 136
Lorelei, 303
Loring, Eugene, 192
Lorraine, Lillian, 91–92
Lortzing, Albert, 40, 58
Losch, Tilly, 147, 149
Lost in the Stars, 196
Loudon, Dorothy, 314, 343
Louisiana Purchase, 165,
    184, 186
Love Birds, 138
Love Life, 196
Love's Lottery, 81
Lucky, 157
Luders, Gustav, 74, 76–77,
    84, 90, 100
Ludmila, Anna, 128
Luescher, Frank, 97
Lugosi, Bela, 137
Lulu Belle, 134
Lund, Art, 218
Lute Song, 192
Lynde, Paul, 244–45
Lyons, Julius J., 44

MacDermot, Galt, 293–94,
    318–19, 322–23, 325

MacDonald, Christie, 55, 61,
    75, 78
MacDonald, Jeanette, 141
MacGrath, Leueen, 220
Mack, Andrew, 54–55
Mack, Cecil, 150
Mack and Mabel, 312
MacMahon, Aline, 127, 133
MacMurray, Fred, 148
MacRae, Gordon, 270
Madam Moselle, 100
Madcap Princess, A, 77
Mlle. Modiste, 83, 97, 138
Maffitt, James S., 22
Magdalena, 189–90
Magic Melody, The, 138
Maid in the Moon, The, 61
Maid of Athens, The, 95
Major Charles, 77
Make It Snappy, 126
Malcolm, Donald, 247
Maltby, Richard, Jr., 311
Mame, 273, 297
Mamoulian, Rouben, 162,
    197, 215
Mam'selle Napoleon, 90
Man in the Moon, The, 61
Man in the Moon, Jr., The,
    61
Man of LaMancha, 296–97,
    315, 317, 347, 348
*Man Who Owns Broadway,
    The*, 87
Man with Three Wives, The,
    95
Manhattan Mary, 152
Manheim, Ralph, 318
Mann, Theodore, 316
Manning, Irene, 193
Mantle, Burns, 111
Marbury, Elizabeth, 121
Marchetti, Young, 6
Margetson, Arthur, 183–84
*Marie Dressler's All-Star
    Gambol*, 112
Marion, George, 87
Markova, Alicia, 183
Marks, Walter, 264
Marquis, Don, 225
Marre, Albert, 271, 296
Marriage Market, The, 119
Marschner, Heinrich, 40
Marsh, Howard, 138, 157
Marshall, Pat, 224
Martens Family, 15
Martin, Ernest, 210, 216, 245,
    266
Martin, Florence, 118
Martin, Hugh, 257

Martin, Mary, 49, 179, 185,
192, 196, 200, 212, 230,
269–70
Martin, Ralph, 186
Martin, Virginia, 262
Marx Brothers, 141
Mary, 137
Mascagni, Pietro, 59
Mason, Marilyn, 276
Mass, 306
Massey, Blanche, 66
Massey, Daniel, 282
Massey, Ilona, 181
Massine, Léonide, 171, 189
Masteroff, Joe, 282, 285–86
Masterson, Peter, 326–27
Mathias Sandorf, 30
Matons, Bill, 165
Matteson, Ruth, 167
Matthews, Edward, 162
Matthews, Jessie, 145, 147
Mature, Victor, 196
Maugham, W. Somerset, 172
May Wine, 159
Maytime, 102
McCardle, Andrea, 314
McCarthy, Joseph, 309
McCarthy, Justin Huntly, 138
McCarty, Mary, 336
McCoy, Bessie, 109
McCracken, Joan, 210
McCreary, Wayman C., 43
McCullough, Paul, 132
McGinley, Phyllis, 188
McGowan, John, 154
McGuire, Dorothy, 170
McHale, Duke, 174
McHenry, Nellie, 33, 94
McIntyre, Frank, 98
McKayle, Donald, 264, 328
McKechnie, Donna, 304
McLellan, C. M. S., 98–99
McLerie, Allyn, 213
McMartin, John, 335
McNair, Barbara, 316
McNally, John J., 23, 38
McQueen, Armelia, 311
McQueen, Butterfly, 170
Me and Juliet, 210–11, 221
Mecca, 104, 136–37
Medcraft, Russell, 182
Medford, Kay, 244–45
Medium, The, 197
Meehan, Thomas, 302, 314
Meet the People, 168
Meller, Raquel, 145
Menotti, Gian-Carlo, 82, 197
Mercer, Johnny, 215, 222–23, 262

Mercer, Marian, 277
Mercouri, Melina, 264
Merman, Ethel, 49, 152–53,
155, 172, 178–79, 182,
185–86, 214, 231–32,
259, 272, 314
Merö-Irion, Yolanda, 188
Merola, Gaetano, 95
Merrick, David, 221, 228–29,
230, 240, 269, 271–72,
275–76, 278–81, 312,
344
Merrill, Bob, 237, 240, 258,
268, 303, 344
Merry Countess, The, 96
Merry Monarch, The, 58
Merry Mount, 59
Merry War, The, 46
Merry Widow, The, 58, 70, 74,
81, 85, 87–89, 93, 94, 95,
98, 140, 189, 197
Merry World, The, 69
Messager, Andre, 81
*Messenger Boy from Mars,
The*, 70
Mestayer, William A., 24, 34,
54
Metaxa, Georges, 171
Metcalfe, James S., 86
Mexican Hayride, 183
Michaels, Sidney, 254
Michell, Keith, 278
Michener, James, 200
Middleton, Ray, 186, 195
Midnight Bell, A, 37
Midnight Frolic, 128
Mielziner, Jo, 148, 167, 172,
175, 186, 189, 191, 199,
209, 216, 218, 220
Mikado, The, 42, 43, 44, 46,
48, 50–51, 53, 54, 104,
166
Milk and Honey, 271
Miller, Alice Duer, 173
Miller, Flournoy, 224
Miller, Marilyn, 49, 107–8,
110, 125, 139–40, 153–
54, 165
Miller, Robin, 296
Miller, Susan, 187
Million Dollars, A, 78
Millman, Bird, 130
Millöcker, Karl, 42–43, 45,
46, 53–54, 58–59, 80, 83,
160
Mills, Florence, 135
Mills, Stephanie, 329
Mimic World, The, 92
Miner, Henry C., 51

Minnelli, Liza, 285, 345
Minnelli, Vincente, 172, 181
*Minnie Palmer's Boarding
School*, 34
Minturn, Harry, 169
Miracle, The, 180, 197
Miranda, Carmen, 181
Miss Bob White, 88
Miss Hellyett, 58
Miss Information, 121
Miss Innocence, 91
Miss Liberty, 213–14
Miss 1917, 114–15
Mr. Lode of Koal, 92, 135
Mr. President, 257–58
Mr. Wonderful, 224–25
Mistinguette, 126, 145
Mitchell, Abbie, 162
Mitchell, David, 302
Mitchell, James, 194, 225
Mitchell, Julian, 36–37, 79,
95, 98, 109–10, 126
Mitchell, Norma, 182
Mitzi, 96, 124
Mod Donna, 295
Moffat, Graham, 71
Molnár, Ferenc, 199
Molyneux, Eileen, 109
Monckton, Lionel, 66, 67,
74–76, 94, 140
Monnot, Marguerite, 279
Monroe, George W., 116
Monte Carlo, 67
Monte Cristo, Jr., 27
Montgomery, David, 79, 84,
97, 99
Montgomery, Robert, 144
Moore, Charlie, 72
Moore, Douglas, 197
Moore, Florence, 111, 131,
132
Moore, Grace, 132, 160
Moore, Melba, 292
Moore, Sam, 215
Moore, Victor, 85, 153, 154,
161, 178, 179, 184
Moran and Mack, 131, 145
Morehouse, Ward, 84
Morgan, Frank, 149
Morgan, Helen, 150, 157, 173
Morgan, Roger, 322
Morison, Patricia, 184
Morley, Christopher, 11
Moross, Jerome, 165, 226
*Morris Gest's Midnight
Whirl*, 127
Morse, Robert, 240, 275, 303
Morse, Woolson, 56–57, 58
Mortimer, James, 11

Moss and Fontana, 150
Most Happy Fella, The, 208, 218, 228
Mostel, Zero, 191, 284, 288, 317
Mother Goose, 80
Moulan, Frank, 95
Moylan, Mary Ellen, 192
Mullenhowen Brothers, 3
Mulligan Guard, The, 35
Murray, Mae, 91, 100
Murray, Wynn, 174
Music Box Revue, 132
Music in My Heart, 189
Music in the Air, 158, 212
Music Is, 344
Music Man, The, 208, 241, 265, 278
Musser, Tharon, 336, 343, 345
My Darlin' Aida, 224
My Fair Lady, 208, 237, 238–40, 253, 254, 255, 257, 278, 296, 300, 307, 348
My Innocent Boy, 72
Myerberg, Michael, 192
Myrtil, Odette, 159

Naldi, Nita, 108
Namara, Marguerite, 95
Nanon, 46–47, 51
Nash, N. Richard, 261, 269
Nash, Ogden, 197
Natwick, Mildred, 172
Naughton, James, 305–6
Naughty Marietta, 84, 97, 138
Neff, Hildegarde, 220
Nel Giappone, 105
Nelson, Gene, 335
Nemiroff, Robert, 328
Neptune's Daughter, 82
Never Homes, The, 116–17
New Faces, 167–68
New Faces of 1952, 234
New Girl in Town, 235, 237–38
New Moon, The, 159
New Yorkers, The, 155
Newley, Anthony, 279, 317
Newman, David, 267
Newman, Phyllis, 259, 304
Nic Nax of 1926, 144
Nichols, Mike, 284, 346
Nielson, Christine, 55, 100
Night In Paris, A, 145
Night in Spain, A, 145
Night in Venice, A, 145

Night with the Pierrots, A, 106
Nightcap, 271
Nightclub Cantata, 319
Nightingale and the Rose, The, 131
Nina Rosa, 159
Ninety in the Shade, 120–21
No for an Answer, 169
No, No, Nanette, 111, 141, 300, 307–9, 315, 348
No Strings, 274, 305
Nobody Home, 121, 123
North, Sheree, 276
Norton, Elliot, 237
Norton, Frederick, 115
Norworth, Jack, 111
Novelty, with the Laying of the Atlantic Cable, 5
Novotna, Jarmila, 188
Nowak, Adolph, 44
Nype, Russell, 214
Oakie, Jack, 127
O'Brien, Jack, 330
O'Connell, Hugh, 163
Odds and Ends of 1917, 111
Odets, Clifford, 201, 263–64
Oenslager, Donald, 178
Of Thee I Sing, 66, 141, 154, 160–62, 163, 165, 175, 215, 223, 243
Offenbach, Jacques, 12, 22, 39, 42–43, 46, 47, 49, 58, 83, 180–81, 203, 256
Oh, Boy, 122–23
Oh, Kay, 153
Oh, Lady, Lady, 123
Oh, Look, 124
Oh, My Dear, 123
Oh! Oh! Delphine, 97–98
Oh, Please, 146
Oh, What a Lovely War, 278, 281–82
O'Hara, Jill, 277
O'Hara, John, 176, 213
O'Horgan, Tom, 293, 322–25
O'Keefe, Walter, 181
O'Keeffe, Georgia, 324
Oklahoma!, 3, 66, 98, 168, 194, 197–99, 200, 202, 208, 210, 215, 218
Olaf, Pierre, 228
Olcott, Chauncey, 50
Old Dutch, 116
Oliver, 278, 280
Oliver, Edna May, 122, 157
Olivette, Nina, 152
Olsen, George, 126, 137, 152

Olsen, Ole, and Johnson, Chic, 181, 183, 344
O'Malley, Rex, 179
On a Clear Day You Can See Forever, 254–255
On the Town, 36, 187–88, 202, 232, 303–4
On the Twentieth Century, 304–5
On Your Toes, 173, 204, 212
Once Upon a Mattress, 226–27
One Damned Thing After Another, 156
One for the Money, 167, 176
110 in the Shade, 268, 269, 278
One Touch of Venus, 192, 196
Only Girl, The, 97
L'Opéra de Quat' Sous, 194
Orbach, Jerry, 225, 248, 269, 277, 340
Orchid, The, 66, 76
Osato, Sono, 187
Osterman, Lester, 260
Ostrow, Stuart, 284, 321
Ouina, 28
Our Goblins, 53
Out of this World, 219
Over Here!, 311
Over Night, 121
Over the Top, 102
Oy-Ra, 119

Pacific Overtures, 300, 333–34, 339
Padlocks of 1927, 144
Padula, Edward, 244
Page, Ken, 311, 316
Page, Ruth, 132, 189
Paige, Janis, 236
Paint Your Wagon, 223
Pajama Game, The, 208, 235, 316, 348
Pal Joey, 66, 176–77, 186, 199, 212–13, 275–76, 316–17, 348
Palmer, Harry, 8, 11, 24
Palmer, Minnie, 34
Palmer, Peter, 222
Panama, Norman, 222
Panama Hattie, 179
Panjandrum, 56, 57, 75
Papp, Joseph, 294–95, 316, 318–20, 341
Parade, 165–66, 271
Pardon My English, 162
Paris, 177
Parisian Model, The, 90

Park Avenue, 172
Parker, Eleanor, 316
Parker, H. T., 51, 53
Parks, Bernice, 191
Parlour Match, A, 37
Parsons, Estelle, 317
Party with Comden and Green, A, 304
Passing Show, The, 38, 54, 64, 68, 69, 102, 106–8, 110, 111, 116, 126, 132–33, 145, 181
Pastor, Tony, 3, 4, 47, 50, 68, 70
Patchwork, 32
Patience, 41, 49
Paulton, Harry, 52
Payne, John, 309
Peace, 295
Peacock, Bertram, 138
Pearl, Jack, 145, 150
Peep Show, 185
Peerce, Jan, 284
Penn, Arthur, 263
Pennington, Anne, 109–10, 114–15, 126, 129, 144
Pepita, or, The Girl with the Glass Eyes, 50
Perfect Fool, The, 129
Peter Pan, 230
Peters, Bernadette, 296, 304, 312–13
Peters, Paul, 165
Petrova, Olga, 94
Pflueger, Carl, 60
Philemon, 321
Pickwick, 278
Picon, Molly, 271
Pidgeon, Walter, 240
Piff! Paff!! Pouf!!!, 80
Pink Lady, The, 74, 97–98
Pins and Needles, 166–67, 188, 276
Pinza, Ezio, 200, 228
Pioneer Days, 82
Pipe Dream, 208, 210–11, 221
Pippin, 19, 321, 328, 339–41, 347
Pirates of Penzance, The, 41, 50
Pixley, Frank, 76, 78
Pixley, Gus, 68
Plain and Fancy, 240–41
Platinum, 346
Platt (Platoff), Marc, 187
Pleasures and Palaces, 274, 291

Plume de Ma Tante, La, 228–229, 278
Pocahontas, 6, 19, 32
Pockriss, Lee, 253
Poitier, Sidney, 221
Pollock, Arthur, 147, 148, 159
Pollock, Channing, 110
Polly, 48, 50
Polonaise, 189
Pons, Helene, 174
Poor Jonathan, 53–55, 59
Poor Little Ritz Girl, The, 142
Pop, 24–25
Poppy, 137
Poretta, Frank, 317
Porgy and Bess, 141, 151, 162–63, 169, 190, 223–24, 300, 329–30
Porter, Cole, 124, 128, 131, 147, 153, 155–56, 177–79, 182–84, 203, 213, 219–21, 336
Portfolio Revue, 321
Powell, Eleanor, 152
Powell, Jane, 309
Power, Tyrone, 115
Powers, James T., 34, 38, 67
Powers, Tom, 122
Pratt, John, 169
Present Arms, 156
Presley, Elvis, 243, 280–81
Presnell, Harve, 265
Preston, Robert, 241–42, 254, 269–70, 312, 344
Pretty Mrs. Smith, 96
Prettybelle, 303
Previn, André, 255
Price, Gerald, 225
Price, Gilbert, 306
Price, Leontyne, 223
Price, Michael, 315
Price, Vincent, 261
Prince, Harold, 235–37, 242–43, 278, 282–83, 285–87, 289–90, 291, 297, 305, 306, 331–39, 340, 345
Prince of Grand Street, The, 344
Prince of Pilsen, The, 76
Princess Ida, 41, 50
Princess Nicotine, 50, 68
Princess of Trebizonde, The, 49
Princess Pat, The, 97
Priorities of 1942, 68, 181
Prochnik, Bruce, 280
Promenade, 295

Promises, Promises, 268, 275–77, 278, 341
Pruette, William, 54
Puck, Eva, 131
Puerner, Charles, 59
Puritania, 59
Purlie, 291–92
Puzzles of 1925, 128

Quaker Girl, The, 94, 106
Queen of the Movies, The, 119
Queen's Lace Handkerchief, The, 53
Quintero, José, 318

Rado, James, 293, 322
Rae, Charlotte, 225
Rag Baby, A, 36–37
Ragland, Oscar, 99
Ragni, Gerome, 293, 322–23
Rahn, Muriel, 192
Rainbow Girl, The, 124
Rainmaker of Syria, The, 62
Raisin, 328, 347
Raitt, John, 236, 287
Ramsay, Remak, 304
Randall, Carl, 110, 123, 125, 132, 172
Randolph, James, 316
Rape of Lucretia, The, 197
Rasch, Albertina, 62, 146, 149, 159, 180, 196, 204
Rasely, George, 115
Rathburn, Roger, 309
Ravel, Gabriel, 15
Ravel Family, 5–6, 10, 14, 15
Raye, Martha, 190, 272
Raymond, Helen, 122
Razaf, Andy, 310
Red Canary, The, 120
Red, Hot and Blue, 178
Red Hussar, The, 50
Red Mill, The, 84
Red Petticoat, The, 118–19
Red Rose, The, 117
Redgrave, Lynn, 344
Redhead, 238, 291
Reed, Florence, 115
Reed, Richard, 168, 173
Reed, Roland, 51
Reed, Vivian, 310
Regina, 197
Rehan, Ada, 45
Reiff, A., Jr., 15
Reinhardt, Max, 102–4, 106, 110, 114, 115, 136, 159, 180, 188

Relyea, Marjorie, 78
Renault, Francis, 126
Reunion in New York, 168
Revenge with Music, 171
Revill, Clive, 278, 280
Revue of Revues, The, 105
Revuers, The, 230
Rex, 302
Rey, Federico, 181, 187
Reynolds, Debbie, 309
Reynolds, James, 126
Rhapsody in Black, 150
Riabouchinska, Tatiana, 10,
    189
Rice, Edward E., 10, 12, 13,
    19–27, 33, 34, 48, 54, 56,
    59–60, 66–67, 72–73,
    77
Rice, Elmer, 196
Rice, Sarah, 338
Rice, Tim, 323–24
Rich Mr. Hoggenheimer, The,
    76
Richards, Jess, 304
Richardson, Ian, 307
Richman, Harry, 144, 150
Richmond, Ada, 70
Rigby, Harry, 280, 308–9
Riggs, Lynn, 197
Riggs, T. Lawrason, 124
Rigl, Betty, 10
Rinehart, Mary Roberts, 138
Rio Rita, 158
*Rise and Fall of the City of
    Mahagonny, The*, 317
Ritchard, Cyril, 230, 256, 279
Ritchie, Adele, 68
Rivera, Chita, 224, 234,
    244–45, 340
*Roar of Greasepaint—The
    Smell of the Crowd, The*,
    278, 279–80
Rob Roy, 100
Robber Bridegroom, The,
    321, 326
Robber of the Rhine, The, 59
Robbins, A., 101, 182
Robbins, Jerome, 168, 172,
    187–88, 209, 227, 230,
    231, 234–35, 236, 283,
    291, 303–4, 316, 317
Roberta, 23, 172
Roberts, Alexander, 310
Roberts, Anthony, 276
Roberts, Arthur, 65
Robertson, Guy, 180
Robertson, Tom, 57
Robeson, Paul, 173

Robin, Leo, 229
Robin Hood, 44, 59, 100, 104
Robinson, Bill, 150, 169
Rockwell, Doctor, 131, 183
Rodgers, Mary, 226–27, 346
Rodgers, Richard, 2, 134, 142,
    153, 156–57, 158, 172,
    173–77, 186, 197, 199–
    200, 208–13, 219, 221,
    227, 242, 243, 249, 254,
    273–74, 301–3, 305,
    313, 336, 348
Rogers, Ginger, 272
Rogers, Gus and Max, 54, 81
Rogers, Jaime, 264
Rogers, Stanley, 127, 145
Rogers, Will, 110, 126
Roi Malgré Lui, Le, 58
Roly-Poly, 71, 111
Romberg, Sigmund, 96,
    101–2, 108, 128, 138–
    39, 142, 153, 159, 190
Rome, Harold, 166, 167, 185,
    188, 227–29, 275–76
Rooney, Pat, Sr., 218
Ronzani Troupe, 5, 6
Rosalie, 153
Rosalinda, 159, 188–189
Rose, Billy, 111, 150, 158,
    173, 183, 191
Rose, George, 307
Rose, Marie, 118
Rose Girl, The, 136
Rose Maid, The, 96
Rose Marie, 138, 246
Rose of China, The, 136
Rose of Persia, The, 80
Rosenfeld, Sydney, 44, 45,
    46, 51, 68
Rosenthal, Jean, 271
Ross, Adrian, 87
Ross, Jerry, 236–37
Ross, Robert, 162
Roth, Lillian, 276
Rothschilds, The, 301–2
*Round New York in 80 Min-
    utes*, 69
Routledge, Patricia, 261, 306
Royal Family, The, 55
Royal Middy, The, 45, 47, 51
Royale, Ted, 245
Royce, Edward, 114, 122, 140
Rubens, Paul, 74, 94, 119,
    121, 140
Rubin, Cyma, 308
Rubinstein, Anton, 60
Ruby, Harry, 156
Ruby, Thelma, 227

Ruddigore, 53, 54
Ruggles, Charles, 108
Rule, Janice, 256
Runaway Colt, A, 37
Runaway Girl, A, 67, 88
Runaways, 320
Runaways, The, 79–80
Running for Office, 85, 87
Runyon, Damon, 216–17
Russell, Lillian, 4, 23, 47–50,
    54, 56, 58, 59, 70–71, 81
Russell, Robert, 240
Russell, Rosaline, 232–33,
    255
Ryan, Robert, 257
Ryan, Sue, 181
Rychtarik, Richard, 189
Ryley, J. H., 41
Ryskind, Morrie, 154, 160–
    62, 223

Sablon, Jean, 181
Saddler, Donald, 308, 309
Sadie Thompson, 172
Sager, Carole Bayer, 343–44
Saidy, Fred, 221, 256
Sail Away, 257
St. John, Florence, 65
St. Louis Woman, 222
Saint Subber, Arnold, 219
Saks, Gene, 305
Sallert, Ulla, 254
Sally, 91, 139–40
Sally, Irene, and Mary, 137
Salsbury, Nate, 16, 24,
    31–34, 36, 53, 66, 94
Salvation, 294
Sambo, 295
San Francisco Minstrels, 3,
    31
San Toy, 79
Sanderson, Julia, 94, 95,
    119–20
Sandhog, 226
Sandrich, Mark, Jr., 254
Sands, Dorothy, 133
Sangalli, Rita, 10, 14
Santley, Joseph, 123, 132, 139
Sappington, Margo, 316
Saratoga, 222
Sari, 96
Saroya, Bianca, 100
Saturday Night, 287
Sauter, Eddie, 292
Savage, Henry W., 87, 89, 95,
    96
Savo, Jimmy, 166, 174
Savoy, Bert, 115, 117, 127, 130

Sawyer, Ivy, 123, 132, 139
Scannell, George P., 62
Scheff, Fritzi, 55, 83
Schenck, Joe, 114
Schmidt, Harvey, 247–48, 269–70, 321
Schoenfeld, Gerald, 348
Schuller, Gunther, 330
Schumann-Heink, Ernestine, 81
Schwartz, Arthur, 133, 148–49, 171–72, 215–16, 255–56, 336
Schwartz, Stephen, 340, 345–46
Scorsese, Martin, 345
Scott, Bonnie, 275
Scott, Hazel, 181
Scott, Leslie, 223
Scott, Raymond, 192
Scruggs, Earl, 325
Sea Cadet, The, 45, 46, 51
Seabrook, Thomas Q., 69
Seal, Elizabeth, 278
See America First, 124
Seeley, Blossom, 106, 116, 131
Seesaw, 341
Segal, Vivienne, 114, 123, 138, 175, 176, 199, 213
Selwyn, Arch, 135, 137, 147, 171
Serenade, The, 82, 189
Sgt. Pepper's Lonely Hearts Club Band on the Road, 325
Serpentine, 11
Sesostra, 106
Set to Music, 160
Seven Ages, The, 25–26
Seven Lively Arts, 183–84
1776, 291–92, 321
Shapiro, Mel, 318
Sharaff, Irene, 185, 196, 209, 211, 216
Sharkey, 176
Sharpe, Albert, 193
Shaw, David, 238, 253
Shaw, Mary, 183
Shaw, Oscar, 122, 132
Shaw, Robert, 183
Shawn, Dick, 260
She Loves Me, 268, 282, 287, 332
Shean, Al, 96, 126
Sheldon, Sidney, 238
Shelton, Reid, 314
Shenandoah, 300, 313, 315, 347

Sherman, Hal, 132
Sherman, Hiram, 276
Sherman, Richard and Robert, 311
She's a Good Fellow, 139
She's My Baby, 156
Shevelove, Burt, 188, 288, 308
Shinbone Alley, 224–25
Sho-Gun, The, 76
Short, Hassard, 131, 132, 149, 180, 183, 185, 192, 224
Show Boat, 66, 123, 131, 135, 157–58, 173
Show Girl, 154
Show Is On, The, 172
Show Time, 182
Shubert, Sam S., Lee, and J. J., 54, 69, 92, 95, 96, 97, 100, 102, 104, 105, 106, 110, 111, 112, 113, 118–19, 126, 128, 131, 136, 138, 139, 144, 145, 159, 168, 171, 172, 180–81, 191, 223, 319, 345, 348
Shuffle Along, 135, 224, 310
Side by Side by Sondheim, 305
Sidney, Robert, 185
Siegmeister, Elie, 190
Silk Stockings, 220, 222
Sillman, Leonard, 167–68
Silverman, Stanley, 318
Silver, Lew, 128
Silvers, Phil, 222, 258–59
Simon, Neil, 262, 276–77, 291, 303, 343–44
Simon, Robert A., 159
Simple Simon, 157
Sinclair, Robert, 174
Sing for Your Supper, 168
Sing Out, Sweet Land, 190
Sing Out the News, 166–67
Singin' in the Rain, 220
Siren, The, 95
Sirène, La, 11
Sissle, Noble, 135, 224, 310
1600 Pennsylvania Avenue, 306
Sklar, George, 165
Skyscraper, 266
Sleeping Beauty and the Beast, The, 80
Slezak, Walter, 228
Sloane, A. Baldwin, 79
Small, Charlie, 329
Small Wonder, 188
Smiles, 153
Smith, Alexis, 335, 346

Smith, Betty, 215
Smith, Edgar, 70, 105
Smith, Harry B., 44, 77, 95, 96, 109, 120
Smith, Mildred, 191
Smith, Muriel, 192
Smith, Oliver, 159, 187–88, 191, 211, 239, 252, 254, 255, 271–72, 273, 307
Smith, Paul Gerard, 224
Snake Charmer, The, 47
So Long, Letty, 124
Sobel, Bernard, 70
Solomon, Edward, 46, 48–50
Something for the Boys, 182
Something's Afoot, 315
Sometime, 101
Somewhere Else, 100
Sondheim, Stephen, 230, 235, 264, 274, 287–90, 291, 297, 303, 331–39, 340, 345
Song of Norway, The, 189, 219
Song of the Flame, 142
Sons o' Fun, 181
Sorcerer, The, 43, 50
Soudeikine, Sergei, 162, 167
Soul Kiss, The, 91
Sound of Music, The, 208, 212, 243, 278
Sousa, John Philip, 58, 59, 113–14
South Pacific, 2, 98, 197, 200, 201, 202, 204, 208, 210, 211, 243
Sovey, Raymond, 174
Spencer, Kenneth, 173
Spencer, Willard, 43
Spewack, Bella and Sam, 184
Sporting Days, 82
Spring Chicken, The, 140
Spring Is Here, 154
Stadlen, Lewis J., 332
Stafford, Marion, 108
Stange, Stanislaus, 61
Star and Garter, 185
Star Gazer, The, 96
Stars in Your Eyes, 172, 175, 199
Steele, Tommy, 280–81
Stein, Joseph, 224, 240, 282, 284, 287, 307
Stein, Leo, 106
Stephenson, Mabel, 68
Stepping Stones, 140
Stern, Ernest, 103
Stetson, John, 51
Stevens, Ben, 57

Stevenson, B. C., 50
Stevenson, Katherine, 118
Steward, Ron, 295
Stewart, Michael, 243, 244, 264, 268, 271–72, 303, 305–6, 312–13
Stockton, Frank R., 44
Stolz, Robert, 42
Stomp, 294
Stone, Allene, 140
Stone, Dorothy, 140
Stone, Ezra, 185
Stone, Fred, 79, 84, 97, 99, 128, 140
Stone, Peter, 266, 291, 301, 303
Stop the World–I Want to Get Off, 278, 279–80, 317
Story, Wilbur S., 19
Stothart, Herbert, 142
Strada, La, 268
Straight Tip, A, 38
Strang, Lewis C., 53, 55
Straus, Oskar, 89, 94, 189
Strauss, Johann, Jr., 42, 45, 46, 53, 58–59, 80–81, 83, 87, 89, 96, 114, 159, 180, 188, 203
Stravinsky, Igor, 183
Straw Hat Revue, The, 168
Street Scene, 196–97
Streets of Paris, The, 181
Streisand, Barbra, 258–60, 276
Strike Me Pink, 153
Strike Up the Band, 154–55, 161
Stritch, Elaine, 257
Strouse, Charles, 243–44, 263–64, 266–67, 314, 346
Stuart, Leslie, 78, 140
Student Prince, The, 102, 139
Styne, Jule, 229–32, 258–61, 303
Subways Are for Sleeping, 259, 278
Sues, Leonard, 187
Sugar, 303
Sullivan, Arthur, 22, 34, 39–42, 43, 46, 47, 48–49, 50–51, 53, 56–57, 64, 74, 80, 100, 124, 134, 161, 166, 169
Sullivan, Dan, 261
Sullivan, Jo, 218, 225
Sullivan, Maxine, 170
Summer Widowers, The, 116

Sumurun, 102–4, 106–7, 110, 115, 118, 180
Sunny, 140
Sunny River, 159
Sunshine Girl, The, 94
Suppé, Franz von, 40, 42, 45, 46, 58, 100, 160
Suratt, Valeska, 117
Swados, Elizabeth, 319
Sweeney Todd, 300, 337–39
Sweet Adeline, 158
Sweet and Low, 150
Sweet Charity, 268, 277, 291
Sweet Little Devil, 141
Sweethearts, 97, 189
Swenson, Inga, 254, 269
Swerling, Jo, 216–17
Swing It, 168
Swing Mikado, The, 166, 169
Swingin' the Dream, 170
Swiss Cottage, The, 9

Tabasco, 61–62
Tabbert, William, 228
Take a Chance, 152–53
Take Me Along, 240, 278
Talisman, The, 62
Talva, Galina, 214
Tamale Boys, 68
Tamara, 173
Tamiris, Helen, 133, 186, 190, 216, 241
Tandy, Jessica, 270
Tangerine, 137
Tanner, James T., 67
Tar and the Tartar, The, 59
Tashman, Lilyan, 110, 114
Tate, Neal, 295
Tauber, Richard, 189
Taylor, James, 346
Taylor, Laurette, 256
Taylor, Tom, 40
Tchaikovsky, Peter Ilyitch, 189
Tebelak, John-Michael, 324
Telephone, The, 197
Tell Me More, 141
Tempest, Marie, 50, 59
Templeton, Fay, 23, 26, 70, 85, 173
Temptation, 105
Tenderloin, 282, 287
Ter-Arutinian, Rouben, 238
Terkel, Studs, 345–46
Terris, Norma, 157–58
Terry, Edward, 65
Tester, Ruth, 148
Texas, Li'l Darling, 215, 222
Texas Steer, A, 37

Texsmith, Vaughn, 78
They're Playing Our Song, 343–44
This Is the Army, 185
This Year of Grace, 146
Thomas, Hugh, 248
Thomas, John Charles, 95–96, 100, 107, 108
Thomas, Tasha, 329
Thompson, Fred, 158
Thompson, Jay, 226
Thompson, Julian F., 177
Thompson, Lydia, 12, 14, 16–19, 20, 21, 27, 64
Thompson, Randall, 133
Thomson, Virgil, 197
3 for Tonight, 244
Three Musketeers, The, 159
Three to Make Ready, 167
Threepenny Opera, The, 225, 300, 317–18
Three's a Crowd, 148–49
Throckmorton, Cleon, 11
Through the Years, 153
Thurston, Ted, 270
Tierney, Harry, 125, 309
Tietjens, Paul, 79
Tilkins, Felix, 75
Tiller Girls, 126, 140, 147
Timbuktu!, 317, 348
Time for Singing, A, 268
Tin Soldier, A, 36–37
Tinney, Frank, 106, 109, 115, 118, 120, 124
Tip-Toes, 141
Tip-Top, 128
Todd, Michael, 169, 185
Tommy, 323
Tone, Franchot, 197
Too Many Girls, 139, 175
Top Banana, 222–23
Top-Notchers, 181
Topol, 284
Topsy and Eva, 137
Toreadors, The, 75
Touch, 325
Toumanova, Tamara, 10, 172
Tourists, The, 77
Tourists in the Pullman Palace Car, The, 24, 34, 35
Tours, Frank, 105, 124
Tovarich, 253
Trama, Johnny, 222
Traubel, Helen, 211
Treacher, Arthur, 150, 181
Treasure Girl, 154
Tree Grows in Brooklyn, A, 215, 242

Treemonisha, 329–30
Trentini, Emma, 84, 100
Trial by Jury, 40
Trip to Chinatown, A, 37–38, 118, 202
Trip to Coontown, A, 36, 72
Trip to Japan, A, 82
Truex, Ernest, 122
Tucker, Sophie, 179
Tudor, Antony, 192
Tumble In, 138
Tune, Tommy, 326–27
Tunick, Jonathan, 277, 333, 337–38
Two by Two, 301
Two for the Show, 167
Two Gentlemen of Verona, 316, 318–19
Tyler, Judy, 210–11
Tyne, George, 225
Tyrolean, The, 59

Udell, Peter, 292, 313
Uggams, Leslie, 258, 260–61
Uhry, Alfred, 326
Ullman, Liv, 302
Under Many Flags, 113
Unger, Gladys, 96, 119
Unsinkable Molly Brown, The, 265–66
Up in Central Park, 159, 190
Urban, Joseph, 110–11, 114, 125, 127–28, 130, 136, 148, 150, 153, 158, 171, 183
Urquhart, Isabel, 52

Vagabond King, The, 138
Valentina, 183
Vallee, Rudy, 180
Vamp, The, 260
Van and Schenck, 114, 125
Van, Bobby, 309
Van, Gus, 114, 125
Van Dyck, Dick, 243–45
Van Heusen, Jimmy, 266
Van Peebles, Melvin, 327–28
Vandross, Luther, 329
Vassar, Queenie, 75
Vaughan, Kate, 65
Vaughan, Theresa, 26
Vecsey, Armand, 136
Velez, Lupe, 179
Velvet Lady, The, 138
Vera Violetta, 106
Verdon, Gwen, 220, 236–38, 291, 340

Vereen, Ben, 324, 340
Verne, Jules, 28, 30, 171, 183
Véronique, 81
Very Good Eddie, 121–23, 300, 315, 347, 348
Very Warm for May, 173
Via Galactica, 325
Vicar of Bray, The, 48–49
Vie Parisienne, La, 47, 189
Vienna Life, 80–81
Villa-Lobos, Heitor, 190
Villella, Edward, 316
Vinay, Ramón, 181
Virginia, 48, 180
Voegtlin, Arthur, 24, 105, 107, 108, 113, 116
Vokes Family, 16, 32, 94
Volinine, Alexander, 104
Vroom, Lodewick, 188

Wagner, Robin, 305, 324–25, 343
Wahl, Walter Dare, 222
Waissman, Kenneth, 311
Wake Up and Dream, 135, 147
Walburn, Raymond, 288
Waldman, Robert, 326
Walk with Music, 190
Walker, George, 135
Walker, June, 197
Walker, Margaret, 78
Walker, Nancy, 186, 187
Walking Happy, 266
Wall, Max, 227
Waller, Thomas "Fats", 310–11
Wallop, Douglass, 236
Walsh, Mary Jane, 175
Walters, Lou, 181
Walton, Ray, 210, 236
Walton, Tony, 285, 341, 345
Waltz Dream, A, 89
Wang, 44, 53, 55–57, 104
Wanted, 321–22
Warfield, David, 69
Wars of the World, 112, 113
Wasserman, Dale, 296
Watch Your Step, 120
Waters, Ethel, 150–51, 165, 171, 182, 190
Watson, Harry, Jr., 90
Watson, Susan, 244, 254, 270, 309
Watts, Richard, 130, 155
Wayburn, Agnes, 78
Wayburn, Ned, 106–7, 114, 126, 128

Wayne, David, 193
We, Us and Company, 34, 54
Weatherly, Tom, 147–48
Weaver, Fritz, 254
Webb, Clifton, 109, 148, 156–57, 164, 171, 179
Webber, Andrew Lloyd, 323–24
Weber, Joe, 27, 38, 54, 61, 64, 70–71, 79, 81–82, 85, 93, 97, 111, 112
Webster, John, 33
Wedding Day, The, 54, 56
Weede, Robert, 218, 271
Weidman, Charles, 62, 165, 190, 204
Weidman, Jerome, 242, 275–76, 282
Weidman, John, 333–34
Weill, Kurt, 165, 180, 187, 194–97, 225, 317–18
Weinstock, Jack, 275
Weiss, George, 224
Welles, Orson, 169, 183–84
Well-Fed Dora, 21
Wells, Carolyn, 95
Werba and Luescher, 97
Wescott, Marcy, 175
West, Mae, 101, 106, 118
West Side Story, 208, 230, 234–35, 242, 260, 282, 287, 296, 306
What Makes Sammy Run?, 275–76
What's in a Name, 136
What's Up?, 193
Wheatley, William, 8–9, 11
Wheaton, Anna, 123
Whedon, John, 215
Wheeler, Bert, 126, 159, 182
Wheeler, Hugh, 309, 332, 334
Where's Charley?, 210, 216, 316, 348
Whiffen, Thomas, 40
Whirl of Society, The, 106
Whirl of the World, The, 108–9
Whirl-I-Gig, 71
White, George, 69, 106, 115, 129–30, 144, 152, 180
White, Miles, 190, 199, 240
White, Onna, 240, 242, 273, 280, 292
White, Sammy, 108, 131
White Fawn, The, 11–12, 14, 19
White Horse Inn, 180
Whitehead, O. Z., 167

Whiteman, Paul, 126, 157, 310
Whiting, Jack, 187
Whiting, Richard, 129
Whitmore, Vida, 118
Who, The, 323
Whoop-Dee-Doo, 81
Whoopee!, 300, 315, 347
Wife Hunters, The, 117
Wild Rose, The, 77
Wildcat, 261
Wildflower, 141
Wilder, Jo, 225
Willard, John, 122
Willett, John, 318
Williams, Bert, 92, 110, 125, 135, 310
Williams, Fred, 45
Williams, Hattie, 75
Williams, Hope, 155
Williams, Jesse, 60
Willson, Meredith, 241–42, 265–66
Wilson, Billy, 310
Wilson, Dooley, 190
Wilson, Francis, 48, 49, 52–53, 58, 59, 75, 85
Wilson, John C., 184
Wilson, Marie, 78
Wilson, Maud, 44
Wilson, Sandy, 245–46
Wiman, Dwight Deere, 147–48, 159, 172–73, 175
Windust, Bretaigne, 193
Windy City, 191
Winninger, Charles, 111, 125, 141, 157
Winsome Widow, A, 118

Winsome Winnie, 77
Winter, Edward, 277
Wisdom, Norman, 266
Wise, Jim, 296
Wish You Were Here, 227–28
Witch of Salem, A, 59
Without the Law, 71
Wittop, Freddy, 187, 271–72
Wiz, The, 300, 328–29
Wizard of Oz, The, 79–80, 83, 97, 262, 317
Wodehouse, P. G., 99, 115, 122–23, 136, 153, 158, 247
Wolf, Rennold, 110
Wolin, Judd, 328
Wonder Bar, The, 160
Wonderful Night, A, 159–60
Wonderful Town, 232–33, 235, 242
Wood, George, 6
Wood, Peggy, 97, 111
Woods, A. H., 95
Woodward, Charles, 337
Woolf, Walter, 138
Woollcott, Alexander, 152, 154, 159
Woolley, Monty, 159
Woolsey, Robert, 159
Words and Music, 307
Working, 345–46
World of Pleasure, A, 109
Wright, Robert, 219
Wrightson, Earl, 196
Wyler, Gretchen, 220
Wynn, Ed, 101, 108, 128–29, 152, 157, 181
Wynn, Keenan, 167

Yancy, Emily, 306
Yankee Circus on Mars, A, 82
Yankee Doodle Dandy, 69
Yeamans, Annie, 36
Yellen, Sherman, 301–2
Yeomen of the Guard, The, 53
Yip, Yip, Yaphank, 124, 184–85
Yordan, Philip, 191
You Never Know, 179
Youmans, Vincent, 141, 152–53, 308
Your Own Thing, 294
Yours Is My Heart, 189
Yukiro, 317

Zaltberg, Charlotte, 328
Zanina, 45–46
Zell, Violet, 99
Zeller, Karl, 59
Ziegfeld, Florenz, Jr., 37, 78, 81, 89–92, 97, 109–11, 114–15, 118, 125–26, 128, 137, 139–40, 145–46, 150, 152–54, 156–59, 180, 319
Ziegfeld Follies, 37, 69, 74, 81, 87, 90–92, 106, 109–11, 116, 125–26, 128, 129, 130, 132, 133, 136, 138, 139, 145–46, 147, 150, 156, 158, 180–81, 188, 259
Zig-Zags, 15
Zipprodt, Patricia, 283, 286, 341
Zorba, 268, 287
Zorina, Vera, 175, 184

CECIL SMITH

"The man who took the pains to write this comprehensive history of musical comedy has, surely, a genuine affection for his subject. His love, however, is not blind. Cecil Smith has never been an easy man to please. As dramatic and musical comedy critic of the *Chicago Tribune* and, more recently, the musical comedy editor of *Theatre Arts*, he has kept his standards high and overpaid no one with compliments. His opinions are very much his own and his expression of them is never ambiguous. It is the honesty and individuality of his views which distinguish this book." —Oscar Hammerstein II, reviewing the book in the *New York Herald Tribune*.

Cecil Smith was known primarily as a serious music critic. After graduate study in the Department of Music at Harvard, he joined the faculty of the University of Chicago, and from 1943 to 1946 was Chairman of its Department of Music. For seven years he was music critic for the *Chicago Tribune* and during several of those years also its drama critic. Coming to New York in the 1940s, he became music critic for *The New Republic,* associate editor of *Theatre Arts Monthly*, and editor-in-chief of *Musical America.* He taught a course in music and its relation to dance at the Martha Graham School of the Dance, and for quite a few of his New York years wrote the program notes for all new music performed by the New York Philharmonic Orchestra. Following a season as guest music critic for the London *Daily Express,* Cecil Smith was invited to become its regular critic, and his informed and witty articles were considered among the best English music criticism of the period.

GLENN LITTON

Glenn Litton is an Executive Producer for Public Television's WGBH in Boston, where his work has included *The Advocates* and *The Stravinsky Series*. A long-time aficionado of musical comedy, he has directed musicals for various regional theatre companies. He holds a Ph.D. in English Renaissance drama and has published articles on Shakespeare, the New Journalism, film, and drama, as well as on musical theatre.